Contraception

A History of Its Treatment by the
Catholic Theologians and Canonists

Contraception

A History of Its Treatment by the
Catholic Theologians and Canonists

John T. Noonan, Jr.

The Belknap Press of
HARVARD UNIVERSITY PRESS
Cambridge, Massachusetts
1966

Second Printing

Library of Congress Catalog Card Number 65–16687
Printed in the United States of America

DECANO PROFESSORIBUSQUE SCHOLAE IURIS

PATRIBUSFAMILIAS EXEMPLARIBUS

NECNON ALTERIS AMICIS MEIS

UNIVERSITATIS NOSTRAE DOMINAE

ACKNOWLEDGMENTS

Ann Reynolds, Harvard University, has checked my citations and the sources used. The following persons have replied to requests for particular information: the Reverend Antonio de Aldama, S.J., Roman Archives of the Society of Jesus; Professor Morton Bloomfield, Harvard University; Professor James Brundage, University of Wisconsin; Henry Chadwick, Regius Professor of Divinity, Oxford University; Professor Eric Cochrane, University of Chicago; Dr. Joseph Dorsey, Peter Bent Brigham Hospital; Professor Jean-A. Dugauquier, Walincourt, France; Professor John Freccero, Cornell University; John T. Gilchrist, University of Adelaide; Jacoba Hanenburg, University of Groningen; Dr. André Hellegers, The Johns Hopkins Hospital; Stephan Kuttner, Professor of Catholic Studies, Yale University; the Right Reverend Charles Lefebvre, Auditor, Sacred Roman Rota; Dr. John Rock, Professor of Gynecology, Emeritus, Harvard Medical School; the Reverend John W. Scheberle, C.S.C., University of Notre Dame; the Reverend Michael Sheehan, C.S.B., Pontifical Institute of Mediaeval Studies, Toronto; the Reverend Alfons M. Stickler, S.D.B., Pontificio Ateneo Salesiano.

Professor Charles Fried, Harvard Law School, read and criticized the manuscript. Ralph Lazzaro, Harvard Divinity School, and the Very Reverend Ivo Thomas, O.P., University of Notre Dame, have read the book critically in proof. Others have scrutinized individual chapters: Professor Ludwig Bieler, University College, Dublin; Professor Giles Constable, Harvard University; David Daube, Regius Professor of Civil Law, Oxford University; the Reverend John Dunne, C.S.C., University of Notre Dame; the Reverend John C. Ford, S.J., the Catholic University of America; Keith Hopkins, London School of Economics; the Right Reverend Philip Hughes, University of Notre Dame; John M. Kelly, Trinity College, Oxford; Dean Joseph O'Meara, Jr., Notre Dame Law School; Professor Robert E. Rodes, Jr., Notre Dame Law School; Marie Sabin; and William Sabin. Mary Lou Kistler typed the manuscript.

To these persons, all of whom generously, many of whom laboriously, have contributed to this book, I express my warmest thanks.

John T. Noonan, Jr.

Rome, March 25, 1965

CONTENTS

PART THREE

INNOVATION AND PRESERVATION
1450–1750

PART FOUR

DEVELOPMENT AND CONTROVERSY
1750–1965

Indi al cantar tornavano; indi donne
   gridavano e mariti che fuor casti,
   come virtute e matrimonio imponne.

E questo modo credo che lor basti
   per tutto il tempo che 'l foco li abbrucia.

Purgatorio 25.133–137

ABBREVIATIONS

AAS *Acta Apostolicae Sedis, Commentarium officiale* (Rome, 1909—).

ASS *Acta Sanctae Sedis in compendium opportune redacta et illustrata* (Rome, 1865–1908).

CC *Corpus christianorum: Series latina* (Turnhout, Belgium, 1953—).

CSEL *Corpus scriptorum ecclesiasticorum latinorum* (Vienna, 1866—).

DTC *Dictionnaire de théologie catholique* (Paris, 1903–1950).

GCS *Die griechischen christlichen Schriftsteller der ersten drei Jahrhunderte* (Leipzig, 1897—).

LTK *Lexikon für Theologie und Kirche,* ed. Michael Buchberger, 2nd ed. (Freiburg im Breisgau, 1957—).

Mansi G. D. Mansi, ed., *Sacrorum conciliorum nova et amplissima collectio* (Florence, 1759–1767; Venice, 1769–1798).

PG *Patrologia graeca,* ed. J. P. Migne (Paris, 1857–1866).

PL *Patrologia latina,* ed. J. P. Migne (Paris, 1844–1865).

INTRODUCTION

THIS BOOK is an investigation of the teaching of the theologians and canonists of the Catholic Church on contraception. It sets out the history of this teaching, and in this process attempts to discover the reasons for the positions taken. The history of a question is itself a work of criticism. Answers are critically compared. Assumptions, made explicit, are analyzed. Other questions are brought to light. I attempt here such a criticism, bringing together the criticisms of the theologians and canonists themselves, and considering what further questions might appropriately have been raised.

"Contraception" is a term which could be applied to any behavior that prevents conception. Sexual continence is contraceptive in effect; sexual intercourse when an ovum will not be fertilized avoids procreation as much as intercourse where a physical barrier is used to prevent the meeting of spermatozoa and ovum. How has some behavior now generally approved by Catholic moralists been discriminated from other acts of contraception which have been condemned? Questions of this sort will be dealt with.

My focus is not, however, on a single term, but on the ideas and values clustered into a doctrine on contraception. Seen from one aspect, the doctrine is a reply to the question, "On what terms may the generation of human life be controlled?" Considered from another aspect, it is an answer to the question, "Under what conditions may human beings have sexual intercourse?" From another, it responds to the inquiry, "What revelation of God or what laws of nature are relevant to sexual conduct?" The way of putting and answering these questions is what I am investigating.

An account of this kind is not identical with that full exploration of the factors of the moment which is the province of the writer of horizontal history. To relate in detail the circumstances, for example, that led St. Albert the Great to describe three methods of contraception belongs to the biographer of St. Albert; all the forces that made Pope Sixtus V decree the penalties of murder for contraception are the domain of the social historian of sixteenth-century Rome. No historian describes all the factors, for he does not know them all; of necessity there is choice and emphasis. Here I have tried to catch the most significant pressures and events that affected the doctrine on contraception. There is an advantage to looking at a single set of concepts over two thousand years. Ideas have their own consistency, their own logic; and this internal logic controls, in good part, those who handle them. To look at this vertical context is to gain not only a sense of the strengths and weaknesses of the concepts, but an insight into their role and purpose, as a man's character may best be seen in studying his life from birth to death.

This study, in focusing on a group of concepts, is primarily concerned with standards, theories, and the expression of values. Such a concern needs no justification to anyone who believes that the history of human ideas is the larger and better part of any history we have. In addition to its interest as a portion of that larger history, the development of theory on contraception has its special claims. As an attempt to set out what the purposes of sexual behavior should be, the tradition I explore uniquely combines appeals to divine instruction, natural laws, and psychological and social consequences. Is there any comparable effort, assiduously sustained within the same general framework for over nineteen hundred years, to express in rational terms a standard of sexual behavior?

The meaning of theory, however, is properly understood only when one determines what conditions it responds to. Consequently, I have described the contraceptive means known to different eras, and what can be inferred as to their diffusion and employment. The data here set forth, gathered from the canon law, the manuals for confessors, the commentaries of theologians and canonists, and medieval medical books and herbals, substantially alter the picture formerly drawn of contraceptive practice. In particular, the period between 400 and 1600 will be seen to be marked by a possession and use of contraceptive means which previous accounts have not suggested. It was in the face of this contraceptive practice that the doctrine upon it was promulgated in western Europe.

The theory, then, will not be viewed as an abstract logic developed without reference to existing habits. I shall set out both the practice to which doctrine responded and the steps taken to alter the practice. The effort at enforcement tested the seriousness with which the theory was intended. Unlike a history of secular law, however, where the meaning of a rule may be measured by its effective sanctions, the history of a moral doctrine must be, chiefly, an account of what was taught. The application of a moral rule is effected primarily not by agencies of compulsion but by an individual's accepting it in his heart. If a moral teaching is violated, it may still have been "effective" if it played a part in the moral consciousness of the violator. The diffusion of a moral doctrine, and the external embodiment and enforcement of it, may be gauged; the principal effect of the doctrine, its effect on conscience, must largely be inferred from the terms in which it is proposed.

The believers to whom a moral doctrine is addressed will range from the devout to the conformists to the rebellious. Partly as a function of faith, partly as a function of other psychological attributes such as attitude to authority, partly as a function of social environment, the acceptance of the doctrine will vary. At no time, I suppose, has a specific moral teaching put forward by the theologians been received in an identical way by all the faithful. The seriousness with which a doctrine is taken by different persons and groups is a matter of estimate. The range of reaction in the audience may be presumed to have affected the enunciation of the doctrine itself. When the theologians speak to a community of various degrees of faith, various degrees of moral sensitivity, various degrees of education, they may use language unsuitable for more intimate dialogue, and, in the words of the Talmud, they may "build a fence around the Law," setting up outer ramparts to keep an inner treasure secure.

The assent of human beings, which gives effect to a doctrine, is not to a single set of propositions, but to the Christian faith. Within this faith there are beliefs on the Bible, grace, original sin, the sacraments, sexuality, marriage, the value of human lives, the purpose of human existence. These beliefs or doctrines structure the propositions on contraception. I have noted the points of most significant impingement, without writing a history of the other relevant doctrines. However tight the relation, however close the dependence on the Christian framework, the teaching on contraception has had its own set of problems, concepts, articulations: its own history.

The larger doctrinal context may be at least indicated. Far more difficult is the fair presentation of the teaching on contraception by a series of propositions. Can the doctrine be rationally dissected without caricaturing it? Analysis approaches from the outside, not seeing the heart within. A moral doctrine must be grasped affectively. "Give me a lover," says St. Augustine, expounding another Christian teaching, "and he will understand me." The meaning of the doctrine is grounded in a charity which escapes analysis. The propositions live, acquire force, make sense, only for the man animated by a love of God and his neighbor. Such objection, at any rate, could be urged against the adequacy of my account, which cannot reach this love beyond analysis. Nonetheless, there is a large amount of rational construction in the doctrine, and much of it is based on appeal to the experience of all men. The construction can be examined for its articulateness, its logic, its consistency. The appeal to experience can be tested for its accuracy and adequacy. The literary antecedents of the rules may be established; the role played by hostile influences can be determined. If only the bare bones of doctrine appear, if the secret vital sap is still missing, the limitation may be noted without abandoning the task of rational analysis, indispensable if love of God and neighbor is to receive rational direction in an organized community.

The sources of this history are, first, those who shaped the foundations: the largely anonymous writers of the Old Testament, the Evangelists, and St. Paul, together forming one category of writing accepted by the Catholic faith as inspired, and Philo, the Stoics, and the writers of the Talmud, who contributed to early Christian attitudes toward sexual intercourse. After taking stock of these early influences, and the Gnostic movements against which the Christians reacted, I examine the ideas as they developed — not abstractly, but in the minds of distinct individuals. The dominant figures are few, indeed perhaps only one: St. Augustine. Next to him, with an importance gained largely through his prestige in other matters, stands St. Thomas. After him may be mentioned the wisest of scholastic writers on sexuality, St. Albert the Great, and the most critical, Martin Le Maistre. A few other able men stand out: Clement of Alexandria, St. John Chrysostom, Thomas Sanchez, Peter de Ledesma. The rest of the theologians writing on this subject are skilled commentators or collectors; they add very little to the basic discussion of the problems, but perpetuate the teaching and provide a setting in which the men of genius function. Original insight or penetrating criticism within the tradition is rather rare. The work of individuals merges with that more collective organ of teaching, the legislation of the Church. Here the decretals of Gregory IX and the collections of Burchard of Worms, Ivo of Chartres, and Gratian have been of special importance. Yet the development of doctrine is not mere accretion or the simple unfolding of the logic of an idea. The process involves conflict, variety, and personal decision. It is not immaterial to consider where, by whom, when, and how the formulas were repeated. I do not purport to relate the views of all the thousands of theologians who have written on the subject. But I believe that the authors selected include the original, the influential, the representative, and the critical; and where an author of one of these classes is silent on a problem, his silence is often as significant as his speech.

Are these writers and legislative enactments to be equated with "the Church"? There is a tendency among some historians to make the identification, to say that the Catholic Church taught this or did that, when all that one can be certain of is that particular men, baptized Christians, occupying a particular role in the ecclesiastical system, did this or taught that. The Church, of course, to teach at all, must teach not only by the extraordinary pronouncements of ecumenical councils or Popes, but also by its ordinary organs, the bishops, who will rely on the common opinions of the theologians. Yet no great original theologian, not even an Augustine or a Thomas, has been able to write extensively on theology without writing what later has been determined to be heresy. Only the

Church is free from error. What is the teaching of the Church becomes itself a theological question.

Obviously, an answer to a theological question within the competence of the Church cannot be given by a book of this kind. An historian may recount, however, what was the teaching of individual theologians and the degree of acceptance apparently accorded the teaching by the hierarchy and the faithful. A history may suggest what may be regarded as ephemeral error and what has become part of the normative rules. The frequency with which fallacies, some of a scientific, some of an analytical character, infected the views of particular writers on our subject may, moreover, serve as a useful reminder of how little the individual theologian is immune from mistake. A knowledge of biology, everyone would agree, was not included in Christian revelation; what the absence of reliable biological information involved for the formulation of moral doctrine becomes concretely apparent in this study. In addition, I suppose, no one would maintain that the immunity of the Church from error was a guarantee that the theologians were right in the reasoning by which they reached their conclusions. This study will provide opportunity for marking the distinction.

The key terms in my history are tension, reaction, option, and development. All of these metaphors imply that a human process is going on, that what is happening is not the unilateral action of God making His Will increasingly evident. If one wants to see a providential pattern of development, nothing in my description precludes such a view; but such a task of theological interpretation is not my purpose. I prescind from the divine influence on the development and suppose at each stage that there were human choices to be made. Thus I would not consider "God so willed it" a sufficient answer to the question, "Why was marriage considered a sacrament?" Some questions of this kind I have not examined because the theological answer, "divine institution," constituted something already taken as a datum for the teaching on contraception; but I have proceeded on the assumption that historical investigation of secondary causes could be fruitful in exploring similar questions which also have theological solutions.

As I do not look at doctrinal development as an automatic unfolding of the divine will, neither do I approach it as a process determined by forces capable of quantification. "Tension" and "reaction" are physical terms which may carry unintended implications of mechanical response. There was tension within the Catholic doctrine arising from the value placed on procreation and the conflicting value placed on education. In using the term "tension" I do not imply that one value had to give way. The Catholic teaching on marriage was a reaction to the organized Gnostic opposition to all procreation. By saying "reaction" I do not mean that the formation of the counter doctrine was inevitable, but that such doctrine had to be asserted if certain values prized by some Christians were to be preserved. "Tension" and "reaction" are ways of signaling the existence of human choices which had to be made at the cost of suppressing some possible alternatives. The existence of these options is at the heart of the history of the doctrine. The options were presented in different ways, at different times, in environmental conditions and under theological auspices which varied and which went far toward determining the response to them. The Church had to choose among them, its freedom being ultimately limited only by its own understanding of its constitution and the commandments it had to keep.

The propositions constituting a condemnation of contraception are, it will be seen, recurrent. Since the first clear mention of contraception by a Christian theologian, when a harsh third-century moralist accused a pope of encouraging it, the articulated judgment has been the same. In the world of the late Empire known to St. Jerome and St. Augustine, in the Ostrogothic Arles of Bishop Caesarius and the Suevian Braga of Bishop Martin, in the Paris of St. Albert and St. Thomas, in the Renaissance Rome of Sixtus V and the Renaissance Milan of St. Charles Borromeo, in the Naples of St. Alphonsus Liguori and the Liège of Charles Billuart, in the Philadelphia of Bishop Kenrick, and in the Bombay of Cardinal Gracias, the teachers of the Church have taught without hesitation or variation that certain acts preventing procreation are gravely sinful. No Catholic theologian has ever taught, "Contraception is a good act." The teaching on contraception is clear and apparently fixed forever.

The teaching, however, has not been proposed without reasons. It has not been unrelated to other doctrinal propositions. It has not been isolated from the environment in which Christians live. If the teaching were constant while the reasons, related doctrine, and environment changed, it would not be the same teaching that these reasons, doctrine, and environment now supported. A closer examination of the teaching may show that it does not possess an abstract constancy and independence. It has developed. There has been tension, and there has been reaction. Have the options selected made all further choice unnecessary or impossible?

Often the makers of legal or moral rules do not make explicit the innovations and departures from the past which characterize the development of doctrine; the historian does not share this institutional inhibition. My function is not to prophesy what further mutations may occur. But, marking the circumstances in which the doctrine was composed, the controversies touching on it, the doctrinal elements now obsolete, the factors favoring further growth, this study may provide grounds for prophecy.

PART ONE

SHAPING OF THE DOCTRINE

50–450

CHAPTER I

CONTRACEPTION
IN THE ROMAN EMPIRE

U NLIKE MANY ACTS on which moral judgment has been passed, contraception requires a knowledge of technique. Even the most elementary contraceptive behavior calls for the possession of some biological information; mechanical methods rest on some awareness of physiology; chemical preparations demand a further mastery of pharmacology. If these kinds of technical knowledge were nonexistent, there would be no acts of contraception for moralists to judge. The effectiveness of existing technique, and the distinction between it and means used to control birth by producing abortions, are also germane to the moral evaluation, as are the extent of the diffusion of the practice, and the motives of those who employ it. The judgments made by Christians on contraception in the first four centuries can be understood only if the existence, effect, and use of contraceptive technique in the Roman Empire are appraised.

The existence of contraceptive technique in the pre-Christian Mediterranean world is well established. The oldest surviving documents are from Egypt. Five different papyri, all dating from between 1900 and 1100 B.C., provide recipes for contraceptive preparations to be used in the vulva. The Kahun Papyrus has three different formulas: pulverized crocodile dung in fermented mucilage; honey and sodium carbonate to be sprinkled in the vulva; and a substance, whose name is now undecipherable, to be mixed with mucilage and sprinkled in the vulva. In the Ebers Papyrus it is said that pregnancy may be prevented for "one, two, or three years" by a recipe of acacia tips, coloquintida, and dates, mixed with honey, to be placed in the uterus. The Ramasseum Papyrus IV reports that to prevent pregnancy crocodile dung should be placed on moistened fibers in the opening of the uterus. A recipe to prevent pregnancy given in the Berlin Papyrus is fumigation of the uterus with the seed of a particular grain.

In the Carlsberg Papyrus the contents of the recipe are lacking, but the contraceptive purport of a formula is evident.[1]

These prescriptions, aimed at blocking or killing the male semen, were rational ways of attempting contraception. Some of the substances mentioned, like coloquintida and sodium carbonate, appear in contraceptive prescriptions in much later European literature. It is not unreasonable to suppose that some form of this ancient lore was in existence in early Christian times. But the Greek and Roman writers do not use the unsystematized Egyptian material directly.[2] The papyri are relevant here only in revealing a culture where contraception was already a matter of medical technique. The desire to prevent pregnancy by artificial means will be found even more characteristic of the society the Christians knew.

THE KNOWLEDGE AVAILABLE

JEWISH INFORMATION

The practice of coitus interruptus, intercourse followed by withdrawal and semination outside the vagina, is close to being a self-evident method of contraception. Its early practice among the Hebrews is testified to by Genesis 38:8–10, the story of Onan. The prevalence of this simple method in the world the early Christians were familiar with is suggested by several references in the Babylonian version of the Talmud that go back to at least the first century of the Christian era.[3] In *Yebamoth* ("Sisters-in-Law") 34b the Gemara refers to the practice during the first twenty-four months of lactation; the act is described euphemistically as "threshing inside and winnowing outside." The text is third century or later; the statement is attributed to the first-century Rabbi Eliezer. In *Niddah* ("The Menstruant") 13a there is a quotation of Rabbi Johanan ben Nappaha, the founder of a school at Tiberias in the third century, on the deadly sin of Onan, and the sin here is clearly his contraceptive act.

Pessaries are spoken of several times. In *Yebamoth* 35a, Rabbi Jose is said by the third-century Babylonian, Rabbah, to believe that a harlot will use an absorbent to prevent conception. Rabbi Abaye suggests that a proselyte to Israel will also take contraceptive steps, so that she can be sure that her child is born after she has been received. Similarly, he indicates, a slave about to be freed will not want to conceive before her

---

[1] All these recipes are translated in Hildegard von Deines, Hermann Grapow, Wolfhart Westerndorf, *Uebersetzung der medizinischen Texte* (*Grundriss der Medizin der alten Aegypten* IV, Berlin, 1958), pp. 277–278.

[2] See Hermann Grapow, *Von der medizinischen Texte* (*Grundriss der Medizin der alten Aegypten* II, Berlin, 1955), pp. 3–4.

[3] All the following references to books of the Talmud are to *The Babylonian Talmud*, translated into English under the editorship of Isidore Epstein, 35 vols. (London, 1935–1952).

freedom. A parallel passage in *Kethuboth* ("Marriage Contracts") 37a implies that a captured woman will use a contraceptive to prevent conception before she is sure of her future status. It is not definitely said that the proselyte, the slave, and the captive will, like the harlot, use "absorbents," though this may be implied. Abaye himself comments simply that "a woman playing the harlot turns over to prevent conception," that is, attempts to expel the semen by postcoital exercise. An absorbent of flax or hackled wool is also mentioned in the fourth-century Gemara on *Niddah* 45a, and its use as a pessary is indicated. *Niddah* 3a, in passing, refers to a discussion by Shammai, a rabbi of the second century B.C., of the problem of determining the time when menstruation begins for a woman using a contraceptive absorbent which soaks up the menstrual flow. Sterilization of some sort was also known: the Talmud mentions women who have been "split," in a context which does not explain the operation but indicates a sterilizing effect (*Yebamoth* 17a).

Another type of contraceptive measure referred to by the Talmud is "root potions." This is mentioned in *Shabbath* ("Sabbaths") 110a–110b, not as a contraceptive but as a cure for jaundice; it is incidentally noted that two thirds of a cup of this mixed with beer will sterilize, apparently permanently. The cup of roots is described by Rabbi Johanan ben Nappaha as a mixture of Alexandrian gum, liquid alum, and garden crocus. A smaller dosage of the same potion mixed with wine is said to have a fertilizing effect on a menstruant. *Yebamoth* 65b, in an express discussion of the moral duty of procreation, tells the story of Judith, the wife of Rabbi Hiyya (circa A.D. 330), who, troubled by difficulty in bearing twins, took a potion that made her sterile permanently. The Tosefta, a fifth-century compilation independent of the Talmud, refers to a "cup of roots" which, drunk, will make a man or woman sterile (*Yebamoth* 8:4).[4]

In short, the means of contraception known to the Jewish communities included not only coitus interruptus, but postcoital ejection, occlusive pessaries, sterilizing potions, and sterilizing surgery. The pessaries and potions seem to be of later date than coitus interruptus, and may reflect Hellenistic influence and the diaspora's encounter with the pagan world. Probably the effectiveness of these methods varied widely. Coitus interruptus was a sure means of contraception if the withdrawal was duly effected; the pessaries and the surgery could have worked; postcoital ejection had a chance of success.

The potions are the most difficult to evaluate. As they are a type of contraceptive which constantly recurs in this history, I will summarize here what can be guessed today as to their effectiveness. In the course of

[4] *The Tosefta According to Codex Vienna, with Variants from Codex Erfurt, Genizah Mss. and Editio Princeps* (Venice, 1521) (New York, 1955).

history over a hundred different plants have been reported to contain substances affecting human fertility. Reports of such plants come from every continent in the world. Some sixty of them have been identified, and tentative estimates made of their contraceptive properties. Some of the plants appear to have properties effecting temporary sterility, and would be true contraceptives. Others are abortifacients, disturbing implantation or gestation, although in some cases, taken in smaller amounts, these abortifacients might only affect conception.[5] The most successful instance of experimental tests of a "root potion" have been performed on a desert plant, *Lithospermum ruderale*, used by the Shoshone Indians of Nevada as a contraceptive. "Most investigations support the view that some orally active material is present in Lithospermum which causes a reduction of reproductive capacity." [6] Other tests in 1955 of the seed of the legume *Psoralea corylifolia* have shown it to have antifertility effects when used in the diet of adult female mice. *Polygonum hydropiper*, when administered as a dry powdered whole plant, temporarily impaired the fertility of male and female mice and produced sterility in female guinea pigs, apparently through effect on the gonadotropic functions of the pituitary.[7]

These experiments, of course, tell us nothing about the contraceptives so often described in the literature here investigated as "root potions," "herb potions," or merely "potions." But the experiments do show that contraception is possible by means of distilled or crushed plants. Without being able to determine accurately whether the potions used by a given society were effective, we can say that the use of plant potions to affect fertility was a rational method of trying to achieve temporary sterility.

GRECO-ROMAN INFORMATION

Turning from papyri preserved by chance and references interspersed in the moral argumentation of the rabbis, we may now consider certain works of a professedly technical character, which deal with contraception as a matter of scientific interest. These works are of two general kinds: books on the phenomena of nature, and books explicitly concentrating on medical topics. In the first group are two rather different books: Aristotle's *History of Animals,* and Pliny's *Natural History.* The first established Aristotle's reputation as an observer of biological phenomena, and from the fourth century B.C. until the seventeenth century was a highly regarded scientific work. The other, by Pliny the Elder (A.D. 23–79), contained a great garnering from other works, popular superstition,

[5] Henry de Laszlo and Paul S. Henshaw, "Plant Materials Used by Primitive Peoples to Affect Fertility," *Science* 119 (1954), 626.

[6] H. Jackson, "Antifertility Substances," *Pharmacological Reviews* 11 (1959), 151–152.

[7] *Ibid.*, pp. 152–153.

and the writer's own experience. It was the Roman world's best approximation to an encyclopedia of science.

In the second group, composed of books intended to impart medical information, the earliest are *The Nature of Women* and *Diseases of Women*. Both are anonymous products of what is conventionally designated as the school of Hippocrates, in the fifth century B.C.[8] A much later Greek authority is the *Materia medica* of Dioscorides of Cilicia, a collection of pharmaceutical information from earlier Greek sources, made about A.D. 75. Much of it is paralleled by Pliny.[9] Of far greater importance is the *Gynecology* of Soranos of Ephesus. Soranos, who practiced medicine in Rome between A.D. 98 and 138, was a physician with an excellent knowledge of past medical theories, and the most judicious authority on childbearing in the Roman epoch.[10] *Gynecology* is the principal fount of contraceptive information for the Empire, for the Arabs, and, through the Arabs, for medieval Europe. Later works are substantially dependent on Soranos and Dioscorides. Among them are the *Books for Eunapius* of Oribasios, and *Medicine*, by Aëtios of Amida.[11] These books exhibit the persistence of contraceptive information in the later Empire. Oribasios was a well-known doctor in mid-fourth-century Constantinople. Aëtios was the court physician of the Emperor Justinian (527–565) and a count of the Empire.

Potions are the first form of contraceptive mentioned by any of the classical writers, and the type most often mentioned. In the Hippocratic writings a potion is the only contraceptive described. It is a drink of *misy*, which could mean either a plant called a truffle or copper from Cyprus; the plant would seem more likely to have been effective, but later writers appear to understand the word as "copper." It is clearly distinguished from an abortifacient. It is also clearly intended to achieve only temporary sterility: it is said to be effective for one year (*The Nature of Women* 93; cf. *Diseases of Women* 1.102).

The first-century writers on pharmacology are familiar with a variety of contraceptive potions. Dioscorides lists the following: willow leaves in

[8] Hippocrates, *Oeuvres complètes*, ed. and trans. E. Littré (Paris, 1839–1861), vols. VII and VIII.

[9] Dioscorides, *Materia medica*, ed. C. G. Kuhn, *Medicorum graecorum opera* XXV (Leipzig, 1829). On the probable borrowings of Pliny and Dioscorides from a common source, see W. H. S. Jones's Introduction to vol. VI of the Loeb Classical Library edition of Pliny's *Natural History* (Cambridge, Mass., 1951), pp. xvii-xviii.

[10] On Soranos see J. H. Waszink, in his edition of Tertullian, *De anima* (Leiden, 1947), pp. 25*-30*. Citations are to the edition of Soranos by Johannes Ilberg in *Corpus medicorum graecorum* IV (Leipzig and Berlin, 1927). An English translation of the *Gynecology* has been made by Owsei Temkin (Baltimore, 1956). I have generally followed Temkin's translations of technical words.

[11] Oribasios, *Libri ad Eunapium*, ed. Joannes Raeder, *Corpus medicorum graecorum* VI, part 3 (Leipzig and Berlin, 1926); Aëtios of Amida, *Medicine*, ed. S. Zervos (Leipzig, 1901), book 16.

water (*Materia medica* 1.135);[12] the leaves of barrenwort (*Epimedium alpinum*), finely ground and taken in wine after menstruation (4.19); the roots of the brake, a fern (4.184); ostracite, a kind of clay, to be drunk for four days after menstruation (5.164). Besides these varieties, there are two whose use seems to have been suggested by an association of ideas between a sterile metal and sterility: iron rust and iron slag (5.93, 94). All of these potions are apparently intended as temporary sterilizers. Of the mixture based on leaves of barrenwort, Dioscorides says explicitly that it will work only for five days. There are potions which apparently will sterilize completely: barrenwort taken plain (4.19); asparagus (2.151); the bark of white poplar taken with the kidney of a mule (1.109); rennet of hare drunk for three days after menstruation (2.21). Pliny, interested though he is in pharmacopoeia, gives only one prescription for a contraceptive potion, and that cautiously: a drink of rue, which is also an abortifacient, is "said to impede generation" if boiled with rose oil and an ounce of aloes (*Natural History* 20.51.142–143).

Soranos deals with potions under the heading, "Ought One to Make Use of Abortifacients and Contraceptives, and How?" (*Gynecology* 1.19.60–63). He is far more selective than Dioscorides, admitting only three types: a mixture of panax sap, rue seed, and Cyrenaic sap coated with wax and drunk in wine; a mixture in wine of wallflower seed, myrtle, myrrh, and white pepper, to be drunk for three days; rocket seed and cow parsnip mixed in oxymel. He warns that "these medicines" — apparently designating thereby the several potions just described — "not only impede conception, but also destroy what is already conceived." He adds that they also cause a heavy head, indigestion, and vomiting.

Oribasios gives variants of the fern root and willow leaf potions in Dioscorides and adds another recipe of cabbage blossoms in wine. These drinks are to be taken after coitus (*Books for Eunapius* 4.114). The prescription of postcoital use suggests an intention to have the drinks work either as contraceptives or as abortifacients. Aëtios repeats the Cyrenaic sap potion of Soranos. Moreover, Cyrenaic sap in water and wine, drunk once a month, will prevent conception and cause menstruation. He recommends copper water in which iron has been extinguished, possibly because of his understanding of Hippocratic *misy*; it is to be used by women, especially after menstruation. A mixture of aloes, stock seed, ginger, pep-

---

[12] The association of willows with barrenness is ancient. In the *Odyssey* 10.510, Homer describes willows with an adjective that can be translated either as "fruit-losing" or "fruit-destroying." Aristotle declares that, unlike most living things, "the willow and the poplar bear no seed" (*The Generation of Animals* 1.18, 726a). A collection of classical authorities treating the willow as a symbol of barrenness or as a way of achieving infertility has been made by Hugo Rahner, S.J., "Der Weide als Symbol der Keuschheit in Antike und im Christentum," *Zeitschrift für katholische Theologie* 56 (1932), 231–246.

per, and saffron drunk after menstruation is also effective. Other plant potions are prescribed: poplar root, to be drunk once a month during menstruation; black ivy berries in water and wine after menstruation, as long as the woman wants to remain sterile; willow bark mixed with honey. A potion for men is also given: the burned testicles of castrated mules drunk with a willow potion (*Medicine* 16.17).

A second kind of contraceptive method familiar to the ancients was a blocking of the entrance of the sperm to the uterus. Describing the ways generation may be aided and the ways it may be impeded, Aristotle notes that, if the lips of the cervix are smooth, conception is difficult: "Wherefore, since if the parts be smooth conception is impeded, some anoint that part of the womb on which the seed falls with cedar oil, ointment of lead, or frankincense and olive oil." [13]

Dioscorides lists mixtures of peppermint juice or of sicklewort with honey as apparently effective pessaries (*Materia medica* 3.36, 136); he also speaks of the application of alum to the uterus (*ibid.* 5.122). Soranos is familiar with the use in the uterus of old olive oil, honey, juice of the balsam tree, or cedar gum, alone or together with white lead; also alum or galbanum with wine. Soft wool in the mouth of the uterus is also effective. He goes on to generalize on the contraceptive effect of any means which either astringently or occlusively results in closing the mouth of the womb, and adds that astringents can also affect the sperm by "extracting another fluid from it" (*Gynecology* 1.19.61). He lists varieties of these vaginal suppositories: wool soaked in pine bark and tanning sumac (*Rhus coriaria*) dissolved in wine; a mixture of cimolite and root of the panax; various mixtures of pomegranate and gallnut; moist alum and the inside of pomegranate rind applied with wool; pomegranate peel, gum, and oil of roses; pulp of dry figs and sodium carbonate (*ibid.* 1.19.62). Oribasios prescribes as a pessary only coronilla seed injected into the vagina (*Books for Eunapius* 4.114). Aëtios, following Soranos on this point, speaks of the pine bark, pomegranate, and fig pessaries. He declares that a mixture of pomegranate and gallnut works without fail (*Medicine* 16.17).

A third kind of contraceptive is salve or ointment to be applied to the male genitals. Either the ointment is believed to act as a spermicide, or it is intended to function, like the pessaries, to close the uterus on penetration into the vagina. One of the materials to be used is one used also as a pessary: cedar gum (Dioscorides, *Materia medica* 1.105; Pliny, *Natural History* 24.11.18). Oribasios speaks of the juice of hedysarum, a form of wild mint, for this purpose (*Books for Eunapius* 4.114). Aëtios recommends the use of alum, pomegranate, and gallnut triturated with vinegar or brine (*Medicine* 16.17).

[13] Aristotle, *History of Animals* 7.3, 583a.

In addition to these three chemical or mechanical ways of blocking conception, there was belief in a sterile period for women. The Hippocratic school had decided that the period most likely to be fertile occurred just after menstruation (*The Diseases of Women* 1.38). Soranos held that "the uterus, being congested at the time of menstruation, is well adapted for the evacuation of the blood which has flowed into it, but it is un-fitted for the reception and retention of the seed"; a few women may conceive while menstruating, but the menstrual period is not "the proper time as derived from scientific considerations." The time before menstruation was also unsuitable for conception because the uterus was already "receiving material," and so would have difficulty in receiving the seed. "The best time for fruitful intercouse is when menstruation is ending" (*Gynecology* 1.10.36). This mistaken fixing of the moments of high fertility was made a basis for contraceptive advice. Indeed, the first of the several contraceptive measures which Soranos prescribes is avoidance of "sexual intercourse at those periods which we said were suitable for conception" (*ibid.* 1.19.61). He was followed literally by Aëtios (*Medicine* 16.16).

Three types of contraceptive physical movement are mentioned by the ancient writers. Herodotus reports that Pisistratus, the sixth-century tyrant of Athens, "did not want to have children by his new wife and so had intercourse with her not according to custom" (*nomos*).[14] Either coitus interruptus or anal intercourse is meant. Lucretius notes the use of turning movements by prostitutes to avoid conception.[15] Soranos recommends that a woman hold her breath, then immediately rise, squat, sneeze, and wash; he suggests that she also drink some cold water (*Gynecology* 1.19.61). His formula seems to be based on a combination of hygienic experience and a belief held in ancient India that control of the breath is somehow related to control of the semen.[16] He was followed verbatim by Aëtios of Amida (*Medicine* 16.16).

Finally, there is the wearing of amulets possessing special properties. Dioscorides speaks of women wearing contraceptive amulets of asparagus or heliotrope (*Materia medica* 2.151, 4.190). Pliny, who loves a good story whether he believes it or not, says that he would recommend to women "who in their fecundity, teeming with children, need some such relief" the wearing of an amulet made from a certain kind of spider. Two worms are to be extracted from the spider, tied in a deerskin, and placed on one's person before sunrise; or so, he says, Caecilius told us in his *Commentar-*

[14] Herodotus, *History of the Persian Wars*, ed. and trans. A. D. Godley, Loeb Classical Library (Cambridge, Mass., 1922–1928), 1.61.1.
[15] Lucretius, *De rerum natura*, ed. C. Bailey (Oxford, 1921), 4.1269–1275.
[16] On the Indian beliefs see Mircea Eliade, *Yoga: Immortality and Freedom*, trans. Willard Trask (New York, 1958), pp. 53–56, 134, 247–249; on their antiquity see pp. 294–364.

ies (*Natural History* 29.27.85). Soranos scouts the use of amulets (*Gynecology* 1.19.63). But his firm opinion did not destroy popular trust in such purely magical means. As late as the sixth century, Aëtios recommends an array of amulets such as the tooth of a child, a worm from a marble quarry, and henbane seed diluted by mare's milk and carried in a stag's skin (*Medicine* 16.17).

The prevalence of amulets may suggest that no method could have been very good. The indiscriminate lumping of magical, doubtful, and probably effective methods in an author like Aëtios is remarkable. On the other hand, the Hippocratic writers and Aristotle are restrained and precise in what they recommend, and Soranos distinguishes clearly between the advantages of different methods. There is no reason to doubt that postcoital exercise and movement, various pessaries, and the ointment for male use all had some, if not invariable, success. What has been said of the Hebrew potions applies here: potions based on roots could have affected the pituitary gland. The most striking omission in the scientific works of Greco-Roman authors is coitus interruptus. Was this method too evident to need description or too unacceptable to be recommended? Its absence does emphasize that the main effort was to control fertility through the woman. Failure to describe it may, arguably, also reflect confidence in the techniques given as adequate.

Several other general characteristics of classical lore on contraception are relevant to the Christian reaction. Contraceptives were discriminated from abortifacients in theory. In practice it was difficult to distinguish between the abortive and contraceptive effects of some potions, and according to the most authoritative writer, Soranos, this difficulty attended every potion he would recommend. Use of the sterile period, precoital pessaries, postcoital exercise, and gum for the male genitals were all intended to work only contraceptively. All of the latter methods, however, did involve an attack on the sperm; even the sterile period was supposed to be sterile because the menstrual flow would affect the seed.

It is also germane to the Christian judgment that almost all the methods used were intended to achieve only temporary sterility. Only a few potions were apparently intended to sterilize permanently. The other potions and all the other means proposed were ways by which pregnancy might be postponed for a given time.

Finally, the close association of magic and contraceptives should be remarked. The herb potions were "rational" methods of achieving control of fertility in the sense that there could be a causal relation between the properties of the herbs and the consequences for the female reproductive system. But the herbs were the special resources of the magician. The homeopathic basis of a number of the potions — the sterile willow causes sterility, sterile iron causes sterility — is one of the oldest forms of magic.

The distinction we would make between amulets and potions was one which would occur only to a highly sophisticated writer like Soranos. In popular estimation the herbal potions seemed as mysterious and magical in their effect as any amulet.

PRACTICE

How widely was contraceptive information disseminated in the Empire? How much was contraception practiced? Actual testimony to the use of contraceptives is hard to find. The earliest record of practice outside of Genesis is Herodotus' account of Pisistratus. He avoided procreative intercourse "because he already had adolescent children and because the family of the Alcmeonids was said to be under a curse" (*History* 1.61.1). Apart from this hearsay report by a good historian, one must infer the extent of the practice from a number of factors which are open to different interpretations.

One possible limitation on the diffusion scarcely existed: most writers do not speak of any moral objection to the dissemination of contraceptive information. The Hippocratic oath rejecting the use of some forms of abortion is famous;[17] no similar pledge was made as to contraception. Aristotle, describing the contraceptive use of cedar oil in a biological work, might have found moral comment inappropriate; but he does approve of abortion as a way of preventing excess population (*Politics* 7.16, 1335b), so that presumably he did not object to less drastic techniques. In the *Republic*, Socrates in sketching a kind of pastoral paradise notes in passing that the inhabitants would not beget too many offspring "lest they fall into poverty or war" (Plato, *Republic* II, 372c). This light and glancing recognition of social reasons for avoiding conception does not amount to formal endorsement of contraception, but at least indicates that contraception would have been acceptable to Plato for reasons of state. Pliny in his book of popular science does not scruple to set out the contraceptive properties of plants, although he says it is "right" (*fas*) for him to recommend a contraceptive only for women already teeming with children (*Natural History* 29.27.85).

Soranos does show sensitivity to certain moral considerations. Discussing abortion, he says that some hold that abortion is never proper, others that abortion is not to be used to conceal the consequences of adultery or to maintain feminine beauty, but that it can be employed when birth is dangerous or is likely to be impeded by some physical condition in the mother. A parallel dispute exists over the issue of contraceptives. Soranos does not declare his own position except obliquely,

---

[17] *Oath*, in Hippocrates, *Medical Works*, vol. I, ed. and trans. W. H. S. Jones, Loeb Classical Library (Cambridge, Mass., 1957), p. 298.

who survived their name days, or two who lived three years, or one w
lived to the legal age of marriage (fourteen for a boy, twelve for a girl

The purpose of the law to stimulate reproduction in the more succe
ful members of society is emphasized by the intricate provisions on
rights of a patron against the estate of a person he had freed. Norma
the patron had the right to claim against the freedman's estate if
freedman died intestate or excluded him from the will. However, by
Lex Papia, if the freedman left 100,000 sesterces and one child, the mas
took only one-half; if two children, the master took only one-third;
three children, the master took nothing (Gaius, *Institutes* 3.41–42).
freedwoman had to leave four children to defeat the patron, and he s
took one-fifth (*ibid*. 3.44). The daughter of a patron succeeded to
rights against a freedman's estate only if she had three children (*ib*
3.46). It was debated whether the daughter's right prevailed against
freedman with four children (*ibid*. 3.47). If a woman freed a ma
she had some rights against his estate if she had two children, and fu
rights if she had three children (*ibid*. 3.50).

The "right of children" (*ius liberorum*) determining these privileg
is expressed generally as consisting in three children for a free woman, fo
children for a freedwoman (Gaius 1.145, 1.194). These moderate numbe
appear to constitute the most that Roman officials could expect. Pli
records as a minor prodigy a procession to the Capitol of a humble free
man from Fiesole, Gaius Crispinus Hilarus, with his 8 children, 27 grand
children, and 18 great grandchildren (*Natural History* 7.13.60). Crispin
was apparently chosen out of all Italy as an astonishing example c
fecundity, and his children do not seem to have maintained the pace
at least in terms of surviving offspring. Despite legislation and propaganc
such as this honoring of a fertile patriarch, three children constitute
a large family.

The purpose of marriage, according to Roman law, was the procreatio
of children; government officials praised procreation as a civic duty; th
Stoics saw it as a moral purpose; but, unlike the Hebrews, the ordinar
upper-class Romans were not convinced that many children were among

[22] Ulpian, *Tituli XXVIII* 16.1, 17.2, and 18, *FIRA* II, 278–280.
The law was suspended in particular cases by the emperor's conceding to a
childless or unmarried man" the right of "parents with three children" (see, e.g.,
ny, *Epistles* 10.95). The law also applied in different ways in parts of the Empire.
us a papyrus from Egypt of about A.D. 150–161, the code of regulations of the
ologus, the chief financial minister in Egypt for the emperor, provides that any
eritance of an unmarried man over sixty is confiscated and that Romans who are
married and childless and own property worth more than 100,000 sesterces also
not inherit. If they have less, they inherit (*Code of the Idiologus*, secs. 27 and
The code adds, "If a woman is fifty years of age, she does not inherit; if she is
nger and has three children, she inherits; if a freedwoman has four children, she
rits" (secs. 33–38). (*FIRA* I, 474–475.)

by saying that contraception is surer than abortion (*Gynecology* 1.19.60–61). Some physicians may have taken an ethical stand against any use of contraceptives; others probably followed the ideal of not prescribing contraceptives in aid of criminal or frivolous purposes. Yet the sense of responsibility in Soranos, who was strongly influenced by Stoicism, may not have been typical. Other doctors must have known no restraints.

In the Christian era of the Empire, there seems to have been no new inhibition to the dissemination of contraceptive techniques.[18] Oribasios was suspect in religion, a friend of that emperor Julian to whom his excoreligionists gave the epithet "the Apostate"; his writing on contraception could be treated as typical only of the pagans who remained. But Aëtios was a physician at the court of Justinian, the foremost Christian lawgiver of the Empire. Somewhat more explicitly than Soranos, it is true, Aëtios does introduce his discussion of contraceptives by speaking of cases in which pregnancy is dangerous or birth difficult, so that "for these women it is preferable that they should not become pregnant." This word of explanation given, he seems to have no reservation about listing contraceptive means. He does not retain the remark of Soranos that some consider their use to be never permissible.

Physicians, then, throughout the life of the Empire could obtain information on contraception, and probably felt free to impart it if the medical indications made prevention of pregnancy advisable. Economic or social reasons for preventing conception are not discussed by the medical writers; doubtless different ethical judgments existed as to the propriety of contraception on such grounds. How widely the medical information was disseminated is a matter of conjecture. Apothecaries would have known Dioscorides. The small literate class would often enough have had access to manuscripts of Aristotle and Pliny. The impression remains that knowledge of the variety of precise techniques described in the works just reviewed would have been the prerogative of the rich.[19] Others would have had to depend on information passed by word of mouth, folk custom, and popular superstition. Some of the methods used were well adapted to this kind of transmission. If a slave of the Hebrews could use a

[18] The leaders of the Western Church seem to have had the greatest regard for Soranos. Tertullian draws on his treatise *The Soul* to write his own treatise; see, e.g., Tertullian, *De anima* 6.6 (Waszink ed., p. 8), and the examination of Tertullian's borrowings from Soranos by Waszink, pp. 30*–39*. Augustine quotes an anecdote about Soranos, describing him as "medicinae auctor nobilissimus" (*Against Julian* 5.14.51, *PL* 44:813).
[19] The poor abandon their children; rich women "deny their own fetus in their uterus and by parricidal potions extinguish the pledges of their womb in their genital belly," says St. Ambrose in the fourth century (*Hexaemeron* 5.18.58, *CSEL* 32¹:184). By those potions he definitely means abortifacients and probably includes contraceptives. At a minimum, his statement supports what might otherwise be guessed, that the potions, costing money, would be the prerogative of those able to afford them.

wool pessary, such a simple expedient may have been used by many women in the classical world. Coitus interruptus was a method requiring only moderate sophistication to adopt. It was a method at least suggested to anyone familiar with the Old Testament. The concern of the Talmud with coitus interruptus — a concern unparalleled in the preceding centuries of Jewish history — suggests that the Jews were faced with its practice in the diaspora, in the Roman world. The methods of prostitutes must have been widely known, and concubinage with slaves must have both promoted the use of contraception and spread the knowledge of contraceptive techniques.

The availability of contraceptive information, then, while conjectural, is probable for many persons. Apart from the four kinds of users described by Soranos, and the motives described by Herodotus, who would want to use this information? Consider, first, the slaves who made up a substantial part of the Empire's population. Here there is no hard evidence, and one is left to speculation. It may be that the conditions of slavery created a psychology unfavorable to the bearing of children. Denied legal recognition of any marriage, and knowing that their children would be born into slavery too, many slaves must have refused to bring offspring into their unhappy world. It has, indeed, been argued that one unspoken reason for the later transition to serfdom was that serfs were more likely to reproduce themselves. Opposed to this speculation is the guess that parenthood might have an increased psychological value to some slaves, as it does to some poor people today. Moreover, a kind of psychological sophistication is required to take steps to prevent procreation from occurring. Further, slaves from the Hellenistic part of the Mediterranean world were often men of some education as well as business talent and did not lead miserable lives. Many of them were emancipated by their owners for one reason or another; the laws *Aelia Sentia* and *Fufia Caninia* of Augustus were necessary to regulate these manumissions. Calixtus, the pope who was to have a part in the first controversy over contraception, is probably a fair example of the kind of entrepreneurial slave who could achieve freedom in the empire. Whether the absence of freedom affected the desire for self-perpetuation in these educated and enterprising men more or less seriously than in the drawers of water taken from Gaul and Iberia must be a matter of speculation. It seems reasonable, however, to conclude that to want a large number of children in a slave existence would at least be an unlikely desire, and that slaves would often have had motives for practicing contraception.[20]

At the other end of society, as early as the first century the legislation of

[20] The speculation that the slaves did not reproduce themselves has been most strongly urged by Adolphe Landry, "La Dépopulation dans l'antiquité," *Revue historique* 177 (1936), 1, 5. A modern sociologist speculates in much the same way, with a little hard evidence, that slave conditions in the American South led to an aversion

Augustus reflected concern with a falling birth rate in the upper class Two enactments, the *Lex Julia de maritandis ordinibus* of 18 B.C. an the *Lex Papia Poppaea* of A.D. 9 (usually referred to jointly as the *L Julia et Papia*), represent an earnest, if mild, effort to stimulate birt among the governing group by a system of modest rewards and penalt By this legislation the childless were disqualified from holding cer high offices, such as praetorships or provincial governorships. These p sions were circumvented by arranged adoptions, but the Senate legis against this abuse in 62.[21] Secondly, the *Lex Julia et Papia* denie right of inheritance to an unmarried male over twenty-five and married female over twenty. It further provided that a childless person could only take one-half of what was willed him. These pr were not very stringent, as inheritance from ascendants or desc within three degrees was excepted, at least by interpretation of The legislation bore most heavily on inheritances between spo couple were childless, and the husband between 25 and 60 and between 20 and 50, either could inherit only one-tenth of the p his spouse. Exceptions were made for spouses related to each o six degrees of kindred, and immunity could be obtained fro peror: the exceptions suggest that the law had enough bite ingenuity to work to soften its effect. Another exemption high infant mortality: the couple is immune if they bore t

to childbearing and to careless killing of infants by parents who had (Melville J. Herskovits, *The Myth of the Negro Past*, New York, 194

On the other hand, in the somewhat more humane conditions of t American Negro population increased considerably over the number slave trade (Robert R. Kuczynski, *Population Movements*, Oxfor Marcel R. Reinhard, *Histoire de la population mondiale de 1700 à* p. 346). There is no law that slave populations must decrease. O mission policy and on the large number of children of slaves wh men, see Tenney Frank, "Race Mixture in the Roman Empire," *Review* 21 (1911), 698–699. The laws *Aelia Sentia* and *Fuf* Gaius, *Institutes* 1.18, 42–47, in vol. II of *Fontes iuris romani an* tore Riccobono et al. (Florence, 1941–1943), hereafter cited

As far as the slaveowners were concerned, it is argued pregnancy meant interruption of work, and, because of partic infant mortality among slaves must have been even higher rate. Moreover, child-raising meant expense. Thus, if slaves by conquest, economic considerations were against breedir business. On the other hand, a healthy slave child was a weighing the cost in underemployment of his mother, and t his value by giving the owner a right to damages if he v One small piece of evidence on slaveowner attitudes in a when Rome was very weak is a sermon of Caesarius of slaveowner would be shocked at her slaves' using con *CC* 103:196).

[21] Tacitus, *Annals* 15.19. The law also apparently barre public celebrations. See the decree of the Senate in 17 the secular games, *FIRA* I, 273–274. How such a law not very clear.

the marks of a happy union.[23] Tacitus, writing about A.D. 116, reports that Augustus' laws failed to increase marriages and the rearing of children: "childlessness prevailed" (*Annals* 3.25). This statement by a Roman official, very well informed albeit at times tendentious, must carry considerable weight, written as it is in a context where he is objecting to the informers spawned by the financial penalties of the laws. Pliny the Younger, in a letter of about A.D. 100 seeking political support for the son of a friend, Asinius Rufus, notes as one of the father's merits that he has fulfilled the function of a good citizen in having "several children," and this "in an age when even one child is thought a burden preventing the rewards of childlessness" (*Letters* 4.15).[24] The implication here is that the adulation and financial benefits to be expected by a childless person from those hoping to be his heirs outweigh the light penalties of the Augustan laws.

Later amendments of and commentary on the *Lex Julia et Papia* continue to reflect a modest standard for fertility. Hadrian gives a right of inheritance from her children to a woman who has the *ius liberorum*, that is, who has borne three children (*Institutes* 3.3.2).[25] The jurist Paul teaches that under the law a freedman is relieved from rendering services or gifts he had promised to give his patron in consideration of his freedom, if he becomes the parent of two children (*Digest* 38.1.37). The Emperor Severus decrees in 203 that one may be excused from the onerous duty of being a guardian or curator by having a certain number of children: three in Rome, four in the rest of Italy, five in the provinces (*Codex* 5.66.1). The differing standard arguably reflects Roman favoritism rather than higher provincial fertility; by modern standards even the provincials are not expected to raise big families to win the exemption.

The birth rate of the aristocracy was a concern for the government in the first century.[26] In the second century serious plagues, such as that of

[23] Gordon Williams, "Some Aspects of Roman Marriage Ceremonies and Ideals," *Journal of Roman Studies* 48 (1958), 16, 28.

[24] C. Plinius Caecilius Secundus, *Epistularum libri decem*, ed. R. A. B. Mynors (Oxford, 1963).

[25] References to the *Corpus juris civilis* are as follows: *Institutiones*, ed. Paul Krueger; *Digesta*, ed. Theodor Mommsen and Paul Krueger; *Codex*, ed. Paul Krueger (16th ed., Berlin, 1954).

[26] Arthur E. R. Boak, *Manpower Shortage and the Fall of the Roman Empire in the West* (Ann Arbor, 1955), pp. 15, 113. Jerome Carcopino says childlessness had increased by the end of the first century (*Daily Life in Ancient Rome*, trans. E. O. Lorimer, New Haven, 1940, p. 90). A study of the *Corpus of Latin Inscriptions* shows what the author calls "a startling inability" of first-century noble families to perpetuate themselves (Frank, "Race Mixture," p. 704). One classicist, Fritz Schulz, very sweepingly attributes the "catastrophic" decline of the Roman nobility in the last century B.C. and the similar decline of the new aristocracy to "birth-control in the form of the 'one or two child families'" (*Classical Roman Law*, Oxford, 1951, p. 106). Schulz offers no direct evidence for this statement; he refers to the 1949 *Report of the Royal Commission on Population* on the effect of birth control in modern England.

166–180, and a variety of wars adversely affected the population. If the recruitment of the barbarians to fill the army, a policy begun under Hadrian, is ambiguous evidence of depopulation, it is at least some index that the population was not generating any surplus. In the third century the towns of the empire in the West began to decline, even in Britain. By the fourth century there is a considerable decline in the cultivation of land in Italy and Africa, and the settlement of the barbarians as *coloni* within the empire is again evidence of at least a failure of the Empire's population to grow. A main factor in the population problem was the low life expectancy. Using the fragmentary and limited data provided by Latin inscriptions chiefly in Africa and the Danubian provinces, it has been calculated that female mortality was significantly higher than male mortality, and that many women did not live through childbearing age. It has further been calculated that in Roman Africa, adult mortality "approximated to that of rural China, early twentieth century India, or a Victorian slum"; and that infant mortality "was of the order perhaps of 200 to 250 per 1000." On the Danubian frontier or among the slaves at Carthage, adult mortality was proportionally worse.[27] As to other factors affecting the population, it is difficult, if not now impossible, to determine whether other factors such as diet, health, and genetic mutation also played a part. Yet with allowance made for all other causes, it is not unreasonable to conclude that the fall in population was also due to, and therefore evidence of, the deliberate avoidance of conception and childbearing. Certainly the special concern directed to conscious control of the birth rate of the governing class reflected contemporary recognition that the problem was not simply the result of wars or plagues.[28]

The want of men produced a crisis. Each child was valued as a citizen "born for the state" (*Digest* 37.9.1.15). Yet the Empire in its first three

[27] A. R. Burn, "Hic Breve Vivitur," *Past and Present* 4 (1953), 9.

[28] In *Manpower Shortage and the Fall of the Roman Empire,* Arthur Boak argued that depopulation was evident in the Empire by the second century (p. 11). His arguments were sharply criticized in a review by M. I. Finley, *Journal of Roman Studies* 48 (1958), 156–162, who pointed out that all Boak had shown was a shortage of men in given jobs which the government wanted filled, not necessarily an absolute population shortage. In particular, he noted that there are policy reasons besides population shortage for building an army of aliens. Finley did not deny that the population of the Western empire declined in the third century (*ibid.,* p. 162). A. E. H. Jones, in his review of Boak, also agreed that a decline occurred in the third century and that an acute labor shortage was clear in the fourth century, by which time taxation did not leave the peasants means enough to rear many children (review in *English Historical Review,* 2nd series, 9 (1957), 380–381).

On depopulation of towns in England, see R. G. Collingwood and J. A. L. Myres, *Roman Britain and the English Settlements,* 2nd ed. (London, 1937), p. 180. On depopulation in the West in the fourth century, see the texts cited by Dudden, *The Life and Times of St. Ambrose* (Oxford, 1935), I, 96, and the general evaluation by Adolphe Landry, *Traité de démographie* (Paris, 1945), p. 50.

centuries did nothing to check infanticide or the abandonment of children by their parents. Unwilling or unable to interfere in family life, the government's main recourse was the positive encouragement of the *Lex Julia et Papia*. With this view of the possibilities of official action dominant, it is a remarkable indication of the problem created by abortion and by contraception that any laws were enacted which had some relation to those practices.

The background for the law lies in the association of potions of contraception and magic. There are traces of this association in earlier Roman law. Writing in the second part of the first century, Plutarch said that Romulus in his original laws for Rome had enacted "a severe law" permitting a husband to divorce his wife, not only for adultery, but for "medicine in regard to children." Plutarch's testimony need not be accepted literally. He was a moralist with a strong desire to encourage a better attitude toward parenthood, as his *Affection Toward Children* shows. But he may have been familiar with a Roman tradition along these lines. It is hypothesized, too, that the *Twelve Tables* of ancient Rome had a provision forbidding administration of "medicine," for Gaius in his commentary on the *Twelve Tables* qualifies the term (*Digest* 50.16.326).[29] In both the tradition preserved by Plutarch and in Gaius the key word is "medicine" — in Greek *pharmakeia*, in Latin *veneficium*. In both languages the term means use of "magic" or "drugs." The ambiguity of the term, which is preserved in each language although different roots form the words, is deliberate, and reflects the attitude of Greco-Roman culture. Drugs are intimately associated by this culture with magic; the users of Greek or Latin see no need to have two words to differentiate magic and the drugs. The ambiguity of the term, then, is inherent. A univocal translation suppresses one of the two meanings suggested by the word in most contexts. I adopt the suggestion advanced by Clyde Pharr that the English term which best preserves the ambiguity is "medicine" used in the sense in which a North American Indian medicine man makes medicine.[30] The term "medicine" in respect to children primarily designates abortifacients. But the definition by Gaius of *venena* or *medicamenta*, preserved in Justinian's *Digest*, describes "medicine" as "that which when employed changes the nature of that to which it is employed" (*Digest* 50.16.236). Probably contraceptive drugs fall

[29] Plutarch, *Romulus* 22 in *Parallel Lives*, law set out in "Leges regiae: Romulus" 1.9, *FIRA* I, 8; Gaius, *On the Twelve Tables*, set out in "XII Tabulae" 8.25, *FIRA* I, 63. Plutarch's "Affection for Offspring" is in the Loeb Classical Library *Moralia*, vol. VI, ed. and trans. W. C. Helmbold (Cambridge, Mass., 1939), pp. 331–357.

[30] In general, I here follow Clyde Pharr, "The Interdiction of Magic in Roman Law," *Transactions and Proceedings of the American Philological Association* 63 (1932), 272–273.

within this broad definition and within the intention of the ancient law-makers to prevent a woman from affecting her fertility without her husband's consent.

By the third century the ancient law described by Plutarch was no longer relevant to divorce, and the exact scope of the fragments surviving from the Twelve Tables is not clear. By this time the chief legal usage of "medicine" was in the Cornelian Law providing capital punishment for assassins and medicine men (*veneficii*), enacted under Sulla in 81 B.C. but still basic criminal legislation. Commenting on the law, Marcian, a third-century jurist, noted that drugs (*medicamenta*) are of different kinds. Sometimes they are used to cure; sometimes they are used to produce love; these uses are not condemned by the statute.[31] Sometimes they are used to kill a man. It is this use of these evil drugs which the statute forbids. As Marcian expounds the law in force in his day it is not directed to the protection of infant life; in Roman law a fetus was not a man (*Digest* 25.4.1.1; 35.2.9.1) and so its destruction would not be within the law, which is directed only at the deliberate killing of a man by weapon or drug.

Within the law, however, according to Marcian, is the irresponsible sale of hemlock, salamander, wolfsbane, pine-caterpillars, hare's ear, mandrake, and Spanish fly. It is inferable that these are regulated only because they may be dangerous to life, as we know that wolfsbane, salamander, and Spanish fly were so regarded (Pliny, *Natural History* 27.2.4; 29.23.74; 29.30.93). To this point, the law as it stands in the early third century seems to have nothing to do with abortion or contraception. But Marcian adds, "By a decree of the Senate, exile to the islands is provided for her who, not with a bad intention, but giving a bad example, gives a medicine for conception (*ad conceptionem*) as a result of which the woman receiving the medicine dies." The usual interpretation of this text is that the medicine in question is meant to aid conception, that it is a potion for fecundity.[32] This interpretation assumes that conception would be desired. But conception could also be undesired. The phrase *ad conceptionem* can be interpreted to mean a "medicine for conception,"

---

[31] "Potions of love" and "love drink" were not euphemisms for contraceptives. For a typical list of these herbal aphrodisiacs with magical properties see Ovid, *Ars amatoria*, ed. E. J. Kenney (Oxford, 1961), vol. II, lines 415–423.

[32] E.g., Theodor Mommsen, *Römisches Strafrecht* (Leipzig, 1899), p. 637: "Mitteln gegen die Unfruchtbarkeit"; *The Civil Law*, trans. S. P. Scott (Cincinnati, 1932), IX, 60: "producing conception." The text reads: "Sed ex Senatus consulto relegari iussa est ea, quae non quidem malo animo, sed malo exemplo medicamentum ad conceptionem dedit, ex quo ea, quae acceperat, decesserit" (*Digest* 48.8.3).
There is possibly a parallel reference to this criminal law in the civil law. Under the *Lex Aquilia* giving an action for damages for various injuries, a midwife was liable if a woman died to whom she had applied (*supposuit*) a drug (*medicamentum*) with her own hands (*Digest* 9.2.9, Ulpian citing Labeo). It would seem again that the medicine could have been either to aid conception or to prevent it.

by saying that contraception is surer than abortion (*Gynecology* 1.19.60–61). Some physicians may have taken an ethical stand against any use of contraceptives; others probably followed the ideal of not prescribing contraceptives in aid of criminal or frivolous purposes. Yet the sense of responsibility in Soranos, who was strongly influenced by Stoicism, may not have been typical. Other doctors must have known no restraints.

In the Christian era of the Empire, there seems to have been no new inhibition to the dissemination of contraceptive techniques.[18] Oribasios was suspect in religion, a friend of that emperor Julian to whom his ex-coreligionists gave the epithet "the Apostate"; his writing on contraception could be treated as typical only of the pagans who remained. But Aëtios was a physician at the court of Justinian, the foremost Christian lawgiver of the Empire. Somewhat more explicitly than Soranos, it is true, Aëtios does introduce his discussion of contraceptives by speaking of cases in which pregnancy is dangerous or birth difficult, so that "for these women it is preferable that they should not become pregnant." This word of explanation given, he seems to have no reservation about listing contraceptive means. He does not retain the remark of Soranos that some consider their use to be never permissible.

Physicians, then, throughout the life of the Empire could obtain information on contraception, and probably felt free to impart it if the medical indications made prevention of pregnancy advisable. Economic or social reasons for preventing conception are not discussed by the medical writers; doubtless different ethical judgments existed as to the propriety of contraception on such grounds. How widely the medical information was disseminated is a matter of conjecture. Apothecaries would have known Dioscorides. The small literate class would often enough have had access to manuscripts of Aristotle and Pliny. The impression remains that knowledge of the variety of precise techniques described in the works just reviewed would have been the prerogative of the rich.[19] Others would have had to depend on information passed by word of mouth, folk custom, and popular superstition. Some of the methods used were well adapted to this kind of transmission. If a slave of the Hebrews could use a

[18] The leaders of the Western Church seem to have had the greatest regard for Soranos. Tertullian draws on his treatise *The Soul* to write his own treatise; see, e.g., Tertullian, *De anima* 6.6 (Waszink ed., p. 8), and the examination of Tertullian's borrowings from Soranos by Waszink, pp. 30*–39*. Augustine quotes an anecdote about Soranos, describing him as "medicinae auctor nobilissimus" (*Against Julian* 5.14.51, *PL* 44:813).

[19] The poor abandon their children; rich women "deny their own fetus in their uterus and by parricidal potions extinguish the pledges of their womb in their genital belly," says St. Ambrose in the fourth century (*Hexaemeron* 5.18.58, *CSEL* 32^1:184). By those potions he definitely means abortifacients and probably includes contraceptives. At a minimum, his statement supports what might otherwise be guessed, that the potions, costing money, would be the prerogative of those able to afford them.

wool pessary, such a simple expedient may have been used by many women in the classical world. Coitus interruptus was a method requiring only moderate sophistication to adopt. It was a method at least suggested to anyone familiar with the Old Testament. The concern of the Talmud with coitus interruptus — a concern unparalleled in the preceding centuries of Jewish history — suggests that the Jews were faced with its practice in the diaspora, in the Roman world. The methods of prostitutes must have been widely known, and concubinage with slaves must have both promoted the use of contraception and spread the knowledge of contraceptive techniques.

The availability of contraceptive information, then, while conjectural, is probable for many persons. Apart from the four kinds of users described by Soranos, and the motives described by Herodotus, who would want to use this information? Consider, first, the slaves who made up a substantial part of the Empire's population. Here there is no hard evidence, and one is left to speculation. It may be that the conditions of slavery created a psychology unfavorable to the bearing of children. Denied legal recognition of any marriage, and knowing that their children would be born into slavery too, many slaves must have refused to bring offspring into their unhappy world. It has, indeed, been argued that one unspoken reason for the later transition to serfdom was that serfs were more likely to reproduce themselves. Opposed to this speculation is the guess that parenthood might have an increased psychological value to some slaves, as it does to some poor people today. Moreover, a kind of psychological sophistication is required to take steps to prevent procreation from occurring. Further, slaves from the Hellenistic part of the Mediterranean world were often men of some education as well as business talent and did not lead miserable lives. Many of them were emancipated by their owners for one reason or another; the laws *Aelia Sentia* and *Fufia Caninia* of Augustus were necessary to regulate these manumissions. Calixtus, the pope who was to have a part in the first controversy over contraception, is probably a fair example of the kind of entrepreneurial slave who could achieve freedom in the empire. Whether the absence of freedom affected the desire for self-perpetuation in these educated and enterprising men more or less seriously than in the drawers of water taken from Gaul and Iberia must be a matter of speculation. It seems reasonable, however, to conclude that to want a large number of children in a slave existence would at least be an unlikely desire, and that slaves would often have had motives for practicing contraception.[20]

At the other end of society, as early as the first century the legislation of

[20] The speculation that the slaves did not reproduce themselves has been most strongly urged by Adolphe Landry, "La Dépopulation dans l'antiquité," *Revue historique* 177 (1936), 1, 5. A modern sociologist speculates in much the same way, with a little hard evidence, that slave conditions in the American South led to an aversion

Augustus reflected concern with a falling birth rate in the upper class. Two enactments, the *Lex Julia de maritandis ordinibus* of 18 B.C. and the *Lex Papia Poppaea* of A.D. 9 (usually referred to jointly as the *Lex Julia et Papia*), represent an earnest, if mild, effort to stimulate births among the governing group by a system of modest rewards and penalties. By this legislation the childless were disqualified from holding certain high offices, such as praetorships or provincial governorships. These provisions were circumvented by arranged adoptions, but the Senate legislated against this abuse in 62.[21] Secondly, the *Lex Julia et Papia* denied the right of inheritance to an unmarried male over twenty-five and an unmarried female over twenty. It further provided that a childless married person could only take one-half of what was willed him. These provisions were not very stringent, as inheritance from ascendants or descendants within three degrees was excepted, at least by interpretation of the law. The legislation bore most heavily on inheritances between spouses. If a couple were childless, and the husband between 25 and 60 and the wife between 20 and 50, either could inherit only one-tenth of the property of his spouse. Exceptions were made for spouses related to each other within six degrees of kindred, and immunity could be obtained from the emperor: the exceptions suggest that the law had enough bite to put legal ingenuity to work to soften its effect. Another exemption suggests the high infant mortality: the couple is immune if they bore three children

to childbearing and to careless killing of infants by parents who had not desired them (Melville J. Herskovits, *The Myth of the Negro Past*, New York, 1941, p. 103).

On the other hand, in the somewhat more humane conditions of the Old South, the American Negro population increased considerably over the number brought in by the slave trade (Robert R. Kuczynski, *Population Movements*, Oxford, 1936, pp. 6–7; Marcel R. Reinhard, *Histoire de la population mondiale de 1700 à 1948*, Paris, 1949, p. 346). There is no law that slave populations must decrease. On the liberal manumission policy and on the large number of children of slaves who had become free men, see Tenney Frank, "Race Mixture in the Roman Empire," *American Historical Review* 21 (1911), 698–699. The laws *Aelia Sentia* and *Fufia Caninia* appear in Gaius, *Institutes* 1.18, 42–47, in vol. II of *Fontes iuris romani anteiustiniani*, ed. Salvatore Riccobono et al. (Florence, 1941–1943), hereafter cited as *FIRA*.

As far as the slaveowners were concerned, it is argued by Landry that slave pregnancy meant interruption of work, and, because of particularly inadequate care, infant mortality among slaves must have been even higher than the high general rate. Moreover, child-raising meant expense. Thus, if slaves were easily obtainable by conquest, economic considerations were against breeding them as a deliberate business. On the other hand, a healthy slave child was a valuable possession, outweighing the cost in underemployment of his mother, and the *Lex Aquilia* recognized his value by giving the owner a right to damages if he were injured (*Digest* 9.2). One small piece of evidence on slaveowner attitudes in a period late in the Empire when Rome was very weak is a sermon of Caesarius of Arles. He suggests that a slaveowner would be shocked at her slaves' using contraceptives (*Sermons* 44.2, *CC* 103:196).

[21] Tacitus, *Annals* 15.19. The law also apparently barred the unmarried from certain public celebrations. See the decree of the Senate in 17 B.C. modifying this rule for the secular games, *FIRA* I, 273–274. How such a law could have been enforced is not very clear.

who survived their name days, or two who lived three years, or one who lived to the legal age of marriage (fourteen for a boy, twelve for a girl).[22]

The purpose of the law to stimulate reproduction in the more successful members of society is emphasized by the intricate provisions on the rights of a patron against the estate of a person he had freed. Normally the patron had the right to claim against the freedman's estate if the freedman died intestate or excluded him from the will. However, by the *Lex Papia*, if the freedman left 100,000 sesterces and one child, the master took only one-half; if two children, the master took only one-third; if three children, the master took nothing (Gaius, *Institutes* 3.41–42). A freedwoman had to leave four children to defeat the patron, and he still took one-fifth (*ibid.* 3.44). The daughter of a patron succeeded to his rights against a freedman's estate only if she had three children (*ibid.* 3.46). It was debated whether the daughter's right prevailed against a freedwoman with four children (*ibid.* 3.47). If a woman freed a man, she had some rights against his estate if she had two children, and full rights if she had three children (*ibid.* 3.50).

The "right of children" (*ius liberorum*) determining these privileges is expressed generally as consisting in three children for a free woman, four children for a freedwoman (Gaius 1.145, 1.194). These moderate numbers appear to constitute the most that Roman officials could expect. Pliny records as a minor prodigy a procession to the Capitol of a humble freedman from Fiesole, Gaius Crispinus Hilarus, with his 8 children, 27 grandchildren, and 18 great grandchildren (*Natural History* 7.13.60). Crispinus was apparently chosen out of all Italy as an astonishing example of fecundity, and his children do not seem to have maintained the pace, at least in terms of surviving offspring. Despite legislation and propaganda such as this honoring of a fertile patriarch, three children constituted a large family.

The purpose of marriage, according to Roman law, was the procreation of children; government officials praised procreation as a civic duty; the Stoics saw it as a moral purpose; but, unlike the Hebrews, the ordinary upper-class Romans were not convinced that many children were among

---

[22] Ulpian, *Tituli XXVIII* 16.1, 17.2, and 18, *FIRA* II, 278–280.

The law was suspended in particular cases by the emperor's conceding to a "childless or unmarried man" the right of "parents with three children" (see, e.g., Pliny, *Epistles* 10.95). The law also applied in different ways in parts of the Empire. Thus a papyrus from Egypt of about A.D. 150–161, the code of regulations of the *idiologus*, the chief financial minister in Egypt for the emperor, provides that any inheritance of an unmarried man over sixty is confiscated and that Romans who are unmarried and childless and own property worth more than 100,000 sesterces also do not inherit. If they have less, they inherit (*Code of the Idiologus*, secs. 27 and 32). The code adds, "If a woman is fifty years of age, she does not inherit; if she is younger and has three children, she inherits; if a freedwoman has four children, she inherits" (secs. 33–38). (*FIRA* I, 474–475.)

the marks of a happy union.[23] Tacitus, writing about A.D. 116, reports that Augustus' laws failed to increase marriages and the rearing of children: "childlessness prevailed" (*Annals* 3.25). This statement by a Roman official, very well informed albeit at times tendentious, must carry considerable weight, written as it is in a context where he is objecting to the informers spawned by the financial penalties of the laws. Pliny the Younger, in a letter of about A.D. 100 seeking political support for the son of a friend, Asinius Rufus, notes as one of the father's merits that he has fulfilled the function of a good citizen in having "several children," and this "in an age when even one child is thought a burden preventing the rewards of childlessness" (*Letters* 4.15).[24] The implication here is that the adulation and financial benefits to be expected by a childless person from those hoping to be his heirs outweigh the light penalties of the Augustan laws.

Later amendments of and commentary on the *Lex Julia et Papia* continue to reflect a modest standard for fertility. Hadrian gives a right of inheritance from her children to a woman who has the *ius liberorum*, that is, who has borne three children (*Institutes* 3.3.2).[25] The jurist Paul teaches that under the law a freedman is relieved from rendering services or gifts he had promised to give his patron in consideration of his freedom, if he becomes the parent of two children (*Digest* 38.1.37). The Emperor Severus decrees in 203 that one may be excused from the onerous duty of being a guardian or curator by having a certain number of children: three in Rome, four in the rest of Italy, five in the provinces (*Codex* 5.66.1). The differing standard arguably reflects Roman favoritism rather than higher provincial fertility; by modern standards even the provincials are not expected to raise big families to win the exemption.

The birth rate of the aristocracy was a concern for the government in the first century.[26] In the second century serious plagues, such as that of

[23] Gordon Williams, "Some Aspects of Roman Marriage Ceremonies and Ideals," *Journal of Roman Studies* 48 (1958), 16, 28.

[24] C. Plinius Caecilius Secundus, *Epistularum libri decem*, ed. R. A. B. Mynors (Oxford, 1963).

[25] References to the *Corpus juris civilis* are as follows: *Institutiones*, ed. Paul Krueger; *Digesta*, ed. Theodor Mommsen and Paul Krueger; *Codex*, ed. Paul Krueger (16th ed., Berlin, 1954).

[26] Arthur E. R. Boak, *Manpower Shortage and the Fall of the Roman Empire in the West* (Ann Arbor, 1955), pp. 15, 113. Jerome Carcopino says childlessness had increased by the end of the first century (*Daily Life in Ancient Rome*, trans. E. O. Lorimer, New Haven, 1940, p. 90). A study of the *Corpus of Latin Inscriptions* shows what the author calls "a startling inability" of first-century noble families to perpetuate themselves (Frank, "Race Mixture," p. 704). One classicist, Fritz Schulz, very sweepingly attributes the "catastrophic" decline of the Roman nobility in the last century B.C. and the similar decline of the new aristocracy to "birth-control in the form of the 'one or two child families'" (*Classical Roman Law*, Oxford, 1951, p. 106). Schulz offers no direct evidence for this statement; he refers to the 1949 *Report of the Royal Commission on Population* on the effect of birth control in modern England.

166–180, and a variety of wars adversely affected the population. If the recruitment of the barbarians to fill the army, a policy begun under Hadrian, is ambiguous evidence of depopulation, it is at least some index that the population was not generating any surplus. In the third century the towns of the empire in the West began to decline, even in Britain. By the fourth century there is a considerable decline in the cultivation of land in Italy and Africa, and the settlement of the barbarians as *coloni* within the empire is again evidence of at least a failure of the Empire's population to grow. A main factor in the population problem was the low life expectancy. Using the fragmentary and limited data provided by Latin inscriptions chiefly in Africa and the Danubian provinces, it has been calculated that female mortality was significantly higher than male mortality, and that many women did not live through childbearing age. It has further been calculated that in Roman Africa, adult mortality "approximated to that of rural China, early twentieth century India, or a Victorian slum"; and that infant mortality "was of the order perhaps of 200 to 250 per 1000." On the Danubian frontier or among the slaves at Carthage, adult mortality was proportionally worse.[27] As to other factors affecting the population, it is difficult, if not now impossible, to determine whether other factors such as diet, health, and genetic mutation also played a part. Yet with allowance made for all other causes, it is not unreasonable to conclude that the fall in population was also due to, and therefore evidence of, the deliberate avoidance of conception and childbearing. Certainly the special concern directed to conscious control of the birth rate of the governing class reflected contemporary recognition that the problem was not simply the result of wars or plagues.[28]

The want of men produced a crisis. Each child was valued as a citizen "born for the state" (*Digest* 37.9.1.15). Yet the Empire in its first three

[27] A. R. Burn, "Hic Breve Vivitur," *Past and Present* 4 (1953), 9.

[28] In *Manpower Shortage and the Fall of the Roman Empire*, Arthur Boak argued that depopulation was evident in the Empire by the second century (p. 11). His arguments were sharply criticized in a review by M. I. Finley, *Journal of Roman Studies* 48 (1958), 156–162, who pointed out that all Boak had shown was a shortage of men in given jobs which the government wanted filled, not necessarily an absolute population shortage. In particular, he noted that there are policy reasons besides population shortage for building an army of aliens. Finley did not deny that the population of the Western empire declined in the third century (*ibid.*, p. 162). A. E. H. Jones, in his review of Boak, also agreed that a decline occurred in the third century and that an acute labor shortage was clear in the fourth century, by which time taxation did not leave the peasants means enough to rear many children (review in *English Historical Review*, 2nd series, 9 (1957), 380–381.

On depopulation of towns in England, see R. G. Collingwood and J. A. L. Myres, *Roman Britain and the English Settlements*, 2nd ed. (London, 1937), p. 180. On depopulation in the West in the fourth century, see the texts cited by Dudden, *The Life and Times of St. Ambrose* (Oxford, 1935), I, 96, and the general evaluation by Adolphe Landry, *Traité de démographie* (Paris, 1945), p. 50.

centuries did nothing to check infanticide or the abandonment of children by their parents. Unwilling or unable to interfere in family life, the government's main recourse was the positive encouragement of the *Lex Julia et Papia*. With this view of the possibilities of official action dominant, it is a remarkable indication of the problem created by abortion and by contraception that any laws were enacted which had some relation to those practices.

The background for the law lies in the association of potions of contraception and magic. There are traces of this association in earlier Roman law. Writing in the second part of the first century, Plutarch said that Romulus in his original laws for Rome had enacted "a severe law" permitting a husband to divorce his wife, not only for adultery, but for "medicine in regard to children." Plutarch's testimony need not be accepted literally. He was a moralist with a strong desire to encourage a better attitude toward parenthood, as his *Affection Toward Children* shows. But he may have been familiar with a Roman tradition along these lines. It is hypothesized, too, that the *Twelve Tables* of ancient Rome had a provision forbidding administration of "medicine," for Gaius in his commentary on the *Twelve Tables* qualifies the term (*Digest* 50.16.326).[29] In both the tradition preserved by Plutarch and in Gaius the key word is "medicine" — in Greek *pharmakeia*, in Latin *veneficium*. In both languages the term means use of "magic" or "drugs." The ambiguity of the term, which is preserved in each language although different roots form the words, is deliberate, and reflects the attitude of Greco-Roman culture. Drugs are intimately associated by this culture with magic; the users of Greek or Latin see no need to have two words to differentiate magic and the drugs. The ambiguity of the term, then, is inherent. A univocal translation suppresses one of the two meanings suggested by the word in most contexts. I adopt the suggestion advanced by Clyde Pharr that the English term which best preserves the ambiguity is "medicine" used in the sense in which a North American Indian medicine man makes medicine.[30] The term "medicine" in respect to children primarily designates abortifacients. But the definition by Gaius of *venena* or *medicamenta*, preserved in Justinian's *Digest*, describes "medicine" as "that which when employed changes the nature of that to which it is employed" (*Digest* 50.16.236). Probably contraceptive drugs fall

[29] Plutarch, *Romulus* 22 in *Parallel Lives*, law set out in "Leges regiae: Romulus" 1.9, FIRA I, 8; Gaius, *On the Twelve Tables*, set out in "XII Tabulae" 8.25, FIRA I, 63. Plutarch's "Affection for Offspring" is in the Loeb Classical Library *Moralia*, vol. VI, ed. and trans. W. C. Helmbold (Cambridge, Mass., 1939), pp. 331–357.

[30] In general, I here follow Clyde Pharr, "The Interdiction of Magic in Roman Law," *Transactions and Proceedings of the American Philological Association* 63 (1932), 272–273.

within this broad definition and within the intention of the ancient law-makers to prevent a woman from affecting her fertility without her husband's consent.

By the third century the ancient law described by Plutarch was no longer relevant to divorce, and the exact scope of the fragments surviving from the Twelve Tables is not clear. By this time the chief legal usage of "medicine" was in the Cornelian Law providing capital punishment for assassins and medicine men (*veneficii*), enacted under Sulla in 81 B.C. but still basic criminal legislation. Commenting on the law, Marcian, a third-century jurist, noted that drugs (*medicamenta*) are of different kinds. Sometimes they are used to cure; sometimes they are used to produce love; these uses are not condemned by the statute.[31] Sometimes they are used to kill a man. It is this use of these evil drugs which the statute forbids. As Marcian expounds the law in force in his day it is not directed to the protection of infant life; in Roman law a fetus was not a man (*Digest* 25.4.1.1; 35.2.9.1) and so its destruction would not be within the law, which is directed only at the deliberate killing of a man by weapon or drug.

Within the law, however, according to Marcian, is the irresponsible sale of hemlock, salamander, wolfsbane, pine-caterpillars, hare's ear, mandrake, and Spanish fly. It is inferable that these are regulated only because they may be dangerous to life, as we know that wolfsbane, salamander, and Spanish fly were so regarded (Pliny, *Natural History* 27.2.4; 29.23.74; 29.30.93). To this point, the law as it stands in the early third century seems to have nothing to do with abortion or contraception. But Marcian adds, "By a decree of the Senate, exile to the islands is provided for her who, not with a bad intention, but giving a bad example, gives a medicine for conception (*ad conceptionem*) as a result of which the woman receiving the medicine dies." The usual interpretation of this text is that the medicine in question is meant to aid conception, that it is a potion for fecundity.[32] This interpretation assumes that conception would be desired. But conception could also be undesired. The phrase *ad conceptionem* can be interpreted to mean a "medicine for conception,"

---

[31] "Potions of love" and "love drink" were not euphemisms for contraceptives. For a typical list of these herbal aphrodisiacs with magical properties see Ovid, *Ars amatoria*, ed. E. J. Kenney (Oxford, 1961), vol. II, lines 415–423.

[32] E.g., Theodor Mommsen, *Römisches Strafrecht* (Leipzig, 1899), p. 637: "Mitteln gegen die Unfruchtbarkeit"; *The Civil Law*, trans. S. P. Scott (Cincinnati, 1932), IX, 60: "producing conception." The text reads: "Sed ex Senatus consulto relegari iussa est ea, quae non quidem malo animo, sed malo exemplo medicamentum ad conceptionem dedit, ex quo ea, quae acceperat, decesserit" (*Digest* 48.8.3).

There is possibly a parallel reference to this criminal law in the civil law. Under the *Lex Aquilia* giving an action for damages for various injuries, a midwife was liable if a woman died to whom she had applied (*supposuit*) a drug (*medicamentum*) with her own hands (*Digest* 9.2.9, Ulpian citing Labeo). It would seem again that the medicine could have been either to aid conception or to prevent it.

as aspirin is "for a headache." The law would then affect the sale of contraceptives. There is the further consideration that these contraceptive
potions were more likely to produce sickness than drugs given to produce
fertility. This interpretation may be strengthened by considering a text
taken from the jurist Paul, now inserted in the section of the *Digest* dealing with punishments (48.19.38.5). Paul says that those who give "a
drink for love or abortion" are to be punished by exile, if of the upper
classes, or by the mines, if of the lower class. The punishment applies
even though they have not acted with malice (*dolo*); they give a "bad
example." If a man or woman affected by the potion dies, the death
penalty is to be invoked. This passage suggests that the current form
of the Cornelian law punishes abortioners and dealers in aphrodisiacs for
their "bad example." The bad example is the use of magic. In the same
way the aspect of the law noted by Marcian punishes the bad example
of medicine men using drugs to promote or to prevent fertility, at least
if the person receiving the potion dies. That the same law should cover
both contraceptives and drugs for fertility need not be considered an eccentricity of an ancient law; in a not too dissimilar fashion, as will be seen
in Chapter XIII, the present Swiss criminal code punishes the obscene
promotion of contraceptives and of devices to prevent venereal disease.

It may be argued, then, that the second-century Empire legislated
against both abortifacient and contraceptive drinks where death resulted
to the consumer. This kind of legislation is primarily a protection of existing adult life. Its secondary effect, however, in discouraging the sale of
powerful drugs which might occasionally kill a woman, should not be
overlooked. It made dealers in abortifacients and contraceptives act at
their peril. How much it was enforced is not known. What the text on
medicine suggests is that, almost as much as the widespread use of abortifacients, the use of contraceptive potions was officially recognized as a
bad example in the state.[33]

One other kind of behavior with contraceptive effect was punished by

[33] On the frequency of abortion, see J. H. Waszink, "Abtreibung," in *Reallexicon
für Antike und Christentum*, ed. Theodor Klauser, I (Stuttgart, 1950), 57; Franz Joseph
Dölger, "Das Lebensrecht des ungeborenen Kindes und die Fruchtabtreibung in der
Bewertung der heidnischen und christlichen Antike," *Antike und Christentum: Kultur-
und religionsgeschichtliche Studien*, II (Munich, 1930), 37–44. Seneca praises his own
mother because, unlike some, she has not "crushed the conceived hopes of children
within her entrails" (*Ad Helviam matrem de consolatione* 16.1).

It would seem that the law against abortion had a wider scope than abortion by
potion if the father objected. In Marcian it is stated that the Emperors Severus and
Antoninus decreed that if a woman procured an abortion in herself (the means not
being specified) she should be exiled, "for it may be considered dishonorable for a
woman to deprive her husband of children with impunity" (*Digest* 47.11.4). Does this
reason for the rule limit it to cases where the father objects? Ulpian reports the same
decree without reference to the reason (*Digest* 48.8.8). It may be that Ulpian, or the
quotation in the *Digest* from Ulpian, has enlarged the statute.

law, probably because of its association with certain Eastern religious cults. By decrees of Hadrian, to render a man impotent became an offense subjecting to the death penalty both the operating physician and the man seeking it for himself (*Digest* 48.8.4.2, 48.8.5; cf. 48.8.3.4). The barrier was not absolute, for the prefect of a province could license voluntary castration.[34]

References of the imperial age are not many, if the Christian and Jewish references to it are not counted. In literature from an earlier age, abortion is mentioned in the *Truculentus* of Plautus as a likely action for a pregnant prostitute to take. There may also be a punning reference to the contraceptive means employed by prostitutes: "Your deeds and hearts are soaked in poison and bitter vinegar" (*acerbo aceto*).[35] In the classical period, abortion alone is mentioned by such a sophisticated authority on sexual mores as Ovid (*Amores* 2.13–14, a fervent attack on abortion; *Fasti* 1.621–624, an historical anecdote; *Heroides* 11.37–42).[36] Juvenal speaks of a rich woman's "arts and medicines" (*medicamenta*) which "make sterile and lead to the killing of men in the womb" (*Satires* 6.595–597).[37] The word *medicamenta* is so general that either contraceptives or abortifacients could be meant. Unquestionably he is speaking of abortion, but it is not clear whether his reference to sterility does not include contraceptive acts.

Contraception was not likely to be a topic of dramatic interest where society found no moral issue in the act. From the poems, novels, and drama of the United States in the twentieth century, it would be difficult to derive any notion of the widespread practice of contraception. Except in a dramatic presentation of a Catholic family, such as Gabriel Marcel's play *Croissez et multipliez,* birth control is not likely to present grounds for struggle or comment. The absence of reference to the subject in Roman classical literature is perhaps best understood as due to a general calm acceptance of contraceptive practices.[38]

The existence of contraceptive methods in the world from which the Christians came is established: by the Old Testament, by the Talmud, by

[34] See the story of a Christian youth who sought such permission, told by St. Justin, *Duae apologiae* 1.29, ed. Gerard Rauschen (Berlin, 1911).

[35] Plautus, *Truculentus,* ed. and trans. Paul Nixon, Loeb Classical Library (Cambridge, Mass., 1938), line 179.

[36] Ovid, *Amores,* ed. E. H. Kenney (Oxford, 1961). Ovid, *Fasti,* ed. and trans. James George Frazer, Loeb Classical Library (Cambridge, Mass., 1931). *Heroides,* in Ovid, *Heroides and Amores,* ed. and trans. Grant Showerman, Loeb Classical Library (Cambridge, Mass., 1925).

[37] Juvenal, *Satires,* in *Juvenal and Persius,* ed. and trans. G. C. Ramsay, Loeb Classical Library (Cambridge, Mass., 1924).

[38] Keith Hopkins is publishing an article in the Spring 1965 issue of *Classical Quarterly* which will contain further proof of contraceptive practice in the Roman Empire.

Aristotle, by Pliny, by the physicians, and by imperial law. Coitus interruptus, potions, pessaries, spermicides, genital salves, postcoital exercises, the sterile period — a very wide range of possible techniques was known. The extent to which contraception was practiced is far more conjectural. From the prevalence of more brutal forms of population control, from the fragmentary indications of population decline, from the presumed psychology of slaves, from the great interest of imperial law in encouraging members of the more successful classes to raise at least three children — from these circumstantial and comparatively slight data, the inference may be drawn that contraception was a social phenomenon in the Roman empire of which the Christians could not have been ignorant. What judgment did the Christians give upon it?

CHAPTER II

THE SCRIPTURAL STRUCTURE AND
EXTERNAL SOURCES OF DOCTRINE

THE TEXT of a sacred document is not so important as the interpretation it is given. The Catholic community has generally recognized that the vital meaning of a biblical passage is that which the community, the Church, gives it. Yet if a book is regarded as sacred, inspired by God, as the Bible is regarded by Catholics, the texts themselves must remain a guide, a criterion rebuking extravagant hypotheses, a treasury to which the speculative theologian or legislating bishop must return. In a process that can only be seen historically as interaction, the Word of God is interpreted by the community, while the community returns again and again to the Scriptures to purify and deepen its understanding.

To engage in any interpretation of Scripture, then, is to venture into theology. The opposite procedure of collecting texts and letting them speak for themselves results in forcing each reader to be his own theologian. In this history I shall try to set out the texts which seem to me most immediately relevant to the Church's understanding of marriage, sexual intercourse, and procreation. To the extent that I elaborate on these texts I shall be elaborating a theology, but one which seeks to be rooted historically in the significance given the texts as they were accepted in the community.

THE OLD TESTAMENT

The Old Testament provides a structure which is basic to the understanding of the Christian development of a sexual ethic. The structure may be resolved into four propositions, elementary and of sweeping breadth. Woman is a person, like man. Marriage is good, and is the ordinary state in which man and woman are sexually related. Fecundity is good. Sexual acts are not necessarily good.

The basic themes are struck in the two accounts set out in Genesis.[1] The yahwist tradition of Genesis 2, earlier than that of Genesis 1, affirmed:

> Then the Lord God said, "It is not good that the man is alone; I will make him a helper like himself."
> . . . And the rib which the Lord God took from the man, he made into a woman, and brought her to him. Then the man said, "She is now bone of my bone, and flesh of my flesh. She shall be called Woman, for from man she has been taken." For this reason a man leaves his father and mother, and clings to his wife, and the two become one flesh.   (Gn 2:18, 22–24)

The post-Exilic, priestly narration of the Creation proclaimed:

> Male and female he created them. Then God blessed them, saying, "Increase and multiply; fill the earth and subdue it."   (Gn 1:27–28)

The formula "increase and multiply" is also used of the creatures of sea and air in Genesis 1:22, and so may be intended only to register the fact of multiplication. But the value placed on human fecundity by the Old Testament as a whole is evident. The blessing by God with the divine direction to multiply is repeated after the Flood (Gn 9:1). Fruitfulness is a divine reward. The author of Deuteronomy tells Israel that God "will love and bless and multiply you; he will bless the fruit of your womb . . . no man or woman among you shall be childless" (Dt 7:13–14). A similar promise is made by God in Exodus 23:26. The blessing of a marriage is, "May the Lord make this wife come into your house like Rachel and Lia, who between them built up the house of Israel" (Ru 4:11).[2]

Is the emphasis on the number of children as well as on the ability to have children? Abraham and his family are several times promised a posterity "numerous as the stars" (Gn 15.5, 26:4), or "as the sands on the seashore" (Gn 22:17), or "countless" (Gn 16:10). The contexts and emphasis suggest a concern with the ultimate number of the descendants, rather than with the size of the immediate family. Sara's one son is sufficient to assure Abraham that God is fulfilling his promise (Gn 21:1). Yet, in an age when infant mortality was high, concern with one's ultimate descendants would lead to desire for a family large enough to guarantee

---

[1] For scriptural quotations, I have generally used *The Holy Bible, Translated from the Latin Vulgate* (The Douai-Rheims Bible as revised by Challoner), but I also have eclectically resorted to the Confraternity Edition (New York, 1953) and to the books now translated in *The Holy Bible, Translated from the Original Languages with Critical Use of All the Ancient Sources by Members of the Catholic Biblical Association of America*, 5 vols. (Paterson, N.J., 1952–1964). Where, however, there is substantial divergence between these translations and *La Sainte Bible*, translated into French under the direction of the Ecole Biblique de Jérusalem (Paris, 1956), I have followed the latter. On the approximate dates and sources of Gn 1:27–28 and Gn 2:18, 22–24, I follow Roland de Vaux's commentary in *La Sainte Bible*.

[2] On the value placed on fecundity, see also Roland de Vaux, *Les Institutions de l'Ancien Testament* (Paris, 1958), I, 71–73.

some sons surviving beyond puberty. The biblical account, focusing on a privileged line, only indirectly suggests that if a big posterity was a blessing, so was a big family. Job, in his enviable state before his misfortunes, and again in his happy, restored condition, is shown as having seven sons and three daughters (Jb 1:2, 42:13).

Accompanying the value placed on procreation is a disinterest in virginity. Only one Old Testament figure is presented as unmarried by choice: Jeremias (Jer 16:2). His decision may be understood as a symbolic acting out of the sterility about to befall Israel. The Old Testament has no word for bachelor.[3]

The praise of fecundity does not obscure altogether a perception of personal values in marriage. The note is already struck in Genesis 2. The prophets, beginning with Osee 1–3, offer a conception of the relationship of God to his people modeled on the marital relation. Yahweh is depicted as a husband linked to a faithless wife (Jer 2:20–25, 31:2–6, 21–22; Ez 16:8–59). In Second Isaias 54, the relation reveals greater depths: out of love Yahweh forgives the infidelity. The focus is theological, but the image used is drawn from contemporary notions, and at the same time serves to provide a model for behavior in human marriage.

The Song of Songs, written in the post-Exilic age, concentrates almost exclusively on the personal relation between the lover and his beloved. "All mine is my true love, and I all his" (2:16). Human sexual love here has a value independent of fertility. In a more sober domestic vein the praise of a good wife in Proverbs is not of her fruitfulness, but of her prudence and the loving confidence her husband has in her (Prv 31:11), but it is made clear that she is fruitful (Prv 31:28).

In the world of the Old Testament woman is not treated as the complete moral equal of man. Polygamy is permitted. Slave concubinage is allowed. An unmarried man who takes an unmarried girl and has intercourse with her is to be fined and forced to take her as a wife, but if a girl has secretly been unchaste, she is to be stoned (Dt 22:13–29). Divorce may be obtained only by a husband (Dt 24:1–4).

True, moments of tenderness, personal encounter between man and woman, or passion are recorded. Although the account of the origins of Israel is primarily the history of the tribes, one may abstract from the major purpose of the narrative to observe what were considered to be possible motivations for human action. Jacob is so moved by Rachel's beauty that he is willing to serve his prospective father-in-law, Laban, for seven years, "and they seemed to him but a few days, so much did he love her" (Gn 29:20). Yet, in this polygamous society, love is neither exclusive nor more important than procreation. At Laban's insistence Jacob takes the elder sister Lia before he takes Rachel, and later, when

[3] See Lucien Legrand, *The Biblical Doctrine of Virginity* (New York, 1963), p. 29.

Rachel is barren, she gives her slave girl to Jacob so that she may vicariously beget children through her slave (Gn 29:22–28, Gn 30:1–5). A later story tells of David and his several wives, Micol, who "loved him" (1 K 18:20, 28); Abigail whose enterprising betrayal of her first husband impressed him (1 K 25:23–42); and Bethsabee, whose beauty moved him to adultery and murder (2 K 11:2–17). The man to whom Micol was given during David's quarrel with Saul weeps when David takes her back (2 K 3:16). David consoles Bethsabee when their first child dies (2 K 12:24). It would be foolish to deny that even in a polygamous society personal emotions could have a place. Yet fertility remains more important than love. When Elcana asks his sterile wife Anna, "Am I not better to thee than ten children?" neither she nor the narrator of the story agrees. Anna declares she is "an exceeding unhappy woman," and she remains so until the Lord makes her fertile (1 K 1:1–28). Personal encounters would be apt to be as fugitive as David's. The major factors of male domination prevented the establishment of an ethic which would make a personal relationship in marriage a value superior to fecundity.

The Old Testament also contains a strain which qualifies its positive acceptance of sexuality. Woman embodies an attraction which may cause disaster. Eve and Dalila are temptresses to sin (Gn 3:1–17, Jgs 16). Bethsabee is the occasion of David's fall, Thamar of Amnon's (2 K 11–12, 2 K 13). Ritual continence may be a way of gaining divine favor, as in 1 Kings 21:5 and Exodus 19:15. In Psalms, sexuality is associated with sin: "In guilt was I born, and in sin my mother conceived me" (50:7). A man is "unclean" if he has "an emission of seed," or if he has ordinary marital intercourse (Lv 15:16, 18). Ritual purification is necessary after menstruation and after childbirth (Lv 16:28, 12:1–8). In the much later story of Tobias and Sara, from the Jews of the diaspora, sexual desire is contrasted with the desire for procreating descendants and is condemned as a motive for marriage (Tb 8:7); a demon, who may be intended allegorically as the demon of lust, kills the earlier husbands of Sara, who do not observe this distinction.

I cite the above texts on sexuality because, whatever the intention of their authors, they will furnish support to one stand of Christian thought, mistrustful of sex. Similarly, I cite the texts stressing the personal values of marriage because, in the long run, they too will play a part in the Christian judgment on marriage. But the most obvious and commanding message of the Old Testament is that marriage and the procreation of children are eminently desirable human goods, which God has blessed.

This structural emphasis on procreation is far more influential for Christian writers than the solitary and celebrated text which is so often cited in controversies over contraception. That text is Genesis 38, a fragment of yahwist provenance giving an account of the origins of the Judean tribe. Er, the first son of Juda and Sue, was married to Thamar, but was slain by the Lord for an unspecified act of wickedness. The text continues at verses 8–10:

Then Juda said to Onan, "Go to your brother's wife, perform your duty as brother-in-law, and raise up seed for your brother." Onan knew that the descendants would not be his own, so whenever he had relations with his brother's wife, he let [the seed] be lost on the ground, in order not to raise up seed for his brother. What he did displeased Yahweh, who killed him also.[4]

Juda's command to Onan reflects a patriarchal society in which the father selects his son's wife; and Onan's act is disobedient to his own father's command. It has sometimes been argued that Onan's action violated the levirate law which provided that a brother must beget children from a dead brother's widow, so "that his name may not be blotted out from Israel" (Dt 25:5–10). But this law refers to a situation where the father is dead, and the brothers are holding land in common; the duty to beget offspring is imposed in order to maintain the share of the deceased brother by letting a son begotten of his widow step into his place. The only penalty provided by the levirate law set out in Deuteronomy is a form of public infamy — the widow spits on a defaulting brother and takes his sandal (Dt 25:9). The story in Genesis is older, the situation different because the father is alive, and the offense is viewed more gravely.[5] Onan's offense, it will also be observed, consisted in repeated acts, not an isolated action, and was committed with the purpose, not of limiting his offspring, but of avoiding all procreation by Thamar.

The reason which the narrator believed explained Onan's punishment has been variously stated by modern exegetes.[6] Most obviously, in the

---

[4] I follow the translation in *La Sainte Bible*. The Hebrew omits the words "his seed." Most English translations supply it. *La Sainte Bible* reads, "il laissait perdre à terre." On Jerome's translation used in the Vulgate, see Chapter III below.

[5] David Daube, "Consortium in Roman and Hebrew Law," *Juridical Review* 62 (1950), 72–73, 79, 89, 96.

[6] A convenient summary of the positions taken by the exegesis is given by A. M. DuBarle, "La Bible et les Pères ont-ils parlé de la contraception?" *La Vie spirituelle* 15, Supplement (1962), 575–576: (1) Punishment for the contraceptive method used—John Skinner, *A Critical and Exegetical Commentary on Genesis* (New York, 1910); Otto Procksch, *Die Genesis* (Leipzig, 1913); Benno Jacob, *Das erste Buch der Tora: Genesis* (Berlin, 1934); Johannes Hempel, *Das Ethos des Alten Testaments* (Berlin, 1938); W. H. Griffith Thomas, *Genesis, A Devotional Commentary* (Grand Rapids, Mich., 1946); E. C. Messenger, *Two in One Flesh* (Westminster, Md., 1949), III, 55–56. (2) Punishment for lack of family affection — August Dillmann, *Die Genesis* (Leipzig, 1882); Hermann Gunkel, *Genesis übersetzt und erklärt* (Göttingen, 1910); Otto A. Piper, *Die Geschlechter: Ihr Sinn und Geheimnis in biblischer Sicht* (Hamburg, 1953); Gerhard von Rad, *Das erste Buch Mose* (Göttingen, 1953). (3) Punishment for violation of the levirate law — Heinrich Holzinger, *Genesis erklärt* (Freiburg, 1898); Joseph Chaine, *Le Livre de la Genèse* (Paris, 1951); Joseph Fletcher. *Morals and Medicine* (Princeton, 1954); Pierre Grélot, *Le Couple*

context of a story of the descent of the tribe, Onan had broken a law designed to perpetuate the name of the elder son. He had disobeyed his father. He had also shown a want of family feeling and at the same time displayed an introverted egotism. Moreover, he had appeared to accept the obligation placed upon him to marry his widowed sister-in-law, but by his acts he had frustrated the purpose of the obligation. Finally, his contraceptive behavior itself may have seemed wrong to the narrator. Was Onan punished for his disobedience, for his lack of family feeling, for his egotism, for his evasion of an obligation assumed, for his contraceptive acts, or for a combination of these faults? Comparison with breaches of the later levirate law suggests that death was an improbable punishment for mere breach of this law.[7] That contraception as such is condemned seems unlikely. There is no commandment against contraception in any of the codes of law.

A comparison between the provisions on other sexual matters and on contraception points up the omission. A man is unclean if he has an emission of seed, but he is not condemned on this account but merely required to bathe (Lv 15:18). On the other hand, some sexual acts in marriage are severely condemned by the law. Marital intercourse in menstruation is treated on a par with adultery (Ez 18:6, Lv 18:19); it is a crime requiring that husband and wife "be cut off from their people" (Lv 20:18). It is surely strange that this act should be so severely and definitely punished and the illegality of contraception left to inference, if the compilers of the Pentateuch believed contraception to be unlawful.

It can scarcely be surmised that there was no occasion to legislate on contraception. The story itself shows that coitus interruptus was a practice known by at least the first millennium B.C. The Egyptian documents reflect the practice of contraception in a country that had great cultural influence on the Jews. The people of Israel knew no immunity from the sexual customs of their neighbors. There is explicit post-Exilic legislation against homosexuality, against bestiality, and against temple prostitution (Lv 18:22, 20:13, 20:15–16, Dt 23:18). If these acts had to be prohibited by law, it seems unlikely that, in the absence of clear prohibition, the Jewish people would have believed that coitus interruptus or the use of contraceptives was immoral.

These considerations — the lack of any commandment, the contrast

---

humain dans l'Ecriture (Paris, 1962), p. 39. (4) Punishment for egotism and the contraceptive act — Paul Heinisch, Das Buch Genesis (Bonn, 1930); Roland de Vaux, La Sainte Bible, p. 46, footnote d. (5) Punishment for accepting an obligation of the law and then evading the duty imposed by it — S. R. Driver, The Book of Genesis (New York, 1904).

[7] J. P. Schaumberger, "Propter quale peccatum morte punitus sit Onan?" Biblica 8 (1927), 209–212; C. F. De Vine, "The Sin of Onan, Gen 38, 8–10," Catholic Biblical Quarterly 4 (1942), 323.

with other explicit regulations on marriage, the evident need to restrain other forms of sexual misconduct — support the view that contraception is not the act for which Onan was killed. The story nonetheless furnished a striking example by which later commentators, Jewish and Christian, could demonstrate the sinfulness of contraception.

THE NEW TESTAMENT

The Gospels give preeminence to a single value in human behavior: love. The commandments of love are Old Testament commandments: "Love the Lord, your God, with all your heart, and with all your soul, and with all your strength" (Dt 6:5); "Love your neighbor as yourself" (Lv 19:18). But they are singled out, emphasized, made decisive in the Gospels: "On these two commandments depend the whole law and the prophets" (Mt 22:40). The teaching is repeated by Paul: "The greatest of these is charity" (1 Cor 13:13). The commandment to love one's neighbor is made both universal and specific; the neighbor is not only the fellow tribesman, but an alien or an enemy or any man met in distress (Lk 10:29–36; Mt 5:44). Finally, the example of Jesus is seen as the embodiment of the law of love: "This is my commandment, that you love one another as I have loved you" (Jn 15:12). The commandment, in terms of this pattern, is "a new commandment" (Jn 13:34).

This commandment of the Lord to love as he loved has proved to be the difficult commandment. Who would say that many individual Christians have ever observed it? At an institutional level it would seem to have been occasionally neglected. In a code of specific duties, even between spouses, and in the severe enforcement of this code, the spontaneity, freedom, creativity of love would seem sometimes to have been sacrificed to an ethic alien to love.

What love was, was nowhere specified in the Gospels. Even Pilate did not put the question. The meaning had to be found in the example of the Lord and in some collections of moral rules endorsed by him. It has taken twenty centuries for Christian experience and meditation to develop what the Church holds to be the central meaning of love. Numerous interpretations, of which the crusades and inquisitions are salutary examples, have been tried and discarded. The process of development, of perfecting the demands of love, indeed, continues.

In the course of this development the moral rules of the Gospels and Epistles played a part. Was Christian love totally without law? Or was Christian love the most rational development of human potentialities, in the ordering of which law was indispensable? There is constant tension in the early Christian community between a belief that all acts are possible to the Christian and a belief that some acts are unworthy of a man.

The moral rules lessened spontaneity and creativity, while they functioned to give a content to love.

In the course of the development in later centuries, both the basic commandment of love and the more specific rules functioned as touchstones — sometimes obscured, but always returned to. Moreover, the command to love had a force by which more particular injunctions of the New Testament itself were tested. St. Paul enjoins the Corinthians not to engage in litigation (1 Cor 6:7) and, eight verses later, to avoid intercourse with harlots (1 Cor 6:15). The author of Timothy tells slaves to obey their masters (1 Tm 6:1–2), and the author of Ephesians 5 tells wives to respect their husbands (Eph 5:33). Why did not Christians hold that lawyers were as bad as prostitutes? Why did they not find slavery as sacred an institution as marriage, and consider the injunction to slaves to obey their masters as binding as the injunction to wives to respect their husbands? As neither an individual nor a society has ever existed which has taken all the texts of Scripture with equal literalness, such questions are not to be answered from the texts alone. The answer has to be found in the living response of the Christian community — a response to the environment, physical and social, but also a response to the person of the Lord and his basic commandment of love. In the long run — and the long run is, of course, a vague concept — it has been difficult for a particular rule to keep its vitality if it is seen to work against the commandment of love. The whole process of development consists in this searching, in this testing of particular laws by the law of love. If the rules relating to marriage have been treated with a reverence not accorded the texts on lawyers or on slaves, it is partly because the channeling of sexual behavior is of more pervasive significance for a society, but it is also partly because of the close relationship believed to exist between the laws of marriage and the law of love.

The more particular texts of the New Testament which form the doctrine on sexuality, in which the rule on contraception is born, may be analytically reduced to eight themes: the superiority of virginity; the institutional goodness of marriage; the sacral character of sexual intercourse; the value of procreation; the significance of desire as well as act; the evil of extramarital intercourse and the unnaturalness of homosexuality; the connection of Adam's sin and the rebelliousness of the body; the evil of "medicine."

The texts of the New Testament on marriage must be understood in terms of the teaching of the New Testament on virginity. It is the teaching on virginity which was a radical break from the Old Testament, which to many early Christians overshadowed the teaching on marriage, and which put marriage in a place where, as it were, it had to justify its own existence. The value assigned procreation in the early development of doctrine can only be understood in terms of the value assigned virginity by the Gospels and St. Paul.

In the most Jewish of the Gospels, Jesus speaks of those who have "made themselves eunuchs in view of the kingdom of heaven," and it is added, "Let him take it who can take it" (Mt 19:12). This teaching occurs in a chapter which also teaches that the kingdom of heaven belongs to little children and that it is difficult for the rich to enter (Mt 19:13–25). This sequence of themes suggests that virginity, like poverty and child-likeness, is a sign proclaiming the advent of the kingdom. Matthew 22:30 reports that Jesus said that "at the resurrection they will neither marry nor be given at marriage, but will be like the angels in heaven." Matthew 1:18–25 recounts the virgin birth of Jesus.

The emphasis on virginity is even stronger in Luke, the gospel influenced by Paul. According to Matthew 10:37 the follower of Christ must love him more than his parents or his children. In Luke, the teaching is presented, with typical Lucan rhetoric, that the follower must "hate" his parents and his wife, as well as his children, his brothers and sisters, and his own life (Lk 14:26). Luke connects this renunciation with a statement of what will be a principle of Christian asceticism, later invoked for the married as for virgins: "He who does not carry his cross and follow me cannot be my disciple" (14:27). A reward is promised to those who leave house or parents or brothers or wife or children for the sake of the kingdom (Lk 18:29). The rhetoric of these texts has not been urged to support suicide or dissolution of a family. They do, however, reflect Luke's tendency to see a wife as an encumbrance. Similarly, Luke expands the teaching of Matthew 22:30 on marriage and the resurrection:

> The children of this world marry and are given in marriage. But those who shall have been accounted worthy of that world and of the resurrection from the dead neither marry nor take wives. For neither shall they be able to die any more, for they are equal to the angels, and are sons of God, being sons of the resurrection.   (Lk 20:34–36)

The narration of the virgin birth is an important element of Luke's teaching on virginity. Mary "knew not man," and the angel told her that Jesus would be conceived by "the power of the Most High" (Lk 1:30–37). Mary's hymn celebrates the power of God to make her virginity fruitful (Lk 1:46–55). It has been persuasively argued that Luke intends to draw a parallel here between the Spirit who can bring the Messiah out of barren flesh and the Spirit who can bring the Messiah out from the dead. Virginity in the archetypal case of Mary, Luke implies, is the Christian way of fecundity, as the cross is paradoxically the way of life.[8]

The connection of the kingdom, the resurrection, and abstinence from

---

[8] Legrand, *The Biblical Doctrine of Virginity*, pp. 43–44.

marriage appears again in Apocalypse 14:1–5. The 144,000 who are the perfect number of redeemed have not been "defiled with women; for they are virgins." The saved have already lived as the resurrected. Is this meant literally? Apocalypse 7 presents a similarly perfect number of the redeemed as all martyrs. It does not seem that the author means to make both martyrdom and virginity necessary for salvation. But he does mean to exalt both martyrs and virgins.

Jesus himself is presented by the Evangelists as endowed with a holiness that excludes not only sin but even any consideration of marriage. The very reticence of the Gospels on the subject responds to a sense that there would have been something radically incongruous in postulating its possibility for Jesus. As Christian meditation has focused on the person of Jesus as the person to imitate, this example has been a powerful teaching on virginity.

The fullest explicit treatment of the values at stake is in Paul. With a full awareness of the reversal of values in the kingdom, Paul transmutes Genesis 2:18 and proclaims, "It is good for man not to touch woman" (1 Cor 7:1).[9] Virginity is preferable to marriage: "I would that you were all as I am myself" (1 Cor 7:7). Paul continues this theme in an eschatological context in which he declares, "the time is short":

> I would have you free from care. He who is unmarried is concerned about the things of the Lord, how he may please God. Whereas he who is married is concerned about the things of the world; and he is divided. And the unmarried woman, and the virgin, thinks about the things of the Lord that she may be holy in body and spirit. Whereas she who is married thinks about the things of the world, how she may please her husband.   (1 Cor 7:32–34)

There appears to be a deliberate contrast between the consecration of the virgin, "holy in body and spirit," and the divided spirit of a spouse. The difference between the contemplation of Mary and the busyness of Martha, described in Luke 10:38–42, is, perhaps, not without a parallel here.

The exaltation of virginity, the disinterest in procreation, the ambiguity of the texts on the marriage of the "resurrected," must all be considered if the sexual ethic of the first several centuries of Christianity is to be understood. If these texts had stood alone, Christianity could have taken

---

[9] It has been, in recent times, argued that the correct understanding of this passage is as a reply by Paul to a query of the Corinthians, in the course of which he quotes them. The text would then read, "Now concerning the things whereof you wrote me, 'It is good for man not to touch woman.' However, for fear of fornication, let each man have his own wife and let each woman have her own husband" (1 Cor 7:1–2). There are no apodictic arguments against the insertion of this punctuation which makes the sentence the Corinthians' and not Paul's. However, this interpretation was not known to the Fathers or the later Christian writers who were influenced by the passage. For the argument in favor of the interpretation, see Max Thurian, *Marriage and Celibacy*, trans. Norma Enerton (London, 1959), pp. 66–67.

the position on procreation that Gnosticism and Manicheanism were to take. The texts did not stand alone; but they could be read alone. Their existence accounts for much of the initial Christian approach to marriage.

Yet the Gospels also taught that marriage as an institution is good. Jesus reaffirms the teaching of Genesis 1 and Genesis 2 on the divine origin of matrimony (Mk 10:7–8, Mt 19:4–6). John, who does not report these affirmations, shows Jesus performing his first miracle at a wedding feast (Jn 2:1–12). Luke, who shows such small regard for marriage, does report Jesus' condemnation of remarriage after divorce, a condemnation implicitly carrying with it a sanction of the first marriage (Lk 16:18). Joy at a marriage is used several times to illuminate the relation of Christ to his people (Mk 2:19–20, Mt 25:1–13, Jn 3:29). In Apocalypse 21:2 and 9 the Old Testament theme of Yahweh as the bridegroom of Israel in a monogamous marriage is repeated with Christ as the bridegroom of his people.

The theme of the Lord as bridegroom receives its most elaborate development in Ephesians 5:25–33, where ecclesiological and marital doctrine are intertwined:

Husbands, love your wives, just as Christ also loved the Church and delivered himself up for her, that he might sanctify her, cleansing her in the bath of water by means of the word, in order that he might present to himself the Church in all her glory, not having spot or blemish. Even thus ought husbands also to love their wives as their own bodies. He who loves his own wife, loves himself. For no one ever hated his own flesh; on the contrary, he nourishes and cherishes it, as Christ also does the Church (because we are members of his body). "For this cause a man shall leave his father and mother and cleave to his wife, and the two shall become one flesh." This is a great mystery—I mean in reference to Christ and to the Church. However, let each one of you also love his wife just as he loves himself; and let the wife respect her husband.

Of all New Testament texts on marriage, this passage most fully specifies the meaning of the general commandment to love in the particular case of husband and wife.[10]

Not only is marriage itself presented as good; sexual intercourse is presented as holy. It is the fleshly unity of spouses which is emphasized in Ephesians as the symbol of the relation of Christ and Church. The holiness of marital intercourse is contrasted by St. Paul with the unholiness

---

[10] The authorship of Ephesians 5 has traditionally been ascribed to St. Paul. This attribution has been seriously challenged. Outside of Catholic circles probably a majority of American and Continental scholars reject it. Opinion among British scholars seems more favorable; see C. Leslie Mitton, *The Epistle to the Ephesians* (Oxford, 1951), p. 2. Mitton himself says, "We must recognize that its authenticity was never for a moment in doubt in the early Church." It is because it is an epistle attributed to Paul that its doctrine on married love has such influence as it has on the theologians and canonists.

of extramarital intercourse: he who has intercourse with a harlot makes "the members of Christ the members of a harlot" (1 Cor 6:16). Christians, Paul exhorts, "present your bodies as a sacrifice, living, holy, pleasing to God" (Rom 12:1). The special holiness of the Christian use of sex is inculcated by other epistles: "Learn how to possess your vessel in holiness and honor, not in the passion of lust like the Gentiles who do not know God" (1 Thes 4:4).[11] The Christian wives of unbelievers are admonished to be of "chaste behavior," and Christian husbands are told to "pay honor to the woman as the weaker vessel and as coheir of the grace of life" (1 Pt 3:2, 7).

The valuation of marriage as good and of intercourse as sacred is not linked in the Gospels to procreation. The words of Genesis "Increase and multiply" are not repeated when Genesis is cited in Mark 10 and Matthew 19 to establish monogamy. Sexual procreation is, however, used as a symbol. A mother's "joy that a man is born into the world" is used by John as the image of the joy the disciples will feel at Christ's return (Jn 16:21). The image, an echo of Isaias 26:17, would not have been chosen in a community which did not value procreation itself. In Ephesians, immediately following the great passage on the mystical significance of marriage, children are told to obey their parents (Eph 6:1); again procreation is assumed to be proper although its value is not emphasized.

Besides the indirect evidence of approval of procreation by the early Christians, there is a single direct text, whose Pauline authorship has been much disputed.[12] The author strikes a simple and characteristically Old Testament note. Women are not to teach or to exercise authority over men. Eve was deceived, not Adam. Yet, if faithful and modest, women will be saved "through motherhood" (1 Tm 2:15). This teaching occurs in a letter where the author warns against deceitful teachers, who, among other things, "will forbid marriage" (1 Tm 4:3). Although Paul in 1 Corinthians 7:8 advises widows not to remarry, the younger widows are now told to marry and "bear children" (1 Tm 5:14). A battle is already joined with the early Gnostics. In this context the single direct teaching on procreation in the New Testament seems a late effort to correct a misunderstanding that Paul's earlier emphasis on virginity has fostered.

[11] 1 Thes 4:4 has been variously interpreted as meaning that an unmarried man is to get a wife to avoid fornication; that a married man is to possess his own wife in purity; that a man is to possess his body in sanctification; that the married should respect their own wives and the unmarried marry wives in a spirit of consecration and honor.

[12] The genuineness of 1 Timothy is ably attacked by P. N. Harrison, *The Problem of the Pastoral Epistles* (Oxford, 1921). E. K. Simpson, *The Pastoral Epistles* (London, 1954), seems to establish a preponderance of evidence in favor of its authenticity. The epistle was accepted, in any event, by the early Church. It is recognized in the Muratorian canon; reminiscences from it are found in Justin Martyr and perhaps in earlier Christian writers (Simpson, p. 3).

The most famous passage on marital intercourse has no reference to procreation, nor does it deal with the sacral aspect that Ephesians illuminates. This text occurs in 1 Corinthians where St. Paul is answering in impromptu fashion the inquiries of his recent converts at Corinth. Is virginity mandatory? appears to have been one inquiry. The reply of Paul, commending virginity, has been given above. Yet, Paul stresses, virginity is not commanded. Marriage is an acceptable outlet for those "unable to control themselves." "It is better to marry than to burn" (1 Cor 7–10).

Paul goes on to lay down what many later Catholic writers, ignoring Ephesians 5, would find to be the heart of the Catholic doctrine on marital intercourse. He writes:

Let the husband render to his wife what is due her, and likewise the wife to her husband. A wife has not authority over her body, but her husband; the husband likewise has not authority over his body, but his wife. You must not refuse each other, except perhaps by consent, for a time, that you may give yourselves to prayer, and return together again lest Satan tempt you because you lack self-control. But this I say by way of concession, not commandment.
(1 Cor 7:3–6)

In the light of later disputes, one omission is notable in this passage. Nothing is said of intercourse for the purpose of procreation. Nothing is said of any purpose with which marital intercourse must be undertaken.[13]

The substantive content of this passage is remarkable for its stress on marital intercourse as something which is due, which is owed as a debt is owed.[14] The Vulgate will correctly translate the term as *debitum*, debt, and if generations of canonists will delight in this injection of legalism into matrimony, responsibility for the term rests with Paul. Probably to assert the equality in this matter of husband and wife, he has hit on a formidably juridical formulation of a personal relation. This firm insistence not only on the rightness but on the duty of sexual relations will serve to mark off the Catholic view of sexuality from that of the sectarian spiritualists who disdain the body. Whether the duty asserted is paramount over other marital values will be answered only in the course of centuries.

[13] The prevailing Catholic exegesis of this passage has been to read "the concession" as referring to marital intercourse; see Ceslaus Spicq, *La Première Epître aux Corinthiens*, in *La Sainte Bible*, ed. Louis Pirot and Albert Clamer (Paris, 1946). However, it has been urged that verse 6 is more properly understood as referring to the preceding verse's injunction to practice temporary continence. If one assumes that the Corinthians to whom Paul was writing were practicing a false asceticism, it makes sense for him to warn against taking his injunction to continence as a commandment; see Thurian, *Marriage and Celibacy*, pp. 69–70.

[14] The Greek word for *debitum* is *opheile*. The term is used by Paul elsewhere to indicate what is owed to governmental authority (Rom 13:7). The substantive is also used in Mt 18:32 to designate what is due a creditor in the parable of the stern master.

The capital point, even in Paul's account in 1 Corinthians, is that marital intercourse is, at a minimum, lawful for a Christian. As such, it is distinguished from a variety of sexual acts which are sins. One theological reason for condemning extramarital intercourse has been remarked: its infringement of the holy unity of Christ and the believer. There is further the teaching in Matthew that Jesus demands a higher standard of sexual morality than that set by the Old Testament:

You have heard that it was said to the ancients, "Thou shalt not commit adultery." But I say to you that anyone who so much as looks with lust at a woman has already committed adultery with her in his heart.   (Mt 5:27–28)

The passage reflects a concern with mental acts which, in various forms, will run through the treatment of sexual morals by Christians.

The holiness found in marital intercourse is most sharply distinguished by Paul from sexual behavior which is "against nature." The Gentiles, who do not have the Mosaic law, "show the work of the law written in their hearts" (Rom 2:15). But some pagans have behaved idolatrously; God has given them up

in the lustful desires of their heart to uncleanness, so that they dishonor their own bodies among themselves — they who exchanged the truth of God for a lie, and worshipped and served the creature rather than the Creator who is blessed forever, amen. For this cause God has given them up to shameful lusts; for their women have changed the natural use for that which is against nature, and in like manner, the men also, having abandoned the natural use of the woman, have burned in their lusts one toward another, men with men doing shameless things and receiving in themselves the inevitable recompense of their perversity.   (Rom 1:24–27)

A few exegetes have contended that the exchange of "natural use" for "unnatural" is intended to include anal intercourse within marriage. If this interpretation were true, Paul's sentence would be the most specific New Testament text on one form of contraceptive conduct. The prevailing exegesis, however, appears to be that Paul is using the term "unnatural" in a Hellenic and Stoic meaning. The exegetes conclude that as he condemns the homosexual acts of men, so he condemns also the lesbian acts of women.[15] The "nature" used as a criterion is a purposefulness, an order for man, discoverable in the universe. It is not identical with each and every impulse experienced by man. Paul writes in the same epistle, "It is not what I wish that I do, but what I hate that I do" (Rom 7:15). What is "natural" is not what happens, but what man's constitution requires.

[15] Hermann L. Strack and Paul Billerbeck, *Kommentar zum Neuen Testament aus Talmud und Midrash*, 3rd. ed. (Munich, 1961), vol. III, *Die Briefe des Neuen Testament und die Offenbarung Johannis*, pp. 68–69, notes the rabbinic usage, which could extend the meaning to "unwonted ways" in marriage. The more common Greek meaning is noted in, e.g., Otto Michel, *Der Brief an die Römer* (Göttingen, 1955), p. 59.

The requirements of nature are thus introduced by Paul as essential in living the Christian life of love.

There is in this exposition of nature another concept introduced, that of original sin, the sin of Adam. "Through one man sin entered into the world" (Rom 5:12). Sin still dwells in Paul: "I see another law in my members, warring against the law of my mind and making me prisoner to the law of sin that is in my members" (Rom 7:23). Paul does not specify this "sin in my members" as sexual rebelliousness, nor does he associate Adam's sin and its perpetuation with anything specifically sexual. His words will, however, provide later generations of Christians a starting point for reflections which tie together Adam's fall, sexual stirrings, and sexual sin.

Use of nature as a standard to measure licentiousness is not unconnected with a distrust of magic, including an aversion to *pharmakeia,* the use of drugs ordinarily associated with magic. Writing against the licentious members of the community in Galatians, and possibly using a standard list of moral failings, Paul denounces their licentiousness, then *pharmakeia* (5:20). Similarly, Apocalypse 9:21, describing the sinners who were not saved, says, "And they did not repent of their murders or of their *pharmakeia* or of their immorality or of their thefts." In Apocalypse 21:8, the *pharmakoi,* those who practice *pharmakeia,* are condemned by the Lord after He condemns fornicators. Outside the heavenly city, says Apocalypse 22:15, are "the dogs and the *pharmakoi* and the fornicators and the murderers and the idolaters and everyone who loves and practices falsehood." There is only one other passage in the New Testament where *pharmakoi* or *pharmakeia* appears. This is in Apocalypse 18:23, describing the fall of Babylon, who by her *pharmakeia* had led astray all the nations of the earth. Here magic is clearly meant. In every other case, to translate the term as "magic," "sorcery," or "witchcraft," as is commonly done in English translations such as the Douay, King James, Goodspeed, and Catholic Confraternity translations, is to resolve an ambiguity inherent in the meaning. As the discussion in Chapter I indicated, *pharmaka* embraces potions used to affect life or birth. The Vulgate preserved the ambiguity by translating *pharmakeia* as *veneficia,* and *pharmakoi* as *venefici.* The roughly contemporary usage by Plutarch in *Romulus* 22 shows that *pharmakeia* in respect to children was an idea familiar to the Greeks. We cannot now resolve the ambiguity, but can only conclude that the New Testament in these passages does record a hostility to "medicine" and "medicine men." Whether this hostility is based on the pagan, magical association of the drugs or on their purpose as well cannot be apodictically determined. Although *pharmakeia* covers drugs, one can contend that it includes contraceptive potions only if one assumes that the early Christians regarded such potions as evil. There were a vast variety of potions used to kill, to make a man love, or to make a man hate (Philo, *The Special Laws* 3.94). There was, moreover, a sense in which *pharmakon* could mean a helpful drug. In chapter 20 of his celebrated letter to the Ephesians, St. Ignatius of Antioch spoke of the community "breaking the one bread, which is the *pharmakon* of immortality." There is, in short, "good medicine" and "bad medicine." One cannot tell from the condemnations of *pharmakeia* presented in the New Testament whether only certain of the drugs used for evil purposes were condemned, whether all were condemned, or whether a contraceptive potion fell within the category of "bad medicine."

These particular texts of the New Testament on virginity, marriage, intercourse, sin, "medicine," provide the basis from which doctrine bearing on contraception is developed. It is apparent that the texts themselves emphasize different and sometimes contrasting values. The relationship between the texts could not be settled by simple inspection of them. Was Paul's view of marriage as a permitted sexual outlet to be given more or less weight than 1 Timothy's more positive affirmation of salvation through motherhood? Was Matthew on eunuchs to be taken literally? These kinds of questions were implicit in the collection of writings constituting Scripture, and they were not answered at once. It is evident that procreation as the primary purpose of marriage is not emphasized in these writings. It is also evident that several topics relevant to our subject were not expressly touched on: the intention with which intercourse in marriage may be sought; the lawfulness of marriage by the sterile; the role of pleasure in marriage. No more was contraception itself expressly treated. Any doctrine on the subject claiming to be Christian had to be constructed from inferences based on the New Testament texts we have cited, the Old Testament teachings which were retained, and the great commandments of love. This work of construction was the work of the Christian community.

The construction was not a purely theological enterprise. It was not undertaken in a vacuum, removed from other religious, philosophical, and social strivings. The state of medical knowledge was one factor in the development of theory on marital intercourse. The predominant institutional modifications of monogamous marriage in Roman society, namely, slave concubinage and easy divorce, affected the values which Christians would stress in marriage. Contemporary Jewish thought and contemporary Stoic thought formed other patterns limiting the impact of the Gospels. Gnostic speculation created a current to which Christians reacted.

Within the intellectual and social context of the Roman Empire, the vital acts of selection, discrimination, emphasis, and application of the biblical texts were performed. In this collaboration between the Christian community and the written word, under the pressures generated by Roman life, the teaching on contraception took shape.

THE STOIC IDEAL

Turning now to the secular intellectual influences on the doctrine, we look at material whose influence, if more transitory, was as real as that of Scripture. If the Stoic writings did not occupy a privileged position, if consequently they were not to be consciously returned to by later generations seeking renewal, they had a powerful grip on the minds of many of the ablest Christians; and as the writings of the Fathers incorporating Stoic doctrine were frequently returned to, the teaching of the Stoics was not without its impulse of life long after Stoicism had perished. Stoicism was in the air the intellectual converts to Christianity breathed. Half consciously, half unconsciously, they accommodated some Christian beliefs to a Stoic sense.

Perhaps one might suppose a fundamental incompatibility between the law of love and basic Stoic tenets. The Stoics distrusted emotion; viewed dependence on others with scorn; measured in terms of justice, not love. Yet they also cherished virtues of a less disillusioned character. Stoic universalism could buttress Christian brotherhood. Stoic rationality might be linked to the purposefulness of the redeemed Christian. The Christians shared with the Stoics, or took from them, the assumption that there was a natural law by which acts unworthy of human beings might be judged.

The Stoic approach to sexuality apparently had a particular appeal for Christian moralists. The Stoics sought to control bodily desires by reason, to the end of being rationally self-sufficient, dependent on no external force. A typical Stoic such as Epictetus considered immoderation in bodily activities irrational, for it made a man dependent on his own body (*Enchiridion* 41).[16] The Stoic watchwords were nature, virtue, decorum, freedom from excess. The Christian intellectuals adopted these guides to sexuality without adopting the Stoic goal of rational self-sufficiency. Logically, a Stoic might have condemned marriage as another form of coerced dependence on another. But moderation and respect for nature curbed Stoic logic. Passion in marriage was alone suspect. Marriage must have another basis. Plainly that basis was its necessary part in the propagation of the race. By this standard of rational purposefulness, self-evident and supplied by nature, excess in marital intercourse might be measured. This view of marriage was to seem right and good to many Christians.

[16] Epictetus, *Enchiridion*, in vol. II of *Epictetus*, ed. Heinrich Schenckl, trans. W. A. Oldfather, Loeb Classical Library (Cambridge, Mass., 1928).

In the first century the clearest formulation of Stoic marital doctrine is made by Musonius Rufus, the influential teacher in Rome of Epictetus, the younger Pliny, and a number of other Romans from the governing class. Musonius taught that marital intercourse was morally right only if its purpose were procreative; intercourse for pleasure within the limits of marriage was reprehensible.[17] His doctrine joined the Stoic distrust of pleasure and the Stoic insistence on purpose.

Seneca, that experienced first-century Stoic rhetorician and states-man, proclaimed:

All love of another's wife is shameful; so too, too much love of your own. A wise man ought to love his wife with judgment, not affection. Let him con-trol his impulses and not be borne headlong into copulation. Nothing is fouler than to love a wife like an adulteress. Certainly those who say that they unite themselves to wives to produce children for the sake of the state and the human race ought, at any rate, to imitate the beasts, and when their wife's belly swells not destroy the offspring. Let them show themselves to their wives not as lovers, but as husbands.[18]

The neo-Pythagoreans, themselves imbued with Stoic doctrine, held the same views on marriage. "It is particularly well established," says a Pytharogean treatise spuriously ascribed to Ocellus Lucanus, "that we have intercourse not for pleasure but for the purpose of procreation . . . The sexual organs are given man not for pleasure, but for the mainten-ance of the species" (*The Nature of the Universe*, sec. 44).[19] From an originally pagan collection of gnomic wisdom came the epigram, "An adulterer is also everyone who is shameless with his own wife." [20] Sym-bolic of Stoic influence, the epigram, in a variation of it by St. Jerome, was destined to echo through a thousand years of Christian writing on marriage.

The prevailing doctrine in these highly respectable, morally earnest circles thus favored the restriction of sexual activity by rules of reason appealing to nature. These authors had sought a purpose for sexual ac-

[17] Musonius Rufus, *Reliquiae*, ed. O. Hense (Leipzig, 1905), sec. 63.

[18] Seneca, *Fragments*, ed. Friedrich G. Haase (Leipzig, 1897), no. 84. This passage is found only in Jerome, *Against Jovinian* 1.49. It is contained in a section where Jerome introduces the teaching of Aristotle, Plutarch, and "our Seneca." He does not identify specific quotations from Seneca, and it is doubtless impossible to demon-strate that he has not sharpened the passage, although this is unlikely if the work was well known. Haase claims the passage here quoted as obviously from Seneca; he ascribes it to a lost treatise entitled *Marriage*. The reference to imitating the beasts by not destroying the offspring is understood in later literature as an injunction not to have intercourse in pregnancy.

[19] *Ocellus Lucanus*, text and commentary by Richard Harder (Berlin, 1926).

[20] *The Sentences of Sextus*, Greek and Latin texts edited by Henry Chadwick (Cambridge, 1959), no. 231. Chadwick shows that the final compiler of the collec-tion of these sayings later used in Christian circles was himself a Christian; he rejects as improbable Jerome's identification of Sextus as a Pythagorean. The original collec-tion, however, was made by a pagan (p. 137).

tivity, and they had found it in the biological function. The suspicion they felt toward affection and dependence excluded the expression of love as a purpose. The supreme norm for them was not love, but nature.

If one asks, then, where the Christian Fathers derived their notions on marital intercourse — notions which have no express biblical basis — the answer must be, chiefly from the Stoics. In the case of such an early and influential teacher as Clement of Alexandria, the direct descent is obvious; his work on the purposes of marriage is a paraphrase of works of Musonius.[21] In the second century, Origen's standard for intercourse in pregnancy is clearly Seneca's. In the third century, Lactantius' remarks on the obvious purpose of the generative faculties echo Ocellus Lucanus. In the fourth century, Jerome's most austere remarks are taken from Seneca. It is not a matter of men expressing simple truths which common sense might suggest to anyone with open eyes. It is a matter of a doctrine consciously appropriated. The descent is literary, the dependence substantial.

Contraception itself was, of course, implicitly excluded by the Stoic doctrine. There is one explicit statement by Musonius Rufus, in which he argues directly against contraception with an appeal to civic responsibility and family pride:

The lawgivers, who had the same task of searching out and finding what was good for the city and what bad, and what helped or harmed it, did not they also all consider that it was most beneficial to their cities to fill the houses of the citizens, and most harmful to deplete them? They considered that childlessness, or small families, of citizens was unprofitable, while to have children, and in fact many children, was profitable. Therefore they forbade the women to induce miscarriage, and punished those who did not obey; therefore they forbade them to court childlessness and to prevent conception; therefore they set prizes for those with many children, both husbands and wives, and made childlessness subject to penalties. How then could it be that we are not acting unjustly and unlawfully, when we do things contrary to the wish of these lawmakers, godly and god-favored men, whom it is considered good and useful to follow? And we act against their wish when we prevent our women from having many children. How could we not be sinning against our ancestral gods and against Zeus, protector of the family, when we do such things? For just as he who mistreats a guest sins against Zeus the protector of the rights of hospitality, and he who acts unrighteously to a friend, against Zeus the god of friendship, even so whoever acts unrighteously toward his family line sins against his ancestral gods and against Zeus protector of the family, who watches for sins against the family: and he who sins against the gods is impious. And indeed one can see that it is good and profitable to rear children, when he considers how a man with many children is honored in the city, and how he shames his neighbors, and is the most powerful among his equals, if they are not equally blest with children. For just as a man with many friends is more powerful than a friendless man, likewise a man with many children is more powerful than one who has no children, or few; and the more so, as a son

[21] Paul Wendland, *Quaestiones Musonianae* (Berlin, 1886), p. 35.

stands in a closer relationship than does a friend. It is right to consider as something special and wonderful a man or woman with large family seen among assembled sons and daughters. One could not see any procession in honor of the gods so beautiful, nor any sacred choral dance of dancers moving in fine measure so worth looking at, as a procession of many children leading the way in the city of their father or mother, and leading their parents by the hand, or in some other fashion carefully ministering to them. What sight is more splendid than this? What is more enviable than these parents, especially if they are good people? With whom would one more fervently join in praying for good things from the gods, or more heartily strive to achieve what they have done? [22]

This appeal to civic virtue and this emphasis on the desirability of a big family will not be found in the early Christian approach. Nonetheless, the Stoic opposition to contraception is clearly a precedent for Christian opposition.

To be sure, the Christian view of contraception might have been much the same if Stoicism had never existed. The Stoic doctrine on marriage would never have been received if there were not other strands of thought in the Christian community to which it was congenial. Before Clement, Origen, or Jerome, the law of nature had been invoked by St. Paul to determine sexual vice. Values in the Jewish heritage of the Christians were confirmed by the Stoic teaching. The statement that the rational use of sexual faculties is a procreative one is not the same as the Old Testament statement that fecundity is highly desirable. The ideas do, however, harmonize; and either might have been sufficient basis for rejecting contraception. But what Christian sexual doctrine would have been without the influence of Stoic teaching is a speculative construction. In fact, the Stoic view of marital intercourse, the stress on procreative purpose, the failure to connect intercourse and love, were profound influences on the Christian approach; the doctrine on contraception, as it was fashioned, largely depended upon them.

THE JEWISH HERITAGE

The Jewish heritage is, of course, much more than the scriptural statements and the attitudes engendered by them which we have already examined. There was the living Judaism from which many Christian leaders came. The legacy of this Judaism is the Talmud, the Tosefta, and the Midrash. Put together as definitive collections in the fifth century, these works testify to values and ideas probably current in the period of nascent and growing Christianity. I cite their texts embodying moral judgments on contraception as indicative of valuations which Christians coming from a Jewish milieu would have known and found acceptable.

[22] Musonius Rufus, "Should All Children Born be Brought Up?" as quoted in Stobaeus, *Florilegium* 75.15, in Musonius, *Reliquiae*, ed. Hense.

In the Babylonian Talmud, *Niddah* 13a has a stern condemnation of masturbation, and the third-century Palestinian rabbi Johanan ben Nappaha is quoted: "Whoever emits semen in vain deserves death." To say that a person deserves death is a way of expressing strong disapproval, but to estimate its force one should bear in mind that the Talmud also teaches that one who admires a beautiful tree while discussing Scripture "deserves death." An association of ideas, often to be met with in later Christian literature, is made between an act destroying the seed and homicide. The punishment of Onan is cited, and in addition Isaias 57:5, which speaks of the idolatrous sacrifice of children, is found apposite: it is cited as condemning the "pressing out" of children, that is, apparently, the destruction of children in the waste of human semen. Finally, *Niddah* 13b links the loss of the seed to a Messianic theme: Rabbi Jose states that the Son of David will not come until all the souls of the unborn have been born. Christianity necessarily will reject this idea, in recognizing the coming of the Messiah; but this supernatural reason for encouraging fecundity would seem to have a basic kinship with the medieval Christian theme of fecundity increasing the population of heaven.

Two other books of the Babylonian Talmud explicitly touch the question. *Yebamoth* 34b cites rabbis who teach that the acts both of Onan and of his older brother Er were unnatural. *Shabbath* 110b states that Rabbi Hanina prohibited castration, and cites Leviticus 22:24, prohibiting an offering of castrated animals, as equally prohibitive of castration of men. The same section of *Shabbath* speaks of the sterilizing potion of roots, and, without expressly condemning the drink, seems to imply that the prohibition of castration extends to consumption of such potions. However, a dictum of Rabbi Johanan seems to imply that sterilization indirectly achieved, without affecting the genital organs, is permissible.

There is, then, a tendency apparent in the Talmud to permit exceptions to the rule on contraception. It is permitted by some authorities if the woman's health is endangered or if it is important to postpone conception to preserve the religious or social status of the potential child. Thus coitus interruptus is justified by Rabbi Eliezer when a woman is lactescent, as according to nature (*Yebamoth* 34b). The opinion is a curious foreshadowing of the stand of some twentieth-century Catholic theologians defending the use of progesterone pills in lactation because nature does not intend women to be fertile while they nurse. Similarly Rabbi Bibi, in the presence of Rabbi Nahman, a teacher in Babylon about 330, is reported to permit the use of an "absorbent" or pessary by a nursing mother and also by a pregnant woman and an eleven-year-old girl (*Niddah* 45a). These two cases might be interpreted ironically: contraception is permissible only when conception is impossible. But the Gemara understands all three cases literally and gives reasons. The nursing mother is permitted to prevent pregnancy lest it affect the weaning of her child. The expectant mother is permitted to avoid a second pregnancy which will turn the first into an abortion. The eleven-year-old girl, one year below the legal age of marriage, and above the age where conception is impossible, is permitted to avoid a pregnancy which would affect her health. In *Yebamoth* 35a, which speaks of the proselyte and the captive and the slave uncertain of their fate using contraceptive measures, there may be the implication that, in these special circumstances where a postponement of birth is desirable, contraception by a woman is permissible. A dictum, not assigned to any rabbi and not attached to any clear context, proclaims, "Let, however, a preventive measure be made in respect of a proselyte and an emancipated slave." It is not clear why the emancipated slave should use contraceptives, unless the view is that she will engage in illicit intercourse and her illegitimate children should be prevented. No judgment is given on the behavior of the harlot who expels seed after coitus; but approval seems implicit.

In *Yebamoth* 65b the story is told of Judith, the wife of Rabbi Hiyya, who had twins, one of whom developed more quickly than the other as a fetus; in consequence she suffered agonizing pain in childbirth. After her recovery she came in disguise before her husband and asked, "Is a woman commanded to propagate the race?" "No," he answered. Relying on the decision, she drank a sterilizing potion. When Hiyya later found out that it was his own wife and that his own ruling had deprived him of more children, he is reported to have said, "Would that you bore unto me only one more issue of the womb." Hiyya's ruling is preserved in the Tosefta, of which he was the principal author. Here the text gives a generality and explicitness to his statement that the story in the Talmud, with its emphasis on the medical reason for his wife's action and the ironic consequence of Hiyya's opinion, obscures. The Tosefta reads, "A man is not allowed to drink a cup of roots in order to become sterile, but a woman is allowed to drink a cup of roots to become sterile" (*Yebamoth* 8.4). In comparison with the general attitude and cautious casuistry of the Talmud, the Tosefta appears simple and radical in its solution.

Two other related questions are discussed in the Babylonian Talmud: the duty of propagation and the limits of permissible behavior in marriage. Not surprisingly, opinion is divided on both questions. The controversies are of interest, because in each case Christian converts could have been adherents of the more rigorous school. The Mishnah in *Yebamoth* 65b says that only a man "has a duty to propagate the race," but Rabbi Johanan ben Beroka holds that both man and woman have the duty. The Gemara in the same section also reports a conflict of opinions. The Mishnah in *Yebamoth* 61b states that "a man shall not abstain from the performance of the duty of propagation of the race unless he already has children." Shammai is cited as saying this means two male children, Hillel that it means a boy and a girl. The Gemara, discussing the Mishnah text, speaks of a man, after he has completed his duty, as being free to marry a sterile wife, but says nothing explicitly or even indirectly suggesting that the man is now free to practice coitus interruptus.

The problem of birth control might have been much to the fore, if the low requirements of procreation were considered in conjunction with the teaching on the duty of intercourse. The Midrash, *Mekhiltha*, interpreted Exodus 21:10 (asserting that a man who takes another wife may not deny food, clothing, or conjugal rights to his first wife) as imposing a duty of conjugal intercourse.[23] The Mishnah, *Kethuboth* 61b, said that, according to Rabbi Eliezer, the time for conjugal duty for men of independent means was every day, for laborers twice a week, for ass-drivers once a week, for camel-drivers once in thirty days, for sailors once in six months. If a man took a vow not to have intercourse with his wife, the period could not be more than two weeks according to the school of Shammai, more than one week according to the school of Hillel.

As to permissible forms of marital intercourse, Rabbi Johanan is reported in *Nedarim* 20b ("Vows") as saying, "A man may do all that he will do with his own wife." The context suggests an approval of at least anal intercourse. But other authorities are cited who criticize intercourse not in the usual way. Even a posture in which the woman is above the man is condemned by the second-century Rabbi Johanan bar Dahabai (*Nedarim* 20a).

The interpretation given the story of Onan in the Talmudic literature was probably bolstered by *The Testament of the Twelve Patriarchs*, a popular set of stories written perhaps as early as 100 B.C. In the narrative attributed to him, the patriarch Juda amplifies the account of Genesis 38:8–10 as follows:

And after these things my son Er took to wife Tamar from Mesopotamia, a daughter of Aram. Now Er was wicked, and he was in need concerning Tamar because she was not of the Land of Canaan. And on the third night an angel of the Lord smote him. And he had not known her, according to the evil craftiness of his mother, for he did not wish to have children by her. In the days of the wedding feast I gave Onan to her in marriage, and he also in wickedness knew her not, though he spent with her a year. And when I threatened him, he went into her, but he spilled his seed on the ground according to the command of his mother, and he also died through wickedness.[24]

The story has some ambiguity. Er is not said to have attempted intercourse, while Onan not only attempts intercourse but spends a year with

[23] *Mekhiltha* 85a (Vienna, 1865), Ex 21:10.
[24] "The Testament of Judah" 10:1–5, *The Testament of the Twelve Patriarchs*, in R. H. Charles, *The Apocrypha and Pseudepigrapha of the Old Testament* (Oxford, 1918), II, 318–319.

Thamar. The acts constituting the specific sins of Er and of Onan could be argued. But, like Genesis 38, the story, whatever its author's intention, has a plot which could be used didactically to illustrate the evil of coitus interruptus. By no means as authoritative for the Jews as Scripture or the Talmud, the *Testament* was to have a long history among Christians.

Early Christians may also have been influenced in their views on marital morality by the practices of the Essenes. This small Jewish community, estimated at no more than four thousand by Philo, lived on the margin of Palestinian civilization about the beginning of the Christian era. As a community living an ascetic life, it functioned as an exemplar. Josephus writes that some Essenes maintain celibacy, while "another order" of them marries. The married "do not approach those with child, showing that they marry not for self-indulgence, but for the procreation of children." [25] Josephus, writing in a Roman intellectual milieu, may have had some interest in putting Stoic doctrine in Essene mouths; his work at least is evidence of what would strike a Romanized Jew as an ascetic ideal.

Philo, the foremost philosopher of the first-century diaspora, may be taken as a final example of Jewish thought on marriage at the time of Jesus and St. Paul. Neither a rabbi nor a friend of Christians nor an ascetic sectarian, Philo is an intellectual responding to the best philosophy of the day, conscious of Jewish doctrine, desirous of setting out the rules of the Old Testament humanely and reasonably as natural and just. Not himself a Stoic, and rejecting the Stoic extirpation of all emotions,[26] Philo condemns "the passion of love" as the origin of countless calamities, and the desire for bodily beauty as the source of lustful wickedness (*The Special Laws* 4.85–90).[27] Explaining the Mosaic law on adultery, Philo anticipates Seneca's famous dictum on adulterous love within marriage: "Now even natural pleasure is often greatly to blame when the craving for it is immoderate and insatiable . . . as the passionate desire for women shown by those who in their rage for sexual intercourse behave unchastely, not with the wives of others, but with their own" (*ibid.* 3.2.9).

Philo does not say here what it means "to behave unchastely," but in a retelling of the story of Joseph in Egypt he has Joseph explain to Putiphar's wife the difference between marital intercourse for procreation and intercourse for the unlawful purpose of pleasure (*Joseph* 9.43). In his

[25] Josephus, *The Jewish War*, ed. and trans. H. St. John Thackeray, Loeb Classical Library (Cambridge, Mass., 1961), 2.120, 160.

[26] On Philo's relation to Stoicism, see Harry Austryn Wolfson, *Philo* (Cambridge, Mass., 1948), II, 276.

[27] All references to Philo are to the texts printed in the Loeb Classical Library edition with English translations by F. H. Colson (Cambridge, Mass., 1935–1939): *De specialibus legibus* in vols. VII and VIII thereof, *De Josepho* and *De Abrahamo* in vol. VI.

exposition of the story of Abraham, God blesses married couples who have intercourse for children; He punishes those whose intercourse is "disordered" and "limitless" (*Abraham* 137).

With the agricultural metaphors favored by the Stoics Philo attacks the homosexuals. "Like a bad husbandman," the homosexual "spends his labor night and day on soil from which no growth at all can be expected." The revulsion from pagan pleasure-seeking, the need to set a single standard for sexual behavior, pushes Philo to a position not taken by anyone before him: the condemnation of marriage with women known to be sterile. If a woman turns out to be sterile after marriage, a man may be excused who does not divorce her; familiarity with the woman extenuates his sin in retaining her. But if a woman has been proved to be barren in an earlier marriage, a man who marries her "ploughs hard and stony land"; he acts for lust alone and is condemnable. Of such men Philo says, "Those persons who make an art of quenching the life of the seed as it drops stand confessed as the enemies of nature" (*The Special Laws* 3.36). At no point does Philo apply this doctrine to contraception directly; the whole thrust of what he says is against contraception absolutely.

Philo's teaching on intercourse in menstruation is an objection to the contraceptive effect of such intercourse. Leviticus 18:19 and Ezechiel had forbidden intercourse during menstruation without explanation. He explains the prohibition on the ground that conception is impossible. The fresh menses make the womb moist; the humidity "paralyzes the seminal nerve forces" (*The Special Laws* 3.6.32). In this reading, Leviticus 18:19 could become a general prohibition of contraception. Philo, however, does not so extend it.

The position of Philo is particularly instructive. Here is a man writing at the beginning of the Christian era, the Jewish writer most sensitive to Greek thought, a virtuous man developing the law of the Old Testament in the Gentile world of Alexandria. Without Christian influence he sets out a doctrine on marital relations very close to that which the Christian Fathers will adopt. In his philosophical and exegetical methods Philo is a strong influence on the second-century generation of Christian intellectuals; he is also their predecessor, if not their guide, in these matters of marital ethics.

The New Testament taught that the supreme law for Christians was to love one another as the Lord had loved them. Human beings were to be loved — but the New Testament provided no information as to when a being became human. It communicated the command to love men; those who followed the commandment would be impelled to discover who "men" were. On marriage and marital intercourse the New Testament provided a variety of perspectives, from the view in 1 Corinthians of marital intercourse as a sexual outlet, to the belief in 1 Timothy in salvation through childbearing, to the proclamation in Ephesians of the symbolism of marital love. Marriage was good; virginity was better. What these propositions meant had to be worked out. Some kinds of sexual desire and intercourse were unholy, even unnatural. The implications of these teachings had to be developed. The Old Testament, which was accepted as part of the Christian inheritance, blessed fertility. It also presented a number of commands on sexual usage such as the prohibition of intercourse in menstruation. The Jewish interpretation contemporary with early Christianity taught that in Genesis 38 coitus interruptus was condemned by God. The Stoic intellectuals found in procreative purpose the only measure by which lawful sexual behavior could be distinguished from lust. Philo agreed. In the blending of Stoic doctrine with the more rigorous beliefs of Jewish intellectuals, what was to be the dominant view of marital intercourse among the Christian Fathers was already formed.

The teaching on contraception springs from a combination of the doctrinal elements just reviewed. That these elements were, in fact, fashioned into a teaching on contraception was not an inevitable result. Development of doctrine is rarely a logical necessity. It is a response of the Christian community to meditation on the Scripture and to the pressures of the environment. Both Scripture and environment confine the options. But there are usually options. The selection is a creative choice which may be observed but not completely accounted for.

In the case of contraception the major texts on marriage, 1 Corinthians 7 and Ephesians 5, said nothing that dictated the development. The high valuation of virginity was accompanied by a disinterest in the growth of the Church by physical propagation. The New Testament teaching on love invited freedom, particularly in accordance with Ephesians 5, in the expression of love between man and wife. Why were the rules on contraception adopted? The shape the teaching took depended not only on the texts of Scripture and the doctrines current in intellectual circles of the first century which the Christians found congenial; it depended also on those forces which the Christians identified as alien and enemy. To these antithetic attitudes and movements the next chapter is addressed.

CHAPTER III

GNOSTICS, PAGANS, AND THE

ALEXANDRIAN RULE

HE FORMATION of early Christian doctrine on contraception is largely
a response to two major attitudes prevalent in the Greco-Roman
world. One attitude was religious and therefore, I believe, of greater
concern to religious men. It was an attitude hostile to all procreation. It
was the position of the Gnostics. The other attitude was less defined,
more generally secular. It consisted of indifference to the preservation of
embryonic and infant life. It was the attitude of many pagans. Connected
with it, although distinguishable, was an indifference to male promiscuity
and to the sexual exploitation of other persons.

In opposition to these attitudes, the Christians adopted the Jewish-
Stoic rules and a specific condemnation of contraception. The extreme
positions against which they reacted had a major effect on the formulations they adopted. An understanding of the Christian consciousness is
inadequate unless the Christian view of the forces and beliefs which
seemed antithetical to their position is grasped. To a consideration of
these counter forces we now turn, and first to a consideration of a movement not only antithetical but competitive — the religious tendencies embraced under the general heading "Gnosticism."

The Gnostic movement, which caused such a profound reaction in
nascent Christianity, coupled Iranian myths, Jewish mysticism, and Jewish
magic; it was nourished by Greek and Chaldean philosophical and mystical speculation; and, finally, it appealed to the freedom from law proclaimed by Christ and St. Paul. It incorporated a number of Christian
personages, symbols, texts, and even doctrines. By the third century a
Christian might regard a Gnostic creed as only a variation on certain
pagan myths. But especially in the first two centuries, the Gnostics, believing that they had a better understanding of Christ than the orthodox
one, did not hesitate to press their interpretation on those whom they may
have regarded as an opposing school. Often enough they were successful.
The reaction of orthodox Christianity to Gnosticism, then, was not the

pure disdain felt for some pagan cults. It was a reaction to an active, proselytizing interpretation of the Christian mysteries; a reaction to a religious force which, before it was vanquished, left its impress on early Christian thought.[1]

"Gnosis" was a good word, meaning "knowledge." The orthodox claimed to have the "knowledge" of revelation; but the "gnosis" of those labeled Gnostics was a special knowledge higher than that of ordinary Christians. Gnosticism itself was not unitary, but a series of movements claiming such knowledge. In the first two centuries the Gnostics were usually found in individual schools consisting of a teacher and disciples; by the third century they were often organized over more than one region as a sect. The names of the schools and sects, and the sources of their beliefs, are many. Preoccupied with religion and controlled by neither a central ecclesiastical authority nor a canonical scripture, the Gnostics produced a variety of doctrinal and moral formulations. For our purposes, however, in all this variety of doctrine there was one significant common theme. Virtually without exception, the Gnostics challenged marriage as a child-related institution.

ORGANIZED OPPOSITION TO PROCREATION

A spectrum of possible moral positions on sexual intercourse might range as follows from left to right (the terms are used without political prejudice):[2]

		Doctrine	*Advocates*
Left:	1.	Intercourse in all possible ways is mandatory for salvation.	Believers in all possible experience
	2.	Intercourse in any way is permissible for anyone.	Strict antinomians

[1] On Gnosticism and Christianity in the first century, see Robert M. Grant, *Gnosticism and Early Christianity* (New York, 1959); Walter Frei, *Geschichte und Idee der Gnosis* (Zurich, 1958); Hans Jonas, *Gnosis und spätantiker Geist* (Göttingen, 1954). For a view stressing the differences between Gnosticism and orthodox Christianity see Jean Doresse, *Les Livres secrets des gnostiques d'Egypte: Introduction aux écrits gnostiques coptes découverts à Khénoboskion* (Paris, 1958), p. 367. In the posthumously published work of a great scholar, Arthur Darby Nock, the statement is made that the relationship of Gnosticism to Christianity "may fairly be called the crucial issue today in the study of early Christianity." "Gnosticism," *Harvard Theological Review* 57 (1964), 255. Nock's view is that the newly discovered Gnostic texts "vindicate completely the traditional view of Gnosticism as Christian heresy with roots in speculative thought," a heresy which arose at a time when orthodoxy had not yet taken shape by conflict and contrast (p. 274).

[2] The Gnostics themselves used "left" and "right" to designate, respectively, the lower and higher elements; see François M. M. Sagnard, *La Gnose valentinienne et le témoignage de St. Irénée* (Paris, 1947), pp. 544–545. Cf. Mt 25:33.

	Doctrine	*Advocates*
	3. Intercourse is permissible for anyone as long as procreation is avoided.	Dualists
Center:	4. Intercourse for women is decent only in marriage; intercourse for men is permissible with wives, concubines, prostitutes.	Conventional Roman society
	5. Intercourse in marriage alone is permissible; within marriage there are no limits or specific purposes.	Much of Old Testament
	6. Intercourse in marriage alone is permissible provided it is not against nature.	A few Church Fathers
Right:	7. Intercourse in marriage alone is permissible and then only for procreation.	Stoics
	8. Virginity is preferred, but intercourse in marriage, for procreation only, is permissible.	Most Church Fathers
	9. Intercourse is never permissible.	Strict ascetics

The extreme left was considered by the orthodox writers to be occupied by the Gnostics, with the modification that the orthodox believed that adherents of 1 and 2 opposed procreation. Position 9 was, in the Christian view, also occupied by the Gnostics, except that the orthodox suspected that in practice it was more like 3. The Christian reaction was substantially against the three positions of the left.

Gnosticism, as a special mixture of Christian theology and sexual morality, was ancient, contemporaneous with St. Paul and the composition of the Gospels. The characteristic Gnostic claims of a higher knowledge and freedom from moral law were the frequent subject of vehement refutation by Paul; it is evident that they penetrated some of the earliest Christian communities. As early as 1 Corinthians, St. Paul has to tell the new converts that incest is not permitted, a sin which both gentiles and Jews would have condemned, so that its acceptance by the community must have been due to an antinomian self-confidence. This, Paul says, is not the way "of keeping festival" (1 Cor 5:1–8). Paul earnestly warns them that, while "all things are lawful," "the body is not for immorality" (1 Cor 6:12–13). In Romans, Paul may not be merely putting a rhetorical question but answering an argument when he asks, "Shall we continue in sin that grace may abound?" (Rom 6:1). He may be refuting a real contention when he declares, "Therefore, brethren, we are debtors not to the flesh" (8:12). There is no condemnation for "those who are in Christ Jesus," on one significant condition, that they "do not walk according to the flesh" (8:1). In Philippians, Paul speaks of Christians whose "glory is in their shame," who are "enemies of the cross of Christ" (3:18). In

Galatians, he warns his readers "not to use liberty as an occasion for sensuality" (5:13). In Ephesians 5, there is plain opposition to persons in the community who permit and practice sexual immorality: "Let no one lead you astray with empty words." A fornicator or one guilty of other sexual misbehavior has no part of Christ (5:5–7). The recipients of the letter are urged to have no part in these "unfruitful works of darkness." Of what these others do "in secret," "it is shameful even to speak" (5:11–12).

In the later epistles to Timothy, Gnostics appear to be the object of renewed warning. In 1 Timothy Gnostics are attacked by means of a prophecy of those who will "give heed to deceitful spirits and the doctrines of devils." These men "will forbid marriage and will enjoin abstinence from food" (1 Tm 4:1,3). Against the Gnostic teaching it is asserted that women will be "saved by childbearing" (1 Tm 2:15). In 2 Timothy 2:18, Hymeneus and Philetus are denounced for saying that "the resurrection has already taken place," a belief which was probably a postulate of antinomian behavior. The faithful are urged to shun "those who make their way into houses and captivate silly women who are sin-laden and led awry by various lusts, ever learning yet never attaining knowledge of the truth" (2 Tm 3:6–7).

In Apocalypse there is twice a fierce denunciation of "Nicolaites." The church at Ephesus hates "the works of the Nicolaites, which I also hate" (Ap 2:6). But the church at Pergamum has "some who hold the teaching of the Nicolaites." They are likened to those who "hold the teaching of Balaam, who taught Balak to cast a stumbling-block before the children of Israel, that they might eat and commit fornication" (Ap 2:14–15). The danger of antinomian license is also warned against in Jude: "certain men have stealthily entered in," who "turn the grace of God into wantonness" (Jude 4). They are "sensual men, not having the Spirit" (19). They walk "according to their lusts" (16). The things "they know by instinct like the dumb beasts become for them a source of destruction" (10). They sin, in particular, at banquets where they stain their feasts of love (12). Against them is invoked the example of Sodom and Gomorrah, which "committed sins of immorality and practiced unnatural vice" (7).

Similar urgent warning permeates 2 Peter. Among you there will be "lying teachers who will bring in destructive sects" (2 Pt 2:1). Sodom and Gomorrah were destroyed "as an example to those who in the future should live impiously" (2:6). These men (the tense becomes present) are "like irrational animals" (2:12). "They regard as pleasure their delight in revelry; they are spots and blemishes, they abound in wantonness while banqueting with you. They have eyes full of adultery and turned unceasingly toward sin" (2:13–14). They "entice with sensual allurements of carnal passion those who are just escaping from such as live

in error" (2:18). They are, in addition, guilty of distorting certain difficult passages in St. Paul "to their own destruction" (3:16). In both 2
Peter 2:15 and Jude 11 the persons warned against are said to have followed the way of Balaam, so that the rabbinical elaboration of Numbers
22–24, which Apocalypse uses, seems to be the standard comparison for
these licentious Christians. As the Talmudic tradition conveys this story,
Balaam is guilty of "practicing magic by means of his genitals" (Rabbi
Johanan and Rabbi Mar Zutra as quoted in the Babylonian Talmud, San-
hedrin 105a). The connection of sexual crime and magic made in the
Talmudic story is precisely what the orthodox impute to the Gnostics.

"Gnostic" was the later description of this current of thought contemporaneous with the gospel. The orthodox Christians of the second century
traced the intellectual descent of the Gnostics they encountered to these
rivals of the apostles. Simon Magus, who was teaching in Samaria when
St. Peter met him, according to Acts 8:9–24, was seen as the first Gnostic.
The Nicolaites whom the Apocalypse decried were seen as bearers of the
Gnostic word.[3] The accuracy of these second-century descriptions could
be debated; they testify to the antiquity of the competition.

In the second century the Gnostic current exerted strong pressure on
the still nascent Church. As Christian intellectuals began to speculate on
the data of apostolic times, the danger may have been particularly acute.
Gnosticism threatened to engulf the Christian centers of thought at
Alexandria and at Rome. The first orthodox authority on Gnosticism, that
is, the first Christian to analyze the Gnostic beliefs as systems, was Clement of Alexandria. According to Jerome "the most learned of the Fathers,"
this converted philosopher wrote near the end of the second century in
the city which was both a hotbed of Gnostic speculation and the center
of Christian theology. As the Alexandrian school's view of marriage was
to exercise a dominant influence on later Christian thought, Clement's
view of the Gnostic competition is of peculiar importance.

On the extreme right were the Gnostic ascetics, who relied on their
exegesis of certain texts of the New Testament. Their most prominent
representative was Tatian, a disciple of St. Justin. Justin had thought it
laudable for a Christian youth to show the baselessness of Roman
beliefs about Christian promiscuity by seeking legal permission to castrate himself (Apology 1.29), but he had never condemned marriage as
such. After Justin's martyrdom in 169, Tatian became the leader of those
known as the Encratites, "the self-controlled." For them marriage was
corruption and fornication (Tatian, Perfection According to the Saviour,
as quoted by Clement, Stromata 3.12.90, GCS 15:237). Another leader of

---

[3] Irenaeus, The Pretended Gnosis 1.23.1, 1.26.3, PG 7:670, 687. Irenaeus' work
bears the title Against the Heretics in PG 7. I adopt the title restored to it in Doresse,
Les Livres secrets, p. 5.

this current of thought was Julius Cassianus, who wrote a book entitled *Abstinence or Eunuchry*.

The ascetic Gnostics placed great reliance on a fifth Gospel, *The Gospel According to the Egyptians*. Clement's attitude toward it is instructive. It is not among "the four Gospels which have been handed down to us" (*Stromata* 3.13.93, GCS 15:238). Yet he does not stamp the work apocryphal, as he does another gospel circulated in the community, and he is always at pains to provide an exegesis for the texts from it which the Gnostics use to disparage marriage. There are five such texts which Clement knows. The first is a dialogue between Jesus and Salome. She asks, "How long shall men die?" Jesus answers, "As long as you women bear children." Writers like Julius Cassianus take this as an implicit injunction to defeat death by ceasing from procreation. Clement resorts to allegorical explanation. By "as long as women bear children" the Lord meant "as long as desires are active" (*Stromata* 3.9.64–67, GCS 15:225–226). A second text is this: the Saviour says "I came to destroy the works of the female." The Gnostics say "female" means "desire" and "works" mean "birth and corruption." Clement answers them by saying that the Lord has in fact destroyed the works of desire; desire is not merely sexual, but encompasses such things as greed for money. And, though desire is destroyed, "birth and corruption" "must necessarily continue until the achievement of complete separation and the restoration of the elect" (*Stromata* 3.9.63, GCS 15:225).

A third saying from the *Gospel According to the Egyptians* was pressed by Julius Cassianus: Salome asked the Lord when those things about which she asked would be known, and he replied, "When you trample on the gown of shame, and when the two become one, and the male female, and the female male." Cassianus urged that the text supported the ideal of eunuchry, "freed from the coupling of members." Clement again invoked allegory. By "male" was meant "anger," and by "female" "desire." The ideal is a man who unites wrath and desire in obedience to reason (*Stromata* 3.13:92–93, GCS 15:238–239).

The *Gospel According to the Egyptians* reported Salome as saying "I would have done better had I never given birth to a child." The Lord replied, "Eat of every plant, but eat not of that which has bitterness in it." In its context, the saying of the Lord could have been intended as reinforcement of Salome's regret. But Clement gives the text a rude twist and argues that it means that the Christian is free to marry or not, apparently adopting the theory that what is "bitter" depends on the subjective disposition of the believer (*Stromata* 3.9.66, GCS 15:226).

The four Gospels themselves offered texts which the ascetics used and which Clement was forced to explain. In Matthew 24:19 and Luke 21:23 are the lines, "But woe to those who are with child or have infants at the breast in those days." In the Coptic version of the *Gospel of Thomas*, contemporary with Clement though not cited by him, similar words are used: "For there shall be days when you will say, 'Blessed is the womb that has not conceived and those breasts which have not given suck.'" [4] It is evident from the use of these lines in a Gnostic gospel, and from Clement's treatment of the verses in Matthew and Luke, that ascetic Gnostics found here a repudiation of childbearing in the days when the kingdom had been established. It might seem easy enough to say that Matthew and Luke were talking about the days following the fall of Jerusalem. But this kind of tying of the Gospel to concrete historical happenings was not much in favor. The best Clement can do with the texts is to say "they are to be interpreted allegorically" (*Stromata* 3.6.49, *GCS* 15:219).

The same theory that Christians are now living the life of the kingdom appears in the use of another text favored by the ascetics, Luke 20:35, "But those who shall be accounted worthy of that world and of the resurrection from the dead, neither marry nor take wives." But, said Clement, this verse refers to the resurrected (*Stromata* 3.12.87, *GCS* 15:236). And "if, as they say, they have already attained the state of resurrection, and on this account reject marriage, let them neither eat nor drink" (*Stromata* 3.6.48, *GCS* 15:218). Clement refuses to accept a morality based on the assumption that Christians are no longer men.

Julius Cassianus interpreted as a commandment not to marry, the words of Jesus on those who made themselves eunuchs in view of the kingdom (Cassianus as reported by Clement, *Stromata* 3.13.91, *GCS* 15:238). A completely literal interpretation of this saying of the Lord is attributed by Clement to the followers of Basilides, a teacher in the Christian community in Alexandria about A.D. 120, although Clement, possibly for tactical purposes, does not charge Basilides himself with the doctrine (*Stromata* 3.1.1, *GCS* 15:196).

Reliance was also placed by the ascetics on Luke 14:20: "I have married a wife and cannot come" is the excuse of one who fails to heed the invitation to the wedding feast and who therefore "will not taste of my supper." Clement noted that this "was an example to convict those who for pleasure's sake were abandoning the divine command" (*Stromata* 3.12.90, *GCS* 15:238). A more far-fetched interpretation was pressed by the ascetics in behalf of their position: "Do not lay up for yourselves treasures on earth where rust and moth corrupt" (Mt 6:19). The text, it was urged, was a prohibition of procreation, which brought into being

---

[4] *The Gospel of Thomas*, according to the Coptic text Chenoboskion X, in *New Testament Apocrypha*, I, ed. Wilhelm Schneemelcher, trans. Robert McL. Wilson (Philadelphia, 1963). *Thomas* twice has the equivalent of Mt 10:37, Lk 14:26: the follower of Christ must hate his parents and brother and sister. But, unlike Lk 14:26, it does not say that the follower must hate his wife (vv. 55, 101). Is this omission because wives were not permitted to members of the community?

what was certain to be corrupted. On this argument Clement commented simply, "But the Saviour did not refer to begetting children" (*Stromata* 3.12.86, *GCS* 15:236).

Above all, the example of Jesus himself was alleged: "They proudly say that they are imitating the Lord who neither married nor had any possession in this world, boasting that they understand the gospel better than anyone else." Clement, with some awkwardness, explained why the example of the Lord need not be followed. First, he had his own bride, the Church. Secondly, he was "no ordinary man that he should also be in need of some helpmeet after the flesh." Third, "it was not necessary for him to beget children since he abides eternally and was born the only Son of God" (*Stromata* 3.6.49, *GCS* 15:218).

Paul was appealed to less than one might suppose, if Clement is to be believed. In his *Perfection According to the Saviour* Tatian, however, interpreted 1 Corinthians 7:5 as condemning sexual intercourse. This difficult exegetical operation was achieved by stressing the phrase, "lest Satan tempt you because you lack self-control." To lack self-control, said Tatian, is to seek intercourse. The married couple are not to give in to this temptation, but to return together again to renounce their rights over each other's body (Tatian as reported by Clement, *Stromata* 3.12.81, *GCS* 15:232–233). Other Gnostics, and perhaps Tatian himself, pointed to the more obvious text in 1 Corinthians 7:1, "It is good for man not to touch woman." Clement felt the objection and resorted to explanation and qualification: "When the apostle says it is good not to touch woman, he speaks not to those who chastely use marriage for procreation alone, but to those who were desiring to go beyond procreation, lest the adversary raise a strong blast and arouse desire for alien pleasures" (*Stromata* 3.15.96, *GCS* 15:240). Clement further answered from the example of the apostles: Paul was married, Peter had children, Philip had children and gave them in marriage (*Stromata* 3.4.52–53, *GCS* 15:220). The statement on Paul appears to be an exegesis of 1 Corinthians 9:5 and Philippians 4:3. This forced interpretation reflects the pressure the ascetics had brought to bear on those trying to defend marriage.

All of this argumentation shows how a strong case could be made from the New Testament for total celibacy, and how the way of meeting this case, without abandoning a moral stance, appeared to be by the insistence that marriage, too, had a purpose, the procreation of the race. The need for finding a purpose was immensely increased by the antinomian beliefs and practices of Gnostics of the left.

The strain of antinomianism which had been assailed by the later epistles of the apostolic age continued to disfigure the Christian image in the Roman world. To Tacitus and to Pliny the Younger, the Christians are known only for their "vices" (Tacitus, *Annals* 15.44, Pliny, *Epistles*

10.96). The word chosen by these conventional Romans to describe their acts, *flagitia*, suggests sexual excess as well as atheism. It is against this cultured pagan belief in Christian immorality that Justin urged his example of the good Christian youth who would have castrated himself (*Apology* 1.29). In the Alexandria of Clement a variety of antinomian factions appeared within the Church. The most important was that of Carpocrates and his son Epiphanes. They believed that women should be common property. For this position, they cited the example of Nicholas, who brought his beautiful wife before the apostles and declared that anyone might marry her, putting into practice the saying, "One must abuse the flesh." They misused the eucharistic feast ("I would not call their meeting an agape"), for, after eating, "they have intercourse where they will and with whom they will." Against them Clement invoked the "prophetic" warning of Jude. Carpocrates was, nonetheless, considered to be a Christian, for Clement was compelled to ask, "And how can this man still be reckoned among our number?" (*Stromata* 3.4.25, 3.2.8, GCS 15:207, 199).[5]

Other Gnostics also abused the Christian agape: "There are some who call Aphrodite Pandemos [physical love] a mystical communion . . . They have impiously called by the name of communion any common sexual intercourse . . . These thrice-wretched men treat carnal and sexual intercourse as a sacred religious mystery, and think that it will bring them to the kingdom of God." To justify their libertine ways, they appealed to Matthew 5:42, "Give to him who seeks." They derived their doctrine from a work which Clement stamped as apocryphal, whose opening passage he quoted, "All things were one, but as it seemed good to its unity not to be alone, an inspiration came from it, it had intercourse with it, and it made the beloved." These men apparently claimed the patronage of Valentinus, for Clement was obliged to contend that Valentinus himself spoke "only of acts of spiritual union." Against these believers, Clement quoted Ephesians 4:20–24 and 5:1–11 and Matthew 5:28 (*Stromata* 3.4.27–29, GCS 15:208–209).

Another group, followers of Prodicus, took for themselves the name of Gnostics. They regarded themselves as "Lords of the Sabbath" and "royal sons" who were bound by no law. In secret they committed adultery (*Stromata* 3.4.30, GCS 15:209–210). Moreover, the followers of Basilides "do not live purely, supposing either that they have the power even to commit sin because of their perfection, or indeed that they will be saved by nature even if they sin in this life because they possess an innate

---

[5] At one time skepticism ran high as to the existence of Carpocrates and his son, who Clement reported had died at seventeen and was the object of a cult, but the prevailing opinon now seems to accept Clement's view as essentially accurate; see John Ernest Leonard Oulton and Henry Chadwick, *Alexandrian Christianity* (London, 1955), pp 26–27.

election." Taking the name of Christ, they "live lewder lives than the most uncontrolled heathens" (*Stromata* 3.1.3, *GCS* 15:196–197).

All of these antinomian groups claimed to proceed from an interpretation of the Gospel. A fourth group also claimed to be Christian, but derived their moral position chiefly from their metaphysics. These were Marcion and his followers. Marcion, a church reformer bitterly opposed to acceptance of the Old Testament, had been excommunicated by the Roman Church in 144 and had thereupon set up a competing organization with a hierarchy and a form of Christian liturgy. His own adherence to Gnostic dualism has been disputed.[6] But there is no doubt that the doctrine of his church on marriage was hostile to marriage, and Clement believed that Marcion himself regarded birth as an evil because the world was evil. Many of the ancient Greeks, Clement pointed out, thought birth was a misfortune because of the ills which beset man, but their opposition was not to creation as such. In contrast, the Marcionites found that "nature is evil." "Therefore, not wanting to fill a world made by this creator, they want to abstain from marriage, resisting their creator" (*Stromata* 3.2.12, *GCS* 15:200–201). The Marcionites are accused of hostility to marriage, but not promiscuity. Another unnamed group of dualists followed to a licentious conclusion the doctrine that the created world is the evil work of the God of the Old Testament. As this evil God said, "Thou shalt not commit adultery," they defied him by breaking this law. Why, of all the commandments, Clement asked rhetorically, is this the one they choose to manifest their opposition by breaking? (*Stromata* 3.4.34, *GCS* 15:211).

This seething Alexandrian world where, within the Christian community itself, marriage was scorned as sinful or as useless was the world where a moral middle way was sought by the dominant figures of the patristic period. But this view of dangers at each extreme was not confined to Alexandria. It appeared equally in the West in the writing of Irenaeus, a native of Smyrna who became a priest of Lyons, in Tertullian, the most ardent Christian apologist of the second century, and in the work called the *Elenchos* or *Refutation of All the Heresies*, ascribed to Hippolytus, a priest of Rome. In Irenaeus' book, *The Pretended Gnosis Unmasked and Refuted*, written about 190, an even sharper sense of the Gnostic menace prevailed than in Clement's work. Irenaeus may have been less informed or less careful about his sources than Clement; he attributed directly to Basilides and Valentinus teachings which Clement only ascribed to followers who misinterpreted them.[7] But Valentinus had

[6] Adolf von Harnack, *Marcion: Das Evangelium vom fremden Gott* (Leipzig, 1923), pp. 135–136.
[7] Opinions differ on the trustworthiness of Ireneaus' account of Valentinus and Valentinian doctrine. Quispel considers Irenaeus reliable (G. Quispel, "The Original Doctrine of Valentine," *Vigiliae Christianae* 1 [1947], 44); Chadwick considers him

taught at Rome after 136, and Clement may not have been informed on his teaching there; moreover, there was an obvious polemical temptation not to attack a distinguished man himself, but his followers' distortions. Even in Clement, Valentinus was charged with teaching that Christ had a purely spiritual nature, a view which Clement associated with a belief that creation is evil (*Stromata* 3.17.102, *GCS* 15:243). In any event, Basilides, Valentinus and Saturninus, their Syrian teacher, appeared to Irenaeus all equally guilty of antinomianism. As what is crucial for the Gnostic influence on doctrine is not so much the beliefs taught by the opponents of orthodoxy as the beliefs the orthodox thought their opponents taught, so the conviction of Irenaeus that there had been a long historical chain of Gnostics threatening the Christian community is of paramount significance in understanding the position reached by orthodox moralists on marriage.

According to Irenaeus, Saturninus and Basilides taught that the practice of all lusts was a matter of indifference, while at the same time saying, "Marrying and bearing are from Satan" (*The Pretended Gnosis* 1.24, PG 7:675–678). Valentinus held that the spiritual man, the true gnostic, was not bound by the moral law governing "animal men." The spiritual man, initiated into perfect knowledge of God, had that freedom from law which Paul preached. The spiritual man could not sin: "It is impossible for the spiritual man ever to be corrupted." Secure in this belief, the followers of Valentinus, reported Irenaeus, committed the acts stigmatized as sins by orthodox morality. They committed fornication and adultery, often seduced the women they instructed, and, living together as brothers and sisters, frequently got the sisters pregnant (*The Pretended Gnosis* 1.6, PG 7:506–510). Indeed, the Valentinians gave a special significance to intercourse. They said, "Whosoever being in this world does not so love a woman as to obtain possession of her is not of the truth nor shall he attain to the truth" (*ibid.* 1.6, PG 7:510). This emphasis on copulation was linked with a religious myth: the emission of seed by the spiritual men hastened the coming of the Pleroma, the fullness of the divine hierarchy of aeons (*ibid.* 1.6, PG 7:511).[8] In the

---

poorly informed on Basilides and Valentinus (Oulton and Chadwick, *Alexandrian Christianity*, p. 30).

[8] For other examples of Gnostic use of Jn 3:29 ("the friend of the Bridegroom"), see *A Coptic Gnostic Treatise contained in the Codex Brucianus*, with translation and commentary by Charlotte A. Baynes (Cambridge, Eng., 1933), p. 153.

In the myth of the Pleroma the emission of seed is spoken of directly. Other Gnostic myths speak of the particles of light scattered in the universe which will come to the Treasure of Light, e.g., the *Pistis-Sophia*, trans. Carl Schmidt in *Koptisch-gnostische Schriften* I (Leipzig, 1905; 2nd ed., Berlin, 1954).

The particles of light are seen by a modern commentator as a substitution for human semen. The sperm is observed as light or pneuma, because it is a fire-bearing substance; see Geo Widengren, *Mani und der Manichäismus* (Stuttgart, 1961), p. 62.

Pleroma the spiritual men would be married to angels (*ibid.* 1.7, *PG* 7:511). The Valentinians seemed to be equally a danger to Tertullian observing them in Rome. The Valentinians have made mysteries "sacred to pandering." They are a large crowd, filled by many ex-Catholics. Their founder, Valentinus, was a man of ability and eloquence, who had reason to believe he would be chosen bishop (*Against the Valentinians* 1 and 4; *CSEL* 47:177, 181). If Tertullian is talking about the Roman bishopric, it appears that only because a confessor, one who had suffered persecution for the faith, became the rival and successful candidate was the Church spared Valentinus as Pope.[9]

Two other antinomian groups were attacked by Irenaeus, who assigned to both the same rationale for their actions: they believed the essential thing was to have every possible experience. In this way Irenaeus analyzed the Carpocratians, who, in fact, he asserted, concentrated on sexual experience, performing acts "which we cannot believe or even conceive in our minds" (*The Pretended Gnosis* 1.25.4, 2.32.2, *PG* 7:682–683, 827). So, too, were the Cainites, who claimed that an angel conducted them in all their acts (*ibid.* 1.31.2, *PG* 7:705).

The continuation of ascetic Gnostics was noted by the *Elenchos*, especially in its description of the Naasenes. For them, the "new man" was "androgynous," so that generation was no more. They did not mutilate themselves, but they advocated a kind of holy nudity. To be perfect it was "necessary to take off your clothes and become spouses deprived of virility by the original spirit." [10] Sexual coitus was "completely abominable and forbidden," for it tied man to the material world (*Elenchos* 5.7.14 and 15, 5.8.44, 5.9.10–11, *GCS* 26:82, 97, 100).

The androgyne was, indeed, characteristic of Gnostic theology whether of the right or of the left. One of the most common Gnostic characters is an androgynous divine being who plays an essential role in the creation of the world. Examples are the Valentinian myth of the self-multiplying unity cited by Clement; Sophia ("wisdom"), otherwise known as Prounikos ("the lascivious one"), in the myth of the Ophites as reported by Irenaeus (*The Pretended Gnosis* 1.30.3, *PG* 7:695); and Sophia-Pansophos and the Adam of Light in the Gnostic work, the *Epistle of Eugnostos the Blessed*.[11] The androgynous ideal was proclaimed for man in such Gnostic works as the *Gospel of Thomas*. The final verse of *Thomas* contained this emphatic teaching: "Simon Peter said to them, 'Let Mary go

---

[9] Chadwick treats as certain the candidacy of Valentinus for bishop of Rome (Oulton and Chadwick, *Alexandrian Christianity*, p. 15).

[10] For a similar text teaching that nudity is the way to the kingdom of heaven, see *The Gospel of Thomas*, v. 37.

[11] Doresse, *Les Livres secrets*, p. 211. Another example is the Anthropos, a divine androgynous being of the Sethians, *A Coptic Gnostic Treatise*, sec. 3, p. 17; sec. 5, p. 24.

forth from among us, for women are not worthy of the life.' Jesus said, 'See, I will lead her that I may make her male, so that she may become a living spirit like you males. For every woman who makes herself male shall enter the kingdom of heaven.' " [12] In *Thomas* "to become male" seems to be a prescription to achieve an androgynous condition. The androgyne, elevated to the status of an ideal being, was the symbol and exemplar of a humanity which had transcended procreation by the blending of the sexes.[13]

That an androgynous being is not sexually procreative, that a dualist belief in the evil of the world excludes procreation, that an ascetic ideal that the celibate alone enjoy the kingdom of God — all of these Gnostic positions evidently are incompatible with the perpetuation of the race by procreation. The incompatibility of Gnosticism of the left with such perpetuation may not be so evident. There is nothing in the formal theory of antinomianism — there scarcely could be — which condemns it. The Valentinians, according to Irenaeus, did get girls pregnant. Yet the whole thrust of the antinomian current was to devalue marriage, to deprive marital relations of any particular purpose, and to value sexual intercourse as experience and not for the procreation which might follow. When antinomian thought is rebuked in the New Testament, it is associated with sterility, and, although the sterility described is primarily spiritual, the choice of language which suggests physical sterility may not be entirely arbitrary. In Jude 12 and 13 the Gnostic enemies are described as "clouds without water, carried about by the winds; trees in the fall, unfruitful, twice dead, uprooted; wild waves of the sea foaming up their shame; wandering stars for whom the storm of darkness has been reserved forever." In 2 Peter 2:17 they are called "springs without water and mists driven by storms; the blackness of darkness is reserved for them." When the followers of Valentinus make a ritual of sexual intercourse as a way of entering the kingdom, when the followers of Carpocrates seek sexual intercourse of all kinds as the necessary condition of salvation, the notion

---

[12] This gospel also has an expansion of the saying from the *Gospel According to the Egyptians* quoted by Clement: The disciples ask, "If we then be children, shall we enter the kingdom?" Jesus says to them, "When you make the two one, and when you make the inside as the outside, and the outside as the inside, and the upper side as the lower, and when you make the male and the female into a single one, that the male be not male and the female not female; when you make eyes in the place of an eye, and a hand in place of a hand, and a foot in place of a foot, an image in place of an image, then you shall enter" (*Gospel of Thomas*, v. 22).

[13] Rabbinic tradition also viewed the ideal first man, Adam, as androgynous: "Male and female he created them" (Gn 1:27) and "called *their* name Adam" (Gn 5:1–2); see David Daube, *The New Testament and Rabbinic Judaism* (London, 1956), pp. 72–74, 441. Philo, *De opificio mundi* 24.76, has this interpretation. Daube finds echoes of this belief in the New Testament texts against divorce, and in Eph 5:32 with its reference to a "great mystery."

of marriage as the orderly way of propagating the race seems to have totally disappeared within these segments of the Christian world.

The Gnostic threat continued in a diminished form into the first quarter of the third century, but by this time the Gnostic approach was no longer a major rival to the orthodox interpretation. By the early fourth century such Gnostic sects as existed seemed reduced to the hidden existence of the sect encountered by Epiphanius in Egypt in 332. Yet the substantial disappearance of Gnosticism occurred only as Manicheanism spread in the fourth century, and, for our purposes, the Manichean doctrine was a continuation of the Gnostic tradition. The Gnostic movements accompanied the first several hundred years of Christian thought, competing with it and attempting its infiltration. The Gnostic approach to sexual morality could at no point be lightly dismissed.

The appeal of Gnostic doctrine on marriage to Christians may be suggested by the case of Tertullian, a lawyer who scorned the fables of Gnostic theology. Converted to the Catholic Church from paganism in 193, he had definitely broken with the Church by 215 to join the adherents of Montanus. The Montanists, Tertullian found, were "spirituals" in contrast with the merely "physical" pagans and the merely "psychic" Catholics. The Montanist quarrel with the Church was not specifically over sexual morality. Yet Tertullian as a Montanist made marital morality an issue, teaching that marriage after the death of one's spouse was absolutely unlawful (*Monogamy* 1.4, CSEL 76:44). He stopped just short of condemning intercourse in any marriage, and seemed uncertain why it was ever permitted (*ibid.* 3.2, CSEL 76:46–47). If Tertullian had such difficulty with the ordinary orthodox teaching, the attraction of Gnostic doctrine may be gauged. Tertullian was a zealous anti-Gnostic. His attempt to find a "spiritual" man superior to the ordinary member of the Church reflected the attitude which led others to Gnosticism. A basic question for him was, What is the significance of marriage and marital intercourse for the new man the Christian has become? If this one-time champion of orthodoxy, to whom all of Western patristic theology is so deeply indebted, wavered, much more must ordinary Christians have been attracted by the powerfully simple answers of the Gnostics.

The Gnostic appeal rested, in part, on the similarity of Gnostic attitude to the Christian stress on virginity. The words and example of the Lord Jesus, the teaching of St. Paul, had been enthusiastically accepted by many of the early Christians. If the Alexandrian Gnostics appealed to the example of Jesus, they only carried further what orthodox believers did. The strong devotion to virginity in the first several centuries may be measured by the praise directed to it by writers of the fourth century, when Christianity was established as the state religion and the Parousia was not viewed as imminent. In the East, St. Gregory of Nyssa declared that a virgin is "deified" (*Virginity, PG* 46:319). St. John Chrysostom said that it renders "mortals like angels." Marriage is a nest for birds who cannot fly. Who can make the journey to heaven encumbered by a wife and family? (*Virginity, PG* 48:540, 545, 567). In the West, St. Ambrose taught that St. Paul "did not have a commandment, but he did have an example." The Lord speaks to a virgin the words of the Song of Songs, "Come from Lebanon, my spouse." "A virgin," Ambrose declared, "marries God" (*Virgins* 1.23, 38, 52, *PL* 16:195, 199, 203. Ambrose invoked Luke 23:29, "For behold, days are coming in which men will say, 'Blessed are the barren, and the wombs that never bore, and breasts that never nursed'" (*ibid.* 1.26, *PL* 16:196). Jerome recalled Matthew 24:19: "But woe to those who are with child or who have infants at the breast in those days" (*On Ephesians* 5.24, *PL* 26:564–565). These verses in which the Gnostics had found much comfort were now cited as advice in favor of virginity in the Christian era.

Not only was virginity praised and preferred outside of marriage; it was exemplified in marriage by Mary and Joseph. When Helvidius denied that Mary remained a virgin after the birth of Christ, and referred to the several texts speaking of "brothers of the Lord," Jerome attacked him as a blasphemer (*Against Helvidius: The Perpetual Virginity of Blessed Mary* 16, *PL* 23:210). Joseph was "guardian of Mary rather than husband" (*ibid.* 19, *PL* 23:213). The virginal marriage of Mary and Joseph was set forth as an ideal pattern. The holy wives Jerome knows have "in the very relationship of marriage imitated the chastity of virgins" (*ibid.* 21, *PL* 23:214).

In seeking to work out some guidance for the faithful, the instincts of those recognized as orthodox were on the side of prudence, restraint, "puritanism" as to sexual intercourse even where it might occur lawfully in lawful marriage. A number of Christian Fathers advised, with various degrees of emphasis, against having marital intercourse on feast days or on days on which the Eucharist was to be received. In this way a fence was built to screen the agape from the profanation to which the Gnostics of the left had put it. In the fourth century the demand became insistent that priests, if married, should not have intercourse with their wives. St. Ambrose taught it; Pope Siricius (383–399), in one of the first decretals, announced the rule to the bishops of Gaul; the Council of Carthage in 419 legislated the rule.[14]

[14] Ambrose, *De officiis* 1.50.248, *PL* 16:104–105; Siricius, *Letter, PL* 13:1184:85; Council of Carthage, canon 70, *Discipline générale antique*, I² ed. Perikles Joannou (Pontificia commissione per la redazione del codice di diritto canonico orientale, *Fonti* IX; Rome, 1962). For patristic references to refraining from intercourse on feast days or before communion, see Dominikus Lindner, *Der Usus Matrimonii* (Munich, 1929), pp. 76–78.

The danger that this kind of position could move to one of condemnation of marriage, even in the fourth century, may be illustrated by the history of Eustathius of Sebaste in Armenia. At one time a friend in good standing of St. Basil, he and his followers were condemned in 340 by the synod of Gangra in Paphlagonia because they had rejected marriage as un-Christian. The council anathematized those "who keep virginity as from a horror of marriage," and wives who have left their husbands "because they despised marriage." [15]

Irenaeus reproached Gnostics who claim to live together as brother and sister without being married. But this custom appeared in Christian communities. It is persuasively, although not conclusively, argued that St. Paul recognized and approved the practice in his first letter to the Corinthians (1 Cor 7:36–38).[16] The practice appeared in third-century Africa, where it was criticized by St. Cyprian (*Letters* 4.4, CSEL 3¹:475): It existed in Greek communities known to St. John Chrysostom, who objected to it because of the dangers to chastity presented (*Against Those Who Have Virgins Under Their Protection At Home*, PG 47:495–514): Even in fourth-century Rome, the custom in Catholic circles was encountered by Jerome (*Letter 22, To Eustochium*, CSEL 54:161–162). Thus among small groups of Christians, for four centuries, a custom con-

---

[15] Council of Gangra, canons 1, 9, and 14, in *Discipline générale antique*, ed. Joannou, pp. 82, 93, 95.

[16] The argument depends on the translation. The standard Vulgate translation makes it a father-daughter relation: "But if any man thinks that he incurs disgrace with regard to his virgin, since she is over age, and that it so ought to be done, let him do what he will; he does not sin if she should marry. But he who stands firm in his heart, being under no constraint, but is free to carry out his own will, and has decided to keep his virgin — he does well. Therefore both he who gives his virgin in marriage does well, and he who does not give her does better."

The critics of this translation contend that it makes the vital decisions here turn on the father's decision to keep his daughter a virgin, and there is nothing in the Christian context which would give such power to a father or make it praiseworthy for him "to stand firm in his heart" in his intention to keep his daughter a virgin. It is, accordingly, argued that the relationship is between a man and a virgin who is under his protection and probably living with him. The phrase "since she is over age" is replaced by "since he is overcome by his vitality." "If she should marry" is replaced by "let them marry," a better translation, for the Greek verb is plural. "Gives his virgin in marriage" and "does not give her" is replaced by "marries his virgin" and "does not marry her." This last translation is the weakest point in the argument; it involves a wrenching of the ordinary Greek word for "giving in marriage." For the arguments in favor of this interpretation, see J. Héring, *La Première Epître de saint Paul aux Corinthiens* (Neûchatel, 1949), pp. 60–62; Max Thurian, *Marriage and Celibacy*, trans. Norma Emerton (London, 1959), pp. 73–75; contra, Ceslaus Spicq, *La Première Epître aux Corinthiens*, in *La Sainte Bible*, ed. Louis Pirot and Albert Clamer (Paris, 1946).

It is of interest to note that Clement of Alexandria understood the relationship to be that of father and daughter (*Stromata* 3.12.79, *GCS* 15:231). But his interpretation was undoubtedly affected by the battle against the Gnostics.

tinued whereby the sexes were associated, procreation was excluded, and virginity idealized.

With this kind of valuation placed on virginity outside of marriage, or within it, the Gnostics appealingly claimed to posses the true teaching which rejected marriage, or at least procreation, altogether. The Gnostics forced several questions on the Christians. If the Gnostic ascetics were wrong in forbidding marriage, while the Gospels extolled virginity, what was the purpose of marriage? If the Gnostic dualists were wrong in saying that the imprisonment of spiritual man should not be perpetuated by procreation, what was the value of procreation? If the antinomian gnostics were wrong in saying that the spiritual men were above all laws, what laws bound the Christian?

Not everyone might ask such questions or think them important. "Common sense" had, no doubt, its answers. But what was "common sense" in a community redeemed by a resurrected man who was the incarnate Son of God? What answers held? If the Christian community was to be a community at all, some answers were needed. On his way to what he rightly believed would be martyrdom in Rome, St. Ignatius, bishop of Antioch, attempted one answer. In the last letter of his life, written to Polycarp (Irenaeus' mentor), Ignatius issued warnings against Gnosticism of the left and of the right: "Flee from evil acts, but rather preach against them. Speak to my sisters that they love the Lord and be content with their husbands in flesh and in spirit." Promiscuity in the form of spiritual marriage was thus rejected. At the same time continence was lawful, if not boasted of; if one boasted of it, "he was polluted." For those who wished, marriage was right. There was one condition, that marriage be with the consent of the bishop, so "that the marriage be according to the Lord and not according to lust" (Ignatius, *To Polycarp* 5, *PG* 5:724). Marriage within the Church: this was the possible middle way; to proclaim it may have sufficed for the needs of many Christians. But in a community many of whose most brilliant members were intellectual, theological, disputatious, this plain answer did not go far enough. If marriage within the Church was good, why was it so?

THE CHRISTIAN RESPONSE

THE AVAILABLE RESOURCES

To answer the questions Gnosticism forced on the Christians, second-century intellectuals like Clement of Alexandria and Irenaeus had three resources: the New Testament, the Old Testament, and the law of nature. The New Testament could be used to show that some kinds of sexual behavior were not allowed even the redeemed Christian. The antinomians were denounced often enough, but what positive ethic replaced their liberated acceptance of all sexual acts as good? The difficulties may be suggested by the straits to which Clement of Alexandria was reduced. Arguing against the Gnostics, he thought that the best text blessing marriage that he could draw from the Gospels was the saying of the Lord, "For where two or three are gathered together for my sake, there I am in the midst of them" (Mt 18:20). Clement asked, "Does he not mean by the 'three' husband, wife, and child?" Yet he admitted the text could be also expounded allegorically so that the "three" meant flesh, soul, and spirit (*Stromata* 3.10.68, *GCS* 15:226–227). There was, in fact, only the single text ascribed to Paul, 1 Timothy 2:15. Clement did as much as he could with it, speaking of the Christian layman, and saying "*he* shall be saved by childbearing (*Stromata* 3.12.90, *GCS* 15:237). But this single text favoring fertility was a slender reed to rely on against the several New Testament passages extolling virginity.

Ephesians 5 provided a basis for seeing marital intercourse in terms of the demands of marital love. This option was generally not selected. Sexual acts and love were not associated. This dissociation was a fundamental choice made by the early Christian writers. How explain it? By the Christian emphasis on virginity, by a yielding to the Gnostic distrust of sexuality, by a social structure in which marriages were not often made from love? Each of these factors played a part in making another rule seem more attractive.

Much later, in the fourth century, love and marriage were associated by St. John Chrysostom. Speaking on Ephesians 5, Chrysostom dwelt with eloquence on its injunction of love between spouses. As St. Paul said, husbands are to love their wives as Christ the Church. Let no husband say, "He was Christ, He was God." A husband is to love his wife to the point of giving his life for her. Marriage where the husband loves his wife is "marriage according to Christ." A wife is "the source and occasion of all joy." Chrysostom quoted the text used in Ephesians, "the two shall become one flesh." He continued, "and after the seeds are mixed, a child is born; then the three are one flesh" (*Homily 20 on Ephesians* 5, *PG* 62:137, 141, 140). These words were immediately followed by a statement on the relation of Christians to Christ, "So we become one flesh with Christ by participation." If Christians are united to Christ in one flesh, it might be inferred that the "one flesh" of spouses and child also is a way of embodying love. There is the undeveloped germ of a theory on the union of man and wife in fruitfulness as symbolizing the union of Christ and Church. Chrysostom himself added that Paul teaches us to love our wives as ourselves, because husband and wife are "one body." He quoted 1 Corinthians and exclaimed, "You see how zealously he unites flesh to flesh and spirit to spirit. Where are the heretics? If marriage were of those things which are abominated, he [Paul] would not speak of spouses, nor exhort one to this by saying, 'A man shall leave father and mother.' Nor would he have added, 'I speak in Christ and the Church'" (*ibid., PG* 62:141–142).

An answer to the Gnostics in terms of Ephesians was, then, possible. Chrysostom, however, was a man of the fourth century. His predecessors had not made the same choice. Even he was aware of a social structure that made a treatment of marriage based on love somewhat incongruous. The "great mystery" of which Ephesians speaks is that a man should leave his parents "and bind himself to her he has not even seen and with whom he has nothing in common, and prefer her to all others" (*ibid., PG* 62:140; cf. Chrysostom, "What Sort of Wives are to be Chosen," *PG* 51:230). In a society where the occasions of such mysteries were common it is not surprising that marriage was rarely analyzed in terms of love.

Sturdier, more tangible, commoner reasons were needed, or so at least the Christians of the second century seem to have thought, if the Gnostic view of marriage was to be successfully opposed. The demands of Ephesians 5 must have seemed unreal; the requirements of love, too much. The Old Testament seemed a stronger position from which to answer the Gnostics. As a result, it was under constant Gnostic attack. Typical is the statement of Basilides as reported by Irenaeus, "Christ came to destroy the God of the Jews" (*The Pretended Gnosis* 1.24.2, *PG* 7:675). The controversy strengthened orthodox devotion to Old Testament ethics without the Gnostics' being persuaded by the authority of the Jewish Scripture.

The greatest reliance in argument, then, had to be placed on the law of nature, the concept sanctioned by Paul in Romans 2:15, developed by the Stoics, invoked by Philo. Irenaeus taught expressly that the liberation effected by Christ did not abrogate the natural law: all precepts of nature are common to Christians and Jews, and only receive an increase and completion in the morals of Christians (*The Pretended Gnosis* 4.13.1, *PG* 7:1007). Clement constructed a natural law of marriage from Stoic elements so that he could contrast purposeful procreation, the natural measure, with both license and forced abstinence (*Stromata* 3.6, 3.12, *GCS* 15:216–222, 231–238). Nature became the ground on which the orthodox stood, the measure by which they measured.

Three different, if related, senses of nature may be observed in Christian argumentation on sexuality. One sense appeared in the comparisons essayed by a number of writers such as Athenagoras, Origen, Clement, Ambrose, between the sexual process and the sowing of a field. Without being completely articulated, the Stoic conviction was present that a pattern discovered in a process uncontaminated by human sin or error is "natural." Man might safely translate this discovered law into human behavior. A second sense appeared in the importance attached to animal behavior. What the animals do is "natural." The notion occurred in Seneca, in Clement, in Ambrose, and in Jerome quoting Seneca. Like the first meaning, this sense reflected a belief that universal patterns, of use to man, can be discovered where human sin has no part. It went beyond the first meaning in assuming a close continuity between animals and men. Implemented by much more exact methods of observation, much modern psychology incorporates the same assumptions. In a third sense nature was a structure discerned in the human body. What particular organs did was observed. "Eyes are to see with." The more obvious function of a particular organ was "natural." The analysis of the function tended to be isolated from a consideration of the organ in relation to the person as a whole. What was natural for an organ was taken as self-evident; no demonstration was attempted or believed necessary.

In each sense of the term, the "natural" was selectively chosen. An agricultural phenomenon was considered where human effort was completed by physical forces; the example of human beings damming a river to prevent a flood was not used as an example of "nature." Not all animal behavior was found appropriate to follow; the hyena, for instance, popularly supposed to have a set of organs serving a sexual but not a generative purpose, was an example to avoid (Clement, *Paedagogus* 10.85, *GCS* 12:209). The human sexual organs functioned for a variety of purposes; some of them were "unnatural."

It is, I suggest, evident that the appeal to a given "nature" was a way of teaching. The invocation of "nature" reinforced positions already taken. The "natural" was discriminated from the "unnatural" by considerations, often unarticulated, of a more general philosophical or religious character. To call an act natural expressed what man should be, not what animals did or particular organs could accomplish. In the Christian writers of these early centuries, however, as in their Stoic predecessors, the pedagogic function of "nature" was not sharply distinguished, and "nature" was appealed to as a discovered pattern, a self-evident argument.

The use of Stoic values contained in the appeal to nature served, finally, not only to answer the Gnostics. It was a way of reacting to the general secular social environment in which the search for sexual pleasure often seemed to Christian writers to be heedlessly and uncontrollably pursued. In a world in which slave concubinage flourished, divorce by mutual consent was easy, and homosexuality was frequently practiced the Christian writers found the opposite of the holy control recommended by the Gospels and St. Paul. The test of procreative purpose seemed to many Christians, as it had to the pagan Stoics and to reflective Jews like Philo, the measure by which sexual promiscuity might be rationally criticized.

The reaction to secular sexual license operated to reinforce the commitment to the Stoic-Jewish rules which the Gnostic polemic had made appear essential.[17]

THE ADOPTION OF THE STOIC RULE

"We Christians," said St. Justin in his celebrated explanation of Christian belief to a skeptical second-century world, "either marry only to produce children, or, if we refuse to marry, are completely continent" (*Apology for Christians* 1.29, PG 6:373). Christians, the Greek philosopher Athenagoras declared in his address to the emperor in 177, marry only to produce children. Adopting an agricultural metaphor, he added that Christians consequently avoid intercourse in pregnancy: "as the husbandman, throwing the seed into the ground, awaits the harvest, not sowing more upon it, so the procreation of children is the measure of our indulgence in appetite" (*Legation on Behalf of Christians* 33, PG 6:965). To the pagan Romans, Minucius Felix argued: "By choice we are bound by the bond of a single marriage with the desire of procreating" (*Octavius* 31.5, CSEL 2:45).

These statements were made in apologies designed to set off the good points of the Christians. The Stoic doctrine presented was current in intellectual circles. The image used by Athenagoras was as old as Philo. The statements are evidence of a self-consciously developing orthodox rule on marriage. They are not conclusive on the internal discipline of the community. None of them indicates the degree of guilt attached by the community to violation of the ideal.

In the second-century Alexandrian development of Christian morals, the influence of Philo and the Stoics is evident. Clement declared that the Christian law is for "husbands to use their wives moderately and only for the raising up of children" (*Stromata* 3.11.71.4, GCS 15:228). "To have coition other than to procreate children is to do injury to nature" (*Paedagogus* 2.10.95.3, GCS 12:214). In Clement this view was linked to his basic position that desire as such was evil. "Desire" was, he had admitted to his Gnostic opponents, a work which the Lord had destroyed. It is the purposeful, nondesirous act of intercourse which he defends: "A man who marries for the sake of begetting children must practice continence so that it is not desire he feels for his wife, whom he ought to love, and so that he may beget children with a chaste and controlled will" (*Stromata* 3.7.58, GCS 15:222–223). Love is not excluded, but love is viewed as totally distinct from sexual desire or sexual action. "The human ideal of continence, I mean that which is set forth by Greek philosophers, teaches that one should fight desire and not be subservient

---

[17] On the Christian view of the sexual promiscuity of the pagan world, see Rom 1:24–28; Tertullian, *Apology* 1.9, CSEL 69:23–27.

to it so as to bring it to practical effect. But our ideal is not to experience desire at all." This ideal, he added, was possible of achievement only through God's grace (*Stromata* 3.7.57, GCS 15:222). In the next generation Origen, the most influential exegete and speculative theologian of the East, taught — in expounding allegorically the meaning of circumcision for Christians — that the truly circumcised does not commit adultery and that he has intercourse with his wife "only for the sake of a posterity" (*Third Homily on Genesis* 6, GCS 29:47).

The emphatic character of this requirement was made plain in both Clement and Origen by their repetition of the Stoic denial of a right to intercourse in pregnancy. When the matrix is actually occupied with a fetus, "it is wicked to trouble nature by breaking out superfluously in demanding lust." The closing of the matrix is a denial of further coitus. Like a farmer, one may sow only where the soil admits seed (Clement, *Paedagogus* 2.10.93, 102, GCS 12:213, 218). Clement used Philo's agricultural metaphor. Origen adopted Seneca's comparison with animals: there are some women "who, like animals, serve lust without any restraint; indeed I would not compare them to dumb beasts. For beasts when they conceive know not to indulge their mates further with their plenty" (*Fifth Homily on Genesis* 4, GCS 29:62).[18]

The dominance of the Alexandrian view is shown by the *Didascalia*, a collection of canons emanating from Syria about 220–250 and later believed to be "apostolic canons," dictated by the Apostles. After condemning sodomy, bestiality, fornication, and adultery, the *Didascalia* forbids intercourse with a pregnant wife (6.28).[19] Such an act, it is explained, is not to produce children, but for pleasure; as such, the implication seems to be, it is self-evidently bad.

The Stoic marital ethic was accepted. If intercourse when nature itself prevented impregnation was wicked, it would seem, a fortiori, that intercourse would have been regarded as seriously sinful when a human agency made fruitful insemination impossible. Contraception stood condemned by the express conditions required for any lawful intercourse.

East or West, there appear to have been only two very prominent dissenters from the Stoic view.[20] In the late third century Lactantius gave

---

[18] This trust in the continence of pregnant animals seems to have been general in the ancient world: "Except for women, few pregnant animals copulate" (Pliny, *Natural History* 7.11.42).

[19] *Didascalia Apostolorum*, ed. Richard Hugh Connolly (London, 1929). On date and origin, see P. Galtier, "La Date de la Didascalie des Apôtres," *Revue d'histoire ecclésiastique* 42³ (1947), 315.

[20] Both Clement and Origen cite the Pauline texts on marriage as a remedy for incontinence, but make no effort to relate the Pauline view to their own teaching on procreative purpose (see Clement, *Stromata* 3.15, GCS 15:240–242; Origen, *On Matthew* 14.23, GCS 40:339). When Origen says the Holy Spirit is not present in the act of intercourse, he is deliberately contrasting ordinary, sinless acts such as this with special occasions, such as prophesying, where the Holy Spirit is present (*Homily 6 on Numbers* 21.24, PG 12:610).

a value to the Pauline purpose of intercourse as remedy for incontinence. He wrote, "Whoever cannot control his affections, let him keep them within the limits of a lawful bed." The passage by itself would be ambiguous, but Lactantius went on to discuss intercourse in pregnancy. God has made other female animals reject their mates when pregnant, but He "has made woman suffer her husband lest, when their wives repel them, husbands be driven by lust to seek eleswhere and so doing not keep the glory of chastity" (*Divine Institutes* 6.23.13, 26, *CSEL* 19:566, 568). This rejection of animal behavior and of the Stoic norm is the only opinion I have encountered in any Christian theologian before 1500 explicitly upholding the lawfulness of intercourse in pregnancy. Yet even Lactantius did not give the practice complete approval. The wife does not sin, but neither can she be considered as having "the virtue of modesty" (*pudicitia*).

More importantly for doctrine on contraception, Lactantius was also a defender of the position that nature proclaims the normal purpose of intercourse. In a passage he did not bother to reconcile with his Pauline interpretation of marriage, he exclaimed: "God gave us eyes not to see and desire pleasure, but to see acts to be performed for the needs of life; so too, the genital part of the body, as the name itself teaches, has been received by us for no other purpose than the generation of offspring" (*Divine Institutes* 6.23.18, *CSEL* 19^1:567). God has implanted a sexual instinct in all animals, so that, impelled by "this most burning desire," they can "propagate and multiply the species" (*ibid.* 6.23.2, *CSEL* 19^1:565). Apparently, then, Lactantius would have rejected any intentional frustration of the normal purpose.

In the fourth century, St. John Chrysostom defended the Pauline view and largely ignored the Stoic notion. Preaching at Constantinople, Chrysostom taught, "There are two reasons why marriage was instituted, that we may live chastely and that we may become parents." Today, after the Resurrection, a Christian may become a parent spiritually, "so there is one occasion for marriage, that we may not commit fornication" (*On Those Words of the Apostle, "On Account of Fornication,"* PG 51:213). In taking this view, Chrysostom indicated that intercourse in old age is not blamable, although it is presumably not procreative; intercourse in pregnancy and by the sterile are implicitly justified by his doctrine.[21]

No special consequences for contraception, however, were derived from

---

[21] Preaching against avarice, Chrysostom also remarks, "There is no great reason to have money, while there is great reason to have wives to preserve chastity: hence no one blames a man who has lawful intercourse with his wife into old age, but all blame him who accumulates money" (*Homily 5 on the Epistle to Titus*, PG 62: 689). Chrysostom is not entirely consistent. Attacking adultery, he says that wives were married to husbands "for companionship and the procreation of children" (*Homily 5 on 1 Thessalonians*, PG 62:426).

Chrysostom's defense of unprocreative intercourse. He had a distinctive theory of his own on procreation. It is not the marital act which produces children: "It is the word of God saying increase and multiply. And witnesses to this are those who have used marriage, but have not become fathers" (*ibid.*, *PG* 51:213). Boldly, without nuances, Chrysostom stated a belief which will be found hidden in many Christian views of marital intercourse. The generative act is sacral. To interfere with it — so runs the implicit corollary here — would be to attack the work of God. As will be seen, Chrysostom regards contraception as worse than homicide, a mutilation of nature.

In the West, Ambrose, bishop of Milan, the then capital of the western Empire, and Chrysostom's somewhat older contemporary, stated the sacrality of intercourse in terms that joined it to the familiar Stoic rule on procreative purpose. Explaining why Elizabeth was embarrassed at having a child in her old age (Lk 1:24), Ambrose declared,

Youths generally assert the desire of having children and think to excuse the heat of their age by the desire for generation. How much more shameful for the old to do what is shameful for the young to confess. For even the young who temper their hearts to prudence by divine fear, generally renounce the works of youth when progeny have been received. And is this remarkable for man, if beasts mutely speak a zeal for generating, not a desire for copulating? Indeed, once they know the womb is filled, and the seed received by the generative soil, they no longer indulge in intercourse or the wantonness of love, but they take up parental care. Yet men spare neither the embryo nor God. They contaminate the former and exasperate the latter. "Before I formed you in the womb," He says, "I knew you and sanctified you in your mother's womb." To control your impatience, note the hands of your Author forming a man in the womb. He is at work, and you stain with lust the secret of the sacred womb? Imitate the beast or fear God. Why do I speak of beasts? The land itself often rests from the work of generating, and if it is often filled with the seeds thrown by the impatient eagerness of men, it repays the shamelessness of the farmer and changes fertility to sterility. So even in the elements and the beasts it is a shame to nature not to cease from generating.[22]

In this view, the generative purpose is barely excuse for intercourse when generation is possible. Intercourse for the old or for the pregnant is not only shameful but unnatural, for generation is impossible.

The Alexandrian doctrine on procreation was also enthusiastically embraced by St. Jerome. The marital act, he taught, was lustful unless for procreation (*On Galatians* 5, *PL* 26:443). In his diatribe against Jovinian, a monk so insensitive to the desirability of virginity as to marry, Jerome adopted the saying from Sextus we have already noted. Sextus had recently been translated into Latin by Rufinus of Aquileia, then a friend of

---

[22] Ambrose, *Exposition of the Gospel according to Luke* 1.43–45, *CSEL* 32⁴:38–39). Ambrose uses "senex" for old. *Senex* usually means over forty, but can mean over fifty, when contrasted with *juvenis* or *adolescens* by Latin authors.

Jerome. He apparently believed, and Jerome followed him in believing, that "Sextus" was the sainted Pope Sextus II, martyred in 258. Invoking this revered authority, Jerome made his phrase more caustic. Where Sextus had said, "An adulterer is also everyone who is shameless with his own wife," Jerome said, "An adulterer is he who is too ardent a lover of his wife," and he continued with the quotation from Seneca we have already cited (Chapter II, note 18).[23] These biting phrases, preserved by Jerome, and in medieval times attributed to him, will ring through the centuries, repeated by commentators on Christian marriage. "Not as lovers, but husbands." "Imitate, at any rate, the beasts." "With judgment, not affection." These will be the watchwords of those defending the procreative function of intercourse.

Jerome also brought into the Bible itself a version of the Stoic-Jewish rule on procreation. Through his monumental translation, his words were to be the words in which most Europeans for a thousand years were to know the Scriptures, the language which the Catholic Church was to use as its common text for fifteen hundred years. What Jerome contributed to doctrinal development by his work here is doubtless his most significant contribution.

In translating Tobias, Jerome is supposed to have used an Aramaic manuscript, now lost, and the earlier Latin text. The translation was made with some haste; Jerome remarked, perhaps with some exaggeration, that he had done it in "a day" (*Preface, PL* 29:26). The story in its original form embodied some speculation on marital intercourse; Tobias, the successful husband of Sara, succeeds where preceding husbands have been destroyed by demons. His success presumably has some connection with his statement to the Lord, "And now it is not pleasure which I seek in taking my sister" (Tb 8:9). But the connection was not spelled out in the original version. Meditation in Alexandrian terms added to the text, and it is these additions which Jerome's work transmitted in the standard Bible of the Catholic West.

In this version, the angel Raphael warns Tobias of whose who in matrimony shut out God from their mind and "give themselves to their lust as the horse and mule." To avoid the disasters of his predecessors, Tobias is told to be continent for three nights after marriage and then "to take the

---

[23] Sextus was probably, in fact, a Christian philosopher who, between 180 and 210, had reworked an ancient set of gnomic sayings (Henry Chadwick, *The Sentences of Sextus*, Cambridge, Eng., 1959, pp. 137, 159). His work was already known in the Church in Origen's day; it was to circulate in the next two centuries as a treasury of Christian wisdom. Jerome later identified Sextus as "a Pythagorean," without changing his appreciation of the sentiment (Oulton and Chadwick, *Alexandrian Christianity*, p. 119).

Among the sayings of Sextus which Jerome might have used, but did not, is this: "You know that marrying and procreating children is the worst thing, yet if, as one knowing battle to be the worst thing, you wish to fight, marry and procreate children" (no. 230 b). Also this: "Do nothing for lust [*libido*] alone" (no. 232).

virgin with the fear of the Lord, moved rather for love of children than for lust" (6:17–22). Tobias later prays, telling the Lord, "Thou knowest that not for fleshly lust do I take my sister to wife, but only for the love of posterity" (8:9). Those three additions were made. The quotation of Genesis 2:18, "It is not good that man be alone," which might have supported a nonprocreative purpose in marriage, was eliminated. The version as given by Jerome was an explicit endorsement of the procreative purpose as the sole proper purpose in intercourse.[24]

PROCREATIVE PURPOSE AND INCREASE OF POPULATION

The stress on procreative purpose in sexual intercourse did not arise from any special valuation placed on the increase of population. Procreation rationalized and measured the sexual impulse; to find it good implied that the addition of human beings to the world was good. Yet classical Christian literature made no effort to develop any doctrine that the increase of population was itself good.

At least four grounds might have existed for favoring population growth. One was social and secular. The Empire was in danger; more men were needed; underpopulation was a social menace. This aspect was never considered by the early writers. Not only when Christianity was a "slave religion," not only when it was persecuted, but after its establishment, concern with the social order was never advanced as a reason for having children. Indeed, the Christians were so insensitive to the problem of underpopulation that one of the first evidences of Christian influence on Roman law is a decree of Constantine of January 31, 320, terminating part of the Augustan legislation encouraging procreation. Celibates, male and female, were now to be treated "as though married," and "no person shall be considered childless." Exception was made only for the continuation of restriction on inheritance by childless couples (*Codex Theodosianus* 8.16).[25] The special privileges of the large families and the exception penalizing childless couples were both ended by a later decree of September 4, 410 (*ibid.* 8.17.2, 3). Christian influence prevailed in these matters, although no change dictated by Christian sensibility was made in the law on abortion. Of course, it was harder to prevent abortion than to remove disabilities of the celibate; but the area in which Christian valuations triumphed has nonetheless some significance. Protection of virginity was given priority over the encouragement of population growth.

A second possible ground for increasing the number of Christians was to increase the population of heaven. The more Christian souls the better, this argument might have run. It was not made. A third approach would

---

[24] For the text restored in a translation following the Hebrew, see *La Sainte Bible*, Ecole biblique de Jérusalem (Paris, 1956). For Jerome's version, see *Biblia Sacra iuxta latinam vulgatam versionem ad codicum fidem*, ed. H. Quentin (Rome, 1926).

[25] *Theodosiani libri XVI cum constitutionibus Sirmondianis*, ed. Theodor Mommsen and Paul M. Meyer, 3rd ed. (Berlin, 1962), I², 418.

have been in narrower ecclesiastical terms. The Christians were few, the pagans many. How could the Church build itself better than by Christians' propagating other Christians? This view of propagation was not widespread.[26] Finally, might there not have been a metaphysical conviction that the more manifestations of rational good the better, hence the more human beings the better? If man is the image of God, it might have been added, it is good to multiply the image. Rational human beings are the glory of the cosmos, the reflection of God's glory. This kind of consideration was not advanced. All of these ideas, which were to occur to Christians of later centuries as reasons for opposing contraception, do not seem to have been developed in the first four centuries of Christianity.

This is not to say that some of these considerations which were not articulated did not have some bearing on the doctrine that was adopted. If the world had in fact been perishing from overpopulation, who can suppose that the Stoic rule on procreative purpose would have seemed so eminently sensible, even though some writers, as the example of St. Jerome will show, might have stubbornly supported it? If there had not been a belief in the heavenly destiny of Christian souls, the bringing of children into this world might have been viewed as a disaster. If the multiplication of rational man had not been valued as a good, procreation would have been an exercise without meaning. Valuation of procreation cannot be absolutely separated from increase of population. But the values justifying procreation were never turned into an argument for augmenting the number of people in the world. The reason is not hard to find: it lies in the preeminent value put upon virginity.

The prevailing Christian view of population appeared in St. Basil's exegesis of "Increase and multiply" (Gn 1:28). The text, said Basil, means that man is to increase from infancy to maturity until he governs the world by reason. God has given animals, too, a command to multiply. The difference between the two commands is that man's growth is to be in reason (*Orations* 1.17–18, PG 30:25–28). Animals grow "by bodily increase" and "their multitude of children." "We increase spiritually and multiply by good works" (*Orations* 2.2, PG 30:44).

The Christian disinterest in descendants was such that it must frequently have been a stumbling block for converts from the Jewish world where fertility was so esteemed. The Christian historian, Eusebius, writing in the early fourth century, has a hypothetical questioner asking why, if the Christians have the same religious roots as the Jews, do the Chris-

<hr>

[26] In Methodius (d. 311) the growth of the Church in size and beauty is explicitly contrasted with an understanding of "Increase and multiply" in terms of carnal procreation (*Symposium* 3.8 opposing the view of 1.1, GCS 27:27). On the other hand, St. Ambrose says that the Church should rejoice in generation because "the number of the devout people is increased" (*Exposition on Luke* 1.30, CSEL 32⁴:29).

tians "neglect" "marriage and the procreation of children?" Eusebius had
three basic answers. One is the eschatological difference: the Jews were
concerned with the beginning; we Christians are concerned with the end.
In Paul's phrase, "the time is short." In these days, we have no need to
care as they did. A second answer is that the Jewish holy men were few
and had to procreate to have others to whom to pass the revelation. But
in our time there is no need for doctors and preachers of the word to
have physical offspring when "innumerable crowds" seek the Gospel, and
Christian teachers give birth to "divine and incorporeal offspring." A third
reason is that Christians have so many outside pressures to disturb their
worship of God (as Jews had not) that they have no leisure (between
business and worship) to raise a family (*The Gospel Demonstration*
1.9, *PG* 22:77–81).

The eschatological reason for virginity, already present in St. Paul, was
retained by writers like Eusebius although the Parousia no longer seemed
imminent. "The last days" are here whenever the world actually ends,
for Christ has come. In the same way "the world is full," for humanity
is redeemed.

"The world is full" is even sometimes stated as a literal observation on
population. Arguing against the Pythagorean theory of transmigration of
souls, Tertullian urged that if this theory were true, the population of the
world would be unchanging. But, in fact, the population is increasing:
"The highest testimony is matter of common knowledge: We are burdensome to the world. The elements scarcely suffice us. Our needs press.
There are complaints among all. For now nature will not support us.
Pestilence, famine, wars, and the swallowing up of cities are deputed, indeed, as remedies, as haircuts for the growth of the human race"(*The
Soul* 30.4).

Jerome, echoing Tertullian, said, "The world is already full and the
earth does not hold us" (*Against Helvidius* 21, *PL* 23:215).[27] These observations do not accord with other data on the Roman Empire in 200 or
in 380. They do reflect the Christian disinterest in increase of population.

In Jerome the procreative requirement in intercourse was still insisted
on even though he believed the world was overpopulated. The extreme
Christian position on population was taken by St. John Chrysostom. Marriage was instituted after the Fall as a solace for death so that man, who
now must die, could continue in his descendants. After the Resurrection,
death has no hold. "The whole world is full." We journey to a better life.
There is no need of descendants: "Now a spiritual form of giving birth
has been introduced, a better kind of birth, a more useful support to old

[27] Another echo is the anonymous *Epistula de castitate* 14.4, ed. Carl Paul Caspari,
in *Briefe, Abhandlungen und Predigten aus den Zwei letzten Jahrhunderten des kirch-
lichen Alterthums und dem Anfang des Mittelalters* (Oslo, 1890), p. 155.

age" (*On Those Words of the Apostle, "On Account of Fornication"* 3, *PG* 51:213). In this analysis, procreation was an answer to death. The answer is no longer needed when death is conquered and heirs are spiritual. Chrysostom's approach, logically stated, led to the question, "If procreation is not necessary, why is it good?" He did not ask the question. When he dealt with the positive prevention of procreation, he fell back on the Stoic view of nature. His theory remained as the outer limit of the orthodox disinterest in population.

The primary interest of Christian writers in these first three centuries was not in more persons, but in spiritually better persons. When the Church was small, a mere handful among a multitude, virginity was preferred. When the Church embraced what its representatives deemed to be the whole world, virginity was preferred. The exhortations to virginity were addressed to those most likely to respond to spiritual injunctions, to those most likely to raise good Christian children if they had them. The Church was not to increase by number, but in quality.

The emphasis on perfection through virginity marks the sharpest contrast with the valuation of numbers for their own sake. But the Christian interest in education of offspring which becomes evident in the second century equally establishes this point. In the letter of Clement, bishop of Rome, to the Corinthians written near the end of the first century, he presented the "paedeia of God," that is, the educational ideals of Christ, as the sum of the written Christian tradition, as the teaching which must guide Christians who would be a community (*First Letter to the Corinthians* 52). When Clement of Alexandria wrote his *Paedagogus,* it was to show Christ to be the true *paedagogus,* as the true educator. There is a heavenly reward not for the person who procreates indiscriminately, but for him "who has procreated children according to the Logos and who has educated them and instructed them in the Lord" (Clement, *Stromata* 3.15, *GCS* 15:241). This fundamental incorporation of the Greek ideals of education was effected by the Alexandrian Christian school of theology, by Clement and Origen, the founders of Christian philosophy.[28] With these views of the nature of man, Clement and Origen could not have found mere multiplication of progeny an end in itself.

The procreative requirement in intercourse thus stopped short of a plea for propagation. The evaluation of virginity cut across the valuation of procreation. Procreative purpose was valued as a rational control of marital intercourse, as an answer to the Gnostic attack on intercourse. The

---

[28] I summarize in this paragraph views of Werner Jaeger which, expressed in many of his writings, are most succinctly and eloquently summed up in his *Early Christianity and Greek Paideia* (Cambridge, Mass., 1961), esp. pp. 22–26, 37–67, 116–118. The edition of Clement of Rome used is that in *Opera patrum apostolorum,* ed. Francis X. Funk (Tübingen, 1887), vol. I.

connection between procreation and an increase of population was not explored.

INDIFFERENCE TO LIFE

A commandment directed to the control of sex might also have a justificatory rationale in terms of its protection of life. The statement of Seneca against intercourse in pregnancy is a case in point. Such intercourse is condemned as an irrational use of the sexual organs. It is also represented as endangering the fetus. The double rationale was kept by Ambrose and Jerome.

A second case shows the development of the life-protecting rationale for a commandment which appears in the Old Testament without explanation. Intercourse in menstruation is there designated as a capital offense for husband and wife. Some Christian writers repeated the condemnation without analysis (e.g., Chrysostom, *On 1 Corinthians 7, PG* 51; *Didascalia* 6.28). Philo's explanation that conception was impossible does not seem to have been used. The developed Christian view was to see the prohibition not as a mysterious and inexplicable ordinance of God, but as a protection for the child. St. Jerome wrote, "If a man copulates with a woman at that time, the fetuses conceived are said to carry the vice of the seed, so that lepers and gargantuans are born from this conception, and the corrupted menses makes the foul bodies of either sex too small or too big" (*Commentary on Ezechiel* 6.18, *PL* 25:173). It was a common belief that children conceived in menstruation were born sickly, seropurulent, or dead (Pliny, *Natural History* 7.15.67). The protection of future life became the articulated basis for the prohibition of the act as serious sin.

The rule on contraception will be seen to have this double aspect: in part the outgrowth of a theory of sexual control, in part justified as a protection of life. The interest in preserving life should be distinguished from the interest in limiting sexual promiscuity. As in the case of the requirement of procreative purpose, the Christian rule is best understood as a reaction.

The conventional Roman attitude on fetal and infant life was strikingly callous. Seneca refers to the drowning of abnormal or weakly children at birth as a commonplace Roman phenomenon and as a reasonable kind of action (Seneca, *De ira* 1.15).[29] Suetonius speaks casually of the exposure of children by their parents, with the implication that the act entirely depends on the will of the parents (Suetonius, *Gaius Caligula* 5).[30] In a generally uncomplimentary account of the Jews, Tacitus finds

[29] Seneca, *De ira,* in *Moral Essays,* ed. and trans. John W. Basore, Loeb Classical Library (Cambridge, Mass., 1928).

[30] Suetonius, *De vita Caesarum,* ed. and trans. J. C. Rolfe, Loeb Classical Library (Cambridge, Mass., 1920).

it remarkable that they do not kill children who are born after the father had made his will, that is, children born when the parents no longer want offspring as heirs (*Histories* 5.5).[31]

The governmental interest in population seemed confined to encouraging reproduction of the upper classes. Indifference to what a parent did with his offspring was general. The *patria potestas*, the father's legally recognized absolute power over the life of his children, had been limited in historical times to a paternal right to punish older children for their crimes, and custom limited its exercise.[32] It was not, however, until November 16, 318, under Constantine, that the killing of a son or daughter by a father was made a crime of parricide (*Codex Theodosianus* 9.15.1). It was only after more than half a century of Christian establishment that the killing of an infant was, on February 7, 374, declared by law to be homicide (*ibid.* 9.14.1). The very loose law on abortion was never changed even in Christian times. The law decreed no punishment for the killing of a fetus with paternal consent if the mother was not injured and poisons were not employed (see Chapter I). There was no criminal penalty for abandonment of a child. Infanticide, abandonment, and abortion were all permissible, and the failure of the law to intervene, though men were needed, shows how ingrained were these parental rights to dispose of nascent life. To this established attitude the Christian moralists reacted with vigor.

The Christian reaction had Jewish roots. The Hebrew text of Exodus 21:22–23 dealt with abortion accidentally caused and provided a fine for the man accidentally responsible. No effort was made to deal with intentional abortion. In the diaspora a development occurred. The Septuagint significantly expanded the teaching. If the fetus is "formed," when the abortion occurs, "life shall pay for life." Still not dealing with intentional abortion at the parents' request, the text showed a new willingness to treat a fetus as human.

The new insight of the Septuagint was developed by Philo. He repeated the teaching of the Greek and by implication expanded it to cover intentional abortion by parents. He went on, "This ordinance carries with it the prohibition of something else more important, the exposure of

---

[31] Cornelius Tacitus, *Historiae*, ed. and trans. John Jackson, Loeb Classical Library (Cambridge, Mass., 1931).

[32] Theodor Mommsen, *Römisches Strafecht* (Leipzig, 1899), p. 618. A law of pre-Republican days punished the abandonment of children by fine. It seems to have fallen into desuetude. It is this law which Tertullian apparently refers to when he speaks of easily evaded "laws" against infanticide (*To the Nations* 1.15). See Mommsen, *Römisches Strafrecht*, p. 619.

In another context, it is explicitly stated that a fetus is not a man: Papinian on whether a fetus in the womb of a slave shall be given a value in applying the Falcidian law (*Digest* 35.2.9); cf. Ulpian's statement in regard to the right to inspect a pregnant woman if her husband suspected her of being pregnant "partus enim antequam edatur, mulieris portio est vel viscerum" (*Digest* 25.4.1.1).

infants, a sacrilegious practice which among many other nations, through their ingrained inhumanity, has come to be regarded with complacence" (*The Special Laws* 3.20.110). Infanticide, Philo noted, is now commonly practiced by parents strangling their infants, drowning them with attached weights, or exposing them in deserted areas to wild beasts and carnivorous birds. These parents are guilty of murder, and the greatest abomination of all, the murder of their own children. Their crime also has a sexual aspect. They stand "self-condemned" as lovers of pleasure: "For they are pleasure lovers when they mate with their wives not to procreate children and perpetuate the race, but like pigs and goats in quest of the enjoyment which such intercourse gives" (*ibid.* 3.20.113).

The ethical perceptions of Philo were incorporated in the positions of the early Christians. In the mid-second century, St. Justin proclaimed, "We have taught that it is the act of wicked men to abandon even newborn children." We do not wish "to be killers of men" by such acts (*Apology for Christians* 1.27, 29, PG 6:369, 373). Half a century later Tertullian asserted that abandonment of infants to beasts, drowning of newborn infants, and general infanticide were widespread among the pagans (Tertullian, *To the Nations* 1.15, CSEL 20:85; *Apology* 9.7–8, CSEL 69:24). The Christians, on the other hand, were forbidden to destroy even a fetus (*Apology* 9.8). Over a hundred years later, Lactantius cast the same reproach against the pagans: "They strangle children born of them, or, if they are too pious for that, they abandon them" (*Divine Institutes* 5.9.15, CSEL 19:427).

The Christian opposition to abortion is strong testimony to this Christian concern for life. As early as the *Didache* or *The Teaching of the Twelve Apostles*, the Way of Death is that of "killers of children" (*Didache* 5.2). In *The Letter of Barnabas*, probably an early-second-century document, the command is set out plainly: "Thou shalt not kill the fetus by an abortion or commit infanticide" (*Letter of Barnabas* 19.5).[33] In the second century Athenagoras and Clement of Alexandria attacked abortion with zeal.[34] Two apocryphal but orthodox works, the *Apocalypse of Peter* and the *Apocalypse of Paul*, testified to popular Christian abhorrence of the abortioner.[35] In the third century abortion was rigorously and directly condemned by Tertullian and Cyprian.[36] The fourth-century

---

[33] *Doctrina duodecim apostolorum; Barnabae epistula*, ed. Theodor Klauser, Florilegium Patristicum (Bonn, 1940).

[34] Athenagoras, *Legation for Christians*, PG 6:969. Clement of Alexandria, *Paedagogus*, 2.10.96.1, GCS 12:215.

[35] *Apocalypse of Peter* in Montague Rhodes James, *The Apocryphal New Testament*, corrected ed. (Oxford, 1953), pp. 506 (fragment in Clement), 509 (Akhmim fragment), 515 (Ethiopian text). *Apocalypse of Paul* 40, *ibid.*, p. 545 (treating of God's punishment of parents after their death for acts of abortion and infanticide by drowning).

[36] Tertullian, *Apology* 9.8; Cyprian, *Epistles* 52.2, CSEL 3¹:619.

compilation, the *Apostolic Constitutions*, condemned the killing of a formed fetus (7.3.2.).[37] Abortion was even the subject of conciliar action, although in a context limited to a connection with sexual sin. A local Spanish council at Elvira, circa 300, condemned it with a penalty of exclusion from communion till death.[38] The Council of Ancyra in 314 provided ten years of penance for women who fornicate and then "destroy" the product of their intercourse. This council of twelve Eastern bishops presided over by Vitalis, bishop of Antioch, acted for the Eastern provinces of Syria and Asia Minor; its canons were much cited in later conciliar legislation, East and West. The Council noted an earlier practice, apparently followed in the East also, of excluding such sinners from communion till death.[39]

Climactically and sweepingly, the canons of St. Basil, which were to be the basic legislation of the Eastern church, condemned without qualification all women who commit abortion, whatever the state of development of the fetus. The penalty is that of Ancyra: ten years' penance.[40] In the West, St. Jerome described the mother who commits an abortion as a parricide (*Letter 22, To Eustochium, CSEL* 54:160).

Combating the prevailing indifference, the Christians taught that all life must be inviolate, and, using the terms the law reserved for the killing of adults, they charged that not only the destruction of existing life but the interruption of the life-giving process was homicide and parricide. They were led to attach sanctity not only to life but to the life-giving process.

THE CHRISTIAN MEANING OF "HOMICIDE"

If this desire to protect life is understood, the significance of the terms in which the Christian writers criticize contraception is illuminated. It will be found that the words applied to contraception are "parricide," "worse than murder," "killing a man-to-be." One might think that these terms either reflect an erroneous biology which identifies man with the seed, or show that the writers are not speaking of contraception at all. Neither alternative is correct. The Christian writers are using this language rhetorically and morally, just as, rhetorically and morally, they attacked abortion as homicide or parricide. A review of (a) the relevant

---

[37] *Didascalia et Constitutiones Apostolorum*, ed. Francis X. Funk (Paderborn, 1905).
[38] Mansi 2:16.
[39] Canon 21, Mansi 2:519. For the influence of Ancyra, see Roger John Huser, *The Crime of Abortion in Canon Law* (Washington, 1943), p. 21. For a summary of patristic texts, see Constancio Palomo Gonzalez, *El Aborto en San Augustin* (Salamanca, 1959).
[40] St. Basil says, "A woman who deliberately destroys a fetus is answerable for the taking of life. And any hairsplitting distinction as to its being formed or unformed is inadmissible with us" (*Letters* 188, PG 32:672).

theories of classical biology, (b) the leading theories on ensoulment of the fetus, and (c) Roman legal terminology confirms this conclusion.

Classical biology. Three theories of procreation existed, all of them assigning the major role in procreation to the male seed. According to Aristotle, the male seed was the active form; the female menses provided the passive matter on which the form worked (*Generation of Animals* 1.20, 729a, 2.3, 737a). The view was general in the Roman world that the male seed combined with the female menses to make a fetus. It is asserted by Jerome (*On Ephesians* 5.30) and by Augustine (*On Genesis According to the Letter* 10.18.32). It appears to be the theory of the Hellenized Jew who wrote the Book of Wisdom (*Wis* 7:2), and of Lactantius (*The Worker of God* 12.6). The theory is assumed by Clement of Alexandria (*Paedagogus* 1.6.39, *GCS* 12:113). The theory in its strict Aristotelian form gives the male seed the shaping role. In the looser way in which it became popular in the classical world, the theory drops the philosophical contrast between form and matter, and the female contribution seems more important. But the male seed has a kind of primacy.

A second theory, held by many Stoics, was that the male sperm contains moisture and "pneuma." In the uterus this pneuma combines with the pneuma of the woman, so that the soul of the embryo springs from both parents, but the body only from the father's seed. A third theory omits any reference to the pneumatic contribution of the woman. The uterus is merely a depositary for the male seed. This appears to be the view of Soranos, who defines "conception" as "the prolonged hold on the seed or an embryo or embryos in the uterus from a natural cause" (*Gynecology* 1.12.43).[41] This theory accords with Soranos' frequent comparisons of the act of procreation to the sowing a field (e.g., *ibid.* 1.35.6, 1.36.1): a seed is deposited, which gets nourishment from the soil or mother, but which is only being fed, not taking substance from its depositary. The Stoic agricultural metaphor on intercourse, adopted by Philo and later Christian writers, reflects this theory.

If a Christian writer adopted Soranos' view, as Tertullian does in *The Soul*, he would have reason to invest the male seed with special significance. Under the other theories he would have had a general notion that male seed was important. But under no theory was the male seed itself equal to a "man," for under no theory was it maintained that the seed already had a soul.

Theory on ensoulment. That no classical writer literally identified semen with man is clear from a consideration of the leading theories on ensoulment.

---

[41] See the excellent exposition of all three theories by Waszink in his edition of Tertullian's *De anima*, pp. 342–346. Waszink concludes that Tertullian adopts the position of Soranos.

In Aristotle, a fetus becomes human forty days after conception if the fetus is male, ninety days after conception if the fetus is female (*History of Animals* 7.3). A similar view may underlie the prescription in Leviticus 12:1–5 that a woman must spend forty days in becoming purified if she has given birth to a boy, eighty days if she has given birth to a girl.

Divergent theories apparently underlie two versions of an Old Testament verse. In Exodus 21:22, according to the Hebrew text, if a man accidentally causes an abortion, "life is given for life" only if the mother dies; the death of a fetus is not treated like the killing of an adult human being. It seems to be supposed that the fetus is at no point a man. In the Septuagint version of Exodus 21:22, the text prescribes the penalty of "life for life" if the embryo is "formed." By "formed" may be meant what Aristotle means. This view is adopted by Philo. A third theory appears in Tertullian. He argues that the embryo, after conception, has a soul, and that it is man (*homo*) when it attains its final form (Tertullian, *The Soul* 25.2, 37.2).

Jerome's translation of the Old Testament followed the Hebrew in Exodus 21:22 and opened the possibility of treating the fetus as at no point of development human. The prevailing Christian understanding, however, seems to have followed the Septuagint in distinguishing between an unformed and formed stage. This view was evidently held by Jerome himself. Writing on another question to Algasia, one of his many female questioners, he notes, " . . . seeds are gradually formed in the uterus, and it is not reputed homicide until the scattered elements receive their appearance and members" (*Epistles* 121.4, CSEL 56:16).

Augustine reflects the continuing controversy among Christians; commenting on Exodus 21 in a version based on the Septuagint, he says,

> Here the question of the soul is usually raised: whether what is not formed can be understood to have no soul, and whether for that reason it is not homicide, because one cannot be said to be deprived of a soul if one has not yet received a soul. The argument goes on to say, "But if it has been formed, he shall give soul for soul" . . . If the embryo is still unformed, but yet in some way ensouled while unformed . . . the law does not provide that the act pertains to homicide, because still there cannot be said to be a live soul in a body that lacks sensation, if it is in flesh not yet formed and thus not yet endowed with senses. (*On Exodus* 21.80, CSEL 28²:147)

It is abundantly clear from these discussions that the most anyone contends is that ensoulment occurs at conception; the dominant view is that the fetus becomes a man only when "formed." The moment of formation appears to be the forty-day period set for Aristotle for males, and the eighty-day period suggested by Leviticus for females. In the light of such views on the fetus, no one could have confused the seed with a man or meant to say that destruction of the seed was literal homicide.

The Roman terms for murder. In the second and third centuries, *parricidium* was the aptest word to use if intentional unlawful killing of a relative was being alleged. *Parricidium* was the specific term for the unlawful killing of a close relation such as a parent or brother. It did not apply to the killing of a fetus or newborn infant by its parent.[42]

When the second- and third-century Christians apply the term "parricide," then, they do so in a conscious effort to enlarge the legal meaning to condemn what they believe is morally wrong. Thus Tertullian, who is particularly sensitive to legal nuances, does not hesitate to call parricides parents who kill their own infants (*Apology* 9, *CSEL* 69:23–27). Similarly Lactantius treats parents abandoning their infants as parricides (*Divine Institutes* 6.20.21–24, *CSEL* 19²:559). It is not a difficult step to extend this moral usage of the term further. Thus Lactantius treats homosexuals as parricides: his implication is that they destroy potential human beings (*ibid.* 6.23.10, *CSEL* 19²:566). It is entirely in keeping with this approach to treat the users of contraceptives and abortifacients as parricides or homicides. The description is neither biological nor legal, but moral. The essential Christian position is put by Tertullian in an attack on pagan abortion: "To prohibit birth is to accelerate homicide, nor does it matter whether one snatches away a soul after birth or disturbs one as it is being born. He is man who is future man, just as all fruit is now in the seed." [43] The protection of life leads to the prohibition of interference with life at the fetal stage. It is only one step to extend this protection to the lifegiving process.

The need to protect life, the need to defend procreation — these are the needs which guide the development of Christian thought on contraception. The impetus which leads to the adoption of the Stoic-Jewish rule on procreative purpose and the impetus which leads to the treatment of destruction of the fetus as homicide or parricide produce the condemnation of contraception.

THE CONDEMNATIONS OF CONTRACEPTION

The possible, probable, and express condemnations of contraception in the first three centuries of Christian thought are now to be reviewed. The actual statements are few. Their rationale has been stated in anticipation.

[42] *Homicidium* does not appear to have been used by the classical jurists, so that *parricidium* also could have the broad meaning of any intentional killing (see Mommsen, *Römisches Strafrecht*, p. 613).

[43] *Apology* 9.8, *CSEL* 69:24. Tertullian does not appear to be referring to contraception as well as abortion. He has just declared the Christian position on abortion only. When he speaks of a soul "being born" (*animam nascentem*) he apparently refers to birth. It is in this sense that he speaks of the time of a soul being born (*temporibus animae nascentis*) in *The Soul* 37.3.

Their significance as witness to doctrine may be more easily gauged after the exact texts have been examined.

In the *Didache* or *Teaching of the Twelve Apostles* 5.2 there is set out a Way of Life and a Way of Death. The Way of Death is filled with sins, of which one is *pharmakeia* or "medicine"; another sin is use of the magic arts. The evil men who follow this way are "killers of offspring, corrupters of the mold [*plasma*] of God." This catalogue of sins overlaps to some degree. One may suppose that the author repeats his thought, emphasizing magic arts by "medicine," and "killers of offspring" by "corrupters of the mold of God." If, however, the work is interpreted as noting different aspects of related sins, it may be argued that "medicine" here means drugs used as abortifacients or contraceptives, and that "destroyers of the work of God" means those committing abortion or contraception. The same teaching is repeated in the Two Ways as it appears in the later *Epistle of Barnabas* 20. Again, as with the references to *pharmakeia* in the New Testament, one could be sure that contraceptive drugs were included only by assuming that the community thought them evil. The date of the *Didache* itself has been much disputed, but if the most recent monograph on it is followed, the Two Ways is a document of early apostolic times, and contemporary with the composition of the Gospels; it is probably at any event a first-century document.[44] What is particularly striking is that it is clearly an anti-Gnostic document. Chapters 11 and 12 are devoted to distinguishing orthodox apostles and prophets from false ones. Its warning against "medicine" is in a context where the enemies of the Way of Life are also practitioners of the magic arts.

In the second-century works there is indicated an opposition to sexual conduct in marriage which would have a contraceptive effect. The *Epistle of Barnabas* 10.8 uses the weasel as the symbol of men who "work iniquity with their mouth in their uncleanness" and women "who work iniquity with their mouth." Oral intercourse is meant, for, the letter says, "this animal conceives by the mouth." Justin tells of a Christian convert married to a man who sought to satisfy his lusts by copulating with her "against the law of nature and against what is right." Her family asked her to stay with the man, and she stayed suffering his violence and hoping to improve his morals. But they moved to Alexandria, and he projected

[44] The early date of the *Didache* and especially of *The Two Ways* is strongly argued by Jean-Paul Audet, *La Didachè: Instructions des Apôtres* (Paris, 1958), p. 197. Theodore Camelot agrees that at least a date no later than A.D. 100 has been established; "Didache," *LTK* 3:369. Audet believes the edited form of the *Didache* came from an apostolic mission at Antioch; he draws attention to the anti-Gnostic thrust of the *Didache* and connects the enemies it aims at with Simon Magus of Acts 19 (Audet, p. 201).

"worse things." Lest she be a participant in "injuries and impieties," she left him. Justin clearly approves her conduct (*Apology* 2.1).

In the *Paedagogus,* or *The Educator,* of Clement of Alexandria, a work intended to instruct Christians in moral conduct, Clement wrote: "Because of its divine institution for the propagation of man, the seed is not to be vainly ejaculated, nor is it to be damaged, nor is it to be wasted" (*Paedagogus* 2.10.91.2, GCS 12:212). This text was immediately preceded by an exhortation not to commit adultery. It was immediately followed by the statement that Mosaic law forbade intercourse in menstruation lest "what is soon to be a man" be polluted, and by a further statement that intercourse in pregnancy was forbidden. The train of thought follows that of Philo in *The Special Laws.* Just as Philo's denunciation of the waste of seed could be taken broadly to condemn contraception, so Clement could be read broadly as criticizing contraception. But his context seems to limit the text to a criticism of intercourse in menstruation, which will damage the seed, and intercourse in pregnancy, which will waste it.

A third possible reference to contraception occurs in the *Octavius* of Marcus Minucius Felix. This late-second-century dialogue by a Roman lawyer was intended to persuade cultivated pagans of the reasonableness of Christianity. It contrasted the decent behavior of Christians with the conduct of pagan women who "by drinking drugs extinguish the beginning of a future man, and, before they bear, commit parricide" (*Octavius* 30.2, CSEL 2:43).[45] The drugs Minucius describes could be either contraceptives or abortifacients. The effect of the act — "extinguishing the beginning" — could indicate an act either of contraception or of abortion. "Parricide," in the sense of Roman law, would not, in either case, have been committed; as a strong denunciation, the epithet could apply to either. It may be that Minucius intended to cover both possibilities. His statement is ambiguous testimony on contraception.

The first fairly clear reference to contraception by a Christian writer is in the *Elenchos,* or *Refutation of All the Heresies,* written between 220 and 230.[46] The book contains a scathing attack on Pope Callixtus, an ex-slave with a criminal past, who is treated as a usurper of the Roman

---

[45] Minucius here is very close to Tertullian, *To the Nations* 1.15 and *Apology* 9.6, which speak only of abortion and infanticide. Whether Tertullian drew on Minucius, or vice versa, has been argued but not decided; see Johannes Quasten, *Patrology* (Westminster, Md., 1950–60) II, 159. A strong case for the dependence of Tertullian on Minucius is made by Marta Sordi, "L'apologia del martire romano Apollonio, come fonte dell' *Apologeticum* di Tertulliano e i rapporti fra Tertulliano e Minucio," *Rivista di storia della Chiesa in Italia* 18 (1964), 169–188.

[46] The *Elenchos* or *Philosophoumena* was attributed at the time of its modern recovery in 1851 to St. Hippolytus, the rival of St. Callixtus for the Roman bishopric. Recent scholarship has challenged this attribution; see Doresse, *Les Livres secrets,* p. 3. The majority view still seems to support the attribution; see R. Gögler, "Hippolytos," *LTK* 5:378–379.

bishopric. Among the innovations introduced by this pretender is said to be "concubinage" between Christian free women and their slaves. Presumably a more charitable interpretation would be that the bishop of Rome had permitted Christian marriages between these persons which the law did not recognize.[47] The consequence of this innovation, according to the *Elenchos*, is that "as, on account of their prominent ancestry and great property, the so-called faithful want no children from slaves or lowborn commoners, they use drugs of sterility or bind themselves tightly in order to expel a fetus which has already been engendered" (*Elenchos* 9.12.25, GCS 26:250). This conduct, the critic of Callixtus concludes, is "adultery" and "murder." Adultery stigmatizes the relationship; "murder," the acts of contraception and abortion.

This first record of Christians using contraceptives employs the technical term for contraceptive found in Soranos, *atokiois pharmakois*, "anti-bearing drugs." Although such drugs could also be abortifacient, as Soranos testifies, it appears that they were primarily meant as contraceptives. The categorization of "murder" is not stronger than the Talmud's or Philo's characterizations of destruction of semen.

The *Elenchos* assumed that its point was made against Callixtus when it had shown where his tolerance had led. It assumed that all Christians would recognize that contraception is murder. Its confidence may argue to a common belief. On the other hand, the *Elenchos* is argumentative and polemical. Its spirit is rigorist. Its interpretation of the position of Callixtus on marriage is extreme. Whether it gives an accurate reflection of Christian belief on contraception is at least subject to question.

Two particular kinds of acts with contraceptive effects are noted pejoratively by Lactantius. Writing about A.D. 300, he contrasts the conduct of Christians with that of those who commit incest, sacrilege, murder, prostitution, and sodomy, and who are climactically charged with committing oral intercourse and self-castration (*Divine Institutes* 5.9.17, CSEL 19:427). Lactantius finds it unnecessary to spell out why these acts are evil. In the sixth book of *The Divine Institutes*, entitled "The True Religion," Lactantius speaks of a Christian who is too poor to raise a large family. The only solution for such a man is absolute continence (*ibid.* 6.20.25, CSEL 19:559). This is the first reported reference to a Christian for economic reasons not wanting children. Contraception is not mentioned, although

---

[47] The exact legal status in A.D. 200 of a marriage of a woman and her slave is not clear. Legislation under Constantine refuses to recognize a marriage of this kind and treats it as an "affair" (*rem*). The penalty is death for both (*Theodosian Code* 9.9.1). At the same time the law refers to a woman "married" (*nupta*) to a slave before enactment of the legislation. Mommsen mentions no criminal law prohibiting the marriage before Constantine (*Römisches Strafrecht*, p. 686). I would conclude that in 200 the pressure on the women to conceal their marriages was social rather than legal.

abortion, infanticide, and child abandonment are noted as alternatives which no Christian could accept.

In the fourth century Christianity became the established religion of the Empire. In the flowering of Christian literature which followed, themes are developed which were present in early times but never so fully articulated. The evidence of judgment on contraception is not markedly more abundant than in the second and third centuries. The texts available, however, do present a clearer statement of the basic positions.

The need to oppose a Gnostic reading of the Gospels' view of sexuality is shown by one act of the first ecumenical council, Nicea, in 325. The first canon of the Council prescribes that those who have voluntarily castrated themselves are not to be ordained as clerics and, if already ordained, are to function no longer (Mansi 2:668). The council thus put the Christian belief in a nature which should not be mutilated in opposition to the theory of ascetic Gnosticism which made the avoidance of intercourse desirable at any cost. This opposition was enlarged on later in the century by St. John Chrysostom. Those who castrate themselves "stand with the Manichees"; these suppose that the Creator has made a mistake (*On Galatians* 5, PG 61:688–669). Moreover, they do the work of "murderers" (Chrysostom, *Homily 62 on Matthew* 19, PG 58:599).

Castration is an extreme form of contraception. Contraception in a narrower sense was charged to a Gnostic group by St. Epiphanius. Epiphanius, a native of Palestine, in his late teens journeyed to Egypt in search of spiritual instruction. He encountered a group of secret Gnostics, who instructed him in their doctrine and showed him their books, while beautiful girls, members of the sect, invited him to be saved by intercourse with them. He resisted their wiles and reported their existence to the bishop, who had about eighty of the Gnostics expelled from his diocese. Epiphanius returned to Palestine, founded a monastery, and was in 367 elected bishop of Salamis in Cyprus. In his sixties he wrote a long analysis of all known heresies, the *Panarion*, or *Medicine Chest*, in book 26 of which his Egyptian experience is related (GCS 25:297–298).

The Gnostics described by Epiphanius assigned to nonprocreative sexual acts a central place in their religious rites. In a ritual meal they offered to God human semen and menses and then fed upon them (*Panarion* 26.4, GCS 25:280–281). Semen was procured by coitus interruptus, by masturbation, by homosexual intercourse, depending on the subgroup involved (*ibid.* 26.11.10, 26.11.1, 26.13.1, GCS 25:288–292). Among these Gnostics a virgin was one who had experienced intercourse up to the male ejaculation but had not experienced intromission of the seed (*ibid.* 26.11.10, *GCS* 25:290). A subgroup called the Phibionites attached a special value to coitus and sought to perform 365 such acts with 365 women, each act corresponding to one of the Gnostic archons (*ibid.* 26.9.6–8, *GCS* 25:286). Another antinomian Gnostic group, the Carpocratians, made a practice of oral intercourse (*ibid.* 27.4.6, *GCS* 25:305). At points Epiphanius ascribes all this behavior to animal lust, but fundamentally his position is that the practices are organized on a religious basis. They are, as he puts it, "the rites and ceremonies of the devil" (*ibid.* 26.14.6, *GCS* 25:294).

Are these descriptions of organized orgies to be taken as phantasms of the aged monk, or wild exaggerations of his teen-age recollections? Epiphanius had access to the Gnostic writings at the time he composed his own work; he quotes the *Gospel According to the Egyptians*.[48] He appeals to the confirmation of his information by other credible men (*Panarion* 26.18, *GCS* 25:298–299). He makes rather careful distinctions between the Gnostic subgroups. The numbers he finds involved are small. It is difficult to conclude that he is completely imagining what he describes. There were some practices Irenaeus found impossible to imagine and did not describe. But the religious value assigned acts of coitus by some of Epiphanius' Gnostics is not greater than the place the Valentinians give to coitus in the accounts of Irenaeus and Tertullian. What is new in Epiphanius is the explicit emphasis on contraception.

Some skepticism as to Epiphanius' details may, of course, be salutary. The numbers of Gnostics involved seem, in any event, insignificant. But Epiphanius' account has a twofold significance. Looking backwards, Epiphanius makes explicit what Christians found to be the connection between Gnostic morality and contraceptive behavior. The statement of this connection makes concrete and clear a belief implicit in the earlier orthodox writers. For Epiphanius himself, and for later Christian writers like Augustine who will consult his work, these Gnostics are a symbol. Their religious practice of intercourse was the antithesis of Christian marital conduct; their behavior was the ultimate case of intercourse disjoined from procreation.[49]

The passages where Epiphanius condemns the contraceptive acts of

[48] Epiphanius refers to this gospel as *The Gospel of Philip*. Doresse identifies it as *The Gospel of the Egyptians*, otherwise known as *The Book of the Great Invisible Spirit* (Doresse, *Les Livres secrets*, p. 243). The text Epiphanius quotes seems to be a declaration against procreation: "I have known myself and I have collected myself from all places. I have not borne sons for the prince, but I have plucked out his roots and collected the scattered members in one" (quoted in *Panarion* 26:13, *GCS* 25:292).

[49] An even greater significance to this branch of Gnosticism might be found, if it should prove to be connected, even in a degenerate form, with the movement called tantrism which swept India in the fourth century. There are many suggestive paral-

the Gnostic group reflect passion, shock, outrage; they testify to the depth of the orthodox reaction. The contraceptive conduct is criticized with a generality sufficient to cover any contraceptive intercourse, but the context of Epiphanius confines the criticism to the ritual practice: "They exercise genital acts, yet prevent the conceiving of children. Not in order to produce offspring, but to satisfy lust, are they eager for corruption" (*Panarion* 26.5.2, *GCS* 25:281). This practice is "most foul impurity." The "devil has plunged them into a deep whirlpool." They commit "enormities." Their abhorrence of children is "the worst conduct and crime."

The anti-Gnostic epistle of the New Testament, 1 Timothy, is invoked against them. The New Testament epistle on natural law, Romans 1, is used to condemn them (*Panarion* 26.16.2–4, *GCS* 25:296). And for the first time in an important patristic writer the story of Onan is used to condemn contraception. These Gnostics who have intercourse without seminal intromission "imitate that immense and frightful crime of Sela

---

lels between some forms of Gnosticism and the account of tantrism given by Mircea Eliade. I will summarize some of the relevant passages:

"It is said of him who accomplishes the *khecarimudra* that his 'semen never wastes away, when he is in the embrace of a beautiful woman . . . As long as the *khecarimudra* is firmly adhered to, so the semen does not flow out.'" (Mircea Eliade, *Yoga: Immortality and Freedom,* trans. Willard Trask (London, 1955), p. 134, quoting the *Dhyanabindu,* a late Upanishad of the second century.)

"We must not forget that *maithuna* is never allowed to terminate in an emission of semen. *Bodhicittam notsrjet,* 'the semen must not be emitted,' the texts repeat." (*Ibid.,* p. 267, describing the tantrist process of *maithuna,* that is, sexual union without insemination.)

"The *Goraksa Samhita* (61–71) states that during the *khecarimudra* the *bindu* (sperm) 'does not fall' even if one is embraced by a woman . . . All these texts insist upon the interdependence between the breath, psychomental experience, and the *semen virile.*" (*Ibid.,* pp. 248–249, describing Hatha Yoga as it appears in the works of the twelfth-century yogin Gorahknath.)

The Sahajiya is a profound mystical movement which includes tantrism; and, as in tantrism, "sexual union is understood as a means of obtaining 'supreme bliss' (*mahasukha*), and it must never end in seminal emission." (*Ibid.,* p. 266.)

"The yogin 'should draw back up again with the *medhra* (the *bindu* discharged in *maithuna*)' and the same act of reabsorption must also be performed by the woman." (*Ibid.,* p. 249, quoting the *Hathayogapradipika,* III, 82.)

There was a "metaphysical ambiguity" in tantrism that encouraged excesses. The *Guhyasamaja-tantra* teaches that the tantrist may lie, steal, commit adultery; for all contraries are illusory (Eliade, p. 204). But even if those who understood or practised tantrism imperfectly were often accused of orgies, the pure tantrist sought salvation, and *maithuna,* the practice just described, was the way of salvation. In this union the woman became a goddess, the man a god. In the perfect control of thought, breath, and semen, the sexual union became cosmic and eternal. The tantrists said that Buddha himself obtained immortality by practicing *maithuna* (*ibid.,* p. 263). With tantrism went a discovery, a glorification of woman; and in some regions there was associated with the cult of the Divine Woman a type of adulterous love. Thus, in seventh-century Bengal there were "courts of love" where the merits of conjugal love were compared to those of adulterous love, always to the triumph of the latter (*ibid.,* p. 264).

with Thamar" (*ibid.* 26.11.11, *GCS* 25:290).[50] The Gnostic Origenians, who repudiate marriage, also "perpetuate that crime which Onan son of Juda is said to have committed" (*ibid.* 63.1.4, *GCS* 31:399).

The Gnostics of Epiphanius, then, constituted the classic case in which contraception was condemned: ritual intercourse where insemination was avoided on dogmatic grounds. This archetypal practice was the rejection of three fundamental propositions to which orthodoxy was committed: that creation was good, that marriage was good, that the perpetuation of the species was good. Epiphanius gives the ultimate, concrete cases of rejection. The dogmatic propositions of the Gnostics, which these cases embodied, had for three centuries excited the orthodox leaders and occasioned their commitment to the Stoic-Jewish rules on intercourse.

Contraception for hedonistic, not religious, reasons was attacked by the bishop of Constantinople. Preaching about 390 on the fashion in which Christian marriage festivities should be conducted, St. John Chrysostom turned from his plea for decorum to say a word against prostitution and contraception:

Why do you sow where the field is eager to destroy the fruit? Where there are medicines of sterility? Where there is murder before birth? You do not even let a harlot remain only a harlot, but you make her a murderess as well. Do you see that from drunkenness comes fornication, from fornication adultery, from adultery murder? Indeed, it is something worse than murder and I do not know what to call it; for she does not kill what is formed but prevents its formation. What then? Do you contemn the gift of God, and fight with His laws? What is a curse, do you seek as though it were a blessing? Do you make the anteroom of birth the anteroom of slaughter? Do you teach the woman who is given to you for the procreation of offspring to perpetrate killing? That she may always be beautiful and lovable to her lovers, and that she may rake in more money, she does not refuse to do this, heaping fire on your head; and even if the crime is hers, you are the cause. Hence also arise idolatries. To look pretty many of these women use incantations, libations, philtres, potions, and innumerable other things. Yet after such turpitude, after murder, after idolatry, the matter still seems indifferent to many men—even to many men having wives. In this indifference of the married men there is greater evil filth; for then poisons are prepared, not against the womb of a prostitute, but against your injured wife. Against her are these innumerable tricks, invocations of demons, incantations of the dead, daily wars, ceaseless battles, and unremitting contentions.

(Homily 24 on the Epistle to the Romans, PG 60:626–627)

The means of birth prevention are "medicines" — the Latin *venena* is an approximate equivalent. It is unspecified whether they are oral or external, temporary or permanent, nor is a clear distinction made between abortifacients and contraceptives. It would seem that both were included

---

[50] "Sela" is apparently a slip of the pen for "Onan," made either by Epiphanius or an early manuscript, unless there was a story current about Thamar and Onan's younger brother Sela which Gn 38 does not contain.

as agents preventing birth.[51] Two aspects of this denunciation of contraception are striking. First it is made by a priest preaching to his flock, the Christians of Antioch. Second, the reason given for condemning contraception is equally applicable whether contraception occurs in fornication or in marriage.

In a second sermon, on avarice, a sin that concerned Chrysostom more than sexual failings, he spoke again of contraception. Men who are avaricious and desirous to avoid children as a burden "mutilate nature, not only killing the newborn, but even acting to prevent their beginning to live" (*Homily 28 on Matthew* 5, PG 57:357). The expression "mutilate" may suggest castration. The prevention of life could possibly include abortion. More probably, however, contraception alone is meant, the basic idea being that it is a mutilation of nature in preventing the beginning of life. The act denounced plainly takes place in marriage, as Chrysostom indicates that but for the man's avaricious nature, children would be desired.

In the West, St. Ambrose spoke of potions used in marriage in the course of a commentary on Genesis, but at a rather unexpected place. Commenting on the variety of birds whose creation is described by Genesis, he exclaimed, "Let men learn to love their children from the pious custom of crows." Crows sedulously cared for their tender young. But "the women of our race" are different. The poor abandon their offspring. The rich, "lest their patrimony be divided among several, deny their own fetus in their uterus and by a parricidal potion extinguish the pledges of their womb in their genital belly, and life is taken away before it is transmitted" (*Hexameron* 5.18.58, CSEL 32¹:184). Does this statement relate only to abortifacients? Given the belief that the fetus was not "ensouled" or "vivified" at once, the reference to life not yet having been transmitted is not decisive. Ambrose seems to speak of potions acting on an embryo already in the womb. Probably he did not have in mind a clear distinction between an abortifacient and a contraceptive potion. To users of potions preventing life he applied the condemnation "parricide." From the context where protection of inheritance is the object of these acts, it is probable that any use of the potions in marriage is what is condemned.

The basic thought of Ambrose — that it is wrong to take life before it is given — appears in a famous letter of Jerome which deserves special

---

[51] Dubarle argues that "the crime which is murder and worse than murder must be abortion," although he notes that medicines of sterility refers to contraceptives. A. Dubarle, "La Bible et les pères ont-ils parlé de la contraception?" *La Vie spirituelle* 15, Supplement (1962), 599. But it would seem that the contrast is between killing a human being and, what Chrysostom finds is worse, sterilizing nature. Similarly Chrysostom says that those who castrate themselves are "homicides" (*Homily 62 on Matthew*, PG 58:599).

attention because of its later authority. Jerome, a Catholic from the provinces, had spent a youth of sexual license, reformed, lived in the desert as a monk, and appeared in 382 in Rome, where, now in his mid-thirties, he won the regard and trust of Pope Damasus. The moment was a high one for the Church; only two years before, the emperors by official decree had "adjudged demented and insane" all heretics from the Catholic Church (*Theodosian Code* 16.1.2). Damasus enjoyed official recognition no predecessor had ever had. Jerome, as his secretary and as a man of great talent, was a figure in society. The aristocratic Roman world was still divided between Catholics and pagans; pagans were a majority, but the Catholics were conscious of making headway. Jerome quickly took a leading role among the Catholic upper class. One great admirer was Paula, a Catholic descended from an ancient Roman line, who had been married at about twelve and who, now in her early thirties, was a widow with five children. Jerome became the spiritual mentor of the family. The oldest daughter, Blesilla, was carefully instructed by Jerome, but, somewhat to his annoyance, married, only to be widowed in seven months. Jerome was determined to encourage her next-oldest sister, Eustochium, to persevere as a virgin. She was his star pupil in learning Greek and Hebrew; she was virtuous as well as bright. She was, he declared, the first noble Roman woman to seek to live as a virgin dedicated to Christ. To encourage her Jerome wrote a small treatise on virginity; and so as to not waste his labor on one mind alone, he did nothing to prevent its circulation; indeed, he had included in it many thrusts at elements of Catholic high society in Rome of which he disapproved, and these thrusts were not intended to go unread. In a passage of particular verve, he deplored the number of virgins who fell daily, the many women of distinction who were lost to the bosom of Mother Church. "You may see," he announced, "a number of women who are widows before they are wives." Some of these pranced about, hiding their unwanted pregnancy with concealing dress. There were those even less scrupulous: "Others, indeed, will drink sterility and murder a man not yet born." Finally, there were those who, after they conceived, used poisons to commit abortions: these were parricides, and, as sometimes the abortifacient was fatal to themselves, they went condemned to judgment as adulteresses, killers of their children, and killers of themselves. Yet this kind of Christian woman has an answer. "All things are pure to the pure," they say. "My conscience is enough for me." These girls parade about the streets with loose-bound hair, low-heeled shoes, flying capes, and a loosejointed walk, drawing after them the eyes of a crowd of young men. They have, Jerome concludes, their admirers; he is not one (*Letter 22, To Eustochium* 13, CSEL 54:160–161).

The evidence of Christian practice offered by this letter to a teen-ager is mixed. Evidently contraception was known and practiced in fashionable Catholic circles. Jerome denounces it in strong terms, but in a passage which mixes indignation at abortion with scorn of teen-age dress. The inference to be drawn from the Catholic reaction of the day to Jerome's little tract is also of some relevance. It made him generally unpopular. Some felt that he had confirmed what most respectable old pagan families felt about the morals of Catholics. Jerome himself described his book as one "that was stoned" (*Letters* 52.17, *CSEL* 54:440). But however malicious and exaggerated the Catholic society of Rome in 385 thought his gibes, his words were the ones which survived to posterity. There, in unmistakable language, contraception was described as a form of homicide.[52]

THE SCRIPTURAL TEXT

There was a general failure to invoke the story of Onan, which Jewish rabbis had already used against contraception. Origen expounded Genesis 38 only in an allegorical fashion (*Selections on Genesis, PG* 12:129). St. Ambrose commented on Genesis without alluding to the text. St. John Chrysostom himself spoke of the death of Onan, "who had shown himself to be evil," without connecting his fault with contraception (*Homilies on Genesis* 62.1, *PG* 54:533). St. Ephraem (306–373), a Syrian contemporary of Epiphanius, said that Onan acted out of both hate for his brother and love for Thamar, and was killed for "his bitter trick," an explanation with some of the ambiguities of the original text.[53] Only St. Epiphanius gave a plain interpretation of the text as a condemnation of contraception, and he did so only in the context of his anti-Gnostic polemic.[54]

St. Jerome did not find Onan apposite to his denunciation of potion-drinking. It is to Jerome, however, that is owed a translation of Genesis 38:8–10 which was to make it a powerful text in later times against con-

[52] The above summary is based on Jerome's own letters and their analysis by Ferdinand Cavallera, *Saint Jérôme, Sa vie et son oeuvre* (Louvain, 1922). Jerome's birth-date is calculated by Cavallera, II, 10. References to his stormy youth in his letters are collected, II, 72–73. Paula's biography is given by Jerome in a letter to Eustochium on her death (Letter 108, *CSEL* 55:306–351). The contemporary Catholic reaction to Jerome's letter on virginity is summarized by Cavallera, I, 108. On the relations between Catholic and pagan families in Roman society, see P. R. L. Brown, "Aspects of the Christianization of the Roman Aristocracy," *Journal of Roman Studies* 51 (1961), 1–12.

[53] St. Ephraem adds the information that Juda sent Thamar away because she was suspected to be the cause of the deaths of both Onan and Er. St. Ephraem, *In Genesim et in Exodum commentarii* 34.1, Syriac text and Latin translation by R. R. Tonneau, *Corpus scriptorum christianorum orientalium*, vol. 153 (Louvain, 1955), p. 81.

[54] It might be observed that Thamar is in the Davidic line of ancestry of the Messiah according to Mt. 1:3, so that Christian commentators had occasion to consider Gn 38 and opportunity to note Onan's failure to participate in the Davidic line.

traception.[55] In three important particulars Jerome established a version which was different from the version today accepted as the best version of the Hebrew. In two of these three cases his translation is significantly different from the Old Latin text he had before him. (1) Jerome's translation speaks of Onan "entering" (*introiens*) Thamar, thereby failing to indicate that the practice was repeated, not an isolated action. The Old Latin had similarly used a verb indicating a single action (*introisset*). (2) Jerome supplied the word *semen* omitted by the original and by the Old Latin as the object for "spilled." (3) Most important of all, he appeared to make Onan's act the reason for God's punishment: "God slew him because he did a detestable thing" (*rem detestabilem*). The Hebrew said because he "did not please God." The Old Latin said "he appeared evil before the Lord"; in neither is there the same focus on an act. The term "destestable" is apparently derived from an earlier commentary by Zeno of Verona (circa 360) where Onan and Er are said to be "detestable" symbols of their pride and idolatry (Zeno, *Tractatus* 2.14, *PL* 11:434–436). It is a harsh word of denunciation, not elsewhere employed by Jerome in his translation of the Bible. The total effect of Jerome's emendations was to make the passage a strong text against contraception. It incorporated Jerome's judgment of the practice.

The importance given the text by Jerome might indeed be connected with his friendship with Epiphanius. At a venerable age Epiphanius had come to Rome in 382 to attend the council held by Pope Damasus. He was Paula's guest and thereby joined the circle closest to Jerome. In 385 he in his turn was host in Salamis to Jerome and Paula on their way to Bethlehem (Jerome, *Letters* 108.6, 7, *CSEL* 55:310–313). Jerome speaks of "*Papa* Epiphanius, the five-tongued one," with warmth and admiration (*Against Rufinus* 3.6, *PL* 23:483). He was thoroughly familiar with the *Panarion*, which was completed in 377 (*Heresies* 66.20), and he translated the Pentateuch about 400.

ANAPHRODISIACS

The attitude of the Fathers to potions attacking or preventing life may profitably be compared with their attitude to anaphrodisiacs.[56] Origen

---

[55] Jerome's translation reads: "Ille sciens non sibi nasci filios introiens ad uxorem sui fratris sui semen fundebat in terram ne liberi fratris nomine nascerentur et idcirco percussit eum Dominus quod rem detestabilem fecerat" (*Biblia sacra,* ed. Quentin). For the Old Latin text, see *Vetus latina,* ed. Peter Sabatier, rev. Erzabtei Beuron (Freiburg, 1942).

[56] These passages on the willow and chaste tree have been collected and analyzed by Hugo Rahner, S.J., in terms of Christian adoption of pagan symbol, "Die Weide als Symbol der Keuschheit in der Antike und im Christentum," *Zeitschrift für katholische Theologie* 56 (1932), 231; Hugo Rahner, *Griechische Mythen in christlicher Deutung* (Zurich, 1945), pp. 390–413.

is at the fount of this teaching. Commenting on a reference to the willow and the chaste tree in the Septuagint version of Exodus, Origen declares, "In power as in name these plants are those of chastity" (*On Exodus* 9.4, *GCS* 29:244). Commenting on Ezechiel, he teaches that it is written that all believers will receive "the willow crown" (*On Ezechiel* 1.5, *GCS* 33:330). In these references the willow, associated with sterility by Greeks like Homer and Aristotle, was made to figure as a symbol of Christian chastity. The chaste tree (*agnos* in Greek) had already been identified by pagan tradition as a symbol of chastity. According to legend, at the Thesmophoria, the autumnal harvest festival at Athens, the maidens, who were supposed to remain chaste, scattered leaves of chaste tree where they slept (Pliny, *Natural History* 24.38.59); now in Origen it operated as a talisman of chastity.[57] Origen's use was expanded by Methodius, a Christian teacher in Lycia near the end of the third century and the author of a Platonic dialogue on chastity.[58] The work stands out among patristic writings by having only women (fourteen in all) as its characters. One participant in the dialogue, Theopatra, explicates Psalm 136:1, "On the willows of that land [Babylon] we hung up our instruments." By instruments, she said, "they mean their bodies, which they have hung up on the branches of chastity." She further explained of the willow that "if you drink its flower steeped in water it extinguishes whatever arouses carnal desires and passions within us, even to the point of making a person utterly sterile and rendering ineffectual all efforts at procreation" (*Symposium* 4.3; cf. 4.9). None of the other maidens present appeared to think that this anaphrodisiac-contraceptive was a curious symbol of Christian chastity. Indeed Theopatra was allowed to make without challenge the completely inaccurate statement that Scripture everywhere uses the willow as a symbol of chastity (4.3). Tusiane, another girl in the dialogue, combined the Athenian festival with Leviticus 23:40 where in the Septuagint the Jews were told to take branches of chaste tree at the Feast of the Tabernacles. This, she said, was a mystic foreshadowing of "the great Feast of the true Tabernacle in that new creation where there will be no pain, when all the fruits of the earth will have been harvested, and men will no longer beget or be begotten" (9.1).

The Greek lead was followed in the West. Ambrose, in the same com-

[57] Frazer speculates that the chastity of the maidens at the Thesmophoria was connected with their responsibility for sowing the harvest seed. James G. Frazer, *The Golden Bough*, 3rd ed. (London, 1933), vol. I, part V, "Spirits of the Corn and of the Wild," p. 116.

[58] In his introduction to his translation of the *Symposium*, Herbert Musurillo, S.J., remains skeptical about all the other legends we have of "St. Methodius," and admits only the possibility that he may have been a bishop and martyr. Methodius, *Symposium*, trans. H. Musurillo (Westminster, Md., 1958), p. 5. I follow Musurillo's translation here.

mentary on Luke in which he so vigorously denounces intercourse during pregnancy, made a reference to Psalm 136:2 and expounded the willows of the Psalm as symbols of abstinence and chastity (*On Luke* 2.70, *CSEL* 32⁴:78). Ambrose did not mention the contraceptive property of willow, but if he considered willow merely as an anaphrodisiac, he probably thought it acceptable. In his review of the works of creation in Genesis he commented on hemlock as that means by which "the furies of lusts generally shrivel," and, as he was pointing to the beneficent uses of all creation, he appeared to accept this anaphrodisiac effect (*Hexameron* 3.9.39).

Two points are suggested by these tolerant views of anaphrodisiacs. One is that the association of herbal potions with magic did not lead to a condemnation of all potions. The anaphrodisiacs were potions which were acceptable. The second is that not all forms of interference with the processes of the human body seemed intolerable. The sexual instinct, it seemed, might be stupefied without violation of the fundamental nature of man.

THE SIGNIFICANCE OF THE CONDEMNATIONS

There are at least two ways of evaluating the significance of the patristic statements taken as a whole. On the one hand, it may be argued that the *Didache* and the *Epistle to Barnabas* convey the same opposition as Galatians and the Apocalypse to all "medicine." This opposition is made precise in the *Elenchos* condemnation of "medicine" used to prevent conception. The teaching is reaffirmed by Jerome and John Chrysostom and probably by Ambrose. The use of drugs in marriage is explicitly condemned by Ambrose and John and, in effect, distinguished by Ambrose from permissible anaphrodisiacs. That it is hard to tell whether some condemnations relate to abortifacients or contraceptives is understandable because in fact abortifacients and contraceptives were hard to distinguish. Similarly "magic" and "drugs" were sometimes not distinguished because they were bound together in practice. Coitus interruptus, a form of contraception not favored by the Greco-Roman medical writers, received less attention. It is implicitly rejected in Justin's condemnation of unnatural behavior in marriage, and in the rejection of oral intercourse by the *Epistle to Barnabas* and Lactantius. It is explicitly condemned by Epiphanius, and his judgment on it as a religious ritual is reaffirmed by Jerome when he uses "detestable" to describe the same practice in the marriage of Onan.

On the other hand, it may be said that no one addresses himself solely to the sinfulness of a single contraceptive act by a married person with reason not to have more children. Of those who condemn contraceptive potions in marriage, Chrysostom and Ambrose link their use to avarice or hardheartedness. The *Elenchos* condemns potions only in a relationship which its author did not regard as marriage; Jerome condemns potions used by fornicators. Epiphanius condemns coitus interruptus only as a rite. Jerome gives no judgment on it independent of his understanding of Scripture. Oral intercourse or the unnatural intercourse spoken of by Justin cannot be identified with all forms of contraceptive acts. The "medicine" rejected by the *Didache* and Barnabas may be rejected by them because of its association with magic or with fornication; there is no indication in them, any more than in the New Testament, that contraceptive drugs are specifically meant, while they condemn abortion with some explicitness. Indeed, the comparison with the testimony on abortion is especially striking. The condemnations there are many and clear. They are express and direct, not in passing or inferential. The act is often condemned on its own account, not just as an adjunct to fornication. Several of the condemnations occur in documents meant to teach the faithful. There is church legislation against the act. The penalties involved — exclusion from communion for life or for ten years — establish that the sin was regarded as a serious one depriving the sinner of his right to be with the community. There is no reason for believing that a means like coitus interruptus was not more effective than many abortifacient potions. Of persons who would commit abortion, it is probable that at least some would at any rate attempt contraception. If abortion is so often castigated, and contraception so little, contraception cannot have been regarded generally as a major offense against God.

On the other hand, when writers do refer to contraception as evil they do so with an evident air of introducing no novelty, of expecting acceptance of their criticism. Abortion could have seemed a more obvious evil to attack even if an equally strong view of contraception were held. The common doctrine on the requirement of a procreative purpose in intercourse was presented to the faithful by writers like Clement, Origen, Lactantius. This doctrine necessarily excluded contraception, although it did not determine whether contraception was a major or minor sin. Most moralists may have been content to rest on their presentation of this teaching.

The position of the first three centuries on contraception is, then, enmeshed with the Alexandrian commitment to the Stoic rule on procreative purpose and the Stoic view of nature. Remove those parts of the testimony, and what is left is the contention that contraception attacks life — a contention with much claim to be heard when embryonic life needed protection, but not intended literally. Beyond this protection of existing life lies the assumption that the life-giving process is itself sacred, a cooperation with God immune from interference; St. John Chrysostom alone expresses this position distinctly.

This was the state of the doctrine on contraception when the Church experienced a trauma as profound as that of Gnosticism — the competition of the Manichees — and when a writer appeared who, comprehensively and passionately, synthesized his own experience, the Stoic rule on procreation, the teaching on original sin, the need to protect life, into a rule on contraception: St. Augustine.

CHAPTER IV

THE MORALS OF THE MANICHEES, AND ST. AUGUSTINE

ORROWING MUCH from the Gnostics, something from Christianity,
and a good deal from Iranian folk religion, the prophet Mani (216–
277) founded a new religion, bequeathed it a scripture, and sealed his
testimony of a new revelation by his martyrdom. Begun in Babylon, the
religion spread before his death to Egypt, Palestine, Rome; by the mid-
fourth century it was in Asia Minor, Greece, Illyria, Italy, North Africa.
Like Christianity, Manicheanism was a religion with a canonical scripture: it possessed the seven books of Mani. Like Christianity, it claimed to
be universal: its hierachy and apostles spread throughout the Roman
world. Like Christianity, it accounted for the religions on which it drew
by explaining them as incomplete predecessors: Mani was the last in a
chain of revelation. Like Christianity, it was a missionary faith; Christians
were among its converts, and its most famous convert was to be the most
influential teacher of the Catholic Church on marriage, sexuality, and
contraception.[1]

THE TEACHING OF MANI AND THE MANICHEES

What did the Manichees believe on marriage and sexuality? The basic
structure was set for them by Mani's theology; for Manicheanism was at
once a theological explanation of the world and a plan of conduct for
salvation. In *The Fundamental Epistle*, Mani, "by the the providence of
God the father, an apostle of Jesus Christ," proclaimed, "In the beginning
there were two substances divided from each other." One was the realm
of God the Father, "the kingdom of light." The other was "the land of

[1] A good account of Mani and Manichean doctrine is Henri-Charles Puech, *Le Manichéisme* (Paris, 1949).

boundless darkness." [2] This fundamental division between light and darkness was the basis for explaining the whole development of the universe.

The King of Darkness, attracted by the splendor of the light, invaded the Kingdom of Light. He was met by an evocation of the Father called "Primitive Man," a supernatural being of light. In a duel of Primitive Man and his sons with the King of Darkness and his sons, the forces of light were vanquished and then devoured by their opponents. In this way the light was imprisoned. This imprisonment was the basic fact for Manichean morality.[3]

The Father evoked the Living Spirit, or Demiurge, who rescued Primitive Man himself, but left mixed with the sons of the King of Darkness the light which they had absorbed in devouring the sons of Primitive Man. The Living Spirit then made the earth and sky, using the carcasses of some of the defeated sons of darkness, or Archons, as material. From some of the Archons he drew light and made the sun and moon of pure light.[4]

[2] *The Fundamental Epistle* of Mani in its Latin version, as quoted by Augustine, *Contra epistolam quam vocant fundamenti* 5, 13, 15, *CSEL* 25^1:197, 209, 212. The importance of this book may be gauged by Augustine's remark that "it contains almost all that you [Manichees] believe" (*ibid.* 5, *CSEL* 25^1:197). Felix, a Manichean opponent of Augustine, is quoted as saying, "It is the beginning, the middle, and the end" (*Contra Felicem* 2.1, *CSEL* 25^2:828).

[3] The substance of this paragraph is not present in the Latin quotations of Augustine. It follows the Syriac version of *The Fundamental Epistle* quoted by Theodore bar Khôni, *Scholia* (translated in Henri Pognon, *Inscriptions mandaïtes des coupes de Khouabir* (Paris, 1898), pp. 178–186 (hereafter *Scholia*). This work has been analyzed by Franz Cumont, *Recherches sur le manichéisme*, vol. I: *La Cosmogonie manichéenne d'après Théodore Bar Khôni* (Brussels, 1908). Cumont, pp. 5–6, takes the position that both Augustine and Theodore are dealing with the same document. He prefers Theodore's version, because the Syriac is closer to the original Mandaean. There are, as will be seen, some considerable differences between the two. I do not see how we can be certain that Theodore, writing in the early eighth century, did not have a version much changed from the original.

There is a third account of Manichean theology in the *Fihrist*, or *Register of the Sciences*, of Muhammad ibn Ishaq ibn al-Nadim, written in Arabic in 987–988. The work has been edited and translated by Gustav Flügel in *Mani, seine Lehre und seine Schriften* (Leipzig, 1862); this version is hereafter cited as *Fihrist*. The *Fihrist* is derived from unknown earlier sources; its author is familiar with a number of works attributed to Mani. Cumont identifies *The Letter of the Two Princes*, referred to by the *Fihrist*, as *The Fundamental Epistle* (*Recherches*, p. 5). The *Fihrist* agrees with the Latin and Syrian versions in the basic doctrine that Light and Darkness were divided from each other at the beginning of the world; that the Darkness invaded the Light; that the King of Light made Primitive Man; and that the Prince of Devils defeated Primitive Man (*Fihrist*, pp. 86–87). It also agrees in teaching that the present world was made as a way of freeing light from the Dark (*ibid.*, p. 89). It does not have the story of the devils devouring the sons of Primitive Man.

[4] The Syriac version of Theodore bar Khôni is followed (*Scholia*, pp. 188–192). "Living Spirit" and "King of Darkness" are the Syriac terms; "Demiurge" and "Prince of Darkness" are the terms used in the west.

According to the Latin version of *The Fundamental Epistle*, the Prince of Darkness then generated the first human being, in order to produce a figure of light like one of the glorious appearances of the Father. The generation occurred in three steps: The Prince commanded the remaining sons of darkness to copulate. He devoured the offspring thereby produced. He copulated with his own wife and brought forth man. Man was thus sired by the darkness, but he has within himself some light derived from the light once within the sons of darkness.[5]

In the Syriac version of *The Fundamental Epistle,* the Father took pity on the light still imprisoned in the defeated Archons. He sent a third evocation, the Messenger, to liberate the light in the Archons. The Messenger, also known as the Virgin of Lights, was androgynous. He appeared to the male Archons as a girl, to the female Archons as a boy. His beautiful appearance aroused the concupiscence of the Archons, and they responded by emitting the light that they had absorbed. At the same time, and in proportion to the light released, "the sin" in the male Archons was separated from them and fell; it became the origin of trees. The female Archons, already pregnant, were stimulated to abort by the beauty of the Messenger. The abortions fell to the ground and became the origin of animals. The animal abortions desired to imitate the form of the Messenger and were advised by Ashaqloun, son of the King of Darkness. Following his plan, they let themselves be eaten by Ashaqloun and his female friend Namräel. Ashaqloun and Namräel copulated and brought forth Adam and Eve, the first human beings. In this account, as in the Latin version, man has a demoniacal sire, but his connection with the light is more tenuous.[6]

The story of "the seduction of the Archons" appears in a different way in Book 7 of *The Treasure* of Mani. Here it is not connected with the generation of man, but only with the rescue of the light and the fall of some light particles which become earthly seeds. The account reads as follows:

Then the blessed Father, who has ships of light as lodging-places and dwellings according to their magnitudes, by virtue of his innate clemency brings the help by which he is released and freed from the wicked bonds and difficulties and torments of his vital substance. And so by his invisible nod he transforms those virtues of his that are contained in the brightest of the ships, and makes them visible to the opposing Powers, which have been assigned to the various

---

[5] Here the Latin version is followed as quoted by Augustine in c. 46 of *De natura boni,* ed. A. Anthony Moon (Washington, 1955).

[6] The Syriac version (*Scholia*, pp. 187–192). A similar account is given in Friedrich C. Andreas and Walter B. Henning, *Mitteliranische Manichaica, aus Chinesisch-Turkestan,* Sitzungsberichte der Preussischen Akademie der Wissenschaften, Phil.-hist. Klasse (Berlin, 1932), p. 194. The *Fihrist* has man originating from the copulation of the Archons with Force, Covetousness, Concupiscence, and Sin (*Fihrist,* p. 90). It does not have the story of the seduction of the Archons.

tracts of the sky. And since those Powers are of both sexes, some masculine and some feminine, he therefore orders the aforesaid virtues to appear some in the form of naked youths to the opposing female Powers, others in the form of luminous maidens to the opposing males; for he knows that these hostile Powers, because of the deadly and most vile lust innate in them, are easily caught and made subject to those beautiful forms that appear to them, and in this way are destroyed. Yet you may know that this blessed Father of ours is the same as his Virtues, which of necessity he changes into the virgin likeness of youths and maidens: he uses them as the weapons, and through them he fulfills his will. The ships of light are filled with these divine Virtues, which are set before the infernal race in the likeness of mates, and which speedily and easily accomplish what they intend in the same instant that they think of it. Therefore, when reason demands that these divine Virtues appear to the male Powers, they immediately appear to them in the form of most beautiful maidens; and when they approach the females, putting off their womanly appearance they show themselves in the form of naked youths. And at this beautiful vision the ardor and lust of the hostile Powers increases; and in this way the bond of their worst thoughts is loosed, and the living soul, which was held captive in their limbs, thus released, makes its escape and mingles itself with the pure air. And there the thoroughly cleansed souls ascend to the ships of light, which have been prepared for them as transport and conveyance to their native land. But that part which still bears the strains of the hostile race is broken up by the heat and descends bit by bit, and is mixed with trees and the other things that are planted and all things that are sown, and is infused with various colors.[7]

This, the version known to the West, embodied the myth which Augustine will come to see as the epitome of sexual usage religiously dedicated to a nonprocreative end. The androgynous agents of the Father here provoke lust, and the provocation of lust results in emissions which

[7] *The Treasure*, as quoted by Augustine, *The Nature of the Good* 44. There is a third main version of the seduction of the Archons. In this account the story is a myth of the origin of death. When the sons of Darkness are moved by lust, they sweat and their sweat becomes rain; they are also angry at human beings and send pestilence on earth and, cutting the tie that binds men to superior beings, bring about the deaths of men. Hegemonius, *Acts of Archelaus* 9, *GCS* 16:13–15, followed by Epiphanius, *Panarion*, PG 42, and by Cyril of Jerusalem, *Catecheses* 6.34, PG 33. Which of the three accounts variously preserved in Theodore bar Khôni, Augustine, and Hegemonius was the original version of Mani? Possibly he wrote different versions in different books. We can only believe that the Latin version of the *Treasure* was the one more general in the West. The basic legend goes back to Zervanian folk religion (Geo Widengren, *Mani und der Manichäismus*, Stuttgart, 1961, p. 62). On the relation to the myth of the Valentinian Gnostics, see Jean Doresse, *Les Livres secrets des gnostiques d'Égypte* (Paris, 1958), p. 67.

Other references to the androgynous Virgin of Lights are frequent in Manichean literature: e.g., Mani's prayer to, among other beings, the Virgin of Lights, in *Manichäische Homilien*, ed. and trans. Hans Jacob Polotsky (Stuttgart, 1934), p. 53. So too praise of "the beloved daughter of her Father, the blessed maid of Light [?], who puts to shame by her ineffable beauty the powers that are full," in *A Manichean Psalm Book*, II, ed. and trans. C. R. C. Allberry (Stuttgart, 1938), p. 2. A Chinese Manichean reference to the Virgin of Lights occurs in strophes 42 and 43 of the Tunbuang Chinese MS, trans. Tsiu Chi, *Bulletin of the School of Oriental Studies* 11 (1943), 179.

free the light. The relationship between this narrative of divine behavior and human conduct will become the subject of Augustine's analysis.

In both versions of the origin of man, some light is imprisoned in the world and in man, light which is from the Father. How is it to be rescued? Man's part in the rescue is the center of Manichean morality.

Light could be released by eating. If one of the Elect ate bread, vegetables, or fruit containing seeds, he effected a release of the light particles within the food.[8] The release of light also could be effected or impeded by sexual actions. The analysis of man by Mani as a being composed of light particles in a body originally generated by demons determined what sexual actions were efficacious and what were obstructions. As the first human beings were generated by the Prince of Darkness, so, Mani taught in *The Fundamental Epistle*, "we see the nature of evil become the framer of bodies, deriving from bodies the generative forces to fashion them." [9] Procreation is the evil act of evil.

Many Manichean statements on sexual behavior which have survived, like many Gnostic statements, are apparently close to Christian teaching on virginity and continence.[10] Their meaning becomes ambiguous only in the light of the Manichean myths. They can be read as expressions of a devotion to bodily purity, or they can be read as expressions of hostility to procreation as a perpetuation of the light's imprisonment.

Thus, in the fourth century, the "Psalms to Jesus" say, "The gifts of Matter I have cast away . . . I have known my soul and this body that lies upon it, that they are enemies to each other . . . The bitter darts of lust, the murderers of souls, thou hast not tasted, thou, o holy son undefiled" (*A Manichean Psalm Book* 247, p. 55; 248, p. 56; 254, p. 64). The "Psalms of the Bema" of the same period proclaim, "[A sinner is] he for whom lust has soiled the whiteness of his clothes . . . The lust of the sweetness that is bitter I have not tasted" (*ibid.* 241, p. 45; 247, p. 55). The "Psalm to the Trinity" finds "the purity of virginity" the "sign of the holy Spirit" (*ibid.*, p. 115). Another fragment contrasts the excellence of virginity to mere continence (*ibid.*, pp. 179–181).

---

[8] Augustine, *The Nature of the Good* 47, CSEL 25². In *The Morals of the Manichees*, Augustine relates how the Manichees avoid flesh and drink (*De moribus Manichaeorum* 13.27, PL 32:1356). But they favor bright-colored vegetables, as indicating more light within. He asks (*ibid.* 16.39, PL 32:1362), "Where do you get the doctrine that part of God, as you call it, exists in corn, beans, cabbages, flowers, and fruits?"

[9] As quoted by Augustine, *The Nature of the Good* 46, CSEL 25².

[10] The *Fihrist* purports to set out the ten commandments of Mani for the Auditors, including a commandment against adultery. The Auditors are also commanded to observe the three seals, one of which is a seal against sexual lust. Those entering the Manichean religion (i.e., the Elect) are said by the *Fihrist* to have to be able "to tame concupiscence and covetousness, and to leave the eating of flesh, the drinking of wine, and marital intercourse." If they are unable to do this, it is implied that they stand in the position of Auditors, who should at least try to master their covetousness and sensuality (*Fihrist*, pp. 94–95).

The *Kephalaia*, or "Chapters," a Coptic Manichean text, says of the ordinary catechumen, "he keeps his bed pure through continence on all Sundays." But he is also reproached: "You are at all times in sin, and you pass your life in eating and drinking, in concupiscence for a woman, for gold and silver." On the contrary, the perfect catechumen is told, "You find a woman in the house with you, and you are with her as a stranger." It is good to hate one's body.[11]

There is little in these expressions which might not be matched in some orthodox Christian writer. The addressing of prayers to Jesus and the Trinity, the appeal to the Spirit, seem orthodox. The very similarity is what made the Christians particularly apprehensive or exasperated. Occasionally sentiments are expressed that suggest the difference from orthodoxy. The Continent and the Virgin are contrasted with the Married. Each has a "cry." For the Married, "Her cry . . . is to defilement . . . Shame to this lover of sin that repents not while she is in the body" (*A Manichean Psalm Book*, p. 181). The Continent cries, "I did not make my Lord be born in a womb defiled" (*ibid.*, p. 175). A fragment in the *Kephalaia* implies that intercourse of every kind is "fornication" (*Kephalaia* 78, p. 190). No orthodox writer could have called marriage sin, disparaged procreation as the defiling birth of the divine substance, or denounced all intercourse as fornication.

The depth of the Christian reaction to Manichean morality cannot, however, be estimated from inspection of the few Manichean statements on sex which have survived. These texts suggest how close yet how far the Manichees were from being Christians; they indirectly confirm that the orthodox did not invent the morality they attributed to Manichees. They tell us nothing of how well the Christians understood the teaching of the Manichees. I do not think we can be certain now of knowing how the Manichees actually behaved. There is reason to suppose that sectarian differences developed within Manicheism.[12] But we can be certain of what the Christians believed the Manichees taught and did. It is this Christian reaction which enters the history of Christian doctrine on marital intercourse. In the encounter with the Manichees the Christians found the encounter with the Gnostics prolonged or re-enacted. The rules safeguarding procreation and marriage were again the line of orthodox defense.

---

[11] *Kephalaia*, ed. and trans. Carl Schmidt (Stuttgart, 1935–1939), 91, p. 233; 88, p. 220; 91, p. 228; 83, p. 200.

[12] The *Fihrist* gives some evidence of the kind of schisms and heresies that might have been expected to develop, although, of course, its evidence is very late. Thus it refers to the Manichean heretics called Dunjâwarier living near the Oxus in the eighth century. It also refers to one sect of Manichees, the Mâsìja, who believe that something of the Light will remain imprisoned in Darkness even at the end (*Fihrist*, pp. 97, 90).

THE REACTION OF THE ORTHODOX

The orthodox, in general, reacted to the Manichean threat with vehemence. After about three hundred years of conflict with Gnostics, the Catholic theologians were prepared to analyze and refute this new dualism; and, as the Church was now accepted by the imperial government, the interests of the Empire reinforced theological considerations. East and West, the Catholics repudiated the Manichean dogma dissociating sexual activity and procreation. For the great speculative theologians in the age following the Christian triumph with Constantine, the Manichees were not the major concern. The intellectually exciting controversies were over the Trinity. Later in the century neither Chrysostom nor Ambrose was preoccupied with the Manichean challenge. But when the theologians who were primarily aroused by more theoretical issues looked at problems of sexual ethics, the Manichees were the group they marked as those whose pattern of conduct most challenged orthodox standards.

Sometime between 325 and 348, Hegemonius, a Christian in Asia Minor, gave a probably fictitious account of a debate between Mani and Archelaus, said by Hegemonius to be the Catholic bishop of Charchar in Mesopotamia.[13] The words attributed to Mani were intended as a summary of Manichean doctrine. On marriage, Mani was made to say this:

> If you truly consider how the sons of man are generated, you will not find the Lord the creator of man, but the creator is another who is of that nature of which there is no builder nor creator nor maker, for only his own wickedness bore him. The intercourse of you men with your wives comes from this kind of happening. When you are satiated with fleshly food, your concupiscence is excited. The fruits of generation are in this way multiplied — not virtuously nor philosophically nor rationally, but from a mere satiety of food and from lust and fornication.   (Hegemonius, *Acts of Archelaus* 16, GCS 16:26–27)

Here the Manichean myth of the events preceding the creation of man is followed: procreation is the result of eating and concupiscence. Intercourse is plainly treated as fornication. The King of Darkness is seen as the author of generation.

A little later St. Epiphanius drew on these *Acts* as a true account of a

---

[13] On the date and the authenticity of the *Acts of Archelaus,* see Johannes Quasten, *Patrology* (Westminster, Md., 1950–1961), III, 357–358. The book is directed against the *Treasure* of Mani, and its real title was "The True Treasure or Disputation held in Charchar, Mesopotamian city, between Bishop Archelaus and Mani."

Other opponents besides the Catholics identified the Manichees as foes of marriage. On Mani's home grounds in Persia the Zoroastrians in the mid-fourth century attacked the Manichees for their opposition to marriage; see *Acts of the Zoroastrian Religion,* trans. A. V. Williams Jackson in *Researches in Manicheanism with Special Reference to the Turfan Fragments* (New York, 1932), pp. 204–215.

debate with Mani (*Panarion* 66.26, *GCS* 37:57–60). The *Acts* had a retelling by Mani of the story of the seduction of the Archons. Epiphanius added his own characteristically tart comment: "In constructing this androgynous devil he puts forward his own concupiscence and lust" (*ibid.* 66.52, *GCS* 37:89). The androgyne was again seen as the symbol of non-procreative sexuality.

In Bostra in Asia Minor the Catholic bishop Titus wrote, sometime after 363, a tract entitled *Against the Manichees*.[14] The Manichees "contemptuously vituperate the procreation of children and desire that there be bodily intercourse without procreation." Reason, Titus argued, demonstrates the necessity for the procreation and education of children.

> But indulging in pleasure more frequently, they [the Manichees] hate the fruit that necessarily comes from their acts; and they command that bodies be joined beyond what is lawful and restrict and expel what is conceived and do not await births at their proper time, as if birth alone were dangerous and difficult.   (*Against the Manichees* 2.33, PG 18:1197)

Sexual intercourse without procreative purpose and abortion are thus charged to the Manichees; coitus interruptus and anal intercourse may also be ascribed to them by the phrase "beyond what is lawful."

St. John Chrysostom, writing circa 386–397, lumped Mani with the Gnostics Marcion and Valentinus.[15] All were heretics who praised virginity for the wrong reason. They condemned marriage and the created world as evil. Consequently, "The continence of the heretics is worse than all lust. The latter only does injury to man. The former contends with God and offends his infinite wisdom. Such snares does the devil lay for those who cultivate him" (*Virginity* 5, PG 48:537). Chrysostom invoked against these opponents of marriage the familiar anti-Gnostic text on procreation in 1 Timothy 4. Twice when he condemned self-castration, he compared its practitioners to Manichees, who calumniated creation and treated the Creator as evil (*Homily 62 on Matthew* 17, PG 58:599; *On Galatians* 5, PG 61:668).

These Catholic writers agreed that the central teaching of Manicheanism was opposition to procreation. In Epiphanius and Titus this opposition was explicitly associated with indulgence of lust. The Manichean pattern as it appeared to orthodox eyes repeated the Gnostic pattern. A dualist theory of creation, a real or pretended asceticism, a hatred of pro-

---

[14] On the date see Quasten, *Patrology* III, 359–360.

[15] On the date see H. Musurillo, "Some Textual Problems in the Editing of the Greek Fathers," *Studia Patristica* 3 (1962), 92.

In his commentary on Galatians, Chrysostom ranks the Manichees with those "accusing the works of God" and declaring matter to be evil (*On Galatians* 5, PG 61:668). The Manicheans say that the builder of the world is a devil (*Homily 8 on 2 Corinthians*, PG 61:455).

creation — these were the familiar elements which opposed the orthodox beliefs in God the creator, virginity as only a counseled way of perfection, continence as compatible with marital intercourse, procreation as good.

In the West, about 380, well before he had met Augustine, Ambrose associated the Manichees with the Gnostics, and invoked the old story of Balaam to characterize them. Balaam recommended using beautiful women to seduce men from their religious duties, Ambrose instructed Chromatius, bishop of Aquileia. Apocalypse 2:14 and 15 comdemned such men. The sacrilege that Balaam instigated "appears to be that of the Manichees, who mix and unite sacrilege and foulness" (*Letters* 50, PL 16:1208). This was an epitome of orthodox reaction to Manichean sexual behavior.

The orthodox revulsion to Manichean doctrine was intense. To label a man a Manichee was to stamp him an enemy of Christian morals. Three examples may illustrate the depth of the orthodox reaction and its effect on theological thought. In 380 two Spanish bishops, Instantius and Salvien, and a rich Spanish layman, Priscillian, were suspected by other Spanish Catholics of unorthodox behavior with women and of undue private asceticism. A council at Saragossa showed the hierarchy perplexed and divided; the bishops contented themselves with condemning the practice of women who went to night meetings to listen to strangers read, as well as unusual patterns of fasting and Eucharistic devotion (Canons 1–5, Mansi 3:633–634). The two suspect bishops then consecrated Priscillian as bishop of Avila, and the three proceeded to Italy to plead their case with Pope Damasus. They were preceded by charges from other Spanish bishops that they were Manichees. They solemnly denied the charge and anathematized Mani and his works. Their enemies were ahead of them with an imperial rescript removing them as Manichees from their bishoprics. The pope's doors were closed to them (Instantius, *Letter to Damasus*, Tract 2, CSEL 18:39–40). Tried by a church synod in Gaul, Priscillian appealed to the secular authorities and was eventually tried in Trier in 385 under Maximus, a Spanish general who was attempting to take over the imperial government. In the first Christian use of capital punishment to suppress Christian heresy, Maximus had Priscillian executed. There was considerable criticism, even from the orthodox, and in his insecure political position Maximus felt the need to justify himself with the bishop of Rome. Priscillian and his associates, he told Pope Siricius, "admitted to the crime of being Manichees"; they confessed to "shameful things of which we cannot speak without blushing" (*Letter from the Emperor Maximus to His Father Siricius*, CSEL 35:91). This statement by a Roman general of what he would blush to tell scarcely needs to be taken at its word; it is, however, revealing of what an aspirant to the emperorship thought would be persuasive with the church authorities at Rome. To claim to have killed a Manichee must have seemed a very plausible defense for executing a bishop.[16]

A second example of the use of the term "Manichee" is this. When Jovinian declared virginity to be no more pleasing to God than marriage, and doubted the perpetual virginity of Mary, Ambrose assembled a synod at Milan to look into the matter. Evidently the orthodox stand favoring virginity must have been characterized as "Manichean," for Ambrose and his fellow bishops responded by saying that the "real Manichees" were Jovinian and his followers. The reasoning here was not spelled out, but the implicit thought was that in not giving honor to the humanity of Jesus in his Virgin Mother, Jovinian and company were, in effect, rejecting the goodness of human nature. The orthodox bishops concluded, "It is the impiety of the Manichees which the most clement Emperor has abominated, and all who have met them have run from them as from a plague" (Ambrose, *Letters* 42, PL 16:1176). The Emperor responded to this denunciation of a Manichee — there were no laws against those questioning the virginity of Mary — by prescribing that Jovinian be beaten with leaden whips and exiled to the island of Boa (*Theodosian Code* 16.5.53).

A third example of the use of "Manichee" in orthodox circles is less sanguinary. When Jerome advised Eustochium to lead the austere life of a Christian virgin, he was aware that she might be taunted by teen-age Catholic acquaintances of less exacting standards. This crowd of girls, Jerome said, called anyone with a sad, pale face a Manichee (*Letter 22, To Eustochium* 13, CSEL 54:161). Even at this level of popular misuse a Manichee was one whose behavior by its deviation from normal acceptance of life smacked of a repudiation of the goodness of creation.

The odium attached to Manichean morality was reflected in imperial legislation. It has sometimes been supposed that the accusation of sexual crimes was a stock charge against heretics. On the contrary, nothing like the charges made against the Manichees was advanced against the theologically more dangerous Arians. The attack on Manichees as enemies of the race by reason of their sexual morals was specific to them and to Gnostic groups with similar dualist tendencies. It was because of their combination of moral and religious dogma that the Manichees were

---

[16] A good modern estimate of Priscillian is given in F. Homes Dudden, *The Life and Times of St. Ambrose* (Oxford, 1935), I, 237. The effort of Adhémar D'Ales, S.J., to show a covert Manicheanism in the writings attributed in *CSEL* to Priscillian is not persuasive (see D'Ales, *Priscillien et l'Espagne chrétienne à la fin du quatrième siècle*, Paris, 1936, pp. 92–93). I do, however, follow D'Ales (p. 75) in assigning these works to Bishop Instantius. An older view of Priscillian is found in Marcelino Menéndez Pelayo, *Historia de los Heterodoxos españoles* (1880; reprinted Madrid, 1956), I, 150–157.

viewed as a menace by imperial governments. The first decree against them dates from about 320, but was not apparently influenced by Christian beliefs. Issued from Alexandria to the proconsul for Africa, the decree replied to his report. Manichees has been found using "medicines" (*venena*). These persons had come from Persia, where they had committed numerous crimes; they were now attempting to corrupt "the more innocent Roman nature" by Persian ways; they were a "new and unheard-of sect hostile to the older religions." Destruction by fire was prescribed for their leaders and their books, death for their followers, imprisonment in the mines for those of their converts who ranked as distinguished citizens (*Fontes iuris romani anteiustiniani*, II, 580–581).

By Augustine's day this sweeping edict was not being enforced in any systematic way; neither he nor any of the Manichean leaders he mentions seems to sense any danger of serious punishment from the law, although the leaders were aware that a malcontent Manichee might denounce them to the authorities. Beginning in 372, however, a series of decrees by Catholic emperors launched a more persistent campaign to destroy the Manichees. The legislation is of interest in a variety of ways. First, it revealed something of the orthodox view of Manichean rites. The decree of 381 struck at Manichees meeting "in unlawful and profane *coitiones*"; the term was, perhaps deliberately, ambiguous, meaning either "assembly" or, as in the *Theodosian Code* 15.8.2, "coitus." The same decree, issued at Constantinople, forbade Manichees to establish their "customary tombs of deadly mysteries" (*Theodosian Code* 16.5.7); presumably the Manichees, like the Christians of an earlier day, were meeting in catacombs. Second, the law reflected concern with Manichean teaching and a desire to prevent contagion from Manichean example. The decree of 372 prohibited Manichees from assembling for worship, confiscated their meeting places, and specially penalized Manichean teachers (16.5.3). The law of 383 forbade proselytizing by Manichees and other heretics (16.5.11). Legislation of 389 exiled Manichees from the entire Roman Empire and "especially from the city of Rome" (16.5.18). Legislation of 425 banished Manichees from Rome and "from the sight" of any city (16.5.62, 64). Third, against the Manichees was deployed the same device that the now-abolished *Lex Julia et Papia* had once applied against celibates. By terms of the decree of 381, no Manichee might inherit or bequeath property (16.5.7); the law was modified in 382 to permit bequests to agnates (16.5.9); a much stronger decree was enacted in 407 providing for outright confiscation of Manichean property in favor of the next of kin if the latter were not Manichees and denying to Manichees the legal right to buy, sell, or make contracts (16.5.40). Fourth, the Manichees were pursued with special intensity by the emperors. Other heretics were also attacked by law. There were a whole series of decrees relating to the Eunomians, an ultra-Arian group with ascetic tendencies, beginning in 389 with an imperial order that "the Eunomian eunuchs may not inherit or bequeath"; but the law on the Eunomians was in constant flux, being revised, repealed, re-enacted, repealed, between 389 and 410 (16.5.17, 18, 23, 25, 27, 49). The Manichees were pursued with substantial consistency. For seventy years decrees poured out against them. It was in the spirit of this sustained persecution that, in the long enumeration of proscribed heresies in a decree of 428 issued in Constantinople, the Manichees climaxed the list as "those who have arrived at the lowest depth of wickedness" (16.5.65). Fifth, the law contained evidence of shirking if not downright opposition by officials favorable to the Manichees. The legislation of 382 ordered the Praetorian Prefect in Constantinople to appoint investigators and not to apply to informers against the Manichees the penalties of the law against informers (16.5.9). A decree of 399, issued from Milan, ordered the vicar for Africa to seek out "the detestable criminals," the Manichees. However, in 407 the emperors had to complain of "the evil sloth of judges, the connivance of office staffs, and the contempt of municipal senates" in not enforcing the laws against the Manichees and the Donatists. The officials were now to be fined if they disregarded the law. Moreover, the government turned to the Church for aid in enforcement. Bishops were to be furnished men from the secret service, men who "know that the measure of the statutes must be observed in all respects and so will immediately report to the judges." With their help, the bishops were empowered to prevent heretical rites from being held in cemeteries (*Sirmondian Constitutions* 12). Sixth, the enlistment of the bishops in enforcing this decree "for the support of human morals and religion" reflected the harmony of the interests of state and church in suppressing the Manichees. This union of interests was most strikingly exhibited in a decree directed from Rome to the proconsul of Africa in 407. If an accused person, however deep-dyed a Manichee or heretic, would now adopt the Catholic creed, his simple profession of Catholic faith might absolve him from the guilt he had incurred in violating imperial law (*Theodosian Code* 16.5.41). In 444 a special investigation held before the Senate and Pope Leo the Great compelled a Manichean bishop to confess "all the secrets of their [the Manichees'] crimes." Acting together, the Pope and the Emperor drove the Manichees from Rome, and the Pope instructed the bishops of Italy to give them no respite anywhere (*Letters* 7 and 8, *PL* 54:620–624).

The sum total of these imperial enactments between 372 and 444, designed to support and protect the Catholic Church against what appeared to be its most wicked foe, justify the conclusion that, whatever the preoccupations of speculative theologians, the institutional Church had experienced a severe challenge and responded to it vigorously, employing the resources of the Empire. This experience of the Church as a whole was concentrated and dramatized in the life of St. Augustine.

THE EXPERIENCE OF ST. AUGUSTINE

The reaction of St. Augustine was, in its essentials, no different from that of Titus or of John Chrysostom. Yet there were important differences. Augustine, unlike the Greek Catholics, had been the pupil of the Manichees. He had spent eleven years of young manhood as a Manichean Auditor, from age eighteen to twenty-nine, his faith gradually declining from active interest to tepidity. He once had credited Mani's account of the universe, Mani's vision of evil, Mani's teaching on sex.[17] When Augustine spoke against the Manichees he spoke as one twice a convert, once to Manicheanism, once from it. He analyzed their morality with knowledge of the books of Mani, familiarity with the teaching of contemporary Manichean bishops, intimacy with Manichees whose fellow he had been. As his knowledge of Manicheanism was greater, so was his revulsion deeper. There were, doubtless, Manichean imprints Augustine never effaced from his mind; his concern with evil, his concern with sexuality, were Manichean preoccupations. But the greater effect of his Manichean experience was reaction. To the morals of the Manichees which rigorously condemned procreation, which separated intercourse and procreation, he opposed an ethic which bound intercourse to procreation and found marital procreation good.

Two books composed in the first year after his baptism as a Catholic Christian proclaim the reaction. They are *The Morals of the Manichees* and *The Morals of the Catholic Church*. They were written, Augustine states specifically, to refute the Manichean claims of continence.[18] In *The Morals of the Manichees*, Augustine declares that the Manichees are opposed to marriage. They are opposed to marriage, because they are opposed to procreation which is the purpose of marriage. They permit marriage, it is true, to their Auditors, the multitude of followers or catechumens who are not held to the standards of the Elect. These marriages of Auditors, however, the Manichees attempt to deprive of substance, for they advise the Auditors to avoid procreation. Augustine recalls the advice given and evaluates its significance in a passage which turns into a major attack on contraception:

---

[17] Augustine says of himself, as he writes against the Manichees, "All those fictions which by daily custom hold you bound and tied I carefully sought, I attentively heard, I fearfully believed" (*Against The Fundamental Epistle* 3, CSEL 25¹). In the *Confessions* Augustine gives the history of his long connection with the Manichees (*Confessiones* 3.6, 5.7, CSEL 33:50–53, 98–100).

[18] Augustine, *Retractationes* 1.6.1, CSEL 36:28.

Is it not you who used to warn us to watch as much as we could the time after purification of the menses when a woman is likely to conceive, and at that time refrain from intercourse, lest a soul be implicated in the flesh? From this it follows that you consider marriage is not to procreate children, but to satiate lust. Marriage, as the marriage tablets themselves proclaim, joins male and female for the procreation of children. Whoever says that to procreate children is a worse sin than to copulate thereby prohibits marriage; and he makes the woman no more a wife but a harlot, who, when she has been given certain gifts, is joined to man to satisfy his lust. If there is a wife there is matrimony. But there is no matrimony where motherhood is prevented; for then there is no wife. (*The Morals of the Manichees* 18.65, PL 32:1373)

The method of contraception practiced by these Manichees whom Augustine knew is the use of the sterile period as determined by Greek medicine. The Manichees, despite their keen interest in avoiding procreation, had acquired no better information. Probably they explained the disappointments which this advice must have entailed as due to some failure to watch the period closely.

In the history of the thought of theologians on contraception, it is, no doubt, piquant that the first pronouncement on contraception by the most influential theologian teaching on such matters should be such a vigorous attack on the one method of avoiding procreation accepted by twentieth-century Catholic theologians as morally lawful. History has made doctrine take a topsy-turvy course. Yet Augustine's words are confined by a context. It is against men who would prevent all procreation that his biting phrases are deployed. The Manichean concern "lest a soul be implicated in the flesh" is an objection to every act of generation.[19]

A second attack on Manichean contraception is made by Augustine a dozen years later. It occurs in a treatise responding to an anti-Catholic polemic of Faustus, a Manichean bishop. In writing against Faustus, Augustine is answering a man he knew well and for whose intellectual integrity he had some regard, although he had found his knowledge disappointingly limited.[20] Augustine's tone is polemical. Yet the accusation of contraceptive practice, for reasons of Manichean dogma, is asserted as a charge whose truth Faustus must admit.

In his criticism of Catholics, Faustus had used a standard Gnostic and Manichean technique for discrediting the Old Testament. He had made much of the sexual misconduct of the Old Testament prophets and patriarchs. Many of them, Faustus observed, he would not care to have

[19] One of the foremost modern authorities on Manicheanism refers, rather reservedly it seems, to "accusations of Malthusianism" made against the Manichees by Augustine (Puech, *Le Manichéisme*, p. 186). Widengren also appears not to credit Augustine (*Mani und der Manichäismus*, p. 99). But on this point I see no reason at all to doubt Augustine's strong and repeated charges, based, in part, on his own experience as an Auditor, and made directly to Manicheans who would have discounted his apologetic for Christianity if he were plainly wrong.

[20] *Confessions* 5.6–7, CSEL 33:96–99.

dinner with; Osee, for example, had married a prostitute. Augustine answers, the Manichees "would have been better pleased that the woman continue to be a prostitute so as not to bring their God into confinement than that she become the wife of one man and bear children" (*Against Faustus* 22.80, *CSEL* 25^1:682–683). By "their God" Augustine means the particles of light which are of the same substance as the Father, according to *The Fundamental Epistle*.[21]

Faustus had charged Abraham with sexual crimes. Augustine answers:

> For thus the eternal law, that is, the will of God creator of all creatures, taking counsel for the conservation of natural order, not to serve lust, but to see to the preservation of the race, permits the delight of mortal flesh to be released from the control of reason in copulation only to propagate progeny. But the perverse law of the Manichees commands that progeny above all be avoided by those having intercourse, lest their God, whom they complain is bound in every seed, should be bound more tightly in what a woman conceives. Therefore their God by a shameful slip is poured out rather than bound by a cruel connection. Abraham did not burn with an insane madness for having progeny, but the Manichean is delirious with an insane vanity of avoiding progeny. Hence, Abraham, keeping the order of nature, did nothing in human coitus except to give birth to a man; the Manichee, observing a perverse fable, fears nothing in any kind of copulation except that his God be captured.
> (*Against Faustus* 22.30, *CSEL* 25^1:624)

"Pouring out" in a "shameful slip" is apparently a direct charge of practicing coitus interruptus. This is the first condemnation of the practice by a theologian in the West, and like the condemnation by Epiphanius in the East it is directed at coitus interruptus practiced on religious grounds. A few pages later Augustine discusses the story of Onan, but, rather surprisingly in such an argumentative tract, foregoes the opportunity to apply it to the Manichees. He comments only that Er, the older brother of Onan, is etymologically the symbol of active evil; while Onan symbolizes one who does not do the good he is capable of. Both are sinners, but Er is worse (*ibid.* 22.84, *CSEL* 25^1:687).

The criticism of Manichean teaching on marriage is repeated at various points in Augustine's refutation of Faustus. The criticism is always the same. Denying procreation, the Manichees "make the bridal chamber a brothel" (*ibid.* 15.7, *CSEL* 25^1:430). In a comprehensive denunciation, closely paralleling his denunciation in *The Morals of the Manichees* but omitting reference to the sterile period, Augustine declares,

[21] This phrase is a logical deduction from Mani's teaching that the light imprisoned in man originally came from the Father of light; and, to judge from *The Morals of the Manichees*, c. 39, the phrase may have been used by the Western Manichees. But there is a polemical flavor to Augustine's use; it is not clear that Manicheans customarily made such a direct identification of light in them with God. In the debate at Hippo between the Manichean Felix and Augustine, Felix is clearly reluctant to admit the identification (*Against Felix* 2.20–21, *CSEL* 25^2:849–851).

The consequence is that you violate the precept, You shall not commit adultery. For what you most of all detest in marriage is that children be procreated, and so you make your Auditors adulterers of their wives when they take care lest the women with whom they copulate conceive. They take wives according to the laws of matrimony by tablets announcing that the marriage is contracted to procreate children; and then, fearing because of your law, lest they infect a particle of God with the foulness of their flesh, they copulate in a shameful union only to satisfy lust for their wives. They are unwilling to have children, on whose account alone marriages are made. How is it, then, that you are not those prohibiting marriage, as the Apostle predicted of you so long ago, when you try to take from marriage what marriage is? When this is taken away, husbands are shameful lovers, wives are harlots, wedding beds are stews, fathers-in-law, panders.

(*Against Faustus* 15.7, CSEL 25^1:429–430)

The Manichees are for Augustine the archetypal advocates of contraception, and his judgments on contraception must be read against the background of his judgment on the Manichees.

The importance of the Manichean position on procreation in Augustine's own religious evolution is indicated in a letter to a Manichean Auditor, Secundinus. Secundinus, a stranger to Augustine, had, about 400, written him a letter of exhortation with the intention of winning this famous man back to the true religion. Augustine, ignoring the letter's occasional acerbities, replied in great earnestness, generously seeking to show his correspondent the roots of his own Manichean errors. His answer, he was to remark later, was the best of all his writings on the Manichees. At the outset Augustine tells Secundinus why he himself had quit them. It was out of fear of the words of the apostle Paul in 1 Timothy 4. The Manichees seemed then to him to be the hypocrites who come proscribing marriage and the use of foods (*Against Secundinus* 2, CSEL 25^2:906). The issue between Catholic and Manichean morality is then joined over the Catholic adherence to the Old Testament. Secundinus, a pious Manichee, cannot believe that Augustine really believes what is in this book. He quotes as evidently evil, shockingly immoral, the command of Genesis, "Increase and multiply" (*To Augustine*, CSEL 25^2:896). Augustine sees that the evil is self-evident only in terms of Manichean dogma: "You are shocked because you do not want the fetters of your God to be multiplied." Secundinus recalls with horror the story of Osee's marriage to the prostitute. Augustine comments,

I know what your indignation comes from. It is not so much the prostitute who shocks you, as that fornication is changed to marriage and converted to marital modesty. You believe your God to be bound by tighter bonds of flesh in the procreation of children. You think prostitutes spare God, because they take steps not to conceive in order to serve lust, freed from the burden of bearing.

(*Against Secundinus*, CSEL 25^2:938–939)

For the Manichees, prostitution, with its usual accompaniment of contraception, is preferable to marriage with procreation. This is not hyperbole, wild declamation, ignorant hearsay. It is what Augustine, an old Manichee, can say seriously to a believing Manichee whom he is trying to convert. The doctrine of Mani on the imprisonment of the light makes this moral conclusion inescapable.

The dogmatic separation of intercourse from procreation seemed bad enough to Augustine after he had accepted 1 Timothy. But his reaction was turned to revulsion by an additional belief he later acquired, that some Manichees practiced coitus interruptus in a religious rite. The gradual hardening of this suspicion confirmed and intensified his detestation of contraception.

As early as his first book against the Manichees Augustine mentions a current suspicion that the Elect engaged in a ritual in which human semen was eaten in order to free part of God from imprisonment in the seed. The rumor ran that the ceremony was concealed from the Auditors to avoid shocking them (*The Morals of the Manichees* 18.66, *PL* 32:1373). Yet Augustine says that he himself knew personally only of occasional lapses in chastity by individual members of the Elect. These cases, which had scandalized him as a young convert to Manicheanism, are not asserted to have any doctrinal basis (*ibid.* 19, *PL* 32:1373–1376).

Two years later in a debate held in the baths of Sassius, Fortunatus, a Manichean priest of Hippo, challenged Augustine as a former Manichee to admit the purity of the Manichean conduct he had observed. Apparently Augustine had no desire to discuss contraceptive practice in this public forum. He evaded the challenge; he had been only an Auditor, and the charges of immorality ran against the Elect, of whom he could not testify (*Disputation with Fortunatus* 2–3, *CSEL* 25^1:84–85).

Seven years later Augustine gives more credence to the repeated rumor. A Christian in Rome has told him that both in Paphlagonia and in Gaul Manichees have confessed before judges that they have engaged in the ritual emission and eating of semen. Augustine's main emphasis is that the practice is a logical deduction from the story of the Archons told in *The Treasure*. Men are in the position of the princes of darkness because their bodies come from them. If the light was released by the seduction of the princes, if androgynes played the central role in the release, cannot the process be repeated? "These unhappy men read this, they say it, they hear it." Some Manichees, Augustine believes, go on to act upon it, taking the myth as an exemplary pattern. The Manichees themselves, if asked, answer that such conduct can only be that of apostates from their church. Augustine does not question the good faith of this answer; but he adds, "Even if they do not do it, whoever do practice it do so from these books" (*The Nature of the Good* 45, 47, *CSEL* 25²:886–887).[22]

In his reply to Faustus, no accusation of ritual conduct of this kind is made against this man Augustine knew well. He does say, however, that the story of the seduction is a reprehensible example. He marvels that God "needs such baseness to be freed" (*Against Faustus* 15.7, *CSEL* 25¹:431).

Twenty-eight years later Augustine returns to the charge. In an imperial inquiry before the tribune Ursus at Carthage, a girl not yet twelve and "a sort of Manichean holy woman" have testified to participating in a Manichean ritual in which intercourse took place, semen was emitted onto grain, and the mixture was eaten "as a eucharist." Similar testimony has been taken in other inquiries by Catholic bishops. Augustine again notes the Manichean protest that such rituals are not part of orthodox Manicheanism. The ritual is followed only by a heretical Manichean sect, the Catharists. Augustine does not reject the protest. He merely returns to his settled suspicion of *The Treasure*. It is from Mani's book that "the baseness flows which the Manichees deny is theirs" (*Heresies* 46, *PL* 42:36).

The popular rumor, the report of the Christians in Rome, the second-hand accounts of official inquiries, the stories of a child and a probably scared woman cannot be taken as establishing that even the Cathar sect practiced the rites ascribed to them.[23] Augustine's main point, however, is less historical than psychological. In Augustine's mind the case was the paradigm of Manichean behavior. Here intercourse without intromission of semen was invested with a positive religious value, intercourse which was intentionally nonprocreative was treated as sacred. The myths of Mani had created a Manichean view of sexuality. They had shown androgynes as divine; they had celebrated the emission of semen without sexual union; they had treated the actual production of offspring as disaster inflicted by the powers of darkness. A pattern opposed to marriage, heterosexual union, procreation of children, had been set up. Against this pattern, whether it was only embodied in teaching or

[22] Augustine understands the myth of the seduction of the sons of Darkness, described in the Latin *Treasure* as involving a release of "evils," to involve in fact an emission of seed. This conclusion is stated bluntly by his friend and fellow bishop, Evodius, in *On Faith, Against the Manichees* 17, *CSEL* 25²:957–958: "What else does it mean except that through the genitals of the devils the divine majesty finds ways of escape?" In a ninth-century Persian résumé of Manichean doctrine the term "seed" is used in a version of the myth like that quoted by Augustine. See Cumont, *Recherches*, p. 60.

[23] The evidence is criticized and doubted by Prosper Alfaric, *L'Evolution intellectuel de Saint Augustin* (Paris, 1918), I, 164–165. The evidence is credited by Moon in his edition of *The Nature of the Good*, pp. 240–242, 253–254. Puech believes that among some Gnostic sects the myth had been tied to practice, but that the Manichees are found to have such practices only by enemies attributing to them the behavior described in the myth (*Le Manichéisme*, p. 173).

whether it was also embodied in practice, Augustine reacted. Against it he developed his understanding of Catholic doctrine on marriage, intercourse, procreation.

The doctrinal reaction was not the only force at work in Augustine's mind. Doubtless no creative theologian has taken up the basic concepts of sexual morality without putting something of his own sexual experience into his treatment. But an almost universal reticence has prevented his readers from seeing the vital roots in personal experience of the ideas he set out. Many hundreds of theologians, moreover, have used the basic concepts mechanically, unmindful of their meaning for living human beings. Augustine is a creative theologian, and while he adopts the concepts of the past, he has been willing to reveal, at least up to a point, the sexual experience which animates his understanding of them. For this very reason, perhaps, Augustine's formulas were destined to be accepted for more than a thousand years.

All the years he was a Manichee, from eighteen to twenty-nine, Augustine had lived with a girl he would not marry. By her he had a son whom they gave the name Adeodatus, "Given-by-God," a name which, bestowed by a Manichee, has a curious and ironic ring. After this child, conceived in the first year of their relationship, they did not have another. Throughout the eleven-year period the union was a stable one, and Augustine was faithful to this one woman (*Confessions* 4.2, *CSEL* 33:64–65).

Augustine's attraction to the girl is evident. With delicacy he never gives her name. With a mixture of egotism and regard for her reputation he reports that when she left him she swore she would never know another man. His love for her is not so clear. She was, he says, "torn from his side." He means that at the age of twenty-nine he gave in to the pressure of his dominating mother, Monica, who arranged for him to be affianced to a socially acceptable girl. The idea of marrying his companion of eleven years seems not to have been considered (*ibid.* 6.13–15, *CSEL* 33:136–138).[24]

It is from this close sexual union, in which selfless love seems to have had little part, that Augustine drew both positive and negative elements of his idea of marriage. He tells how his relationship was so established that his friend Alypius envied it, for, as it seemed to Augustine then, his situation lacked only "the honorable name of marriage." Yet the honor that "comes from the duty of well-ordered life together and the having of children" had little influence with him. Only the slaking of his lust bound him (*ibid.* 6.12, *CSEL* 33:135–136). The experience was am-

[24] Without apparent foundation, the suggestion is made by some modern apologists, more anxious to defend Augustine than he himself was, that there was some legal barrier to his marriage with the girl: e.g., Henri Marrou, *Saint Augustine and His Influence through the Ages*, trans. Patrick Hepburne-Scott (New York, 1957), p. 24.

biguous: on one hand, guilt in intercourse where procreation was not a purpose, guilt in intercourse where Manichean ways of avoiding procreation may have been used; and, on the other hand, a sense that he had what marriage had to give except a permanent bond and the procreative purpose. Eighteen years after he had left the girl and become a bishop, is there not a reminiscence of this relation when he speaks of an unmarried man and an unmarried woman living together? Suppose, he says, the man lives with her for a time until he finds one "whom he can marry as an equal": such a man is an "adulterer." But suppose the woman "remains faithful to him and, after he has taken a wife, does not plan to marry and is prepared to refrain absolutely from such an act": she is a sinner, but "I could not easily bring myself to call her an adulteress" (*The Good of Marriage* 5.5, *CSEL* 41:193–194). It is the old relation which he evokes; his old mistress he cannot condemn as he condemns himself. It is the relation which guides his approach to marriage.

Having had this guilt-ridden experience of sexual intercourse in a quasi-permanent union, Augustine believed there was nothing rational, spiritual, sacramental in the act of intercourse itself. The words of Genesis, repeated by the Lord Jesus, repeated by St. Paul, were that in intercourse man and wife became "one flesh." In intercourse, said Augustine, man "becomes all flesh" (*Sermons* 62.2, *PL* 38:887). Sexual intercourse in marriage is the greatest threat to spiritual freedom: "I feel that nothing more turns the masculine mind from the heights than female blandishments and that contact of bodies without which a wife may not be had" (*Soliloquies* 1.10, *PL* 32:878). If marital intercourse was tolerable at all — and it must be if the Manichees were wrong — there must be some good, some purpose, some reason external to the marital act itself. From an experience of the sterile seeking of lust for eleven years, Augustine turned to the Stoic analysis of marriage in terms of procreative purpose.

THE GOOD OF MARRIAGE

In 400, the same year that he wrote against Faustus, Augustine wrote another book. It is not directly addressed to Manichean questions. But the Manichees are the heretics whose opposing views Augustine mentions by name, and the discussion he undertakes proceeds against the background of the Manichean attack on procreation. Augustine's principal intent is to demonstrate to those who attack marriage what its values are, and at the same time to show the limits of these values, and how they are achieved in marriage. The book is pointedly entitled *The Good of Marriage*.

The work begins on a grandly social note:[25]

[25] There is an echo of Chrysostom's view that marriage may be a remedy for death, and it is stated that if man had not sinned (thereby bringing death into the world)

Since every man is part of the human race, and human nature is something social and possesses the capacity for friendship as a great and natural good, God for this reason willed to create all men from one, so that they might be tied together in their society, not only by the similarity of race, but also by the bond of blood. (*The Good of Marriage* 1, CSEL 41:187)

Man is not the child of the devil. Men are not particles of light inhabiting evil bodies. They are beings joined in blood and body to each other. God, man's creator, wills his perpetuation in marriage. The Lord Jesus Christ has blessed marriage by condemning divorce and by attending the wedding feast at Cana (*ibid.* 3, CSEL 41:190). But, apart from the divine blessing, why is marriage good?

In a climactic chapter, Augustine gives his answer in a succinct formula:

All these are why marriage is good: offspring, fidelity, symbolic stability [*proles, fides, sacramentum*]. (*Ibid.* 29.32, CSEL 41:227)

Each term in this classic formula needs a note of exegesis.

Offspring, Augustine finds, are the first and obvious good. "What food is to the health of man, intercourse is to the health of the race" (*ibid.* 16.18, CSEL 41:210–211). "Offspring," however, does not mean mere physical multiplication of human beings. In the context of the opening chapter, the value of offspring appears as the friendly society of the human race created by the marital engendering of children. More specifically, for a Christian the good of offspring means the generation of members of Christ. It is for this reason that the intention of a Catholic couple to marry and have children is more valuable than the preservation of virginity by "the impious" (*ibid.* 8.8, CSEL 41:198).[26] As Augustine's later commentary *On Genesis* expresses it, by offspring as a good is meant not merely their procreation, but "the receiving of them lovingly, the nourishing of them humanely, the educating of them religiously" (*On Genesis According to the Letter* 9.7, CSEL 28¹:276).

By *fides*, literally faith, is meant a value more closely approximated by the English word "fidelity." Fidelity means not only keeping from intercourse with others, but paying the marital debt. Married persons owe each other "not only fidelity in sexual intercourse for the purpose of procreating children but also the mutual service, in a certain measure, of sustaining each other's weakness, for the avoidance of illicit intercourse" (*The Good of Marriage* 6, CSEL 41:195).

Augustine uses the term *sacramentum,* here translated "symbolic sta-

---

the purpose of marriage might not have been to produce children (*The Good of Marriage* 2.2, CSEL 41:188). But the logical implications of this view are not worked out as they are in Chrysostom.

[26] In a later work Augustine similarly contrasts the superiority of Catholics to the virginity of "heretics" — probably a thrust at the Manichees (*Marriage and Concupiscence* 1.4.5, CSEL 42). As he says here, "By offspring I mean not merely that they be born, but that indeed they be reborn" (*ibid.* 1.17.19).

bility," for the third value of marriage. Later usage was inevitably to identify the term with "sacrament" in the more specific sense of a sacrament instituted by Christ. The later meaning is not entirely alien to Augustine's thought. He proposes this value as a result of reflection on the indissolubility of Christian marriage. The bond made for the purpose of procreation cannot be set aside if procreation is impossible. A couple who "know they will have no children" cannot be divorced so that one spouse, if fertile, could have children by another. A man who has dismissed his wife for adultery is not permitted to remarry, even though he cannot now have children. What is there in Christian marriage which, unlike pagan marriage, unlike Jewish marriage, makes the bond unbreakable? Augustine gives this answer: Christian marriage is a *sacramentum*, that is, it is a symbol of stability (*ibid.* 7, CSEL 41:196–197).[27]

There is, in this analysis, no mention of love between husband and wife, no citation of Ephesians 5. There has also been dropped from the final formula an idea that Augustine had advanced in chapter three. We do speak, he had remarked, of the marriage of old people; procreation cannot be the purpose. There must be, then, another value, the good of "mutual companionship between the two sexes" (*ibid.* 3, CSEL 41:190). This perception is not incorporated into the classic Augustinian formula.[28] Neither love nor marital friendship is tied to offspring or fidelity or *sacramentum*. The main thrust of Augustine's approach ap-

---

[27] One study distinguishes four usages of *sacramentum* in Augustine: 1. A mysterious property of marriage, not explained. 2. A sign or symbol: as "the sign [*sacramentum*] of several women married to one man in the Old Testament signified the future people to be subject to God, . . . so the sign [*sacramentum*] of single marriages of our time signifies the unity of all of us subject to God to be in a single heavenly city" (*The Good of Marriage* 18.21). 3. An indissoluble bond: Paul has said marriage is a *magnum sacramentum* in Christ and the Church; "But what is then great in Christ and the Church, this is little in each individual husband and wife, but yet a bond [*sacramentum*] of inseparable unity" (*Marriage and Concupiscence* 1.17.23). 4. A seal: marriage remains despite desertion or divorce; it "remains for the purpose of punishment . . . for a certain seal [*sacramentum*] is affixed" (*The Good of Marriage* 7). See Nicholas Ladomérszky, *Saint Augustin, docteur du mariage chrétien* (Rome, 1942), p. 121. "Sacrament" is not used in the later theological sense; see also Joseph Mausbach, *Die Ethik des heiliges Augustinus* (Freiburg im Br., 1909), II, 323. On the use of "sacrament" by Augustine in other contexts, see C. Couturier, " 'Sacramentum' et 'mysterium' dans l'oeuvre de S. Augustin," in H. Rondet et al., *Etudes Augustiniennes* (Paris, 1953).

[28] One phrase of Augustine's on marriage is used in much later times to indicate that marriage may be for companionship. In marriage, he says, there is a "solace for humanity" (*humanitatis solatium*). But this phrase is tied by him to a sentence in which he is saying that for Christians marriage is now "a remedy for infirmity, in some, indeed, a solace for humanity" (*De bono viduitatis* 8.11, CSEL 41:317). In short, he slightly expands his view that marriage is a remedy for concupiscence.

The marriage of the aged was a problem not unknown to Roman law. Tiberius had amended the *Lex Julia et Papia* to prohibit men over sixty from marrying; Claudius abrogated the amendment (Tacitus, *Annales* 3.28; Suetonius, *Claudius* 23 in *De vita Caesarum*).

pears in his exegesis of the text of Genesis where God has said that it is not good for man to be alone. Why? asks Augustine, and he answers, "I do not see what other help woman would be to man if the purpose of generating was eliminated" (*On Genesis According to the Letter* 9.7, *CSEL* 28¹:275).

Of the three goods of marriage, however, procreation may be dispensed with, not only for the aged, but for those who wish to be continent. As virginity is preferable to marriage, so continence in marriage is preferable to intercourse. Spouses are progressively better as they learn to refrain from coitus by mutual consent. "In these days, indeed, no one perfect in piety seeks to have children except spiritually" (*The Good of Marriage* 3.3, 8.9, 17.19, *CSEL* 41:190–191, 200, 213). Continence is thus a higher value than procreation, for procreation may be rejected to achieve it. But continence is not a higher value than fidelity. If one spouse seeks the marital debt, the other must join in intercourse (*ibid.* 6.6, *CSEL* 41:195). Fidelity is an absolute in a way in which procreation is not.

The three values analyzed are advanced by Augustine as the constituents of "the good of marriage." What is their relation to marital intercourse? The correspondence between the goods of marriage and the goods of marital intercourse, as Augustine develops them, is less than perfect.

Symbolic stability, *sacramentum*, is never related to intercourse. Offspring are assigned an absolute value. The Stoic rule is accepted without acknowledgment of its derivation. Only sexual intercourse "for the sake of procreating" is fully lawful. The comparison of intercourse with eating is turned to illustrate the rule:

> What food is for the health of a man, intercourse is for the health of the species, and each is not without carnal delight which cannot be lust if, modified and restrained by temperance, it is brought to a natural use. What is unlawful food in supporting life, this is fornication or adulterous intercourse in seeking offspring; and what is unlawful food in the wantonness of the belly and gullet, this is unlawful intercourse seeking in lust no offspring; and what is for some the immoderate seeking of lawful food, this is that pardonable intercourse in spouses. (*The Good of Marriage* 16.18, *CSEL* 41:210–211)

The fault involved in not having a procreative purpose is not a lethal one. It is not, Augustine says, adultery or fornication. Yet an unmarried woman living in a sexual relationship with an unmarried man and only wanting children may be less of a sinner than some matrons who seek marital intercourse "not for progeny, but intemperately" (*ibid.* 6.6, *CSEL* 41:194–195). In general, the sin is what the Apostle Paul in 1 Corinthians 7:6 permits by "pardon" (*indulgentia*, as the Vulgate has it). It is a sin, but a small sin (*ibid.* 10.11, *CSEL* 41:203).[29]

---

[29] Augustine distinguishes between major sins (*crimina*) and small sins (*minuta* or

In later works Augustine reaffirms these conclusions on intercourse without procreative purpose. Such intercourse is the kind of sin, he says in a sermon, that may be cleansed by ordinary acts of Christian charity such as almsgiving (*Sermons* 9.11.18, *PL* 38:88). Indeed, he is willing to entertain the argument that 1 Corinthians 7:6 means there is no sin at all. It might have been possible, he says, in a later treatise, that intercourse without procreative purpose should not be thought a sin. But he rejects the argument: "It would have been 'possible,' I said, that this should not be thought a sin, had not Paul added, 'But I speak this by way of concession, not by commandment.' And now who will deny this to be a sin, when admittedly those who do this have only a concession made on apostolic authority to excuse them?" (*Enchiridion* 78.21, *PL* 40:269).[30] Paul is effectively turned against himself to establish the Stoic rule.

The sin of nonprocreative purpose is, one might suppose, a common one. Augustine himself so supposes. It is easier to be chaste alone than to use marriage only to produce children; hence many Christians prefer virginity to marriage. Married Christians of Augustine's acquaintance fail to observe the rule: "Never in friendly conversations have I heard anyone who is or who has been married say that he never had intercourse with his wife except when hoping for conception" (*The Good of Marriage* 13.15, *CSEL* 41:208). The experience of the faithful is not regarded as a relevant datum.

The approach of Augustine requires both the objective possibility of procreation and the subjective intent to procreate. There is one exception to these absolute requirements. It serves to relate the marital good of fidelity to intercourse. If, says Augustine, one spouse seeks intercourse, fidelity requires a response. One cannot be continent without the other's consent. Hence, although the intention now is not procreative, "there is no sin in returning the conjugal debt" (*ibid.* 6.6, 7.6, *CSEL* 41:195). The workability of this distinction between an initiating spouse and a responding spouse is not explored. Paul's legal term "debt" is made the basis for a new, legalistic, moral distinction. Fidelity cuts across the procreative requirement, but as fidelity has such a limited content, the exception created does not destroy the rule.

The way Augustine has justified marital intercourse might be described in the categories of a later age as an exercise in double effect. In the marital act there is the satisfaction of sexual desire, a result which Augus-

---

quotidiana). See M. Huftier, "Le Péché selon S. Augustin et selon S. Thomas," doctoral dissertation in theology, University of Lille, 1957, p. 456.

[30] Cf. *Marriage and Concupiscence* 1.14.16, *CSEL* 42:229: "Since copulation with the intention of generation is not culpable, as it is proper to marriage, what does the Apostle concede by way of pardon, except this: that married persons, not containing themselves, demand the debt of the flesh from one another, not from a wish of progeny, but from the pleasure of lust."

tine does not treat as good, and there may also be the achievement of the good of procreation and the good of satisfying a just demand. These goods are great enough to say that marital intercourse is lawful when these purposes are sought.

The insistence on the general rule of procreative purpose recognizes that departure from it does not involve grave sin. Some forms of intercourse, however, are "against nature." The terms of condemnation at least suggest that Augustine regarded anal and oral intercourse as gravely evil:

> The natural use, when it slips beyond the nuptial bond, that is, beyond the need of propagating, is pardonable in a wife, condemnable in a prostitute. A use against nature is execrable in a prostitute, but more execrable in a wife. The ordination of the Creator and the order of the creature is of such weight that, in things of which the use is permitted, exceeding the measure is far more tolerable than a single or rare excess in things not permitted . . . Hence one sins far less in being uxorious than in being a very rare fornicator. Yet when a husband wants to use a member of the wife not permitted to be used for this, it is more shameful if the wife permits it to happen to her rather than to another woman. (*The Good of Marriage* 11.12, CSEL 41:203–204)

The heart of the Augustinian position is the old rule of Philo and the Stoics, buttressed by their appeal to a nature whose purposes are evident. Augustine did not invent the doctrine. He gave it its classic form. He synthesized, to a degree, the requirements of procreative purpose with the requirements of fidelity and indissolubility. For a thousand years and more the Augustinian formulas guided the Church in the West. From A.D. 400 to the present, the Augustinian terms *proles, fides, sacramentum* have, with much development, served to define for Catholic theologians the good of marriage.

CONCUPISCENCE AND MARRIAGE

Augustine had worked out his basic position by 400, while the Manichean challenge was still strong in his mind. The doctrine stood by itself before he enunciated, in response to the new challenge of Pelagius, his views on grace, original sin, concupiscence, and sexuality. The Pelagian controversy, however, did serve to bring out assumptions latent in *The Good of Marriage*, and the positions now articulated did buttress and confirm the main analysis of *The Good of Marriage*. Special connections between original sin, concupiscence, and intercourse were set out which made marriage seem all the more in need of procreative justification.

At the time Augustine wrote, two views were discernible in the Christian tradition on the connection of original sin and sexual behavior. The Alexandrian authors had seen a connection which was close and almost palpable. Clement, responding to ascetic Gnostic contentions that the original sin was intercourse, replied with a distinction. The sin committed by Adam was not in having intercourse but in having it too soon. He fell because he was tricked by the serpent "to procreate children sooner than was right" (*Stromata* 3.17.103, *GCS* 15:243). In this sense Adam "yielded to concupiscence" (*Protrepticus* 11.111.1, *GCS* 12:78). The consequence of Adam's sin, according to Clement, was a tendency, innate in man, to sin and to pleasure. By "pleasure" Clement seemed to mean principally sexual pleasure. In somewhat the same vein, Origen found original sin to have affected, in particular, man's appetite for food and for sex (*On Romans* 5.7, *PG* 14:1035). Associated with this approach was a belief that the generative act had a special function in the transmission of original sin. The words of Psalm 50:7, "For behold I was conceived in iniquities and a sinner my mother bore me," were construed to support the view that not only is original sin inherited but it is the sexual character of generation which transmits the sin (e.g., Ambrose, *Apology on David* 1.11.56, *CSEL* 32²:337–338).

The alternative approach emphasized none of these close connections between original sin and sexuality. Chrysostom did not go beyond the letter of Genesis in seeing original sin instigated by the devil; he did not give the sin a specifically sexual character. St. Athanasius said the sin had consisted in turning from the contemplation of God to the contemplation of man. Ambrose, an adherent in some respects of the first approach, simply identified the first sin with pride.[31]

The relation of original sin to sexual concupiscence in contemporary human beings was also unmentioned by a number of prominent theologians, such as St. Athanasius, St. Basil, St. Gregory of Nyssa. St. John Chrysostom found concupiscence to be a consequence of the Fall, but did not find concupiscence itself inherently unmeasured: "Concupiscence is not a sin, but when it loses its measure and does not keep itself within the limits of marriage but seeks other objects, adultery occurs — not by concupiscence, but by the immoderate desire of concupiscence" (*Homily 13 on Romans* 1, *PG* 60:508). In this approach the special appropriateness of sexual generation as the instrument of transmitting original sin was not emphasized.

All the elements of the question — original sin, its transmission to succeeding generations, the disobedience of the body — had been present in Paul. But in the literature before Augustine it is difficult to say that the development of Paul which associated sexual acts and original sin was dominant. No firm and comprehensive union of the several elements had been made. In the battle with Pelagius, Augustine established such a synthesis.

[31] For a survey of development, see A. Gaudel, "Péché originel," *DTC* 12¹:330–371.

Like his teaching on marriage, Augustine's views in this instance are rooted in his own experience. At the time he had received the illumination which led to his conversion, he was still held back by lust. In a passage which reveals how much he understood Paul in terms of his own struggle, he writes,

> Whence this monstrousness? And why is it like this? Let your mercy enlighten me, and I will ask if perhaps the hidden punishments of men, the most dark griefs of the sons of Adam, can answer me. Whence this monstrousness? And why is it like this? The mind gives the body an order and it is obeyed at once. The mind gives itself an order, and it is resisted . . . And thus there are two wills in us, because neither one of them is whole, and what is present to one is lacking to the other. (*Confessions* 8.9, *CSEL* 33:187–188)

Reflecting his own conflict, Augustine's formulas had vitality. Incorporating a human experience which Christians of this era wanted explained in theological terms, his approach won general acceptance among the Christians of the West.

The teaching of Pelagius, a British layman, as seen by opponents within the Church, was a kind of naturalism, stressing the athletic vigor of the human will to combat sin. His position appeared to make man self-sufficient without supernatural grace. It seemed to assume that original sin had not been transmitted in any way from Adam to his descendants, and that concupiscence was not present in the contemporary Christian. An optimism about human capabilities banished suspicion of sexuality. The position taken by Pelagius challenged the personal experience, the Manichean preoccupation with evil, and the reading of Christian tradition of Augustine.

In 418, after both a council at Carthage and Pope Zosimus had condemned Pelagius, Augustine wrote a work which explored the central Pelagian question as it bore on marriage. With his usual skill at evoking an issue in a title, he called his book *Marriage and Concupiscence*. Dedicated to Count Valerius, a Christian layman in power, it was designed to show how Catholics differed from the Manichees on the one hand and the Pelagians on the other. The Manichees, as Augustine interprets their mythology, say that marriage is sinful because man born from it is a child of the devil, stained by original sin. The Pelagians say that not only is marriage lawful, but no man born has the sin of Adam. The Catholics say that marriage is good, yet "man, born through concupiscence, brings with him original sin" (*Marriage and Concupiscence* 1.1, *CSEL* 42:211–212). Marriage was to be shown as good, concupiscence as evil, and marital intercourse as a mixture of good and evil.

What is concupiscence? It is not original sin, but the inevitable effect of the original sin inherited by the descendants of Adam. It is a force in the flesh of the baptized, even after original sin has been effaced by baptism. In the unredeemed, concupiscence is equivalent to sin.[32] For all men, the exercise of concupiscence is the means by which original sin is transmitted. If Adam had not fallen, there would have been no "concupiscence of the flesh" in generation.[33] Now it accompanies generation, and "is not from the Father but from the world" (*ibid.* 1.18.21, *CSEL* 42:233). It is sometimes identified with the "heat" which accompanies every copulation, sometimes with the "confusion of lust" (*libido*).[34]

Augustine offers evidence for the existence of concupiscence, "the law of sin," in man. Man's generative parts will not obey reason (*ibid.* 1.6.7, *CSEL* 42:218–219). In the act of copulation this disobedience is manifest: "Although conjugal copulation to generate offspring is not itself a sin (because the good will of the mind controls the pleasure of the body instead of following pleasure's lead, and the human judgment is not subjugated to sin) yet in the use of the generative act the wound of sin is justly present" (*ibid.* 1.12.13, *CSEL* 42:226).

Augustine, then, argued against the Manichees that procreation is good, against the Pelagians that concupiscence is not good. If one reaches a goal limping, the attainment of the goal is good, the limp is not (*ibid.* 1.7.8, *CSEL* 42:220). Substantive evil in man does not exist, yet, because of original sin and concupiscence, man needs grace.

The analysis by Augustine was much circulated. It brought a reply from Julian, the former bishop of Eclanum in Italy, who had been deposed for his failure to subscribe to the condemnation of Pelagius. Julian, as Augustine reported in a counterreply, directly charged the former Manichee with continuing to teach Manicheanism (*Against Julian* 1.3.5, *PL* 44:643). He attempted to pin Augustine to one of two unacceptable alternatives: the original sin which Augustine declared present in every infant born of man must be caused either by parents who were baptized Christians, or it must be caused by the marital act itself; either the bap-

---

[32] After baptism "the concupiscence of the flesh" remains, "but it is not imputed as sin" (*Marriage and Concupiscence* 1.25.28, *CSEL* 42:240).

[33] As to the character of original sin itself, Augustine followed Ambrose in identifying it with pride. As to how all men could have sinned in Adam, Augustine found a real unity between him and all humans through the generative seed: "In Adam all sinned, since in his nature, by virtue of that power by which he could generate them, all were still one" (*The Merits of Sinners and the Remission of the Sins of Infants* 3.7.14, *CSEL* 60:141).

[34] "Concupiscence" is normally used by Augustine in an evil sense: "This custom of speaking obtains that if avarice (*cupiditas*) or concupiscence (*concupiscentia*) is spoken of and no modification is added, it cannot be understood except in an evil meaning" (*The City of God* 14.7.2, *CSEL* 40²:14).

Concupiscence, used by Christians like Clement of Alexandria, was also a favorite Manichean term. How widespread was the Manichean usage is illustrated by an early medieval Chinese Manichean tract in which "Concupiscence" appears as a female demon; Ed. Chavannes and P. Pelliot, "Un traité manichéen retrouvé en Chine," *Journal asiatique* 18 (1911).

tized were still sinners and agents of evil, or the marital act itself was evil. Either position was Manichean, not Christian.

Augustine, in a new memorandum to Valerius, held his position. He refused to accept either alternative. The diversity of the sexes, sexual intercourse in marriage, human fecundity, were all good. But there was also "the concupiscence of the flesh which is not from the Father, but from the world, and the prince of that world is the devil" (*Marriage and Concupiscence* 2.5.14, CSEL 42:265). The "prince of that world" and "concupiscence" as an active force sounded Manichean. But Augustine reacted to the charge of Manicheanism much like a Socialist today being called a Stalinist. Socialists and Stalinists may share a Marxian distrust of capitalism; they may even have a common view of an ultimate utopia. But how that utopia is reached, and the freedom of man in reaching it, create vital distinctions. Augustine and the Manicheans shared a suspicion of sexuality. The ideal purity of the Manichean Elect may not have differed radically from Augustine's ideal of virginity. But on the means by which the ideal was to be achieved, and on the freedom of man in choosing his course, there was vital disagreement. For Augustine, man was free to procreate, and procreation was good. To call his doctrine Manichean was to pay a dangerous compliment to the Manichees (*Against Julian* 1.2.4, PL 44:643). Commitment to procreation is the central moral tenet which marks off Augustine from Mani.

The upshot of Augustine's strong emphasis on the role of concupiscence is a reinforcement of the requirement of procreative purpose for lawful intercourse. It is procreative purpose which makes good an act in which lust is present. The old Stoic arguments are again marshaled to support what appears here only as Christian theologizing. The example of birds and animals who act to propagate their kind rather than to satisfy their lust is invoked (*Marriage and Concupiscence* 1.4.5, CSEL 42:215). The comparison with eating is refurbished: food must be tasty enough to eat, but beyond the necessity of eating for sustenance, "there is lust, there is evil, which must not be yielded to, but resisted" (*Against Julian* 4.14.67, PL 44:771). Mortal sin may even occur in marital intercourse, if one is "intemperate" in his lust. This "intemperateness" is apparently a lack of restraint beyond what St. Paul pardons. In intemperate lust, says Augustine, invoking the old opinion of Seneca and ascribing it to Ambrose, one is an adulterer (*Against Julian* 2.7.20, PL 44:687). The Stoic comparisons are swept into the anti-Pelagian synthesis. The account of generative purpose is solidly embedded in the theology of original sin. Concupiscence is proved by psychological observation; marital intercourse is found to need a saving purpose; procreation is theologically established as the good which justifies the marital act.

The results for the doctrine on contraception were largely indirect.

There is, however, one passage in *Marriage and Concupiscence* which deals specifically with the subject. It reads:

It is one thing not to lie except with the sole will of generating: this has no fault. It is another to seek the pleasure of the flesh in lying, although within the limits of marriage: this has venial fault. I am supposing that then, although you are not lying for the sake of procreating offspring, you are not for the sake of lust obstructing their procreation by an evil prayer or an evil deed. Those who do this, although they are called husband and wife, are not; nor do they retain any reality of marriage, but with a respectable name cover a shame. They give themselves away, indeed, when they go so far as to expose the children who are born to them against their will; for they hate to nourish or to have those whom they feared to bear. Therefore a dark iniquity rages against those whom they unwillingly have borne, and with open iniquity this comes to light; a hidden shame is demonstrated by manifest cruelty. Sometimes [*Aliquando*] this lustful cruelty, or cruel lust, comes to this, that they even procure poisons of sterility [*sterilitatis venena*], and, if these do not work, extinguish and destroy the fetus in some way in the womb, preferring that their offspring die before it lives, or if it was already alive in the womb to kill it before it was born. Assuredly if both husband and wife are like this, they are not married, and if they were like this from the beginning they come together not joined in matrimony but in seduction. If both are not like this, I dare to say that either the wife is in a fashion the harlot of her husband or he is an adulterer with his own wife.

(*Marriage and Concupiscence* 1.15.17, CSEL 42:229–230)

This vehement passage, so rich in the antitheses dear to Augustine, is a fundamental text. It is the only passage in Augustine dealing with artificial contraceptives. It is one of two passages in Augustine on contraception where the explicit context does not restrict the denunciation to the Manichees. It provided later canon law with its term for contraceptives, "poisons of sterility." Under the heading *Aliquando,* it was to become the medieval locus classicus on contraception. Formally, unequivocally, passionately, Augustine here condemned contraception practiced by the married.

Some further commentary may be helpful. The "homicide" argument favored by Jerome and Chrysostom is not relied on. There is a close association in Augustine's mind, and in contemporary practice, of infanticide, abortion, and contraception. The association gives a sting to his critique. But the acts are distinguished. The fetus in the womb, not yet alive, is the fetus in the forty days before ensoulment. The "poisons of sterility" are intended to achieve their deadly effect before conception; the other means are used if they fail, and a fetus has been conceived. The reference to obstruction of offspring by an "evil prayer" (*malum votum*) is puzzling. Perhaps it refers to magical efforts at contraception; perhaps it simply means a prayer against conception or a desire to avoid it.

Does the analysis condemn isolated acts of contraception or only the practice of contraception? Does it embrace parents who only limited the number of their offspring but who did not prevent all procreation? It is difficult to answer these questions on the basis of this text alone. The words directed in criticism of contraception, "lustful cruelty or cruel lust," seem directed at persons who do not want to be parents at all. If the persons Augustine has in mind are the Manichees, a practice of contraception is what is attacked. His effort in *Marriage and Concupiscence* to dissociate his doctrine from Manicheanism would make this reading plausible, except that nowhere else are the Manichees charged with using artificial contraceptives. If this text is read in conjunction with Augustine's general doctrine on the generative purpose of marital intercourse, it would be a fair inference that he means to condemn each and every act of marital contraception. It might still be argued that the very strong terms of the text would not apply to individual acts. Yet considering the intense repugnance Augustine expressed to single acts of "unnatural" intercourse, one may well conclude that single acts of contraception could easily be condemned by him in these terms.

When Augustine used the term *venena* he was doubtless aware of the Scriptural connotation. It is *veneficia* which are denounced by Galatians 5:20, Apocalypse 9:21, 21:8, 22:15. With his profound knowledge of the Bible, this usage in the Latin translation of his day would have been in his mind. He was probably aware, moreover, of the Roman law against *veneficia*. This passage is, then, capable of two interpretations. One may appeal to it to show that St. Augustine understood the Scripture to condemn contraceptive drugs as *venena;* or one may contend that Augustine condemned contraceptive drugs partly because they were "medicines," that is, drugs with magical associations. One might further argue that, if Augustine believed the passages in the New Testament clearly applicable, he would have actually cited them at some point to condemn contraception.

There is one further discussion of contraception by Augustine. It is in an answer of about 419 to a Christian inquirer, Pollentius, who wanted his opinion on the remarriage of an innocent party after divorce from a spouse guilty of fornication. Augustine upheld the position that no remarriage was possible even for the purpose of procreating children, remarking, "In this time of refraining from embrace it is not necessary to beget children." Yet he does not wish to be misunderstood: once married, one may not avoid children. It is lawless and shameful to lie with one's wife where the conception of offspring is avoided: "This is what Onan, the son of Juda, did, and God killed him for it." You may marry to give an outlet to your incontinence, "but you ought not to temper your evil so that you exterminate the good of marriage, that is, the propagation of children" (*Adulterous Marriages* 2.12.12, *CSEL* 41:396).

Augustine's reference to the scriptural story is the first use of the fate of Onan by a prominent theologian as an argument against contraception in marriage. It is an exegesis of considerable, although not controlling, authority for later writers. Augustine's main objection rests on his teaching on the procreative purpose of marriage.

In Augustine, Stoic observation on the procreative function of intercourse is incorporated into an analysis of the values of marriage. The "natural good of marriage" is intercourse for procreation (*Marriage and Concupiscence* 1.4.5, *CSEL* 42:215). "The procreation of children is the first and natural and lawful reason for marriage" (*Adulterous Marriages* 2.12.12, *CSEL* 41:396). The natural purpose is vindicated against Manichean attack. It enables Augustine to justify marital intercourse despite the presence of concupiscence, which his anti-Pelagian polemic insists is its accompaniment.

Committed to the procreative rationale, Augustine is the enemy of contraception. He condemns the Manichean use of the sterile period and the Manichean use of coitus interruptus. He finds in the myths of Mani and the practice of the Catharists the pattern of all intercourse where, on religious grounds, insemination is avoided. Generalizing his specific responses to the Manichean attack on procreation, he condemns the use of contraceptive poisons as destructive of any marriage. He cites the punishment of Onan as warning and example.

Augustine's own experience molds his view of marriage and gives vitality to his formulas. The two great intellectual controversies of his life feed his thought. The Christian reaction to a religion so comprehensively articulated as to win such an intelligent religious spirit as Augustine would, in any case, have been violent; the reaction is traumatic when the leading authority on sexual matters has himself been a Manichee. The Christian view on original sin and concupiscence was already ambiguous in its implications for sexuality before Augustine. After the conflict of Pelagius and Augustine, sexual intercourse was clearly in a suspect position, stained by concupiscence, forced to justify itself by a procreative purpose. There are latent contradictions in Augustine; there are in every synthesis which reconciles competing values by recognizing them to a point and no further. Anselm, Aquinas, Luther, each can find texts in him supporting his views. These divergent interpretations need not detain us here. In his mind, Augustine had achieved a balance which saved Christian marriage, explained the effect of original sin, rejected Manicheanism. This balance, centering on the procreative requirement, was to be preserved for a thousand years in the Christian West. By its terms, it necessarily excluded and condemned contraception.

What if the one other option available had been adopted? Suppose the guide had not been St. Augustine but his contemporary, St. John Chrysostom, who had had no experience of concubinage, no initiation into Manicheanism, no battle with Pelagius. Suppose the doctrine had been adopted that marriage was no longer for procreation since the Resurrection had defeated death, that love was a value which the union of husband and wife incorporated and symbolized, that original sin and concupiscence had no special association with sexuality. Would it have made any difference for the doctrine on contraception? If the other teachings of Chrysostom had also been adopted, that the marital act is sacral and that the interruption of the procreative process is worse than murder, no concrete difference for the rule of contraception would have followed. It can scarcely be denied, however, that if Chrysostom's ideas had become the leading ones in theological development in the West, a different theological tone, a different way of looking at marriage might have led to different results in the active rethinking of theology, which, after the period of preservation of Augustine from 500 to 1100, was to take place on Augustinian terms.[35]

[35] The East by no means committed itself to Chrysostom. St. Cyril of Alexandria (d. 444) defended marriage as wholly good only when used for procreation (*Adoration in Spirit and Truth* 15, PG 68: 690). Intercourse is regularly soiled by original sin and by the seeking of pleasure: "In sins was I conceived," Ps 50:7 (*ibid.* 15, PG 68:1008; *On Psalm 50 7*, PG 69:1092). Of Onan himself Cyril observes briefly, "He broke the law of coitus" (*Critical Comments on Genesis 6*, PG 69:309).

PART TWO

THE CONDEMNATION INGRAINED

450–1450

CHAPTER V

THE LESSONS OF THE MONKS

THE DOCTRINE of the Fathers, so brilliantly synthesized by St. Augustine, received a sharper, simpler, rougher presentation in the next several centuries, from approximately 500 to 1100. The transmission was largely the work of monks. They brought to their task a strong respect for tradition and an accompanying disinterest in speculation; at the same time, within the supernaturalist, traditional framework they accepted, they were rationalists in a mechanical way: they wanted a strict accounting for the purpose of each human act; they wanted specific proscriptions of immoral conduct and concrete sanctions for each violation of the code. Partly as a projection of their own experience of monastic organization, they insisted on collective standards for all Christians; partly as a reaction to an age of enormous disorder, they valued rules. In the specific area of sexual behavior, they were fearful and inclined to extreme rigor; their distrust was usually not tempered by any clear appreciation of marriage. Augustinian sexual pessimism, an impassioned and delicately balanced personal synthesis, gave way to a monastic code even more pessimistic and severe. In the formation of this monastic code the patristic teaching against contraception was given precise and legal form. These monks were, often enough, bishops, and bishops who were not monks gave their support to the monastic understanding of marital morality. It cannot be successfully argued that the monastic code was worked out by persons with no pastoral responsibilities or sympathies. The code responded to what seemed to be crying evils of the day. Nonetheless, the standard by which these evils were measured, and the perception, empathy, and insight which the authors of the law possessed, had been chiefly shaped in a monastic environment.

How is one to understand the repeated opposition to contraception during this long chapter of Christian history? The opposition is not difficult to rationalize as a social necessity in an age of dwindling population, when military barbarism and the lack of medical resources made life even more precarious than in the Roman Empire. No contemporary analysis was made in terms of population needs or deficiencies. But one overlooks the constructive, order-building interests of monks and bishops, if this retrospective rationalization of their purpose is thought to have had nothing to do with their attitude. The Augustinian analysis of contraception as a destruction of the goods of marriage was not used. It was Jerome's analysis of the contraceptive act as homicide which was employed. The description is puzzling, as the most usual contraceptive was a potion affecting the woman and not acting upon the male semen. Was this description adopted because potions were the usual contraceptive and Jerome specifically referred to drinking sterility? Did it reflect the difficulty of distinguishing contraceptives from abortifacients? Was it favored as a forceful and dramatic way of impressing immature Christians with the seriousness of the act? All of these questions might be answered affirmatively, and the cumulative reasons for the choice of Jerome's approach would together reflect a half-conscious desire to place high protective walls about life and the life-giving process. The scarcity of men stimulated this desire.

A different kind of reason for condemning contraception was its association with pagan superstition. Throughout this period the term for magic, *maleficium*, was often used as a synonym for a sterilizing act, and in this term the old opposition to "medicine," to *veneficium*, was continued. Opposing magic generally, the Christian leaders opposed contraception specifically.

Lastly, there was hostility to sexual behavior lacking rational justification. There was the usual Christian teaching against adultery and fornication, with which contraception was sometimes connected. More important, there was marked antipathy to certain sexual acts in marriage — anal or oral intercourse, and coitus interruptus. Was this reaction an echo of the Stoic-patristic view of nature, or did it reflect Celtic and Germanic traditions of what was natural, or was it the judgment of Christians considering such acts afresh in the light of the general Christian teaching on human sexuality? As criticism was directed not only against particular kinds of nonprocreative acts, but against procreative acts where the position in intercourse was other than that of the man on top of the woman, elements of tribal lore seem to be incorporated into the teaching. The criticism as a whole may still be understood as an effort to introduce into marital relations a rationality whose roots were Stoic and patristic.

These general observations may be given a more tangible quality by a review of sixth-century ecclesiastical action against contraception, and by a consideration of the teaching of the penitentials.

SIXTH-CENTURY ECCLESIASTICAL ACTION

Individual bishops such as Chrysostom, Epiphanius, and Augustine had taught against contraception. A different and stronger stand developed when action was taken bearing a more corporate stamp.

The first bishop to exhort an entire province to turn against contraception was Caesarius, bishop of Arles from 503 to 543. Born in Chalon-sur-Saône in Burgundy in 470, Caesarius had been a monk of Lérins. He became bishop of what was the primatial see of Gaul, a meeting point of German and Roman culture, and the leading ecclesiastical center north of Italy. Under Arian Visigoths (503–507) and under Arian Ostrogoths (508–536), Caesarius remained the pastoral leader not only of his province, but of southern, central, and eastern Gaul and the territories of the Rhône, exercising the moral and social leadership of a metropolitan bishop in lands where the invasions had left the Church as the most stable authority. Pope Symmachus (498–514) urged him to have a care for "the affairs of religion, both in Gaul and in Spain" (*Epistles* 9, *PL* 62:66). Caesarius took the Pope at his word, and outdid it. According to his admiring friend and biographer, Cyprian of Toulon, the emissaries of Caesarius were dispatched to bring counsel to the bishops not only of Gaul and Spain, but of Italy itself (Cyprian, *Life of Caesarius* 5, *PL* 67: 1021). He was the genius behind thirteen church councils held between 506 and 541, and his influence extended not only to the Ostrogoth but to the Frankish episcopate. His preoccupation was moral reformation, and the thirteen councils strove vigorously to establish some moral norms. The history of penance in sixth-century Gaul is the history of his work.[1] Among Christians in a turbulent age St. Caesarius was the strong man. In the teaching on contraception, as one of many topics to which a sixth-century reformer might address himself, Caesarius left his stamp.

The morals of the people of Arles were, in Caesarius' estimation, poor. Concubinage, especially concubinage with slaves, abounded. The harassed bishop would have excommunicated all who had concubines, but, he observed, there were too many in this situation (*Sermons* 42.5, *CC* 103:188; *Sermons* 43.5, *CC* 103:192). Possibly by way of compensation, he reacted to the widespread indifference to Christian teaching on fornication by insistence on a rigid standard of marital morality. He committed himself totally to the Augustinian view that the sole lawful purpose of marital intercourse was procreative; to depart from it was at least venial sin. He appealed to Psalm 50:7 and Exodus 19:15, texts which implied that all intercourse was unholy. He went further. Adopting the old

---

[1] Cyrille Vogel, *La Discipline pénitentielle en Gaule des origines à la fin du VII*ᵉ *siècle* (Paris, 1952), p. 85. On the reforming activity of Caesarius generally, see pp. 80–87.

agricultural analogy, he took it to a new extreme. He declared, "No land could give lawful fruit which in a single year was frequently sowed. Why does one do in his own body what he would not do in his own field?" (*Sermons* 44.3–6, *CC* 103:196–199). Not only sterile intercourse but repeated intercourse seemed un-Christian by this stern measure.

At some undetermined time in his long episcopate, Caesarius addressed a letter to the other bishops and priests of his province on the pressing moral problems of the day. He exhorted his brothers to preach Christian morals to the people. After denouncing abortion as homicide, he continued:

> Who is he who cannot warn that no woman may take a potion so that she is unable to conceive or condemns in herself the nature which God willed to be fecund. As often as she could have conceived or given birth, of that many homicides she will be held guilty, and, unless she undergoes suitable penance, she will be damned by eternal death in hell. If a woman does not wish to have children, let her enter into a religious agreement with her husband; for chastity is the sole sterility of a Christian woman.
>
> (*Letter*, printed as *Sermons* 1.12, *CC* 103:9)

The epigrammatic ending is worthy of Augustine: Chastity is the sole sterility of the Christian. Only women are spoken of as guilty of committing contraception; only potions are considered as the form of contraceptive in use. The homicide analysis, one might suspect, is taken from Jerome's epistle to Eustochium, and a citation from the same letter in a sermon (51.4) by Caesarius confirms that he was familiar with Jerome's text. He expands Jerome's charge in a deceptively juridical fashion: the potion taker is guilty of a multiplicity of homicides. But is every act of intercourse after taking the contraceptive a new sin of homicide, or is it supposed that the first act of intercourse would have been fruitful and that succeeding acts of intercourse would have occurred in pregnancy? The bishop does not deal with these questions, which he leaves to God. The ultimate force of his warning is moral, not judicial.[2]

[2] According to the Council of Agde in 506, at which Caesarius presided, "homicides" (*homicidae*) were to be excommunicated unless they had given "the satisfaction of penance" (Council of Agde, Canon 37, Mansi 8:331. Penance in sixth-century Gaul was an arduous affair. It meant, in effect, civil death, and, most relevantly for the sin of contraception, it meant interdiction of all conjugal intercourse. This interdiction lasted during the penance and, according to the only surviving authorities, continued in effect after reconciliation to the Church (Vogel, *La Discipline pénitentielle*, pp. 117, 154). As a result, Agde itself counseled against giving penance readily to the young (Canon 15, Mansi 8:327); for the young might fail in their penance, and the state of the sinning penitent was considered worse than that of the sinner who had not attempted penance. Penance was usually reserved for the old or those about to die (Vogel, *La Discipline pénitentielle*, p. 118).

In the light of these facts, if Caesarius meant to say that contraception should canonically be treated as homicide, he was giving those guilty of it a choice between excommunication and the practical end of their marriages.

On the anticontraceptive texts of Caesarius, see also the commentary of A. M.

Three sermons of Caesarius carried out his own injunction to preach on the subject to the faithful. In one he attacked "diabolical" and "deadly" potions which prevented conception. He pointed out that a woman would not want her female slaves or tenants to use them, and asked, "With what conscience . . . does she herself refuse to bear those who could be Christians?" (*Sermons* 44.2, *CC* 103:196). In a second sermon he developed a rationale. It is an interference with God's will for the sterile to seek to become fecund "by herbs or diabolical marks or sacrilegious amulets." It is equally against God's will to avoid fecundity by contraceptive potions (*Sermons* 51.4, *CC* 103:229). In both sermons, he repeated his formula: so many conceptions prevented, so many homicides. In the third sermon, he dealt explicitly only with abortion, but spoke of a motive which might also have animated contraception. Some women, after they have had "two or three children," resort to abortion, "fearing lest perhaps if they have more children they cannot be rich." The remedy suggested for avoiding this sin is the same one proposed in Caesarius' letter to the province: a pact of continence between wives and husbands (*Sermons* 52.4, *CC* 103:231–232).

Perhaps the most striking aspect of these three sermons is that the hostility to using herbs to cure sterility appears as keen as the hostility to their use to prevent fecundity. Birth is in God's hands. It would be, I think, a mistake to view this approach as primarily an antipathy to artificial intervention of any sort in the life-giving process. It is chiefly an opposition to magical means. The herbs were condemned as the stock-in-trade of pagan magicians; their pagan character was objectionable, whatever use they were put to. Contraception fell under this rubric of magic, although it was not solely as magic that it was condemned.

As no legislation against contraception had been specifically enacted by a council, the collections of conciliar canons made in the West between 450 and 550 have nothing on the subject. They contain only the canon of the council of Ancyra on abortion. Thus it is with the two versions of collections made by Dionysius Exiguus (d. 540), a Scythian monk, at the request of the bishop of Salone;[3] with the *Editio prisca* or Italian Collection made about 450; with the Gallic version made near the end of the fifth century and with the *Epitome hispanica* based on it; with the Quesnel Collection used in sixth-century Gaul; with the *Abridgment of Canons* of Ferrandus, a deacon of Carthage, made about 546.[4]

Dubarle, "La Contraception chez Césaire d'Arles," *La Vie spirituelle* 16, Supplement (1963), 515–519.

[3] See Paul Fournier and Gabriel Le Bras, *Histoire des collections canoniques en occident* (Paris, 1931), I, 24.

[4] For the *Prisca* and Dionysian 1 and 2 collections, the Gallic version, and the *Epitome hispanica* see *Ecclesiae occidentalis monumenta juris antiquissimae*, ed. Cuthbert H. Turner (Oxford, 1907), vol. II. The Quesnel Collection is printed as

The absence of enacted law was drastically remedied by St. Martin of Braga (d. 579). Martin, a native of the Roman province of Pannonia on the Danube, from which Jerome had also come, had visited the Holy Land and then decided to undertake missionary work as a monk in the West. He founded the monastery of Dumium near Braga, the capital of the Sueves who controlled the northwest corner of the Iberian peninsula, and became a bishop in 556, the same year in which, thanks partly to his missionary endeavor, the Sueves turned from Arianism to Catholicism. Five years later he played an active part in the first council of Braga, and by 572 had become archbishop of Braga, in which capacity he presided at a second council in 572.[5]

Martin's activity against contraception took place against a background of Manichean danger. After the execution of Priscillian the movement fostered in his name became in fact affected by Manicheanism. The see of Astorga in Spain was held in succession by two bishops, father and son, with Priscillianist tendencies.[6] In the 440's Leo the Great approved the installation in Astorga of a bishop of firmly Catholic views, Turribius, and wrote to him to instruct him on the current errors of the Priscillianists: "They condemn marriage and have a horror of the procreation of the newborn, in which, as in almost all things, they agree with the profanity of the Manichees; so, as their morals prove, they detest conjugal copulation, for there is no freedom for baseness where matrimonial chastity and offspring are respected" (Leo, Letters 15.7, PL 54:683). The heresy, clearly a problem in 447 when Leo wrote, was still a major problem for the church in Iberia in 572. The first council of Braga moved energetically to its repression, and Priscillianism, rather than the defeated Arian heresy, was the chief business of the council. A series of canons condemned the Manichean view of the diabolical creation of the world. Canon 11 dealt with the Manichean view of procreation: "If anyone condemns human marriage and is horrified at the procreation of the new-

---

Codex canonum ecclesiasticorum et constitutionum sanctae sedis apostolicae, PL 56:359. Its place of composition was either Arles or, more probably, Italy; see Eligius Dekkers, Clavis patrum latinorum (Sacris erudiri III; new ed., 1961), no. 1770. For Fulgentius Ferrandus, Breviatio canonum (PL 67:957), the date of 546 is given by Dekkers, Clavis patrum latinorum, no. 1768.

[5] Martin was the adaptor of a lost work of Seneca, and under Martin's name this Formula vitae honestae or De quattuor virtutibus cardinalibus helped to spread Stoic moral teaching in medieval Europe. As late as 1544 it was being used in France as a schoolbook. See Claude W. Barlow, ed., Martini episcopi Bracarensis opera omnia (New Haven, 1950), pp. 3–7. All references will be to this edition of Martin's works.

[6] Adhémar D'Ales, Priscillien et l'Espagne chrétienne à la fin du quatrième siècle (Paris, 1936), p. 23. Philastrius, bishop of Brescia, had reported near the end of the fourth century that there were at that time in Spain many Manichees and "Abstainers" who said that creation was evil (Philastrius, De haeresibus, PL 12:1175–1176, 1196–1197).

born, as Mani and Priscillian, let him be anathema" (First Council of Braga, in Martin, *Opera*, p. 108).

With Manicheanism in the air, concern to protect conception from attack was understandable. Martin, who had known a more established Christian civilization, drew up a list of canons for the instruction of Nitigisius, archbishop of Lugo, and the other bishops of this out-of-the-way corner of Christendom. He presented the canons as authentic church legislation from the East. He, however, either had encountered new versions in the East, or did not hesitate to make improvements. Among the canons given he offered this deliberate expansion of the canon of Ancyra to cover contraception, and to cover its practice in marriage as well as in fornication:

If any woman has fornicated and has killed the infant thence born or has desired to commit an abortion and kill what she has conceived, or to take steps so that she may not conceive, either in adultery or in legitimate marriage, the earlier canons decreed that such women might receive communion at death; we, however, in mercy judge that such women, or other women who are accomplices of their crimes, should do penance for 10 years.
(*Chapters from the Synods of the Eastern Fathers 77*, in Martin, *Opera*, p. 142)

The first apparent church legislation against contraception is thus an interpolation. Enjoying the sponsorship of a saint who also came to hold the prestigious metropolitan see of Braga, Martin's canon was accepted as the work of the venerable fourth-century council. The text circulated as that of Ancyra wherever Martin's collection was used; and other collections drew on Martin. Of the latter, the most important to adopt the canon was the *Spanish Collection* of about 666.[7]

Accurate versions of Ancyra continued to circulate. The collections made before 585 had the unchanged text. The unaltered collection of Dionysius Exiguus was sent by Pope Hadrian I to Charlemagne in 774, and, with papal and imperial backing, it enjoyed a commanding position. Yet while St. Martin's concoction was not in every collection, it was influential enough to be often cited. The collection sent by Hadrian to Charlemagne was regarded as the law of the Frankish kingdom. But in the *Capitula* of Radulf, archbishop of Bourges, written about 850, it is Martin's version which is used (c. 41, *PL* 119:723).[8]

The continued success of this spurious canon can be explained as a blind copying of available authorities or as a response to conditions which required a canon against contraception. Whichever account is

---

[7] *Spanish Collection, PL* 84:385. *El Codice Lucense de la Colección canonica Hispaña*, ed. Gonzalez (Burgos, 1954).

[8] For the dates see Roger Huser, *Abortion in Canon Law* (Washington, 1943). Martin's collection as a whole is also referred to by the Council of Langres in 859; see Carlo De Clerq, *La Législation religieuse franque* (vol. I, Louvain, 1936; vol. II, Antwerp, 1958), II, 403.

correct, the acceptance of the text as official church legislation did in truth commit the ecclesiastical organization, in Iberia at least, to firm condemnation of such conduct. Like the pastoral of Caesarius, Martin of Braga's canon invoked, as well as witnessed, corporate opposition to contraception.

At Rome itself no explicit teaching on contraception appeared, but authoritative support was given to a new doctrine on marital intercourse, so austere in its demands that contraception would have been unthinkable for those accepting it. The new doctrine was the work of St. Gregory, known to posterity as "the Great," the last doctor of the patristic Church, the first strong medieval pope. Gregory was a former praetor of Rome, who had renounced his secular career to become a monk. Pope from 590 to 604, he found himself the leader of the Church in the ruins of Roman civilization; and his reaction to moral ruin was exacerbated by his already acute sensibility. He took a solemn and austere view of marital morals, which out-Augustined Augustine.

In his *Pastoral Rule*, Gregory provided a chapter on "How the Married and the Celibate Are To Be Admonished." The married were to be admonished that they might copulate only to produce children. This was merely Augustine. But Gregory went further. Not only is pleasure an unlawful purpose in intercourse, but if any pleasure is "mixed" with the act of intercourse, the married have "transgressed the law of marriage." Their sin, to be sure, is as small a one as the nonprocreative purpose in Augustine; it may be remitted by "frequent prayers." But sin has been committed. The guilty married have "befouled" their intercourse by their "pleasures" (*Pastoral Rule* 3.27, PL 77:102).

The same doctrine was repeated in an even more celebrated letter of Gregory to St. Augustine, archbishop of Canterbury. The authenticity of the letter has been doubted, but not, I think, disproved.[9] If considered ungenuine, it would have less authority today. But it was ascribed by Bede to Gregory and from 730 on was accepted by the Middle Ages as Gregory's teaching, and its content does not differ from the *Pastoral Rule*.

[9] M. Deanesley and P. Grosjean advanced the theory that the letters which appear in Bede's *Ecclesiastical History* as a response from Gregory had, in fact, been a collection edited at Canterbury by Nothelm, a priest and later archbishop. Question Eight, from which the statement on marriage comes, was supposed by them to be a homily given at Canterbury, probably by Archbishop Theodore, drawing on authentic work of Pope Gregory. "The Canterbury Edition of the Answers of Pope Gregory I to St. Augustine," *Journal of Ecclesiastical History* 10 (1959), 1–43. Their methods and conclusions were effectively criticized by Paul Meyvaert, "Les *Responsiones* de S. Grégoire le Grand à S. Augustin de Cantorbéry," *Revue d'histoire ecclésiastique* 54 (1959). Meyvaert noted, in particular, that Bede had the material in the letter as early as 721, and concluded that the question of Gregorian authenticity was still open (pp. 889, 894). It might be added that Bede, a cautious authority, testifies positively that Gregory wrote the letter (Bede, *Ecclesiastical History* 2.1, ed. C. Plummer, Oxford, 1896).

Augustine, sent by Gregory to evangelize England, had asked the Pope's advice on what to teach "the rude English people": could a man enter a church or receive communion after marital copulation, if he had not first washed himself? Gregory's answer, as reported in the celebrated letter, was an emphatic negative. The way it was done in Rome was otherwise. Moreover, there was a reason. Miraculously a man might have intercourse without sin, as one might be in fire without burning. But miracles did not usually attend marital intercourse; sin was to be expected. His doctrine, Gregory asserted, was neither a condemnation of marriage, nor new:

> Saying these things we do not assign fault to marriage. But because this lawful mingling of spouses cannot be done without pleasures of the flesh, one is to abstain [from entering the church at once]. This pleasure cannot be without fault. For not of adultery nor of fornication, but of lawful marriage was he born, who said, "Behold I was conceived in sins, and in delights my mother bore me," Psalm 50.7. (*Epistles* 11.64, *PL* 77:1196–1197)

In this teaching the Stoic distrust of pleasure was pushed to the limit. A barrier was set against the consideration of marital values other than procreation; consideration of a value such as love was blocked. By this rigid doctrine that only the procreative purpose was pure, interference with procreation was, in a formidable a fortiori way, excluded.

Gregory wrote when Manicheanism, no longer a threat, was more than a memory. The Priscillianist crisis dealt with by Braga had occurred in his lifetime. He himself wrote to Cyprian, the governor of the papal estates in Sicily, that he should pursue the Manichees he found and "recall them to the Catholic faith" (*Letters* 5.8, *PL* 77:729). He warned John, bishop of Squillace, that Manichees from Africa were getting ordained in Italy (*Letters* 2.37, *PL* 77:575). He solemnly judged the book of an Eastern monk, Athanasius of Istauria, to be Manichean (*Letters* 6.14, *PL* 77:805). In his letter to Augustine in England, he taught that a pregnant woman might be baptized — a teaching which seems implicitly designed to forestall a Manichean error. In his commentary on Job, he contrasted the Catholic middle way with Jovinian's repudiation of virginity and Mani's condemnation of marriage (*Moralia* 19.18, *PL* 76:115). This consciousness of Manichean morality, and of the distinction between it and Catholic morality, does show that, even in finding intercourse unavoidably befouled by light sin, Gregory maintained the central orthodox position that procreation was good. By carrying the Alexandrian-Augustinian rule one step further, he not only rejected the Manichees but even more firmly barred contraception. In the context of his doctrine on intercourse, contraception would have appeared as a monstrous denial of the single excuse for coitus. Gregory's doctrine sealed, at the highest level, the opposition to contraceptive acts. Enhanced in authority by Gregory's personal prestige and increasing in importance as the papacy increased in authority in the Middle Ages, this doctrine assured the absolute condemnation of contraceptive practice by the entire ecclesiastical organization.

The stress on procreative purpose should not be confused with a stress on population. The liturgy approved by Gregory for use in Rome is instructive. Outside of the prayers for a marriage, there seems to have been little stress on increase of the faithful by large families. In the Good Friday service the prayer for the catechumens indicated that the Church increased by "new offspring" in the sense of new catechumens, that is, persons educated in the faith. In the service for a wedding, procreation was linked with religious education. The prayer of blessing for the spouses asked God that "the children of adoption be multiplied," that is, children of the New Law. The prayer asked that "what generation puts forth to the splendor of the world, regeneration may lead to the increase of the Church." Offspring were not the same as regenerated offspring. A short prayer at the *Pax Domini* referred to marriage as ordained by God for "the propagation of the human race." A closing blessing was imparted to the new wife: "May she be as lovable as Rachel to her husband, as wise as Rebecca, long-lived and faithful as Sara." The fecundity of none of these Old Testament women was referred to. The prayer continued, "May she be grave with decorum, venerable with modesty, taught in heavenly doctrines. May she be fruitful in offspring. May she be approved and innocent." Surely in this list of virtues fertility held no preeminence.[10]

THE LESSONS OF THE PENITENTIALS

Caesarius, Martin, Gregory — these monks become bishops gave voice to a corporate opposition to contraception. This doctrine was also transmitted, and inculcated, by those peculiarly monastic instruments, the penitentials. These works consisted of an arrangement of sins by subject matter, together with prescribed penances. Sometimes anonymous or pseudonymous, they are an expression of monastic standards of what is sinful and the gravity of the sin. How often the prescribed penances were

[10] *The Gregorian Sacramentary under Charles the Great, Edited from Three MSS of the Ninth Century*, ed. H. A. Wilson (London, 1915). On its authenticity see Annibale Bugnini, "Sacramentario," *Enciclopedia cattolica* 10:1567.

A later document from Rome reflected more stress on procreation. In 866 Pope Nicholas I replied to points of doctrine raised by the Bulgarians and had occasion to describe the Roman wedding ceremony. The blessing of the wedded couple, he said, was "according to the example by which the Lord blessed the first humans in Paradise, saying to them, 'Increase and multiply.' Similarly Tobias, before he came together with his wife, is described as praying to the Lord with that prayer" (*Letters* 97, *PL*, 119:980).

enforced is not clear; doubtless a good deal depended on the devoutness of the community and the penitent. The penitentials are most clearly a witness to the moral judgments of the monastic writers. But as the monastic writers were the chief expositors of the moral ideas of this period, these judgments helped shape the mentality, the ethic, of western Europe.

It will be convenient first to list the penitentials used; second, to indicate the contraceptive practices they describe; and third, to note the sanctions they invoke.

THE PENITENTIALS USED

Sixth Century

St. Finnian	Irish
St. Columban	Irish

Seventh Century

Cummean	Irish
St. Theodore of Tarsus	Anglo-Saxon
Canons of Gregory	Anglo-Saxon

Eighth Century

The Irish Collection of Canons	Irish
St. Bede	Anglo-Saxon
Egbert	Anglo-Saxon
Pseudo-Bede	Anglo-Saxon
Old Irish	Irish
Merseburg A, B, and C	Frankish
St. Hubert	Frankish
Pseudo-Egbert	Anglo-Saxon

Ninth Century

Halitgar	Frankish
Pseudo-Vigila	Spanish
Martène	North or Middle Frankish
Pseudo-Theodore	Frankish
Pseudo-Cummean	Frankish

Tenth Century

Regino of Prüm, *Churchly Disciplines and the Christian Religion*	German

Eleventh Century

Burchard of Worms, *Decretum*	German

All of the penitentials examined, with the exception of the *Old Irish*, are in Latin. The earliest are of Irish provenance. The first is by one of the famous abbots of the monastic springtime of Ireland, although it is uncertain whether the author is St. Finnian, abbot-bishop of Clonard, or St. Finnian, abbot of Morville. The second is an adaptation of Finnian by St. Columban (d. 615), the missionary from the monastic school of Bangor who brought the Christian gospel back to areas of Burgundy, Switzerland, and northern Italy. The later Frankish penitentials, the *Merseburg* group and *St. Hubert* (named for their places of discovery in

Merseburg and St. Hubert, a monastery in the Ardennes) are eighth-century derivations from Columban. The later Irish compilations represent markedly different currents from the earlier works. The penitential of Cummean, bishop of Clonfert (d. 662), is based on Cassian's arrangement of the eight deadly sins. The two eighth-century penitentials are products of later monastic revivals. The *Irish Collection* was made in the early eighth century at Iona off the coast of Scotland. The *Old Irish* was composed in Gaelic about 780 at the center of eighth-century reform, the monastery of Tallaght near the present city of Dublin.[11]

Another set of penitentials was developed in the formative years of the Anglo-Saxon church. The first goes back in some form to St. Theodore, a Greek monk originally from Tarsus sent from Rome to become archbishop of Canterbury (669–690) and the effective organizer of the church in England. The *Canons of Gregory* are also ascribed to him. Both works may have been arranged as penitentials after his death. A second penitential bears the name of St. Bede, the monk of Wearmouth and Jarrow and church historian extraordinary, who in 1899 was recognized as a Doctor of the Church. A third is attributed to the leader of the church in the north, Egbert, archbishop of York from 731 to 767. The authenticity of these Anglo-Saxon works, and of particular texts within the collections, is not beyond dispute. The penitentials assigned to Pseudo-Bede, Pseudo-Egbert, Pseudo-Theodore, and Pseudo-Cummean are established to be later continental works.

Three of the later penitentials are by leaders of the church on the Continent. Halitgar was bishop of Cambrai and a leader in the Frankish church after Charlemagne; the work, also known as the Roman Penitential, is ascribed to him with probability; it dates from about 830. Regino, an early-tenth-century abbot of Prüm in Lorraine, wrote about 906. Burchard, who composed his *Decretum* about 1010, was bishop of the important ecclesiastical center of Worms; his work marks a transition from

---

[11] The editions of the penitentials used are as follows: Regino and Burchard are from *PL*. The *Irish Collection of Canons* is from *Die irische Kanonsammlung*, ed. F. W. H. Wasserschleben (Leipzig, 1885). Finnian, *Old Irish*, Columban, and Cummean are from *The Irish Penitentials*, ed. Ludwig Bieler (Dublin, 1963). All of the others are from *Die Bussordnungen der abendländischen Kirche*, ed. F. W. H. Wasserschleben (Halle, 1851).

On the dating, authors, and authenticity of the penitentials, see the editions cited, except for Pseudo-Bede, Pseudo-Cummean, Pseudo-Egbert, and Pseudo-Vigila see Dekkers, *Clavis patrum latinorum*, pp. 419–421. Bieler corrects Wasserschleben's dating of 690 for the *Irish Collection of Canons* to 725 (*The Irish Penitentials*, p. 23). On Bede, see M. L. W. Laistner, "Was Bede the Author of a Penitential?" *Harvard Theological Review* 31 (1938), 263, and John T. McNeill and Helena M. Gamer, *Medieval Handbooks of Penance* (New York, 1938). A ninth-century date is assigned the *St. Hubert* and *Merseburg* penitentials by H. J. Schmitz in his edition of them, *Die Bussbücher und das kanonische Bussverfahren* (Düsseldorf, 1898). This date has not been generally accepted; see Gabriel Le Bras, "Penitentiels," *DTC* 12¹:1169–70.

the penitential to the more elaborate collection of canons which the next age will develop into a science. The other Continental penitentials are anonymous or pseudonymous. Vigila was a ninth-century Spanish monk, to whom the Pseudo-Vigila is attributed. The Martène penitential is named for its first editor.

THE PRACTICES CONDEMNED

Indisputable reference to contraception is not earlier than the eighth century. The contraceptives described are potions, and it is regularly assumed that they will be used by women. The *Irish Collection of Canons*, a particularly well-organized compilation of scriptural, patristic, and conciliar decisions, devotes two chapters of a section entitled "Womanly Questions" to abortion and to contraception. Chapter 3 quotes Jerome on "drinking sterility." Chapter 4 has a criticism, reminiscent of Caesarius of Arles, of women taking "diabolical drinks by reason of which they can no longer conceive." Its formula "so many conceptions prevented, so many homicides" is that of Caesarius.

Merseburg B (c. 13) and *St. Hubert* (c. 56) denounce potions taken by a woman "in order not to conceive or to kill what she has conceived." An echo of Martin of Braga is evident. *Merseburg C* (c. 3) refers more generally only to a woman "making herself an enemy to herself not to have children." *Martène* (c. 47) repeats the quotation of Jerome on drinking sterility. Pseudo-Vigila (c. 45) uses the formula of Caesarius of Arles to condemn women for preventing conception by potions. Regino of Prüm speaks of preventing conception or generation by drinks or other means (*Churchly Disciplines* 2.5.8–9, *PL* 132:282). This text is repeated by Burchard (*Decretum* 17.57, *PL* 140:933).

The references to potions are interwoven with references to magic, and it seems that the magical means spoken of were usually herbal potions. The significance of these magical potions for contraceptive practice may become evident in an exegesis of the term *maleficium*. Etymologically, *maleficium* means "evil-doing." Often it is used to mean "magic"; and *malefici*, those who perform *maleficium*, are viewed as sorcerers, Wherever used, the terms *maleficium* and *maleficus* carry this implication of magical means.[12] But in addition to its broad and vague meaning of magic,

[12] The original source for the penitentials' condemnatory references to magic appears to be the fourth-century Roman law, *Theodosian Code* 9.16, "De maleficis et mathematicis et ceteris similibus." Here a definition of *maleficus* runs as follows: "A magician or one accomplished in magic arts, who by popular custom is called *maleficus*" (9.16.6). An exemption from criminal penalty is made for magicians who keep storms from damaging crops, but the *interpretatio* of this law says, "*Malefici* or enchanters or senders of storms, or those who by the invocation of demons disturb the minds of men, shall be punished with every kind of penalty" (9.16.3).

The Theodosian provisions were adopted by the Visigoths in the *Liber judiciorum* or Laws of the Visigoths, put out under King Erwig in 681: see 6.2, "Of Magicians

maleficium sometimes refers more specifically to an act causing an abortion or producing sterility with magical, that is, diabolical, help. In the sense of an act causing either an abortion or sterility, it is used by Egbert, who speaks of a woman "killing some others by her magical evil-doing art [*arte maleficia*], that is, by drink or by some art" (7.7). The same text is repeated in Pseudo-Bede 15.3 and Pseudo-Theodore 6.6. As the placing of the text in a section dealing with infanticide makes clear, the reference to killing of "some others" is to a destruction of progeny. In short, *maleficium* has the ambiguity of *veneficium* in classical Latin, and is sometimes specified to indicate abortion or contraception.

In the unmistakable sense of a contraceptive or sterilizing act, *maleficium* first appears in the secular law. In the revision of the Salic Law of the Franks made under Guntram (567–593), title 19, "De maleficiis," section 4, reads as follows: "If a woman has committed *maleficium*, so that she cannot have infants, she will be judged liable to a fine of sixty-two gold *semis*." [13] Here *maleficium* consists in a contraceptive act performed on herself by a woman, and the notion of hostility often connected with magic has been dropped. The text, I think, is strong evidence of a specific sense for *maleficium* of "sterilizing magical act" in addition to its general meaning.

One other text is of capital significance in explicitly giving a very similar special sense of *maleficium*. Pseudo-Bede asks: "Have you drunk any *maleficium*, that is, herbs or other agents so that you could not have children?" (Pseudo-Bede, "The Order for Giving Penance," 30). In this sentence *maleficium* is not the sterilizing magical act, but the sterilizing magical potion.

---

and Those Consulting Them, and Poisoners," *Leges Visigothorum*, ed. Karl Zeumer (Hannover, 1902), *Monumenta Germaniae historica: Leges nationum germanicarum* I. But the Visigoths add to the offenses connected with magic the use of poison (*venenum*) to kill a person (6.2.3). The Visigoths thus associated *maleficium* with the giving of poison, although not defining *maleficium* in these terms. In the penitentials there is sometimes the same approach as the Visigoths': both poisoning and the sending of storms are treated as cases of *maleficium*. For example, the *St. Hubert Penitential* 20 and Halitgar 5.3 each take *maleficium* to mean the magical sending of storms.

McNeill and Gamer in their English translation of a number of the penitentials invariably translate *maleficium* as "magic" (*Medieval Handbooks of Penance*, e.g., pp. 252, 274). This translation fails to catch the specific meaning of *maleficium* where it is used not to mean magic in general, or the magical sending of storms, but the magical causing of sterility.

The penitentials do not, I believe, distinguish between magic causing sterility and magic causing impotence. The distinction is a later refinement.

[13] *Pactus legis salicae*, ed. Karl A. Eckhardt (Hannover, 1962), p. 82. *Monumenta Germaniae historica: Leges nationum germanicarum* IV¹. In the earlier version of the Salic law under Clovis (507–511), this same title 19 deals with "giving herbs to drink" which kill the person taking them. Many manuscripts treat this act as a *maleficium*. The revision of the law quoted above adopts and expands this usage: the giving of herbs to sterilize is now a *maleficium*.

Of only slightly less import is a text in Burchard which uses *maleficia* and herbs as parallels. He speaks of women who, to kill what has been conceived or to prevent conception, use *"maleficia* and herbs" (*Decretum,* 19.5, *PL* 140:972). This text catches the generic similarity of contraceptive herbal potions and other forms of magical contraceptives.

These references to contraceptive *maleficium* are clear. Like the texts on potions, none of the texts from the penitentials is earlier than the eighth century. There is, however, an earlier chain of texts where the meaning of *maleficium* is "poison causing an abortion," but where reference to any sterilizing act might be meant. These references begin with the penitential of Finnian. Penance is prescribed for a cleric or a woman who is a *malefica* or a man who is a *maleficus,* who deceives anyone by *maleficium.* Such an act is "an immense sin," to be punished by six years of penance (no. 18). But if the culprit did not cheat anyone, but "for wanton love gave to someone," the penance is only a year (no. 19). Finnian then says if a woman has destroyed (*perdiderit*) her fetus by *maleficium,* she shall do penance for approximately three years. In each case the act described is the use of magical potions. The third case involves abortion; the second the use of an aphrodisiac without abortive effect; the first is uncertain and seems to involve something less than the intentional killing of an adult, for the ordinary seven-year penance for killing by a cleric (no. 23) is not applied.

St. Columban puts these three sections together and revises the language as follows:

> If one has destroyed another by his *maleficium,* let him do penance on measured bread and water for three years and for another three years abstain from wine and meat, and then in the seventh year he may be received into communion. If anyone becomes a *maleficus* to excite love, however, and destroys no one, let a cleric do penance a whole year on bread and water, a layman half a year, a deacon two years, a priest three years. In particular, if through this one cheated a woman of her fetus, let each one increase his penance by six terms of forty days, lest he be guilty of homicide.   (Columban B6)

Here, it may be argued, is an attempt to deal with three distinct cases. The first, the most serious, is the hostile bringing about of the destruction of another. The second, much more lightly punished, is "for love," *pro amore,* that is, to excite love in someone else; an aphrodisiac potion is employed.[14] "Without destroying anyone" means that the magic has no

---

[14] In this interpretation I follow Ludwig Bieler's translation of *pro amore* as "to excite love" (*The Irish Penitentials,* p. 101). This interpretation seems to me to be confirmed by the *St. Hubert Penitential* 11, classifying the case under a separate heading, "Illicit Love." The aphrodisiac use of potions is most clearly spelled out in Pseudo-Egbert: "If someone uses poisons for the sake of someone's love, and gives any to someone in food or drink, or uses incantations of any kind, that thereby their love may increase, let him fast half a year, if a layman, with bread and water Tuesdays and Wednesdays, and no meat other days" (4.18).

unintended side effects. This situation is contrasted with the third case, where a woman is deprived of offspring and the culprit is guilty of homicide unless he performs an increased penance; in this case the potion has operated as an abortifacient.[15] It might be possible to argue that contraception is also envisaged. "To cheat of a fetus" may be used in the sense of depriving one of what is expected. The later *Old Irish Penitential* understands the penalty to run only against abortion.[16] But this later understanding is not absolute proof. The text is repeated with unimportant variants in the *St. Hubert Penitential* 10–11, Halitgar 5.1–2, *Merseburg A*, 9–10, and Pseudo-Cummean 7.1–2. In the last two works the words for "poison" and "poisoner" are indifferently substituted for *maleficium* and *maleficus*, confirming the view that the magic is supposed to work by poisonous potion.

This review of the texts not only serves to establish the close association between abortion and magic, between contraception and magic, and between poison, abortion and contraception; it may also suggest that with the authors of the penitentials, as with Caesarius of Arles, opposition to magic reinforces the opposition to contraception. Contraception is not condemned merely as magical, but the hostility to it has added force from the orthodox Christian distrust of pagan magic.[17]

The type of contraceptive employed suggests other observations on the effects and the effectiveness of the potions. Probably, as with the Greek potions described by Soranos, it was difficult to determine whether a potion operated as a contraceptive or as an abortifacient. Burchard speaks of herbs which either produce an abortion or, if conception has not yet taken place, prevent conception (*Decretum* 19, PL 140:972). But while this practical difficulty in distinguishing effects was felt, many authors make a point of distinguishing contraception from abortion; and from the *Irish Collection of Canons* to Burchard, both abortion and contraception are condemned.

The effectiveness of the contraceptives is, of course, highly speculative. It is easy to dismiss as superstitious a belief that magic will cause sterility; it is not so easy to assess the force of magic which takes the form of

[15] Bieler translates Columban's phrase here as "has produced abortion" (*The Irish Penitentials*, p. 101).

[16] *Old Irish Penitential*, ed. D. A. Binchy, in Bieler, p. 272. The result is rather like the Cornelian law against poisoners.

[17] The diocesan statute of Gerbald, bishop of Liège (787–810), condemns sorcerers (*sortilogi*) and "poisoners, that is, women who give some potions to cut out embryos (*partus*) and make magic so that their husbands will love them more" (Statute, ed. De Clerq in *La Législation religieuse*, I, 360).

For an account emphasizing the penitentials' association of contraception with abortion, fornication, and adultery. see R. S. Callewaert, O.P., "De middeleeuwse biechtboeken anticonceptionele praktijken," *Tijdschrift voor theologie* 4 (1964), 254, 272–274.

herbal drinks. If herbs had some effect on female fecundity among the Hebrews, the Romans, and the North American Indians, it seems more likely than not that they worked for the Franks, Celts, and Anglo-Saxons.

Meaningful variation and fresh formulation are some evidence that the penitentials were not merely repeating academic learning, but passing moral judgment on existing contraceptive practice. Another bit of evidence on this point is the secular legislation. The revised Salic law, quoted above, is, as far as I can determine, the oldest surviving text of a law specifically aimed at contraception; and, as the law presumably is dealing with sterilization achieved by the herbal potions, it is temporary self-sterilization which is legislated against. The significance of this law is not great in the absence of any knowledge about its enforcement. It may merely reflect an ecclesiastical injection into the law, not a response to a social exigency. But if ecclesiastics believed secular legislation would be helpful, probably some practice of self-sterilization was current. In contrast, the Visigothic and the Anglo-Saxon laws condemn abortion, but are silent on the prevention of conception.

The prevalence of contraceptive practice is related to that other question equally crucial for the evaluation of the condemnations articulated: What were the motives of the users? The penitentials provide a fair amount of information. Four kinds of motives appear. One group of users are unmarried women who wish to avoid pregnancy. They are aimed at by the *Irish Collection of Canons*, which puts its quotation from Jerome under the heading "Simulated Virgins and Their Morals" ("Womanly Questions," 3.3). This perennial problem is referred to three centuries later by Bishop Burchard of Worms, who speaks of prevention of conception by women "fornicating and attempting to conceal their crime" (*Decretum* 19, "Interrogatory," PL 140:972).

A second group are those resorting to magic to cause sterility out of hostility. The texts on *maleficium* already inspected imply that herbs causing sterility might, at least on occasion, be foisted on an unwary neighbor. Regino speaks of prevention of generation or conception out of "meditated hatred" (*Churchly Disciplines* 89, PL 132:301). Third, chapters 79 and 80 of Pseudo-Vigila distinguish drinking a potion "for chastity" from "doing this in order not to have children." Where the potion is "for chastity," presumably it acts as an anaphrodisiac, destroying sexual desire; the text does not, however, distinguish the type of potion, but only the motive.

Finally, and most interestingly for the modern observer, an economic motive for not wanting children is recognized. This recognition occurs in a discrimination made among penances on the basis of the economic status of the penitent. The distinction is made first in connection with infanticide. If a woman killing her child were a *paupercula* or *pauperina*, a "poor little woman," the penance was to be half that for a mother not in this condition. So taught Theodore (1.14.25–26). The teaching also was set out in the *Canons of Gregory* 102–103. No explanation was given; apparently the difficulties of nourishment and rearing for a *paupercula* were obvious enough without comment. Theodore was followed literally by Pseudo-Cummean 6.9–10, *Martène* 51.13–14, Pseudo-Theodore 6.6.

Meanwhile, Theodore's distinction had been adopted by Bede in determining the penalty for abortion: "It makes a big difference if a poor little woman does it on account of the difficulty of feeding or whether a fornicator does it to conceal her crime" (4.12). The same rule was followed for abortion by Pseudo-Theodore 6.4.

The economic reasons which would prompt infanticide or abortion would seem to operate with equal force to stimulate recourse to contraception. Clear texts speaking of the motive in association with contraception are not found before Burchard. There is, however, a relevant chain of texts which begins with Egbert; he speaks of a woman "destroying others by her art of *maleficium*, that is by potion or some art." The penance for this destructive magic is approximately halved if the woman is a *paupercula* (7.7–8). Egbert is dealing in this chapter with the sins of women in marriage, so the "others" referred to are presumably the woman's progeny; the economic distinction also makes sense only on this assumption. It is not evident whether abortion or contraception, or both, are meant. Egbert is followed by Pseudo-Bede 15.3 and *Martène* 77.4.

The first entirely unambiguous reference to contraception committed on account of poverty is in Burchard. It is an instructive conflation of Caesarius of Arles, Martin of Braga's version of Ancyra, and Bede:

> Have you done what some women are accustomed to do when they fornicate and wish to kill their offspring, act with their *maleficia* and their herbs so that they kill or cut out the embryo, or, if they have not yet conceived, contrive that they do not conceive? If you have done so, or consented to this, or taught it, you must do penance for ten years on legal feriae. But an ancient determination removed such from the Church till the end of their lives. For as often as she impeded a conception, so many homicides was a woman guilty of. But it makes a big difference whether she is a poor little woman and acted on account of the difficulty of feeding, or whether she acted to conceal a crime of fornication.
>
> (*Decretum* 19, PL 140:972)

This compound text at last connects the rule developed for abortion and infanticide to contraception: poverty extenuates, although it does not justify the crime. Burchard's question and observation could be interpreted as merely a logical extension of Bede. But that the extension was made at all affords us, I believe, some evidence of contemporary mentality and practice: contraception for economic reasons seems as likely to Burchard as it did to Caesarius of Arles.

Almost always it is assumed that the users of contraceptive potions or magic will be women. *The Irish Collection of Canons* typically puts the matter under "Womanly Questions"; Burchard's interrogations on the subject are directed solely to female penitents. Exceptions occur. The anaphrodisiac of Pseudo-Vigila seems probably meant for a man. *Maleficium*, by means other than potions, might affect male fecundity: the possibility is made explicit in Regino's reference to "something" preventing a man from "generating" (*Churchly Disciplines* 2.89, PL 132:301). But it seems arguable that an effect on the male is visualized here only from a hostile source. In other words, there is no text clearly speaking of a man intentionally using a sterilizing potion. That the sin of self-sterilization is normally regarded as a female one may have had some unarticulated influence on the firm monastic reprobation of it; contraception as practiced in these ages was often a refusal by a woman to perform the chief role society had assigned to her.

It would be misleading to stop at the condemnation of potions. There were also prohibitions of various forms of marital intercourse in which procreation was intentionally avoided. In these condemnations it is male behavior which is usually criticized, although sometimes both spouses seem to be comprehended in the condemnation.

Coitus interruptus is rarely mentioned. In over a hundred quotations from the Bible in the various Irish penitentials, there is no citation of Genesis 38.[18] The greatest scriptural scholar of Anglo-Saxon England, Bede, made no reference to marriage in his commentary on this text in Genesis, following instead Augustine's allegorical treatment of Onan as a type of useless human being who did not contribute what he could (*On the Pentateuch*, PL 91:266). The absence of more widespread allusion to Onan argues an absence of widespread use of his method of contraception.

The most definitively dated reference to the sin occurs not in a penitential but in diocesan legislation which is substantially the work of Theodulphus, bishop of Orléans. Theodulphus, a Visigoth who was one of the leaders of the Carolingian renaissance, was bishop of Orléans from 798 to 818; the legislation dates from about 813. Under the caption "Irrational fornication" a variety of sexual sins are dealt with. Immediately preceding a denunciation of masturbation, the law states: "It is called uncleanness or the detestable sin not to lie naturally with a woman, whence it is read that Onan, son of Juda, was struck by God when, having entered into his wife, he poured out his seed on the earth." [19]

The references to Onan in the penitentials may precede or follow this

---

[18] See the list of scriptural references in Bieler, *The Irish Penitentials*, pp. 288–289.

[19] The Second Diocesan Statute of Theodulphus, bishop of Orléans, ed. De Clerq in *La Législation religieuse*, I, 338.

Carolingian literary interest in the Bible. *St. Hubert*, c. 57, castigating the act, describes it as "the spilling of seed in coitus with a woman as the sons of Juda did to Thamar." "The sons of Juda" supposes that Er as well as Onan committed the act. The condemnation is particularly striking as it occurs in a sentence which first deals with a woman taking potions "so that she does not conceive or kills the conceptus"; the same penance is applied to each one of these acts — contraception by the woman, abortion by the woman, withdrawal and ejaculation by the man. *Merseburg B* 13 is identical with *St. Hubert*.

Other forms of nonprocreative sexual behavior in marriage are much more frequently mentioned. Oral intercourse (described as putting *semen* in the *os*) and anal intercourse (described as *a tergo*) are often vigorously denounced. There is also condemnation of departure from an assumed norm of coital position: the posture *retro* by the man is regularly condemned. The particular penitentials in which these practices are noted are listed below in connection with a consideration of the penances assigned them. If quantity of references is some index of concern, and if concern has some relation to practice, oral and anal intercourse were more common than coitus interruptus.

Of all the penitentials only the seventh-century work of Cummean of Clonfert, which represents a different current from all the others, has nothing on contraception by potion, *maleficium*, or objectionable intercourse in marriage. If *maleficium* includes contraception in the penitentials, evidence of condemnation of contraception goes back to sixth-century Ireland and seventh-century England. If this conclusion is rejected, contraception is first condemned by the penitentials in eighth-century Ireland and the kingdom of the Franks; the condemnations are repeated on the Continent in the ninth, tenth, and eleventh centuries. In view of the small amount of writing in these ages, and the sparseness of surviving documents, this handful of texts is evidence of a consistent opposition to acts preventing conception.

SANCTIONS

Acts preventing conception are invariably treated as serious sins. This spiritual condemnation is the gravest sanction imposed by the penitentials.

In addition to the spiritual condemnation, fixed penances are attached to the sins. It is difficult to say how literally they were applied. The set penances probably give a false impression of rigidity. There must have been much variation in accordance with the quality of devotion of a particular community; it is difficult to believe that seven- or fifteen-year fasts could have been successfully imposed except in very devout areas. As the *De arreis*, an Irish monastic work of the eighth century, shows, a system of commuting the fasts to shorter periods of prayer was eventually invented in Ireland and spread to the continent.[20] As early as Theodore, a range of penalties from seven years to life was specified for the same act; presumably the confessor was free to choose according to his discretion. Some standard mitigations were established, as for the *paupercula*. Burchard distinguished between the "canonical penance" and what he prescribes "according to mercy" (19.5, *PL* 140:952). One may still suppose that, in the heyday of the penitentials, in a devout community built about a monastery, the penalty set for a contraceptive act was regularly applied, even if the fast was then commuted to prayers.

The great value of the prescribed penances, for our investigation, is that they afford some measure of the gravity with which contraception was regarded as compared to other sins. For this reason, in the chart on the next page, which lists the penances prescribed for abortion and for various forms of contraception by eighteen of the penitentials, I have given also the penances imposed for homicide. The periods of time referred to are regularly periods of fasting on bread and water. The numbers designate years unless days are indicated. By embryo I mean here a fetus under forty days. By dorsal intercourse is meant coitus with the woman on top of the man.

From the sampling offered in the chart, some generalizations may be made; I would not contend that more than a rough index to attitudes is provided. Anal or oral intercourse is treated as a serious sin by everyone who mentions such behavior. Many writers prescribe a more serious penance for it than for homicide committed by a layman; without exception, such acts are treated as more serious than the abortion of a fetus under forty days. This discrimination suggests that protection of life is less a motive to the authors of the penitentials than the control of lust.

Why is dorsal intercourse punished at all? The patristic classics had not attacked it as sinful, and, unlike the other forms of objectionable intercourse, it did not preclude procreation. In the light of later medieval commentary, one may guess that a belief was current that it somehow impeded procreation. Hence, the light forty-day penances were assigned, with heavier penances added if procreation was habitually hindered. The punishment of this position as sinful is a development of the notion of what is "natural" in human intercourse. The standard of animal behavior is here rejected; indeed, Burchard attacks the dorsal position contemptuously as "doglike" (*Decretum* 19.49).[21]

The patristic standards are not only developed; there is general indifference to some acts the Fathers had thought sins. Intercourse in

[20] "The Old Irish Table of Commutations," ed. Binchy, in Bieler, ed., *The Irish Penitentials*, p. 277.

[21] *Decretum*, in *Bussordnungen*, ed. Wasserschleben. This text is not in *PL*.

A Comparative Chart of Penances

	Intentional homicide	Abortion	Contraception by potion	Coitus interruptus	Anal intercourse	Oral intercourse	Dorsal intercourse
Finnian (6th century)	7 for cleric (no. 23)	3 if by *maleficium* (no. 19)					
Columban (late 6th c.)		1⅔ if by *maleficium* (B6)					
Theodore (690–710)	7 for layman (1.4.4)	3 40-day periods, or 1 if embryo (1.14.24, 27)				7 or 15 or life (1.2.15)	
Canons of Gregory (690–710)	7 for layman (c. 112)				15 (c. 107; cf. 93)	3 (c. 100)	
Bede (before 735)	4 for layman (4.2)				4 (3.39)		40 days (3.38)
Egbert (ca. 750)	4–5 for layman (4.11)				7 if custom (7.10)		3 if custom (7.10)
Merseburg A (680–780)	10 for cleric (c. 1)						
Merseburg B (680–780)				2 (c. 13)			
Merseburg C (680–780)	7 for fratricide (c. 15)	7 if by *maleficium* (c. 3)					
St. Hubert (680–780)	10 (c. 1)		10 (c. 56)	10 (c. 56)			
Pseudo-Bede (ca. 750)	4 for layman (13.1)	1 (14.1)	7 (15.3)		3 (8.1)		40 days; 7 if custom (8.1, 3)
Old Irish (ca. 780)						5; 7 if custom	
Pseudo-Egbert (ca. 800)	7 (2.1)	7 or 10 (2.2, 4.21)			10 (4.68)	7 or life (4.68,10)	
Halitgar (ca. 830)	3 or 7 for layman (1.1, 4)	3 (7.2); 240 days if by *maleficium* (5.2)					
Pseudo-Theodore (9th century)	life for layman (6.11)	10; 1 if embryo (6.4)			3; 7 if custom (16.19)		1; 3 if custom (16.19)
Pesudo-Cummean (9th century)					15 (3.10, 12)	7 or life (2.14)	40 days (3.11)
Pseudo-Vigila (ca. 850)	22 (c. 27)	4 (cc. 41, 43)	12 (c. 80)		15 days* (c. 57)		
Burchard (ca. 1010)	40 days for 7 (*Interrogatory*)	10 on legal feriae (*Interrogatory*)	10 on legal feriae (*Interrogatory*)		10 (107)		5–40 days (17.56, 59)

* Possibly a scribal error.

pregnancy is warned against by Finnian, but he provides no penalty (c. 46). Pseudo-Theodore gives a forty-day penance for intercourse in the last three months of pregnancy (2.2), but most of the penitentials, including Columban's, which is based on Finnian, ignore the subject. Similarly, Finnian says that a couple who are sterile should observe continence (c. 41); but he gives no penalty. His rule is repeated only by Cummean 2.28 and by Pseudo-Vigila 68. The other penitentials are silent. The indifference to these two topics represents a rejection of the Augustinian insistence on procreative purpose. None of the penitentials here reviewed deals with the absence of procreative purpose as a sin. The failure of Augustine to win more support in this area might be due to the continuation in Celtic ecclesiastical circles of a strain of Pelagian optimism. Pope John IV felt it necessary to write the Irish bishops in 640 to decry "the poison of the Pelagian heresy" which was "reviving among you." He solemnly warned them that man could not avoid sin without God's grace; he added the words of Psalm 50, "in sins my mother bore me" (John, *Letter*, in Bede, *Ecclesiastical History* 2.19).

A similar independence of patristic lore is shown in the general treatment of intercourse in menstruation as a light sin. A forty-day penance is set for it in the *Canons of Gregory* 107, Bede 3.37, *Merseburg A* 96, Pseudo-Cummean 3.13. A thirty-day penance is set by Pseudo-Theodore 2.2.5 and a mere twenty days by the *Old Irish Penitential* 2.36. This leniency toward what Jerome considered a major sin affords an instructive comparison with the reception accorded his stricture against "drinking sterility."

Contraceptive potion drinking is always treated as a serious sin by those who deal with it, but no clear pattern of comparative severity emerges. *Merseburg B* 13 and Pseudo-Vigila 80 show that such an act was not always punished as homicide, even though Pseudo-Vigila 45 uses a variant of the formula "so many conceptions prevented, so many homicides." Occasionally, as in Pseudo-Bede 15.3 and in Burchard, such potion drinking is treated as worse than premeditated homicide.

Even more inconsistency appears in the prescription of penance for the performance of sterilizing *maleficium* or "cheating of offspring." Some authors apparently assimilate this act to contraception (Pseudo-Bede 15.3), others to homicide (*Merseburg C* 3). Generally, it seems to receive a somewhat lesser penalty than an aggressive act toward another adult, probably on the theory that it is less sinful to sterilize oneself than to sterilize another (Finnian 20, Columban 20, *Merseburg A* 10, *St. Hubert* 11, Pseudo-Theodore 6.6).

Despite a lack of scientific precision or thorough consistency, the general pattern is, I suggest, clear. Selectively, the penitentials have drawn on the Fathers to condemn conduct thwarting procreation. Analysis is not attempted; the term "nature" is not used. But a standard of natural marital intercourse is implicitly invoked. Departures from it preventing procreation are major sins. Contraception by potion is treated like homicide, although not as identical with it; the life-giving process is to be free from interference. The opposition to magic plays a part, but a subordinate part, in this opposition to contraception.

In addition to the sanctions of penance, other kinds of sanctions may be seen operative in the penitentials. They employ the sanction, as much social as spiritual, of classifying the use of potions or sterilizing *maleficium* as "homicide." This course is chosen in the *Irish Collection*, Pseudo-Vigila, *Martène*, and Burchard. Equally evocative descriptions are applied to the objectionable forms of marital intercourse. Theodore puts anal intercourse on a par with intercourse with animals and describes oral intercourse as "the worst of evils" (1.14.22, 1.2.15). Bede classifies anal intercourse as "sodomitic crime" (3.39).

This type of sanction by categorization had been used by the Fathers. A different type of sanction now appears for the first time: inquiry. In a secular legal system, inquiry would usually be considered only a prelude to sanction, although even secular interrogations have sometimes appeared punitive in themselves. In a spiritual system, it seems proper to understand inquiry as itself a sanction: deterrence of sin is aimed at when a potential sin is asked about; and actual sin receives a preliminary punishment in being the subject of inquiry.

The use of inquiry as this sort of spiritual sanction becomes common only with the growth of private confession and penance in the West. The penitentials provided not only a tariff of penances, but a list of sins about which confessors could interrogate their penitents. Some interrogation probably was customary before an injunction to inquire was expressed in writing. It is not, however, until the eighth century that there is evidence of explicit instruction to a confessor to inquire about contraception. Then, in Pseudo-Bede, in the "Order for Giving Penance," 30, the confessor is told to ask the penitent, "Have you drunk any *maleficium,* that is herbs or other agents, so that you could not have children, or have you given it to another . . . ?" Theodulphus, the early ninth-century bishop of Orléans, instructs his priests to inquire in confession about fornication, a sin which includes coitus interruptus in his legislation.[22]

The fullest evidence of confessional interrogation is late, in the early-eleventh-century *Decretum* of Burchard. His entire nineteenth book is on penance, and here he advises confessors as to the questions they should "mildly and gently" ask (19.4, PL 140:950). He has nothing relevant in his questions on homicide, but he comes to a set of interrogatories which "specially pertain to women." Here follow inquiries on lesbianism, stimu-

[22] De Clerq, *La Législation religieuse,* I, 338.

lation of the vagina by instruments, bestiality, and incest, culminating in the question on abortion and contraception quoted earlier. It would seem unlikely that the question described by him was put in these exact terms to any penitent. But it would seem probable that where time and opportunity permitted, and reason for suspicion existed, a priest instructed by Burchard would have asked a woman penitent about her involvement with contraception.

A different type of inquiry, public rather than private, seems to be envisaged by Regino of Prüm. In his tenth-century work, a bishop is given questions to ask on a pastoral visit to a village of his diocese. The bishop is to question: "Is there any woman who has killed her own husband or any man by poisoned herbs or deadly potions, or taught another to do this? Is there any man or any woman who has done this so that a man cannot generate or a woman conceive, or who has taught another to do such a thing?" (*Churchly Disciplines and the Christian Religion* 2.5.8–9, PL 132:282).

There is also the development of sanctions against cooperators in contraception. Martin of Braga's version of Ancyra had begun this effort to reach the accomplices. In every case where sterilizing *maleficium* is not hostile magic, but an effort to achieve sterility desired by the woman affected, there is cooperation in the woman's sin; the penitentials reach this cooperation by treating the *maleficium* as sinful, although usually less serious than taking a potion oneself. Pseudo-Bede 15.3 treats as equally guilty the consumer and giver of herbal potions. Regino and Burchard go even further, at least by their terms, reaching not only the accomplice in the act, but one who has "taught" how to commit abortion or contraception; the penalty Burchard sets is the same as for the act itself (19, *PL* 140:972). If Regino and Burchard are taken literally, their questions on "teaching" are the first explicit ecclesiastical efforts to control the dissemination of contraceptive information.

THE INFLUENCE OF THE PENITENTIALS

The penitentials are important evidence on the state of the teaching on contraception for a period of six centuries. Blunt, vigorous in doctrine, and unsubtle in articulation, they are testimony to the dominant ecclesiastical opinion in this vast span; they are some indication of what was taught the Christian people and of what married couples may have learned to believe.[23]

[23] The penitentials also had an influence on the Eastern Church. Early twentieth-century Russian Orthodox writers speculated that the penitentials found in the medieval Orthodox church came originally from Eastern sources, but the prevalent opinion today appears to be that the ninth-century apostles of the Slavs, Saints Cyril and Methodius, brought with them versions of the Carolingian penitentials.

The single most influential legacy of this period for the doctrine on contraception is a text which will become, in the thirteenth century, canon law as the decretal *Si aliquis*. The text incorporates many of the factors we have examined separately. It is first encountered in Regino of Prüm, after he has listed questions to be asked by the bishop on his pastoral visitation. Regino states:

If someone [*Si aliquis*] to satisfy his lust or in deliberate hatred does something to a man or woman so that no children be born of him or her, or gives them to drink, so that he cannot generate or she conceive, let it be held as homicide."

(*Churchly Disciplines and the Christian Religion* 2.89, PL 132:301)

It is not clear in this context that the contraceptive act condemned may occur in marriage. "To satisfy his lust" might suggest fornication accompanied by contraception. Yet one might be believed to act lustfully by using contraceptives in marital intercourse. "In deliberate hatred" refers to hostile magic. The phrase is roughly equivalent to "with malice aforethought," and in this sense is used in other canons to describe intentional murder (e.g., *ibid.* 2.95, PL 132:302). It is unclear if the text applies to self-sterilization; it seems more naturally to read as directed only toward the sterilizing of another person, so that the person condemned by the text is the purveyor of contraceptives or the spouse who urges a contraceptive potion on his mate. "Do something" seems intended

---

H. F. Schmid, "Pénitentiels byzantins et occidentaux," *Actes du VI Congrès international d'études byzantines* (Paris, 1950), pp. 359–363.

The earliest Greek penitential (erroneously attributed to John the Abstainer, a sixth-century patriarch of Constantinople) was written sometime between the end of the eighth century and the end of the tenth century (Emil Herman, S.J., "Il più antico penitenziale greco," *Orientalia christiana periodica* 19 (1953), 71, 85. One version of this work denounces as a very serious sin "the drinking of a drug, as a result of which one cannot further procreate" (*Penitential*, PG 88:1904).

A penitential of the Armenian Church, written by David of Ganjak (d. 1140) in Caucasian Albania, has a strong denunciation of coitus interruptus: "Certain evil men, in the course of fornication or in order to spite their wives, act contrary to Creation, that is, they spill the seed of procreation which the Lord established for the increase [of His creatures], which act is cursed by the church of God. If anyone is possessed by the Evil One and does this many times, he shall be classed among the murderers. But the vardapets, considering his heavy penance, may reduce the period." *The Penitential of David of Ganjak,* trans. C. J. F. Dowsett (*Corpus scriptorum christianorum orientalium* CCXVII; Louvain, 1961), no. 54. David also says that "unmarried prostitutes who take drugs to prevent pregnancy are counted among those who kill their child in the womb," while "sterile women who take drugs to induce pregnancy shall repent one year, for God is the Creator of nature" (*ibid.,* no. 53).

David's editor, Dowsett, thinks it unlikely that he had any direct contact with Anglo-Saxon or Irish penitentials. Would this Armenian work reflect an older Eastern tradition? The statement on the use of drugs by prostitutes is not far from St. John Chrysostom, *On Matthew* 5; the statement on coitus interruptus as a way of "spiting one's wife" is not far from St. Ephraem's description of the act as "a bitter trick."

as a vague and comprehensive inclusion of sterilizing *maleficium*. "Give to drink" specifies the usual form of contraception, and is the only means specified in the interrogatory for the bishop which has the parallel questions (above, page 167). The established categorization of such acts as homicide completes the condemnation.

The subsequent popularity of *Si aliquis* is owed not to Regino but to Burchard. Almost a century later, he incorporated this text in his *Decretum*, describing it as "canon 30 of the Council of Worms" (17.57, *PL* 140:933). Worms was an important ecclesiastical center in Carolingian times, and the meeting place over several centuries for the synods of neighboring bishops. It is possible that a synod enacted *Si aliquis;* the text has a legal form. The nearest approximation to the subject, however, is canon 35 of the Council of Worms of 868, and this canon, as preserved, deals only with abortion (Mansi 15:876). It may be urged that the records of these gatherings are not complete, and that Burchard, as bishop of the conciliar meeting place, may have had access to a text now lost. In any event, with the extra weight of synodal authority attached to it by Burchard, *Si aliquis* was known to the later Middle Ages.

Burchard also made one significant contribution to the understanding of *Si aliquis*. He did not treat it as primarily governing a magical process or primarily concerned with hostile sterilization: he did not put it in the book "On Incantations and Auguries" nor in the book "On Homicide." He treated it as a canon involving a sexual offense, by placing it in the book "On Fornication." By this arrangement Burchard seems to make the canon relate only to contraception outside of marriage. However, he did not himself understand it so narrowly. Where he prescribes interrogation for the sin of contraception, he does not restrict the inquiry to unmarried women (*Decretum* 19, "Interrogatory," *PL* 140:972).

Si aliquis came from the penitentials, and it was preserved in the law of the Catholic Church until 1917. Its emphasis on potions, its vague reference to magic, its classification of contraception as homicide, and its use to condemn sexual sin — all these aspects faithfully reflected the approach of the penitentials to the subject. In this chief text there was a concentration of elements characteristic of the monastic era.

A traceable legacy, *Si aliquis* is only a symbol of the greater impact of the whole teaching of the monks on married sexuality. For six centuries the canons and the penitentials had expressed a code of behavior which the monks both as writers and as bishops had attempted to inculcate. Their efforts were not without fruit in forming the consciousness and the conscience of the new Europe. Their work was not so abstract or so unresponsive to real problems as to repel the pastors who used it. The teaching of the patristic age was transmitted, the basic role of procreation in marriage was preserved. But while transmitted, the teaching was transformed into a code, a code with new elements and emphases. When the theologians of a more speculative age came to consider questions of marital morality, they found already established in theological opinion and, it may be inferred, in popular belief, that oral or anal intercourse was horrible, that the dorsal posture for the male was objectionable, that contraceptive potions had magical associations and were evil. The resulting rules on sexual conduct were so deeply ingrained that the theologians of the twelfth and thirteenth centuries seemed to have no option. They had to rationalize what they had received. When joined to a revived Augustinianism, the lessons of the monks, so long and so vigorously inculcated, formed a marital morality not easy to dislodge.

CHAPTER VI

THE CANONISTS, THE CATHARS,
AND ST. AUGUSTINE

ARTIN OF BRAGA and Burchard of Worms had put out prohibitions of contraception purporting to be the work of councils.
Their work had circulated with considerable authority; but these episcopal
collections were not actions of the pope or the universal Church. A new
stage was arrived at when a canon against contraception appeared in
a papally authorized collection. In the development from the late-eleventh
to the mid-thirteenth century this new peak of opposition to contraception was reached.

Three factors played a part in the development. They were the tradition incorporated in the penitential and conciliar documents of the past;
the rebirth of Augustinianism; and the reaction to the Cathars. All three
elements, I suggest, were indispensable in determining the positions
finally taken. In one respect, the development which occurred was only
a continuation of the procedure of the preceding centuries: it consisted
in the collecting and republishing of venerable authorities. But there was
a difference. The collections were made with increasing theological and
legal sophistication. The collectors were becoming aware of the need to
choose among authorities and to reconcile conflicts among canons and
among Fathers. The new sophistication was associated with a greater
familiarity with patristic writings, and it was accompanied by the emergence of Augustine as a dominant authority. The Augustinian analysis
of marriage now tended to supplant the meager teaching of the penitentials. The doctrine on contraception would not have been what it
was if the penitentials, the canonical collections, and Augustine had not
existed. It would not have been focused in the fashion it was focused if
the Cathars had not challenged the basic assumptions of the Christian
sexual ethic.

THE DEVELOPMENT OF THE *LOCI CLASSICI*

As theology began to become again an object of study, a new collection of authorities was made by Ivo, bishop of Chartres from 1091 to 1116. An active churchman, devoted to the great cause of the Gregorian reform, Ivo was apparently dissatisfied with the *Decretum* of Burchard. About 1094, he set out to make a bigger and more contemporary *Decretum*, incorporating most of Burchard and the newer legislative texts and organizing them in a fashion more responsive to the needs of the day.[1] Burchard was no longer to provide the authorizations. On sexual morals, the chief reliance of Ivo was on Augustine. He dropped *Si aliquis* and instead used five Augustinian texts. The most important of these was a verbatim quotation from Augustine's *Marriage and Concupiscence* denouncing the use of "poisons of sterility" (*Decretum* 10.55, PL 161:706, quoting the passage translated above, p. 136, beginning with the word *Aliquando*). Augustine's polemic, detached from its context, was given in the form of legislation. The passage was now presented as a canon, to be henceforth designated, from its opening word, as *Aliquando*. Ivo thereby put into the stream of theological speculation a classic and neglected denunciation of artificial contraception; at the same time, he implicitly advanced the view that contraception was a sin against marriage, not a form of homicide.

A second text from Augustine, an expressly anti-Manichean statement from *Against Faustus* (quoted above, p. 122) was reproduced by the *Decretum*: as Manichees eliminate children from marriage, Manichean "husbands are shameful lovers, wives are harlots" (*Decretum* 8.82, PL 161:601). A third canon against contraception in general was made by a repetition of Martin of Braga's version of the canon of Ancyra (*Decretum* 10.181, PL 161:744).

Ivo also took three texts from Augustine directed at unnatural intercourse in marriage; the formula, used twice to describe the sin, is "use of a member not granted for this" (9.110, 128, PL 161:687, 690). A broader passage made a fusion of *Marriage and Concupiscence* 2.20 and *Against the Second Answer of Julian* 5.17 under the caption, "It is more serious to sin against nature than to commit adultery (Augustine, *Against Julian*)": "A use which is natural and lawful in marriage is unlawful in adultery. To act against nature is always unlawful and beyond doubt more flagrant and shameful than to sin by a natural use in fornication or adultery, as the Holy Apostle contends as to both men and women" (*Decretum* 9.106, PL 161:685–686). This language was comprehensive

[1] On the date, authenticity, and intentions of the *Decretum*, see Paul Fournier and Gabriel Le Bras, *Histoire des collections canoniques en Occident* (Paris, 1931), II, 82, 105–106, 113–114.

enough to cover not only use of an unnatural part of the body for intercourse, but also coitus interruptus. It probably should be understood as
condemning any intercourse where the form of the sexual act prevented
insemination.

The work of Ivo was one milestone in the formation of the canonical
approach to contraception. It brought to the attention of the new theological schools the canon which, with the ancient prestige of Ancyra, condemned contraception. More importantly it brought to the subject the
declarations of Augustine. At the beginning of a new era for Western
theology Augustine's words upon the prevention of conception were set
forth as the rule. Ivo or his school made *Aliquando* yet more available in
another collection of canons, the *Collection of Three Parts* (3.20.15). It
was also embodied in the *Caesaraugustan Collection* (4.63), compiled
1100–1120 in Languedoc or Northern Spain.[2]

In the first half of the twelfth century the old view of contraception
as homicide was also current. As the reform movement gathered strength
in Italy with German support, the *Decretum* of Burchard was widely
used.[3] Here *Si aliquis* was the principal text against contraception. At
the crucial date in the middle of the century when the most influential
collections of texts were made, the editor-compilers could have chosen
Si aliquis, Aliquando, Martin of Braga's version of Ancyra, or some other
text among the several in Ivo and Burchard relating to contraceptive
behavior. They chose *Aliquando.*

The decisive collections and the critical decisions were made by two
men: the Camaldolese monk, Gratian, and the bishop of Paris, Peter
Lombard. Their choice of patristic and conciliar lore, organized in the
way they thought appropriate, with the emphases, questions, and comments they believed germane, was to be the staple fare for centuries for
canonists and theologians. Gratian finished his compilation at Bologna
about 1140. Peter, another north-Italian, completed his work in Paris between 1154 and 1157, and often followed Gratian's lead; but Peter was
judicious enough in picking and choosing from Gratian to make his selective approval of a text in Gratian carry independent weight.[4] As an un-
official but universally accepted compilation of canonical authority,
Gratian's *Harmony of Discordant Canons,* popularly known as the *De-*

---

[2] See, on *The Collection of Three Parts* or *Tripartita, ibid.,* II, 104–105; on the
Caesaraugustan Collection, ibid., II, 283–284.

[3] See J. Joseph Ryan, *St. Peter Damiani and His Canonical Sources* (Toronto,
1956), pp. 160–162.

[4] Peter Lombard came to France in 1134 and stayed at Rheims, where he won the
friendship of St. Bernard (Bernard, *Letters* 410, *PL* 182:618–619). He moved on to
Paris to continue his studies, and by 1142 was a master of renown. The composition
of the *Sentences* proceeded as he taught. It seems now established that the definitive
form of the work was achieved between 1154 and 1157. See Philippe Delhaye,
Pierre Lombard: Sa vie, ses oeuvres, sa morale (Montreal, 1961), pp. 14–23.

cretum, was to be treated as part of the basic law of the Western Church until the enactment of the new *Code of Canon Law* in 1917.[5] As the textbook of theology commonly used in the universities until about 1550, Peter's *Sentences* was of about equal influence in theology; over twelve hundred theological treatises are commentaries on the *Sentences.*[6] Lombard's work made *Aliquando* familiar to every student of theology, as Gratian's made it known to every student of canon law. If Augustine is the most important single authority on contraception, and if a single statement of his is to be taken as the epitome of his doctrine, then the use of *Aliquando* by Gratian and Lombard is the most important teaching on contraception in the Middle Ages.

The text is presented in both under almost identical headings. Gratian's heading is "They are Fornicators, Not Spouses, Who Procure Poisons of Sterility" (*Decretum* 2.32.2.7). Lombard's lead sentence is "Those who indeed procure poisons of sterility are not spouses but fornicators" (*Sentences* 4.31.3).[7] Each embeds the text in a discussion of the Augustinian goods of marriage, and each follows it with a chapter on abortion. The effect is to distinguish carefully the specific fault of contraception from the specific fault of abortion, and to place centrally within the teaching on marriage Augustine's passionate rejection of contraception as destructive of the marital relation. Although the text is not elaborated beyond the headnote, nor buttressed by other explicit patristic or canonical testimony, one could not ask for a more basic condemnation, or one more strategically placed, than *Aliquando* as it appears in the *Decretum* and the *Sentences.*

Gratian and Lombard also dealt with marital behavior where the form of the sexual act precludes insemination. Gratian composed the canon *Adulterii malum,* with this introduction, paralleling Augustine and Ivo: "The evil of adultery [*Adulterii malum*] surpasses fornication, but is surpassed by incest; for it is worse to sleep with one's mother than with another man's wife. But the worst of all of these things is what is done contrary to nature, as when a man wishes to use a member of his wife not conceded for this" (2.32.7.11). The passage concludes with an exact quotation of Augustine from *The Good of Marriage* (above, p. 131, the three sentences beginning "The natural use"). The apparent focus is on anal and oral intercourse, but the quotation from Augustine speaks broadly of any marital intercourse "against nature," and this phraseology

[5] On the peculiar status of Gratian, see Stephan Kuttner, *Harmony from Dissonance: An Interpretation of Medieval Canon Law* (Latrobe, Penn., 1960), pp. 15, 27.

[6] F. Stegmüller, *Repertorium commentariorum in Sententias Petri Lombardi* (Würzburg, 1947).

[7] The editions used are: Gratian, *Decretum,* in *Corpus juris canonici,* ed. Emil Friedberg, 2 vols. (Leipzig, 1879–1881); Peter Lombard, *Libri IV Sententiarum,* ed. the Fathers of the College of St. Bonaventure, 2nd ed. (Quaracchi, 1916).

may have been sufficient to include coitus interruptus. The text is placed by Gratian in a discussion of the "degrees of fornication." Lombard adopted *Adulterii malum* and awkwardly tucked it into a chapter on "vows" where the marriage vow happened to be discussed (4.38.2). In neither Lombard nor Gratian is *Adulterii malum* as strategically placed to provoke analysis as *Aliquando*.

The attention of both Gratian and Lombard to contraception stands out in some contrast to the neglect of the topic by one other standard work and by several immediate theological predecessors. What was to be accepted after about 1150 as the *Glossa ordinaria,* or usual commentary accompanying the Bible, had only the allegorical comment on Genesis 38:7–10, the story of Onan, which Bede and Augustine had made: Onan represents the man who is useless because he does not use the goods he has.[8] A similar silence on contraception characterized the work of such active theologians of the next generation as Hugh of St. Victor (d. 1141) and Peter Abelard (d. 1142). Walter of Mortagne, who wrote slightly before Lombard and was much used by him, had a single sentence condemning unnatural intercourse with "any woman" (*Summa of the Sentences* 7.3, *PL* 176:156).[9]

Why did Gratian and Lombard take up the question at all? It would be easy to say that Gratian merely followed texts he had at hand in existing collections of canons, and that Lombard followed Gratian. But why was Lombard interested in the problem when Walter of Mortagne, from whom he had drawn most of his material on marriage, said so little on the subject?[10] Why did Gratian prefer the broad language of *Aliquando* on contraception and marriage to the more juridical text of *Si aliquis* making contraception murder? No certain answer can be given. If *Aliquando* had not been in the earlier canonical collections, it would not have been in the great collections. But its appearance, as I shall attempt to show shortly, is not unrelated to the spread of Catharism.

In the development following Gratian, there are only small additions to the analysis by the new kind of ecclesiastical writers who are self-consciously canonists. The *Paris Summa* (circa 1170), a commentary on Gratian, lets the citation of *Aliquando* pass without comment or explanation.[11] The *Summa* by Paucapalea of the same period is similarly silent.[12] But Rufinus, bishop of Assisi, in his *Summa decretorum,* cites *Si aliquis*

---

[8] The Gloss was formerly ascribed to Anselm of Laon. It is now recognized to be the work of his pupil, Gilbert the Universal, later Bishop of London, and others. See Beryl Smalley, *The Study of the Bible in the Middle Ages* (Oxford, 1952), p. 60.

[9] On Walter of Mortagne and his authorship of Book 7 of the *Summa,* see Marcel Chossat, *La Somme des Sentences* (Louvain, 1923), p. 71.

[10] On Lombard's use of Walter, see Claude Schahl, *La Doctrine des fins du mariage dans la théologie scholastique* (Paris, 1948), p. 60.

[11] *Summa parisiensis,* ed. Terence McLaughlin (Toronto, 1952).

[12] *Die Summa des Paucapalea,* ed. J. F. von Schulte (Giessen, 1891).

while expounding *Aliquando* (2.32.2.7).[13] The greatest of commentators on Gratian, Huguccio, writing a little later, has a full explication of the text (*Summa* 2.32.2.7).[14] *Aliquando*, he makes clear, deals with three cases: the first is contraception; the second, abortion within the first months of pregnancy; the third, abortion in the final stages of pregnancy. *Si aliquis*, he finds, is also relevant. Huguccio's work may be merely the kind of exposition and collation to be expected of a careful commentator, but more probably his attention to the canon reflects a perception of current problems. The standard *Gloss* on Gratian, an early-thirteenth-century work, is very close to Huguccio, except that it omits the cross-reference to *Si aliquis* (2.32.2.7).[15]

Despite their mention of *Si aliquis*, both Huguccio and Rufinus understand that the basic offense of contraception is its destruction of the goods of marriage. The users of the poisons of sterility "do not commit the crime of fornication; . . . conducting themselves in the manner of fornicators, they are no less guilty than fornicators" (Rufinus, *Summa* 2.32.2.7). They "are judged as adulterers in that they do not want children to be born" (Huguccio, *Summa* 2.32.2.7). Concerned to link the use of contraceptives with an effect on marriage, Huguccio makes what is his most dramatic contribution to the development of canon law on contraception, the suggestion of a new sanction. Augustine had stated that the users of the poisons of sterility were not truly married. Should one conclude that their marriage is null? No, says Huguccio, the marriage remains valid if the intention to use the poisons arose after marriage. But antecedent intention is different. "If both were such from the beginning of the marriage," they had an intention radically opposed to the substance of marriage. Consequently, "there was no marriage between them." The corrupt intention made entry into marriage impossible, just as a monk could not enter the monastic state vowing monastic poverty but adding the condition that he keep some property for himself (*Summa* 2.32.2.7).

There is one ambiguity in this analysis. Building on the words of Augustine, Huguccio emphasizes antecedent intention to use the poisons; but he speaks of the intention as held by both. Does he mean an actual mutual agreement to the use of the poisons rather than a private intention? Elsewhere, he speaks of a "condition or agreement on the extinguishing or avoiding of offspring" (*Summa* 2.32.2.4). It seems probable that, for him, the intention of "both" is equivalent to an agreement; but he does not explore the possible distinction.

The *Glossa ordinaria* on Gratian follows Huguccio's language on the nullifying effect of an agreement, antecedent to marriage, to prevent off-

---

[13] Rufinus, *Summa decretorum*, ed. Heinrich Singer (Paderborn, 1902).

[14] MS, Munich, Staatsbibliothek, Cod. lat. 10247.

[15] *Glossa ordinaria*, *Corpus juris canonici* (Venice, 1605).

spring by poisons of sterility (2.32.2.4). Bernard of Pavia, writing a collection of decretals between 1191 and 1198, refers in addition to the nullifying effect of a promise to "avoid children by evil acts" (*Summa* 4.5).[16] In the early thirteenth century, an important theologian at Paris, Robert of Courçon, again refers to a promise "to procure poisons of sterility"; such a promise nullifies a marriage.[17]

The controlling force of *Aliquando* in theological circles is illustrated by a case put by Peter Cantor, one of the masters of theological disputation in late-twelfth-century Paris. A woman has suffered a rupture of the navel (*umbilicus*) in a previous childbirth. The doctors say that if she bears another child, she will die. May she "procure sterility" for herself? Peter resolves this difficult case brusquely: "This last thing is not at all lawful, because this would be to procure poisons of sterility; that is prohibited in every case." [18] Peter does not cite the canon by name, but as he develops no rationale for his answer and rejects the woman's case so bluntly, he must consider *Aliquando* dispositive.

Contemporaneously with the canonical commentary on Gratian, the modern literature for priests hearing confession continued to follow the approach of earlier works of this genre by using *Si aliquis*. In the *Penitential* of Bartholomew (1140–1184), bishop of Exeter, *Si aliquis* is appended to the true text of Ancyra under the heading "Those Committing Abortion." [19] Apparently Bartholomew derived *Si aliquis* from Burchard, for he refers to it as the act of the Council of Worms. Another slightly later use of *Si aliquis* was made about 1200 by Robert of Flamborough, a penitentiary of the abbey of St. Victor in Paris. This experienced confessor cites it in his *Penances and Confessions*.[20]

---

[16] Bernard of Pavia, *Summa decretalium*, ed. E. Laspeyres (Regensburg, 1860). Gandulf, a predecessor of Huguccio at Bologna, speaks of "a pact to procure poisons of sterility" as nullifying; he quotes *Aliquando*. *Magistri Gandulphi Bononiensis sententiarum libri quatuor*, ed. Johannes von Walter (Vienna, 1924), 4.223, pp. 510–511.

[17] Robert of Courçon, *Summa theologica*, Paris, Bibliothèque Nationale, MS. 15524, fol. 132r, quoted by Pedro Abellán, *El fin y la significación sacramental del matrimonio desde S. Anselmo haste Guillermo de Auxerre* (Granada, 1939), p. 105.

[18] Peter Cantor, *Summa de sacramentis* 350, ed. Jean-A. Dugauquier (Louvain, 1965), III², 463–464. In *Quaestiones et miscellanea e schola Petri Cantoris* (W manuscript, fol. 188r; edition in preparation by Jean-A. Dugauquier), it is reported that Peter Cantor's opinion on the case mentioned was given in order to counter "the opinion of some saying that the woman could procure poison of sterility and so return the debt when she was certain that she could not conceive." The reason given here for Peter's answer is that she "would be the killer of her own offspring." Professor Dugauquier has not been able to identify the "some" who held that poison of sterility might be used. I am indebted to Professor Dugauquier for the citations to these works, both of which are in the process of publication.

[19] Bartholomew, *Penitential*, ed. Adrian Morey in his *Bartholomew of Exeter* (Cambridge, Eng., 1937), p. 61.

[20] Robert of Flamborough, *Liber de penitentiis et confessionibus* 5.259, "Those Preventing the Conceptus," in the manuscript being used for an edition in prepara-

In 1230, the Dominican Raymond of Pennaforte began, at the direction of Pope Gregory IX, to make a collection of authoritative decrees; modified from time to time, his work was to become the law of the Catholic Church for the next 685 years. Raymond drew heavily on Burchard's *Decretum*. In the new *Decretals* he adopted *Si aliquis* with a slight variation in word order and inserted it as chapter 5 of book V, title 12, "Voluntary and Chance Homicide." It read as follows:

HE WHO DOES MAGIC OR GIVES POISONS OF STERILITY IS A HOMICIDE.

If anyone to satisfy his lust or in meditated hatred does something to a man or woman or gives something to drink so that he cannot generate, or she conceive, or offspring be born, let him be held a homicide.[21]

With the inclusion of *Si aliquis* in this papally sponsored law for the universal Church, the official opposition to contraception reached its apogee.

Like *Aliquando*, the canon focused on artificial, external means of preventing reproduction. Texts referring to coitus interruptus — such as Augustine on the sin of Onan in *Adulterous Marriages* — were ignored. The legislation was not against all nonprocreative intercourse, but against the use of artificial contraceptive means.

Raymond and Gregory completed their work on contraception by adding a new decretal, probably composed by Raymond and approved by Gregory. Its place in book IV of the *Decretals* suggests its derivation from Bernard of Pavia, whose book IV had a title, "Conditions Set in Marrying," which treated the condition, "You will avoid children by evil arts," as a condition "indecent and repugnant to the substance of marriage." To show that this condition nullified the marriage, Bishop Bernard appealed to *Aliquando* and to a number of texts from the Roman law, of which the most relevant was *Digest* 17.2.3, teaching that a partnership was null which was entered into with a fraudulent intent excluding good faith (*Summa of Decretals* 4.5.3). The new decretal, now issued by the Pope, was entitled "Conditions Set." It read:

If conditions [*Si conditiones*] are set against the substance of marriage — for example, if one says to the other, "I contract with you if you avoid offspring," or "until I find someone more worthy in honor or riches," or "if you give yourself over to adultery for money" — the matrimonial contract, as much as it is favored, lacks effect; although other conditions set in matrimony, if

---

tion by Francis Firth, C.S.B., to whom I am indebted for the exact text. For Robert's use of Huguccio, Bartholomew of Exeter, and Ivo of Chartres, see Francis Firth, "The 'Poenitentiale' of Robert of Flamborough," *Traditio* 16 (1960), 550.

[21] *Corpus juris canonici*, ed. Friedberg. In Burchard, "or offspring [cannot] be born" is governed by "does something"; here it is governed by both "does something" and "gives something to drink."

they are base or impossible, ought, because of the favor for marriage, to be held as if not added. (*Decretals* 4.5.7)

The schematization of the canon is clear: an instance is given contrary to each of the three goods of marriage — offspring, sacramental indissolubility, fidelity. Huguccio's specific reference to an agreement to use poisons of sterility has been broadened to the more comprehensive, if less concrete, agreement "to avoid offspring."

The course of development which finally leads to papal adoption of *Si aliquis* can be regarded as a purely literary sequence in which an oft-repeated text receives the ultimate recognition of incorporation in the *Decretals*. The papal creation of *Si conditiones* may be explained as adaptation of the work of Bernard of Pavia. A similar explanation of the use of *Aliquando* by Ivo, Gratian, and Peter Lombard is possible: the text can be understood as used because it was there, the authoritative voice of a revered ancestor. This simple explanation is not without merit in accounting for the action of writers with immense respect for past authority. Yet it does not wholly explain why interest existed in the problem confronted by the texts, or why, when selection was made — and each compiler exercised choice in his compilation — these particular texts were chosen.

Respect for tradition was not only directed toward preservation of the past; when a new situation had to be met, an ancient text, if roughly appropriate, was preferred to new legislation. Law itself was regarded as a static, given rule, which was "discovered" in the past. The tradition of the Church, as theology understood it, was a fixed deposit. Both jurisprudential and theological views combined to favor use of ancient authority where a new problem had arisen. If old texts were used, it was not simply because they were old and available; it was because they were old and relevant to a new situation. In the case of the canons on contraception the old formulas were relevant for one prime reason: the re-emergence of religious groups opposed to procreation.

THE OPPONENTS OF PROCREATION

In the early tenth century, Bogomil, a Bulgarian priest, had articulated a form of Gnostic doctrine whose dualist opposition to the material world entailed an opposition to procreation. The connection of this doctrine with earlier Gnosticism or with Manicheanism appears to lie in doctrinal similarities, not in direct descent.[22] Bogomil found disciples in Bulgaria, and his followers were soon organized as a church. From Bulgaria, Bogomilism spread to the Eastern Empire's capital, Constantinople, and then

---

[22] Henri-Charles Puech and André Vaillant, *Le Traité contre les Bogomiles de Cosmas le prêtre*, Travaux publiés par l'Institut d'Etudes Slaves, No. 21 (Paris, 1945), p. 28.

swept westward to Bosnia.[23] By the early eleventh century there were religious teachers in western Europe whose doctrine was largely derived from the Bogomils.[24]

A rash of reports by chroniclers testify to the presence of heretics opposing procreation. A "Manichean" is reported in Aquitaine in 1018. What we can now identify as Bogomil doctrine, and a specific denial of marriage, is observed in early-eleventh-century Orléans. In Arras, sometime before 1025, an Italian, Gandulf, is preaching the rejection of marriage. At Monteforte, between Turin and Genoa, an organized community appears where marriage is discouraged, and where a married man is to treat his wife as a mother or sister. In Châlons about 1045 heretics opposing marriage appear.[25]

Other reports of heretics are less specific, but it is conjectured that they, too, represent Bogomil influence. Thus heretics with "secret doctrine" are reported in Toulouse in 1022.[26] The Council of Rheims in 1049, a gathering of some twenty bishops and almost fifty abbots, presided over by the Pope himself, Leo IX, excommunicated "the new heretics who have emerged in Gallic territory" and those who accepted office from them, gave service to them, or defended them. "It equally condemned the sodomites" (Mansi 19:742). In 1056 eighteen bishops at Toulouse excommunicated those having "participation or association with the heretics and the excommunicated" and those attempting to defend them (Mansi 19:849).

Between 1056 and 1100 there is no information on the heretics. It has been conjectured that the chroniclers lost interest in the subject, or that reform movements in the Church attracted men who would have continued the heresy, or that the heretics kept quiet and proselytized discreetly.[27] It seems to me that the last alternative is the most probable, especially in the light of twelfth-century developments. Whatever the true explanation of the silence is, a heresy with Bogomil tendencies could not have seemed a major problem at the time Ivo of Chartres made his collection of canons. His collection puts no special emphasis on the anti-

[23] Steven Runciman, The Medieval Manichee, A Study of the Christian Dualist Heresy (Cambridge, Eng., 1947), pp. 117–120.

[24] Arno Borst, Die Katharer, Schriften der Monumenta Germaniae Historica, 12 (Stuttgart, 1953), pp. 71, 72, 77.

[25] Ibid., pp. 74–79.

[26] Ibid., p. 74.

[27] The alternatives are discussed by Borst, pp. 80–82. He favors the second, and rejects a strict continuity between the eleventh- and twelfth-century movements.

I have followed Borst in applying the term "Cathars" only to the twelfth-century heretics. What I emphasize is the continuity of the orthodox reaction to attacks on marriage. This orthodox stand is all the more understandable if Borst's theory is not accepted, and one follows Antoine Dondaine in seeing a continuity between eleventh- and twelfth-century movements. "L'origine de l'hérésie médiévale," Rivista di storia della chiesa in Italia 6 (1952), 57, 63.

Manichean texts. At the same time, writing a generation after the synods of Rheims and Toulouse had been concerned with heretics with Bogomil tendencies, he could not have found wholly academic the texts of Augustine attacking Manichean opposition to procreation. The Bogomil current would have given a relevance to this doctrine that it would otherwise have lacked.

In the second quarter of the twelfth century a new ideology appears which is opposed to procreation. It is the code of courtly love sung by many of the troubadours of Languedoc and Aquitaine. The relation of the troubadours to an heretical church is a much controverted question.[28] Of the troubadours whose names are known, none were active before 1100, only six before 1150; the large number of known troubadours after 1150, though a sampling, is indicative of the time their activity reached its climax.[29] They became an influential force at the same time that the Cathars came above ground. They appeared in the area of Cathar domination, southern France. Not every troubadour was a Cathar; some were

[28] C. S. Lewis emphasized the "sudden" appearance of courtly love at the end of the eleventh century in Languedoc. He noted that this appearance of "a rival or a parody of the real religion" was as yet unexplained. *The Allegory of Love* (Oxford, 1936), pp. 2, 11, 18. Denis de Rougemont, in a work distinguished equally by its display of brilliant intuition and its disdain for documentation, argued that courtly love reflected a Cathar ideology "both in its surreptitious opposition and its overt opposition to the Christian conception of marriage." He found in the insistence of the troubadours on love without insemination a parallel to the tantrism of India. *Love in the Western World*, rev. ed., trans. Montgomery Belgion (New York, 1956), p. 117. Mircea Eliade notes the parallel between tantrism and courtly love practices, including the cult of the woman, in his study of Indian religion, *Yoga: Immortality and Freedom*, trans. Willard R. Trask (New York, 1958), p. 264.

A. J. Denomy rejected De Rougemont's theory on the grounds that the Cathar dualism could not "provide a basis for the moral code of Courtly Love" nor would the Cathars have viewed "with favor a doctrine that exalted fornication and adultery." A. J. Denomy, "Fin' Amors: The Pure Love of the Troubadours, Its Amorality, and Possible Source," *Medieval Studies* 7 (1945), 184. Denomy postulated derivation of the basic themes of courtly love from Avicenna's *Treatise on Love*, while admitting that there was no translation of Avicenna available to Latin-reading persons before the middle of the twelfth century (p. 205). Denomy's supposition as to a source has not won acceptance; see Theodore Silverstein, "Andreas, Plato, and the Arabs: Remarks on Some Recent Accounts of Courtly Love," *Modern Philology* 47 (1949), 117–126. Nor have studies of Arabic influence been able to show more than an adaptation of Arabic lyric forms; see Alois Nykl, *Hispano-Arabic Poetry and Its Relations with the Old Provençal Troubadours* (Baltimore, 1946), pp. 380, 385 ff, although Nykl argues that the substance of troubadours' poetry is influenced by Arabic and especially Andalusian-Arabic influence (p. 395).

One must either agree that Lewis' conclusion "unexplained" still holds, or see some connection with an heretical ideology. Denomy has well put the terms of the question in "Fin' Amors," p. 206, without giving the answer his question calls for. I suggest that he mistakenly believes that the ideals of the Cathar Perfect, or priesthood, would have had to be reflected in the songs of the troubadours for Cathar influence to have been at work.

[29] Reto R. Bezzola, *Les Origines de la formation de la littérature courtoise en Occident (500–1200)* (Paris, 1944–1963), II², 316.

orthodox Catholics. Even in the troubadours subject to Cathar influence what is generally found is not the expression of Cathar dogma but the reflection of a Cathar ambience.[30] Yet in their basic attitudes toward sexuality and procreation, a substantial number of the troubadours shared a view that seems to have heretical roots. Praising the love of man for woman, they separated love from marriage; celebrating sexual pleasure, they rejected generative purpose.

The theme of the troubadours is *fine amour*, pure love. Pure love is carnal love, love of a man for a woman, extramarital love which terminates in sexual acts.[31] As sung by the leading poets of the mid-twelfth century, it is distinguished by its avoidance of insemination of the woman. Thus, for example, Jaufré Rudel, prince of Blaye in Aquitaine, celebrates the lesson he has learned from a departure from the principles of pure love: henceforth he will not be too hasty and will bed with his beloved clothed rather than naked.[32] Cercamon writes that he cannot continue to live "if I cannot kiss her and hold her near me naked in a curtained room." [33] Marcabrun attacks a false sensual love which is practiced by the many, but his "true love" is itself sexual.[34] Bernart Marti declares, "When I am naked in her dwelling and I hold and caress her flanks, I know of no emperor who, in comparison to me, may acquire greater worth, or have more of pure love." [35] Bernart de Ventadorn describes every embracing of his love except insemination as an act of pure love.[36]

The pure love of the troubadours gave an outlet to the sexual affectivity unrecognized by orthodox theology. It rejected the procreative purpose which was central to the orthodox ethic of sexuality and the orthodox view of marriage. Supported by and influencing the most civilized elite of the new Europe, the nobility of southern France, these poets made a major effort to dissociate sexual intercourse from procreation. In

---

[30] Borst, *Die Katharer*, pp. 107–108. Bezzola notes a similar phenomenon in the great love poem *Tristan*, composed about 1200 by Godfrey of Strassburg: the Cathar doctrine is not slavishly set out, but it is a strong influence (Bezzola, *Les Origines*, III¹, 298).

[31] Some authors have tried to show that the love celebrated by the troubadours was not carnal, that indeed, in a poet like Marcabrun, it was the love of God (e.g., Bezzola, *Les Origines*, II², 321). But I believe that those who insist on a realistic reading of the poetry have the better of the argument. The texts showing the carnal quality of the pure love of the troubadours have been collected and given a good exegesis in Denomy, "Fin' Amors." Cf. Andreas Capellanus, *De amore*, ed. Amadeo Payes (Castellón de la Plana, 1930), p. 153, and the assessment of this debated work by Felix Schlösser, *Andreas Capellanus* (Bonn, 1959), pp. 370–382.

[32] *Les Chansons de Jaufré Rudel*, ed. Alfred Jeanroy (Paris, 1924), pp. 9–12.

[33] *Les Poésies de Cercamon*, ed. Alfred Jeanroy (Paris, 1922), p. 7.

[34] Marcabrun, *Poésies complètes*, ed. and trans. J. M. L. Dejeanne (Toulouse, 1909): no. 5; no. 13, ll. 41–48; no. 21; no 25, ll. 78–84; no. 26, ll. 60–66.

[35] *Les Poésies de Bernart Marti*, ed. Ernest Hoepffner (Paris, 1929), p. 31.

[36] Bernart de Ventadorn, *Ausgewählte Lieder*, ed. Carl Appel (Halle, 1926): no. 7, l. 45; no. 24, l. 35; no. 28, ll. 34–40, 52; no. 36, ll. 34–36.

creating a mystique antipathetic to procreation they pressed against the center of the Augustinian tradition.

While courtly love flourished in Languedoc, heresy with a distinct Bogomil cast spread through the Rhineland, Flanders, Champagne, southern France, and northern Italy. Definite reports on the spread of the heretics are made by shocked Catholic clergy during the 1140's. For example, the abbot of the Premonstratensian abbey of Steinfeld, Everwin, writes St. Bernard in 1143–1144 of encountering heretics who, for some reason he has not been able to discover, condemn marriage (*Letters* 432, *PL* 182:678). St. Bernard himself, after visiting the south of France between 1145 and 1147, preaches against men and women who cohabit with each other, claim to be pure, but who keep their doctrine secret. The doctrine is dissembled, but the "devastation" is clear. Men have left their wives, wives their husbands, clerics their churches to join the group (*Sermons on the Song of Songs* 65.4–5, *PL* 183:1091–1092).

The heretics mentioned seem in retrospect to be identifiable as adherents of the dogmas of the Bogomils.[37] The orthodox have at first no name for them. Then they are variously called "Textores" or "Tesserants" (weavers), from their frequency in that group; "Publicani" or "Popelicani," perhaps from "publican"; "Piphli" or "Pifli" from "Popelicani"; "Albigenses" from their concentration in Albi; "Bulgars" from the origin of their doctrine; "Patarines" from an association with an earlier group in Milan. They themselves use the term "Christians" or "Cathars," that is, "the Pure." [38] It is as Cathars that they will be referred to here.

The emergence of the Cathars, marked by the outcry of the 1140's, is hard to understand as a sudden phenomenon.[39] Organized Cathar churches, with a hierarchy, in Cologne and Champagne, could scarcely have grown overnight. Church legislation almost invariably is much behind the ill at which it is directed; it takes repeated experience of a given danger to overcome the institutional inertia. And especially when an ecumenical council of the Church enacts a law, its action is unlikely to have been occasioned by recent and ephemeral events. The reaction of the orthodox was in response to a new stage in an heretical growth already in progress.

By 1139, a level of danger had been reached that drew the attention of an ecumenical council. A serious threat was recognized to exist in a

---

[37] Borst, *Die Katharer*, pp. 89–90.
[38] *Ibid.*, pp. 240–250.
[39] Borst, *ibid.*, p. 90, seems to view the outbreak of heresy as a new wave, "a triumphal procession," carried along by "a scarcely believable enthusiasm." This view corresponds to the fact that the extant reports on the heretics all date from the 1140's. But he offers no convincing explanation why there should have been a sudden outbreak rather than a slow growth, and he himself admits that groups of Westerners may have responded earlier in the twelfth century to the Bogomil doctrine.

religious opposition to marriage. Referring to those who rejected the Eucharist, the baptism of children, the priesthood, and marriage, the Second Council of the Lateran asked the help of secular powers in suppressing the heretics (Canon 23).[40] It is not clear whether the Council had one or several heresies in mind. The beliefs attributed to the heretics are, however, precisely the sacramental views opposed by Lateran IV, which is indisputably dealing with Cathars. Lateran II makes no identification of the heretics. Whoever is meant, there is evident, at the highest level of the Church, a fear of heretical attacks on marriage.

Gratian and Peter Lombard, then, acted in a period when the Cathar church had become a visible success, when the Catholic hierarchy was showing real alarm at the Cathar progress, and when the heretical denial of marriage had become the object of conciliar concern. It is difficult to believe that either sheer chance or sheer traditionalism made the existence of this threat and the choice of *Aliquando* contemporaneous.

What did the Cathars believe about procreation? What did their orthodox opponents think that they believed? The second question is easier to answer and more relevant to an account of the state of mind in which attention was given by the Catholic authorities to texts on contraception. The first question bears on whether the orthodox were victims of an illusion. It is harder to answer because so little Cathar writing has survived. I shall focus on an answer to the second question, noting, as far as determinable, the relation of the orthodox accounts of the Cathars to their actual beliefs.

The Cathars, it was universally agreed by the orthodox, were opposed to "marriage." They did not object to the ceremony of marriage, for they "fictitiously communicate in our sacraments to veil their wickedness." [41]

---

[40] Carl Joseph von Hefele, *Histoire des conciles*, augmented and translated by H. Leclercq (Paris, 1907–1938), V[1], 731–732. Hefele and Leclercq reject the old theory that Arnold of Brescia was meant and suggest that the targets were "principally the partisans of Peter of Bruys and Henry of Cluny" (p. 732, n. 1.). But the only source for Peter of Bruy's doctrine is Peter the Venerable's *Adversus petrobrusianos haereticos*, and this accuses Peter of Bruys of errors on the baptism of children and the Eucharist (*PL* 189:722). It does not accuse him of errors on marriage. Similarly, St. Bernard accuses Henry of Cluny of errors on baptism, but not on marriage (*Letters* 241, *PL* 182:434–436).

[41] The clergy of Lützen to Pope Lucius II (A.D. 1145), *Variorum ad Lucium Papam epistolae* 4, *PL* 179:938.

Two problems in the interpretation of Cathar language were believed by the orthodox to exist. The orthodox believed that the Cathars deliberately concealed their moral doctrine, since secrecy promoted the spread of their heresy. "New serpents have arisen, hiding in corners," wrote the Franciscan David of Augsburg soon after 1252 in *The Inquisition of Heretics*, edited by Wilhelm Preger as *Der Tractat des David von Augsburg über die Waldesier* (Munich, 1878), p. 24.

Related to this concealment was what the orthodox believed to be an ambiguous use of language, a use which in modern political warfare would be called Aesopian. As Western liberals accuse Communists of using "democracy" in an Aesopian sense,

In condemning marriage what they were rejecting was believed to be "the carnal works of marriage." "You say that the fruit about which God warned Adam, that he should not eat of it, was nothing else but the woman whom He created," Eckbert, later abbot of Schönau, accuses them in 1163 (*Sermons Against the Cathars* 5.6, *PL* 195:30). The anonymous *Summa Against the Heretics*, in the late twelfth century, ascribes to the Cathars the teaching that "no one can be saved who in marriage exercises the rights of marriage." [42] Radulf Ardens, preaching at Paris at about the same time, reports, "They say it is as great a crime to enter into one's wife as into one's mother or daughter" (*Sermons* 2.19, *PL* 155: 2011).[43] In a *Disputation Between a Catholic and a Patarine Heretic*, a Catholic dialogue written by a Florentine layman, George, about 1240, the Patarine is made to declare that he does not condemn a chaste marriage as between Christ and the Church; rather, "that dirty business which a man does with a woman in carnally mixing with her, that adultery is what we prohibit." [44]

This orthodox view of Cathar belief was buttressed by declarations of Cathar converts and by witnesses before the Inquisition. Buonaccorso, a former Cathar, denounced his old beliefs before the populace in Milan sometime between 1176 and 1190.[45] The Cathars "believe," he stated, "that in marriage no one can be saved." "The union of Adam and Eve, as they say, was the forbidden fruit" (*Life of the Heretics*, *PL* 204:776). Rainer Sacconi, a self-described "Cathar heresiarch," became a Catholic, a Dominican, and was at his death grand inquisitor of Tuscany.[46] He says in 1250 that "it is the common opinion of all Cathars that carnal marriage is always mortal sin, and that in the future one will not be more severely punished for adultery or incest than for lawful marriage" (*Summa on Cathars and Leonists, or the Poor Men of Lyons*).[47] A witness before the Inquisition in Toulouse in 1247 alleges that the accused called carnal coitus "the forbidden fruit." [48]

so the Cathars were accused of speaking of sexual sins. Thus "adultery" was not the sin of breaking the marriage vow, but any carnal use of marriage, according to the accusation of the *Disputation Between a Catholic and a Patarine Heretic*, c. 2, in the *Thesaurus novus anecdotorum*, ed. Edmond Martène and Ursin Durand (Paris, 1917), V, 1711–1712.

[42] *Summa contra haereticos*, ed. Joseph N. Garvin and James A. Corbett (Notre Dame, 1958), c. 4, p. 66.

[43] On Radulf Ardens, see J. Gründel, "Radulfus Ardens," *LTK* 8:967–968.

[44] *Disputation*, in Martène and Durand, ed., *Thesaurus novus anecdotorum*, V, 1712. On George, see Borst, *Die Katharer*, p. 16.

[45] On Buonaccorso (Bonacursus), see Borst, *Die Katharer*, p. 7. He was not a Cathar bishop, as alleged in *PL* 204:775.

[46] Sacconi was converted in 1245 by St. Peter Martyr (see Borst, *Die Katharer*, p. 19).

[47] In *Thesaurus novus anecdotorum*, V, 1761.

[48] C. Douais, *Documents pour servir à l'histoire de l'Inquisition dans le Languedoc* (Paris, 1900), II, 93. See other citations in Borst, p. 181.

The accuracy of the orthodox analysis is confirmed not only by declarations whose impartiality could be doubted, but by the single Cathar work which has been discovered in its original form. This is the *Book of the Two Principles*, written in the mid-thirteenth century, probably near Bergamo, by a disciple of John of Lugio.[49] The valuable testimony of this work is contained in its implicit assumptions. It is a reflection of a quarrel between the "Albanian" Cathars at Desenzano and the "Garatene" Cathars at Concorrezo near Milan. The Albanians appear as absolute dualists, holding that all creation is the work of an evil principle; the Garatenes are portrayed as defenders of a mitigated dualism who hold that a single good God created all things, but that a fallen angel, the evil principle, now possessed the visible world. The author of the *Book of the Two Principles* is an Albanian, writing to point out his opponents' error. He says that if the Garatenes accept Genesis, with its story of creation and of God making man in his image and commanding man to multiply, they will conclude with the Albanians that there is "one evil creator who created heaven and earth and all other visible bodies" (*Book of the Two Principles*, p. 134). The author imagines that the Garatenes may respond with proofs of a good creator from the New Testament, a book accepted by all Cathars. He anticipates this response by asking: "If a true Lord God in the beginning made man and woman, the birds and the beasts and all other visible bodies, why do you daily contemn the carnal work of male and female union, saying that it is the work of the devil? Why do you not make sons and daughters for your God?" (*ibid.*, p.135). The Albanian author thinks these rhetorical questions a strong argument *ad hominem*: the Garatenes must renounce a central tenet, if they refuse to accept absolute dualism. Indeed, the Albanian urges, the Garatenes in their compromising present position must acknowledge the force of the argument so often raised against them by "the Romans," that they are the hypocritical contemners of marriage predicted by 1 Timothy. If the New Testament shows a good God ruling the world, then procreation is wholesome. This conclusion the Albanian treats as a triumphant *reductio ad absurdum*: "the Garatenes are therefore trapped in their own words" (*ibid.*, p. 135). The consistent assumption of this argument, conducted within the Cathar movement, is clear: carnal procreation is rejected by all Cathars.

The orthodox summary of Cathar doctrine, as we have seen, often puts

---

[49] The *Liber de duobus principiis* was discovered by Antoine Dondaine, O.P., in Florence, and has been edited by him as *Un Traité néo-manichéen du XII⁰ siècle, le "Liber de duobus principiis," suivi d'un fragment de Rituel Cathare* (Rome, 1939). The book is composed of three principal parts: "The Two Principles"; "Compendium for the Instruction of the Ignorant"; "Against the Garatenes." Despite differences in handwriting in the manuscript, Dondaine (pp. 15–16) ascribes the entire work to one author; Borst agrees (*Die Katharer*, p. 261).

the doctrine as an opposition to carnal intercourse in marriage. But only a few orthodox writers seem to have regarded the Cathars as proposing a way of sexual continence. The Cathars were accustomed to urge that Paul meant that any intercourse was fornication when he used the phrase "on account of fornication" in 1 Corinthians 7; Eckbert and George respond to this line of argument (*Sermons Against the Cathars* 5.2, PL 195:28; *Disputation* c. 2). But the Catholic authors seem to believe that the Cathars were only raising objections to the orthodox view of marriage, not seriously defending total continence. A rare exception is the Franciscan Jacob a Capelli, who testifies to the sexual purity of the lives of the Cathars he knows.[50] The common belief of Catholic theologians was that the Cathars tolerated or encouraged sexual license. The Council of Rheims of 1157 accused the "Manichees" of sexual association without marriage (Mansi 21:843). The term employed is *contubernium*, originally used to designate the cohabitation of slaves to whom marriage was legally denied. The term is also employed by St. Bernard to designate what he has seen on his trip to southern France. Bernard describes a colloquy he had with one of these men of "secret doctrine": "I ask one of these: 'Hey, you, my good man, who is that woman and what is she to you? Your wife?' 'No,' he says, 'for that does not accord with my vow.' 'Your daughter, then?' 'No.' 'What then? Not sister, not niece, not related to you in any degree of kith or kin?' 'Not at all.' 'And how do you preserve your continence with her?'" (*Sermons on the Song of Songs* 65.6, PL 183:1092). St. Bernard reports no answer to his last, rhetorical question; he assumes the relation is sexual. About the same time, 1147, Hugh, the archbishop of Rouen, writes against heretics who are similarly traveling around accompanied by women to whom they are not married, claiming for this custom the sanction of St. Paul's example. Hugh finds it a libidinous usage (*Against the Heretics* 3.4, PL 192:1289).

In the middle of the next century, in one of the first handbooks written for inquisitors, the Franciscan David of Augsburg claims that the heretics "say that marriage is sworn fornication, unless they live continently." But in the next sentence he goes on to show that he does not believe that by "living continently" they mean complete continence: "They say that any other unclean lecheries are more lawful than conjugal copulation. They praise continence, but when lust burns they concede that it may be satisfied in any shameful way. They explain the Apostle's 'It is better to marry than to burn' as 'Better by any shameful act to satisfy shameful lust than to be tempted in your heart'" (*The Inquisition of Heretics* 5).

The Cathars were sometimes accused of unnatural vice; from the name

[50] Quoted in Antoine Dondaine, "Nouvelles sources de l'histoire doctrinale du néo-manichéisme au Moyen Age," *Revue des sciences philosophiques et théologiques* 28 (1939), 479.

of their country of origin, Bulgaria, the term "bugger" has entered the English language. In some of these accusations, it is not clear whether homosexual acts alone are meant or whether, as in the usual theological description of the "sin against nature," acts of anal intercourse in marriage are included. The Benedictine Eckbert, for example, in his twelfth-century sermons against the Cathars, alludes to the likelihood of their falling into practices "disagreeing with the law of nature" (*Sermons Against the Cathars* 5.14, PL 195:36). Instances of "perversity" among Cathars are cited by the Inquisition in Toulouse in 1245.[51] The Patarine is accused by George in his *Disputation* (c. 2) "of preferring the sodom-itic vice, or the copulation of men."

In addition to sexual license, the orthodox often charged the Cathars with a theoretical antinomianism in sexual matters. The Cistercian monk, Pierre des Vaux de Cernay, the reporter of the crusade against Langue-doc, claims "certain heretics said that no one could sin below the na-vel."[52] Alan of Lille (d. 1202) accuses "some" of the Cathars of believing that a "man ought to purge himself in every way of what he has from the prince of darkness, that is, from the body; and so everywhere and in every way one should fornicate, to be more swiftly freed from evil nature" (*Against the Heretics of His Time, Especially the Albigensians* 1.63, PL 210:365–366). This is a wild accusation, perhaps inspired by reading Augustine on the Manichees. But as an index to the orthodox mentality it is revealing: the Cathars "condemn marriage"; hence they are believed to value intercourse for its own sake without reference to procreation. These accusations made by the orthodox, flavored with reminiscences of the Fathers and polemically inspired, are not especially strong evidence of what the Cathars actually did or believed. They are not proof of Cathar conduct; they are an illustration of the orthodox view of the issues.

If the Cathars, then, were regarded as opposed to marriage but not averse to sexual behavior, what was considered to be the heart of their position? The orthodox viewed marriage as a union in which offspring were a principal good, and in which intercourse was truly marital only if the act was for the sake of procreation. When the Cathars are said to condemn "marriage" or "the carnal works of marriage," it is procreation that they are accused of attacking. The Catholic says to the Patarine, in George's *Disputation*, "We prove that the pregnant will not be damned, unlike you who whisper that they are damned irremediably if they die before or while giving birth" (*Disputation*, c. 3).

That the Cathar opposition to marriage in fact centered in opposition

<hr />

[51] Célestin Douais, *Documents pour servir à l'histoire de l'Inquisition dans le Languedoc* (Paris, 1900), II, 99.

[52] Pierre des Vaux de Cernay, *Histoire albigeoise*, trans. Pascal Guébin and Henri Maisonneuve (Paris, 1951), I, 17.

to procreation may be confirmed in three ways. First, such opposition appears to have been an important tenet of the Bogomils in the East. In 1211 these were condemned by the Orthodox Council of Tarnovo as follows: "To those who say that a woman conceives in her belly by the cooperation of Satan, that Satan has resided there and withdraws only at the birth of the child, and that he cannot be put to flight by holy baptism but only by prayer and fasting — to those who speak thus, anathema." [53] If the Bogomils in the East are accurately described as believing procreation to be the devil's work, it is probable that the Cathar churches in the West, which stemmed from the Bogomils and retained some ecclesiastical connection with them, had a similar detestation of conception.

Second, the peculiar horror of pregnancy felt by Cathars points to avoidance of procreation as the central tenet of their sexual ethics. According to the ex-Cathar Rainer Sacconi, a mere "sin of the flesh" might be forgiven by means of confession and a new reception of the *consolamentum*, the Cathar sacrament necessary for salvation.[54] But the *consolamentum* could not be given to a pregnant Cathar, even if she were in danger of death.[55] The intensity and persistence of the Cathars' condemnation of marriage must be directed at procreation if there is any connection between their metaphysical and moral positions. Condemning the world as the devil's, they must find pregnancy objectionable when it is the means for perpetuation of the human race.

Third, surviving Cathar literature reveals a total hostility to procreation. In the recent reconstruction by Thouzellier of a Cathar text from its section-by-section refutation in Durand de Huesca, the following attribution of procreation to the devil is made: "The devil has given seed to the children of this world, who are of the flesh of sin, who are born of blood and the will of the flesh and the pleasure of man" (c. 8).[56] The *Interrogation of John*, a Cathar fragment discovered at Carcassonne, teaches that Adam and Eve engendered "sons of the Devil," who perpetuate themselves.[57] The *Book of the Two Principles* itself, as we have seen, objects to "making sons and daughters for your God." True, the polemical purpose of the author does not lead him to discuss intercourse as such, but it is striking that what he relies on so heavily is the conviction that production of human beings is a disaster.

There was some diversity in Cathar theology. Rainer Sacconi dis-

---

[53] Text in Puech and Vaillant, *Le Traité contre les Bogomiles*, p. 345. These authors assert that opposition to procreation was a principal reason, if not the principal reason, for the Bogomils' detestation of marriage (p. 266).

[54] *Summa on Cathars*, in *Thesaurus novus anecdotorum*, V, 1764.

[55] Borst, *Die Katharer*, p. 181.

[56] *Un Traité cathare inédit du début du 13ᵉ siècle: D'après le "Liber contra Manichaeos" de Durand de Huesca*, ed. Christine Thouzellier (Louvain, 1961), p. 96.

[57] Puech and Vaillant, *Le Traité contre les Bogomiles*, pp. 267, 130 n. 1.

tinguished five Cathar churches, each with some distinctive tenet.[58] The *Book of the Two Principles* illustrates what fierce doctrinal controversy could exist between two Cathar groups in the same general region. According to Sacconi, all Cathars opposed "carnal marriage," but it is not necessary to suppose that, during the two-hundred-year period in which the Cathars spread across western Europe, every Cathar church had the same understanding of what was meant by avoiding carnal marriage; still less is it necessary to hold that every Catholic observer of the Cathars accurately reported their doctrine.[59] What is clear is only that the dominant Cathar position involved a rejection of procreation, and that this position was comprehended by the orthodox as the essential Cathar challenge to marriage.

The orthodox found in the Cathar movement a re-enactment of the great Gnostic-Manichean assault on procreation. The trauma of the patristic church was experienced by the medieval church in the century in which its theological speculation had its first growth, the critical century in which canon law took shape. The trauma, having occurred before, was treated with familiar remedies: the invocation of the Old Testament, appeal to Christ's words on divorce and on adultery, ceaseless citation of the anti-Gnostic text 1 Timothy 4, and, above all, restatement of the Stoic-Alexandrian-Augustinian rule on procreation. Explicit connection was not made between the Cathars and the canons on contraception in the compilations. Indeed, the canons dealt with poisons of sterility and potions, and the Cathars do not appear to have been accused by their unfriendly observers of using artificial contraceptives. No showing of a one-to-one correspondence between the canons and Cathar activity can be made. But it is highly probable that the canons, if not aimed directly at the Cathars, are part of the orthodox response to the doctrine of the Cathars. The canons are absolute assertions that marriage and procreation are linked, and that procreation should not be prevented.

The interest in *Aliquando* is attributable to this orthodox reaction.

---

[58] *Summa on Cathars*, in *Thesaurus novus anecdotorum*, V, 1761.

[59] Eckbert of Schönau in 1163 speaks of persons identified by him as Cathars who will permit only the marriage of virgins. But he adds that even these couples must, according to Cathar doctrine, separate before the end of their lives if they are to be saved (*Sermons against the Cathars* 1.2, PL 195:14). He also speaks of other Cathars who, "following Hartuvinus," permit only the marriage of virgins and the procreation of a single child, after whose birth they must separate (*Sermons against the Cathars* 5.11, PL 195:34). Everwin of Steinfeld also reports the existence of an heretical group which permits only virgins to marry (*Letter to St. Bernard*, PL 182:678–679).

It is difficult to see how the notion of marriage for virgins only fits in with Bogomil doctrine, and it is even more difficult to see the coherence of the "one child" rule with Bogomil beliefs. Everwin in his report distinguishes the heretics forbidden to marry from those heretics permitting marriage only of virgins. May we not assume that Eckbert has misidentified another heretical group? Borst, p. 180, however, accepts the statements as true of "the first Cathars."

Gratian's use of it in the *Decretals* followed by only a year or two the denunciation by Lateran II of heretics attacking marriage. Peter Lombard's use of it coincided with official ecclesiastical expressions in a way that points even more strongly to the relationship. By 1148 Lombard was at work on the composition of the *Sentences*, a work finished by 1157 at the latest. He was among the leaders of the church in France, and was himself to be elected bishop of Paris in 1158. If, as is usually the case, there was a time lag between the perceptions of the intellectuals and official action, theological concern with the Cathars was reaching its height in France at the time Lombard wrote. In 1148 a Council at Rheims, with the Pope, Eugene III, presiding, warned against receiving the "heresiarchs and their followers" who were in "Gascony, Provence, and elsewhere" (Canon 18, Mansi 21:718). The Cathars were not mentioned by name, and they were not the major business of the council. But they were already sufficiently worrisome to cause the council to act. By 1157, another council at Rheims, presided over by Archbishop Samson, treated the existence of the Cathars as a principal problem of the church in France. The Cathars were described as "the most impure sect of Manichees." The council declared that they asserted themselves to be purer than others, and condemned marriage. Yet they themselves were guilty of cohabitation (*contubernium*) without marriage. Excommunication and confiscation of goods were prescribed for them, with perpetual imprisonment for their leaders (Canon 1, Mansi 21:843). It is against this background of ecclesiastical anxiety, voiced in a vehement call for repressive action, that Lombard found *Aliquando* at hand and treated it as a vital text on marriage.

That such use of Augustine's work would have been understood by all as being, in the first place, a response to the Cathars may be shown by other contemporary treatment of the Cathars as "Manichees." In 1163 Eckbert of Schönau's *Sermons Against the Cathars* concludes its polemic with a series of Augustinian texts against the Manichees. The sweeping assault on Manichean contraception made by Augustine in *The Morals of the Manichees* is among the texts paraphrased; in Eckbert's words, "If they indulge in marital intercourse, they nevertheless avoid conception and generation by whatever means they can" ("Excerpts from St. Augustine on the Manichees," following *Sermons Against the Cathars*, PL 195:102). It is in the same spirit that Alan of Lille attributes to the Cathars the Manichean belief that a man "ought to purge himself in every way of what he has from the prince of darkness."

The crisis of the Cathars continued to provide both a background for *Aliquando* and an interest in the other canons on contraception which culminated in the insertion of *Si aliquis* in the *Decretals*. The action of Lateran II was only the beginning of a century of public battle, by both religious and secular sanctions, against the Cathars. Another ecumenical council, Lateran III under Alexander III in 1179, noted that there was now in Gascony, Albi, Toulouse, and elsewhere public profession of "the perversity" of the heretics known as Cathars, Patarines, or Publicani. The Council anathematized those protecting them, lodging them, or doing business with them (Mansi 22:232). Two years later, a joint decree issued by Pope Lucius III and Emperor Frederick Barbarossa at a council held in Verona again urged both religious and civil authorities to act against the Cathars and Patarines and other heretics (Mansi 22:476–478).

In 1215, Lateran IV, convoked by Innocent III, took even more severe measures against the Cathars. The goods of lay heretics were to be confiscated. Secular rulers who failed to obey the request of the Church "to purge" their land of heresy were to be excommunicated. Catholics undertaking a crusade to exterminate the heretics would enjoy the privileges of crusaders for the Holy Land.[60] What was in substance an anti-Cathar profession of faith was composed by the Council. It affirmed, "Not only virgins and the continent, but also the married, pleasing God by true faith and good action, will be judged worthy of attaining eternal beatitude."[61]

The link between the anti-Cathar reaction and the canons is circumstantially strongest in the final choice of Si aliquis for the Decretals. The Decretals were composed when papal action against the Cathars was taking its most vigorous form. In 1231 Pope Gregory IX set death by fire as the penalty for Cathars in the states of the Church. In 1233 he invoked against them his new weapon, the Inquisition. It was at his direction that the Decretals were compiled between 1230 and 1234. The Pope was bent on crushing the Cathars, and his right hand in the work on the Decretals was St. Raymond, a leader of the Dominican order which had been founded in 1217 with the primary mission of converting the Cathars. The Dominicans had by their success become the Cathars' most hated enemy; the order was in the front of bitter struggle with them in northern Italy and southern France.[62] One probable consideration affecting Raymond when he selected the venerable text, Si aliquis, and composed the new text, Si conditiones, was the desire to have strong canonical sanctions against behavior which the Cathar doctrine logically entailed.

An analogous process may be observed in popular devotion. Since the time of Gregory the Great, the Ave Maria had been part of the Roman liturgy as a prayer to be said on particular feast days. It had not been prescribed as a prayer which every Christian should know. It did not have the status of the Creed or the Pater Noster. In the twelfth century

[60] Canon 3, Hefele-Leclercq, *Histoire des conciles*, V², 1330–1331.
[61] Canon 1, *ibid.*, p. 1325.
[62] Borst, *Die Katharer*, p. 132.

the Ave Maria emerged as a popular Catholic prayer. In 1198 at the synod of Paris, Odo de Soliac, bishop of Paris, prescribed that priests should exhort the people to pray the "Salutation of the Blessed Virgin" (Mansi 22:681). In the next century the prayer was recommended by a number of local councils.[63] Not all these bodies reacted to a direct Cathar menace; for example, the action of the council of Coventry in 1237 scarcely responded to a Cathar danger. But the conciliar actions did reflect an ideology which the Cathar menace had made prominent in the Church. In 1254, when the Cathars had been destroyed in southern France and a council of Catholic bishops met in the old Cathar seat of Albi to root out the effects of the heresy, the three prayers prescribed to be taught to every child over seven were the Creed, the Pater Noster, and the Ave Maria (Mansi 23:837). The central Cathar tenet was indirectly denied by the prayer, "Hail Mary, full of grace. The Lord is with you. Blessed are you among women, and blessed is the fruit of your womb."

The canons may be understood, then, as an indirect ideological response to an ideological challenge. If the canon law is a type of public teaching even more than a system of organized sanctions, the dramatic and exemplary aspect of the three canons made them particularly appropriate. To agree to avoid children is to agree not to marry. Avoidance of children in marriage is fornication, adultery, or homicide. What could be a more vigorous commentary on the Cathar ethic? The orthodox relived the experience of the Fathers facing the Gnostics, the Fathers facing the Manichees. The orthodox commitment to marriage was reaffirmed by the assertion that procreation was an absolute value in intercourse; contraception was once more condemned without exception.

CENTRAL THEORY ON PROCREATIVE PURPOSE

The development of the presentation of the key texts on contraception has been outlined. Their relation to Catharism has been suggested. But what locks these texts in place is the central doctrine on procreative purpose. The development of this doctrine in the twelfth century is itself a reaction to Catharism and to courtly love. The developed doctrine, vigorously excluding pleasure as a purpose from intercourse, is a most powerful positive teaching against contraception. The basic reason for the existence of the doctrine is the revival of Augustine.

The revival of the Augustinian sexual ethic took tangible form with the heavily Augustinian collection of Ivo. It took its most influential shape in the restatement of Augustine in the *Sentences* of Peter Lombard. Here the Augustinian association of original sin, concupiscence, and

[63] Hefele-Leclercq, *Histoire des conciles*, V² 1734–1759.

the necessity of procreative purpose was expressed in condensed and striking form.

Original sin is transmitted by an act of generation, an act which is preceded by concupiscence. Adam's descendants are in turn infected with concupiscence (*Sentences* 2.25.7; 2.30.8, 10; 2.31.4, 7; 2.32.2). As the result of this transmission of original sin and its consequences, there is "the law of lethal concupiscence in our members, without which carnal intercourse cannot occur." Therefore, "coitus is reprehensible and evil, unless it be excused by the goods of marriage" (*Sentences* 4.26.2). Here the basic Augustinian assumptions are succinctly combined. Concupiscence, the effect of original sin, necessarily reveals its presence in intercourse. Somehow it is peculiarly present, or exercised, in this act rather than, say, in walking, talking, or going to sleep. Because concupiscence accompanies intercourse, intercourse needs to be excused. The excuse is provided by the goods of marriage. These goods are the familar Augustinian triad, *fides, proles, sacramentum* (4.31.1). Of the three, however, only the seeking of the good of offspring is sufficient to excuse intercourse (4.31.5).

Lombard's reaffirmation of Augustine was particularly significant in tacitly rejecting two authorities who favored a nonprocreative purpose in intercourse: Peter Abelard and John Damascene. Abelard (d. 1142) was the most brilliant but least trusted theologian of the preceding generation. With a sexual history almost as turbulent as Augustine's — first the seducer of his pupil, Heloise, then her husband and the father of her child, Astrolabe, then castrated and separated from her — Abelard had worked out a different sort of synthesis. Original sin was a penalty, not a fault. Concupiscence did not make sexual pleasure bad in itself. Marital intercourse might be sought to avoid fornication. Heloise, now abbess of the Paraclete, wrote him, "Can someone sin in what is permitted or even ordered by God?" Abelard took the question to refer to marital intercourse, and, invoking Augustine as his authority, reached the conclusion that if marriage is entered for the procreation of children, it excuses "those acts of intercourse which occur without this intention" (*Problems of Heloise* 42, PL 178:724–725). Among the clean of heart, he tells Heloise, are the married who seek intercourse "not for pleasure and the delight of the flesh in the manner of beasts," but as a "remedy for their incontinence" (*ibid.* 14, PL 178:701).

Abelard is the first married man in the Western Church to contribute to the theology of this issue. His contribution suffered from three weaknesses. He was sufficiently sensitive to the prestige of Augustine to present his own views as Augustine's, a presentation which led to a wrenching of the Augustinian texts. His view of original sin was, at the insistence of St. Bernard, condemned by the Council of Sens in 1140, and the destruction of this part of his approach inevitably impaired his analysis of concupiscence and sexual pleasure. His own personal testimony did not strike his contemporaries as the insight of a repentant sinner now ardent in his love of God, but as the cry of an egotistical academician. His autobiography was not called *Confessions*, but *The Story of My Calamities*. If Abelard had been an Augustine, a different theology of marital sexuality might have carried the day.

The Greek saint, John Damascene, was equally ineffective in influencing the main stream of twelfth-century doctrine. This eighth-century writer had repeated the doctrine of Chrysostom that marriage now, when Christ had ended the reign of death, was only for the purpose of avoiding fornication (*Orthodox Faith* 4.24, PG 94:1207). He thereby eliminated the procreative requirement in intercourse and presented an alternative theory for the Western theologians to consider. The *Orthodox Faith* was translated into Latin by Burgundio of Pisa about 1150, shortly before Peter Lombard wrote. Lombard cited it twenty-seven times. But he took nothing from it on the purposes of marriage; and John's small impact on the textbook of Western theology may be measured by comparing the twenty-seven citations of him with Lombard's nearly a thousand citations of St. Augustine.[64]

A third approach which failed to affect the central Augustinian position was that of Hugh of St. Victor. Courtly love emphasized the joys of the joining of man and woman without biological purpose. A parallel emphasis may be detected in Hugh of St. Victor, but in a sense counter to the poets of courtly love who were his contemporaries. In a context where the sacramental aspect of marriage was developed and where the virginal marriage of Mary and Joseph was exalted, Hugh emphasized the spiritual tie of husband and wife. Their love is the subject matter of the sacrament. The relation of husband to wife symbolizes that of God to the soul (*The Sacraments of the Christian Faith* 1.8.13, PL 176:314–318). Eve was made from Adam's rib "to show that she was created for loving association" (*Sacraments* 1.4.35, PL 176:284). In a work either by Hugh or by an immediate disciple, the generative function itself is explained as dependent on marital love. A man chooses a wife "to be joined with, uniquely and singularly, in undivided love." It is because of the existence of this unique society that God attached to it the duty of generation (*Epistolary Book on the Virginity of Blessed Mary*, PL 176:864).

A trace of Hugh may be found in one of Peter Lombard's personal contributions to his collection. He says, apropos of the marriage of Mary and Joseph, "Marriage is the sign of the spiritual union and the love of

---

[64] Joseph De Ghellinck, *Le Mouvement théologique du XII siècle* (Paris, 1914), pp. 242, 368–369. In contrast, it may be observed that the one Father of the Church whom the Cathars would cite is St. John Chrysostom (Borst, *Die Katharer*, p. 181, n. 3).

souls by which spouses ought to be united with each other" (*Sentences* 4.26.6). But Lombard does not develop the idea, and there is no integration of the ideal of personal love with the purposes of intercourse. Without going outside the framework of his discourse to consider psychological or social factors, one must attribute this lack to Augustinianism. Hugh of St. Victor himself adopted the Augustinian theory of the purpose of marital coitus. Concupiscence infects coitus, which is "per se evil" (*Sacraments* 2.11.7, PL 176:494). Only the procreative purpose excuses coitus completely; to have intercourse to avoid fornication is venial sin. The personal interrelationship involved is totally ignored, and the Augustinian comparison of food and sex is revived. The words of Augustine in *The Good of Marriage* 16.18 are repeated, that "venial copulation in marriage is the same thing as immoderate appetite for lawful food" (*Sacraments* 2.11.10, PL 176:497). In this way the theologian whose tender description of married love offered the greatest promise of a sacramental or a personalist account of intercourse remained a prisoner of Augustine. Lombard echoed his words on the love of man and wife, and, like him, kept this spiritual love effectively separated from intercourse.

The central Augustinian position, then, as adopted by the twelfth-century theologians, treated as venial sin even the Pauline purpose of avoiding fornication. A fortiori, marital intercourse "for delight," "to satisfy lust," "only for the satisfaction of lust" (*libido*), would be sinful. The majority view at mid-century seems to have been authentically Augustinian: such intercourse was only venial sin. So held Gilbert de la Porrée (1076–1154), Peter of Poitiers (1130–1205), Walter of Mortagne (circa 1150), and Peter Lombard himself.[65] This view was check enough on any consideration of contraception. But an even stronger view appears at this time, apparently stimulated by reflection on one text aimed against contraception. Gratian had summarized the usual Augustinian view in a caption: "Immoderate use by the married is not an evil of marriage, but is venial on account of the good of marriage" (2.32.2.3). He had also stated that coitus "beyond the intention of generating" is venial (2.32 *ante* 3). But he had at the same time inserted these words, seemingly derived from a consideration of *Aliquando*: "Those who copulate not to procreate offspring but to satisfy lust seem to be not so much spouses as fornicators" (2.32.2.1). Gratian's professed aim in his work had been to make a "concordance of discordant canons." But in this addition he made a discord, for his comment seemed to say that intercourse "for lust" was as serious a sin as fornication. Gratian also made available the statement of Jerome denouncing intercourse in preg-

[65] Gilbert de la Porrée, *Commentarius in 1 Cor.*, MS, Bruges, City Library, Cod. 78, fol. 33r, quoted in Abellán, *El fin*, p. 46; Peter of Poitiers, *Sententiae* 5.5, *PL* 211:1258; Walter of Mortagne, *Summa Sententiarum* 7.3, PL 176:156; Peter Lombard, *Sentences* 4.31.

nancy, which begins with the quotation of Sextus, "He who is too ardent a lover of his wife is an adulterer" (2.32.4.5). Again, mortal sin
seemed to be the category for a "too ardent love" which was adultery, and
the context even suggested that intercourse where procreation was not
possible was always "too ardent." Finally, Gratian quoted as an absolute
statement Origen's words, "The presence of the Holy Spirit will not be
given at the time conjugal acts are accomplished" (2.32.2.4); Origen's
context, contrasting such acts with prophesying, was lost.

Huguccio, the chief of Gratian's commentators, inclined to a strict
view of sexuality. He explicitly expressed what some texts in Gratian
implied: marital intercourse, "in order to sate one's lust or satisfy one's
pleasure [voluptas] is mortal sin" (Summa 2.32.2.2, dictum "quod
enim . . . "). His view was shared by another leader of the Bolognese
canonists, Bishop Rufinus (Summa 2.32.2.1). A particularly juridical expression of the same position occurs in an anonymous treatise, "Marriage,"
dating from about 1200: marital intercourse "to satisfy lust" is "criminal
and reputed or judged as adulterous." [66]

This violent hostility to pleasure as a purpose was joined, in some
authors, by the belief that any pleasure experienced in intercourse, even
procreative intercourse, was sinful. This doctrine had been that of Gregory the Great. In the twelfth century his position was dourly set forth by
Huguccio. Coitus "can never be without sin, for it always occurs and is
exercised with a certain itching and a certain pleasure; for, in the emission of the seed, there is always a certain excitement, a certain itching, a
certain pleasure" (Summa 2.32.2.1). He characterized this pleasure as
"a very small venial sin."

Huguccio's position was far from unique among the orthodox. It was
shared by Gandulf, a theologian and canonist who was Huguccio's
predecessor at Bologna.[67] More strikingly, it was repeated by one of
the most energetic of medieval popes and a star pupil of Huguccio, Innocent III, writing as a private theologian: "Who does not know that
conjugal intercourse is never committed without itching of the flesh, and
heat and foul concupiscence, whence the conceived seeds are befouled
and corrupted?" (On the Seven Penitential Psalms 4, PL 217:1058–
1059). If an intelligent pope could think the Gregorian analysis so firmly
established as to be the object of a rhetorical question, the theological
popularity of the view in the late twelfth century can scarcely be doubted.

A variety of other opinions existed coming to the same conclusion but
by a more circuitous analysis. Both Peter Cantor and his pupil Cardinal
Courçon divided the act of intercourse into discrete moments. Begun

---

[66] De coniugio, ed. H. Weisweiler from a manuscript coming from Tegernsee, in
Maître Simon et son groupe, De sacramentis, Spicilegium sacrum Lovaniense (Louvain, 1937), p. 100.
[67] Gandulf, Sentences 2.173, 4.248, 4.253 (ed. Walter, pp. 247, 533–534, 556).

for a good purpose, coitus still reached a point where man was submerged in "delight of the flesh." At that point there was venial sin.[68] Another analysis distinguished between enjoying and suffering pleasure. A "holy man," according to William of Auxerre, is rightly displeased with any pleasure he feels in the act of intercourse. In acting without sin to propagate children, he suffers the pleasure just as one eating honey to feed himself might suffer the sweetness of the honey.[69] The stringency of Courçon and Auxerre was particularly striking, as they were willing to admit that the nonprocreative purpose of avoiding a sin of fornication was lawful.[70] Their stringency on pleasure effectively undid their leniency on nonprocreative purpose.

Even Peter Lombard, who was the model of Augustinian moderation, did not totally escape the infection of Gregorian rigorism. He quoted Gregory's famous letter to England, then tried to explain how Gregory's observation was often correct. Intercourse to procreate children is lawful, and, Lombard implies, pleasure experienced in an act with this purpose is not unlawful. But "hardly any can be found still experiencing carnal embraces who do not sometimes come together beyond the intention of procreating offspring." Then there is venial sin (Sentences 4.31.8). In this analysis, apparently any mixing of a nonprocreative purpose with a consciously procreative state of mind leads to venial sin.

On the mildest of these analyses, any departure from a procreative consciousness involved sin. According to the more rigid standards of Huguccio, Gandulf, Innocent III, Cantor, and Courçon, some small sin was inevitable. The significance of this doctrine for our purposes lies in its impact on the doctrine of contraception. If pleasure in intercourse was, in the view of important authorities, always sinful, if the seeking of pleasure in intercourse could be mortal or, at best, venial sin, if love had no relation at all to acts of intercourse, then the notion of deliberately separating coitus from its one justification could not have been considered by any theologian.

The great difference between the orthodox and the Cathars appeared in the link the orthodox kept between procreation and intercourse. Some writers of this period, like Huguccio, thought that they could escape with a different distinction. Was his position, that sin was inevitable in intercourse, heresy? No, answered Huguccio. The heretics said that intercourse could not be without mortal sin. He, on the contrary, held only that the inevitable pleasure was "a very small venial sin" (Summa 2.33.4. 7). This reasoning, while it seems to have satisfied his pupil, who would

---

[68] Abellán, El fin, p. 106.

[69] William of Auxerre, Summa aurea in quatuor libros Sententiarum (Paris, 1500), fol. 288r.

[70] Ibid. 4.4 (fol. 287r); Robert of Courçon, Summa, fol. 154r.

become Innocent III, still logically implied a condemnation of intercourse as involving a small offense against God. If the orthodox writers of the late twelfth century felt far removed from the Cathar position, the difference had to be found in the orthodox belief in procreation. Procreation was a good, and the procreative function of intercourse was not assailed by even the most austere Bolognese canonist. This position was directly opposed to Catharism. Indeed, the unrelenting insistence on procreation as a purpose was a sign of the reaction to Cathar morals. In the welding of intercourse to procreation — even more than in the choice of the three canons on contraception — the reaction to the Cathars left its deepest mark on the doctrine on contraception. In this anti-Cathar context, Augustine was triumphantly reasserted.

The period of revived theological speculation and canonical development which began roughly with Ivo of Chartres reached the end of a stage which is conveniently marked by the issuance of the *Decretals*. By the end of this period the medieval theologians had relived the battle with the Manichees. The Augustinian insistence on procreative purpose had been reasserted as central to the defense of marriage itself; the Augustinian explanation of the goods of marriage and their relation to original sin and concupiscence had become entrenched. Contraception was excluded by theological theory on marriage and intercourse; it was now also condemned by the lawbook of the universal Church. The discipline of the era of the penitentials had become the code of the centralizing papacy. The lines drawn against any form of contraceptive behavior seemed strong and tight and unyielding.

CHAPTER VII

CONTRACEPTIVE TECHNIQUES: MEANS AND DISSEMINATION IN THE HIGH MIDDLE AGES

THE ECCLESIASTICAL CONCERN with contraception is inherited from the Fathers and the penitentials; it is restated in reaction to Cathar ideology. After the establishment of Lombard, Gratian, and the *Decretals* as basic texts, most writers of the thirteenth, fourteenth, and fifteenth centuries phrased their comments on contraception in categories derived from *Aliquando, Adulterii malum,* and *Si aliquis.* It might be supposed that their comments were pure interpretations of the texts, framed without reference to contemporary practices. But that a civilization whose articulated ideals were largely the work of monks and clerics should have had no commerce with contraception would be imagined only by those insensitive to the gap between articulation and achievement. In the present chapter, I will try to suggest the kinds of contraceptive behavior known to the later Middle Ages and to make some estimate of the kinds of persons practicing contraception. The theologians and canonists did not develop their commentaries in an age in which contraception was unknown; they did not theorize without a sense of existing situations.[1]

MEDICAL INFORMATION ON CONTRACEPTION

The course of contraception in medieval Europe is linked to the spread of medical knowledge, and this came almost wholly from the Arabs. From

[1] The unwarranted assumption has sometimes been made that the practice of contraception was negligible in medieval times (see, e.g., Helen Bergues, *La Prévention des naissances dans la famille,* Paris, 1960, pp. 140–141, 211–212). Norman E. Himes writes, "It may even be doubted whether Europeans in the late Middle Ages knew as much about contraceptive medicine as the ancient Hebrews and Egyptians" (*Medical History of Contraception,* Baltimore, 1936, p. 160).

the first European medical school, in the eleventh century at Salerno, to the twelfth-century offshoot of Salerno at Montpellier, the Mohammedan world provided the impulse and the books for European medicine. In making available all that was preserved of ancient lore, these books disseminated the Greco-Roman world's techniques of contraception, amplified by a few Arabian concoctions.

One other source may be noticed at the start: Aristotle's *History of Animals*, containing the text on contraception by cedar oil. Aristotle's treatise was translated from Arabic into Latin by Michael Scot in 1220, and again from Greek into Latin by William of Moerbeke about 1265.[2] Its single, casual reference cannot be compared with the storehouse of information in the Arabic treatises; the latter, moreover, were translated at a much earlier date. But it did provide, under the auspices of the most prestigious philosopher in the Middle Ages, a rational method of attempting contraception.

Of the Arabic texts the most basic was the *Canon of Medicine* by ibn-Sina, known to the Latin world as Avicenna. Written in eleventh-century Damascus, it was translated into Latin at Toledo by Gerard of Cremona or his school about the middle of the twelfth century. For over five hundred years it dominated Western medical thought. One measure of its continued popularity is its survival in at least fifteen incunabular editions.[3] The scholastics sought a standard treatise in every learned field. What the *Digest* was in law and the *Sentences* in theology, such was the *Canon of Medicine* in medicine. For Europeans it was the main textbook until the middle of the seventeenth century.[4] A philosopher of some importance for the West, Avicenna was far more significant for Western science as a teacher of medicine. Learning medicine from him, European physicians incidentally possessed themselves of the contraceptive data of the classical world.

The encyclopedic scope of the *Canon of Medicine* left space for only a few sections on contraception; they provided the essentials of classical lore, with variations and additions.[5] In the pharmacopoeia which composes book II of the *Canon of Medicine*, Avicenna lists the contraceptive properties of several plants. He mentions a spermicide, a pessary, and a talisman. Cedar "corrupts the seed, and when the penis is oiled by it before coitus, it prohibits impregnation"; it also "kills the fetus" (2.2.163, "Chitran"). Mint "placed as a suppository before the hour of coitus pro-

[2] George Sarton, *Introduction to the History of Science* (Baltimore, 1931), II², 494, 716.
[3] *Ibid.*, p. 343.
[4] Charles Singer and E. Ashworth Underwood, *A Short History of Medicine,* 2nd ed. (Oxford, 1962), p. 76.
[5] Avicenna, *Libri canonis medicinae,* in *Opera omnia,* trans. Gerard of Cremona (Venice, 1595).

hibits impregnation" (2.2.495, "Menta"). Sowbread hung about the neck "prohibits impregnation" (2.2.277, "Facaileseus"). Besides plants, other contraceptives are listed in this pharmaceutical section. The rennet of the wood hare drunk with acid three days after the ending of menstruation "prohibits impregnation" (2.2.394, "Lepus sylvestris"). Iron scourings "prohibit impregnation" (2.2.686, "Scoria"). Avicenna seems credulous about the sowbread talisman; in other instances he is more cautious. *Scolopendria*, a form of saxifrage plant, "is said" to prevent impregnation if hung around the neck (2.2.636, "Scolopendria"). Menstrual blood, used as a suppository, will also have this effect, "according to what some think" (2.2.609, "Sanguis").

In book III, where medical procedures are described, contraception is treated as a special subject. Not surprisingly in such a heterogeneous work, there is little correlation with book II. Under the heading "The Prevention of Pregnancy," five forms of contraceptive measures appear:

(1) After coitus, seven to nine jumps backwards by the woman; also sneezing, which "sometimes" helps to make the sperm slippery.

(2) Suppositories in the vagina, to be applied before and after coitus, to be made of cedar oil; or of pomegranate pulp and alum; or of cabbage leaves and cabbage seed, particularly if soaked in cedar oil and mint; or of leaves of the weeping willow soaked in the juice of the weeping willow; or of colocynth pulp; or of equal parts of fresh mandrake, iron dross, cabbage leaves, scammony leaves, and cabbage seed, mixed with cedar.

(3) Oiling the penis with cedar oil, oil of balsam, or ceruse, a method to be used in conjunction with the cedar oil suppository.

(4) Suppositories of pepper or elephant's dung applied after coitus.

(5) A potion of three pints of sweet basil in water.[6]

The first recommendation is only a variant of Soranos, with the specification of a number, probably of magical significance. The second class of contraceptives includes the cedar oil and ointment of lead known to Aristotle and Soranos. The third method is a variant of Aristotle. Other classical prescriptions are altered. Willow leaves, used in a contraceptive potion by Oribasios, are made to function as a pessary. Iron dross, described as part of a potion by Dioscorides and Pliny, is given credit as a pessary. The fourth group, the postcoital suppositories, are not in the main Greco-Roman sources; they are apparently intended to act as

---

[6] There appears to be no substantial difference between the Arabic text translated into English by Himes, *Medical History*, pp. 142–143, and the Latin of both the Strassburg edition (before 1473) and the 1595 edition that I have used in making the foregoing summary. The Arabic text treats separately the oiling of the penis, which the Latin text combines with the treatment of suppositories. It also describes a bindweed pessary, whose omission by the Latin text seems without significance. The correspondence of the Latin and Arabic is testimony to the freedom from censorship of Avicenna's medical work.

spermicides. Class five, potions, is constituted by a single drink, possibly an approximation of the *misy* described in Hippocrates. The contrast with Roman, Celtic, and Germanic interest in potions is striking.

The *Canon of Medicine* also speaks in book III of means of controlling coitus. "Oil diminishes the seed, as does the insertion [*emplastratio*] of leaves of black henbane and white henbane, and henbane placed on the testicles and anus." Other medications to be similarly applied are melons with lead, washed white lead, *chymolea*, and vinegar; and a vaporized mixture of fresh psyllium and crushed lettuce seed, white henbane seed, endive seed, dry coriander, and dried water lily. In the pharmacopoeia of book II, other anaphrodisiacs are listed. Chaste tree, in vaporized form, dries up the seed; spread under one's back, it prevents pollution and impedes erection of the penis; taken by women, it inhibits coital desire (2.2.44, "Agnus castus"). Coriander "breaks the power of coitus and the erection of the penis by drying up the seed" (2.2.143, "Coriandrum"). Rue "dries up the seed and cuts it off and removes the desire of coitus" (2.2.578, "Ruta"). Calamint and camphor are both said to "cut off coitus" (2.2.156, "Calamenthum"; 2.2.133, "Camphora"). Lettuce seed, Avicenna says, "dries up the seed and quiets the desire for coitus (2.2.448, "Lactuca"). The water lily "diminishes pollution and breaks the desire for coitus"; mixed with poppy syrup, it "congeals the seed" (2.2.515, "Nenuphar").

Are these plants contraceptives? It depends on definition. They are intended to affect the desire for coitus by affecting the semen before intercourse. They could, then, be regarded as merely artificial aids to continence. On the other hand, they necessarily prevent not only intercourse, but its fruits. Their purpose is, artificially and deliberately, to depress the physiological and psychological tendencies toward procreation. They differ from other contraceptives only in acting upon sexual drive rather than upon the other physiological components of conception. In the presentation of these anaphrodisiacs by Avicenna a distinction is implicitly made between these plants affecting coital desire and the plants preventing impregnation.

The practice of contraception is also carefully distinguished from abortion by Avicenna. He offers a separate chapter in book III on suppositories and potions by which abortion may be accomplished, entitled "Regimen for Abortion and Extraction of the Dead Fetus" (3.21.2.12). Similarly he distinguishes plants with abortive properties, such as laurel, from those with contraceptive effects. No one familiar with Avicenna would doubt that destruction of a fetus was a different process from prevention of conception, and in Avicenna's presentation there are almost no drugs which have ambiguously abortive or contraceptive effects; cedar is an exception.

Avicenna's basic work was not the only respectable source of contraceptive information in Europe after 1140. The *Book for Almansor* by the Persian al-Razi (Rhazes, to the Latin West) was also translated in the twelfth century by the school of Gerard of Cremona.[7] Like Avicenna, Rhazes listed the contraceptive properties of a few plants, such as cedar, which "so changes the seed that an embryo cannot be generated from it" (3.46). He devoted a chapter to anaphrodisiacs, such as lettuce, vinegar, and other acids, affecting the seed (5.67). Finally, after treating "Things Which Aid Impregnation," he followed this chapter with one on "Things Which Prevent Pregnancy or Produce Abortion" (5.73). His first recommendation is the application of cedar oil, either by the woman after coitus or by the man to his genitals before coitus. If this procedure is followed, Rhazes states authoritatively, "impregnation will not occur." Alternatively, a woman is told to apply after coitus a suppository of rue juice or of pepper. Physical movements are also suggested. If the man withdraws before orgasm by the woman, "the woman will not be impregnated." If the woman jumps backwards after coitus, "the seed will fall out." Rhazes also has a short list of means of producing an abortion (5.73).

Rhazes was actually Avicenna's predecessor, and most of his teaching is included in Avicenna's more comprehensive work; the doctor who knew Avicenna scarcely needed both. But the independent spread of Rhazes' work may be taken as further evidence of the availability of contraceptive information. With Avicenna and Rhazes at hand, medieval physicians had as much information on contraception as Greek or Roman ones.[8]

Indigenous European works, inspired by the basic Arabic authorities, made their teaching even more widely known. How contraceptive information was circulated by this process may be observed, first, in the work of a German theologian writing within a century of the translation into Latin of the Arabic treatises, and then in later European medical works.

---

[7] Rhazes, *Liber ad Almansorem* (Venice, 1497). On the date of translation see Sarton, *Introduction* II², 343. Himes, *Medical History*, p. 136, refers to the book under the title *Quintessence of Experience*.

Himes on pp. 139 and 145–151 lists the following works existing only in Arabic as also containing contraceptive information: 'Alī ibn 'Abbās (d. 944), *The Royal Book*; Sayyid Ismā-'l (d. 1135), *Treasury of Medicine Dedicated to the King of Khwārazm*; Ibn al-Jami (Saladin's Jewish doctor, ca. 1170), *The Book of Right Conduct Regarding the Supervision of the Soul and Body*; Ibn-al-Baitār (1187–1248), *Treatise on Simples*. An Arabic-reading member of the European contingent which remained in the Kingdom of Jerusalem after the First Crusade could have encountered one or another of these works.

[8] The medical authors with whom Chaucer says his Physician in *The Canterbury Tales* is familiar include "Avycen," "Razis," "Ypocras," and "Deyscorides"; *The Complete Works of Geoffrey Chaucer*, ed. F. N. Robinson (Boston, 1957), *Canterbury Tales*, "General Prologue," lines 430–432.

The theologian is Albert the Great (1206–1280), a Dominican, bishop of Regensburg, teacher of Thomas Aquinas, canonized and, as recently as 1931, declared a doctor of the Church. Albert was among those Paris theologians who not only were the dominant intellectual leaders of their age, but were to be the masters of the later Christian scholastics. In this brilliant company Albert was distinguished by his curious and patient attention to natural phenomena and to books about them. His observations on contraceptives occur in two treatises intended as purely scientific encyclopedias: *Vegetables and Plants* and *Animals*. His learning on the subject is largely, though not wholly, derived from Avicenna.

In *Vegetables and Plants*, Albert describes three plants, coriander, lettuce, and rue, and notes the same anaphrodisiac effects which were ascribed to them by Avicenna (6.2.4, 11, 16).[9] But of contraceptives proper he mentions only the talismanic use of scolopendria, and here he makes an interesting variation of Avicenna's cautious "it is said to prevent impregnation." Albert has it, "The magician says that, hung on a woman, it prevents impregnation" (6.2.17).

In *Animals*, Albert analyzes the causes of sterility, so that "medicine may rectify them" (10.1.1).[10] He has already described generation in Aristotelian terms: "When in coitus the two humors, the man's and the woman's, meet in the matrix, the matrix, receiving them, closes, and then the sperm of the male draws to itself the humor of the woman, and forms itself into a ball by encircling itself [with the woman's humor], just as the sperm of the rooster is englobulated by the albumen in an egg" (9.2.4). By the woman's "humor," he has explained, he means what is "equivocally" called the "female sperm" or properly called "menstrual blood" (9.2.3). He appears to believe that this menstrual residue is emitted by a woman in orgasm. In terms of this biology, the causes of sterility are set out. Anatomical difficulties, biochemical deficiencies, human mistakes, and artificial interventions are all listed without any special comment on the difference between merely physical and human factors.

Both the male and the female seed may be responsible for sterility because of excessive heat or cold or dryness. "Moistures" (*humiditates*) can also make the seed "too slippery," so that male and female seed do not adhere, or else can weaken the "virtues" that should attract the seed. Dryness can affect the matrix itself unfavorably, and the meatus may be obstructed. The factors producing these effects of temperature are not specified, except that Albert says that "sometimes" acid foods have a drying or cooling effect on the male seed, and that drinks of cold water may constrict the female pores. Defects in the generative members are

[9] Albertus Magnus, *De vegetabilibus et plantis*, in *Opera omnia*, ed. A. Borgnet (Paris, 1890–1899), vol. X.

[10] Albertus Magnus, *De animalibus*, in *Opera*, vol. XI.

another cause. The penis may be too short, the vulva too wide or narrow, the genital nerves injured, the sperm *vasa* weakened or cut. "Or the testicles may be coated with black henbane or otherwise stupefied" (*ibid.* 10.2.1).

What are described as human "errors" may likewise cause sterility. The natural position for intercourse is with the woman on her back. A lateral position hinders projection of the seed; a position with the woman on top turns the matrix upside down, "so what is in it is poured out." A second error is the man's failure to achieve near-simultaneous "emissions" with the woman. A third error "sometimes happens after coitus when the woman gets up at once and moves, or jumps, or urinates, retaining the urine on the lips of the vulva and making it pass upwards to the mouth of the matrix, for then the seed, being slippery, is mixed with the urine and passes out" (*ibid.* 10.2.1).

One cause of sterility is use of anaphrodisiacs, for such appear to be the acid foods. The henbane ointment is puzzling: in Avicenna its use is said to affect coital desire, and perhaps the same anaphrodisiac use is envisaged by Albert. Other volitional causes of sterility described are strictly contraceptive.[11] Accepting Albert's biological premises, one can at least imagine cases where he could have believed that sterility was the unintentional result of the wrong position in intercourse or of a failure to achieve simultaneous emission. But could anyone have believed that the wearing of saxifrage, or directed urination after coitus, was done with any purpose other than contraception? The information about these acts is information about the accomplishment of contraception. More broadly, his whole account of the factors affecting the male or female seed could be regarded as theory from which specific contraceptives were derivable, or as a generalization of Avicenna's specific contraceptives. As much as Soranos, he has set out a comprehensive account of how contraception may be achieved. Albert's work is of special interest because educated men other than physicians must have read his biological treatise, and because some theologians who may not have read Avicenna must have read him.[12] They could obtain from him a general theory of the working of certain types of contraceptive.[13]

[11] Albert also notes that calamint "provokes menstruation" (*Vegetables and Plants* 6.2.4, *Opera*, X, 228). As the Aristotelian theory of generation made the menses supply the matter for generation, it might be argued that to control menstruation was to control generation. However, it was not at all clear in Aristotelian biology that the matter supplied by menstruation had to be freshly supplied; it seems to have been supposed that any residuum of menstrual blood would suffice. Consequently, control of the time of menstruation was probably not considered to affect the material available for generation.

[12] For example, on another medical topic, St. Thomas cites "Avicenna" when he is actually using not Avicenna but Albert's paraphrase of him. *On the Sentences* 4.31.3, "Exposition of text."

[13] Albert's general reputation as a scientist is probably responsible for the ascrip-

Albert provides less evidence of Arabic influence than the three medical writers now to be examined. These are Arnold of Villanova, John of Gaddesden, and Magnino of Milan. The first of these, Arnold, is the famous Catalan physician and writer of apocalyptic treatises (1238–1311), who taught medicine at Montpellier and acted as a physician for the kings of Spain and for both Pope Boniface VIII and Pope Clement V.[14] In his book, *Simples*, a treatment of the medicinal properties of plants, Chapter 45 lists "Medicines Diminishing Milk and Coitus." These plants are chaste tree, garlic, calamint, camphor, hemlock, gourds, lettuce, portulaca, rue, herb sage, and house leek. Arnold observes of this list, "All these cut off libido, prevent impregnation, diminish milk and menses." This observation is striking in running together anaphrodisiac and contraceptive effects as though any distinction between them was not of much significance. Chaste tree and calamint, which are assigned only an anaphrodisiac property in Avicenna, appear here as capable of "preventing impregnation."

In the *Breviary*, a collection of rules for health and the practice of medicine, probably based on earlier collections, an unidentified writer using Arnold's name sets out a curious hodgepodge of contraceptive information. He contends that "it has been proved" that a woman will not conceive for a month if she places the hoof of a mule on burning coals and lets the smoke from this concoction fumigate her vulva. The fumigation will also restrain menstruation. The effectiveness of a mule's hoof is again extolled in a remedy of willow leaves boiled in water and administered in the morning in a dose of two ladlesful "with a little dust from a mule's hoof": "this prevents conception in a wonderful fashion." An elaborate recipe is given of honey and ass's milk to be "cooked until thick on a slow fire" and worn "in a bit of linen" as an amulet over the navel. The effect here is purely magical: conception will be prevented for as many months as the number of days it has been worn. These remedies invoked the ancient association of sterile animals with the production of sterility. But there are other recipes which appear less fanciful. Avicenna's recommendation of a suppository of elephant dung is reproduced. With a cautious "It is said," a potion of iron dross is recommended as a way of producing perpetual sterility in a woman. The recipe, it is reported, is

---

tion to him of the apocryphal *Secreta mulierum* (Augsburg, 1491). It has a brief chapter, "De impedimentis conceptionis," listing two contraceptive potions.

[14] On Arnold's life, see Juan Antonio Paniagua, *Estudios y notas sobre Arnau de Vilanova* (Madrid, 1963), pp. 70–82. For an appreciation of Arnold of Villanova, see Lynn Thorndike, *A History of Magic and Experimental Science* (New York, 1923–1958), II, 842–847. The edition of Arnold's works used here is the *Opera omnia* (Basel, 1585), containing *De simplicibus* and the *Breviarium*. Paniagua has tentatively determined that *De simplicibus* is genuine and the *Breviarium* apocryphal (*ibid.*, p. 42).

also approved by John of St. Paul;[15] and in fact it is as old as Dioscorides. Potions made from crushed fern root, or sesame juice, or juniper seed mixed with ivy seed, prevent pregnancy. During menstruation a woman may avoid conception on a particular day by eating green mint. Pulverized cabbage seed, applied in the vulva directly after coitus, "will corrupt the seed." Pseudo-Arnold's arsenal of contraceptives, however ineffective they may actually have been, is set out with a good deal of assurance and practical confidence (*Breviary* 3.6). The emphasis on short-term contraceptives is especially striking.

Arnold's younger contemporary, John of Gaddesden (1280–1336), is among the first English writers on medicine. He studied at Merton College, Oxford, and became a successful doctor in London, where he was physician to Edward II. He was in holy orders and had a stall at St. Paul's; doubtless he had had more theological training than Arnold. But he was primarily a doctor.[16] His book, entitled *The English Rose*, or *The Practice of Medicine from Tip to Toe*, had considerable currency at home and abroad. Book II, chapter 17, is "On Sterility." Among the "extrinsic" causes of sterility for a man are lettuce, parsley, henbane, or glowworms, eaten too frequently. For a woman the causes are "the taking of cold things such as cold water and lettuce"; also "jumping backwards or too sudden motion after coitus"; the "receiving of sterilizers" (*sterilizantia*); the frequent eating of deer tongue and heart; the wearing of an agate; the suspension of saxifrage over one's bed; crossing over the menses of another woman, or using them as an ointment; the drinking or wearing of a mule's heart; the injection of mint juice into the matrix after coitus. It is apparent that this list is a haphazard jotting down of all that John has read.[17] The saxifrage talisman is now not to be worn on the neck, as in Avicenna, but hung over the bed. In contrast, the sterile mule's heart is to be carried on the person. The agate is an addi-

---

[15] John of St. Paul was a physician of Salerno. He is tentatively dated by Sarton as flourishing about 1175 (Sarton, *Introduction*, II, 439).

[16] John of Gaddesden, *Rosa anglica: Practica medicinae a capite ad pedes*, ed. and amended by Nicholas Scyllatius (Pavia, 1492). Naming medical books for flowers was the fashion. Gaddesden in his introduction explains that he chose the rose because it has five appendages and because it overtops all flowers. On Gaddesden, see Sarton, *Introduction*, III¹, 880–882. Gaddesden is mentioned by Chaucer as "Gatesden" in his roll of writers in whom his "doctor of physic" is well versed, Prologue to *The Canterbury Tales*, line 434. (There seems to be little foundation for the suggestion of H. H. Bashford, "Chaucer's Physician and His Forebears," *Nineteenth Century* 104 [1928], 237, that Gaddesden is actually the model for Chaucer's avaricious physician.) Gaddesden's works were printed three times between 1497 and 1595. They were also translated into Gaelic in the fifteenth century. A modern edition shows that in the Gaelic translation the descriptions of contraceptives were omitted (*Rosa anglica*, ed. Winifred Wulff, Irish Texts Society 25, London, 1929).

[17] Another example: Avicenna had recommended sneezing after coitus as a contraceptive method. We find John listing among "the cures of sterility" the avoidance of sneezing (*Rosa anglica*, fol. 98r).

tion, from current lapidary theory, to the list of talismans. Yet along with these fanciful notions are included the practical means of postcoital exercise and the probably efficacious use of the mint-juice douche.

What John calls "sterilizers" are set off from a list of anaphrodisiacs. The latter are described in these terms: camphor "impedes erection"; rue, chaste tree, and cumin diminish sexual "swelling," that is, physical impulses to intercourse; fasting on bread and water diminishes the seed (2.17). Yet from John's vantage point all these agents are the same: they effect male sterility.

Contemporary thinking on contraceptives around 1300 may be further gleaned from Magnino, a physician of Milan.[18] Magnino followed Salernan custom in writing a *Regime for Health,* a set of rules for keeping each part of the body in condition. Under the heading of rules "appropriate for the feminine sex," Magnino tells how pregnancy may be achieved, and how it is prevented, sometimes by physiological factors, sometimes "because of the use of things preventing conception." A woman desiring to be fecund "must beware of sterilizers and things impeding conception." Sterility is caused by eating iron filings, mint juice, the matrix of a mule, the rennet of a hare, the heart of a deer, or black peas. Talismans such as a goat's matrix or a piece of jet have the same effect. These amulets are distinguished from a deer's heart, an emerald, a sapphire, which impede coition. Saxifrage suspended over one's bed, the root of the pimpernel, the ear or hide of a mule, are talismans which affect either conception or coition. Eating a bee "makes a woman sterile, but eases birth" (*Regime for Health* 2.7). The content of this list is generally similar to John of Gaddesden's. However, a stronger interest in the properties of stones is reflected; mint juice is considered a drink rather than a douche — an important error; seeds of black ivy are added; and postcoital means of contraception are not mentioned.

Under the heading "The Generative Members," Magnino says that camphor and cabbage seed "cut off" coitus by cooling and drying the seed; so do acid and coriander. Finally, after speaking of the cooling and drying effects of cabbage seed, Magnino says, "Whence, such seed, applied after coitus, corrupts the seed" (*ibid.* 2.6).[19] Here a contraceptive is described which seems traceable to the precoital cabbage-seed suppositories of Avicenna.

More ambiguous are Magnino's prescriptions for those "wishing to be continent," a group he characterizes, without apparent irony, as "vener-

---

[18] On Magnino, see Sarton, *Introduction,* III[1], 854. Sarton reports that there are six incunabula editions of his *Regime for Health.* The edition I use is *Regimen sanitatis* (no date or place); it is no. 10482 in Ludwig Hain, *Repertorium bibliographicum,* 4 vols. (Stuttgart, 1826–1838).

[19] The printed text reads "post cibum" instead of "post coitum"; I amend to make sense.

able" (*ibid.* 3.23). Cold and dry oils, especially oil of henbane or poppy, applied to the genitals, dry up the seed; so will lilies, rue seed, seed of the chaste tree, calamint, milkwort (*euforbium*), myrrh, cumin, hyacinth, and vinegar. Walking barefoot depresses the desire for coitus. A thin, minutely perforated lead plating, bathed in dry and cold oil and worn on the loins, will "much suppress coitus." With the addition of milkwort and myrrh, the plants listed are those whose anaphrodisiac properties are commended by Avicenna. Possibly Magnino is indifferent to whether the effect is anaphrodisiac or contraceptive, but it seems more reasonable to take him at his word, that his recipes are for those desiring continence in the usual Christian sense of abstention from sexual intercourse.

In a section entitled "Suppositories," Magnino speaks of suppositories employed "to resoften the womb and to extract matter from remote and particularly from upper parts." Use to provoke abortion could be encompassed by this vague phrasing, and the possibility is relevant in considering how inhibited by moral scruples Magnino may or may not have been. He also speaks of suppositories composed of "honey sharpened by scammony or milkwort or colocynth" (5.8); it will be recalled that he has specifically treated milkwort as drying the seed, and that the use of scammony and colocynth in a contraceptive compound was mentioned by Avicenna. Contraceptive suppositories may, then, be included in this description. In the following chapter, "Pessaries," Magnino gives four uses for pessaries: to provoke menstruation; to clean the matrix; to restrain the menses; to dispose the matrix to receive the embryo.

In summary, Magnino's practical rules for health provide descriptions of contraceptive amulets and potions, of a cabbage-seed spermicide, and of probably contraceptive suppositories, as well as much information on anaphrodisiacs. His handbook, never prescribing contraception, obliquely gives a variety of ways of attempting it.

With what intention did these medieval writers provide contraceptive information? Avicenna's motive is avowedly therapeutic. Following Soranos' doctrine, he teaches that prevention of pregnancy is necessary when birth will endanger the mother (*Canon of Medicine* 3.21.1.2). The Catholic writers of the thirteenth and fourteenth century discuss the subject without recommending that contraception be employed, yet without any moral condemnation of its use. Pseudo-Arnold appears to provide contraceptive information with a willingness to have it used by whoever sees fit. He is equally free with advice on abortion, and his chapter on contraception is immediately followed by a chapter on how an unmarried girl may appear to be a virgin without actually being one (*Breviary* 3.6).

In John of Gaddesden and Magnino of Milan the listing of contraceptives is purportedly made only so that all causes of sterility will be avoided. The presentation is specious. The kinds of "extrinsic" causes mentioned by these authors are so clearly the result of deliberate human choice that the recital of them cannot be for diagnostic purposes only. John is not aiming to help a doctor whose patient is mysteriously sterile because she has blundered by wearing the heart of a mule; Magnino is not visualizing a patient who has inadvertently used a cabbage-seed pessary or hung saxifrage over her bed. The information is given not to cure sterility but to indicate how contraception is accomplished.

To say as much is not to say that these authors were interested in promoting contraceptive practice. Their work is better understood as the reflection of a spirit that could be called scientific or encyclopedist. Having set out to treat a topic, they wanted to treat it fully. If there was pertinent information in their possession, they wanted to lay it out for their readers. The use of the information was not their concern; they set out what they had. The prime example of this spirit is the work of St. Albert. No one who reads his theological treatment of contraceptives could doubt that he considers contraception a serious sin, yet in his scientific work he abstains absolutely from moral judgment. The objection might be advanced that he does not list all the contraceptives in Avicenna; his reticence must reflect a moral inhibition. But Albert's work is selective and generalizing, not a repetition of Avicenna. With the same calmness and selectivity, Albert notes the abortifacient properties of plants (*Vegetables and Plants* 6.1.16, "Colloquintida"; 6.1.26, "Myrrha"; 6.2.4, "Coriandrum"; 6.2.17, "Scamonea"); with the same imperturbability he describes ways of causing abortion (*Animals* 10.2.2). The rigorous separation Albert makes between morals and medicine is clear in that he does indicate the physical risk for the user in taking certain plants: in *Vegetables and Plants* he indicates the physical danger for the user in taking too much coriander or rue. But he never alludes to the moral danger to the user of an abortifacient or contraceptive, never uses moral categories to describe the accomplished abortion or contraception. He embodies the impartial encyclopedist spirit as he lists the means of contraception.[20]

[20] Another Dominican bishop writing in an encyclopedist spirit is Vincent, bishop of Beauvais, who wrote his *Speculum quadruplex* before 1244. Vincent is noticeably more reticent with contraceptive information than Albert. For example, he writes on the scolopendria and mentions Avicenna but not the contraceptive property Avicenna ascribes to scolopendria (*Speculum naturale* [Douai, 1624] 9.131). But he does give the anaphrodisiac effect of rue: "It restrains and represses lusts and confines and entirely dries up the seed" (10.138). He writes similarly of lettuce (11.16). On jasper, he quotes an unidentified Arnold: "It restrains lechery and prevents conception" (8.77). This statement is the only express contraceptive text I have found in Vincent.

A twelfth-century writer whose work has nothing on contraceptives or abortifacients but something on anaphrodisiacs is St. Hildegard (1098–1179), abbess of Rupertsberg and a woman with a great interest in medicine. Her work *Plants* speaks of "wild lettuce" as used "to extinguish lust in man or woman." *Subtilitatum diversarum naturarum creaturarum* I, *De plantis* 92, PL 197:1165.

DISSEMINATION

If information bearing on contraception had been branded disreputable or illegal, probably its dissemination would have suffered in university medical schools. In fact, the information was provided in a way that assumed every well-educated physician should become familiar with it. The information was given openly in the standard medieval textbook, the *Canon of Medicine.*

The reputation of the native Europeans who repeated or enlarged Avicenna's data is another index to the open circulation of information on contraception. Arnold of Villanova had a somewhat clouded name as to orthodoxy and probity of character, but his presentation on contraception was never made a charge against him. Albert was sometimes credited in popular legend with an occult knowledge, but the sanctity of his life and the soundness of his doctrine were not denied in serious theological quarters. John of Gaddesden and Magnino of Milan appear to have been ordinary physicians, better educated and more articulate than their fellows. Gaddesden was a cleric; Magnino dedicated his work to the Bishop of Arezzo. The respectability of these writers indicates that contraceptive information could be set out without an author's incurring censure. It is true that the form adopted by Albert, John, and Magnino is one in which contraceptive information is presented not as an aid to contraception, but in connection with the causes of sterility or the properties of plants. But throughout the period of his use as a text Avicenna circulated freely, despite his advocacy of contraception on medical grounds. The form used by the European writers did not affect the essential data. From the presentation of the data in these serious works, as well as from the central place of Avicenna, one may conclude that a knowledge of contraceptive technique could have been, and often in fact must have been, possessed in medical circles throughout the later Middle Ages.

How widely was this knowledge further diffused? How often was knowledge put into practice? Our evidence on these points is somewhat parallel to what we have on contraception in antiquity, but the evidence is more abundant. We start from the known fact that medical treatises had the information, and that, thanks to the Arabic contribution, it was more complete than in classical times. Its weakness was the weakness of the classical treatises: lack of discrimination between potentially effective and purely magical or merely useless methods. If John of Gaddesden's book is a fair sample of the knowledge of a well-instructed fourteenth-century doctor, confidence in any contraceptive prescriptions must have been hard to maintain. But this kind of weakness was endemic in all medieval medicine. A more important restraint on use would have been the unwillingness of doctors or druggists to provide the information to patients. There is nothing to indicate that an ordinary physician would not have considered contraception a sin and his cooperation in the sin immoral. To the extent that this moral restraint operated, the information was restricted; but one cannot believe that all physicians or apothecaries observed the proclaimed Christian standard.

From this starting point, that information was available but subject to restriction on moral grounds, we may go on to consider further evidence of contraceptive usage. It will be convenient to divide this evidence under four heads: nonecclesiastical references to contraception; motives and users; ecclesiastical descriptions; demographic surmises.

NONECCLESIASTICAL REFERENCES TO CONTRACEPTION

In Dante's *Divine Comedy*, the approach to anything bordering on contraception is indirect, subtle, allusive. In the *Inferno*, cantos 15 and 16 deal with those who have sinned against nature by sexual sin; in the *Purgatorio*, canto 25 deals with the lustful. Under these headings, in both hell and purgatory, homosexual sinners are punished, but not anyone accused of using contraceptives or engaging in unnatural behavior in marriage. In canto 16 of the *Inferno*, Jacopo Rusticucci complains, "I owe my sorrows to my savage wife," but apparently he means that his wife's unkindness drove him to sodomy.

Two other cantos are of greater relevance. In canto 17 of the *Purgatorio*, the wrathful are described. The first of these is Procne. As Procne's fearful tale had been told by Ovid, her sister Philomela had been raped and mutilated by Procne's husband, Tereus; Procne revenged herself and her sister by killing her own child by Tereus, the six-year-old Itys, and serving him to her husband to eat, ignorant that he was eating their own child. As the slaying of Itys was described by Ovid, the boy called out "Mother, mother!" and clung to her neck. She "did not turn her face" as she killed him (Ovid, *Metamorphorses* 6.639–642). The emphasis in Ovid shifts from Procne's just reasons for revenge to her heartless destruction of her child. Procne might stand, then, as the symbol of all women who kill their own childen. Against the background of the canon law, which treated contraception as homicide, against the background of the theological opinion which held contraception to be a sin of wrath, the gory example of Procne might be considered to symbolize dramatically all those mothers who destroyed life or interfered in the life-giving process. But Dante does not develop this association of ideas. The early commentators, such as Francis Buti, recognized that the allusion was to Ovid, but they, too, made no reference to the canons.

If wrath and contraception were not specially linked, what of lust and contraception? Canto 25 of the *Purgatorio*, devoted to the lecherous, begins with a question of Dante to Statius about the inhabitants of Purgatory. "How can they grow so thin who are not touched by the desire of food in their new state?" The question recalls the teaching of Thomas Aquinas that there is neither generation nor eating for the saved (*On the Sentences* 4.44.1.3.4). Statius replies with a long discourse on the process of generation, the relevance of which is not obvious except against the background of theological teaching that analyzes lechery as a sin against the generative process. Dante and Virgil press on to "the last turning," with an abyss on their right, fire on their left. They encounter the souls being purged in the fire, who sing four songs related to different sins within the species of lechery. They sing the Saturday Matins hymn, *Summae Deus clementiae* (a general prayer against lust); they celebrate virginity, repeating the words of Mary, "I know not man"; they reject fornication in honoring the huntress Diana, who expelled from her band of maidens a nymph who had felt the "poison of Venus"; and finally they sing the praises of "ladies and husbands who were chaste, as virtue and matrimony require." In this last song, there is probably reference to chastity within marriage; the suggestion is that both virtue and the laws of marriage set a standard to be met—the verb used to describe the imposition of these requirements is *imporre*. The standard would presumably be the current standard given in terms of avoidance of nonprocreative sexual acts. But there is no dwelling on the exact laws of intercourse in the fashion of the prevailing theology. Instead Dante continues, in words applicable to all the lustful but specifically following the song on the married, "And this way, I believe, suffices them all the time the fire burns them. With such care, with such medicines, the last wound is healed." Not a detailed set of laws but the examples of the virtuous lead them through the fire; the example of the anonymous crowd of married folk who have lived chastely is enough.

In these passages on the lecherous there is also the use of several images taken from medicine. The maiden touched by Venus has felt her "tosco," a term for poison derived from the Latin *toxicum*. For all the lecherous the wound of lust is now to be healed. "Cura," care, is a medical metaphor, as Raphael Andreoli has pointed out. "Pasti" may be translated "medicines." It becomes "medicamenta" in the fifteenth-century Latin translation of Dante by the Franciscan John of Serravalle. In employing this motif of drugs, Dante, it might be thought, plays off the medicines of virtue against the unmentioned medicines which the laws of marriage reject.[21]

If Dante's method here is evocative, not expository, the most important

---

[21] References to Dante are to *La Divina Commedia*, ed. Giuseppe Vandelli, in *Le Opere di Dante*, Società Dantesca Italiana, 2nd ed. (Florence, 1960), *Inferno* 16.44–45, *Purgatorio* 17.19–21 and canto 25. By the standard commentators, I mean those writers collected in Guido Biagi, G. L. Passerini, and Enrico Rostagno, *La Divina Commedia nella figurazione artistica e nel secolare commento*, vol. II (Turin, 1931). Buti, Serravalle, and Andreoli are cited as they appear in this work at the cantos cited.

English literary work of the Middle Ages deals with contraceptives with a startling bluntness. In the *Canterbury Tales*, "The Parson's Tale" treats of the seven deadly sins, and under the sin of wrath speaks of manslaughter. Among the species of manslaughter is a woman's "drynkynge venenouse herbes thurgh which she may nat concevve." Another form of manslaughter is for a woman to put "certeine material thynges in hire secree places to slee the child." A third form is unnatural intercourse. All of these modes are distinguished from the destruction of a fetus already conceived ("The Parson's Tale," *De ira*, lines 570–580).

The Parson's reference to contraception under "Wrath" follows the canonical classification of the sin as homicide. It is generally supposed that Chaucer in composing this prose sermon was following one or more theological summas, but no evidence has been discovered as to his immediate sources.[22] It may be that he was composing with only a loose adherence to whatever model he had found. Consequently, his reference to contraceptive practice need not be a repetition of some text before him; he may have been exemplifying the canon law by specifying practices he had heard of. Whether he followed a theological text or composed more freely, the words chosen by Chaucer reflect awareness of real problems. *Venena sterilitatis*, poisons of sterility, was the standard canonical phrase for artificial contraceptives in his day; but he chooses a concrete phrase with old Germanic roots: the poisons are herbal potions. The "material things in secret places" is not only more specific than the usual theological term; I have not encountered a single theological or canonical writer who refers so explicitly to contraceptive pessaries. That such indeed are meant, rather than abortifacients, is evident from the fact that this case is distinguished from the killing of an embryo. The word "slay" here is not counterevidence. This term merely carries out the canonical definition of homicide; "manslaughter" is the generic sin of which contraception is a species.[23] From the placing of this sin in the Parson's Tale, something more may be concluded: contraception is not such a common

[22] Hazelton has shown Chaucer's reliance on the *Moralium dogma philosophorum* of William of Conches (Richard Hazelton, "Chaucer's Parson's Tale and the *Moralium dogma philosophorum*," *Traditio* 16 [1960], 255-274). But this work, arranged in terms of the virtues, has no mention of the contraceptives noted by Chaucer under *De ira* and *Remedium contra peccatum luxurie*. *Das Moralium dogma philosophorum des Guillaume de Conches: Lateinisch, altfranzösisch und mittelniederfränkisch*, ed. John Holmberg (Uppsala, 1929).
   Another work postulated as the original source of a small portion of Chaucer's tale is Peraldus, *Summa of Virtues and Vices* (W. F. Bryan and Germaine Dempster, *Sources and Analogues of Chaucer's Canterbury Tales*, Chicago, 1941, p. 724). But Peraldus also has no special treatment of contraception.

[23] "Manslaughter" is, of course, a literal translation of *homicidium*. English law at this time knew no distinction between manslaughter and murder. *Murdrum* was killing in secret; only some kinds of voluntary killing were *homicidium* (Henry de Bracton, *De legibus et consuetudinibus Angliae* 3.2.4, London, 1640; cf. James F. Stephen, *A History of the Criminal Law of England*, 3 vols., London, 1883, III, 35).

or popular sin that it would be natural to allude to it in a bawdy tale like the Miller's; neither is it so exotic or unheard of that the sober and plain-speaking Parson can pass over it in silence. He refers to it in language which Chaucer must have supposed a literate audience in the fourteenth century would understand.

The evidence provided in a work by another layman, Chaucer's contemporary, is less clear. In 1371 the French knight, Geoffrey De La Tour Landry, wrote for his three daughters (married and to be married) a book to instruct them by the example of good and bad women. Assisted by two priests and two clerks, Geoffrey tended to draw his examples from the Bible, though he occasionally salted the narrative with his own experience. Chapter 57 of the *Book of La Tour Landry* is headed "Thamar, Who Was Wife of Onan." It is devoted chiefly to Thamar's later life, but it says of Onan: "Cestui Honain fut trop pervers et felon et de mauvaise vie, laquelle je ne vueil pas toute dire, dont Dieux voulst qu'il en morut soudainement et piteusement." [24] The sin of Onan is recognized as "perverse," but La Tour Landry, who is remarkably blunt about fornication and adultery, makes no further reference to the story and does not even indicate that Onan's sin was sexual. The knight's undeveloped allusion seems to reflect not only inhibition but a belief that the danger of such practices is not widespread.

To turn from literature to law, legal treatises show slight awareness of contraception. In the famous treatise *The Laws and Customs of England,* by Henry de Bracton, chancellor of Exeter Cathedral, there is no mention of contraception, although he treats abortion, produced by a blow or by poison, as homicide if the embryo is "formed" or "ensouled" (3.2.4). Since 1237, *Si aliquis* had been part of the canon law; but Bracton's failure to adopt the canonical position is not surprising. He finished his treatise by 1256, and at this date no major theologian — neither Albert, nor Thomas, nor Bonaventure, nor Hales, nor Middleton — had accepted the *Decretals'* treatment of contraception as homicide.

In the next generation a somewhat different attitude is evident. The anonymous royal official who wrote the law book which derives its name from a prison, *Fleta,* took account of *Si aliquis* on contraception, but, whether through ignorance or design, made unintelligible use of it. He writes: "One is rightly a homicide who has pressed on a pregnant woman or has given her poison or struck her to produce an abortion or to prevent her from conceiving, if the fetus was already formed and ensouled, and similarly he who has given or received poison with this intention of

---

[24] *Le Livre du Chevalier De La Tour Landry pour l'enseignement de ses filles,* ed. Anatole de Montaiglon (Paris, 1854), c. 57. An English translation of La Tour Landry, made by William Caxton himself in 1483, is one of the first books printed in English. In this book Onan appears as "Henam" (see the 1868 edition of Thomas Wright, Early English Text Society no. 33).

preventing generation or conception. A woman also commits homicide if she destroys an ensouled child in her womb by potion and the like" (*Fleta* 1.23).[25] This enumeration added to the crimes treated in Bracton the self-administration of an abortifacient by a woman and the giving and receiving of a contraceptive poison. But the first reference to contraception was unintelligently inserted in a sentence where homicide occurs only if the fetus is formed and ensouled. The author faced the same problem as the canonists on how to reconcile *Si aliquis*, holding contraception to be homicide, and *Sicut ex*, holding that only abortion of a formed fetus was homicide. The canonists, as we shall see, solved the problem by distinguishing the kinds of punishment to be applied. *Fleta* merely garbled the canons.

If one turns from English law to the Roman law of Justinian, which was assumed to be still valid in many parts of Italy, Germany, and France, there is no attempt in the standard *Gloss*, written by Accursius, to expand the reference to contraceptives under the Cornelian law, no reference to the canon law (*Gloss on Digest* 48.8).[26] Accursius maintains the old position that to destroy a young embryo is not homicide. Commenting on the *Digest*'s provision of exile for abortion, he adds that this penalty applies only if the fetus is under forty days; after forty days, the penalty for homicide applies according to the law of Moses or the Pompeian law on parricides (*Gloss on Digest* 47.11.4).

I would conclude from this sampling of English and Continental law that there was little secular interest in contraception as a social menace and little interest in giving literal effect to the canon law's special definition of it as homicide.

A different type of evidence is provided by the herbals. These, indeed, might be classified as medical rather than popular, except they seem intended for a somewhat wider audience than physicians. Probably their chief users were the apothecaries. If I may take a printed and therefore rather late herbal as a specimen, consider the *Herbal on the Powers of Herbs* printed in Vicenza in 1491.[27] An anonymous work, it has a frontispiece consisting of pictures of Avicenna and Arnold of Villanova; and, indeed, so much of its information is derived from them that it is probably fair to treat the work as representative of a period much earlier than its printing. It mentions only one contraceptive outright: the saxifrage hung about a woman's neck. Avicenna's cautious "some think" is repeated in stating its contraceptive power ("Scolopendria"). Control of menstruation by two plants is indicated: coriander restrains it, and rue provokes it ("Coriandrum"; "Ruta"). The effect of "drying up" human

---

[25] *Fleta*, ed. H. G. Richardson and G. O. Sayles (London, 1955).
[26] *Corpus juris civilis* (Venice, 1584).
[27] *Herbolarium de virtutibus herbarum* (Vicenza, 1491).

seed and preventing erection is also ascribed to coriander, while lettuce seed in a potion is said "to be contrary to seed" ("Coriandrum"; "Lactuca"). In the fashion of Arnold of Villanova, these descriptions are vague enough to designate contraceptive effects or anaphrodisiac effects, or both. Rue is cited for a clearly anaphrodisiac effect: it "extinguishes lust" ("Ruta").

These random and incomplete listings of properties affecting conception would seem likely to have been typical of compilations drawn from Avicenna's pharmacopoeia in *The Canon of Medicine*. Not every herbal or book for apothecaries had such contents. I find nothing on contraceptive properties in the *Herbal* of Rufinus, composed between 1287 and 1300 by a monk who was penitentiary of the archbishop of Genoa.[28] *Poisons* by Santes de Ardoino (ca. 1425) and *Poisons* by Antonius Guainerius (d. 1445) treat of plants like coriander and rue with no mention of contraceptive or antilibidinous properties.[29] The *Light of Apothecaries* by Quirico de Augustis, printed in Venice in 1497, has nothing on contraceptive effects.[30] This kind of negative proof suggests that contraceptives were not an essential stock in trade of apothecaries, even if herbals deriving from Avicenna may have encouraged some popular use of plants for contraception.

There does not seem to have been great ecclesiastical concern over the apothecaries. In 1285, the synod of Riez, a town in old Cathar territory, provided for the registration with a civic official of the sale of poisons by apothecaries. It further imposed an excommunication reserved to the Pope for whoever "sells or gives poison or deadly herbs for death or abortion" (Canon 14, Mansi 24:581). Probably "deadly herbs" would have included contraceptives, but it would seem that, if contraception had been a substantial problem, contraceptive use would have been more particularly specified.

The probably limited use of such herbs by apothecaries and physicians may be confirmed for early-fifteenth-century Siena and mid-fifteenth-century Florence from the works of St. Bernardine (1380–1444) and St. Antoninus (1381–1451). In Bernardine's unsparing denunciation of the sins of his fellow citizens, he attacks "the sellers of ointments" (*aromatarii* and *pigmentarii*) who "in syrups and medicines put things they know to be corrupt and harmful," but he says not a word about their selling contraceptives (*The Eternal Gospel* 33.2.7).[31] Bernardine is ordinarily explicit enough on sins in marriage so that he would have stated

---

[28] *The Herbal of Rufinus*, ed. Lynn Thorndike (New York, 1946).

[29] Santes de Ardoino, *De venenis* (Venice, 1492); Antonius Guainerius, *De venenis* (Venice, [1487?]). Santes de Ardoino does say that menstrual blood may make one *maleficiatus*, i.e., impotent (5.25).

[30] Quirico de Augustis, *Lumen apothecariorum* (Venice, 1497).

[31] Bernardine, *De evangelio aeterno*, in *Opera* (Quaracchi, 1950–1963), vol. IV.

clearly that "harmful" meant "harmful to conception" if it had been necessary to denounce such medicines. Similarly in St. Antoninus' careful listing of the habitual sins of different occupations, there is treatment of the sins of "the sellers of ointments" (*aromatarii*). They are charged with selling on feast days and with using false weights, but not with selling contraceptives (*Summa of Theology* 3.8.4.6).[32] In Antoninus' *Confessional* there are interrogatories for different professions. A doctor is to be asked if he performed a therapeutic abortion, but there is no question on contraceptives ("Interrogatory" at "Doctors").[33] However, in the *Confessional*, it is noted of the ointment-sellers, "If they teach or sell what procures abortion . . . or if they sell poisons [*venena*] to those who they believe will abuse them, there is mortal sin" ("Interrogatory," at "Ointment-Sellers"). This text is ambiguous. *Venena sterilitatis* being the ordinary canonical term for contraceptives, it is not clear that "poisons" alone encompasses them, but probably it does embrace them in a context where the sale of abortifacients is first considered. The text would seem, then, to reflect a mild belief on Antoninus' part that apothecaries in Florence might sell herbs capable of being used contraceptively. But it would not seem that the problem was a serious one. If the attitudes of Bernardine and Antoninus are compared with the concern of Regino and Burchard, it will be concluded that "herbal potions" are much less a problem in bourgeois Italy than they had been in barbarian Germany.

MOTIVES AND USERS

Who are reported to use contraceptives? Testimony of some value is offered here by the theologians and canonists. The most unsympathetic user of contraceptives is the enemy who, by potion or magic, attempts to render his victim sterile. This kind of use, embraced under the heading *maleficium* in the penitentials, is apparently not unknown to more sophisticated times. One of the most authoritative of decretalists, Henry of Susa, commonly called Hostiensis, notes this possibility in recalling *Si sortiaris* in Gratian 2.33.1.4. This canon dealt with the annulment of the marriage of a couple made impotent by magic. Their case is cited by Hostiensis to show how sorcery may maliciously affect marriage; *Si aliquis* now reaches this evil. Such sorcery, he adds sententiously, is worked "sometimes by a potion, sometimes without a potion" (*Commentary* 5.12.5).[34]

Specific motives of hostile sterilization are supposed by the best of the

---

[32] Antoninus, *Summa sacrae theologiae, juris pontifici et caesarei* (Venice, 1581).
[33] Antoninus, *Confessionale* (Venice, 1524).
[34] Hostiensis, *Commentaria in quinque libros decretalium* (Venice, 1581).

fourteenth-century canonists, Joannes Andreae (1270–1348), who is, incidentally, the first layman to treat of contraception. He writes, "Perhaps she did not want him or her to have children, that the woman might be displeasing to her spouse, or that she might inherit from him if intestate, or more easily under his will, or something similar" (*New Commentary on the Decretals* 5.12.5).[35] The first case is that of a woman bent on alienating the affections of another's husband; the second brings in the bourgeois economic motives of a good detective story. It is difficult to say that the case is more than the supposition of an ingenious lawyer. In the leading canonist of the fifteenth century, Nicholas de' Tudeschi, known as Panormitanus (d. 1453), Andreae's supposition of sterility caused to assure intestacy is repeated, along with Hostiensis' observation that sorcery can render a man impotent (*Commentary on the Decretals* 5.12.5).[36]

In the more interesting area of contraception practiced by a willing person or couple, economic motivation is as old as the *paupercula* of the penitentials. But not much is said on this motivation by the thirteenth-century canonists and theologians. The decretal *Si aliquis* is taken from Burchard, but Burchard's reference to "the poor little woman" is not picked up — possibly for no better reason than that it occurred in the portion of Burchard devoted to confessional interrogation rather than in the collection of canons where *Si aliquis* was embedded. Of the thirteenth-century writers I have examined, only Hostiensis makes reference to an economic impulse in contraceptive practice, and he only obliquely touches the subject. Commenting on marriage, he warns against contraception and then adds, "Let the offspring be gratefully received whether it be a boy or girl; give thanks to the Creator and do not murmur even in the face of exceeding poverty" (*The Golden Summa* 4, "Marriage," 19).[37]

In the first quarter of the fourteenth century there is the first reference to economic motive by an important theologian. Peter de Palude, a Dominican moralist of standing, notes that the husband's motive in coitus interruptus may be to avoid having "more children than he can feed" (*On the Sentences* 4.31.3).[38] His statement is repeated in the fifteenth century by St. Antoninus of Florence, the German Dominican John Nider,

---

[35] Joannes Andreae, *In decretalium libros novella commentaria* (Venice, 1581). Andreae was not only the author of the *Novella* and a married man, but the father of a daughter named Novella, who, according to an old if disputed story, was talented enough to substitute for him in teaching his classes and beautiful enough to distract his students. For a sympathetic appreciation of Joannes Andreae, "the most erudite of medieval jurists," see Stephan Kuttner, "Joannes Andreae and His *Novella* on the Decretals of Gregory IX," *The Jurist* 24 (1964) 393–408, previously printed with a reprinting (Turin, 1963) of the 1581 edition.

[36] Panormitanus, *In quinque libros decretalium commentaria* (Venice, 1571).

[37] Hostiensis, *Summa aurea* (Lyons, 1542).

[38] Peter de Palude, *In quartum librum Sententiarum* (Venice, 1493).

and the Franciscan Trovamala.[39] This verbatim repetition is, of course, only evidence that Palude did not seem so farfetched that a later writer had to excise or explain his observation. Independently of Palude, Panormitanus also supposes that "some do this because of poverty" (*Commentary* 5.12.5). With such authorities making or repeating the assertion that poverty may lead to contraception, it may be concluded that the case was familiar to the theologians; how often it was encountered in fact is a matter for speculation.

A third kind of motive is therapeutic. In the late twelfth century, the case is put by some scholastics of the woman for whom another pregnancy will be fatal (above, p. 177). The case presented is striking in not being a repetition of one of Avicenna's therapeutic possibilities; the condition of the woman is concretely made the result of earlier birth. Strangely enough, the therapeutic motive is not discussed by any of the later prominent scholastics. Why was there this silence when the text of Avicenna, so widely distributed, ought to have raised the problem, if experience did not? Cases must have often occurred where contraception would have seemed desirable as a way of preventing a pregnancy dangerous to the health of the mother. It would appear that the theologians avoided discussion of a hard question.

Another motive for contraception is the narrowly selfish one expressed by Joannes Andreae: "the woman is such that it is not fitting for her to appear pregnant" (*New Commentary* 5.12.5; followed by Panormitanus, *Commentary* 5.12.5). The sentence embodies the thought, as old as the *Elenchos*, that the person most likely to use contraception is one engaged in illicit affairs. This might be a married woman involved in adultery or a single woman committing fornication. There is also some reference to clerics causing contraceptives to be used. St. Raymond, compiler of the *Decretals* and author of a much-used handbook for confessors, asks if a cleric incurs the sanction of irregularity by providing a woman with a potion to prevent conception. He treats this case together with the case of abortion of a fetus that has not yet received a human soul (*Summa for Confessors* 2.1.4). Since the question is raised by so experienced a canonist as Raymond, to dismiss it as mere academic speculation seems unwarranted. There is a continuous concern with clerics causing abortions, a subject treated in the *Decretals* 5.12.20, *Sicut ex*, and thereafter commented on by the major commentators. Any cleric so faithless to his state as to commit fornication and attempt abortion might well have been tempted to try contraception.

The motives for contraception noted by the ecclesiastical writers may

---

[39] Antoninus, *Summa* 3.1.20; John Nider, *De morali lepra* (Paris, 1490), 5.1, "The Genital Abuses of the Married"; John Baptist de Salis (Trovamala), *Summa rosella* (Venice, 1495), "Debt," 11.

be reduced to these: jealousy or avarice, economic necessity, medical necessity, and shame or social or legal pressure. From second-hand speculation on motive one cannot generalize with assurance; but if a good many people had such reasons, and means of contraception in some form were believed to be on hand, the act of contraception must have been executed or attempted with some frequency.

ECCLESIASTICAL DESCRIPTION

There is no need to duplicate the references to contraception already reviewed, nor to anticipate references to be placed in later contexts. It may, however, be helpful to make two points on the language used by the church writers to describe contraceptive behavior, as these points bear on the frequency with which such behavior is encountered, and to add to these points two medieval estimates of the incidence of contraceptive behavior.

The common practice of the scholastic writers was to identify artificial contraceptives by the comprehensive but blind phrase "poisons of sterility." The repetition of this circumlocution of Augustine is not evidence that the theologians using it were not familiar with particular forms of such poisons. The phrase was an easy way of designating contraceptives without imparting detailed information about them and without becoming involved in an appraisal of their efficacy.

Probably there was variation in the concrete referents the theologians had in mind in using the term. When *Aliquando* was cited by Ivo of Chartres, it seems likely that herbal potions were the only contraceptives he knew. At the time of Gratian and Peter Lombard, Avicenna had just been translated, and it is improbable that his work would have circulated enough for the canonists to have been familiar with his prescriptions. By the late twelfth century, when Peter Cantor discussed therapeutic contraception, there may have been some awareness of Avicenna. By the time of the *Decretals* the *Canon of Medicine* was probably known to theologians and canonists interested in such matters. By the mid-thirteenth century it is evident that Avicenna was available to theologians at Paris, and it is probable that by "poisons of sterility" they meant the means described by him.

Did the ecclesiastical writers actually read Avicenna? The evidence here is slight, and one can only urge the likelihood that a learned man speaking of medical matters would at least have been aware of the general contents of Avicenna's work. The failure to mention it or to name specific means is not evidence to the contrary, if the usage of St. Albert is indicative of the common convention. Albert in his scientific writing is heavily dependent on Avicenna and clearly conversant with his armory of contraceptives. Yet in his theological treatment he uses only the standard phrase "poisons of sterility." A less clear-cut but instructive example occurs in the *Confessional* of Antoninus, which distinguishes intercourse "outside the vessel" from that "within the vessel," where, however, insemination is avoided by the seed's not being received ("Interrogatory" 3.1). Antoninus obviously has in mind some means by which the seed is blocked; but he specifies nothing. The convention of vagueness is established, and I have encountered only a single moral theologian, Martin Le Maistre, in the fifteenth century, who breaks from it. I am inclined to believe that the convention reflects the conviction that the poisons of sterility were somewhat exotic, and, if known, should not be described further. Such a conviction would probably have arisen only if the use of poisons of sterility was, in fact, not widespread.

Did "poisons of sterility" designate means effecting both permanent and temporary sterility? The question does not appear to have been raised. It has been seen that in John of Gaddesden the term "sterilizer" is applied to something intended to cause temporary sterility, and that St. Albert mentions among "the causes of sterility" a coating for the genitals that would be temporary in character. When St. Albert discusses the morality of using poisons of sterility, two suppositions are evident in his prescription for penance. The couple is to be asked not to have intercourse; this advice assumes that the sterility may be for some period or may be permanent. The couple is also to be instructed not to use such poisons again; this assumes that the sterility may not be permanent (*On the Sentences* 4.31.18).[40] One must, I believe, conclude that the medieval theologians saw no moral difference between causing temporary and permanent sterility.

An almost equal vagueness attends the scholastic description of forms of sexual usage which thwart or avoid insemination. The Augustinian text on nonprocreative intercourse, basic because incorporated in Gratian and Lombard, was *Adulterii malum*. The sin therein described is "what is done against nature"; an example specifies the sin, but does not exhaust the possibilities. In the twelfth-century writers there does not appear to be further specification of the act "against nature" in marriage. I take this absence of specificity, which contrasts with the usage of the penitentials, not to indicate a sudden disappearance of particular forms of this sin, but to reflect acceptance of a general phrase conventionally covering all the several forms.[41] The purpose of the conventions is not to disclose ways of sin unknown to the innocent. The ways in which a sin

[40] Albert, *In IV Sententiarum librum*, in *Opera*, vol. XXX.
[41] A valuable book on the history of marital theory in the early Middle Ages, Pedro Abellán's *El fin y la significación sacramental del matrimonio desde St. Anselmo hasta Guillermo de Auxerre* (Granada, 1939), disagrees with this conclusion. Abellán says that in the period of 1164–1220 he has found "not a single clear word" on "the sin of onanism" (p. 138). He adds that there was less need for contraception because "there were not today's demands in feeding a family" (p. 159). In fact, economic mo-

against marriage is committed "I neither wish to write nor do I advise you to reveal," writes Hostiensis in his *Golden Summa* 5, "Penances and Remissions," 49, as he gives advice to a confessor.

In the theological development of the thirteenth century, anal intercourse, oral intercourse, coitus interruptus, and departure from the assumed norm of position in intercourse were all analyzed as instances of the marital sin against nature. I do not believe it anachronistic to assume that the twelfth-century writers had such acts as referents for their catch-all phrase. In many of the later writers, too, the variety of sins comprehended by the "sin against nature" can only be inferred from a study of common theological usage. There is never any attempt to provide a biological description of the acts condemned. Medical terms are eschewed. The vagina is usually described as "the vessel" or "the fit vessel." Ejaculation is often described as "pollution." The term "coitus interruptus" is never employed, but the usual description is "outside the fit vessel." One of the most explicit statements of what the act consists of is given by Bernard of Pavia, commenting on a text of Gratian dealing with impediments to marriage. Under the prevailing rules, one could not marry a person with whom one who was within the prohibited degrees of kinship had had sexual intercourse. Suppose one brother had intercourse in an unnatural way with a woman: was "affinity" created with her, so that another brother could not marry her? Urban II, being asked the question, answered negatively: "extraordinary pollution" was not the kind of intercourse which created the impediment (Gratian, *Decretum* 2.35.3.11). Commenting on this response, Bernard of Pavia defined "extraordinary pollution" as "all pollution which is not done within the vessel fit by nature, that is, within the vulva, whether it be done in some other vessel or outside" (*Summa of Decretals* 4.14.7).

A good example of the variety of acts comprehended by the sin against nature in marriage is provided by Alexander of Hales (1185–1245), one of those scholastics who contributed so much to the thirteenth-century flowering of the University of Paris. Regent in both the faculty of arts and the faculty of theology from 1216 to 1236 and sometime Archdeacon of Coventry, he became one of the first great intellectual recruits to the order of St. Francis. His *Summa theologica* was begun in 1237 and completed after his death.[42] The variety of usage of "natural" in this single work may reflect the composite authorship, but more probably illustrates the shades of meaning clustered about "sin against nature."

Treating "the Sixth Commandment," Alexander says that marital coitus is prohibited, if it is "beyond the natural mode" (3–2.3.2.1.2.6.8.3). If

---

tivation for avoiding offspring is noted throughout the Middle Ages. Abellán does not consider the possibility that the sin against nature includes coitus interruptus.

[42] Alexander of Hales, *Summa theologica* (Quaracchi, 1930–1948). On Hales, see Aquilin Emmen, O.F.M., "Alexander v. Hales," *LTK* 1:306.

this phrase were his sole reference under the Sixth Commandment to the sin against nature in marriage, one might well conclude that Hales either condemned only excessively lustful intercourse or only unusual postures in intercourse. But he also quotes Augustine's phrase in Gratian, "use of a member of the woman not granted for this"; and under the heading "Sins of the Married" he indicates that this kind of intercourse is "the sin against nature" (2–2.3.5.2.1.3.3). Again, one might stop at this definition, if Alexander had not written further. Treating "the sin against nature," here labeled "the greatest sin of the flesh," he speaks of marital intercourse departing from the presumed normal position; such an unnatural act he finds to be sin even if "the vessel is kept" (2–2.3.5.2.1.8.3). Nor can one stop at this additional indication of the sin against nature. Treating of the seven deadly sins, Alexander deals with lechery. Here he says "coitus against nature" is to act like "Lamech, who did not intend to procreate offspring to the worship of God, to which matrimonial union is specifically directed, but copulated to satisfy his lust" (2–2.3.4.2.1.7.2.2). "Lamech" I take to be a slip of the pen for "Onan"; the biblical Lamech, a homicidal son of Cain, has no special relation to marriage (Gn 4:23). Alexander now seems to find the sin against nature to occur in intercourse with the intention not to have children, followed by withdrawal and semination outside the vagina. Yet if one had only his treatment of the Sixth Commandment to judge by, this meaning of "the sin against nature" might not be suspected.

In the most influential definition, that of St. Thomas Aquinas in the *Summa theologica*, the "vice against nature" is one of the several species of lust. It is considered after an analysis of fornication, adultery, seduction, rape, incest, and sacrilege. The vice is itself subdivided into autoerotic acts resulting in genital stimulation (*mollities*); bestiality, or intercourse with animals; sodomy, or intercourse with a person of the same sex; and finally acts where "the natural way of lying together is not kept, either because of using an unfit organ or because of using other monstrous and bestial ways of lying" (*Summa theologica* 2–2.154.11).[43] This concluding definition seems intended to encompass anal intercourse, oral intercourse, coitus interruptus, and departure from the normal position. The term "organ," *instrumentum*, replaces the more usual word, "vessel," used by Aquinas himself in his earlier *Commentary on the Sentences* 4.31; presumably the new term has a more scientific sound.[44] The definitions in the *Summa theologica* do not, however, differ in substance from the earlier work where in marriage the sin against nature is "to omit the fit vessel" or "the fit way instituted by nature as to position."

[43] Thomas Aquinas, *Summa theologica*, Leonine edition (Rome, 1899).
[44] Galen defined an *instrumentum* as "the part of a body capable of performing a complete action. The eye is an organ, but the cornea, iris, and retina are not" (*De methodo medendi* 1.6, in *Opera*, trans. John Bernard Feliciano, Venice, 1560).

The same approach to the sin is taken by the canonists. In his *Golden Summa* Hostiensis says the sin occurs "when a woman is known in a different way from what nature requires." What is such an act? "Everyone naturally knows the way nature demands, and nature itself expounds it." The sin is any semination "outside the vessel" and any departure from the normal mode (*Summa* 5, "Penances and Remissions," 49, "What Questions Can or Should Be Asked by One Hearing Confession?").

St. Thomas, following St. Albert, reserved the term sodomy for unisexual intercourse. Such usage is not universal. In the late twelfth century, Peter Cantor is ambiguous. The sodomites, he says, are like Onan, "who spilled his seed on the earth." His denunciation of the sin of sodomy seems to extend to coitus interruptus (*The Abridged Word* 138, "The Sodomitic Vice," *PL* 205:335).

Sodomy and coitus interruptus are often treated as two varieties of the sin against nature. The Dominican bishop of Lyons, William Peraldus (circa 1274), explicitly adopts this approach. "The sin against nature" occurs when "one contrives or consents that seed be spilled in a place other than that allotted by nature." So defined, the sin is said to comprise both the homosexual acts of the inhabitants of old Sodom and the act of Onan (*Summa of Virtues and Vices* 2.3, "Lechery," 6).[45] A similar approach — possibly indebted to a summa stemming from Peraldus — is found in Chaucer's Parson. As put by the Parson, sinning unnaturally ("unkyndely synne") is an act "by which man or womman shedeth hire nature in manere or in place ther as child may nat be conceived" ("The Parson's Tale," line 577). John Gerson (1363–1429), chancellor of the University of Paris, defines sodomy to include both copulation with a person of the same sex and semination "in a vessel not ordained for it"; a reference to coitus interruptus which shortly follows this passage seems to assimilate it as well to sodomy (*Moral Rules* 99).[46] St. Antoninus puts it even more distinctly in his book for confessors, "A man with a man, a woman with a woman, or a man with a woman outside of the fit vessel, is called the sodomitic vice" (*Confessional*, "Interrogatory" 1.6).

In the thirteenth, fourteenth, and fifteenth centuries there is more attention given to "the sin against nature" than to the use of "poisons of sterility." It is the sin against nature in marriage which is preached against, if preaching is done on marriage; about which inquiry is prescribed in hearing confession; which is apparently the more familiar problem to the theologians. It seems fair to conclude that it was the kind of contraceptive behavior most often encountered.

Two particularly somber judgments on marriage indicate a belief in

[45] William Peraldus, *Summa de virtutibus et vitiis* (Venice, 1497).
[46] John Gerson, *Regulae morales*, in *Opera*, edited by L. Ellies du Pin (Antwerp, 1706), III, 95.

the prevalence of the sin against nature. Both are drawn from the life of a single Italian city-state, first in the fourteenth century, then in the fifteenth; wide generalization of them to the rest of Europe may be unwarranted. In a vision of hell attributed by her confessor and biographer to St. Catherine of Siena, St. Catherine noted as a particular class in hell only one group of sinners: "those who sinned in the married state." [47] The anecdote carries Catherine's judgment on Sienese family life. Herself the youngest of a family of twenty-five, she does not seem to have been obsessed by any particularly morbid distaste for marriage. If such was her vision of hell, she probably had some basis in her knowledge of her neighbors. Half a century later, St. Bernardine of Siena, preaching on marriage, declares, "Of 1000 marriages, I believe 999 are the devil's." [48] Explicitly in Bernardine, implicitly in Catherine, these harsh observations are predicated on the frequency of various forms of the sin against nature in marriage. Artificial contraceptives are not meant; Bernardine would have alluded to them.

To measure by canonical treatment, by the amount of theological argument, by quantity of sermons, contraception throughout this period is by no means so prominent and widespread a sin as usury, a sin which could only be committed by the comparatively small class of people with money to lend.[49] The theological references — apart from the despairing statistics of St. Bernardine — do not suggest that contraceptive behavior was universal. Every canonist writing on book V of the *Decretals* was confronted with *Si aliquis*. Every theologian commenting on the *Sentences* was faced by *Aliquando* and *Adulterii malum*. Much of the discussion is generated by those texts rather than by social exigencies. But there are enough fresh treatments of "poisons of sterility" to indicate that these means are still in use; and there is enough pastoral advice on the sin against nature to suggest that, in the period 1232–1480, many persons in marriage sought intercourse, but avoided procreation.

[47] Raymond of Capua, *Vita de S. Catharina Senensi* 2.7.215, *Acta sanctorum*, ed. Godfrey Henschen, S.J., and Daniel Papebroch, S.J., Bollandists, *April*, vol. III (Rome, 1866), p. 915. Blessed Raymond, Catherine's confessor, the later general of the Dominican order, reports the vision as told to him. "I asked her why that sin which was not more serious than others was so seriously punished." She replied, "Because they do not have as much conscience about it, and consequently not as much contrition, as they have about other sins; also more frequently and often they offend in this sin than in others." In short, the married folk who behave in this way do not usually believe they are committing serious sin. Raymond, who has written Catherine's life in a moralistic fashion, would not seem to have invented this account which suggests how much a matter of course the behavior was. His own judgment is also of interest. Where Thomas had treated the sin against nature as the worst of lechery, Raymond says the sin here is "not more serious than others."

[48] St. Bernardine, *Le Prediche volgari*, ed. Piero Bargellini (Milan, 1936), p. 400.

[49] See John T. Noonan, Jr., *The Scholastic Analysis of Usury* (Cambridge, Mass., 1957), pp. 100–195.

DEMOGRAPHIC SURMISES

The work of demographers is of limited relevance to the establishment of the existence of contraception in the Middle Ages. Its relevance is limited, first, by the data available. Before the late-eighteenth century there are no completely reliable records of population; before the thirteenth century in Mediterranean Europe and the fourteenth century in the North, there are not even reliable documents by which estimates can be made of medieval populations.[50] Second there is a limited significance to the demographic surmises made. A sharp increase in population does not seem compatible with the widespread practice of birth control, especially if the mortality rate remains high. But a stationary or declining population may be caused by such factors as disease, war, the postponement of marriage, as well as by contraception. A population trend downward is at most an index to the probable existence of contraceptive practice.

With these limitations in mind, we may find some relevance in some recent demographic conclusions. It appears likely that the population of western Europe rose more or less continuously from the eleventh century to the end of the thirteenth century. Less established hypotheses are that the population of France increased from about ten million in 800 to seventeen million in the same area in 1328; and that the population of England increased from about 1,100,000 in 1086 to 3,700,000 in 1348. These increases over several centuries seem notable only because of the persistence during this period of a high mortality rate and a general inability to control plagues and famine. A stabilizing tendency is hypothesized as occurring about 1300, and it is supposed that at this point population outran food supply. The Black Death in the middle of the fourteenth century brought about a sharp decline: it is estimated that England suffered a 40 percent decline in population from 1348 to 1377, that Tuscany lost up to two-thirds of its urban population. There is some evidence of a sharp rise in the birth rate in the areas affected by the great plague. In fifteenth-century Brabant and Holland there is evidence of population decline, and there is disputed evidence of decline in fifteenth-century England. No one seems to believe that the rate of population expansion from the eleventh century to the end of the thirteenth century was observable anywhere in the West in the fourteenth and fifteenth centuries.[51]

A few more specific studies have shown these results: two lines of Namur nobility, followed between the years 1000 and 1200, had per

---

[50] Carlo Cipolla, Jean Dhondt, M. M. Postan, and Philippe Wolff, Report, in *IXe Congrès International des Sciences Historiques*, vol. I, *Rapports* (Paris, 1950), p. 56.
[51] *Ibid.*, I, 56–80.

generation an average number of children becoming adults of 5.75 and 4.30, respectively; these averages, given the high rate of infant mortality, imply a much higher birth rate for these families, whose typicality, however, is not established.[52] Of a less individual character are the data on city populations. The cities of western Europe remained relatively small. At the end of the fourteenth century, Florence, Genoa, Bruges, Rome, Brussels, and London all had fewer than 50,000 inhabitants; Naples, Milan, and Venice had over 50,000; Paris may have had as many as 90,-000.[53] One student, Russell, has concluded that the cities failed to reproduce themselves, maintaining their size only by drawing new citizens from the country.[54] It is clear that from 1400 to 1500 they increased very gradually — Rome from 40,000 to 50,000, Florence also from 40,000 to 50,000.[55]

There has been some speculation by demographers and sociologists on the voluntary factors affecting population. Mols, who has studied medieval city populations intensively, hypothesizes that population control was achieved by late marriages.[56] Independently, Homans has argued that in the country in England population limitation was effected by elder sons marrying late and by younger brothers and sisters not marrying at all. Some evidence of these practices, maintained in order to keep a village family's small landholdings from being divided, has been found.[57] This evidence may be fortified by the observation of the leading preacher of fourteenth-century England, the Dominican John Bromyard, that when fornicators are rebuked for not marrying, they reply that "they are poor and so cannot have a wife." Others say they would marry "if they had a house to which they could take her." Still others say they would not have enough to live on with offspring (Summa for Preachers, "Lechery," 28).[58]

[52] Ibid., vol. II, Actes (Paris, 1951), remarks by Génicot, p. 34.
[53] Roger Mols, S.J., Introduction à la démographie historique des villes d'Europe du 14e au 18e siècle (Louvain, 1954–1956), II, 504–505. Mols (pp. 512–513) rejects the figure, formerly estimated by Lot, of 200,000 as the Paris population of 1328.
[54] Josiah Cox Russell, "Late Mediaeval Population Patterns," Speculum 20 (1945), 164.
[55] Mols, Introduction, II, 504–507.
[56] Ibid., II, 542.
[57] G. C. Homans, English Villagers of the Thirteenth Century (Cambridge, Mass., 1941) pp. 125, 137-139.
[58] John Bromyard, Summa praedicantium (Nuremberg, 1485). In Jacques Toussaert, Le Sentiment religieux en Flandre à la fin du Moyen-Age (Paris, 1963), there are several references to contraceptive practices in the fourteenth century: in a bastardy case, the defense was that the alleged father had always avoided procreative acts with the woman (p. 776); diocesan statutes in 1300 and again in 1481 made unnatural copulation a reserved sin (pp. 778, 384); Jan de Weert, a cleric at a charitable institution in Ypres, deplored marriages in which fertility was curbed (p. 383); Baudouin Van der Loren, the "official poet" of Ghent in 1381, wrote a plea that practices avoiding procreation be abandoned (p. 383).

Neither Mols nor Homans mentions contraception. But not all those who put off marriage lived in celibacy. If fornication was often the alternative to marriage, it would seem that contraception must have been sometimes practiced if population control was, in fact, achieved. Why do the fornicators mentioned by Bromyard remain without offspring? Within marriage, the same economic motives that prompted postponement of marrying would have been present to stimulate contraceptive practice. Again, with such motives at work, and a means like coitus interruptus available, we cannot suppose that all married couples would have followed the law of the Church. The stable populations of the cities may not be totally unrelated to St. Catherine's and St. Bernardine's judgments of fourteenth- and fifteenth-century bourgeois family life. At the very least the demographic figures of the fourteenth and fifteen centuries suggest that population control, in forms acceptable or unacceptable to the Church, occurred.

I have presented the evidence for contraceptive practice in the later Middle Ages — the type and availability of information, indications of its dissemination, motives for its use, ecclesiastical discussion of its forms, and population changes possibly affected by it. By no test does contraception appear as a major social problem. After the substantial defeat of Catharism by 1260, no religious hostility to procreation posed a threat of serious depopulation. There were economic reasons for individuals to limit births. But plague, famine, and war affected western Europe often enough in this period so that there was no permanent population pressure. Contraception, if practiced, was an individual decision. It was practiced chiefly to avoid shame or to avoid impoverishment. Not a large social problem, the practice of contraception was a reality of medieval civilization. The medieval theologians dealt not only with the texts of a tradition, but with behavior affecting marriages in their society.

CHAPTER VIII

THE RATIONALE OF THE PROHIBITION

T HE CONDEMNATION of contraception had been reaffirmed, in the context of the reaction against the Cathars, in the twelfth and early
thirteenth centuries. Thereafter, the condemnation appeared as the assertion of authority, as the established doctrine of the Fathers, as the law
set out by the papacy. This authoritative condemnation was applied to
the contraceptive behavior encountered in the later Middle Ages. Yet if
authority existed and dominated analysis, it was not authority of the
strongest kind. No single biblical text had gained undisputed rule over
the field, as had Luke 6:35, "Lend freely, hoping nothing thereby," in
the condemnation of usury. Genesis 38 had been treated sometimes, but
not universally, as decisive. No ecumenical council had spoken on the
subject. No Pope had issued against contraception a letter in his own
name.

What was present was, in substance, this: the teaching of the penitentials and the work of St. Augustine. The bulk of the first had been
winnowed to a single text, *Si aliquis,* with the force of a local council to
sustain it. Ascribed by Burchard to the Council of Worms, it was in
1232 attributed by the *Decretals* to the "Council of Guarnicia." Nevertheless, when it had achieved papal insertion in the *Decretals,* this local
canon of uncertain authorship laid claim to universal authority. As for
Augustine, his prestige in the twelfth-century Latin church was enormous.
By his words alone a tradition against all forms of contraception seemed
established.

The tradition, however, did not rest in the naked assertion of what the
Fathers had said or what the popes had commanded. It was a tradition
set in the context of the orthodox victory over the Cathars and in the
context of a theology of marriage and of original sin. Authority was also

armed with reasons. By the very categories employed, the controlling texts condemned contraception because it was homicide, because it was against nature, because it destroyed the marital relation.

CONTRACEPTION AS HOMICIDE

The tendency to treat contraception as some form of killing was derived from two sources: the literal wording and placing of *Si aliquis*, and the ancient rhetoric that made all destruction of human semen a form of murder. This tendency was checked by a counter approach, based partly on another canon, partly on closer analysis of the acts in question.

At first glance, it appears that the compiler of the *Decretals*, Raymond, must have viewed contraception as homicide. The word which *Si aliquis* used to describe the person performing the sterilizing act was *homicida*, the generic term for a man guilty of deliberately killing another man. The canon was placed as number 5 in title 12, "Voluntary and Chance Homicide," a title dealing with the penalties for intentional, negligent, and accidental killing. It was sandwiched between two canons on cooperation in murder. Canon 4 was composed of an excerpt from St. Jerome dealing with the responsibilities of Herod and Salome for John the Baptist's decapitation. Canon 6 was from a letter to Bartholomew of Exeter, in which Pope Alexander III stated the penance to be assigned the cooperators in the murder of St. Thomas à Becket. The placing of *Si aliquis* suggested that contraception was in the same category as ordinary murder. Moreover, of the two preceding titles, title 10 was "Those Who Kill Their Children," dealing with infanticide, and title 11 punished the abandonment of infants or sick children by their parents. The decretal on contraception was thus fitted into a section of the canon law protecting life. The arrangement recalled the Roman criminal law, where the Code of Justinian dealt with murder, including infanticide, in title 16, parricide in title 17, and magical potions in title 18. This analogy and the context provided by the *Decretals* bespoke a view of contraception as an assault on life.

A contrary view was manifested in canon 20 of the title "Voluntary and Chance Homicide." Canon 20, *Sicut ex*, was a letter of Innocent III to a Carthusian priory about a monk who had caused his mistress to abort. The Pope held that the monk was not irregular if the fetus was not "vivified." [1] The wider significance of the letter arose from the usual rules for imposing irregularity. Irregularity was no mere technical deficiency,

---

[1] Innocent III apparently intended the same distinction between a formed and an unformed fetus that Jerome and Augustine had made (above, p. 90). These two universal authorities had been preserved on this point by Gratian, 2.32.2.8, 10, and Lombard, *Sentences* 4.31.4.

but a state in which the right to perform sacerdotal functions was suspended. It was an extra penalty, applicable to a priest qua priest, and independent of either the penance to be assigned for the sin or the criminal punishment to be applied for the act. Irregularity was automatically incurred by a cleric guilty of homicide (*Decretals* 5.12.6). Hence, if the Carthusian monk was not irregular, the plain implication was that no homicide occurred in a stopping of life prior to the time a fetus received a soul. *Sicut ex* cast doubt on the literalness of *Si aliquis*, which held contraception to be homicide.

Si aliquis and *Sicut ex* could be distinguished as dealing with two different matters: penance and irregularity. This was the way their compiler, St. Raymond, understood them. In his *Summa for Confessors*, written before the *Decretals*, he had explained that irregularity was incurred neither by abortion before the fetus was ensouled nor by contraception. But the penance for anyone performing these acts was the penance for homicide (*Summa* 2.1.4).[2] This nice distinction in penalties still left a doubt whether contraception was regarded as homicide in a true sense. The common position, initiated by Hostiensis in the *Golden Summa* 5, "Homicide," 1, and followed by the *Gloss*, was that contraception was "interpretively" homicide.[3] This analysis assimilated the condemnation of contraception to that of other acts attacking life without going so far as the contention that contraception involved the killing of a man.

There were authors, however, who found the teaching of *Si aliquis* objectionable. Within twenty years of the issuance of the *Decretals*, St. Albert registered, indirectly, his dissent from his fellow Dominican's work. Commenting on *Aliquando* in Lombard, he asked, "What penance is due those who procure poisons of sterility?" If one followed the canon law, the obvious answer was, "the penance for homicide." Albert's answer was: "It must be said that a great penance is to be enjoined; and they are to cease to do such things again; and, if they can be induced, they are to be induced not to use marriage further, for they sin against matrimony.

[2] On the date of Book II of the *Summa for Confessors* of Raymond, see Stephan Kuttner, "Zur Entstehungsgeschichte der *Summa de casibus poenitentiae* des heiligen Raymund von Penyafort," *Zeitschrift der Savigny-Stiftung für Rechtsgeschichte, Kanonistische Abteilung* 39 (1953), 419.

[3] *Glossa ordinaria* on the *Decretals*, in *Corpus juris canonici* (Rome, 1582). Hostiensis fortifies his position by an interesting misinterpretation of Roman law, which he regards as the still valid criminal law of his day. The Cornelian law punished by death the administrator of an abortifacient or love potion if a man or woman should lose his or her life through such an act (*Digest* 48.19.38.5); the reference is clearly to the death of the person taking the potion. But Hostiensis takes the law to refer to the death of the fetus after it has been ensouled. Hence "the laws and canons," he says, "here do not disagree, but concord" — in other words, both punish as murder the killing of a formed fetus.

If they cannot be induced, I do not believe that they can be bound, lest worse happen" (*On the Sentences* 4.31.18).

Albert did not mention *Si aliquis* by name, but he drew from the theory underlying it three arguments against his own doctrine. The first was that the users of the poisons were parricides, that is, slayers of their own children, and should be treated as such. To this Albert answered that there was a doubt whether any child would have been born: neither conception nor birth was certain. The point was an obvious one — presumably as obvious to Albert's predecessors as to himself. Yet no important theologian had so challenged the rhetoric of homicide, which Christian moralists from St. Jerome to St. Raymond had found relevant.

A second objection to Albert's position was this: surely it was a worse sin to render a nature sterile than to kill an infant or two. This argument implied what Chrysostom had said explicitly: the act of sterilizing was worse than murder. Answering, Albert made a distinction. True, the act was worse in the extent of its probable harm; but in the deformity of the act itself, the killing of a human being was more serious. This response was not developed; it did reflect a firm refusal to let prevention of birth be made as wicked as the killing of an existing person.

Finally, Albert considered an objection, drawn from Genesis 38, which was notable in linking coitus interruptus and the poisons of sterility. It consisted of the statement that God killed Onan and Er for their acts. It implied that the death penalty was, in God's eyes, the appropriate punishment for contraception, that therefore contraception was as bad as homicide. Albert did not dispute the exegesis, nor the treatment of different kinds of contraception on the same footing. But he attacked the assumption that contraception was now punishable by death: "God did this to terrorize, but the Church does not punish the contrite except in satisfaction for their crime." What an omnipotent God might do was not a precedent for human action; contraception was not now to be equated with homicide.

Albert's analysis stood out as the only important challenge of medieval theology to *Si aliquis*, and even it was made without explicit reference to the canon. His famous pupil, Aquinas, reflected something of his teacher's position in his own youthful commentary on the *Sentences*. He said laconically that the use of the poisons of sterility "is a serious sin, . . . and one against nature because even the beasts look for offspring" (*On the Sentences* 4.31.2.3, "Exposition of text").[4] "Yet," he noted, "it is less than homicide, for the embryo could still be impeded in another way." In his more mature work Aquinas did not mention the poisons of sterility at all. His silence, interpreted in the light of his early rejection of the

---

[4] Thomas, *In libros Sententiarum*, in *Opera omnia* (Parma, 1852–1873), vol. VII.

substance of *Si aliquis,* may be argued to reflect a continuing dissatisfaction with the canon.

From motives of disagreement or disinterest, a number of other prominent thirteenth-century writers also failed to deal with *Si aliquis.* One of the most significant of the silent authorities was Hostiensis' contemporary and friendly critic, Innocent IV. His commentary on the *Decretals,* completed after his election to the papacy in 1243, simply omitted treatment of 5.12.5 — a regrettable loss, for Pope Innocent IV often showed much common sense in moral matters.[5] Alexander of Hales wrote his *Summa of Theology* late enough to know of the decretal, but he did not mention it. Among the theologians of the mid-thirteenth century, neither the English Franciscan Richard Middleton (fl. 1280) nor the Italian general of the Franciscans, St. Bonaventure (1221–1274), took up *Si aliquis* in dealing with the *Sentences;* and the most brilliant of Franciscan theologians, Duns Scotus (d. 1308), also ignored it.

If none of the great theologians of this theological age was eager to treat contraception as homicide, the more common later analysis followed Hostiensis. Contraception was "interpretively" homicide. This view was adopted by Joannes Andreae (1270–1348), the master of Bologna who was the leading canonist of the fourteenth century (*New Commentary* 5.12). It also appeared in Astesanus, a Franciscan summarizing theological doctrine in 1317 after the great creative period was over (*Summa* 8.9).[6] A somewhat similar stand was taken by Monaldus (d. 1285), another Franciscan summist: the giving of something to prevent conception "is reputed homicide as to penalty of law."[7]

One risk in the analysis fostered by the canons was that an act for which the penance for homicide was appropriate was likely to be regarded as homicide. The qualification that the act was only interpretively homicide was likely to be lost. This happened in one of the few works of canon law by an Englishman, the *Summa of Summas* by William of Pagula. In this fourteenth-century attempt to summarize the multitude of existing summaries, under the caption "Voluntary Homicide" there appeared without explanation a paraphrase of the canon, placing among acts of homicide "the giving a woman to drink so she cannot bear."[8] The same

[5] Innocent IV, *Apparatus super libros decretalium* (Venice, 1540).

[6] Astesanus, *Summa de casibus conscientiae* (Ratisbon, 1780).

[7] Monaldus, *Summa perutilis* (Lyons, 1516), fol. 135r. On the works of Astesanus and Monaldus, and the superiority of Astesanus in terms of sources used, see Josef Georg Ziegler, *Die Ehelehre der Pönitentialsummen von 1200–1350* (Regensburg, 1956), pp. 24, 77.

[8] William of Pagula, *Summa summarum,* Huntington Library, MS. 1368. The identification of this work, ascribed to "William of Padua" or "William of Pugula," has been made by Leonard Boyle, O.P. William probably came from Paull near Kingston-on-Hull. He became vicar of Winkfield, near Windsor, in 1314. In 1322 he became penitentiary for the deanery of Reading and later for the whole archdeaconry

kind of abrupt and unnuanced classification was made by Chaucer's Parson, who is the embodiment of sober piety. The use of deadly herbs and pessaries is a sin of wrath, an act of manslaughter ("The Parson's Tale," lines 570–580). A similar view was taken in a popular fifteenth-century work for confessors, enticingly entitled *Moral Leprosy*, by John Nider (1380–1438), a German Dominican, and sometime dean of the faculty of theology of the new university of Vienna. Among those violating the commandment "Thou shalt not kill" were those who take precautions "by poisons of sterility lest a woman conceive." A somewhat later summa for confessors, written in 1485 by Angelus Carletus de Clavasio, an Italian of the Observantine Franciscans, set out under "Homicide" an abridgment of *Si aliquis*.[9]

This brusque treatment was not universal. In the most influential of fifteenth-century works for confessors, the *Confessional* of St. Antoninus, abortion was treated under homicide, but contraception was not mentioned (Part 1, "The Way of Interrogating Penitents"). Antoninus adopted the same approach in his more elaborate *Summa theologica* (2.7.8). In thus implicitly rejecting *Si aliquis* and the commentary of the canonists, he followed in the path of Albert and Aquinas.

There was, however, another theological current favoring the interpretation of contraception as homicide. It stemmed from the theory, as old as Lactantius, that active homosexuals were "parricides." In the twelfth century Peter Cantor said that the Sodomites were like Onan, "who spilled his seed on the earth." God created male and female to multiply men, "but homicides and sodomites destroy them" (*The Abridged Word* 138, "The Sodomitic Vice," PL 205:334–335). Here "homicide," the term of *Si aliquis*, is apparently used to designate a man guilty of coitus interruptus.

In the next century, Peraldus specifically treated "the sin against nature," which he had defined to include sodomy and the act of Onan, as a sin of wrath. It was, he explained, a form of homicide because "in it is spilled what could be matter of a human body" (*Summa of Virtues and Vices* 2.8, "Wrath," 10). Peraldus, or a source following him, influenced Chaucer's Parson. To sin against nature in marriage by preventing conception is, he declares, to commit a sin of wrath, not of lechery. As in the earlier writers, emphasis is on destruction of the seed: the sinner "sheds his nature" ("The Parson's Tale," line 576). As a woman is believed to have seed, she, too, can commit the sin. The act is a form of manslaughter.

of Berkshire. He wrote the *Summa summarum* about 1325–1327. See W. A. Pantin, *The English Church in the Fourteenth Century* (Cambridge, 1955), pp. 195–196.
[9] John Nider, *De morali lepra* (Paris, 1490), 2, "The Ten Commandments," 7.2. Angelus Carletus de la Clavasio, *Summa angelica de casibus conscientiae* (Lyons, 1505), "Homicidium" 1.7.

In the fifteenth century, Nider takes the same view. A sin against the fifth commandment is to use "abusive means of lechery" to prevent conception (*Moral Leprosy* 2, "The Ten Commandments," 7). An even more important advocate of this theory is Bernardine of Siena, the foremost preacher of his day, a learned, ascetic, and passionate Franciscan. In a fiery series of sermons, *The Eternal Gospel,* Bernardine devotes his fifteenth sermon to "The Frightful Sin Against Nature." He quotes a statement, erroneously attributed at this time to Augustine, which proclaimed, "Those laboring under this vice are killers of men, if not by the sword, yet in fact." Bernardine adds, "Not only are they killers of men, but what is more horrible to think, they must most truly be said to be the killers of their own children." The sin is the sin of men, of women, "and most of all of those constituted in holy matrimony" (*The Eternal Gospel* 15.2.1).

In Bernardine's sweeping denunciation, Lactantius' charge of "parricide" finds its logical extension. In the rhetoric of this tradition there is no patience with Albert's observation that not every act of semination could result in children. There is no heed paid to the refusal of the canonists in *Sicut ex* to treat the abortion of a young fetus as homicide. There is the apparent assumption that each seed is a man in potency. Yet, as in St. Jerome, this assumption may not have been entertained as a biological fact. Bernardine may have believed no more than this: any human seed could be the means of procreating; to destroy it was to destroy potential life.

The tradition which spoke of extravaginal ejaculation as homicide was not the dominant one. It had no canon to commend it. Even those who invoked it did not take the logical step of denouncing all nonprocreative intercourse (for example, in pregnancy) as homicide. That such a tradition should have existed at all was, however, related to the existence of *Si aliquis*. The thrust of the canon was to protect life by condemning attacks by potion on the life-forming process. The condemnation, rhetorically expanded, asserted that all efforts to prevent procreation were destructive of men to be. This rationale for the prohibition of contraception — that life must be protected — was implicit in the categorization of it as homicide. That the categorization was not universally accepted was probably due to Albert and Thomas.[10]

[10] In the Middle Ages, Augustine did not appear as a clear authority against the homicide analysis. The erroneous attribution to him of the statement on unnatural sinners as killers of men has been remarked (see PL 40:1326 on this misattribution). Moreover, the epigram of Caesarius of Arles, "so many conceptions prevented, so many homicides," was also attributed to Augustine. As late as 1657 this saying was believed by the theologians of the University of Louvain to be that of Augustine; see "Certain Assertions of Moral Doctrine Censured by the Faculty of Louvain, May 4, 1657," in Francis Deininger, *Joannes Sinnich* (Düsseldorf, 1928), p. 394.

CONTRACEPTION AS UNNATURAL

The phrase "sin against nature" contains within itself the objection to the act to which it refers. This phrase has been seen to be the standard designation for any marital intercourse resulting in extravaginal ejaculation. Here is a sample of the writers after 1250 who so apply the term: in the thirteenth century, Peraldus (*Summa* 2.3.4, "The Species of Lechery"); in the fourteenth century, Astesanus (*Summa* 2.46, 8.9) and Peter de Palude (*On the Sentences* 4.31.3.2); in the fifteenth century, John Gerson (*Compendium of Theology*, "The Vice or Sin of Lechery," and *The Commandments of the Decalogue* 11), St. Antoninus (*Confessional* 3.1 and *Summa theologica* 3.1.20), Trovamala (*Summa*, "Debt," 11), Nider (*Moral Leprosy* 1.4), and Angelus (*Summa*, "Lechery"). With Peraldus in 1270 and Angelus in 1485 using the same designation without debate, we may feel certain that the basic view of this kind of marital behavior was established in theological circles.

Outside of marriage the sin against nature consisted of masturbation, sodomy, and bestiality. The common characteristic of all these acts was that ejaculation occurred but procreative insemination was impossible. As St. Bernardine put it, the sin was committed by an act of semination "wherever" and "in whatever way" "you cannot generate" (*Seraphic Sermons* 19.1).[11] Such an act was a sin because the inseminating function of the genital act was frustrated; it is this function which is indicated by "nature" in this context.

An objection may be raised to this analysis of the sin against nature, since the term was also applied to departure from "the fit way instituted by nature as to position" (St. Thomas, *On the Sentences* 4.31, "Exposition of text"; *Summa theologica* 2–2.154.11). The "fit way" was with the woman beneath the man. Theologians following Aquinas attacked deviation from this position as unnatural and as mortal sin.[12]

This doctrine appears to refute my account of what the scholastics

[11] Bernardine, *Quadragesimale* "Seraphion," in *Opera*, ed. Jean de la Haye (Venice, 1745), vol. III. Similarly, in the vernacular Bernardine says, "Each time that you have joined yourselves in such a way that you cannot conceive and generate children, there has always been sin" (*Le Prediche volgari*, Milan, 1936, p. 433). The sin is against nature in three respects: it is against the nature of the individual, against the nature of the rational species, against the nature of the animal genus (Bernardine, *The Eternal Gospel* 15, "The Frightful Sin Against Nature," 1.1).

[12] Peraldus, *Summa* 2.3.6; Monaldus, *Summa*, "The Goods of Marriage," fol. 136; Astesanus, *Summa* 8.9, favoring this opinion as "safer"; John Gerson, *Opusculum tripartitum, De praeceptis decalogi*, c. 11, and *Compendium theologiae* 8, "The Sin of Lechery," both in *Opera* (Antwerp, 1706), vol. I; Bernardine, *The Christian Religion* 17.1.1, in *Opera omnia* (Quaracchi, 1950), vol. I.

A milder opinion was that a change from this position to that of "brute animals" was "a sign of mortal concupiscence"(St. Albert, *On the Sentences* 4.31.24). The language sounds harsh, but the emphasis is on "sign." If there is a reason for change

meant by "nature." Here is a teaching which insists on a particular order in sexual intercourse, although insemination does not seem at issue. Undeniably, not the usual concept of nature but mere precedent was the greatest single factor accounting for the acceptance of this teaching. It was adopted because it had become embedded in the theological discussions of married sexuality. It also reflected a belief in the natural superiority of man to woman. Yet there is in this standard, so obviously derived from a special tradition, some connection with the primary insistence on insemination. As dispassionate a scientific observer as Albert, in his biological work, taught that with the woman in a lateral position the seed reached her matrix with difficulty, and that when she was above the man, her matrix was "upside down" and "what was in it was poured out" (*Animals* 10.2). The essential doctrine was as old as Avicenna and consequently as widespread as the *Canon of Medicine*. With the woman above the man "retention of the seed in coition is extremely poor"; moreover, the increased "labor in ejection of the seed" causes genital injury.[13] In the light of this kind of medical opinion, the scholastic insistence on natural modes was a second safeguard or outer bulwark for the teaching on insemination. Nature, it was believed, protected the inseminating function by special postures it had set for human beings. To dispense with this protection was to sin against nature.[14]

What assumptions does the general argument based on nature rest on? Why is it wrong to impede insemination? Why must nature be the ultimate standard? These questions may most fruitfully be explored in the statements of Thomas Aquinas. He articulates what is implicit in earlier writers, and he guides a multitude of his successors.

The basic assumptions of Aquinas are that natural coitus was instituted by God; that the order of nature here is distinguished from the rational order; that natural coitus as instituted by God should not be altered by man. These assumptions are made explicit in an article entitled "Is the Vice Against Nature the Greatest Sin Among the Species of Lechery?" Giving an affirmative answer to this question, Thomas faces the objection that "adultery, seduction, and rape, which are injurious to our neighbor, are seemingly more contrary to the love of our neighbor than unnatural sins, by which no other person is injured" (*Summa theologica* 2–2.154.12,

---

— such as bodily size or pregnancy — the change is justified. This milder view, which still takes one position as "natural," was followed by Peter de Palude, *On the Sentences* 4.31.3; St. Antoninus, *Summa theologiae* 3.1.20.

[13] Avicenna, *Canon of Medicine* 3.20.1.10, "Harmfulness of Coitus, Its Arrangements, and the Evil of Forms."

[14] Magnino of Milan repeats Avicenna's doctrine that genital injury will result from the changed position, and he also calls change of position "against law and custom" (*contra legem et mores*). But he says nothing of its effect on procreation (*Regimen for Health* 3.33).

obj. 1). He meets the objection as follows: "Just as the ordering of right reason proceeds from man, so the order of nature is from God Himself: wherefore in sins contrary to nature, whereby the very order of nature is violated, an injury is done to God, the ordainer of nature." The order of reason is strikingly contrasted with the order of nature. Nature is conceived of in a special way as sacred and unchangeable. Fornication and adultery violate what "is determined by right reason." The sin against nature violates what is "determined by nature." Violation of this natural order is an affront to God, though "no other person is injured."

The sharp distinction between acts that offend the natural order and acts that offend the rational order goes back to a distinction in types of natural law. The fundamental precepts of the natural law are stated by Aquinas to be precepts which can be performed only by rational beings: love God, and love your neighbor (ST 2–1.100.3). Yet he also says that in a strict sense natural law is "what nature has taught all animals" (ST 2–1.94.2). These two formulations represent different conceptions, and Aquinas moves from one to the other. In the case of the sin against nature, the two formulas are reconcilable only by supposing, as Aquinas does suppose, that to depart from the inseminating use of the sexual act is to offend God directly; then both animal nature and love of God are violated.

The difference between the objection to the sin against nature and the objection to other sexual sins recurs in Evil, a work in which Aquinas, while writing the second part of the Summa theologica, sought to explore the nature of sin more intensively and more profoundly.[15] The question is asked, "Is Every Act of Lechery Mortal Sin?" Aquinas answers affirmatively, and the objection is made that fornication between consenting persons cannot be mortal sin, for no one is injured. The objection continues: "Every mortal sin is contrary to charity . . . But simple fornication is not contrary to charity, neither as regards the love of God, since it is not a sin against God, nor as regards the love of our neighbor, since thereby no one is injured" (Evil 15.2, obj. 4).

Aquinas does not deny the major premise of the objection, that every mortal sin is contrary to charity. It is, indeed, a restatement of his position that the fundamental precepts of the natural law are: love God, love your neighbor. Natural law is not violated if injury to God or neighbor does not occur. Accordingly, to meet the objection, he assumes that the normal result of intercourse is offspring. The rights of this unborn child may be asserted when one asks, Who is hurt? The injury done consists in

    [15] St. Thomas Aquinas, De malo, ed. P. Bazzi and P. M. Pession in Quaestiones disputatae (Turin, 1949), vol. II. Grabmann dates both Evil and the second part of the Summa theologica between 1269 and 1272; Martin Grabmann, Die Werke des heiligen Thomas von Aquin (Munich, 1949), pp. 295, 307.

the deprivation of definite parentage, of education in a family, of parental solicitude. "The offspring to be born" is the neighbor offended by fornication.

The postulated offspring explains why fornication is sin. What of the sin against nature, committed by acts where generation is impossible? St. Thomas thrice mentions the sin in *Evil* (15.1, 2, and 3), but he does not consider the objection that the sin does not offend one's neighbor. Apparently he is content to rest on the answer of the *Summa theologica:* God, not neighbor, is offended by the sin. This approach put enormous emphasis on the *givenness* of the act of insemination; the act was invested with a God-given quality not to be touched by rational control or manipulation. By the assertion that to interfere with the process was to offend God directly, the act seemed to be assigned the absolute value of God. Aquinas does not go this far explicitly. Unlike perjury, whose mortal sinfulness is proved by its direct contempt of God in calling Him to witness a lie (*ST* 2–2.98.3), the sin against nature is not expressly said to be mortal because of its contempt of God. Yet if the only person injured by the sin was God, it would appear that the affront to Him constituted the malice of the act.

The givenness of the generative process was supported by the assertion that the generative use of sexuality is what "nature has taught all animals." Yet the scholastics, like the Fathers, appealed to animal behavior only selectively, to confirm views already held. Where the natural posture in intercourse is at issue, human behavior is contrasted with animal behavior, and "animal" becomes a dirty word. To desert the natural position, says St. Albert, is to assume "that of brute animals" (*On the Sentences* 4.31.24). The unnatural positions are "animal, not human," says Astesanus (*Summa* 8.9). St. Thomas himself chooses the word "bestiality" to characterize modes of copulation that depart from the rational norm of position (*ST* 2–2.154.11). In short, human reason is used to decide whether what the animals do is part of the nature unalterably given to man.

The Thomistic analysis takes the biological function of the sexual act as given by God and unalterable by man. It would seem to lead to the conclusion that other uses of the sexual act — intercourse in pregnancy, intercourse with a sterile wife, intercourse by an aged man — are "unnatural." Some development on this point may be discerned in Thomas. In his early commentary on the *Sentences*, he uses some very broad language: "The end, however, which nature intends in copulation is offspring to be procreated and educated, and that this good might be sought it has put delight in copulation, as Augustine says, *Marriage and Concupiscence* 1.8. Whoever, therefore, uses copulation for the delight which is in it, not referring the intention to the end intended by nature, acts against nature; and this is also true unless such copulation is had as can be appropriately ordered to that end" (*On the Sentences* 4.33.1.3). These words, though directed to proving the evil of concubinage, are comprehensive enough to suggest that lack of procreative intention is itself a sin against nature.

In the same way, Thomas identifies an intention to have intercourse for the sake of health as an intention against nature. He is defending the proposition that only a procreative purpose excuses coitus, and he is faced with the objection that an act generally good can become evil only through an evil intention. Hence, if marital coitus is good, a sufficiently good intention is the purpose of health. He replies, "Although it is not evil in itself to intend to keep oneself in good health, this intention becomes evil if one intends health by something that is not naturally ordained for that purpose; for instance, if one sought only bodily health by the sacrament of baptism; and the same applies to the act of coitus" (*On the Sentences* 4.31.2.2, reply to obj. 4). This answer identifies the objective and subjective requirements of lawful coitus. Coitus is naturally ordained for procreation, and nothing else.

In the somewhat later *Summa Against the Gentiles*, however, Thomas teaches that "if, *per accidens*, generation cannot follow from emission of the seed, this is not against nature, nor a sin, as if it happens that the woman is sterile" (3.122).[16] The last statement reflects his settled opinion and the prevailing opinion generally. Intercourse of the pregnant, intercourse of the sterile, intercourse of those lacking a conscious procreative purpose — all these sexual but unprocreative acts are not classified as unnatural. This usage points to what is meant by nature here. In the acts of nonprocreative intercourse accepted as natural, semen can be deposited in the vagina. In the acts stamped as unnatural, insemination has been made impossible. What is taken as sacral is the act of coitus resulting in insemination. The same standard appears in the test for validity of a marriage: it is not inability to generate, but inability to complete coitus, which is ground for nullity.

This convention appears most strikingly in the usual treatment of the poisons of sterility. An exception is Thomas' youthful commentary on the *Sentences*, where the use of such contraceptives was condemned as "against nature, for even the beasts look for offspring" (*On the Sentences* 4.31, "Exposition of text"). The potions did not usually prevent insemination, and to call their use a sin against nature was not to stick to the ordinary meaning of the term. No other major writer did it; the canons did not do it. Thomas himself never repeated this analysis, nor

---

[16] St. Thomas, *Liber de veritate catholicae fidei contra errores infidelium seu Summa contra gentiles*, ed. Cesla Pera, O.P., Peter Marc, O.S.B., and Peter Caramello (Turin, 1961). Grabmann dates this work between 1258 and 1263 (*Werke*, pp. 243, 287).

did he ever subsequently suggest that use of contraceptive potions fell within the sin against nature.

It would, however, be incorrect to suppose that the value placed on insemination in coitus had no reference to its ultimate generative effect. If coitus was taken as sacred, it was because generation was only achievable through this means. If coitus was to be regarded as an unalterable process because of its generative consequences, but not every act of coitus was generative, then a discrimination had to be made between the normal or per se and the accidental. This discrimination was made by Thomas. He postulated as normal an act of coitus which led to generation. This norm was not derived from any statistical compilation. It was the product of intuition, the same intellectual process by which Lactantius had concluded that the purpose of the sexual members was to generate. Because the sexual act might be generative, and because generation was an important function, the theologian intuited that generation was the normal function. A typical or essential act of coitus, which was generative, was therefore supposed. Other acts of coitus which did not achieve this purpose were regarded as generically generative but accidentally frustrated. There were thus three types of seminal ejaculation: (1) acts in which insemination was impossible; these were unnatural; (2) acts in which insemination was possible and conception resulted; these were natural and normal; (3) acts in which insemination was possible, but conception did not occur; these were normal, but accidentally different from the norm.

Thus, in *Evil*, Thomas showed that every act of lechery was mortally sinful because each such act lacked direction to the generation and education of offspring. The objection was made: "It is manifest that from the copulation of a woman who is aged or sterile, generation of offspring cannot follow. But yet this sometimes can be done without mortal sin in the state of matrimony. Therefore also other acts of lechery, from which the generation and due education of offspring do not follow, may be done without mortal sin" (*Evil* 15.2, obj. 14). Thomas replied that "the common law is given not according to particular accidents, but according to common consideration." An act in which generation could not follow "according to the common species of the act" was lechery and sin. This kind of act was distinguished from an act affected by a particular circumstance, such as "old age or infirmity."

Did it make sense to postulate one type of coitus as normal, and to treat every variation from it as accidental, even cases in which it was known that conception was impossible? Did it make sense to say that old age was an "accidental" exception to the ability to generate? Thomas did not ask these questions. Part of the essence of animal sexual behavior was seen by him as generative, and this fixed essence guided his analysis. The postulation of the generative act of coitus as the norm was fundamental to his moral judgments.

The condemnation of acts avoiding insemination as unnatural seems to proceed on assumptions different from those involved in condemning contraception as homicide. There is a possible link between the two. In *Evil* Thomas undertook to establish that every act of lechery was mortal sin. He might have rested on the proposition that each unnatural act was in contempt of the natural order established by God, and so a contempt of God. Instead, however, he had recourse to what seems to be the heart of the homicide theory. He proceeded by comparison. Theft of a valuable property is mortal sin. But "the human seed, in which man is in potentiality, is more closely ordered to the life of man than is any exterior property . . . And therefore disorder in the emission of seed concerns the life of man in potentiality" (*Evil* 15.2). Paraphrasing Aristotle, he added, human seed is "something divine." [17] It is the assault on potential life which makes sins of lechery mortal.[18]

Thomas extended this judgment to all sins of lechery. He did not explicitly apply it to the sin against nature, but the form of his discourse necessarily included the sin against nature. The question may then be raised whether he viewed protection of man "in potentiality" as protection of a particular unborn child. He seemed to do so in his argument against fornication, where the child-to-be-born was the object of injury. It would have been harder to maintain that a child whose conception was deliberately avoided was an entity capable of injury. Such a position does seem to be taken by *Si aliquis*, but *Si aliquis* did not commend itself to Thomas. Moreover, if he found the malice of the sin against nature to consist in injury to the child-to-be-born, it is strange that he did not say so in the *Summa theologica* or in *Evil*.

It may be, then, that "life in potentiality" or "seed" should be understood as standing for the species as a whole. The injury is not to the seed by itself, but to the human species whose conservation is threatened. This is the interpretation urged by Joseph Fuchs, the best of the commentators on Thomas' sexual ethics.[19] This interpretation rests most solidly on a passage in the earlier *Summa Against the Gentiles*. Here Thomas defends the proposition that fornication is mortal sin against anonymous opponents who say that all the various bodily emissions are emissions of what is superfluous. He says, "The seed, although superfluous

---

[17] Thomas ascribes the "something divine" to Aristotle's *Politics*, but it seems to be derived from Aristotle's *Generation of Animals* 2.2, 736b–737a, where he speaks of a substance within the seed which causes it to be fertile, an element which is divine.

[18] In the commentary on Matthew, Thomas says, "You shall not commit adultery: that is against life in potency" (*On Matthew* 19, in *Opera omnia*, vol. X).

[19] Joseph Fuchs, *Die Sexualethik des heiligen Thomas von Aquin* (Cologne, 1949), p. 181.

as to the conservation of the individual, is yet necessary to the propagation of the species, while other superfluities, such as excrement, sweat, urine, and the like, are necessary for nothing. Hence, the emission of the latter concerns only the good of the individual. But not only this is required in the emission of seed; it is also required that it be emitted to be of use in generation, to which coitus is ordained" (3.122). He concludes, "The disordered emission of seed is contrary to the good of nature, which is the conservation of the species."

The good of the species as a whole is again invoked in the *Summa theologica* when Thomas answers the question, "Can the lechery which pertains to the venereal act ever be a sin?" He replies, "The more something is necessary, the more necessary is it that the order of reason be observed in it, and consequently the more vicious is omission of the order of reason. Venereal use, however, as stated, is highly necessary to the common good, which is the conservation of the human race" (*ST* 2–2.153.3). When the objection is made that no injury is done anyone, Thomas replies that injury is done God, "who is the principal master of our body" (reply to obj. 2). He does not allege injury to the specific seed. His answer invokes the assumption that the use of the genitals has been specially established by God; the assumption is restated in the duty to keep one's body as God willed it. In Thomas' mind the gravity of sexual offenses depends on the injury to the welfare of the species, and the person who is specifically offended is God.

In estimating the influence of St. Thomas, it must be added that there is enough ambiguity in some of his statements to support two interpretations. His references to the "life of man in potentiality," taken by themselves, could be understood as adoption of the argument that destruction of the seed is homicide, rather than an argument based on preservation of the species. This ambiguity affects later scholastic writing.

The implications of the argument based on the preservation of the race are worth considering. There was nothing new in it. The Fathers, who had stressed the procreative purpose, were aware that the result of procreation was the maintenance of the species. Augustine had said, "What food is to the health of a man, intercourse is to the health of the race" (*The Good of Marriage* 16.18). Nonetheless, the focus of the Fathers, including Augustine, appeared to be on the rectitude which the procreative purpose conferred on the sexual act, rather than on the result achieved. There was a discernible shift of perspective when Aquinas stressed the preservation of the species as the natural good obtained by intercourse. This shift was no more than suggested; it was not developed. Aquinas did not try to show by statistics that fecundity was socially important; he did not measure right or wrong in intercourse by determining that maintenance of the species was actually dependent on a generative outcome of each sexual act. The statement that preservation of the species requires that coitus be directed to generation is indeed no more than a form of the assumption that procreation is the normal end of intercourse. The end makes a requirement of the way of achieving the end. The difference from the Fathers is the shade of emphasis which is given by substituting "conservation of the species" for "procreation."

That the orientation of Aquinas to existing human society affects his view of the givenness of sexual functions is apparent in his treatment of castration. It is "according to the nature instituted by God that the human body be integral in its members." A decayed member, however, may be cut off "for the welfare of the whole body." Moreover, public authority may maim a person "as a punishment for the purpose of restraining sin." Why is castration for the welfare of the soul, then, objectionable? Aquinas answers that mutilation is permissible only if necessary, and "it is always possible to further one's spiritual welfare otherwise than by cutting off a member, because sin is subject to the will" (ST 2–2.65.1, ad 3). There are two sides to this analysis. Nature is respected as generally unalterable. Yet not only may a diseased organ be sacrificed, but, under some circumstances, society may maim as a punishment. Castration is explicitly rejected only because it is unnecessary. Aquinas' analysis is a nice balance of respect for nature and a rationalistic awareness that, under certain exigencies, a natural function may be sacrificed for a rational good. The balance is against castration. Could a different balance have been struck for acts which inflicted only temporary sterilization? Aquinas does not approach the poisons of sterility in these terms.

The elements present in the Thomistic statements on the sin against nature will be the common, if unanalyzed, assumptions of later scholastic writers. A norm is postulated consisting in heterosexual, marital coitus, the man above the woman, with insemination resulting. This norm is ordained, its naturalness is established by God. Deliberate departure from the norm is unnatural, a direct offense against God. The gravity of the offense arises either from its attack on the human life potentially present in any human seed, or from its impairment of the normal process of preserving the human species.

THE NECESSITY OF CONSCIOUS PROCREATIVE PURPOSE

Explicit criticism of marital acts in which insemination was impossible was normally made in terms of the unnaturalness of the acts. Explicit criticism of the use of the poisons of sterility was usually made in terms of homicide. Both types of behavior were also destructive of marriage as viewed by the prevailing Augustinian theology.

Some authors explicitly developed this theme, which in the twelfth century had been that of *Aliquando* and of the formal, juridical glosses of Huguccio and Rufinus on *Aliquando*. In a work of Alexander of Hales' middle years, written between 1227 and 1229, he stated, "Deliberate avoidance of offspring is evil and per se opposed to the good of marriage" (*Gloss on the Sentences* 4.31.12). It has already been remarked that Albert condemned use of the poisons of sterility as a sin "against marriage." In his first treatment of unnatural marital acts, Thomas speaks of a "usus contra naturam conjugis" (*On the Sentences* 4.31.2.3, "Exposition of Text"). This phrase might be translated "a use against the nature of a spouse." More probably it means "a use of a spouse against nature," for he is commenting on Peter's phrase "a use which is against nature." This interpretation would also accord with his later work where there is no attempt to analyze such acts otherwise than as sins against nature.

To treat contraceptive behavior as a sin against marriage rather than as sin against nature or as homicide was scarcely to take a mild view of the acts involved. Nonetheless, within the range of possible shadings of condemnation, to treat the offense in this light was less severe than to treat it as a direct assault on God-given order or on life. Possibly for this reason, later writers, when they considered contraceptive behavior explicitly, tended to adhere to the more severe categorizations, following Thomas rather than Albert.

While the severe analyses were preferred, the notion that contraceptive acts were contrary to marriage sustained and supplemented the direct criticisms made in terms of nature and life. *Si conditiones* proclaimed that an agreement antecedent to marriage to use contraceptives was grounds for nullity of the marriage. The commentators found unnatural behavior subsequent to marriage grounds for divorce (see below, p. 263). While for analysis here a distinction may be made between the rationale appealing to nature, the rationale based on the protection of life, and the rationale defending the purposes of marriage, a sharp line between them cannot be attributed to the scholastic writers. What was treated as a sin of homicide or what was viewed as an attack on nature was also considered destructive of the marital relation.

As in the twelfth century, so in the thirteenth, fourteenth, and fifteenth centuries, a positive barrier to acceptance of contraceptive behavior was the doctrine on the conscious purpose of intercourse. The unnatural or homicidal quality attributed to a contraceptive act related to the objective characteristics of what was done. The requirement of purpose focused on state of mind. Both objective and subjective criteria absolutely excluded contraceptive behavior. The subjective requirement, however, received fuller elaboration, and appears to have been the object of greater theological concern.

Pure Augustinian doctrine stated that only a procreative purpose freed marital intercourse from sin. Intercourse to avoid committing fornication was venial sin. This position, established in the twelfth century with only a few dissents, was reaffirmed by the classical canonists and theologians of the thirteenth century. The most influential of all, St. Thomas, took this stand in his work on the *Sentences* (4.31.2.2, reply to obj. 2). An historical accident enhanced the significance of this relatively youthful work: Thomas did not live to complete the portion of the *Summa theologica* which would have dealt with the purposes of marriage. Accordingly, the youthful commentary on the *Sentences* had to serve as his final statement on the subjective elements in marital intercourse and, following the arrangement made by Reginald of Piperno sometime after 1274, was commonly reproduced as part of the "Supplement to the *Summa theologica.*" The same position was taken in the confessors' manual of greatest influence in the next two centuries, Raymond's *Summa for Confessors* (4.2.8). The Augustinian doctrine was also adopted by Hostiensis, the preeminent commentator on the *Decretals*. It was subscribed to by the leading Franciscans, Bonaventure and Scotus.[20] It was propagated by the summists Monaldus and Astesanus, and by such commentators on Lombard as Francis Mayron (d. 1326).[21] It was repeated in conventional manuals for confessors of the fifteenth century (Trovamala, *Summa*, "Debt," 3; Angelus, *Summa*, "Conjugal Debt"). In the thirteenth, fourteenth, and fifteenth centuries it was the common teaching.

A special case of nonprocreative purpose was intercourse in pregnancy. Such intercourse was deplored with particular zeal. In "The Monk's Tale" Chaucer finds it appropriate for the monk to say that the virtuous Cenobia would not let her husband, Odenake, have intercourse with her once she was pregnant. She says, "It was to wyves lecherie and shame/ In oother caas, if that men with hem pleyde" (*Canterbury Tales*, "The Monk's Tale," lines 2293–2294). In the thirteenth century, Peraldus cited the elephant as an example of a beast which never had intercourse in pregnancy (*Summa* 1.6, "Temperance," 18), and as late as the fifteenth century Bernardine pointed to the modesty of animals as a reason for avoiding intercourse in pregnancy altogether (*Seraphic Sermons* 19.1).[22]

The dominant tradition on procreative purpose was not unchallenged. One of the best pre-Thomistic theologians, Alexander of Hales, had,

---

[20] Hostiensis, *Summa* 4.2.8; St. Bonaventure, *In libros Sententiarum* 4.31.2.2, *Opera omnia* (Quaracchi, 1882–1902); Duns Scotus, *In libros Sententiarum* [*Opus oxoniense*] 4.26, *Opera omnia*, new ed. according to the edition of Luke Wadding (Paris, 1891–1895), vol. XIX.

[21] Monaldus, *Summa*, fol. 136r; Astesanus, *Summa* 8.9; Francis Mayron, *In quattuor libros Sententiarum* 4.26 (Venice, 1520).

[22] Intercourse in pregnancy was also sinful for a reason other than the violation of procreative purpose; see below, p. 284.

after some wavering, defended intercourse for the nonprocreative purpose of avoiding fornication (*Summa theologica* 2–2.3.5.2.1.3.1).[23] In the fourteenth century, an innovating Dominican archbishop, Peter de Palude (d. 1342), carefully developed an appealing hypothetical. Suppose a man is about to speak for a long time in a private place with a woman who has tempted him before: may he not get "cooled off" (*refrigeratus*) by first having intercourse with his wife? Peter concluded that he might, and he set out the generalization that intercourse to avoid fornication was lawful if, but only if, there were no other means of avoiding the temptation to commit adultery (*On the Sentences* 4.31.2 and 3). In the fifteenth century his rule was adopted by the influential *Summa* of St. Antoninus (3.1.20) and the less important work of the Dominican John Nider (*Moral Leprosy* 5.1, "The Genital Abuses of the Married"). The cautious way in which Palude developed a hypothetical instance, and the cautious way in which his instance is repeated, are proof of the place held by the procreative purpose. A frontal assault on the requirement of procreative purpose was difficult. Only with ingenuity could even the Pauline purpose of avoiding incontinence be defended.

This controversy over the Pauline purpose is of greater theoretical than practical significance. At worst the sin of intercourse to avoid fornication was venial. Consequently, it was not ordinarily the subject of interrogation in the confessional. The wife who had intercourse only for procreation might sometimes be portrayed as an ideal, as Cenobia is portrayed by the Monk in the *Canterbury Tales*. But even such a rigorist on marriage as St. Bernardine did not preach against a spouse who sought intercourse to avoid fornication. Moreover, distinctions introduced as to "payment of the marital debt" had refined determinations of fault to such a degree that they were almost unworkable (see below, p. 285). The significance of the controversy lay in its test of the theologians' commitment to the procreative purpose. Slowly, indirectly, artfully, the pure procreative doctrine was undermined, but only to accommodate the doctrine of St. Paul. If only hesitantly, circumspectly, and arguably could a coital purpose be urged which had the highly moral objective of preventing one's own sin, how much less could any other nonprocreative purpose be justified?

The barriers against contraception by the requirements as to purpose were made still higher by the doctrine on marital intercourse with pleasure as its object. Here the categorizations ranged between venial and

---

[23] Other thirteenth-century supporters of the milder position are the Dominican Hugh of St. Cher in 1230–1232 (*On the Sentences* 4.26) and Robert of Sorbonne (*Treatise on Marriage*, written sometime after 1247). Hugh is quoted and Robert cited in Dominikus Lindner, *Der Usus matrimonii: Eine Untersuchung über seine sittliche Bewertung in der katholischen Moraltheologie alter und neuer Zeit* (Munich, 1929), pp. 123, 129.

mortal sin. The twelfth-century rigorists had held intercourse for delight or pleasure or lust as mortal. But the doctrine did not end with rigorist commentary on Gratian. It was adopted by the bible for confessors, Raymond's *Summa* (4.2.8). It was perpetuated by Monaldus, following Raymond (*Summa*, fol. 136r). It was not just an eccentricity of the canonists. Chaucer found it appropriate doctrine to put in the mouth of his virtuous parish pastor. It is mortal sin, the Parson says, "to assemble" not for children, return of the debt, or avoidance of fornication, but "oonly for amorous love and for noon of the foreseyde causes, but for to accomplice thilke brennynge delit, they rekke nevere how ofte" ("The Parson's Tale," *Remedium contra peccatum luxuriae*, line 942).

Into the fifteenth century, the view persists among rigorists on sexual activity. Bernardine of Siena in his preaching puts the question as follows: Can a husband "use his wife only for delight [*delectatio*] or principally for delight?" A husband will "often" say, "Why can't I take delight in my own goods and my own wife?" But to this plausible complaint Bernardine answers, "She is not yours, but God's." It is a sin — impliedly a mortal sin — to have intercourse "too frequently, with inordinate affection, or with dissipation of one's strength" (*Seraphic Sermons* 19.3).

At the same time the predominance of the milder Augustinian view must be recognized. It labeled the intention to seek pleasure in intercourse as venial. It was held steadily by most of the major theologians: Alexander of Hales, *Summa of Theology* 2–2.3.5.2.1.3.2; Thomas, *On the Sentences* 4.31.2.3; Bonaventure, *On the Sentences* 4.31.2.3; William of Rennes, *Gloss on the Summa of Raymond* 4.2.8;[24] Astesanus, *Summa* 8.9; Durand of St. Pourçain, *On the Sentences* 4.31.4;[25] Peter de Palude, *On the Sentences* 4.31.3; John Gerson, *Compendium of Theology*, "The seven Capital Vices: The Sin of Lechery"; Antoninus, *Summa* 3.1.20. None of these writers suggested any modification or loophole by which the seeking of pleasure or delight could be made lawful; none of them entertained reasoning analogous to that justifying intercourse "to avoid fornication." Pleasure as the purpose of intercourse was firmly branded sin.[26]

Moreover, even these authors entered one caveat to their milder condemnation. For them, as for Jerome, the too ardent lover was an adulterer. In Gratian's law book the polemical Stoic phrase had taken on added gravity and an almost juridical force. The thirteenth-century theologians tried to give content to the vague "too ardent." They held that, when this immoderation was exhibited, mortal sin occurred. Two main stand-

---

[24] William of Rennes, *Glossa*, included in Raymond, *Summa* (Verona, 1744).
[25] Durand of St. Pourçain, *In Sententias theologicas Petri Lombardi* (Lyons, 1595).
[26] See, however, the opinion reported by Richard Middleton, analyzed below in Chapter X.

ards were proposed. One was that immoderate love was present when one preferred sexual union with one's wife to union with God as one's last end; so taught Thomas, *On the Sentences* 4.31.2.3; Bonaventure, *On the Sentences* 4.31.2.3; Gerson, *Compendium of Theology*, "The Seven Capital Vices: The Sin of Lechery"; Bernardine, *The Christian Religion* 18.1. Unless it be supposed that this standard was designed deliberately to contrast with the courtly love cult of the woman, the definition given was not very helpful: every mortal sin was a preference of some finite end to God.

The other standard required a deliberate act of abstraction from actual circumstances. "Would the husband have intercourse with his wife even if she were not his wife?" If so, he was guilty of too ardent love. This hypothetical test, so unlikely to be of practical use, was set out by William of Auxerre, *Summa* 4 (fol. 287v). It was adopted by Alexander of Hales, *Summa of Theology* 2–2.3.5.2.1.3.2; Bonaventure, *On the Sentences* 4.31. 2.3; Astesanus, *Summa* 8.9; Durand of St. Pourçain, *On the Sentences* 4.31.4; Antoninus, *Confessional*, "Interrogatory" 3.1. Antoninus, though recommending the test to a confessor interrogating a married penitent, added drily, "It is, however, difficult to discern and recognize this." Indeed, if the test was to have any meaning, it fused with sins of objective behavior where procreation was frustrated. In this sense, the sin of too ardent love became "to use one's wife as a harlot," a definition ventured in an early work of Albert (*The Sacraments* 9.2.2, reply to obj. 2)[27] and adopted by Thomas (*On the Sentences* 4.31.2.3).

The variability in the standard, and the psychological difficulty of applying the test most favored by the theologians, are irrelevant when one measures the effect of the theological position on our subject. The rejection of pleasure, delight, and ardent love might, paradoxically, be argued to have been a defense of personal values in marriage. The tendency, reported by St. Bernardine, for a man to regard his wife as his property was rebuked. The exploitation of one person "as a harlot" for the satisfaction of the other was condemned. To the extent that this was the impact of the doctrine, it contributed to a development of personal values in marriage destined, in the very long run, to be of relevance to the doctrine on contraception.

The more immediate and more obvious effect of this kind of teaching was to emphasize biological purpose. "Too ardent love" was banned; but no category of "moderate love" was recognized as a purpose in intercourse. Chaucer's Parson accurately reflects the fusion of forbidden acts when he rejects intercourse "oonly for amorous love": the purpose of expressing or receiving love was associated with lack of measure, with sinful excess. Intercourse between married persons just because they were

[27] St. Albert, *De sacramentis*, in *Opera omnia* (Aschendorf, 1958), vol. XXVI.

married was unacceptable. As the Parson puts it, for a man and wife to "rekken of nothing but that they been assembled" is mortal sin ("The Parson's Tale," line 904). The narrow confinement of lawful purpose either to procreation or, at most, to avoidance of incontinence effectively reinforced the tie of intercourse to procreation, and procreation was put forward as the single positive value of intercourse.

If one probes further to ask why the procreative purpose was so valued one must recognize that the Cathar challenge was still a live memory for the major thirteenth-century theologians. Aquinas wrote his commentary on the *Sentences* at the same time that the Council of Albi was mopping up the heresy. But if one asks why the doctrine persisted after the demise of Catharism, and why pleasure was so disdained, one encounters, first of all, the Augustinian theological heritage, secondly a society whose customs did not present a challenge to the theological valuations.

Around the Augustinian synthesis on original sin, sexuality, and concupiscence, there swirled a number of controversies.[28] But no new theory or variation of the synthesis gathered sufficient support, or was expressed with sufficient clarity, to dislodge the Augustinian views at the secondary level at which they related to marriage.[29] Thomas, to take the most prominent example, fused Augustine's theory with the eleventh-century teaching of St. Anselm that original sin is, formally, an absence of original justice, that is, an absence of the rectitude of nature submissive to God. This absence, Thomas taught, occurs "in the essence of the soul or intellective part, where original justice was" (*Truth* 25.6).[30] The effect of the loss of original justice is that, no longer subject to reason, "the inferior powers tend individually towards what is proper to each, that is, concupiscence toward pleasure, irascibility toward wrath, and other powers similarly." There is, in other words, an absence of rational integration of the lower animal powers. Concupiscence is felt especially in the generative members, which are furthest from rational control by nature, and which are the means of transmitting original sin (*ST* 2–1.17.9, reply to obj. 3). Baptism gives grace to the soul, but does not ef-

---

[28] In simplified summation, the positions ranged from Abelard's contention that original sin was debt, a notion that de-emphasized its sexual consequences, to the view of Henry of Ghent that original sin was "a morbid infection existing in the seed" (*Quodlibeta* [Paris, 1518] 1.21). In between, on the side of sexual pessimism, was the view of Peter of Poitiers that "the first movements" toward intercourse were sinful because they arose from the genital organs, which were the agents of transmission of original sin. On the fluctuations in twelfth- and thirteenth-century thinking on the whole subject, see A. Gaudet, "Péché originel," *DTC* 12^1:436–507.

[29] An excellent analysis of the relation of sexuality, original sin, and the goods of marriage, as the questions stood at the time Aquinas wrote, is made by Fuchs, *Die Sexualethik des heiligen Thomas von Aquin*, pp. 53–71.

[30] St. Thomas, *De veritate*, ed. Raymond Spiazzi, O.P., in *Quaestiones disputatae*, vol. I (Turin, 1948).

face the disorder of concupiscence, which remains, not as a sin but as a mark of original sin, in the baptized (*Evil* 4.6, reply to obj. 16).

With this view of concupiscence as marking the sexual acts of every man, Thomas asks, "Should marriage have some good by which it is excused?" Like Peter Lombard, he turns the question into "Should marital intercourse have some good by which it is excused?" He answers:

> No wise man should sustain a loss, without the recompense of an equal or a greater good gained. The choice of something which has some loss attached to it needs the addition of some good which will compensate and so give it order and decency. In the union of man and wife a loss of reason occurs: both because reason is absorbed by the vehemence of delight so that it cannot understand anything during this delight, as the Philosopher says, and because of the tribulation of the flesh which such must bear from solicitude for temporal things, as 1 Corinthians 7 makes plain.
>
> (On the Sentences 4.31.1.1)

Thomas appeals to Aristotle's testimony on "the vehemence of delight." But in his answer to objections he reveals the theological root of this emphasis on the absence of rational control: "the generative force, by which original sin is transmitted, is infected and corrupted" (reply to obj. 1).

In the *Summa theologica* the corruption of the sexual act is even more plainly stated. Thomas is dealing with a hypothetical, uncongenial to many modern minds, but useful to test doctrine: "In the state of innocence would there have been generation by coitus?" [31] Aquinas answers affirmatively, and faces the objection that "in carnal intercourse, more than at any other time, man becomes like the beasts, on account of the vehement delight which he takes therein; . . . before sin there would have been no such intercourse of man and woman." He replies,

> Beasts are without reason. In this way man becomes, as it were, like them in coition, because he cannot moderate the delight of intercourse and the heat of concupiscence by reason. In the state of innocence nothing of this kind would have happened that was not regulated by reason, not because delight of sense was less, as some say (rather indeed would sensible delight have been the greater in proportion to the greater purity of nature and the greater sensibility of the body) but because the force of concupiscence would not have so inordinately thrown itself into such pleasure, being curbed by reason, whose place it is not to lessen sensual pleasure, but to prevent the force of concupiscence from cleaving to it immoderately. By "immoderately" I mean going beyond the bounds of reason, as a sober person does not take less pleasure in food eaten temperately than the glutton, but his concupiscence lingers less in such pleasure.
>
> (ST 1.98.2, reply to obj. 3)

[31] For a good history of the twelfth- and thirteenth-century theological discussion of sexuality and generation in the state of man before the Fall, see Michael Müller, *Die Lehre des hl. Augustinus von der Paradiesesehe und ihre Auswirkung in der Sexualethik des 12. und 13. Jahrhunderts bis Thomas v. Aquin* (Regensburg, 1954).

Taken by itself, this passage would suggest that coitus always involved sin, for "going beyond the bounds of reason" is another way of saying "sin." But Thomas makes clear later (*ST* 2-2.153.2) that he holds that marital coitus can be without sin. Consequently, this passage must be read as merely a strong statement of the force of concupiscence in the act of intercourse. It is this strong and inevitable disorder which makes it necessary for intercourse to be excused, or compensated for, by the good of procreation.

Later commentators, in the light of the controversy with the Lutherans and Calvinists, were able to discern in Thomas an optimism which finds human nature unaffected in its constitutive elements and contrasts with Augustine's vision of a corrupted nature.[32] There is a shift in emphasis from Augustine in his definition of the formal essence of original sin. But Thomas is saturated with Augustinian doctrine.[33] Not only is Augustine a theological master for him; Thomas, whose own chastity was celebrated, looks on Augustine as a man whose analysis of sexual behavior carries with it the testimony of experience. He treats Augustine as his teacher on the effects of sexual acts. He repeats the Augustinian epigram that in coitus man "becomes all flesh" (*On the Sentences* 4.31.2.3, reply to obj. 3). He repeats Augustine on the danger of wifely blandishments and fleshly contact for the human spirit (*ST* 2-2.151.3, reply to obj. 2; 153.2). His formulas on concupiscence are Augustine's. When he takes up the old Manichean argument that marital intercourse is evil because original sin is transmitted by the concupiscence involved, he answers in the words of Augustine in *Marriage and Concupiscence* 1.24.27 (*ST* 2-2.153.2, reply to obj. 4). If the most independent of medieval theologians could not escape Augustine, how much less could most of his successors, confronted by both St. Augustine and St. Thomas?

The theological heritage, then, played a major part in the insistence on procreative purpose. But the theologians did not speak in an environmental vacuum. If they were not husbands or fathers, they were sons and brothers; they had been children. If they did not give greater weight to the place of love in marriage, they may have observed no reason for doing otherwise.

The social structure and courting customs of medieval society were not such as to give personal choice and personal relations the preeminent role they enjoy today. Class barriers severely restricted the choice of marriage partners. For the rural mass, tied to small communities, the choice was yet further restricted by availability. Within the narrow limits

[32] Cf. Gaudet, "Péché originel," *DTC* 12¹:469-471; Fuchs, *Die Sexualethik*, pp. 55-57.
[33] Fuchs, *Der Sexualethik*, pp. 43, 49, 61, 136, 275.

already established by society and geography, personal choice was not encouraged; parental initiative in selection of mates was approved. When Francis Barbaro, an intelligent and refined Florentine of the fifteenth century, urged that daughters be allowed to marry only those they love, the best precedent he could find at hand was the custom of mythical "Cretans" (*Directions for Love and Marriage* 2.1).[34] No social institution provided a structure in which persons could know each other before marriage. It is typical that the knight La Tour Landry warns his daughters that a girl who spoke to him in a friendly fashion when he was a young bachelor seemed too forward to be a decent bride (*Book of the Knight La Tour Landry*, c. 13). Courtship, developed by the troubadours as an aspect of adulterous courtly love, was sometimes spoken of as an ideal preparation for marriage; but courtship as an ideal was service to the lady defined as "great emprise" (*Canterbury Tales*, "The Franklin's Tale," line 732); it was not a meeting of persons. Fancy, the sudden effect of beauty, were not unknown factors in choosing a spouse, but they did not seem to the theologians to play a predominant role. Peter Lombard gives the theological motives for contracting marriage (procreation and avoidance of fornication), but he also discusses three other "decent" motives: the reconciliation of enemies, beauty, riches (*Sentences* 4.30.4). It may be not theological bias but sociological fact that leads him to give beauty this subordinate place and not to speak of love at all. The theologians who commented on the *Sentences* seemed to see nothing incongruous in this enumeration. In the social context provided by medieval institutions it was difficult to believe that personal love often motivated those who wanted to wed.

If marrying for love was neither a theological nor social ideal, married love was an ideal of the theologians. Copulation, observes Thomas, "even among animals creates a sweet society" (*Summa Against the Gentiles* 3.123). Among human persons, "a man loves his wife principally by reason of the carnal meeting," and in the order of charity, this love for his wife, founded on the union of the flesh, is lawfully more intense than his love of his father or mother (*ST* 2–2.26.11). Commenting on Aristotle, and primarily trying to explicate the text, Thomas reveals his own appreciation of Aristotle's characterization of man as a "conjugal animal." A friendship is born between husband and wife based on the delightful in the act of generation; the useful in the building of a household; and the virtuous in the response of one virtuous person to another. Such a friendship, with its threefold base, renders both spouses joyful (*On the Ethics*

---

[34] Francis Barbaro, *De re uxoria* 2.1 (Amsterdam, 1639); English trans. (translator anonymous), *Directions for Love and Marriage* (London, 1677). On the significance of Barbaro's work as the beginning of the approach to marriage by the new Italian humanists, see Gabriel Le Bras, "Mariage," *DTC* 9²:2224.

8.12).[35] As Thomas says on his own account, there is between husband and wife "the maximum friendship" (*Summa Against the Gentiles* 3.123). Bonaventure observes, "In marriage there is a certain singleness of love in which an outsider does not share . . . There is mutual love and therefore mutual zeal, and therefore singleness" (*On the Sentences* 4.33.1.2). He continues a little later, "For there is something miraculous in a man finding in one woman a pleasingness which he can never find in another, as say the experienced" (*ibid.* 4.36.2.2). Even Bernardine, who so often speaks so harshly of sexual sins in marriage, quotes Ephesians 5:25–28 to show that love between husband and wife is natural, and repeats its injunction to husbands to love their wives, as Christ loves the Church (*The Christian Religion* 48.3.3).

A case can be made that the theologians gave stronger valuation to married love than anyone else treating of love in the Middle Ages. The courtly love tradition had developed its ideal outside of marriage. Only gradually did secular literature recognize that love and marriage could coincide; an early and rare example is the twelfth-century poem *Erec*, of Chrétien de Troyes. As late as Dante the courtly love tradition, now put to orthodox uses, dissociates love of a woman and marriage, and the greatest poet of the Middle Ages, who has so much to say of love, has nothing to say of his wife. In the fourteenth century, one may observe in Chaucer the domestication of love. The tale told by the Franklin, a kind of country squire, includes a celebration of "The joye, the ese, and the prosperitee/ That is betwixe an housbonde and his wyf" (lines 804–805). The Parson, too, invokes the ideal married love of *Ephesians* (line 929). No reader of Chaucer would believe that such devoted love is characteristic of his society; but the ideal is being proclaimed. It is the ideal already declared by the theologians.

The theologians of the great theological age, the thirteenth century, were, I would suggest, somewhat in advance of their society in their declarations on the ideal of married love. If they generally phrased their arguments against sexual sins not in terms of this ideal but in terms of an offense to nature or to life, an unarticulated reason for their approach must have been the social acceptance of their arguments. Injury to the illegitimate child-to-be, harm to the potential man, danger to the conservation of the species — these arguments must have seemed more tangible than arguments based on the demands of personal love. The failure to incorporate love into the purposes of marital intercourse was largely a failure of theological analysis. The failure occurred in a society whose

---

[35] Thomas had been anticipated in this friendly commentary on marriage by St. Albert's equally warm commentary on the *Nicomachean Ethics* 1162a in his *Ethics* 8.3.8, *Opera omnia*, ed. A. Borgnet (Paris, 1890–1899), vol. VII.

mating customs made procreation, not love, the most prominent value of marriage.

In this European society, in this theology dominated by Augustine, reason itself appeared to condemn contraception. The contraceptive act destroyed potential life. It frustrated the inseminating function of coitus. It violated the principal purpose of marriage and the principal, if not the only, purpose of marital intercourse. Authority had condemned contraception. The Cathar enemy had been the prototype of a people denying the procreative purpose. Reason now showed that authority was right, that the Cathars were wrong, and that contraception was behavior contrary to the good of man.

CHAPTER IX

SANCTIONS

B Y STAMPING CONTRACEPTIVE BEHAVIOR as mortal sin, the theologians of the high Middle Ages, in agreement with the penitentials and the Fathers, maintained the most serious and most universal deterrent to contraceptive usage by a conscientious Christian. To engage in an act which cut one off from grace, offended God, entailed eternal consequences unless remitted — such a deed might be done by a fallible human, but every Christian trying to love God would do his best to avoid it. No Catholic practicing contraception could consider himself in the state of grace, that is, spiritually alive, open to God; nor could he receive the sacraments, until he had repented of his act. To the extent that the Christian people were informed of the sinful character of the act, and to the extent that they were devoutly seeking their salvation, the branding of contraception as mortal sin must have been the most powerful sanction against its practice.

PENANCE

If the user of contraceptive practices or devices was sorry and confessed, his sin was remitted, but he still had penance to do. What kind of penance was enjoined?

This simple question is not easily answered, for two reasons: the discretionary function of the confessor in imposing penance, and the secrecy of the penance given. In the twelfth century, there was explicit awareness that the confessor acted more as a spiritual doctor than as judge, applying different medicines to spiritual diseases (Alan of Lille, *Penitential*, PL 210:285). The penance was to be adjusted not only to the circumstances of the sin, but to such characteristics of the penitent as his sex, age, marital status, and psychological propensities (*ibid.*, col. 287). A mechanically set penance, per some schedule, was not important. "A rational way of penance is always, as we have said, to be set by the judgment of the priest" (*ibid.*, col. 289). "All penances," says St. Raymond in the leading medieval treatise for confessors, "are arbitrary," that is, within the rational discretion of the confessor (*Summa for Confessors* 3.34.4). "This," he adds, "is custom." [1]

As to secrecy, the general rule was well put in the late twelfth century by Bartholomew of Exeter: "No matter how shameful and abominable," a secret sin was to be purged "by secret confession and secret satisfaction" (*Penitential*, c. 28).[2] The sins involved in contraception, though known to one's spouse, would have been secret within the meaning of this rule; they were not public or notorious. The penances for them would not have been of the public character that public sin required by way of reparation and example.

Consequently, we have neither testimony as to the penances given, nor any sure guide from the theological literature. As was customary for all private sins, the penance would have consisted of prayers, fasts, mortifications, or good works. Probably many confessors accepted Raymond's authoritative interpretation of *Si aliquis*, that the penance for contraception by poisons of sterility should be the same as for homicide; but they would have subordinated it to the general rule of adapting penance to the penitent. In particular, it is unlikely that confessors abandoned the policy, recommended by Burchard, distinguishing between contraception to avoid discovery of fornication and contraception to avoid starvation. Besides the classification "homicide," the other categorizations must have suggested analogies, and a sin variously described as adultery, sodomy, parricide, or vice against nature must have been assigned penances of comparative stringency.

Whatever the penances usually imposed, it would be a mistake to emphasize their deterrent quality. For those with little spiritual sensitivity, a sanction consisting of prayers and fasts could not have held much threat. For the spiritually sensitive who would be most apt to obey the Church's teachings or confess their failure to obey, the sanction contained in the description of the acts as offenses against God was far more compelling than the measures prescribed for reparation.[3]

One exception to this rule, however, existed where the acts were made

---

[1] The prevailing attitude is ably analyzed in Pierre Michaud-Quantin, "A propos des premières 'Summae confessorum,'" *Recherches de théologie ancienne et médiévale* 26 (1959), 270 ff.

[2] The Council of Durham warns against imposing such heavy penances on married persons that their spouses will suspect that they have committed "some hidden and enormous crime"; *Concilia Magnae Britanniae et Hiberniae,* ed. David Wilkins (London, 1737), I, 577.

[3] On the predominance in the canon law of pastoral solicitude and moral teaching over effective employment of coercive means, see Robert E. Rodes, Jr., "The Canon Law as a Legal System — Function, Obligation, Sanction," *Natural Law Forum* 9 (1964), 92–93.

"reserved sins," that is, sins whose absolution was reserved to the bishop of the diocese or to priests specially delegated by him. To reserve the sin was to make absolution from it more solemn and more awkward. It was an action occasionally taken against contraception by local councils or individual bishops. Probably the blanket reservation of "homicide" was not enough to reserve contraception by potion. An instructive example is provided by a canon of the council of Mainz in 1310. The canon reserved to the bishop absolution from "homicide," "sins against nature," and the "*maleficia* of those who bewitch spouses so that they cannot copulate, or who procure the sterility of women or abortion" (Mansi 25:346–347). Both cooperation in a contraceptive act and cooperation in abortion were here described as the results of *maleficia*. Despite the designation of such acts as homicide by *Si aliquis*, it was thought necessary to make special mention of them. The "sins against nature" presumably included all forms of intercourse where insemination was avoided without the aid of a sterilizing potion. Another report on reserved sins of this kind is furnished by Antoninus of Florence. Having defined "the sodomitic vice" to include marital intercourse outside the vagina, he noted that this sin was reserved by "some bishops" (*Confessional*, "Interrogatory" 1.6). This kind of sanction went beyond the ordinary sacramental discipline. It was halfway between a purely spiritual sanction and a social restraint.

CONDEMNATION BY CATEGORY

Suppose that one were not sensitive to one's spiritual state, and that inability to receive the sacraments lawfully meant nothing. Then the hard categorizations of the contraceptive act at least stood as social deterrents. The theologians' categories held a prominent place in the formation of popular valuations. Their categories operated as verbal sanctions.

The theologians and canonists proclaimed that nonprocreative marital intercourse, including coitus interruptus, was a form of the sin against nature. Peter Cantor, John Gerson, Bernardine, and Antoninus assimilated such intercourse to the even uglier category of sodomy. *Aliquando* proclaimed that the users of contraceptives were adulterers. *Si aliquis* condemned them as homicides. Bernardine labeled spouses frustrating insemination "the killers of their own children."

In the ranking of sins of lechery, the sin against nature was said by *Adulterii malum* to be worse than incest. Gratian's ordering was maintained by the standard works of theology. In Thomas' *Summa theologica*, the sin against nature, including the sin in marriage, is the greatest of sexual vices, being worse than fornication, seduction, rape, incest, or sacrilege (2–2.154.12). This abstract ordering of vices is put concretely in preaching by Bernardine: "It is better for a wife to permit herself to copulate with her own father in a natural way than with her husband against nature" (*The Christian Religion* 17.1.1). "It is bad for a man to have intercourse with his own mother, but it is much worse for him to have intercourse with his wife against nature" (*Seraphic Sermons* 19.1).

This kind of ranking contributed to a social attitude; these descriptions functioned as epithets as well as analyses. To the best of their linguistic ability, the medieval scholastics sought to label contraception as an affront to decency, life, and nature. The man who engaged in contraceptive behavior had not only to ignore the spiritual consequences, but to defy the social ideals of his community.

DEPRIVATION OF MARITAL RIGHTS

If one were spiritually and socially insensitive, if one never came to confession or, coming, made incomplete and therefore inefficacious disclosure of one's sins — was he beyond the reach of the canonical sanctions? He was not, if his spouse was dissatisfied with his behavior. The canonists had provided three remedies, three kinds of attack on his marital rights: refusal of intercourse; judicial separation; and, most drastic, annulment of the marriage. The first two are usually spoken of in connection with unnatural intercourse, the last only in connection with the use of artificial contraceptives.

The first remedy — refusal of intercourse — was viewed by the scholastics not as a sanction against the sinful spouse, but as a moral requirement for the innocent spouse (regularly assumed to be the wife) if she would avoid guilt. The universal rule was that active cooperation in the sin of another was itself sin. The rule was applied directly to participation in unnatural intercourse.

In the thirteenth century, Alexander of Hales teaches, "The woman ought not at all to consent to the man in the sin against nature, and if she consents, she sins mortally" (*Summa theologica* 2–2.3.5.2.1.3, "The Sins of the Married," 3). Peraldus in his definition of the sin against nature includes "consent" to the sin of Onan (*Summa of Virtues and Vices* 2.3, "Lechery"). In the fourteenth century, Peter de Palude reports a case where a woman consulted him because her husband sought anal intercourse with her. He advised her that, rather than consent to this behavior, she ought "to let herself be killed, or let her husband commit adultery, or shame himself with a mule" (*On the Sentences* 4.31.3.2). Almost a century later, Gerson, preaching at the French court, says if one spouse seeks something "indecent" in intercourse, the other is to resist "to death" ("Sermon Against Lechery," *Works* [Antwerp, 1706], III, 916). The same doctrine is taught in fifteenth-century Italy by St. Bernardine: if the sin against nature is involved, "you women ought to die rather than consent" (*Seraphic Sermons* 19.1; similarly, *Le Prediche volgari* [Milan, 1936], p. 435). Although her husband threatens to seek other women or other men for intercourse, the wife must stand firm: "I say No, even if the devil will carry him off" (*Seraphic Sermons* 19.3).

These solutions were brusque. No attempt was made to analyze the degrees of cooperation that might be involved. Nor was there discrimination among the varieties of behavior in which insemination is avoided. Alexander, Gerson, and Bernardine all adopted a definition of the sin against nature which included coitus interruptus; apparently they included participation in this act, as well as participation in anal intercourse, within the ambit of their advice.

Si aliquis itself condemned cooperation in giving someone a contraceptive potion. But the canon and most writers said nothing at all on the sin of cooperation in intercourse after sterility had been artificially achieved. Their silence left a gap which can only be filled by considering their teaching on cooperation in other sins. Pope Alexander III, a distinguished canonist, had made a good analysis of the ways of cooperating in murder in his letter to Bartholomew of Exeter on the penances for the cooperators in the murder of Thomas à Becket; an excerpt from his letter, placed next to *Si aliquis*, became a principal canonical text on cooperation (*Decretals* 5.12.6). Cooperation in sins of theft or usury had also often been analyzed. Here the usual question was, Who else, besides the actual thief or usurer, was bound to make restitution? The usual answer was, One who had aided the sin by any of the following: "commanding; counseling; consenting; flattering; sheltering; participating with; being silent; not preventing; not making known," with the proviso that the last three categories applied only to those with official duties relating to the act (St. Thomas, *Summa theologica* 2–2.62.7; Alexander Lombard, *Treatise on Usury* 9).[4] These categories, developed to define the obligation of restitution of property, came to be looked on as the standard types of cooperation.

It is not evident how these categories were actually applied to cooperation in sinful marital acts. The last three categories applied only to governmental officials. Presumably "commanding," "counseling," or "flattering" which led to contraceptive behavior would have fallen within the category of condemned cooperation. But suppose a wife simply did not resist her husband. Was this a sin of "consent" or "participation"? Most authors did not discuss the case; Alexander, Gerson, and Bernardine ap-

---

[4] Alexander Lombard, *Tractatus de usuris*, ed. A. M. Hamelin (Louvain, 1962).

parently considered the wife's nonresistance to be either consent or participation.[5]

Cooperation by a husband whose wife had temporarily sterilized herself does not appear to have been specifically considered by the major authors. The nearest case is that put by Albert when he rejected the attribution of homicide to "those who procure poisons of sterility." He looked only at the joint action of the couple and recommended that they be induced to abstain from intercourse (On the Sentences 4.31.18). He did not say what right to intercourse an innocent husband would have if his wife had used a sterilizing potion. According to the dominant theological doctrine, intercourse where sterility was known was always venial sin. No reason existed for the majority who held that position to make an exception in a case of this kind. Whether the formal guilt of a sin of contraception would also have been incurred by the originally innocent spouse is not clear.

The other possible remedies for contraceptive behavior were analyzed as sanctions. Separation, or divortium a thoro, was a judicial act of an ecclesiastical court. It was provided for in Gratian's Decretum 2.32.5 and in the Decretals 4.19, "Divorces." If it was granted, the innocent party was freed from the duties of cohabitation and the rendering of the marital debt, but was not able to remarry. As set out by the canons, divorce in this limited sense was a remedy only for adultery.

It occurred to the commentators that if the sin against nature was worse than adultery, why should not separation be granted on this ground too? In the twelfth century, Huguccio raised this point in commenting on Gratian, and concluded that "a husband can dismiss his wife, or a wife her husband, if one acts with the other in an unnatural or posterior member" (Summa 2.32.4). The Gloss on Gratian, 2.32.7, on the other hand, included "sodomy" as a ground for separation, but doubted whether "pollution with one's own wife was included." Raymond, knowing this controversy, did not see fit to include the point in the Decretals; in his own Summa adultery remained the only ground for separation. However, the glossator on Raymond, William of Rennes, quoted Huguccio approvingly (4.22.1). The authorities thus remained divided.

Hostiensis ignored the conflict. His contemporary Pope Innocent IV took a stance which represented a compromise: "We do not believe that for the sodomitic vice there can be a separation of beds," he declared. But he made an important exception: divorce was allowable for any "crime"

---

[5] The formula for confession in The Cleansing of Man's Soul speaks of sinful intercourse with a spouse "agein my will." This act, regarded as sinful, seems to be an act of forced cooperation in unnatural behavior. (Anon., The Cleansing of Man's Soul, ed. Charles L. Regan, 1963, typewritten MS in Widener Library, Harvard University, based on Bodleian MS. 923.)

where "the husband wants to draw her [the wife] to that sin" *Apparatus* 5.16). The exception would seem to have swallowed his rule, where unnatural sin was at issue, if the husband sought any cooperation.

Although the canonists were in disagreement, the theologians seemed confident that separation would be granted on this ground. "One can proceed to divorce for the sin against nature," says Thomas (*On the Sentences* 4.35.1.1, reply to obj. 4). If something "indecent" is practiced in marriage, a spouse "may complain, first secretly to her priest or her friends, then to the judge, if she does not find other remedy," says Gerson in the fourteenth century ("Sermon Against Lechery," *Works*, III, 916). Peter de Palude is more ambiguous: divorce is available as a remedy but it should not be granted "particularly if the husband is willing to be corrected" (*On the Sentences* 4.35.7). In the fifteenth century, however, Bernardine is emphatic: "You, priest, when you confess some woman who complains that her husband was abusing her by the sodomitic vice, go immediately to the bishop that he may separate them *a thoro*" (*Seraphic Sermons* 19.1). Later in the century, the Franciscan summist Trovamala says that "sodomy" with one's wife is ground for divorce, if the husband wishes to continue this conduct. As to coitus interruptus, here described as "polluting some woman outside the walls" (*extra claustra*), it constitutes adultery if committed outside of marriage. Trovamala leaves the question open as to whether it is also ground for divorce if practiced by a husband with his wife (*Summa*, at "Matrimonium," 7.1–2).

A great many theologians and canonists did not discuss the case. Thomas himself observed that divorce sought because of the sin against nature was rarer than divorce sought for adultery (*On the Sentences* 4.35.1.1). Bernardine noted the reluctance of some bishops to enforce the laws (*Le Prediche volgari*, p. 435). Probably, as Palude and Trovamala suggested, divorce was only granted when the husband was incorrigible. But in theory, and occasionally in practice, divorce operated as a sanction.

Si conditiones, the climax of a canonical analysis begun with Huguccio, declared that a marriage contract "lacked effect" if conditions contrary to the substance of marriage had been set before the marriage (above, p. 177). The principle of the canon is cited with approval by a number of theologians. The invalidating condition agreed to by the spouses is given with some slight variations: "You will have procured poisons of sterility or will agree to my procuring such poisons" (Scotus, *On the Sentences* [*Oxford Report*] 4.31). "Sterility of offspring will be procured" (St. Bonaventure, *On the Sentences* 4.31.1.3). "You will procure poisons of sterility" (Peter de Palude, *On the Sentences* 4.29.2.3). "You will avoid the generation of offspring" (Trovamala, *Summa*, at "Matrimonium" 5.1). The principle of the canon is broad enough to include any agreement to practice contraceptive behavior of any kind. The tendency, exemplified by Bonaventure and Palude, is to confine it to an agreement to use contraceptives.

Other theologians adopted the broad principle present in Huguccio that intention to avoid children nullified the marriage. In the mid-thirteenth century Richard Middleton treats in this way an antecedent intention "to procure poisons of sterility" (*On the Sentences* 4.31.2.1). At the beginning of the fourteenth century, Astesanus calls null a marriage where the contracting parties "intend not to have children, or not to rear them if God gives them, or to procure sterility" (*Summa* 8.9). It is not clear that this stress on intention is meant to be contrasted with the canon's language of condition. Where both spouses had the intention, the difference between "intention" and "condition" would have consisted chiefly in the formality and explicitness of the latter. If, however, only one spouse had the intention "to procure sterility," a case substantially different from a contractual condition would have been presented.

The difference would have had more importance if attempts had been made to obtain annulments on one or the other ground. But did anyone get an annulment on either ground? Hostiensis and Innocent IV, Joannes Andreae, Panormitanus — the leading canonists of the thirteenth, fourteenth, and fifteenth centuries, respectively — have absolutely nothing to say on the decretal. Must we not infer that *Si conditiones* was useful as a teaching device on the meaning of marriage, but found little or no application? There is other evidence that the canon was not often invoked. The question is never raised whether an agreement to practice coitus interruptus meets the test of *Si conditiones.* Nor is it ever asked whether the sterility sought must be permanent or may be of a kind periodically renewed. The practical questions which frequent application of the canon would have raised do not appear.[6]

Si conditiones is, nonetheless, a significant testimony to the teaching on contraception. Much of the impact of the canon law in general was educational rather than legal. This canon taught in a striking way the incompatibility of marriage and avoidance of offspring. As an independent sanction against contraception, it does not seem to have been a vital force.

---

[6] In another canon, Innocent III dealt hypothetically with a case where a man went through a wedding ceremony but "did not propose to take a wife nor ever to consent to the said person." Such a marriage, the Pope said, would be void (*Decretals* 4.1.26). It would have been possible to treat a marriage in which it was agreed that offspring would be avoided as a similarly fictitious and therefore void marriage. This approach does not seem to have been taken. Moreover, the common canonist teaching was that the rule of Innocent III applied only in the internal forum, i.e., that it could not be invoked to obtain an annulment (*Gloss,* at 4.1.26; Hostiensis, *Commentary* 4.1.26; Andreae, *New Commentary* 4.1.26; Panormitanus, *Commentary* 4.1.26.

COMMUNICATION OF THE SANCTIONS

The principal sanctions of the doctrine were of a fragile spiritual kind, dependent not on courts to enforce, but on hearts to accept. A particular importance thus attaches to the question, How was the doctrine disseminated? Four methods may be distinguished: circulation of the canon law and of theological material in writing; preaching; instruction in the confessional; other oral instruction.

The *Decretum* and the *Decretals*, accepted by the central authority of the Church, were the common authorities of western Europe. Peter Lombard's *Sentences* was the common textbook of theology. Works like St. Raymond's *Summa for Confessors*, Hostiensis' *Commentary on the Decretals*, St. Thomas' *Summa theologica*, were almost as authoritative. More summary treatments such as those of Peraldus, Monaldus, and Astesanus had some currency. The difficulties of manuscript reproduction limited the circulation of all these treatises. But for the cleric at a university or for an erudite fourteenth-century layman like Dante or Chaucer the doctrine on contraception, along with the doctrine on a thousand other topics, was available in them. A limited elite, not a mass, was instructed in this way.

Some of the clergy received some instruction at cathedral schools, friars' schools, or grammar schools. These more elementary institutions may have used a manual like Monaldus' *Useful Summa*. But for this less educated group, as for the literate but theologically unsophisticated laymen who appeared in growing numbers in the fourteenth century, an even simpler sort of literature was necessary.[7] In these writings, not professionally designed for theologians or canonists, a tendency appears to omit references to the poisons of sterility and to speak very generally of sin in marital intercourse. The *Somme le Roi* ("The King's Summa"), written in 1279 by a Dominican, Lorens of Orléans, for Philip the Bold of France, had nothing on the subject of contraception by "poisons." This work was especially popular in England, being translated in 1340 into Kentish dialect by Dan Michael, a monk of St. Augustine's, Canterbury, under the title *Ayenbite of Inwit* ("Remorse of Conscience") and in 1375 into East Midland dialect as the *Book of Vices and Virtues*, and, after six other translations, being printed in 1486 by William Caxton as *The Royal Book*. The translations did not add to the original. Equally silent were the "Instructions" of John Thoresby, archbishop of York, generally known as the *Lay Folks' Catechism*, written in 1357 to give a summary of

---

[7] On the training of the parish clergy in England, see W. A. Pantin, *The English Church in the Fourteenth Century* (Cambridge, 1955), p. 29. On the growth of an educated laity, see *ibid.*, p. 189. A rather harsh assessment of clerical and lay education in fourteenth-century Flanders is made by Jacques Toussaert, *Le Sentiment religieux en Flandre à la fin du Moyen-Age* (Paris, 1963), p. 65.

doctrine to the laity. The anonymous moral treatises *The Cleansing of Man's Soul* (1401), *Jacob's Well* (circa 1415), and *The Doctrine of Sapience* (French original, 1389; English translation, 1489) all had nothing. The omission occurred not only in books aimed at the laity, but in a work specifically directed at the simple priests hired as assistants by the beneficed clergy, *Instructions for Parish Priests*, written about 1400 by John Mirk, prior of the Augustinian priory of Lilleshall, Shropshire.[8] A common characteristic of these books is use of the vernacular. A sense of prudence, whose operation also affects preaching, inhibits reference to the poisons of sterility.

Sins by nonprocreative behavior in marital intercourse are not mentioned in John Thoresby's *Lay Folks' Catechism*. More typical, however, is a cautious generality. As the translation in the *Book of Vices and Virtues* puts it, the sixth branch of lechery is "agens kynde [nature] and agens the ordre of wedloke; for a man may slen hymself with his owne swerd, and also a man may do dedly synne with his owne wif." In *Jacob's Well*, the sixth branch of lechery is described as occurring "Whanne a man delyth wyth his wyif unordynatly and unkyndely [unnaturally], agens the ordynaunce of kynde and of holy cherch" (c. 24); and the image from *The King's Summa* is turned into rhyme:

> As a man may sle him-self, with his owne knyif,
> So he may synne dedly, wyth his owne wyif.

The Cleansing of Man's Soul puts under the sixth category of sexual vice any "unleful voydinge [frustrating] of nature" (Bodleian MS. 923, fol. 68v). It gives a formula for confession of the sin of lechery with one's spouse: "I have used my wijf or housebonde wilfully or agein my will deshonestly in reproeuable maner and ageins Goddes lawe and the holy sacrement of matrimonye, which was a foule horrible synne of lecherie" (fol. 106r). In William Caxton's 1489 translation of the *Doctrine of Sapience*, laymen are warned not to use marriage "dishonestly against the ordinance of nature, for therein they shall sin deadly. A man may slay himself with his own sword or knife" ("Of the Sacrament of Marriage").

[8] Lorens, *Somme des Vices et des Vertus*, MS, Houghton Library, Harvard University. English translations: *The Book of Vices and Virtues*, ed. W. Nelson Francis, Early English Text Society, 217 (London, 1942); *The Ayenbite of Inwyt*, ed. Richard Morris, Early English Text society, 23 (London, 1866). John Thoresby, *The Lay Folks' Catechism*, ed. Thomas Frederick Simmons and Henry Edward Nolloth, Early English Text Society, 118 (London, 1901). There is nothing on the sin against nature in the Wycliffian revision of the work, also printed in this edition. *Jacob's Well*, ed. Arthur Brandeis Early English Text Society, 115 (London, 1900). *The Doctrine of Sapience*, as translated by William Caxton, ed. Joseph Eugene Gallagher, 1962, typewritten MS, Memorial Library, University of Notre Dame. John Mirk, *Instructions for Parish Priests*, ed. Edward Peacock, Early English Text Society, 31 (London, 1868; rev. ed., 1902).

Nothing is specified. No acts are described. No reasons are given except what is implicit in the characterization of the acts. Only the general area of the sin is indicated. As the *Book of Vices and Virtues* puts it, the sin against nature is nameless because it "is so foule and so hidous that [it] scholde not be nempned" ("The Last Branch of Lechery"). This vagueness had the advantages of being discreet and frightening at the same time.

The approach of these books designed for the simpler sort of readers tallies with the kind of inquiry that the works for confessors suggest for use in hearing confession. They are probably a fair indication of how the more elaborate theological doctrine on the sin against nature in marriage was conveyed to the populace.

The evidence on preaching varies somewhat with the time and country. In the early thirteenth century, in France, when the campaign against the Cathars was at its height, Alan of Lille said that a confessor ought not to inquire minutely into sins against nature, lest he give occasion of sin. Moreover, his labor would be otiose, "for now in the whole land has gone forth the sound of the preachers" (*Penitential, PL* 210:286). But this suggestion of much active preaching on the subject is an isolated one.

The clergy faced the dilemma of leaving penitents in ignorance of their sins or informing potential sinners of ways to commit new sins. In this difficulty, priests preached on the subject as little as they instructed the laity in writing. John Mirk's *Instructions for Parish Priests*, in early-fifteenth-century England, says categorically of the sin against nature: "Of it you shall preach nothing" (line 224). A quarter of a century later, in northern Italy, St. Bernardine takes pains to emphasize that a sermon on marital duties is "a rare bird in the land" (*The Christian Religion* 18, *ante* 1). Not only is such a sermon rarely preached, but it "smacks of impudence" for a preacher to broach the topic (*ibid.* 17, *ante* 1).

There are, however, some examples of sermons. Bernardine himself, after his conciliatory introduction, preached vigorously on marriage and sin in marriage. His sermons may not be typical, but they do show what could be said to a congregation by a zealous minister of the gospel. These blunt words to an urban Tuscan audience offer some contrast and some similarity with the sermons of John Gerson to the French court in the preceding century. Both Bernardine and Gerson are less restrained than John Bromyard, the foremost authority on preaching in fourteenth-century England.[9] None of the sermons I have seen deals with the poisons of

[9] How close are we to having the original of any sermon? The vernacular versions of Bernardine's sermons, now edited in *Le Prediche volgari* (Milan, 1936), are based on notes made by Benedetto Bartolomei when Bernardine preached them in 1427. There is a close correspondence between the ideas and often the language used in them and in the Latin versions of Bernardine's sermons. The Latin versions represent revisions by Bernardine after delivery (see the Introduction to the *Opera omnia*, Quaracchi, 1950–1956, vol. I, p. xviii).

sterility. Bromyard refers to the Cornelian law on poison when he deals with homicide, but he has not a word on *Si aliquis* (*Summa*, at "Homicidium," 13).[10] Gerson refers to abortifacient potions, but not to contraceptives. Preaching is confined to the sin against nature.

Bromyard's *Summa for Preachers* says of "the vice against nature" that "it is abominably committed in many ways," and that it is "the greatest sin of lechery" (*Summa*, at "Luxuria," 3 and 13). This brief treatment contrasts with his ample invective against fornication. Onan is not mentioned. In contrast, his wife Thamar is given as an example of a sinner who might have been killed for fornication, a reference to the story of her encounter with Jacob, described in Genesis 38:20 (*ibid.* 6).

Bromyard does not touch on the purposes of intercourse, but he does back into a discussion of procreative purpose in marrying. People wonder, he says, why some couples have no children or have children who die young. This wonder is justified, as marriage is "a sacrament designed by God for the purpose of procreating children." The couples could not have intended this end when they married: it would be "quasi impossible" that they would be frustrated if they had intended God's end. They have sought lust or riches in marriage (*Summa*, at "Matrimonium," 8–10). At this level of popular persuasion, physical evils are moral proofs; the procreative purpose of marriage is confirmed by the very facts that seem to challenge it; and the preacher has had to draw only on his intimate knowledge of God's providence and his confident dissection of human hearts.

John Gerson makes a point against contraceptive behavior, with heavy emphasis on the Roman-law punishment of death by burning for sodomy.[11] Sins preventing insemination in marital intercourse are assimilated by Gerson to sodomy (above p. 226). Preaching against lechery, he attacks the "indecencies and inventions of sinners" in marriage; these acts "sometimes deserve the fire and are worse than if done with women not one's own." He continues, "May a person in any case copulate and prevent the fruits of the marriage? I say that this is often a sin which deserves the fire. To answer shortly, every way which impedes offspring in the union of man and wife is indecent and must be reprobated" ("Sermon against Lechery for the Second Sunday in Advent," *Works*, III, 916). Another sermon, reportedly given before Charles VI at Paris, is on mar-

---

Gerson's sermons are Latin versions of sermons given in French, and are not verbatim (*Opera omnia*, Antwerp, 1706, III, 898).

Bromyard's book is a treasury of topics for preachers, which could be used as a source of ready-made sermons. According to Owst, Bromyard's book contains the themes of mendicant preaching in England between 1230 and 1356 (G. R. Owst, *Literature and Pulpit in Medieval England*, rev. ed., New York, 1961, p. 379).

[10] Bromyard, *Summa praedicantium* (Nuremberg, 1485).

[11] By decree of the Emperor Valentinian in 390, sodomy was to be punished by death by fire (*Theodosian Code* 9.7.6).

riage. The goods of marriage are set forth, including, of course, the good of offspring. Gerson continues: "Against this good is the prevention of children, either before conception, by abusing marriage, or after, by causing an abortion through clothes, dancing, blows, potions, or otherwise" ("On the Sunday Within the Octave of the Epiphany").[12] Here, as so often, contraception and abortion are distinguished, but attacked together. The language is pointed, but, in comparison with Bernardine, restrained.

Enough has probably been quoted already from the sermons of St. Bernardine to convey the accurate impression that he was hypersensitive to sexual sins. The pig in mud is the image he finds appropriate to describe the sinner against chastity: the married, he declares, are sunk in supine ignorance, "like a pig in a trough of mud" (*The Christian Religion* 17, *ante* 1). This all but universal ignorance he will dispel. There are risks in this course, he recognizes. He alludes to the danger of teaching the innocent "the enormities perpetrated in marriage" (*ibid.*). But he opts for relative explicitness. He assures his hearers, "You will see that you will have many sins in this state of matrimony which you have never confessed, nor did you know to be sin or sins" (*Seraphic Sermons* 19, *ante* 1). He rebukes the malice of husbands who, lest their wives learn "such necessary truths," keep them home when he is preaching (*The Christian Religion* 17, *ante* 1).

Bernardine's preaching on acts preventing insemination as acts of parricide has already been described. One more example of his tone may suffice: "Listen: Each time you come together in a way where you cannot generate, each time is mortal sin . . . Each time that you have joined yourselves in a way that you cannot give birth and generate children, there has always been sin. How big a sin? Oh, a very great sin! Oh, a very great sort of sin!" (*Le Prediche volgari*, p. 433).

Bernardine and Gerson were extraordinary men; Bromyard is a more typical medieval priest, although more learned than the majority. After making due allowance for homiletic exaggeration, one can believe Bernardine when he says that the faithful were rarely instructed as he instructed them.

If preaching was not much used to communicate doctrine on contraception, an opportunity for more personal and more discreet education was presented by the sacrament of penance. What we know of instruction by confessors is really what we know of inquiry by confessors, and what we know of inquiry is only of the kind of questions confessors were supposed to ask. As these questions were innumerable, we can be certain that our information is of an idealized character. Rarely, if ever, could there have

---

[12] *Opera*, III, 1000. The occasion of the sermon before the King is given in *Opera*, III, 980.

been time to interrogate the penitent in the fashion literally suggested by the standard works. What this literature must have provided is a guide to the kinds of problems the confessor should expect. If a penitent seemed to be in trouble in a particular area, the text-writers gave the kind of question that might then be put.

The interrogatories in Burchard's *Decretum* were current well into the twelfth century, and his work continued the tradition of the earlier penitentials in listing sexual sins in marriage with some explicitness.

The late-twelfth-century trend is away from this explicitness. In the *Penitential* of Bartholomew of Exeter, the confessor is told to begin, "Dearly beloved, perhaps all the things you have done do not now come to mind, and so I will question you." After this tactful opening, interrogation is to follow in terms of the seven deadly sins and the sins stemming from them. There are no very specific questions on sexual sins, and the priest is warned to ask simply, "Brother, recall if you have committed some sin sometime which was against nature or otherwise very abominable." Such sins are not to be specifically named by the confessor, "for we have heard of both men and women by the express naming of crimes unknown to them falling into sins they had not known" (*Penitential* c. 38).

Looking across the Channel twenty years later, we find the same reticence recommended in the penitentials of Alan of Lille and Robert of Flamborough. If the penitent has confessed to unlawful coition, says Alan, the priest is to inquire whether it was fornication, adultery, incest, or the sin against nature. This inquiry is important, for the sin against nature is the gravest of these sins. But the priest "ought not to descend more minutely," or he may give an occasion of sin to the penitent (*Penitential*, PL 210:286–288). Robert of Flamborough says that the confessor is to ask the penitent "if he has done something against nature."[13]

In 1215, the Fourth Council of the Lateran required, under pain of mortal sin, that all Christians should annually confess and receive communion. This decree, largely confirmatory of existing custom, recognized the central role of the confessor in the enforcement of Christian morality. At some point, at least once a year, there was to be an accounting to him. As a consequence of the Lateran legislation, practical, casuistically oriented writings designed to aid confessors in the discharge of their responsibility multiplied in the thirteenth century and were widely disseminated.[14]

The best example of a thirteenth-century form of interrogation on marital sin is provided by Cardinal Hostiensis under the heading, "What

[13] Robert of Flamborough, *Penitential*, quoted in Josef Georg Ziegler, *Die Ehelehre der Pönitential-Summen von 1200–1350* (Regensburg, 1956), p. 132.

[14] Pierre Michaud-Quantin, "A propos des premières 'Summae Confessorum,'" pp. 268, 275–276, 294; Paul Anciaux, *La Théologie du sacrament de pénitence au XII⁰ siècle* (Louvain, 1949), p. 135.

Questions Can or Should Be Asked by One Hearing Confessions?" Interrogating on lechery, the confessor is to explain the sin against nature by saying, "You have sinned against nature when you have known a woman other than as nature demands." The confessor is not to reveal the different ways in which an act may be against nature. He may proceed "cautiously" in this fashion to interrogate the penitent: " 'You know well the way which is natural. Did a pollution ever happen to you otherwise?' If he says, 'No,' ask nothing further. If he says, 'Yes,' you may ask, 'Sleeping or waking?' . . . If he says, 'Waking,' you may ask, 'With a woman?' . . . If he says, 'With a woman,' you may ask, 'Outside the vessel, or within it, and how?' " (*Summa* 5, "Penances and Remissions," 49).

In a work for confessors attributed to Cardinal Hugh of St. Cher, a Dominican at Paris in the mid-thirteenth century, this sequence of questions is given under the title "Adultery": "Or have you sinned with your own wife against nature?" If the sinner inquires, "What's that — 'against nature'?" the priest may say, "The Lord gave one way which all men hold; wherefore, if you have done other than in that one way you have sinned mortally." A second question is, "Have you known your wife only for the sake of delight? Because you ought to know her only for the sake of generating, or avoiding fornication, or returning the debt." (Hugh, *Confessio debet*)[15]

Other writers do not give a form, but indicate by their observations that in confession there is treatment of the sin against nature. St. Albert introduces his discussion of unnatural marital acts with the apologetic note, "It should be said that shameful questions of this sort should never have to be treated, but the monstrous things heard these days in confession compel one to treat them" (*On the Sentences* 4.31.24). Peraldus urges the confessor to exercise discretion in answering questions on the sin against nature (*Summa* 2, "Lechery"). The most influential work for confessors, St. Raymond's *Summa*, treats of both the poisons of sterility and unnatural marital usage (above, p. 233). But he does not give a form for interrogation on the subject, and it is inferable that he did not expect the priest to initiate interrogation on it. The twelfth- and thirteenth-century works, then, give the impression that only very limited instruction on contraceptive sin would be provided by a confessor. If the penitent is aware that he has acted "against nature," the confessor will help him to specify the sin he is confessing.

Two centuries later in Italy a development is noted which might have been anticipated. Some confessors have quizzed wives about their marital

---

[15] The above quotation is given in Pierre Michaud-Quantin, "Deux formulaires pour la confession du milieu du XIIIᵉ siècle," *Recherches de théologie ancienne et médiévale* 31 (1964), 55. The other confessional work, *Ad habendam*, which he presents here has nothing relevant. Michaud-Quantin believes that *Confessio debet* represents a work of Hugh of St. Cher edited by others.

practices, and the husbands have resented it. As Bernardine reports: "Often a fool woman, that she may appear respectable, will say to her husband, 'The priest asked me about this dirty thing and wanted to know what I do with you,' and the fool husband will be scandalized with the priest" (*Seraphic Sermons* 19, *ante* 1). The upshot of this kind of husbandly outrage has been that the priests have held their tongues; they are, as Bernardine quotes Isaiah, "dumb dogs." Bernardine himself is discontented with this relaxation of vigilance. He urges that the confessor do his duty and inquire.

Inquiry is also recommended by the *Confessional* of St. Antoninus, who is a much more cautious authority on sexual sins than St. Bernardine. On usury, Antoninus often follows Bernardine, his fellow Tuscan and slightly older contemporary. On marital morality, he usually ignores him. In a set of interrogatories developed for particular states of life, Antoninus has, under the heading "The Married," these questions: "First, if he has used marriage beyond the fit vessel. If he did something to avoid offspring. If in an undue way, although in the due vessel, and how" (*Confessional*, "Interrogatory" 3.1).

St. Antoninus' book was the most popular manual for confessors for the next hundred years.[16] In a more local work by a more famous man of the next generation, Girolamo Savonarola, the same position is found: "You are to ask about this sin . . . if it was in the vessel, or in an unfit vessel, or outside of any vessel" (*Confessional*, "Sins against the Sixth Commandment"; "Things Which Are Done in Matrimony").[17]

In the North, in Germany, John Nider's *Manual for Confessors* advises caution in asking about sins of the flesh and sins specifically against nature, "lest something be disclosed to the simple of which they were ignorant." But, with caution, the interrogation is to be made (*Manual* 2.3, "Rules of the Chancellor").[18]

To generalize from this handful of fifteenth-century handbooks, somewhat greater initiative is now recommended in inquiry. Detail never exceeds the lines set by Hostiensis. Inquiry about use of the poisons of sterility is never suggested. Bernardine's remarks show that inquiry of any kind in regard to marriage was often resented, and consequently often omitted by the confessor. I conclude that some instruction was given by confessional interrogation, but that such instruction was neither common nor more than rudimentary.

Apart from communication within the structured situations of preaching or confession, priests must have conveyed the doctrine orally on other

---

[16] Pierre Michaud-Quantin, *Sommes de casuistique et manuels de confessions au moyen âge, XII-XVI siècles* (Louvain, 1962), p. 75.
[17] Girolamo Savonarola, *Confessionale pro instructione confessorum* (Venice, 1524).
[18] John Nider, *Manuale confessorum* (Basel, 1475).

occasions. A priest might be consulted by a laywoman about the marital behavior of her spouse as in the case cited by Palude (above, p. 261). Even where no marital conflict was present, the advice and opinion of the clergy on married life must have been given often enough, and directly or obliquely the clergy must ordinarily have conveyed the basic notion that insemination might not lawfully be avoided or procreation lawfully prevented.

The process of diffusion need not be regarded as entirely vertical, from the canons to the commentators to the ordinary clergy to the people. By the time the basic opinions had been taught by the clerical elite for several centuries — say, by 1150 — they must often have been transmitted by teaching in the family. Theologians-to-be must have derived some first impression of what was "natural" by education, express or implicit, in their homes.

This summary of sanctions suggests two conclusions. The principal sanctions against contraception, the spiritual condemnation of it as sin and the social discouragement of it by pejorative description, depended on communication to be effective. Communication in fact occurred, although in a limited, sporadic, and far from efficient manner. The most educated laity were reached by theological literature. Some of the rest of the laity may have occasionally been informed by preachers, confessors, or moral advisers. To the extent that contraceptive behavior — unlike, say, murder or robbery — was not self-evidently evil, many of the laity must have remained in ignorance of what acts constituted the sin.

The limited communication of the sanctions bears on the doctrinal significance of the medieval teaching. If a doctrine on the conduct of the married laity were known only to the unmarried clergy, the doctrine could scarcely be said to be "taught by the Church." Knowledge of the sin was, in fact, not so confined. On the one hand, the dominant Augustinian view that marital intercourse must have a procreative purpose does not seem to have been widely propagated in either preaching or in hearing confessions. On the other hand, the doctrine on unnatural acts was broadly, if vaguely, disseminated. The warning of the canons against the poisons of sterility was not a dead letter. The doctrine on contraception cannot be said to have been fully, freely, and generally known and accepted by the Catholic laity; neither can it be said to have been known only to the literate clergy. In the intermediate zone that it occupied, it was a teaching destined for development — development both by a more instructed and self-conscious future laity, and by medieval theologians themselves who were aware of values other than those the condemnations of contraception embodied.

CHAPTER X

COUNTER APPROACHES

I N THE PRODIGIOUS EFFORT of the theologians and canonists to work out the theory of inherited Christian morality, it might be expected that ideas would have been championed, by orthodox writers, which challenged the dominant theory; that values would have been recognized which logic could extend to clash with the values upheld by the marriage theory; that practices might be accepted whose acceptance would pose problems of consistency with theory. In this chapter I propose to examine some of the counter ideas, values, and practices current between 1150 and 1450.

THE REJECTION OF POPULATION AS A VALUE

A minority current of medieval theology put a value on multiplying the number of human souls. Its most prominent exponent was Duns Scotus. Putting forward the thesis that "to want to procreate children" is good or bad depending on the circumstances, Scotus constructs an argument that would seem to favor limitless procreation: "through the procreation of offspring the city of supernatural citizens is restored in human nature; and to this end, human nature, as multiplied, is per se ordained; for to this end the All Highest has disposed it according to faith, in order to repair the fall of the angels" (*On the Sentences* [*Paris Report*] 4.28).[1] Taken literally, this proposition would seem to be, the more offspring, the bigger the population of heaven. The theme appears in some preaching: procreation is "to repair the fall of Lucifer in heaven." [2] St. Bernardine speaks of marriage as divinely ordained "to fill paradise" (*The Christian Religion* 48.1.1).

[1] John Duns Scotus, *In libros Sententiarum* [*Paris Report*], in *Opera omnia* (Paris, 1891–1895), vol. XXIV. The accuracy of the Paris report of the opinions of Scotus is questionable; see Auguste Pelzer, *Le Premier livre des Reportata Parisiensia de Jean Duns Scot* (Louvain, 1923), pp. 449–456.
[2] G. R. Owst, *Literature and Pulpit in Medieval England* (New York, 1961), p. 379.

This view of the purpose of marriage received its strongest official approval in a papal bull promulgated by Eugene IV at the Council of Florence, November 22, 1439, celebrating reunion with the schismatic Armenians. The bull, *Exultate Deo*, enumerated and briefly described the sacraments. It said, "Through order the Church is indeed governed and multiplied spiritually; through matrimony it is corporally increased" (Mansi 31:1054). The contrast with holy orders was obviously of a neat, schematic kind. The bull is the medieval high-water mark of the theory of population increase as a value.

The majority of theologians did not accept this view. Typical is St. Thomas, who spoke of "the multiplication of offspring to be educated to the service of God" as a purpose for marriage only for the polygamous patriarchs of the Old Testament (*On the Sentences* 4.33.1.2). Even among the minority, the emphasis on population was not made a direct objection to contraception. Nor did they press their view to the logical extreme of maintaining that the optimal endeavor would be to conceive as many children as possible provided that their baptism was assured. Against this logical extension stood the valuations put on virginity and on the welfare of the child. These factors, which checked even those theologians in favor of increasing the population of heaven, operated with still greater impact on the majority who remained unimpressed with this reason for procreation. Indeed, the stress laid on virginity and on the welfare of the child made it impossible for most thoughtful authors to urge that population as such was a value. An examination of the commitment to these counter values will show the strength of the forces working against the appeal to numbers for their own or heaven's sake.

THE PREFERRED STATUS OF CELIBACY

On the preferred place of committed celibacy, there was complete continuity with the doctrine of patristic times so vigorously set forth by writers like Jerome and Chrysostom. In the new European world, where the monasteries had preserved the remains of Roman culture, where the clergy had organized the universities, where the reformers of moral life came from the religious orders, the emphasis on celibacy received an institutional impetus it had lacked in the Roman era. Celibacy was now the established norm for the Western secular clergy. Much of the work of social and intellectual leadership was performed by men who, as secular priests, or monks, or brothers, were bound to observe complete sexual continence. Almost all of the theorizing on marriage and sexuality was done by men both personally and institutionally committed to the ideal of lifelong continence. That, in this context, scripture and patristic teaching should reinforce personal commitment and institutional exigency, and that theologians should again insist on the superiority of dedicated celibacy, is scarcely surprising.

The existence of an elite, with so much power in the society, and having chastity as one of its badges, could provoke criticism. In the most popular secular poem of the thirteenth century, Jean de Meun has Nature oppose the clerical figures, Astenance-Contrainte and Faus-Semblant, in attacking celibacy and "excommunicating" all celibates (*Le Roman de la rose*, lines 19345–19389).[3] But the celibate ideal was taught everywhere and practiced often in the period from 1150 to 1450. At two levels, the teaching presented values counter to childbearing. At a crude popular level, observable even in a man of Gerson's erudition, the miseries of marriage and of parenthood were deplored, and it was even insinuated that marriage presented more temptations to sin than the maintenance of virginity (e.g., Gerson, *Discourse on the Excellence of Virginity*).[4] At a more refined theological level, the spiritual superiority of the celibate state was emphasized. A writer as sympathetic to married life as Albert was steadfast on this point: virginity is "the sign of whole and uncorrupted love of God, spouse of the soul" (*The Good* 3.3.7, reply to obj. 3). Thomas gave the doctrine both philosophical and theological strength. In a system where the vision of God after death is viewed as the supreme human happiness, of which contemplation in this life is a foretaste, Thomas taught that virginity allowed one "to enjoy contemplation of truth more freely" (*Summa theologica* 2–2.152.2). The dedicated virgin, he taught, is "wed to Christ" (*On the Sentences* 4.38.1.5, reply to obj. 1). For man as an individual, in distinction from man as a species, "it cannot be said good to touch woman" (*On 1 Corinthians* 7.1).[5]

The ideal of virginity had a role within marriage. There was general agreement that the union of Mary and Joseph was a true marriage, although the spouses had remained virgins. Peter Lombard had energetically assembled texts supporting the validity of virginal marriage (*Sentences* 4.26.6); and commentary on these texts faithfully upheld the ideal. "The more free from carnal work, the holier and more perfect it was," said Peter. Thomas added, "As the text [of Peter] states, a marriage without carnal intercourse is holier" (*On the Sentences* 4.26.2.4). Mary, a married virgin, was presented as an exemplar of the superiority of virginity (Thomas, *ST* 2–2.152.4). In how many marriages virginity was preserved or continence sworn is difficult to gauge. A surprising amount of theological and canonical discussion, however, was directed to the

[3] Jean de Meun and Guillaume de Lorris, *Le Roman de la rose*, ed. E. Langlois, 5 vols., Société des anciens textes français (Paris, 1914–1924).

[4] John Gerson, *Discours de l'excellence de la virginité*, in *Opera omnia* (Antwerp, 1706), III, 832–833.

[5] St. Thomas Aquinas, *Super epistolas S. Pauli lectura*, ed. Raphael Cai, O.P. (Turin, 1953).

case of spouses taking a vow of continence. The basic texts on such a vow were provided by Gratian (*Decretum* 2.27.2.19–29) and Peter (*Sentences* 4.27.7–9). The rule was that after a marriage was consummated by intercourse the vow by one spouse was lawful only if consented to by the other. The ample discussion of the rule and its variations may testify only to academic fascination with a problem combining marriage, total abstinence, and promises to God. But, few as the actual cases may have been, the possibility of such conduct, completely thwarting the procreative purpose of marriage, was unanimously viewed with benignity.

The ideal of virginity and the related notion that "the world is full" lost some of their early eschatological flavor, but the patristic view that the Resurrection has inaugurated "the last days" was by no means forgotten. Thomas said of St. Paul's exhortation to virginity that Paul spoke "considering the human race already multiplied, and the people of God already increased, not by propagation of the flesh, but by the generation which is from water and the Holy Spirit, as it is said in John 3" (*On 1 Corinthians* 7.1). At times the eschatological note seemed to disappear in a complacent reflection that, without special effort, the Christian people would maintain itself. Marriage, declared William of Auxerre, was "now permitted, but is not a precept, since the people of God have been increased through the whole world, and innumerable marriages now everywhere generate sons of God to a sufficiency" (*Summa aurea* [Paris, 1500], fol. 6ov). The words can be matched in Eusebius, but contentment with the sufficiency of Christians must have been easier to feel in thirteenth-century France than in the fourth-century Roman world.

In this context of an established Christian society, apparently destined to endure for an indefinite time to come, the duty of perpetuating the species did, however, present a more serious challenge than in the Christian society of the fourth century, where the eschatological orientation was clearer. Astesanus is willing to entertain this hypothetical: Suppose "the world were reduced to such a small number of men that, if some of them kept their chastity, the rest would not yield sufficient multiplication of men for the service of God." Would virginity still be preferred, or would there not be a precept to marry? He answers, "Then matrimonial copulation would be a precept binding on all capable of it" (*Summa* 8.7). Astesanus' answer resolved the question with a radical reversal of theological values. It reflected, albeit hypothetically, a belief in the desirability of continuing the present order quite different from that of early eschatology. This belief is not far from that of Thomas when he answers the question, "Is virginity lawful?" He faces the objection that the command of Genesis, "Increase and multiply," is binding on all mankind. He replies: "The precept given as to generation looks to the whole multitude of men. This multitude must be not only multiplied bodily, but advanced spiritually. Therefore, sufficient provision for the human multitude is made, if some undertake the task of carnal generation" (*Summa theologica* 2–2.152.2, reply to obj. 1). The implication of this answer seems to be that some men must perform the spiritually inferior task of propagating the race, that for them it is a duty. But Aquinas does not go so far as to state this implication. Rather, he returns to the dominant ideal of virginity. In the world in which it is assumed that some men will marry and have children, virginity is the better course to follow, and the Christian who would be perfect is told to take it if he can.

Such sexual continence itself could be viewed as contraceptive. The objection is noted by Thomas in *Evil*. He had based his case against lechery on the ground that "every act of lechery impedes the good of offspring." The objection is put: continence "totally impedes the generation of offspring." His answer is simply this: "In the time of grace there should be more emphasis on spiritual propagation, for which those leading celibate lives are more fitted, and so in this state it is accounted more virtuous to abstain from the act of generation" (*Evil* 15.2, reply to obj. 13). For the higher good of spiritual propagation, carnal generation may, and should, be avoided. In the time of grace, that is, now, after the Redemption, the good of offspring may be sacrificed for the spiritual benefits obtainable by abstinence from intercourse.

In this perspective, population, multiplication of numbers, the big family, were not ideals advocated by most theologians. If emphasis on the spiritual freedom of the celibate stopped well short of an advocacy of birth control, there was a dominant valuation of goods of the spirit which ran counter to any idealization of the quantitative increase of humanity.

THE PERFECTION OF OFFSPRING

Both the spiritual and physical welfare of the child were, in general, preferred to the propagation of many children.

In arguing the sinfulness of fornication, Peraldus observes against the objection that the sin increases the number of men: "God does not set great store on the fewness or on the multitude of men . . . One good man is worth more than a thousand bad men" (*Summa* 1.6, "Temperance," 13).

This standard — that numbers do not matter — is essential to the Thomistic argument against fornication, where the injury done in producing a child without proper parents to educate him is not erased by the merit of the act of generating a human being (*Evil* 15.2, reply to obj. 12). Here it is not the spiritual perfection of existing beings which is preferred to the procreation of new beings, as is the case when virginity is preferred to marriage. Here the position is: It is better not to bear a child than to bear a child injured in his basic educational opportunities.

The term "education," normally used in the context of commentary on the good of offspring, is plainly not equivalent to merely physical rearing. It includes an element of moral and spiritual training.[6] Thomas, it is true, used *educatio* as the equivalent of *nutritio*, in the *Summa Against the Gentiles* 3.122. He also spoke in the *Summa theologica* of the task of husband and wife as consisting of "nourishing the offspring" (3.29.2). But he understood both "education" and "nourishment" analogically. This use is developed with force in his most profound discussion of marriage, his commentary on St. Paul, written in Naples near the end of his life. Here he noted that in some species of animals the female did not suffice for the rearing (*educatio*) of offspring. *Educatio*, "rearing" for an animal, is then deliberately enlarged in its significance. Thomas continues, "Especially, however, in the human species, the male is required for the offspring's education (*educatio*), which is expected not only as to nourishment of the body, but more as to nourishment of soul, according to Hebrews 12:9, 'We had fathers of our flesh, indeed, as teachers (*eruditores*), and we revered them,'" (*On 1 Corinthians* 7.1). A parent is the educator of his child as the teacher who develops his soul.

Repeatedly the theologians teach that the offspring are to be "religiously educated." This is their standard commentary on the meaning of the word "offspring" used in the discussion of the three goods of marriage. "Religious education" meant much more than baptism of the child. Augustine himself had said that he meant "religiously informed offspring" (*On Genesis*, above, p. 127). It is this text which Lombard used in the *Sentences*, adding his own important comment: "Many, therefore, have offspring who lack the good of offspring" (4.31). In other words, the good of offspring (*bonum prolis*), which alone justified marital intercourse, was attained only by seeking children to be spiritually educated. Thus Raymond condemned that desire for children which was a mere desire for heirs: to seek heirs was not to seek the good of offspring for which intercourse was permissible; offspring were to be sought "in order to be religiously formed" (*Summa* 4.2.7). "The good of offspring," said William of Auxerre, "is offspring themselves as they are religiously educated to the worship of God" (*Summa* 4, fol. 287v). In a strong passage, Thomas replied to an argument that intercourse sought without reference to the goods of marriage is not a sin because it is according to nature. Although nature's purpose in intercourse is to in-

---

[6] The translation of *educatio* as "upbringing," adopted by the Fathers of the English Dominican Province in their translation of the *Summa theologica* (New York, 1947), may not sufficiently bring out the analogous way in which Thomas uses the term with the definite implication of moral and intellectual training when human beings are spoken of. The range of analogous meanings is recognized in Roy J. Deferrari and Sister M. Inviolata Barry, *A Lexicon of St. Thomas Aquinas* (Washington, 1948–1949), s.v. "Educatio" and "Educare."

sure the good of the species, this does not excuse the act. To seek off-spring, as nature does, only to preserve the species, is to stay sinfully "in the creature." To be without sin there must be an actual, or at least an habitual, intention to seek offspring "as they are the good of the sacrament of matrimony," that is, as "further ordained to God" (*On the Sentences* 4.31.2.2, reply to obj. 1). Even Scotus, by the terms of his argument that the purpose of marriage is to populate heaven, was driven to say that offspring as an end were good if "the offspring are desired in order to be religiously educated for divine worship" (*On the Sentences* [*Paris Report*] 4.28). The Thomistic argument against fornication as an impairment of the education of the child was based on the child's need of a father "to instruct him" and "to aid him by both internal and external goods" (*ST* 2–2.154.2). The argument made instruction extend well beyond the sacramental initiation into the Christian life. A parent who was an *eruditor* to his child was responsible for a real spiritual and intellectual instruction. His task involved "nourishment" of his soul. The Dominican summist and encyclopedist, Vincent of Beauvais, writing before 1244, said that the "good of offspring" means that the offspring are to be "religiously educated," and that parents fail in this duty if "they do not teach their children in the discipline of the Lord or do not correct sinners." He went on to quote Seneca on the result of *educatio*: "Education and discipline indeed make mores, and each man knows well what he has learned" (*Speculum naturale* 30.41). There is no better practical indication of what the theologians meant by education than the founding and development of the Universities of Bologna, Paris, Oxford, and Cambridge.

The universal acceptance of religious education as an element in the good of offspring is an emphatic rejection of the criterion of quantity. What is valued, in the very definition of the procreative requirement, is children of a certain quality. This quality was vaguely enough defined to be capable of expansion. It was designated by "religious education." The content of "religious education" depended on the cultural development of the age; it could include rudimentary instruction or mature theological explorations. The quality demanded by demanding "religious education" was, then, variable; the principle was established. If the common experience of a particular type of coitus was that this quality could not result from it — so ran the argument against fornication — then it was better that the child not be. Not the physical human being alone, but his prospective existence at some level of spiritual development, justified intercourse.

A similar preference for the welfare of the child appears in the rationalization of the rule against intercourse in menstruation. In the Old Testament such intercourse was an offense deserving of death. In accepting the Old Testament rule as binding moral law, the Christian writers were divided upon the gravity of the sin. Augustine and many penitentials had thought such violation merely venial. The medieval theologians, then, were free to treat the sin as major or as minor, and even, perhaps, free to question whether the Old Testament command still held. The more common opinion, defended by Raymond (*Summa* 4.2.6), Thomas (*On the Sentences* 4.32.1.2.2), and Scotus (*On the Sentences* [*Oxford Report*] 4.32), held that such intercourse was mortal sin. The foundation of this severe position was that children begotten at the time of menstruation were likely to be defective. The repetition of this error, as old as Pliny, about the effect of the menses on the seed has by itself little significance. What is of interest is the stress placed on protection of the child-to-be by the theologians who believe that menstruation may harm the conceptus. The valuation implicit in the rule is: better to regulate conception, better to postpone it, for the welfare of the future child, than to procreate as many human beings as possible.

An exception to this rule was introduced in the thirteenth century. If menstruation is abnormally prolonged, intercourse is permissible. Two reasons are advanced to justify the relaxation. One, consistent with the rule's rationale, is that in such a case the woman is sterile. The other assumes that the abnormal menstruant may be able to conceive and yet justifies the risk to the embryo by noting that otherwise the husband would have "to abstain perpetually" (Thomas, *On the Sentences* 4.32.1.2.2). The second reason puts the marital rights of the husband ahead of the injury to the possible child. The welfare of the future child is sacrificed not to a desire to have more beings in the world but to the personal rights of a spouse.

There is only one case in which Aquinas invokes a principle favoring quantity over quality in offspring. It is in the course of explaining a decretal which enjoins a wife to have intercourse with her leprous husband (*Decretals* 4.8.2). The objection is made, not on behalf of the mother but of the child, "that the disease is frequently transmitted to the offspring." Thomas answers, "Although the offspring is born infirm, yet it is better for it to be thus, than not to be at all" (*On the Sentences* 4.32.1.1). In this case, postponement of conception cannot result in a child in better spiritual and physical circumstances. In this narrow case, Thomas favors generation of a child deprived of the physical integrity due him. Here the judgment "better to be than not to be" applies. This principle, however grandly metaphysical it sounds, is not an absolute, rigorously applied to resolve all moral questions. It is invoked only in the special case in which the ordinary perfection of the child seems unobtainable. "Better to be than not to be" is not a rationale for intercourse where delay will lead to a spiritually or physically better child.

THE COMMON GOOD OF THE CHURCH

A minor case, of some interest for the principles involved, is provided by the decretal *Ex multa*. This decree of Innocent III stated that a man might go on the crusade without his wife's consent and without bringing her with him (*Decretals* 3.34.9). The decree, in effect, suspended the right to procreative acts in the interest of the welfare of the Church. The commentators did not develop the implications of the power of the Church to override the right both to intercourse and to procreation. They were, indeed, reserved in their treatment of the canon. Hostiensis, seeing that the same principle should apply to a woman who wanted to go off on a crusade without her husband, said the law applied when she was "old, and powerful in leading soldiers" (*Commentary* 3.34.9). St. Thomas said, with clear hesitation, "It is sufficiently probable that the wife ought to be willing to remain continent for a time, in order to succor the need of the universal Church" (*On the Sentences* 4.32.1.4, reply to obj. 1). Panormitanus labels the case "a most special one" (*Commentary* 3.34.9). Uncommented on and undeveloped, the principle remained unimpaired, that one spouse could unilaterally put temporal and spatial barriers to any procreative act, if the welfare of the Church required it. The value of the case as precedent for putting such barriers to sexual intercourse as such was weak; sexual intercourse while avoiding procreation would have been a different matter. Nevertheless the priority given to the needs of the Church over the increase of population reflects a scale of values different from that used in reaching the general rule against contraception.

To summarize, in a variety of moral judgments the theologians and canonists showed that population as such was not a value for them. In the doctrines on virginity, celibacy, and continence in marriage, they preferred the perfection of existing persons to the procreation of new life. In the canon on the crusader's vow, they preferred the common good of the Church to procreation. In the teaching on fornication and in the rule on intercourse in menstruation they took the position that it was better that a child not be conceived than that he be conceived with educational or physical deficiencies. In the doctrine on procreative purpose itself they made an integral element of the purpose the religious education of the offspring. These several judgments reflected valuations which could have conflicted with the valuation implicit in the judgments against contraception. The valuations were not compared; the possible conflicts were not, at this time, explored.[7]

[7] The prohibition of intercourse in pregnancy does not relate directly to the conflict between the good of existing offspring and the existence of future offspring, because intercourse in pregnancy would not have been procreative. However, the

THE MARITAL DEBT

"Let the husband render to his wife what is due her, and likewise the wife to her husband." The express words of 1 Corinthians 7 were accepted unanimously by the medieval theologians as making lawful and even mandatory sexual intercourse at the request of one spouse. The "return of the debt" was an established purpose of marital intercourse.

The theologians did not view this position as inconsistent with the majority view that procreative purpose alone justified the seeking of intercourse. One spouse seeking and the other spouse returning was the model of marital relations accepted for analysis. That the theory of procreative purpose made one spouse a sinner, while the other fulfilled his duty, did not appear to the theologians as a weakness in theory. In practice, however, recognition of this second purpose for intercourse impaired the theoretical insistence on procreative purpose. The lenient suggestion was made by Albert that a spouse, guessing sinful desires in the

---

development of reasoning on the prohibition is instructive. The majority of theologians who held that a procreative purpose must be present in intercourse had to hold that intercourse in pregnancy was venial sin. But in the thirteenth century the principal reason for overriding the right to intercourse becomes the danger to the existing fetus. Hence, the case is another one in which the Pauline right to the debt was subordinated to the welfare of existing offspring. The case is also instructive because almost all medieval theologians treat the act as a mortal sin on a basis which later medical knowledge will show to be false.

The development begins from the point where the prohibition of intercourse in pregnancy is formulated in Gratian (*Decretum* 2.32.4.5) and Lombard (*Sentences* 4.31.5). Here, the general rule is stated in the language of Seneca, quoted above, p. 47, attributed by Gratian and Lombard to Jerome. This language combines an emphasis on procreative purpose with an implication of risk to the embryo. What happens in the thirteenth century is a shift of emphasis from procreative purpose to the risk to the child.

Points of the development may be summarized as follows. In 1220–1230, St. Raymond simply cited the rule in Gratian and held coitus in pregnancy to be mortal sin (*Summa* 4.2.8). In 1240, Alexander of Hales taught that it was mortal sin "if there is a strong presumption of danger to the embryo" (*Summa theologica* 2–2.3.5.2.1.3.2, *ad* 8). About 1248, St. Albert noted that pregnancy was the time of greatest concupiscence, for which marriage was meant to be a remedy. He cited Avicenna as teaching that the danger of abortion by coitus was based on the possibility that delight might make the matrix open and the embryo fall out (*On the Sentences* 4.31.22). The danger, Albert said, was particularly acute in the first four months of pregnancy. The implication was that thereafter there might be little risk; and Albert appears to hold only intercourse with risk to be sinful, no more than venially sinful. St. Thomas returned to the usual position that mortal sin was involved, but clearly had learned from Albert. He, too, cited Avicenna's opinion, and said, "It is not always mortal sin except when there is probable fear of the danger of abortion" (*On the Sentences* 4.31.2.3, "Exposition of text"). After Aquinas, this formula is general; there is mortal sin "if" there is or "by reason of" danger of abortion: Peter de Palude, *On the Sentences* 4.31.3; John Gerson, *Sermon on Lechery,* in *Opera,* III, 916; Bernardine, *Seraphic Sermons* 19.1, noting that some say the danger may be at the beginning and the end of pregnancy; St. Antoninus, *Summa* 3.1.20.4; Angelus Carletus de Clavasio, *Summa,* at "Debitum conjugale," 32.

other which were not explicitly revealed, would be "discreet" to treat the situation as one in which he was requested to pay the marital debt; he would not, then, be in the sinful, initiating position (*On the Sentences* 4. 32.4). Thomas adopted a modified form of this opinion: a wife, he said, might seek intercourse by "signs" instead of words, and the husband would, in justice, be bound to respond (*On the Sentences* 4.32.1.2). Moreover, Thomas subsumed all intercourse to avoid adultery by one's spouse under the category of observing the marital duty: it was a "certain return of the debt." These attempts at line-drawing were symptomatic of discontent with the pure procreative theory, but they did not amount to repudiation of it, however abstract and artificial the elaboration of the Pauline "debt" became.

What might have been a more serious problem for the theorists was not discussed by them. This problem was the relation of the "repayment of the debt" to the objective, natural purpose of coitus. If coitus satisfied an obligation of marital fidelity, why was not such satisfaction a natural purpose of coitus? This question was not answered by the distinction between a sinning and an innocent spouse. At issue was not the purposes of two individuals, but the structure, the nature, of a single act. No theologian said that satisfaction of the debt was an unnatural purpose for the act. The alternatives seemed to exist of saying that satisfaction of the debt was a supernatural purpose added to the natural purpose of coitus by virtue of the sacrament of matrimony, or saying that satisfaction of the debt was a natural purpose. By either alternative, in a Christian marriage, coitus would have a structure, a value, independent of generation. Neither alternative was expressed.

In the commentary on the *Sentences*, Thomas says of "matrimony" — not of marital intercourse — that, like every act of virtue, it has two ends, that of the person performing the act and that of the act itself. On the part of the person, the due end is offspring. "On the part of the act itself, it is good in its genus in that it falls on due matter; and thus there is set as a good of marriage fidelity, whereby a man approaches his own wife, and not another woman" (*On the Sentences* 4.31.1.2). This analysis would seem to have been transferable to the act of intercourse. The "end of the act," then, would have been the faithful rendering of intercourse. If a procreative requirement remained, it would have been one relating to subjective intent. There would have been nothing in the nature of the act of intercourse itself requiring ordination to procreation. Why the analysis was not applicable to coitus was not discussed by Thomas.

The insistence on insemination as the natural function of coitus seemed to make sense because of the ultimate relation of insemination to generation. However, as Chapter VIII has shown, what the scholastics treat as natural is the inseminating act, not a necessarily generative act. The unanalyzed, tacit acceptance of "return of the debt" as a natural act confirms that what is regarded as natural is insemination. But if it is asked why insemination is regarded as natural in the sense of being beyond human interference, the only scholastic answer seems to rest on the connection between insemination and generation. If this connection did not exist in the objective structure of a lawful marital act, as they themselves implicitly recognized in dealing with "return of the debt," why should the connection have been insisted on in other possible marital acts? The question was not answered, but, as will be seen, it reappeared in other aspects of the scholastic analysis of intercourse.

THE SACRAMENTAL PURPOSE OF INTERCOURSE

The sacramental end, *bonum sacramenti*, was recognized by everyone as a "good of marriage." Yet only a single prominent author, St. Albert, explored the relation between it and the purpose of intercourse. In his commentary on the fourth book of the *Sentences*, written between 1246 and 1249, he raised the question, "Is all coitus sin?" Answering negatively, he distinguished in the act of marital coitus "the end of nature" and "the end of man." The natural end was "the procreation of offspring, for to this end nature invented it, and for this end it formed the organs in such a way." But the human end was "the end of medicine, and of fidelity to the bed, and of the sacrament." An act of intercourse was both nature's and man's. But "as it is a matrimonial act, it is taken as the act of man more than of nature" (*On the Sentences* 4.31.27). "Medicine" was the same as "remedy for incontinence," the Pauline end of intercourse recognized by a minority of medieval writers. "Fidelity to the bed" was the generally recognized duty of paying the marital debt. But what was the end "of the sacrament"? An earlier passage listed four "causes" of marital coitus: the hope of offspring, fidelity, the healing of infirmity, and "recall of the good of the sacrament" (4.26.11).[8] "Recall" (*rememoratio*) of the sacramental good was apparently now indicated. The meaning of "recall" is open to interpretation. It could have meant a revival of sacramental grace by the act of intercourse, or a recall of the indissolubility of marriage, which was the effect of the sacrament,

[8] "Causes" (*causae*) are used to designate subjective motives. Thus Albert speaks of "the hope of offspring," not "the good of offspring." The four subjective purposes, or reasons why, are complemented by the objective purposes, or ends, of the act of coitus.

or an exemplification of the unity which the sacrament stood for. There was just the germ of a theory here. It was not developed. The idea remained that in some way there was a sacramental value in marital intercourse.[9]

This tentative thought was not consistently kept in view. A possible inference from Albert's analysis was that, considered as a human act, intercourse had primarily a sacramental value. The inference was not drawn. The "human end" of intercourse was set out by Albert in answer to this objection: "Every act frustrated in its essential and natural end is vain and evil, but every copulation performed for the sake of pleasure is of this kind" (4.31.27, obj. 3). In his answer stressing the human end, Albert seemed to be saying: the natural end cannot always be achieved. If the human end is kept, then the act is not evil. The human end suffices. But this response was not pressed elsewhere. In 4.26.11, he taught that hope of offspring must be present concurrently with the sacramental good for coitus to be good. Intercourse to avoid fornication was venial sin. He made no effort to reconcile this position, which put him in accord with the Augustinian tradition, with the answer stressing "the work of man" and the sacramental grace of intercourse described in 4.31.27.[10]

But Albert did not stop his work with his standard conclusions on the *Sentences*. In great old age, after much observation, much more immersion in Aristotle, many more scientific experiments, he wrote his own *Summa theologica*. It contained a single sentence of the utmost interest to our subject. He taught: "There is no sin of matrimonial copulation" (*Summa theologica* 2.18.122.1.4).[11] This sentence occurred not in a defense of marriage, where every orthodox writer would have said that marital intercourse was not itself sinful, but in a discussion of sexual sins, where it was customary to treat the sexual sins possible in marriage. If one read in a theologian today, "There is no sexual sin," one would be startled. Is it less startling for Albert to write in 1275, "There is no sin of marital intercourse"? His contemporaries held that there were a variety of such sins: sins of intention, in seeking pleasure or merely seeking to avoid incontinence; sins of position, in not observing the normal posture; sins against nature, in avoiding procreation. Did Albert sweep all these sins away?

Elsewhere in the same work, attributing the saying to Sextus the Pythagorean, he says, "The too ardent lover of his own wife is an adul-

---

[9] See the excellent commentary of Leopold Brandl, O.F.M., *Die Sexualethik des heiligen Albertus Magnus* (Regensburg, 1955), pp. 171–178.

[10] Brandl makes the same comment (*ibid.*, p. 229).

[11] St. Albert, *Summa theologica*, in *Opera*, ed. Borgnet (Paris, 1890–1899), vol. XXXIII.

terer, that is, he who does not keep the limit of nature, or consider the good of marriage" (2.22.133.2, reply to quest. 2). Evidently he has not rejected the possibility of sin in marriage. The surprising statement that "no sin" occurs in "matrimonial intercourse" must be analyzed with stress put upon the qualification "matrimonial." If the coital act is truly matrimonial, then and only then is there no sin. But what would a truly matrimonial act be? With the help of Augustinian doctrine on procreation the meaning of "matrimonial" could be resolved. But Albert, choosing not to use Augustine, has chosen to leave the question open. Another answer could be given from his own tentative thought in the commentary on the *Sentences:* intercourse is a matrimonial act when the sacramental good is recalled. Yet this analysis was not repeated by Albert, and his last word remained an ambiguous one.

Albert's thought, hesitantly broached, had no immediate sequel. His pupil, Thomas, clearly rejected an independent sacramental value for intercourse. The sacramental good, he said, "pertains not to the use of matrimony, but to its essence"; that is, indissolubility was an effect of the sacrament, but intercourse did not have a sacramental value (*On the Sentences* 4.31.2.2).[12] Developed with greater consistency and assurance, the sexual ethic of St. Thomas eclipsed the teaching of his master and shared in Thomas' generally greater theological prestige. Within the Dominican order and outside it, Thomas was the master. Yet, if references to Albert's theory are rare in the later Middle Ages, can we not ascribe to him some influence in keeping Thomas from extreme Augustinianism? Three later writers, bishops and Dominicans like Albert — Durand of St. Pourçain, Peter de Palude, St. Antoninus — have some trace of the humaneness of Albert's views on marital matters. Is it fanciful to see in them an Albertine inheritance within the Dominicans? Most important of all in the long history of doctrine, Albert had adumbrated an analysis of intercourse which freed it from service to procreation and tied it to the sacrament. If his thought was submerged in his own day, were his ideas lost forever?[13]

[12] On the differences between Albert and Thomas, and especially on Thomas' rejection of the Albertine distinction between the act of nature and the act of man, see Brandl, *Die Sexualethik*, p. 201. When Thomas implies that to seek intercourse for health would be like being baptized to be physically cleansed, there is an echo of the sacramental theory (*On the Sentences* 4.31.2.2, reply to obj. 4).

[13] Brandl comments that Albert's view on the "sacramental" end of intercourse seemed "so erratic" within the context of medieval sexual ethics that it was generally ignored (*ibid.*, p. 171). The first theologian he finds who commented on the theory is Herbert Doms in 1935. Doms used Albert's theory to support his own position, and was not interested in giving a strict historical account of the inconsistencies in Albert. See Herbert Doms, *Du sens et de la fin du mariage*, trans. from *Vom Sinn und Zweck der Ehe* by Paul and Marie Simone Thisse (Paris, 1937), pp. 140–141. Brandl, p. 178, notes that Doms puts a valuation on personal union in intercourse which cannot be found in Albert.

THE MARRIAGE OF THE STERILE

Theory and practice permitted the sterile to marry, and affirmed the validity of their marriages. Known sterility antecedent to marriage could be present, as in the case of a woman past the age of childbearing. Sterility could be discovered after marital intercourse had taken place. Antecedent sterility was not a bar to the marriage, nor discovered sterility ground for annulment.

Theoretical justification followed the suggestion of Augustine that marriage was "the solace of human dignity" (above, p. 128n). The text from Augustine was preserved in Gratian (2.27.1.41). "Solace of human dignity" was then treated by Hostiensis as the principal reason for the aged to marry (*Summa* 4, "Marriage"). Thomas dealt with the objection that a sterile marriage should be dissoluble because in it the good of offspring was not achieved. The general rule of indissolubility still held, he said, for this general rule was for the good of offspring: a plurality of spouses was injurious to their education (*On the Sentences* 4.33.2.1, reply to obj. 2). In short, reflecting the common teaching, he accepted sterile marriages as valid although all the goods were not realized. The unanimous teaching on the marriage of the sterile left these questions unanswered and, indeed, unasked: Why were the sterile permitted to marry, but the impotent denied marriage? Why were the sterile permitted to marry if they could not have intercourse without sin? How could the procreative good be essential to marriage if sterile marriages were valid?

That a line was sharply, if roughly, drawn between the impotent and the sterile was clear. Gratian contained two basic canons. One, of uncertain origin, permitted annulment of the marriage if, because of "the frigid nature" of the man, "copulation was not possible" (*Decretum* 2.33.1.2). The other, a letter of Igmarus, archbishop of Rheims, dating from about 860, annulled a marriage where sorcery (*maleficium*) had hexed the couple so that copulation was impossible for them, although each spouse might be able to have intercourse if joined to a different spouse (*Decretum* 2.33.1.4). These canons were reinforced by the *Decretals*, which devoted an entire title to "The Frigid and the Hexed [*Maleficiati*], and Inability to Copulate" (4.15). The title dealt with physical disabilities to the contracting of a valid marriage. The disqualifying condition described generally by this second set of canons is that a person is "frigid" or "impotent"; occasionally the canons indicate more specific injuries, such as injured genitals (c. 2), or a diseased organ (*instrumentum*) (c. 3).

The theologians were in full accord with the canonists as to the disqualification. Peter Lombard repeated Gratian's canons (*Sentences*

4.34). Thomas described the types of disability as "frigidity," which destroys "the rigor of the members by which the joining of bodies occurs"; "too great warmth," which "dries out a man," preventing "the mixing of seeds"; "tightness on the part of the woman"; and inability to copulate caused by *maleficium* accomplished with the aid of the devil (*On the Sentences* 4.34.1.2 and 3). In short, impotence preventing marriage consisted in inability to ejaculate semen into the vagina, or inability to receive ejaculated semen. The impotent were distinguished from the sterile aged. The aged were presumed to be able to copulate "by nature, or art, or medicine" (Huguccio, *Summa* 2.27.1.41). As Thomas puts it, "although the aged sometimes do not have sufficient heat to generate, they have sufficient heat for carnal copulation" (*On the Sentences* 4.34.1.2, reply to obj. 3).

Both impotence and sterility made generation impossible; but only impotence made marriage impossible. Thomas tried to explain the disqualifying effect of impotence in terms that avoided what impotence and sterility shared in common. Marriage, he taught, was a contract to pay a debt. The debt was intercourse. The impotent could not pay the debt and so were unfit for marriage (*On the Sentences* 4.34.1.2). He did not, however, relate this explanation to the more general theory of marriage as an institution with three goods, one of which was the good of offspring. Saying that the aged could marry, he made no effort to reconcile their inability to generate with what he elsewhere had taught was the purpose of marriage.

Other theologians seemed aware of the problem of justifying the marriage of the aged, but were unable to formulate any solution consistent with the Augustinian analysis of the three goods of marriage. Alexander of Hales contented himself with noting that, although the aged may "have no hope of offspring," they are not deliberately avoiding offspring (*Gloss on the Sentences* 4.31.12). But while this observation distinguished the aged from those who married with contraceptive intent, it scarcely held to the requirement that marriage incorporate a "good of offspring." Scotus openly took a position inconsistent with the three-goods analysis. Offspring, he explained, are only "conditionally" a good of marriage: if "there happen to be" offspring, one is "to receive them gratefully and educate them religiously." But where fertility was not probable, the other two goods of marriage "excused" the marriage (*On the Sentences* [*Oxford Report*] 4.31).

The marriage of the sterile aged was accepted, then, at a price. The willingness to acquiesce in the custom, and the unwillingness to accept the marriage of the impotent, reflected the dominance of Christian practice over theory. Plainly, some old people married. Instinctively — for there was no support in theory for the practice — the theologians shrank from attacking the validity of established custom, beneficent in every respect except its complete departure from the central Augustinian account of what marriage was for. The contrasting attitude toward impotence came from a perspective we have noted before, a focusing on the act in which insemination was possible, not on the act in which generation was possible. Just as the sin against nature was constituted by an act in which insemination, not generation, was impossible, so the obstacle to marriage was not incapacity to generate, but incapacity to inseminate. In both cases, the line was drawn, not in accordance with a valuation which made procreation of first importance, but with a valuation giving preeminence to coitus.

If marriage was indissoluble because of the sacrament, if the ability to bear children was not essential to a valid marriage, it was possible, as a matter of merely logical speculation, to treat the marriage of the impotent like the marriage of the sterile. If marriage could survive the loss of one of its essential goods, why could it not survive the loss of two and remain a sacramental union of male and female friends? If the marital debt could be waived by joint vows of virginity, why was the marriage of the impotent not possible? This kind of speculation was not indulged in, because the theologians had some perception of how intolerable might be the condition of spouses in a marriage where continence was not the result of voluntary choice. The discrimination between the aged and the impotent was a response not to the exigencies of Augustinian theory, but to perceptions of the needs of human beings.

In the distinction made in favor of the marriage of the sterile, there was more than inconsistency with the Augustinian theory of marriage as an institution; there was a challenge to the theory of the procreative purpose of intercourse. If marriage was permissible without the good of offspring, was nonprocreative intercourse permissible? Most of those who insisted on the procreative purpose of intercourse knew no exceptions for the sterile. The result, according to them, was that the aged could marry, but they could not have intercourse without sin. Physical ability to have intercourse was necessary in order to marry validly; but the moral capacity to have intercourse without sin was not necessary.

Did a writer of the stature of St. Thomas accept with equanimity this extraordinary result? There are conflicting statements of his which need exegesis. On three occasions he defended intercourse which was not procreative. In the commentary on the *Sentences*, one ground justifying intercourse with the abnormal menstruant was that there is no danger to offspring "since a woman in that state cannot conceive" (*On the Sentences* 4.32.1.2.2).[14] In *Evil*, the intercourse of the aged was declared to

[14] The Leonine edition of the Supplement to the *Summa theologica* (*Opera* [Rome, 1882–1948], vol. XII) omits this question, and presumably the authenticity is doubtful.

be free of mortal sin, although nothing was said as to whether such intercourse constituted venial sin (*Evil* 15.2, reply to obj. 14). In the *Summa Against the Gentiles* he declared expressly that intercourse with a sterile woman was "not a sin" (3.122). All of these statements conflicted with his acceptance of the Augustinian requirement of procreative intention. One is left with a choice: to say that Thomas never abandoned the requirement of procreative purpose, although he sometimes spoke only of objective requirements of the sexual act, or to say that in the exceptional cases of the aged and the abnormal menstruant he did not insist on the requirement. It has been argued that Thomas rigorously separated his statements about the objective morality of intercourse from his statements on the subjective purpose.[15] The statements on sterile intercourse would apply only to the objective morality of the act. But did Thomas mean to defend such intercourse only to make the defense an empty one by a general doctrine that procreative purpose was subjectively required? Whatever interpretation is true, the strain placed on the pure procreative theory of intercourse is evident.

Two prominent fourteenth-century Dominicans, Durand of St. Pourçain and Peter de Palude, take a step which seems influenced by this kind of strain. Durand of St. Pourçain is unwilling to abandon wholly the procreative purpose. But he is willing to accede to the minority position permitting intercourse in order to avoid falling into fornication, if the "principal" end, children, is not attainable, "as with a sterile wife or with one who cannot now conceive" (*On the Sentences* 4.31.4). Peter de Palude, who is a cautious spokesman for the minority position on intercourse to avoid fornication, explicitly urges that such intercourse is lawful when "the aged and the sterile" have "no other way" to avoid fornication (*On the Sentences* 4.31.2).

The minority position on nonprocreative purpose in intercourse was strengthened by this appeal to the case of the lawfully married sterile. For the Augustinian majority there remained the perplexities created by holding that the sterile could marry but could not have intercourse. Small as the immediate effect on the doctrine was, ignored though the problem was by many authors, the dilemma created by the marriage of the sterile pointed to major inadequacies in the dominant doctrine on marriage.

THE ACCEPTANCE OF PLEASURE AS A VALUE

The Gregorian view that all sexual pleasure was an evil had reached its maximum strength at the end of the twelfth century, when it was

[15] Fuchs, *Die Sexualethik des heiligen Thomas von Aquin*, p. 220.

held by Huguccio and Pope Innocent III. The thirteenth century saw the gradual disappearance of this position which was so embarrassing to the orthodox defense of the holiness of marriage. In the mid-thirteenth century St. Bonaventure could still term "probable" Auxerre's opinion that for marital coitus to be without sin "it is necessary that such delight not please, indeed that it displease reason." But Bonaventure himself rejected the opinion as "too hard" (*On the Sentences* 4.31.2.3). The rehabilitation of pleasure as a positive value, however, had to wait for the triumph of Aristotelian influence. This work was largely the task of Thomas Aquinas.

Aristotle had analyzed pleasure as a subjective sense accompanying the performance of acts. Pleasure was not itself an act, and consequently was not the immediate object of moral judgment in the Aristotelian system, where acts were what were judged. Acts and pleasure, however, were inseparably joined, "since without activity pleasure does not arise, and every activity is completed by the attendant pleasure" (*Nicomachean Ethics*, 1174b). A judgment of the act carried with it a judgment on the attendant pleasure. "The pleasure proper to a worthy activity is good and that proper to an unworthy activity bad" (1175b).

As early as the commentary on the *Sentences* in 1255, Thomas adopted this position. He worked from Robert Grosseteste's translation of the *Ethics*, where *delectatio*, delight, is the term for the Greek *hedone*, translated in modern English as pleasure.[16] "Delight," Thomas taught, "follows operation." "The same judgment is to be made about the delight and the operation" (*On the Sentences* 4.31.2.3). Delight is the complement and the crown of each act, or, Thomas said, echoing Aristotle, "Delight is the perfection of operation" (4.49.3.4.3).

The Aristotelian propositions on pleasure were specifically related by Thomas to the pleasure present in sexual intercourse. As matrimonial coitus is good, so is the pleasure experienced in it: "The delight which occurs in the matrimonial act, although it is most intense in quantity, does not exceed the limits fixed by reason before its commencement, although during this delight reason cannot set the limits" (4.31.2.1, reply to obj. 3). The pleasure experienced in coitus in Paradise would have been still greater than that known by fallen man.

A more thorough rejection of the notion that sexual pleasure was sinful in itself would be difficult to imagine. Thomas even went further than a strict interpretation of Aristotle would have suggested in declaring that God had placed delight in the coital act as an inducement to perform it: "To impel man to the act whereby the deficiency of the species

---

[16] Aristotle, *Nicomachean Ethics*, trans. W. D. Ross, *Works*, vol. IX (Oxford, 1926). Robert Grosseteste's translation is reproduced in St. Thomas, *In X libros ethicorum ad Nicomachum*, in *Opera*, ed. P. Maré and S. E. Fretté (Paris, 1871–1882), vol. XXV.

is aided, He put delight in copulation" (*On the Sentences* 4.31.1.1, reply to obj. 1).

If pleasure was good, if sexual pleasure in particular was good, why was it not lawful to seek such pleasure? Why was it, according to Thomas, at least venial sin to seek pleasure? A contradiction existed between the statement that God intends sexual pleasure to be an inducement and the statement that to act for sexual pleasure in marriage is evil.[17] But Thomas' statement on inducement was a departure from Aristotelian principle, according to which pleasure itself was always attendant upon some act: one acted for the act itself, the pleasure followed. A more truly Aristotelian course was chosen by Thomas in discussing temperance in the *Summa theologica:* "All the pleasurable objects that are at man's disposal are directed to some necessity of this life as to their end. Therefore temperance takes the needs of this life as the rule for the pleasurable objects of which it makes use, and uses them only as much as the needs of this life require" (2–2.141.6). If the virtuous, temperate man acts only for needs, he will experience pleasure as he satisfies the needs, but he will not act for pleasure itself.

Yet, with pleasure rehabilitated, the question might have been raised whether pleasure itself was not sometimes a need. Aristotle himself had presented Aquinas with one form of this question. He had said that man might seek amusement (*paidia*) "as a sort of relaxation." Such amusement, like rest, might be sought for the sake of health. Aquinas commented on this passage in a translation where amusement appears as *ludus* (game). He noted that "a game or rest is not the end, because rest is for operation, so that a man after it may work more vigorously" (*On the Nicomachean Ethics* 10.9). In other words, he agreed that a game or rest was not the last end, but could be a means to another end. In the *Summa theologica*, this view of a game was applied generally to the delightful, and Thomas quoted from the *Nicomachean Ethics* 3.11: "The temperate man desires delightful things for the sake of health or for the sake of a sound condition of body" (2–2.141.6, reply to obj. 2). The question was again silently present, If pleasure were good, why could not sexual delight be sought, not as a last end, but as an intermediate value?

In the Augustinian framework, sexual pleasure, even when recognized as good in itself, was still attended by a loss of reason, due to original sin, which had to be compensated for. But, according to Aristotle, health

---

[17] Fuchs (*Die Sexualethik*, p. 227) comments on the two approaches in Aquinas: "Zweifellos stehen hier zwei verschiedenartige ethische Richtungen wenig vermittelt nebeneinander."

could be a compensating value. We have seen how Thomas as a young commentator on the *Sentences* refused to admit this conclusion, arguing that coitus was naturally ordained to procreation. But this position made the subjective requirement of procreative purpose totally dependent on the assumption that, objectively, lawful coitus had to be procreative. If this objective requirement fell, so did any subjective requirement that procreative purpose alone was permissible. With pleasure recognized as a positive value, the subjective tie of procreation and lawful intercourse was thus in grave peril.

One important author does make available a defense of pleasure as a purpose. This is the English Franciscan, Richard Middleton. Writing about 1272, Middleton puts this defense modestly, not as his own opinion but as that of "some" unidentified theologians. The "more common opinion" is against them. But he does not repudiate their view as untenable. They make three points. The first does away with the objection drawn from Augustine that to seek pleasure is to give in to concupiscence: "To satiate concupiscence and to will moderate delight are not the same." Moreover, Augustine when he spoke of pleasure-seeking as a "fault" (*culpa*) may have meant not "sin" but something less than the primal rectitude of the state of innocence.

The second point is Aristotelian. "Delight" cannot be bad in itself; otherwise to regulate it would not be a virtue. But it is agreed that temperance consists in the moderation of delight. Some say that it would be a sin for a man to eat more than is necessary to preserve his being. This is obviously fallacious: "a man does not sin as often as he eats because of delight in tasting."

The third point is reminiscent of Albert: "Intercourse with one's own spouse is chastity. There is, moreover, the good of the sacrament in the intentions of the users of conjugal intercourse, as long as they keep in mind, actually or by habit, that they would not copulate unless there were the decency of matrimony between them, which is there through the good of the sacrament" (*On the Sentences* 4.31.3.2). Here seems to be a brilliant combination of Aristotle and Albert. Moderate pleasure is good. Augustine is explained away. The probable state of mind of married persons not thinking explicitly of procreation in intercourse is justified. There is a modern ring to the solution which Middleton suggested.

The position reported by Middleton won no more general acceptance than St. Albert's own. What prevailed was the Augustinianism inconsistently incorporated in St. Thomas. It was only two hundred years after Middleton that the Aristotelian analysis of pleasure was restated and consistently applied.

PRACTICES PREVENTING CONCEPTION

None of the counter currents or valuations were led to a point where they became a defense of contraception. There were, however, certain practices, approved by some authors, which interfered with the process of conception. Whether they are to be labeled "contraceptive" or not depends on whether contraception is used as a moral term meaning "a forbidden means of preventing conception" or as a descriptive term meaning "any practice consciously used to avoid procreation." The practices which follow are contraceptive in the latter sense. Why they were not unanimously considered contraceptive in the first sense may provide grounds for reflection.

AMPLEXUS RESERVATUS

To begin an act of coitus, but to withdraw without ejaculation in the vagina, is an act involving the use of sexual organs of man and woman in a way that consciously avoids procreation. If ejaculation follows the withdrawal, the act is coitus interruptus, condemned by the Christian moralists as a sin against nature. If ejaculation after withdrawal is inhibited, the act has been described as *coitus reservatus* or *amplexus reservatus*.[18] Its moral status was not necessarily determined by the judgment on coitus interruptus.

The first reference I have encountered to *amplexus reservatus* by an orthodox authority is in the twelfth century. The authority and his reference are surprising. The authority is Huguccio, and he approves the practice. His discussion occurs in a curious context. He has taken the position that every act of marital intercourse involves venial sin because it involves pleasure accompanying ejaculation. But he also argues that if a man is unmarried and incontinent, he should, to avoid the sin of fornication, marry. Yet if he marries, he will have an obligation to render the marital debt to his wife, if she seeks it, and by such intercourse he will inevitably sin. "And so I seem to be perplexed." What is the answer to this dilemma?

To render the conjugal debt to one's wife is nothing other than to make for her a plenty of one's body for the wifely matter. Hence one often renders the debt to his wife in such a way that he does not satisfy his pleasure, and conversely. Therefore, in the aforesaid case, I can so render the debt to the wife and wait in such a way until she satisfies her pleasure. Indeed, often in such cases a woman is accustomed to anticipate her husband, and when the pleasure

[18] Neither term is used in the writers we are about to examine. The practical possibility of such intercourse has been indicated by such modern writers as Robert Dickinson and Louise S. Bryant, *Control of Conception* (Baltimore, 1931), p. 59.

of the wife in the carnal work is satisfied, I can, if I wish, withdraw, not satisfying my pleasure, free of all sin, and not emitting my seed of propagation.

(*Summa* 2.13)

The passage emphasizes the emission of "the seed of propagation," whereas "seed" is usually employed alone in orthodox writing. There is opposition only to the pleasure associated with the man's generative act; orgasm ("the pleasure of the wife") is not objected to.[19] There is no suggestion that even without ejaculation there would be an experience of some kind of pleasure by the man. The tone of the whole passage is so curiously unorthodox that one wonders if the text is genuine. Yet no doubt has been cast on the manuscripts embodying it.[20] Huguccio seems to be in the position of advocating *amplexus reservatus* as actually preferable to procreation and its necessary accompaniment of venial pleasure.

There is only one kind of literature that at this time recommended *amplexus reservatus*. It is the literature of courtly love, where the height of pure love, *fine amour,* was the kind of act described by Huguccio. It seems highly unlikely that Huguccio, a Camaldolese monk, derived his ideas from the troubadours. As he refers to an aspect of the practice as happening "often," he seems to be drawing not on songs or books, but on customs with which he is familiar. Can one suppose that this kind of practice had become common in some North Italian communities? I see no alternative. Can one suppose further that the technique was originally a Cathar way of preventing conception, which owed its diffusion to Cathar settlements in Northern Italy? Here the evidence is not compelling, but it would not seem that a practice requiring a peculiar discipline, a rigorous training in self-control, would arise spontaneously; and there is nothing in orthodox doctrine which would favor its discovery. Huguccio appears, then, to be referring to a going practice in or near Bologna, possibly originated by Cathars. He makes no attempt to explain how this way of avoiding insemination is distinguished from the sin against nature or the use of the poisons of sterility.

For over a century no major writer mentions Huguccio's position. The silence is puzzling, as the *Gloss* on Gratian, St. Raymond, and Hostiensis were all thoroughly familiar with Huguccio's important commentary.

[19] Louis Janssens states that Huguccio here defends "mutual masturbation"; "Morale conjugale et progestogènes," *Ephemerides theologicae lovanienses* 39 (1963), 800. This characterization does not seem to take account of Huguccio's stipulation that there will be no semination by the man. An exposition of the text, defending the moral lawfulness of what Huguccio describes, is made by C. Tiberghein, "A propos d'un texte d'Huguccio," *Mélanges de science religieuse* 9 (1952), 85–92.

[20] Alfons M. Stickler, S.D.B., who is preparing the definitive edition of Huguccio, has sent me the text he is using (Paris, Bibliothèque Nationale, MS. lat. 3892), with variants. The text reads as translated above.

It might be noted that Rhazes had recommended withdrawal before semination by the woman as a method of preventing conception (Rhazes, *Book for Almansor* 5.73).

One would think they would have approved or condemned his stand. It may be that they were simply unable to understand what Huguccio had in mind when they themselves knew of no such practice among orthodox Christians. The practice is not mentioned by such a knowledgeable and sympathetic writer on sexual matters as St. Albert.

This method of avoiding procreation, untreated in the thirteenth century, is launched under fresh auspices, and as a solution to a different problem, in the fourteenth century. In his youth in Burgundy, or in his travels to Cyprus and Jerusalem, or in his wide experience at the French court, Peter de Palude, the Dominican archbishop, had become familiar with the basic technique. He condemns the use of the method of Onan by a husband who does not want more children than he can feed. He continues: "If, however, with same intention, he withdraws himself before completion of the act and does not emit seed, he does not seem to sin mortally; unless from this perhaps the woman is provoked to semination" (*On the Sentences* 4.31.3.2). Palude's approval is markedly different from Huguccio's. The practice is not proposed out of scruple about pleasure connected with the emission of seed. It appears to be limited to cases of severe economic necessity. In the express denial of mortal sin, there is some implication that the act involves venial sin. There is the added caveat that mortal sin occurs if the woman is "provoked to semination." Probably this phrase means "if orgasm occurs" (below, p. 337). With these qualifications, the practice is accepted by Palude as at least not seriously wrong. It is assumed that withdrawal can be accomplished without subsequent ejaculation or orgasm. There is no discussion of the development of control or the need for discipline. There is also no mention of any authority for the opinion given, nor any attempt whatsoever to develop a rationale for it. The only reasoning is what is implicit in the way the case is presented. The control of semination is the basis of contrast with the sin of Onan. The emphasis on the exceptional economic circumstances justifying the act suggests that the practice could not be lawfully engaged in for pleasure.[21]

---

[21] According to Angelus Carletus de Clavasio, writing about 1480, Palude also hold that in the same circumstances of poverty it is not a mortal sin for a wife after coitus "to urinate or quickly stand up to emit the seed lest she conceive" (Angelus, *Summa angelica de casibus conscientiae*, Lyons, 1505, "Debitum conjugale"). The same position is attributed to Palude by Sylvester da Prierio, *Summa summarum quae silvestrina dicitur* (Bologna, 1514), at the word "Debitum," and by Thomas Sanchez, *De sancti matrimonii sacramento* (Venice, 1737), 9.20. However, Sylvester and Sanchez are probably only copying Angelus.

Did Palude hold this position? The copy of his work on the *Sentences*, printed in 1493, which I have used does not contain this opinion. Neither does a manuscript copy dating from about 1480, formerly in the possession of the Duke of Urbino (MS in the University of Southern California). St. Antoninus, John Nider, and Trovamala do not mention the opinion when they follow Palude literally on *amplexus*

Palude was an important authority to sponsor the practice. In the fifteenth century an even more important authority concurring with him was St. Antoninus. He followed Palude to the letter (*Summa theologica* 3.1.20). He did not put the case in his *Confessional*, thereby denying it the widest possible circulation. But his endorsement in the *Summa* was weighty approbation, of especial importance for later fifteenth- and early-sixteenth-century moral theology.

In two fifteenth-century manuals for confessors Palude was also adopted literally and without comment: the Italian Franciscan Trovamala's *Summa* (at "Debitum") and the German Dominican John Nider's *Moral Leprosy* ("The Genital Abuses of the Married"). Thus, up till about 1480, *amplexus reservatus* had been ignored by many authorities, championed by a few, and attacked by none.

How was the deliberate frustration and interruption of coitus in this practice reconciled with the general stand on acts against nature? The obvious distinction turned on the absence of ejaculation. Where this act did not occur, a sin against nature was not at issue. These questions remained undiscussed: Why was the presence or absence of ejaculation crucial? Why was it permissible to frustrate the whole psychobiological mechanism involved in coitus, so long as ejaculation was avoided? Was there something sacred in the act of emission of seed which put it in a different category from every other act involved in coitus?

ANAPHRODISIACS

Medieval medical works were full of anaphrodisiacs. Intended to affect sexual desire, they interfered with the beginning of the reproductive process. There seems to have been popular confidence in their efficacy.

The Pseudo-Vigila penitential had condemned the use of such potions. But no canon reached them. Nor did any theologian or canonist I have read condemn them or even analyze their effect. If common and not condemned, they must have been accepted as morally harmless. Castration for the sake of avoiding sexual sin was condemned because its purpose was properly achieved by the human will alone. The same reasoning could have been extended to the suppression of a natural drive by potion. No evidence of such reasoning appears. The destruction of sexual desire was not criticized as unnatural.

All of the theories, values, practices, reviewed in this chapter ran counter to the theory and valuation which required that the purpose of lawful intercourse be procreative; which treated the act of coitus as

---

reservatus. One may suppose that in some manuscript copies the opinion described by Angelus had been inserted.

intended by nature to be procreative; which implied that the generative process was an absolute, immune from human interference.

If the counter elements had been assembled into a system of values, a different synthesis from the dominant Augustinian one would have been made. The preference, indicated by the valuation of virginity, for the perfecting of living human beings over the propagating of new beings could have been combined with the judgment, made in regard to fornication and menstruation, that conception was to be postponed for the sake of the well-being of the child. These valuations could have been fortified by the unanimous insistence that only a child who could be religiously educated in a full sense constituted the "good of offspring" which justified intercourse. A combination of these valuations might have led to a valuation favoring birth control.

If the sacramental theory suggested by Albert or the theory of pleasure owed to Aristotle had been fully applied, not every lawful act of intercourse would necessarily have had procreation for its purpose; it would have been possible to regard as lawful some acts of intercourse where conception was impossible. If the implications concerning the natural purpose of coitus which the theory of the marital debt contained had been spelled out, or if the theory and practice permitting the sterile to marry had been extended to justify sterile intercourse, it would not have seemed unnatural to engage in an act of coitus which served no procreative end.

As to means by which birth control could have been achieved, approval of some means required only a small extension of the tolerance extended to *amplexus reservatus* and to the anaphrodisiacs. If what was sinful was the interruption of an act of ejaculation, it would have been possible to use contraceptive potions or douches taking effect after ejaculation, with no greater offense to basic principles than the tolerated practices suggested.

All of this rearrangement of values into a synthesis permitting or favoring contraception was possible. That these theories, values, practices, existed in medieval theology is a large reason why they later played such a strong role in the European consciousness. Their existence testifies to what cannot be emphasized too often. The doctrine on sexuality, as it stood, was a balance — not the logical projection of a single value, but a balance of a whole set of competing values. The balance was weighted at a particular point which excluded contraception. If it held where it did at the height of the Middle Ages, the influence of St. Augustine, the reaction to the Cathars, and the mating habits of the age were together responsible. It was not inevitable that the balance remain so. In what follows we shall see a gradual shift.

PART THREE

INNOVATION AND PRESERVATION

1450–1750

CHAPTER XI

NEW ATTITUDES AND ANALYSES

ETWEEN 1450 AND 1750 the doctrine on the purposes of marital intercourse evolved — not in a straight linear motion, not to a point
of final perfection — but, with difficulties and setbacks, to a new synthesis
distinguishable from the medieval balance. The Augustinian theory of
intercourse was seriously impaired. The idea of limiting intercourse in
order to avoid excessive births was introduced and given theological
approval. *Amplexus reservatus* was increasingly discussed as a lawful
alternative to contraception. The innovations accepted amount to a
partial triumph of the theories and values labeled, in terms of the
medieval synthesis, "counter approaches."

The cultural development broadly characterized as the Renaissance
had some effect on the spirit of students of theology in the years between
1450 and 1520. Sexual ethics was among the subjects freshly examined.
After 1520, the decline of Augustinianism in the course of the Catholic
reaction against Luther and Calvin hastened the decline of the Augustinian theory of intercourse. The perceptible growth of an educated
lay class by the end of the fifteenth century coincided with a new, if
limited, confidence of the theologians in the moral judgments of the laity.
These phenomena, all occurring outside the immediate teaching on
marital morality, explain, in part, why change begins to be visible in the
moral theology of marriage.

Yet the history of thought within a continuing civilization is rarely
marked by radical discontinuities. The true ancestors of the advocates of
change were St. Albert and particularly St. Thomas. In Albert, Augustinian
sexual ethics had been undermined. Thomas had followed Augustine's
teaching on marital sins, but in other fields Thomas had championed a
rationalism which continued to bear fruit at the University of Paris. The
firm distinction between grace and nature, the insistence on the value
of nature, the application of reason to the data of revelation, the Christian
adaptation of Aristotle — these Thomistic accomplishments underlay the
later innovations.

A gap usually exists between innovation and acceptance. Layers of theological thought, old and new, coexist. Between 1450 and 1750, as new theory won its way, the *Decretum* and the *Decretals* were the law of the Church. *Aliquando, Adulterii malum,* and *Si aliquis* were disseminated by printing and were more widely known than in the high Middle Ages. The old commentators, such as Hostiensis, were still authorities. St. Raymond's *Summa* was still a useful guide for confessors. The comparatively recent work of St. Antoninus was an even more popular authority. As Lombard's *Sentences* ceased to be the great textbook of theology, Aquinas' *Summa theologica* acquired a position of relative dominance. Augustine, now competing with his medieval heirs, continued to command attention.

Consequently, the new developments formed at first only a small current in a large stream; that they would become the mainstream was not certain. Yet there is a difference between the historical place of St. Albert and that of the fifteenth-century writers. St. Albert was an innovator, born out of his time; his views, on the whole, were lost in the dominant sweep of thought to which they ran counter. Beginning with the mid-fifteenth century the current ran with the innovators.

The first sign of the new spirit is a work designed for the married laity, *The Praiseworthy Life of the Married,* in effect, a short catechism of moral life for the married.[1] Its author was Denis the Carthusian (1402–1471), a monk of Roermond in the Low Countries. He wrote, his introduction says, at the repeated request of "much beloved" married friends of his. He wrote in Latin because they were "learned" friends; and his manuscript was not printed until 1530. Yet this treatise for a limited audience, which would not have wide circulation till about a century after its writing, reflects the hunger of the educated laity for instruction on their role as Christians. That a Carthusian mystic, later known as "the ecstatic doctor," should have supplied it may seem less surprising if we recall the close association of the Carthusians at the Charterhouse in London with the devout English laity of whom St. Thomas More was the brightest example. The Carthusians, justly retaining an ascetic reputation amidst fifteenth-century complaints of ecclesiastical corruption, furnished an example of devotion to laymen trying to be Christians, and monks like Denis responded generously to the desire of their lay friends for spiritual help.

---

[1] Denis the Carthusian, *De laudabili vita conjugatorum,* in *Opera,* ed. the Monks of the Carthusian Order (Tournai, 1896–1913), vol. XXXVIII. His approach here may be contrasted with his more formal scholastic commentary on the *Sentences.* There he gave Thomas' opinion on the lawful purposes of intercourse and Richard Middleton's opinion on intercourse for moderate delight. He did not repudiate Middleton, but he concluded that the contrary view was "common and more secure and more consonant with that of Augustine" (*On the Sentences* 4.31.1, *Opera,* vol. XXV[1]).

In *The Praiseworthy Life of the Married* there is a moving combination of ancient theological lore with a desire to come to terms with the needs of the Christian couple. Denis begins strongly with the statement that marriage is a sacrament (art. 1) and that the married state is good (art. 2); he at once qualifies his praise by a reminder that celibacy is better, but, having set out fifteen reasons why marriage is good, he does nothing to destroy the basic approval he has given to the married way of life. He goes on to show that the marital act is good, and therefore "the work of charity or spiritual love," when it is performed for the traditional purposes of paying the debt or procreating offspring for the worship of God. He also finds intercourse easy to defend when undertaken to prevent fornication by one's spouse, and he notes that there is a split of authority as to whether intercourse is lawful to avoid one's own incontinence. He takes the usual position that intercourse not kept within natural limits is mortal sin, and paraphrases Jerome, "the too fervid lover is an adulterer" (art. 5). But this standard treatment of love and pleasure in relation to intercourse does not end his concern with this vital subject. He returns to an analysis of love. The love of husband and wife should be "multiple, special, cordial." They should love each other with a spiritual love, desiring each other's salvation; they should love each other with a natural love as fellow creatures; they should love each other with a social love, as human beings who share each other's lives. Should they also love each other with a carnal love, that is, a love based "on sensual delights" and "worldly comforts"? The question he finds a hard one, but he resolves it by appeal to the basic Aristotelian principle which Thomas had set forth but not followed: judgment on a pleasure depends on judgment on the act. The marital act is good. Therefore "the married can mutually love each other because of the mutual pleasure they have in the marital act"; therefore "they are said to love each other lawfully with a carnal love." Denis ends this defense of carnal married love with a reiteration of old warnings against uxoriousness: St. Bridget in her *Revelations* says a man was damned for loving his wife too carnally. Husbands with pretty wives, wives with lovable husbands, ought to be careful (art. 8).

Denis' conclusion was an anticlimax. But in a way unknown to earlier theologians he had undertaken to bring together spiritual and carnal love in marriage. Confined by the categories of scholastic analysis, he had made a notable effort to integrate the kinds of love which bound the married. He had come close to breaking out from the usual account of the purposes of intercourse. He had not done so, however, and his work was more significant for its reflection of the new aspirations of the laity than for its contribution to theological analysis. Denis incorporated a new spirit; writing in a rather obscure monastery, he had not produced a theory, and his work had no immediate impact on the development of theology. A new theory had to be the work of a man placed in the intellectual mainstream.

THE NEW THEORY OF MARITAL INTERCOURSE

The new theory began its life with a man who was thoroughly and typically the product of Parisian intellectualism when the University of Paris was still the center of European theological thought: Martin Le Maistre (1432–1481). Augustine and Aquinas were teachers, too, but neither conveys the impression Le Maistre generates of an academic kind of man. Not Augustine's ardor, not Aquinas' asceticism, but a cool professorial outlook was his dominant characteristic. He brought to the subject of sexual ethics neither the experiences and passion of Augustine nor the strong contemplative love of God of Aquinas, but a predominant fondness for intellectual satisfactions.[2]

[2] Martin Le Maistre (Martinus de Magistris or Martinus Magister), who will appear often in these pages as an important innovator, is an almost totally neglected writer today, but was a celebrated academic figure of his day. Born in 1432 in Tours, of a rich bourgeois family with a tradition of service as magistrates, Le Maistre spent his entire life in university work. A professor first at the College of Navarre at the University of Paris, he was ultimately the light of the new College of Sainte-Barbe. He introduced the study of rhetoric at Navarre, but his great love was ethics. He appears as the university lector on Aristotle's *Ethics* for the year 1470. *Auctarium chartularii Universitatis parisiensis,* vol. III, ed. C. Samaran, E. Van Moé and S. Vitte (Paris, 1935), col. 137. Biographical data are also summarized in *Auctarium chartularii Universitatis parisiensis,* vol. VI, ed. Astrik L. Gabriel and Gray C. Boyce (Paris, 1964), col. 387.

In 1474, the very year in which Le Maistre received the licentiate in theology, a royal ordinance proscribed the teaching of nominalist books, and permitted, by way of leniency, only the retention of single copies chained in the libraries. This political intrusion into academic life had been the work of Louis XI's confessor, one of the outnumbered realists at the University. Le Maistre disregarded the royal decree, teaching Occam and Buridan at Sainte-Barbe with "immense success" (J. Quicherat, *Histoire de Sainte-Barbe,* Paris, 1860-1864, I, 41). Moreover, he himself gained the king's attention and became his almoner. In 1481 he had the satisfaction of seeing the old ordinance repealed and the books released, a direct result of Le Maistre's "pertinacity" (*Auct. chartularii,* III, 471, n. 2).

The spirit of independence that appears in his vindication of the nominalists is reflected several times in the university annals by controversies Le Maistre engaged in over his rights to various preferments and posts. Thus from January 9 to February 18, 1468, he was engaged in a losing contest to establish his election as *receptor* of the French nation at the University (*Auct. chartularii,* III, 65, 66, 69, 73). On June 1, 1473, he was in litigation for the prebend of the church of Saint Cajetan in Tours (*ibid.,* III, 234). In 1480, he entered a contest for the mastership of the College of Navarre, only to lose out — owing to bribery — to an old pupil, John Raulin (Quicherat, *Histoire,* I, 48–49). Martin's attempt to interest the university in vindicating his rights was looked on as unseemly contentiousness by many of his colleagues (*Auct. chartularii,* III, 495).

Not a mild man, then, but a prickly academic one, Martin was still respected by his associates. The chronicles of the German nation describe him as "a venerable and truly knowledgeable man" at the time of his election as Reader on the *Ethics*

By the kind of paradox common in intellectual history, Le Maistre, who owed so much intellectually to St. Thomas, enjoyed the reputation of leader at Paris of the Occamists, the enemies of Thomistic theory. But, in fact, Le Maistre was an eclectic, drawing skillfully on both Aquinas and Aristotle. His book, *Moral Questions,* published posthumously in 1490, is, I believe, the most independent critique of the Christian sexual ethic ever undertaken by an orthodox critic.

What Le Maistre does is to sweep away the Augustinian distinctions on the purpose of marital intercourse and establish the general law-fulness of the marital act. Unlike Albert, he does so without recourse to sacramental theory, on a firm rational footing. In Aristotelian fashion, he deals with the question as a problem of virtue and of finding the virtuous mean between excesses. The mean is "conjugal chastity" — surely a striking combination of concepts, to be echoed almost five hundred years later in the most celebrated papal statement on sexual ethics, *Casti connubii.* As a phrase the term was not new. Bromyard had used it to designate marital fidelity (*Summa for Preachers,* "Lechery," 15). Le Maistre's idea may even be present in Richard Middleton's reference to "conjugal chastity" in his work on the *Sentences* (4.33.4.1), for Middleton clearly works under Aristotelian influence. But Middleton neither defined nor developed the idea. With Le Maistre the Aristotelian concept of virtue as a mean is central and "conjugal chastity" is defined as a mean between immodesty and insensibility. With this virtue as the norm by which to measure subjective intention, Le Maistre advances this humble thesis: "Not every copulation of spouses not performed to generate off-spring is an act opposed to conjugal chastity" ("Seventh Conclusion," *Quaestiones morales* II, fol. 48v). He gives as lawful instances the case, always admitted by theologians as to the responding partner, of render-ing the marital debt; the debated case of avoiding the committing of fornication; the unrecognized case of seeking bodily health; and the new case of "calming the mind." The new last instance is explained in a dis-arming way that almost identifies it with the second situation. "It some-times happens," says Le Maistre, "that the desire of lust is so vehement, and so disturbs the mind, that a man is scarcely master of himself." Then no law prohibits intercourse with the wife "given to him for the sake of solace and remedy."

Proceeding cautiously, Le Maistre is only opening the way to a larger

(*Auct. chartularii,* III, 137). In 1464 he was Rector Magnificus of the University (*ibid.,* vol. II, ed. H. Denifle and E. Chatelain, Paris, 1897, p. 952). An old student of his, celebrating his skill in argument, some thirty years after his death, wrote, "Are you not worthy of immortality, O most moral Martin?" (quoted in Georges Ruhlmann, *Cinq siècles au Collège Sainte-Barbe, 1460–1960,* Paris, 1960, p. 15).

Citations of Le Maistre are to the section "De temperantia" in *Quaestiones morales,* vol. II (Paris, 1490).

position. He confronts directly the majority opinions — marital intercourse for the sake of avoiding fornication is venial sin, intercourse for the sake of satisfying lust or obtaining pleasure is mortal sin — and denies them. As to avoiding fornication, he advances a variant of Peter de Palude's hypothetical: if a man is going to see a woman with whom he had the custom of committing fornication before marriage, and fears that concupiscence will again arise in him, he acts prudently in extinguishing his concupiscence in marital intercourse; "so his own priest or any wise man would counsel him" (fol. 49r). Generalizing the case, he continues: marriage is set up as a remedy for fornication; so the act of intercourse to avoid fornication must be lawful. The end is good, and the means have just been shown to be good.

Le Maistre then advances to his most radical position: "I say that someone can wish to take pleasure, first for love of that pleasure, secondly to avoid tedium and the ache of melancholy caused by the lack of pleasure. Conjugal intercourse to avoid the sadness coming from the absence of venereal pleasure is not culpable" (fol. 49v). There are two ancient authorities often cited to the contrary: Augustine and Aristotle. Le Maistre distinguishes Augustine's position as being opposed only to "immoderate" and to "unnatural" intercourse. Aristotle, he notes, permits the use of the pleasurable when it aids "health and the good condition of body or of soul." He presumably has in mind the passage in the *Nicomachean Ethics*, 1176b, on the seeking of amusement for the sake of health (above, p. 294). The Thomistic interpretation of Aristotle, that pleasure cannot be sought as an end, is implicitly rejected. Pleasure may be sought, if a means to some other end; it is a useful or instrumental good. Is not this "to serve lust," as the old theologians feared? "This is not to serve lust, but to place lust under the yoke of reason" (fol. 50r).

Responding to further objections to his position, Le Maistre contends that it is possible to relate the purposes he defends to the generative purpose, "in that the healthy are more fit for generation." What he recommends will lessen the likelihood of fornication, and this result will also make the spouses more apt to generate, "for by the custom of fornication conjugal love is diminished." To the old objection of Aquinas that in the marital act reason suffers a loss which must be compensated for by "the goods excusing marriage," Le Maistre denies that reason suffers a loss, and asserts that if it does, the loss is immediately made good by the effects, inherent in the act, of lessening the peril of fornication or "keeping or acquiring health." To the objection that pleasure cannot be sought as an end referable to God, he replies, "according to Aristotle, I can use pleasure for an honest end; so, then, I can use it for God" (fol. 51v).

Several times hesitation and caution are apparent. Le Maistre clings closely to the authority of Aristotle as he challenges the regnant theological opinion. At times he appears to concede that seeking pleasure only may be venial sin. Yet after making a concession of this kind, he always opposes to it an alternative Aristotelian analysis which disproves the claim that there is sin. Thus he declares: "Right reason dictates that it is lawful to use such copulation for the sake of pleasure, just as it is lawful for me to use lamb or mutton and, though I suppose both are healthy, to use the lamb when it pleases me more. Nor would Aristotle see any fault in this if the use was moderate" (fol. 51v). The Augustinian comparison of food and intercourse is here turned round with a vengeance.

Le Maistre emphasizes the effect of the old doctrine on the married life of Christian couples; that view — that copulation for the sake of pleasure may be mortal sin — is, "I believe, much more dangerous for human morals." Given that doctrine, a simple man will as readily have intercourse with any woman as with his wife when he feels the impulse to pleasure (fol. 50r). The difficulties caused by the old theory are particularly striking where pregnancy has occurred: "I ask how many dangers do they [my opponents] expose the consciences of scrupulous spouses to, for there is many a one whose wife is immediately made pregnant, and after that has happened, they expose to the danger of mortal sin whoever seeks the debt unless it is certain that he does this to avoid fornication" (fol. 50r).

Appeal to the dilemma of married Christians, joined with the most open, penetrating, and comprehensive application of Aristotelian reasoning to marriage, has led to a sweeping legitimation of the nonprocreative purposes of intercourse. On strictly rational grounds Le Maistre has ended the tie between procreative purpose and lawful intercourse. His work is the beginning of a new stage in the Catholic approach to marriage.

The originality of Le Maistre's accomplishment stands out particularly if one looks at the work of two men who might have been able to make the same kind of analysis: Buridan and Erasmus. John Buridan (fl. 1330) was the predecessor of Le Maistre at Paris who enjoyed the greatest reputation as an Occamist moralist. In his *Questions on the Eight Books of the Politics of Aristotle*, he has only a conventional Augustinian analysis of marriage (7.14).[3] Desiderius Erasmus (1464–1536), the unexcelled humanist of the age succeeding Le Maistre, treats of marriage in *The Institution of Christian Matrimony*. He has much to say in praise of marriage, but no analysis of the purpose of intercourse, and he goes so far in linking the procreative end of marriage with the institution that

[3] John Buridan, *Quaestiones super octo libros Aristotelis Politicorum* (Paris, 1513).

he calls the marriages of the old or the sterile not true marriages.[4] Neither the Occamist leader of the past nor the humanist leader of the future made a case for conjugal chastity of the kind developed by Le Maistre.

Robert Gaguin, one of the most knowledgeable of contemporary university figures, greeted Le Maistre's book as a "remarkable work."[5] But the book did not by itself make a dent on scholastic theology. I have read only two major theologians, Cajetan and Lessius, who cite it at all, and both do so unfavorably. If Le Maistre is legitimately considered the beginning of a new era, it is because the next generation at the University of Paris continued his work and propounded his theses. The chief representative of this spirit is a Scots theologian, John Major (1470–1550), professor of theology from 1505 to 1550 at the Sorbonne, Glasgow, and St. Andrews. Tagged a nominalist like his predecessor, he treated questions of marital ethics with the rationalism of Le Maistre. Between Alexander of Hales and Richard Middleton in the thirteenth century and some American theologians today, Major is one of the rare English-speaking theologians to make a substantial contribution to the theological discussion of marriage.[6]

[4] Desiderius Erasmus, *Christiani matrimonii institutio, in Opera omnia,* ed. Jean Le Clerc (Leyden, 1703–1706), V, 617. Written in 1526, the work was unluckily dedicated to Catherine of Aragon, queen of England.

[5] *R. Gaguini epistolae et orationes,* ed. L. Thuasne (Paris, 1903), I, 399, n. 5.

[6] John Major (Mayor, Mair) was born in Cleghornie, Scotland, of a poor family. He studied at Haddington and then went on to study for a year, 1492–93, at God's House (later Christ's College), Cambridge. The next year he entered the College of Sainte-Barbe at Paris, and received his licentiate in 1494 and master of arts in 1496. He moved on to the College of Montaigu, where Erasmus was a fellow pupil. He then taught logic at the College of Navarre. In 1505 he received the doctorate in theology. His commentary on the Fourth Book of the *Sentences* was published in 1509, when he had become a professor of theology at the Sorbonne. Rabelais satirizes his scholasticism in *Pantagruel,* c. 6, with a book title "Major on the Way of Making Puddings."

In 1518 Major returned to Scotland as regent and professor of theology at the University of Glasgow, canon of the chapel royal at Stirling, and vicar of Dunlop. John Knox was here his pupil. When Major's friend, James Beaton, became archbishop of St. Andrews in 1523, Major transferred to the College of St. Salvator at St. Andrews. In 1525, with Beaton in disgrace, Major returned to Paris for six years. Wolsey offered him a professorship at his college at Oxford, but Major preferred Paris. He returned to St. Andrews in 1531, and in 1534 became Provost of St. Salvator. John Knox refers to him at this time as "holden as an oracle in matters of religion," and tells of an incident in which he defended the right of a friar to preach against the licentious lives of the bishops. See Aeneas J. G. Mackay, "Life of the Author," in John Major, *A History of Greater Britain, As Well England As Scotland,* trans. Archibald Constable, Publications of the Scottish History Society, 10 (Edinburgh, 1892), pp. xix, xxxiii–xxxvii, lix, lxii, lxvi–lxxii, xcv, cvi.

For a somewhat critical account of Major's doctrine on marriage, see also L. Vreecke, C.SS.R., "Mariage et sexualité au declin du moyen âge," *La Vie spirituelle* 14, Supplement (1961), 199, 200, 220–224. On Major as "a figure of the greatest importance" for the Reformation in Scotland, see John Durkan, "The Cultural

In his commentary on the *Sentences,* Major puts the question, "When is it lawful to know one's wife?" He notes, "Here I find great variety among the doctors, and men, in my opinion, far too rigid." It is no sin at all to have intercourse in order to avoid falling into fornication. It would be entirely proper to have intercourse for the sake of one's own or one's wife's health. Aristotle in book 7 of the *Nicomachean Ethics* suggests such action, and nothing in the Bible is contrary. Finally, "Whatever men say, it is difficult to prove that a man sins in knowing his own wife for the sake of having pleasure" (*On the Sentences* 4.31).

From Major's "whatever men say," it may be inferred that Le Maistre's revolutionary thesis had had opposition at Paris. Major meets the opposition with Le Maistre's blend of Aristotelianism and respect for the average Christian couple. Marriage, as Aristotle teaches in the *Ethics,* is not only to produce offspring, "but to provide consolation and other mutual services." Like St. Thomas, Major holds that God put pleasure in intercourse to stimulate the act, but, unlike St. Thomas, Major gives this doctrine full value. It is no more a sin to copulate for pleasure than "to eat a handsome apple for the pleasure of it." Moreover, to take the opposite view is "to convict many married people (as I guess) of sin." What of the sayings of the saints on this point? They must be restrictively interpreted, "lest we damn all spouses." The saints spoke as they did, not because copulation is in itself evil, but because of the propensity it may set up. Some ancient authority is treated even more sharply. Rejecting Augustine's opinion on the venial sinfulness of coition to avoid fornication, Major says that the saints "must be interpreted narrowly where they speak extremely." The old twelfth-century view of Huguccio that all coition involves venial sin is characterized as "most absurd." Yet, self-confident as he is, Major advises restraint in preaching his opinion. Not everything is to be declared "to the crowd." The use of his doctrine will be in hearing confession and giving private counsel (*ibid.* 4.31.1).[7]

The change is not only from Stoic and Augustinian doctrine but from Stoic and Augustinian method. The favorite Stoic comparison with

---

Background in Sixteenth-Century Scotland," in *Essays on the Scottish Reformation, 1513–1625,* ed. David McRoberts (Glasgow, 1962), pp. 281–284.

The work of Major used here is *In quartum Sententiarum* (Paris, 1519).

[7] The influence of Le Maistre and Major may be observed on a pupil of Major, Jacques Almain (1480–1515), who died too young to make a great reputation. Almain had studied at the College of Navarre and in 1511 received the doctorate in theology at Paris. In the spirit of Le Maistre and Major, he observes, "To say that every one seeking intercourse in order to be pleased commits sin seems hard." Temperance is the mean, and sin lies only in excess. "Augustine and others" said there was venial sin in intercourse for pleasure, for excess and "vehemence of affection" frequently occurs. But there is no sin if the mean is kept. *Aurea opuscula omnibus theologis perquam utilia* (Paris, n.d.), "Commentaries on matrimony" 26.1, quoted by Heinrich Klomps, *Ehemoral und Jansenismus* (Cologne, 1964), p. 57.

animals is rejected. Animals may not copulate in pregnancy. But "various animals have various appetites." You prove nothing about women from other animals (*ibid.* 4.31.1). Nor do the logical implications of theological premises provide a touchstone. The key is the experience of Christian couples. When Augustine found in his Christian acquaintance not a single couple who had intercourse only for procreation, he was not in the least deterred from stamping all nonprocreative purpose as sinful. In the different Christian community of fifteenth-century France — much more established in its traditions than that of fifth-century North Africa, and innocent of advocates of Manicheanism — a different approach is valued. On another subject of much importance to the laity, usury, Christian moralists were beginning to look to the custom and practice of good Christian merchants in determining whether a particular contract was sinful.[8] Similarly Le Maistre and Major invoke the experience of Christian married folk to determine workable rules for intercourse, and urge the perils of negative reaction that an unrealistic harshness may engender.

ACCEPTANCE OF THE NEW THEORY

The theory launched by Le Maistre and Major contained elements which later writers, in obedience to the force of traditional treatments, were to take up separately. Doctrine on intercourse to avoid fornication has a different history from that on intercourse for pleasure; these histories will be separately traced.

NONPROCREATIVE PURPOSE

The thesis that the nonprocreative use of marriage is lawful to avoid fornication, already defended by a strong minority of medieval theologians, now became dominant. Some caution was evident in the first part of the century. One of the last of the summists, the Italian Dominican, Sylvester da Prierio (1460–1523), took the limited position of St. Antoninus that such use is lawful only if there is no other way of avoiding the temptation (*Summa*, at "De debito conjugali").[9] But unqualified acceptance was given by the leading moral theologian of the day, Thomas de Vio, Cardinal Cajetan (1469–1534).[10] The most penetrating of moral-

---

[8] See my *Scholastic Analysis of Usury* (Cambridge, Mass., 1957), pp. 199–201, 312–315.

[9] Sylvester da Prierio, *Summa summarum quae Sylvestrina dicitur* (Bologna, 1540). On Sylvester (also known as Sylvester Mazolini or Sylvester Prierias) see M. M. Gorce, "Mazolini, Silvestre," in *DTC* 10¹:474–477.

[10] Cajetan, *Summula peccatorum* (Lyons, 1538). Cajetan had entered the Dominican order at sixteen, studied at Padua, and in 1494 became professor of metaphysics there. In 1500 he became procurator general of the order and moved to Rome. In 1507 he was elected general of the order, and in 1517 he was made a cardinal. He was the adviser of four popes, Julian II, Leo X, Adrian VI, Clement VIII. See P. Mandonnet, "Cajétan," *DTC* 2²:1313.

ists taking St. Thomas as a master, the preeminent theologian of the Church on the eve of the Reformation, this Dominican cardinal adopted the non-Augustinian view with surprising ease in a work directed to confessors (*Little Summa of Sins*, at "Matrimonii peccatum"). In the next generation, the astute Spanish Dominican, Dominic Soto (1494–1560), admitted that the contrary opinion was still "sufficiently probable," but for himself took the non-Augustinian view. With an implicit evocation of Major's appeal to Christian custom, he criticized his opponents who were "accustomed to restrict and restrain the conjugal bed too narrowly" (*On the Sentences* 4.31.1.4).[11] With these three important Dominicans defending the principle, acceptance was won among the theological leaders.

The extent of the shift from Augustinianism in the course of the sixteenth century may be measured in the formulations of a document significant for its authorship, authority, and wide distribution: the Roman Catechism of 1566. The Roman Catechism was one of the major Tridentine efforts to strengthen the Catholic Church. At the direction of the Council of Trent it had been prepared under St. Pius V. Its drafting had been the work of a committee chiefly composed of Dominicans under the presidency of St. Charles Borromeo, the extraordinarily able archbishop of Milan. The aim of the Catechism was to provide standard doctrine for the faithful. In soberly simple form it presented a careful distillation of Counter-Reformation theology.[12]

What the Roman Catechism does is to focus on the purposes of marriage, with the effect of submerging discussion of the purposes of marital intercourse:

The causes for which a man and woman ought to marry should be explained. The first of these, then, is this very partnership of diverse sexes — sought by natural instinct, and compacted in the hope of mutual help so that one aided by the other may more easily bear the discomforts of life and sustain the weakness of old age. Another is the appetite of procreation, not so much indeed that heirs of property and riches be left, but that worshippers of the true faith and religion be educated; this indeed was the chief intention of the holy patriarchs when they married as evidently appears from Holy Writ. [Tobias 6:16, 17, and 22 are quoted.] And this is the one cause why God instituted marriage in the beginning . . .

The third is one which after the Fall of the first parent was added to the other causes, when, because of the loss of justice in which man had been established, his appetite began to fight with right reason; so indeed he who is conscious of his weakness and does not wish to bear the battle of the flesh may use the remedy of marriage to avoid sins of lust. About this the Apostle thus writes, "On account of fornication each man may have his own wife, and each woman her own husband." (Roman Catechism 2.8.13 and 14)

[11] Dominic Soto, *Commentarium in quartum Sententiarum* (Salamanca, 1574).
[12] On the composition and influence of the Roman Catechism, see E. Mangenot, "Catéchisme," *DTC* 2²:1917–1918.

The causes (*causae*) of marriage are both the reasons for its establishment by God, and the reasons why a Christian should marry. The Christian should propose at least some one of them in marrying. He may also, however, be lawfully motivated to marry by riches, beauty, genealogy, the desire for heirs, or similarity of manners (2.8.14).

On marital intercourse the faithful "are to be especially taught two things": (1) "not to have intercourse for the sake of pleasure or lust"; (2) "to abstain from intercourse occasionally to pray" (2.8.33–34). By failing to reprove intercourse to avoid fornication, the Catechism tacitly abandons Augustine; and in its phrasing of the causes of marriage it speaks of "use of the remedy of marriage," a phrase almost positively endorsing intercourse to avoid fornication. The Catechism does not, however, go so far as to say that the three principal causes of marriage are all legitimate purposes of intercourse. The first cause, aid in bearing disadvantages, is left unrelated to intercourse. But the brief treatment of unlawful coital purpose invited the merging of matrimonial and coital purposes. This merger would have to be accomplished by later analysts. At the least, however, the Catechism was a document of the Church, of great authority, in which a doctrine on marital intercourse was taught without mention of the Augustinian insistence on procreative purpose.

The other great Catholic catechism of the age was the *Summa of Christian Doctrine*, completed in 1565 by St. Peter Canisius (1521–1597). This work, designed by the Dutch Jesuit who became leader of the Counter Reformation in Germany and Austria, was one of the major influences in keeping Catholicism alive in these regions. The work had four hundred editions in a hundred and fifty years; speedily translated into German, by 1615 it had been turned into a dozen other vernaculars, including Italian, French, Spanish, English, Polish, Slavic, Czech, Greek, Japanese, and Ethiopian. On marriage, the *Summa* asked, "What is marriage?" and in reply taught that the ends of marriage were "the propagation of the human race for the glory of God; close and faithful association of the spouses with each other; and, moreover, the avoidance of fornication in the weakness of this corrupted nature" (Canisius, *Summa* 4.7, "The Sacrament of Matrimony," 1).[13] There is a subtle shift of em-

---

[13] Peter Canisius, *Catechismus maior seu Summa doctrinae christianae post-tridentina*, ed. Frederich Streicher, S.J., Societatis Jesu Selecti Scriptores, 1 (Rome, 1933). On the influence of the Catechism of Canisius, and its translations, see X. Le Bachelet, "Canisius," *DTC* 2²:1526. The *Smaller Catechism* (*Catechismus minor seu Parvus catechismus catholicorum*) prepared by Canisius in 1559 answers the question "Lastly, what is marriage?" as follows: "The sacrament by which a man and woman, lawfully contracting, enter undivided association of life and are given divine grace, both to receive offspring decently and in a Christian way and educate them, and to avoid sin of foul lust and incontinence" (4.80). The *Smallest Catechism* (*Summa doctrinae christianae per quaestiones tradita et ad captum rudiorum accommodata*), prepared by Canisius in 1556, says of matrimony: "This is rightly

phasis from medieval theology here, where procreation is said to be
"for the glory of God," rather than being treated as a rationalization of
intercourse. Nothing is said on the purposes of intercourse taken as distinct from the purposes of marriage.

The decline of Augustinian pessimism in the later sixteenth century
was related to the broader sixteenth-century controversies concerning
grace, original sin, and concupiscence. The doctrinal development which
occurred in this area, like many other doctrinal developments, is most
easily understood as a reaction, a hardening and clarifying of orthodox
positions in opposition to positions identified as heretical. According to
the Catholic theologians' understanding of Martin Luther and John Calvin, the Protestants used Augustine to support an exaggerated view of the
power of concupiscence and man's depravity after the Fall. In reaction
to these declared opponents of the Roman Church, the Catholic theologians limited the importance of Augustine and relied more on the
rationalism running through St. Thomas. The tight Augustinian synthesis
of doctrine on sexual acts, concupiscence, and original sin was weakened.[14]

An instructive example of this process is provided by the work of Robert
Bellarmine (1542–1611). Bellarmine, a Roman cardinal and the most influential Jesuit theologian of his age, directed the greater part of his
theological writings against the Protestant positions as they appeared to
Catholic critics. The common error of Lutherans and Calvinists, Bellarmine maintains, is to assert that "the corruption of nature or concupiscence which remains in man after justification is truly and properly
a sin from its nature, although not imputed to believers." Thus Luther
contends that "the unavoidable lust of holy parents when they generate
is sin." The correct, orthodox view is that concupiscence or lust is, materially, original sin, but not formally. In one who is cured by justifying
grace, as in baptism, there is concupiscence; but it is a defect, not a sin
(*Controversy on the Loss of Grace* 5.5, 5.8).[15]

In this definition of Bellarmine there is nothing different from Aquinas'
interpretation of Augustine. But St. Robert has a different attitude to St.
Augustine from St. Thomas'. Augustine, he observes, never satisfied
himself on how original sin was transmitted. "Nothing," he quotes Augustine as saying, "more obvious to preach, nothing more hidden to understand." The suggestion present in Augustine that lust transmits original

---

spoken of as a sacrament among Christian spouses and it is assuredly stable and indissoluble throughout life; for it contributes partly to the propagation of the Christian
race, partly to the avoidance of human incontinence" (4.39).

[14] On the Catholic reaction to Calvin and Luther on original sin, see A. Gaudet,
"Péché originel," *DTC* 12[1]:511–523.

[15] Robert Bellarmine, *Controversiarum de amissione gratiae et statu peccati libri sex,*
in *Opera omnia,* ed. Justin Fèvre (Paris, 1873), vol. IV.

sin cannot be taken literally. Nothing fleshly can infect the soul. The correct understanding of the traditional doctrine is that we all sinned in Adam because we all were "in his loins." The transmission of sin occurs only because we are descendants of Adam. Nothing more need be supposed (*Controversy on the Loss of Grace* 4.12). This clear separation of concupiscence from the transmission of original sin marks a development of doctrine.

What has been described in contemporary theological terms as a "moderate optimism" about human nature was propagated by Bellarmine and many of the influential Jesuit moralists who followed him in the seventeenth century. Although Augustine remained an authority, the new approach emphasized that the Fall consisted essentially in the deprivation of original justice and sanctifying grace, but that it did not result in an impairment of any essential constituent of human nature; that disordered concupiscence was an effect of original sin, but that man's sexual tendencies were in themselves natural and good; that original sin was transmitted by generation, but that it was not transmitted specifically by sexual lust or sexual concupiscence. All of these positions could be found in Aquinas and arguably supported by texts from Augustine. But the ensemble, in emphasis and orientation, was anti-Augustinian.[16]

It is not at once evident why shifts in emphasis on matters of a highly speculative character should have as much effect upon more practical matters as shifts in the doctrine on original sin and concupiscence have had on the teaching on marital intercourse. After all, it might be observed, if original sin was transmitted by generation, as all orthodox theologians maintained, did it make any difference if one added that it was transmitted by sexual lust? If, as all agreed, some disorder attached to concupiscence after the Fall, was there any very great difference between identifying this disorder with original sin and calling it a "consequence" of original sin? Questions of this kind do not recognize the fascination that the doctrine on original sin has held for professional theologians, and the extent to which attitudes toward sexuality have crystallized in it. For over a thousand years the Augustinian emphasis on the role of concupiscence in the transmission of original sin and the effect of original sin in making man concupiscent had colored the entire discussion of sexual purpose. When the Augustinian burden was lightened, a different atmosphere and attitude were possible.

The reaction from Augustine produced its own reaction toward Augustine within the Church. This counter movement crystallized in Jansenism. At a doctrinal level, Jansenism was incarnated in 1641 in the posthumous *Augustinus* of Cornelius Jansen (1585–1638), Louvain professor and bishop of Ypres. At this level, it may, perhaps, be understood as Augustine

---

[16] A. Gaudel, "Péché originel," *DTC* 12[1]:541–546.

transported from the fifth century to the seventeenth and restored without allowance for the growth that had occurred in the Church. With the condemnation as heretical, by Innocent X in 1653, of five propositions on grace and redemption taken from *Augustinus,* the theological status of Jansenism was substantially impaired.

Jansenism, however, was not merely a doctrine on grace. As a movement, it represented tones, tempers, attitudes, more than dogma. Jansenism in this loose sense stood for the expression of rigorous views, especially on sexual matters, by many who were in no way disciples of Jansen. At their best, those labeled Jansenists were pious French and Belgian Catholics objecting to an intolerable laxity in moral theory and behavior. At their worst, they had the self-righteousness of Pharisees and the priggish scrupulosity of Puritans. Opposed to relaxation in traditional morality, they were "hards." "The hards were not all Jansenists, but all the Jansenists were hards." [17] As militantly orthodox a theologian as Bishop Bossuet was a "hard," championing a dominantly Augustinian view of concupiscence. The hard line on sexual matters was taken by the majority of the French theologians well into the nineteenth century.

The "hards" insisted on the Augustinian tie between sexual acts, concupiscence, and original sin. They insisted on the sinfulness of initiating intercourse with any purpose other than procreation. These are the positions of the dominant theologians at Louvain and at Douai. At Louvain the rigorists were led by John Sinnigh (1603–1666), an Irishman from Cork, who was professor of theology at the Grand Collège du Saint Esprit from 1637 to 1666 and rector of the university in 1643 and 1660.[18] Sinnigh was an ardent, ascetic Christian, sometimes referred to as "the virgin doctor," a man of simple tastes and life, utterly devoted to the study of theological tradition.[19] In exile from his troubled homeland, his loyalties were to the university, the Holy See, the Church. He was no follower of Jansen, no doctrinaire enemy of Jesuits. But he was the relentless foe of "laxists," whom he accused of making a travesty of the Ten Commandments.[20]

The chosen opponent of Sinnigh was John Caramuel y Lobkowicz,

[17] Quoted in Paul Broutin, S.J., *La Réforme pastorale en France au 17ᵉ siècle* (Paris, 1955), II, 538. In the seventeenth century, a Benedictine cardinal, José Saenz de Aguirre, put it still another way. He said there were three types of Jansenists: (1) those who supported the five condemned propositions from *Augustinus;* (2) those who were for severe moral rules; (3) those who opposed the Jesuits. The first were few, the second many, the third infinite. (Quoted in Klomps, *Ehemoral und Jansenismus,* p. 131.)

[18] "Sinnigh" in the Irish spelling becomes "Shinnick" in Anglicized form and "Sinnichius" in Latin. His moral theology is the subject of Francis Deininger, O.S.B., *Joannes Sinnich: Der Kampf der Löwener Universität gegen den Laxismus,* Abhandlungen aus Ethik und Moral, ed. Fritz Tillmann, vol. 8 (Düsseldorf, 1928).

[19] Deininger, *Joannes Sinnich,* pp. 66–69.

[20] *Ibid.,* pp. 281, 388.

whom he had known at Louvain. Caramuel (1606–1682) had been a child prodigy in mathematics in Madrid, a Cistercian monk, a doctor of theology at Louvain, the suffragan of Mainz, the vicar-general of Prague, a bishop in Naples, and finally bishop of Vivegano in Spain. He was an intellectual — "I exercise my brain fourteen hours a day" — a cosmopolite, an extraordinarily complex, many-sided humanist.[21] Caramuel divided moralists into "Thomists" who said acts were sins because they were evil and "Scotists" who said acts were sins because forbidden by God. Making this rather mechanical interpretation of the ancient schools, Caramuel tended to favor the Scotists, with the result that he made most moral rules look like arbitrary, if divine, prohibitions. In accordance with the view of the Scotists, ejaculation outside of marital coitus was a sin only because God had forbidden it. The Thomists said that an autoerotic act was "an enormous sin." But how was it distinguished from intercourse with a woman who was pregnant or old, "in which generation is equally prevented"? Caramuel implied that the only difference was that God prohibited one act and not the other (*Fundamental Moral Theology* 2.57.3).[22] The form of the old sexual law was kept in this analysis, but it seemed emptied of purpose, dangerously open to the evasions and subterfuges which a purposeless, arbitrary law invites. Against the "new morality" in this and other areas Sinnigh reacted. His firm rejection of any departure from Augustine on procreative purpose must be understood as part of his total rejection of the teaching of "the prince of laxists." [23]

Augustinian rigorism also appeared in representative leaders of the theological faculty at Douai: William Estius (d. 1663), in a commentary on the *Sentences* 4.31.7 and 8; Francis Sylvius (d. 1649), in his *Commentary on Question 49 of the Supplement to the Summa Theologica of St. Thomas;* and the Carmelite, Henry de St. Ignace (1630–1719).[24] The hard line, permitting only intercourse with a procreative purpose, was similarly taken by a number of French and Belgian theologians who had much influence on the diocesan seminaries. Among them were Laurence Neesen (1612–1679), who taught at the seminary of Malines; Louis Hubert (1633–1718), a teacher at the Verdun seminary; Francis Genet (1640–1703), the bishop of Vaisson; and Natale Alexander (1639–1724), a Dominican who was a prominent member of the Paris faculty of

---

[21] V. Oblet, "Caramuel y Lobkovitz," *DTC* 2²:1709–1712.

[22] Caramuel, *Theologiae moralis fundamentalis libri* (Lyons, 1675). Caramuel does make a show of defending the Thomistic position by saying that a pregnant woman could conceive again (*superfoetari*) and that an old woman sometimes conceives. But he does not seem to take these reasons seriously. On the other hand, he does accept and develop the Thomistic objections to fornication (*ibid.* 2.56.2).

[23] Deininger, *Joannes Sinnich*, pp. 229–230.

[24] Estius and Sylvius are quoted in Dominikus Lindner, *Der Usus matrimonii* (Munich, 1929), p. 173. Henri de St. Ignace is analyzed by Klomps, *Ehemoral und Jansenismus*, p. 183.

theology. These writers invoked St. Augustine, St. Thomas Aquinas, St. Jerome, and Clement of Alexandria to demonstrate that the tradition was clear that procreative purpose alone was without sin.[25]

Any author who valued the teaching of St. Augustine and St. Thomas more highly than the practices and values of his Christian contemporaries would have taken this position. A striking instance is furnished by Charles Billuart (1685–1757). Born in the diocese of Liège, he joined the Dominicans at sixteen, and eventually became a teacher at Douai. Three times he was elected provincial of the Dominicans. He combined a reverence for St. Thomas with the rigorism characteristic of Belgian moral theologians of the seventeenth century. In his magnum opus, *The Summa of St. Thomas Accommodated to Contemporary Academic Customs,* he strenuously argued that the only lawful purpose in initiating intercourse was a procreative purpose (*Summa,* "The Goods and Acts of Marriage," 2.2).[26] To the objection that the Church permitted the old and the sterile to marry, Billuart replied that they could marry "intending to live chastely or using marriage by only returning but not demanding the debt" (reply to obj. 5). Since these persons might commit greater sins if they were not married, it was better "to dissimulate" the truth that they will probably commit sin in marriage. "Even their confessors" must practice this dissimulation. To the objection that his position made marriage for anyone a continual occasion for venial sins, a result which was "hard, odious, and in some fashion absurd, according to common practice," Billuart replied, "I know this is true, not indeed precisely by reason of the state of matrimony, but from the corruption of men." An Augustine *redivivus,* a "hard" who would not adjust principle to human behavior, Billuart is a classic specimen of a theologian drawing his moral theology from ancient books.

The French and Belgian clergy were thus largely under the influence of Augustinian rigorism. This influence extended to the English-speaking Catholic world. The Irish had ecclesiastical colleges on the Continent at Santiago de Compostela, Seville, Rome, and Rouen, but the chief centers were at Douai and Louvain. Between 1560 and the French Revolution, Douai and Louvain were the principal places for the instruction of English-speaking priests.[27]

The rigorists waged ecclesiastical war upon the laxists. However, when efforts were made by Louvain to obtain Roman condemnation of a large number of laxist propositions, apparently a proposition on the lawfulness of intercourse to avoid fornication was not among them. In any event,

[25] All of these authors are analyzed by Klomps, *Ehemoral und Jansenismus,* pp. 172–179.
[26] Charles Billuart, *Summa Sancti Thomae hodiernis academiarum moribus accommodata* (Paris, 1827–1831), vol. VII.
[27] Deininger, *Joannes Sinnich,* p. 64.

when, in response to the Louvain efforts, Innocent XI in 1679 condemned sixty-five laxist propositions, this proposition was not included.[28]

The future did not belong to Augustine and Billuart. The approach that was to win acceptance was that of St. Alphonsus Liguori (1697–1787), who was to become in the nineteenth century the most influential single authority on moral theology in the Catholic Church. Liguori, who studied to be a priest only after having been a successful lawyer, was a confessor of great reputation, a zealous missionary to the Italian poor, bishop of the small diocese of St. Agatha, and the founder of the Redemptorist order. In moral theology he was not an innovator like Le Maistre, but he boldly defended opinions he had read which seemed sound to him. He commanded the seventeenth-century literature of moral controversy, reviewing the authorities and arguments with enormous skill. Modest, practical, free from eccentric bias in favor of a single school, he regularly gave his own reasoned choice among the conflicting solutions with discernment and judgment. A man of zealous piety himself, he seemed always afraid of imposing demanding standards on others; no doubt temperament and observation here reinforced each other. Extremely aware that for a theologian to say an act was a mortal sin was to say that the act, unrepented, would result in eternal damnation, he was cautious in what he found to be mortal. In matters involving financial sins such as usury, he was lenient. In sins involving marriage he inclined toward leniency. Liguori was not acclaimed as an indisputable authority in his own day. In reading him, we read what the established doctrine of the nineteenth century was to be, rather than what was accepted by all his contemporaries. But in his sure and balanced summaries of opinion we can see what carried weight with an acute and conscientious master of moral doctrine in the middle of the eighteenth century.

In Liguori the decline of the old Augustinian position on nonprocreative intercourse is evident. As he customarily did in his *Moral Theology*, he used as his text the seventeenth-century German Jesuit, Herman Busenbaum (1600–1668), and he quoted Busenbaum's opinion that there is no sin in intercourse "to avoid danger of incontinence in oneself or one's partner" (*Moral Theology* 6, "Marriage," 927).[29] For his own position, he then gave a cross-reference to his treatment of the purposes of marriage; and ever since 1 Corinthians 7 it had been established that one

---

[28] The Louvain theologians Francis van Vianen, Martin Steyart, and Christian Lupus were sent by Louvain to obtain the condemnation from the Pope. On the affair, see *ibid.*, pp. 53–60; cf. Ludwig Pastor, *History of the Popes from the Close of the Middle Ages, 1305–1799*, trans. E. Graf (St. Louis, 1940), XXXII, 431–432; E. Preclin and E. Jarry, *Les Luttes politiques et doctrinales aux 17ᵉ et 18ᵉ siècles*, in *L'Histoire de l'église*, ed. A. Fliche and V. Martin (Paris, 1955), XIX, 208.

[29] Liguori, *Theologia moralis*, in *Opera moralia*, ed. Gaudé (Rome, 1905–1912). The *Moral Theology* was published in 1748. Revised and augmented, it was republished, in the form here used, in 1753–1755.

of the purposes of marriage was to provide an outlet for sexual impulse. If the purposes of intercourse were merged with the purposes of marriage, the controversy over the lawfulness of seeking intercourse to avoid fornication was terminated by the authority of St. Paul. In effecting this merger, Liguori expanded the approach of the Roman Catechism. He did so without argument or analysis of the old doctrine. But, familiar as he was with past theory in moral theology, Liguori must have decided to orient the long controversy over the purposes of intercourse toward solution. He did so by identifying the purposes of intercourse with the purposes of marriage.

INTERCOURSE FOR PLEASURE, HEALTH, OR LOVE

What of the more radical element in the approach of Le Maistre and Major, the contention that the purposes of intercourse need not be confined to the Augustinian purpose of procreation or the Pauline purpose of avoiding fornication? Their thesis was expressed in the proposition that health or pleasure might be the object of intercourse. This position had no respectable patristic or medieval patrons. It was put forward as a teaching of reason alone, with some citation of Aristotle to support it. It met, for a century, with general hostility. Most of the discussion centered upon intercourse for "pleasure," as "pleasure" was the category in which both health and love were buried. Love as such was not a value related by anyone to intercourse, implicit though a recognition of love might be in an appeal to the experience of Christian couples.

The first important moralist to comment on the new approach was Cajetan, and he committed himself to the position of St. Thomas that pleasure by its very nature could not be a moral objective; pleasure followed action, and the morality of the action had to be what was measured. This principle was invoked by Cajetan where its purport was to show that a sexual act cannot be proved bad by showing the pleasure to be evil (*On the Summa theologica of St. Thomas Aquinas* 2–2.154.12.14). Cajetan appears to have believed equally that an act cannot be shown to be good by showing that good pleasure attaches to it. At least, he crisply and flatly stamps intercourse for pleasure as venially sinful (*Little Summa of Sins*, at "Matrimonii peccatum").

Soto took a similar stand. Citing Aristotle, he refused to admit that pleasure could be an independent end. To eat for pleasure was an "otiose act" and therefore venially sinful; to have intercourse for pleasure was equally purposeless and therefore sinful, all the more so as intercourse perturbed the reason more than eating. A virtuous act was an act pleasing God and meriting eternal life, but it did not seem that intercourse could be such a meritorious act. That intercourse could be a means to physical or mental health was not considered. Major was mentioned by name as the sole supporter of intercourse for pleasure. To follow Major and contemn St. Augustine and "all theologians," Soto concluded, "would be nothing but temerarious" (*On the Sentences* 4.31.1.3).

In 1563 the Council of Trent made one statement formulated in language which introduced a new note. In affirming the indissolubility of marriage, the Council said: "Christ himself has promised the grace which perfects that natural love. The Apostle Paul has indicated this, saying 'Husbands, love your wives as Christ loved the Church'" (Session 24, November 11, 1563, Mansi 33:150). This was the first time an ecumenical council had spoken of the role of love in marriage. The reference to love was subordinated to the main purpose of the decree. There was no connection made between love and intercourse. But the controversy with the Protestants over the indissolubility of marriage had led to a perception that between one of the Augustinian goods of marriage and love there was a basic link. Could theologians have begun to suspect that love also had connections with the other two goods of fidelity and offspring?

In his catechism, Peter Canisius quoted both 1 Corinthians 7 and Ephesians 5 in answering the question, "What is marriage?" The "close and faithful" association of the spouses, however, which he himself put as a purpose of marriage, was only a slight expansion of the traditional purpose of "fidelity" (*Summa* 4.7, "Sacrament of Marriage," 1). He said nothing on love and the purposes of intercourse. The classical position was similarly maintained by the Roman Catechism. We have already seen that the only doctrine it contained on the purpose of marital acts was that they might not lawfully be done "for pleasure or lust." It embellished this teaching by quoting the Stoic lines from Jerome, *Against Jovinian*, "Nothing is more foul than to love one's wife as if she were an adulteress" (2.8.33). There was no suggestion that coitus might also be a way of showing matrimonial love. Teaching "what fidelity in marriage is," the Catechism declared that fidelity meant to love one's spouse as Christ loved the Church, seeking nothing for oneself (2.8.24). It stressed the appropriateness of marriage as the symbol of the love of Christ for the Church, because "husband and wife are bound by the very greatest mutual charity and benevolence" (2.8.15). But despite the substantial importance the Catechism accorded the teaching on marital love of Ephesians, it made no effort to connect the exigencies of love with embodiment in physical acts.

Without a shred of support in earlier theological authorities, Le Maistre's and Major's theses had run against the traditionalism of the theologians and seemed to fail. Augustinianism was weakened, but the only two acceptable purposes for initiating intercourse were procreation and avoidance of fornication. As long as there were only these two lawful categories, and the unlawful category of intercourse for pleasure, no exploration of personal values, no valuation of love in intercourse, was possible.

The anti-Augustinian approach appeared, in new guise, at the beginning of the seventeenth century. Its most skillful expositor was Thomas Sanchez.[30] Sanchez (1550–1610) was one of the new breed of post-Tridentine moralists, mostly Jesuits, who brought to moral theology a new precision, a new subtlety, and a greater rationality. Of these writers, Sanchez was the preeminent authority on marriage. Most moral theologians have been generalists; even St. Augustine and St. Albert treated marriage only as one of a multitude of topics. Le Maistre specialized in the four cardinal virtues. Sanchez was a specialist on marriage. His work *The Holy Sacrament of Matrimony,* published in 1602, was the most comprehensive treatment yet given to all the moral and canonical aspects of marriage.

The Jesuit moralists of this era have had their critics. Pascal, in his famous polemic for the Jansenists, observed of the Jesuit writers on sexual ethics: "Our fathers are more reserved on the subject of chastity. But it is not that they do not treat some rather curious questions rather indulgently, especially for the married or the engaged. I have found on this topic the most extraordinary questions one can imagine. It gave me something to fill several letters; but as you let all kinds of people see my letters, I don't even want to note the citations" (*Provincial Letters* 9).[31]

Sanchez was a writer of the sort Pascal had in mind. *The Holy Sacrament of Matrimony* was not a guide to the most Christian way of life in marriage. Moral theology in the vein of Bishop Burchard, or St. Raymond, or Sanchez, does not set out desirable aspirations; it provides minima of conduct for the instruction of the confessor judging sins. Requirements, designed to establish the very least a Christian can be bound to, are being set. To a conscientious and subtle spirit, analysis, distinction, and nice discrimination appear an indispensable part of his work. Such work will lead to casuistry. But cases, as any student of the common law will testify, are an excellent way of testing principles. Not too many cases, but too few, have been the bane of moral theology. Almost inevitably, in the realm of sexual morality, however, the multiplication of cases leads to "the curious," if this epithet is appropriate for any manifestation of human

---

[30] On Sanchez see *Bibliothèque de la compagnie de Jesus,* ed. C. Sommervogel (Brussels, 1890–1909), VII, 530; Hugo Hurter, *Nomenclator litterarius recentioris theologiae catholicae* (Innsbruck, 1903–1913), I, 414; Felix Trösch, "Das *Bonum prolis* als Eheziel bei Thomas Sanchez S.J. und Basilius Ponce de Leon O.E.S.A.," *Zeitschrift für katholische Theologie* 77 (1955), 1.

[31] Blaise Pascal, *Les Lettres provinciales,* in *Oeuvres complètes,* ed. Fortunat Strowski, vol. II (Paris, 1926). Pascal cites Sanchez by name in Letters 5, 7, 8, 9, but all the references are to Sanchez's *Opus morale in praecepta Decalogi* (Madrid, 1613), not to his teaching on marriage.

behavior. As well ask a textbook in biology to omit reference to the reproductive organs as ask for an examination of sexual morality where a priori notions exclude the "curious."

Sanchez himself entered the Jesuit novitiate at seventeen. His entire life was devoted to the academic and spiritual training of others and to his writing. His personal conduct was marked by asceticism. He knew of the problems of conjugal life only from the numerous people who came to consult him. He approached his subject with this limitation in experience, and with disciplined aloofness. He pursued the hypothetical possibilities so dispassionately, astutely, abstractly, that it is easy to believe that men and women of flesh and blood were not in his mind. Yet, however abstractly, with erudition and exact discrimination he tested the principles of scholastic sexual morality.

On the specific question of purpose in marital intercourse, Sanchez takes this position: if one is in the state of grace and does not intend an evil end, one virtually, although not explicitly, refers what one does to God. A married person in this state of mind seeking intercourse acts virtuously. There is, then, no need to fit the intention of married persons in coitus to one of the categories of purpose. There is no sin in spouses who intend "only to copulate as spouses" (*The Holy Sacrament of Matrimony* 9.8).[32]

This approach eliminated the requirement of procreative purpose or even of a purpose to avoid fornication. The gain was in theory, for the theologians' categories had probably never been effectively communicated to the laity. But to bring theory to a more reasonable approximation of the mental state of an ordinary decent couple was to banish the whole Augustinian analysis. What Sanchez does is to apply to a new degree the methodology of Le Maistre and Major: the touchstone of marital morality is the experience of the Christian couple seeking to love God. Such a couple seek intercourse because they are married. If they are in a state of grace, and enter into intercourse considered to be natural, they do well. Their virtual intention is sufficient.

There is a qualification: "Is conjugal use for pleasure alone a sin?" Sanchez asks, and he answers that such intercourse would be "a perversion of order"; that is, pleasure, which is a consequence of an act, would be treated as an end. The sin would be venial (*ibid.* 9.11). The key word in this question is "alone." The question deals with a hypothetical state of mind in which other ends are excluded. It deals with an abstraction. The couple seeking, by a virtual intention, to serve God while exercising their marital rights are not seeking "pleasure alone."

Sanchez' approach to intercourse did not give a positive value to love. He introduces such a value in an analysis of the morality of acts short of

[32] Sanchez, *De sancto matrimonii sacramento* (Venice, 1737).

coitus. He asks if married persons may indulge in "embraces, kisses, and other touchings customary among spouses to show and to foster mutual love," even though there is a foreseen risk of ejaculation. He exclaims: "How many teachers have I seen asserting it to be mortal among those for whom there is risk of pollution" (*ibid* 9.45.33). He names the authorities against him, who include the more liberal as well as the more conservative theologians of the past; among them are Palude, *On the Sentences* 4.31. 3.2.17; St. Antoninus, *Summa theologica* 3.1.20; Angelus, *Summa*, at "Debitum," 26; Sylvester, *Summa* at "Debitum," 7; Cajetan, *Little Summa*, at "Matrimonium" and at "Questions for Confessors," 6; Soto, *On the Sentences* 4.31.1.4; Navarrus, *Enchiridion* 16.42; Peter de Ledesma, *The Great Sacrament of Matrimony* 49.6. Despite this formidable array, Sanchez takes a different view.

His proof follows. To commit an act which may result in unintended semination is not always evil: so, for example, to eat, although as a result there may be unexpected seminal discharge in one's sleep. There is no dispute about this first step; little about the next one. Even if it is foreseen that semination may occur, an "urgent cause" may justify the risk: it is thus with a confessor hearing confessions of a sexual character; it is thus with a doctor performing a medical operation affecting the genital organs (*The Holy Sacrament of Matrimony* 9.45.4–5). Consequently, to defend the acts in issue, all that is necessary is to show an "urgent cause." That "urgent cause" is the need of a spouse to "show and foster mutual love" (*ibid*. 9.45.37).

As is usual when a substantial innovation is being proposed in moral theology, the new theory is hedged by qualifications. Sanchez says only that the acts would not be "mortal"; he does not speak of venial sin, although if his theory is correct there should be no sin. He says that his defense does not apply to "base" (*turpes*) acts between spouses, probably meaning acts such as anal intercourse. With qualifications he does strike at the central doctrine of past authorities who had seen amatory acts of this kind between spouses as related to coitus and who had justified them as they had justified coitus itself. His predecessors had believed "that those touches are not necessarily among those acts which show love, but that they are preparatory to immediate copulation." But "there is an urgent cause for touches of this kind to show and foster mutual love among spouses, and it would be great austerity, and love would be much diminished, if they abstained from touches of this sort" (*ibid*. 9.45.33–37). Sanchez defends the sexual contacts of spouses apart from coitus, and in doing so he proclaims love as a value.

Why does not Sanchez apply his theory to coitus itself? Why is the "showing and fostering of mutual love" not a purpose of the act of union? Sanchez does not raise such questions. Probably they would have been too bold a break from customary moral speculation. But he has advanced an approach which others will adapt, much later, to coitus.

The comprehensive approach to questions of purpose, advocated by Sanchez, did not terminate the controversy over intercourse "for pleasure." A number of lesser seventeenth-century moralists were ranged on both sides of the question. Among those defending as a "probable opinion" the lawfulness of intercourse "for pleasure" were the Augustinian friar and sometime rector of Salamanca, Basil Ponce de Leon (1570–1629); John Sanchez (d. 1624); and the Jesuits Gaspar Hurtado (d. 1647) and Martin Perez (d. 1660).[33] This opinion was held in the teeth of the Roman Catechism. Antonio Diana (1585–1663), a prominent theologian from Palermo of the new order of Theatines, pursued the path suggested by the approach of the Catechism of fusing the purposes of intercourse and the motives of marriage. The Catechism did not deny that one could marry for beauty. Some theologians would admit that one could marry for pleasure. If one can marry for pleasure, Diana reasoned, one may have intercourse for pleasure (*Moral Resolutions* 3.4.216).[34] The theologians favorable to this opinion were, for this and other approaches to moral problems, invidiously classed as laxists.

In fierce opposition were the Louvain theologians, led by Sinnigh, who classified the opinion permitting intercourse for pleasure as "brutish." All of the Douai writers who opposed any form of nonprocreative intercourse, all of the French writers for seminaries we have reviewed, opposed the teaching.[35] Henry de St. Ignace, the Douai Carmelite, taught that "every carnal pleasure, loved and sought for itself, is immoderate in respect of the end sought." The Paris Dominican Natale Alexander said, "Conjugal intercourse does not lack fault, if it is carried out partly for the sake of generation, partly for pleasure." [36]

The rigorists here waged successful war upon their opponents. The diocesan synod of Namur in 1659 condemned the opinion defending pleasure.[37] The great Louvain mission to Rome of 1677 sought its condemnation along with one hundred other laxist moral views. After a two-year wait, in which two commissions, one of cardinals and one of theologians, examined the opinions, the Holy Office under Innocent XI issued a condemnation on March 2, 1679.[38] The proposition censured ran

[33] These authors are analyzed by Lindner, *Der Usus matrimonii*, pp. 182–184. Ponce de Leon's doctrine is contrasted with that of Thomas Sanchez by Trösch, "Das *Bonum prolis*," pp. 5, 200.

[34] Diana, *Resolutiones morales* (Venice, 1640).

[35] See the authorities cited in notes 24 and 25.

[36] De St. Ignace and Alexander are quoted in Klomps, *Ehemoral und Jansenismus*, pp. 184, 179.

[37] Deininger, *Joannes Sinnich*, p. 230.

[38] *Ibid.*, p. 53. In the course of the delay there was a vigorous onslaught by the opponents of Louvain, which led in turn to an official protest by the Louvain faculty to the Spanish government then ruling the Netherlands.

as follows: "A marital act exercised for pleasure alone lacks entirely any fault and any defect." [39]

This condemnation was little more than a slap on the wrist. According to the usual rules adopted by the theologians for interpreting papal censures, if several notes of censure are attached to several propositions, only the minimal note can be predicated of any single one of the propositions. Here, there were sixty-five propositions condemned, a variety of censures globally applied to them, and the minimum note of censure was "at least scandalous and in practice dangerous." However sharp these words may sound, as words of art they were not especially severe. They characterized not the theoretical soundness of a doctrine — as the words "heretical" or "erroneous" would — but only the prudence of teaching it. Moreover, as a universal affirmative proposition was attacked by the condemnation, the strict terms of the condemnation were logically avoided, if it were taught that "some but not all" intercourse for pleasure alone had fault.

The effect of such a limited papal rebuke depended on how it was received by the theologians. Would it be interpreted as a repudiation of all purposes of intercourse outside of procreation and the avoidance of fornication, or would distinctions be noted in order to cut down the force of the teaching? Contemporary theologians took the second course. Didacus de la Fuente Hurtado (d. 1686) and Dominic Viva (d. 1726) — two Jesuit moralists, representative, if not influential — pointed out that "for pleasure alone" meant "excluding the other purposes of marriage."[40] Such a purpose was condemned; but to act "for pleasure" was not touched by the decree. The same position was taken by the more influential group of Carmelite theologians who wrote under the collective name "Salamancans" (*Course of Moral Theology* 9.3.32–33).[41] With this distinction made, the papal teaching was no different from that of Sanchez. Intercourse "for pleasure" was still theologically defensible.

In the mid-eighteenth century the controversy was still alive. Liguori included two approaches of relevance: a quotation from Busenbaum and a cross-reference to his own statement on the purposes of marriage. Busenbaum had given as permissible coital purposes "health and other extrinsic ends of a decent character" (Liguori, *Moral Theology* 6.927). This terminology was very broad, broad enough to include mental health and possibly comprehensive enough to include love. Busenbaum had, however, introduced two qualifications which seemed to run counter to each other. To seek "health only" was probably venial sin. On the other

---

[39] *Enchiridion symbolorum definitionum et declarationum de rebus fidei et morum*, ed. H. Denzinger, rev. Adolf Schonmetzer, S.J. (Barcelona, 1963), no. 2109. The proposition condemned is taken from John Sanchez, *Selectae et practicae disputationes* 23.25.

[40] Quoted in Lindner, *Der Usus matrimonii*, pp. 186–191.

[41] *Ibid.*, pp. 191–193.

hand, a positive procreative purpose was not only not necessary but "indeed may sometimes be lawfully excluded by a simple desire, for example, by a poor man lest he be burdened by too many offspring" (*ibid.*). If procreation might be positively excluded as a purpose in one's mind, but health alone might not be sought, what other purpose must accompany the purpose of health-seeking? The only other lawful purpose explicitly stated by Busenbaum was the avoidance of "the risk of incontinence." The conclusion that could be drawn was that intercourse undertaken for decent, nonprocreative ends was lawful, even with the positive wish not to have more children, provided there was a purpose of avoiding "the risk of incontinence."

Quoting Busenbaum, and apparently accepting the conclusion implicit in his presentation, Liguori also gave a cross-reference to his own exposition of the ends of marriage, as though an issue involving the ends of intercourse might be decided by examining the ends of marriage. He distinguished three kinds of end: (1) intrinsic and essential; (2) intrinsic and accidental; (3) extrinsic and accidental. There were two ends of the first kind: "the mutual giving with the obligation of returning the debt, and the indissoluble bond." Both indissolubility and the giving of a right to one's body for intercourse were intrinsic ends of marriage. The ends of the second category were the procreation of offspring and the remedying of concupiscence. The ends of the third category were several: "to conciliate feuds, to obtain pleasure, and so forth" (*Moral Theology* 6.882).

This division was framed with some attention to the marriage of Mary and Joseph. They had a valid marriage, because there were present the mutual giving of rights to the body, and indissolubility. Liguori not only noted that Mary and Joseph were validly married although ends of neither the second nor the third kind were present, but that the same conclusion held true of an "old man marrying without hope of procreating offspring nor intending remedy for concupiscence." He declared in language which, taken literally, contradicted the canon *Si conditiones*, "It is certain that if one excludes the two accidental intrinsic ends, he can sometimes contract not only validly but even lawfully" (*ibid.* 6.882). One might marry lawfully, excluding procreation and the remedying of concupiscence. In these strong terms, the challenge to the procreative theory of marriage, always present in the marriage of Mary and Joseph and in the marriage of the sterile, was particularly striking. If the ends of marriage determined the ends of intercourse, as his cross-reference suggested, the question was left unresolved why procreation could be excluded in marriage but not in intercourse.

Liguori went on to discuss marriage as a remedy for concupiscence and held marriage for this purpose to be lawful, if the spouses in contracting did not exclude the end of procreation. The conclusion showed that he was not rejecting *Si conditiones*, although he had just expressed himself in language opposed to it. He then asked if it were lawful to marry "principally for the extrinsic accidental ends such as 'obtaining pleasure.'" He concluded that it was lawful, if the intrinsic ends were not excluded, and if the extrinsic end was "decent." Decent ends were "peace, love among relatives, keeping the family honor, preserving health, and similar things." Indecent ends were "pleasure, or cupidity for riches, or vain honor." Marriage for these ends would be sinfully contracted. If this discussion of matrimonial ends is applied to intercourse, the conclusion must be drawn that intercourse principally for pleasure is sinful. Liguori reached the same conclusion in a question specially devoted to intercourse for pleasure (*ibid.* 6.912). The implication, not made explicit, was that if pleasure were sought but not "principally" or "alone," it would be lawful.

The whole discussion of the decent extrinsic ends is striking in its recognition of such reasons for marrying as "love among relatives" and its careful avoiding of "love between fiancés." At no point in this cataloguing of ends or reasons for marrying does Liguori mention what most people today would suppose was the chief motive. The only reason I can see for his avoidance of what must have been evident in some eighteenth-century matches is his sensitivity to the parallel between the ends of marriage and the ends of intercourse, and his unwillingness to make love an end of the latter. It is not, as we might be almost forced to believe, that Liguori does not have a category of "love between man and woman." In regard to "chaste touchings" between married persons, with risk of ejaculation, Liguori follows Sanchez and says that such acts are lawful provided there is "urgent need for showing signs of affection to foster mutual love" (*ibid.* 6.934). Mutual love will justify these acts, but mutual love is never mentioned as a reason for marriage or for marital coitus.

Liguori reflects a doctrine in transition and in some confusion. Augustinianism is banished. Procreation need not be a purpose of marriage; it may be mentally excluded from acts of intercourse. But pleasure is distrusted, and love unrecognized. The approach of Sanchez, trusting the decent intentions of married couples, has not yet won a dominant position. The methodological reform of Le Maistre and Major has not fully succeeded. Liguori still prefers exercises in the analysis of abstractions to consulting Christian married persons.

At this stage, part of the underpinning of the doctrine against contraception had been removed. Marital coitus was no longer viewed by the leading theologians as necessarily procreative; but no new valuation of marital intercourse had been fully developed. The teaching against contraception, deprived of part of its basis, still stood, and there was no new theological account of intercourse from which a different teaching might be worked out. Moreover, Augustinian doctrine still flourished in

France and Belgium and in the English-speaking Catholic world instructed from France and Belgium. The changes made in the three-hundred-year period between Le Maistre and Liguori were to have an impact on the doctrine on contraception. The impact, however, was to be felt only in much later developments.

VOLUNTARY LIMITATION OF PROCREATION

The desires and experiences of Christian couples had been given qualified, but not complete, recognition in the expansion of the lawful purposes of intercourse. In an analogous way the reasons of Christian couples for not wanting children received some theological acceptance.

The avoidance of intercourse by mutual consent was, of course, an old and approved ideal, but the focus of the ideal was continence, not the limitation of offspring. Palude in the fourteenth century had defended mutually agreed-upon continence for the specific purpose of avoiding more offspring than one could feed. The recognition of economic pressure in relation to decisions on childbearing was also not new. Poverty had been admitted in extenuation, but not in justification, of abortion and contraception. Poverty had justified *amplexus reservatus* by mutual agreement.

What was new in the sixteenth century was the giving of theological preference to economic pressures over that right to marital intercourse which, ever since St. Paul, had been treated as fundamental to marriage and as beyond impairment except where intercourse would endanger the health of offspring, conceived or to be conceived. Even such an innovator as Le Maistre had stated the duty flatly, noting that if a wife should refuse intercourse, "she may be compelled to render it by a judge" (*Moral Questions* II, fol. 49r). Now, in the sixteenth century, poverty and the educational welfare of the offspring were said to limit the basic right and to permit unilateral decision by a spouse as to intercourse.

The new development may have seemed implicit in Palude's position on the legitimacy of mutual continence by reason of poverty, for Sylvester da Prierio, a critic of Palude, went out of his way to deny that a desire "not to be multiplied in offspring" justified refusal of intercourse (*Summa*, at "De debito conjugali"). This negative introduction of the topic into theological debate was countered, in the next generation, by another Dominican, Soto, a theologian with a certain hardy independence. Ignoring Sylvester, Soto developed his novel thesis in three steps. First, it was mortal sin to refuse to render the marital debt. Second, mutual continence was lawful when there was "an abundance of offspring." Third, one spouse alone might refuse intercourse, when there was an abundance of offspring (*On the Sentences* 4.32.1.1). The implied basis for this opinion was the danger to existing and future offspring from an increase in the family; for the rule applied "especially when they are pressed by poverty so that they are unable to feed so many offspring." In this case, at least, refusal of intercourse was not mortal.

By linking his position to the good of offspring, Soto drew to its support the standard theory that the good of offspring was the purpose of intercourse. He still made allowance for the remedial theory of marriage: the duty of intercourse remained paramount if one's spouse was in danger of committing a sexual sin because of the enforced abstinence. The implication even remained that refusal of the debt by the desperately poor might always be venial sin. But, like most theological innovators, Soto was cautious. It was enough to have broken the ice.

The appeal of the new approach may be gauged, paradoxically, by the fact of its being ignored by Navarrus (1493–1586), for Navarrus, Soto's younger contemporary in Spain, was usually a critic of Soto's innovations. Navarrus was aware of the problem; he cited with approval Palude's solution of continence by mutual agreement when more children could not be fed. But he did not mention Soto (Navarrus, *Manual for Confessors* 16.33).[42] This is a case where failure to attack was not far from willingness to accept.

Soto's theory, however, was too much of an innovation to find a place in the catechism of Peter Canisius or in the Roman Catechism. The Roman Catechism recommended continence for the sake of prayer (2.8.34); it said nothing on continence because of poverty. Unselfishness in marriage was recommended (2.8.24), but nothing concretely related unselfishness to intercourse and procreation. The important question of when intercourse might justly be refused was not discussed. In this work destined for a wide audience, the problems of poor married folk were conspicuously avoided.

Uncriticized, but unrecognized and undeveloped, Soto's thesis was explored and expanded in 1592 by Peter de Ledesma (d. 1616). Like Sanchez, Ledesma was the fruit of that renaissance of scholasticism experienced by sixteenth-century Spain. Like Sanchez, too, he was an academic person, a man whose entire adult life was spent in teaching. His *Treatise on the Great Sacrament of Matrimony, According to the Doctrine of the Angelic Doctor in Some Questions of Additions to the Third Part of the Summa Theologica* was the most specialized treatise by a Do-

---

[42] Navarrus, *Enchiridion sive Manuale confessariorum et poenitentium*, in *Opera* (Lyons, 1589), vol. III. Navarrus (Martin Azpilcueta) was a canonist and sometime professor at Toulouse, Cahors, Salamanca, and Coimbra. He was counselor to the King of Portugal, then to Philip II of Spain. He concluded his career in Rome as the adviser of three Popes, Pius V, Gregory XIII, and Sixtus V. See Johann Friedrich von Schulte, *Die Geschichte des Quellen und Litteratur des canonischen Rechts* (Stuttgart, 1875–1880), III¹, 715. On Navarrus' criticism of Soto in regard to usury theory, see my *Scholastic Analysis of Usury*, p. 218.

minican on marriage; it is not unworthy of comparison with the slightly later work of Sanchez.[43]

Under the heading "Matters Attached to Marriage and the Rendering of the Marital Debt," Ledesma put the issue this way: "To avoid detriment in the goods of fortune, or in reputation, or in money, is a spouse excused from rendering the debt? Example: Does a multitude of children excuse, especially if poverty presses the parents?" (*The Great Sacrament of Matrimony* 64.1). He had already noted the case where danger to the fetus was a ground for refusing intercourse in pregnancy; and he had extended the principle of this standard case to one where the mother was lactating, the supposition being that her milk, if she became pregnant, would be dangerous to the suckling. There were, then, reasons based on the physical welfare of existing offspring that excused from intercourse, and these reasons held even, as in the second case, where refusal of intercourse meant postponement of procreation. Ledesma now urged the parity of these cases with a situation "where danger could be feared for the education of children already born, especially when poverty presses the couple." If physical danger to offspring was a reason for refusing, why not danger to their education? This basic argument was supplemented by an argument showing the subordination of the duty of intercourse to other concerns of life. A man might leave home on business without his wife's consent. A man (according to the decretal *Ex multa*) might become a crusader without her agreement. If a man could put business or religion above the duty of intercourse, why could he not also prefer the welfare of his children?

Having raised these questions as arguments, Ledesma concluded with a formal negative. A mere multitude of children was not itself sufficient reason for denying the marital debt. Nor was there sufficient reason if the children were "more numerous" than "is customary among couples," for the number of children which nature permits in one marriage never "exceeds the bounds of matrimony." This formal tautology, however, did not dispose of the question when circumstances were considered. If simple number was not decisive by itself, "the avoidance of notable detriment or the requiring of an outstanding advantage," in either property or reputation, justified refusal of intercourse. The kind of compensating advantage required was what "a prudent man would estimate"; the advantage was to be weighed against the length of time intercourse was denied.

Ledesma then entered into an instructive discussion of the economics

<hr />

[43] Ledesma, *Tractatus de magno matrimonii sacramento super doctrinam angelici doctoris in aliquibus quaestionibus additionum ad tertiam partem* (Venice, 1595). On Ledesma see Jacques Quetif and Jacques Echard, *Scriptores ordinis praedicatorum recensiti* (Paris, 1719–1721), II, 404; Hurter, *Nomenclator litterarius recentioris theologiae catholicae*, I, 270–271.

of intercourse. The test for lawful refusal was not capital in terms of expectable inheritance. If the capital of the parents would, on division on their death, not support one more child, they did not have reason for refusing intercourse. The test was income. Intercourse might not be refused if the couple had income sufficient "to educate the children and instruct them" (*ad liberos educandos et instituendos*). Education — undefined, but designating some kind of moral and intellectual training — was related to the proper number of children to bear. Income in relation to education was proposed as the variable controlling the suitable number. The educational welfare of the children, always incorporated in the definition of the good of offspring, had never before been thus preferred to the duty of intercourse; nor had the relation of education, income, and intercourse ever been so specifically spelled out.

A substantially similar analysis was made a few years later, in 1602, by Sanchez. Intercourse, he said, might be refused "if there is present a probable fear of danger or detriment to offspring already born," or "to avoid great detriment in goods of fortune or in reputation, or to achieve great advantage in them" (*The Holy Sacrament of Matrimony* 9.25). He made no explicit reference to education, income, or inheritances; and, like Ledesma, he left unspecified what advantages in "reputation" might be achieved by fewer children. Presumably he was thinking of persons who would not want to lessen their family status by a division of property among a number of heirs. Advantage to reputation in this way was accepted as prevailing over the Pauline duty of intercourse. The new breed of moralists did not regard a socioeconomic motive as a sin or a shame.

Sanchez further held that a wife might refuse intercourse if it were estimated as probable that "a monster would be born from such intercourse." Such a child would be "a great detriment" for the mother (*ibid.* 9.21.7). This reason was a subtle transmutation of the old objection to intercourse in menstruation. The reason was now personal to the mother. The mother, who would have to suffer the difficulties of rearing a defective child, was permitted to put her feelings ahead of the debt. That it is better to be than not to be was unmentioned, as though this principle were irrelevant to the duty of intercourse.

The significance of allowing economic, social, or personal reasons to override the duty of intercourse is evident. It was ancient doctrine that one purpose of marriage was avoidance of incontinence. The Pauline purpose had been upheld even by the Augustinian tradition, which did not excuse from sin the partner initiating intercourse, but did insist on the duty of response. The Pauline theory had been weakened by the teaching forbidding intercourse in pregnancy. But this exception in favor of the welfare of the fetus had not led to a denial of intercourse at any time when procreation might result. Now the duty of intercourse was diluted in such a way that not only the Pauline purpose of marriage but also the main Augustinian purpose was treated as lawfully subject to frustration. The "counter approaches" of the medieval theologians favored the new interpretation. But it required a wrench of traditional thought to relate these counter values to the marital debt. Earlier theologians had not discussed the question, because no earlier theologian had been temerarious enough to suppose that the education of existing offspring, the social status of the family, or the personal feelings of a mother could be a reason for repudiating the obligation enjoined by St. Paul. Because it was so new, indeed so revolutionary, the new theory, even with the support of such eminent moralists as Ledesma and Sanchez, did not have clear sailing.

In the half century following Ledesma and Sanchez, caution prevailed. Leonard Lessius (1554–1623), the Belgian Jesuit who was the most acute of moralists on usury questions, was completely silent on this important question of marital life, which had economic aspects of the kind he often handled with subtlety in his *Justice and Law and the Other Cardinal Virtues*.[44]

St. Francis de Sales (1567–1622) would have seemed to be a theologian preeminently fitted to express the values of the pious French upper classes. He was the descendant of Savoyard nobility; he had been educated to be a lawyer before he had become a priest; and he had a great ability to make friends among the laity and to empathize with them. In 1607 he began a series of essays on the life of the Christian lay person for Louise de Charmoisy, the twenty-one-year-old wife of Claude de Charmoisy. These essays were revised and combined with others composed for the widow Jane de Chantal (herself the mother of six children in eight years). They were then published in 1609 under the title *Introduction to the Devout Life*, a book, De Sales said, "addressed to people of the world, to courtiers, and others." The book was an immense success among the educated nobility and bourgeoisie. It had a specific section on "The Married State." Yet in this work, designed for the upper classes by one who knew them, not a word was said of the Ledesma-Sanchez theory. Perhaps De Sales did not know it: he complained of his bishopric, Annecy, as a place where books were hard to get. It seems, nonetheless, significant of the prevailing conservatism that nothing like the two Spanish theologians' qualifications on the duty of marital intercourse should have occurred to this perceptive and benign saint.[45]

The theory was analyzed by Paul Laymann (1574–1635), a German

---

[44] Leonard Lessius, *De justitia et jure ceterisque virtutibus cardinalibus libri quatuor* (Venice, 1616).

[45] On St. Francis de Sales see Michael de la Bedoyère, *François de Sales* (New York, 1960), pp. 118–120, 152–158. Citations are to François de Sales, *Oeuvres*, ed. Religious of the Visitation of the Monastery of Annecy (Annecy, 1843–1925).

Jesuit whose *Moral Theology*, published in 1625, was to be for a hundred and fifty years the standard work in theological faculties staffed by Jesuits in the Austrian Empire. Laymann approved the refusal of intercourse only if the family would be reduced to "extreme poverty" by another child. He would not admit the case if it would only be "difficult to feed the children" (*Moral Theology* 5.10.31.16).[46] He failed to deal at all with the question of the children's education as a value. He said, however, "It is better that the offspring be poor and alive than not alive at all." This kind of valuation had been expressed by medieval writers defending intercourse where the offspring might be physically deformed. Used by Laymann, it was an indirect rejection of Ledesma and Sanchez.

In the mid-seventeenth century, Antonio Diana reviewed the authorities, with the question posed as follows: "If there is no danger of incontinence, is it mortal sin not to render the debt in order that offspring not be multiplied?" (*Moral Resolutions* 3.4.213). He interpreted Laymann as holding such refusal mortal sin, Soto venial sin, Sanchez no sin. He did not commit himself, and thereby appeared to be willing to have his reader choose any of the three opinions as probable.

A hundred years later, in Liguori, the same question was put narrowly in terms of the right to refuse intercourse in order to avoid more offspring than one could feed. Liguori ranged Soto, Sanchez, and Ledesma as defenders of such action not only against Sylvester but also against Navarrus and Laymann, whom he rather inaccurately noted as totally opposed. Like Diana, he did not analyze the merits of the arguments, and he made no estimate of the importance to be assigned the education of existing children. Both opinions seemed to him theologically maintainable, but he preferred the negative position on the ground that there was almost always danger of incontinence. In such cases, he seemed to think, the Pauline duty prevailed (*Moral Theology* 6.941).

Liguori's narrow treatment was an anticlimax. What the history of Soto's original opinion had established was this: there were sound grounds in theory for subordinating the most fundamental of marital rights, not only to the physical but to the educational welfare of existing children. If Ledesma's broad exposition of this thesis had not been welcomed, neither had it been attacked. Neither educational nor economic motives for not wanting children had been challenged as sinful. The Soto-Ledesma-Sanchez position had been taken on the most difficult terrain, where the reasons for not wanting children were weighed against the duty of intercourse. If these reasons had weight even here, a fortiori they had weight where the marital duty was not at issue, where both

---

[46] Laymann, *Theologia moralis*, 8th ed. (Bamberg, 1699). Laymann taught moral theology and canon law at Ingolstadt, Dillingen, and the Jesuit house of studies at Munich (Schulte, *Die Geschichte des Quellen*, III[1], 133).

parties by agreement did not want children. No major theologian denied that continence, to avoid too numerous progeny, was lawful.

The possibility was not considered that, if the educational welfare of existing children might be impaired by more offspring, contraception might be practiced. The choice presented was between intercourse with the possibility of procreation and abstinence from intercourse. The development of doctrine was a limited one. Nonetheless, there was now theological opinion recognizing that economic and educational reasons were valid moral reasons for not wanting more children and for suspending the basic marital right of intercourse.

ACCEPTED MEANS OF CONTROL

Anaphrodisiacs, never questioned by the medieval theologians, were equally tolerated and unanalyzed in this later period. Francis de Sales, drawing on Pliny's allusion to the Thesmophoria in his *Natural History* 24.38.59, said that those who slept on chaste tree became "chaste and modest." He clearly believed this usage a laudable one (*Introduction to the Devout Life* 3.13). But anaphrodisiacs were never brought into a discussion of deliberate control of conception. *Amplexus reservatus* was a different matter. It had the support of several Dominican and Franciscan theologians, of whom the most authoritative was St. Antoninus, and it had been attacked by no one of prominence. It had, however, been ignored by even such liberal authorities as St. Albert and Le Maistre. By the middle of the eighteenth century, it was a method generally familiar to the moralists, condemned by some, accepted in principle by others.

The first to attack the practice was the Dominican, Sylvester da Prierio. He outlined the practice as described by Peter de Palude and simply dismissed Palude's approving opinion as "highly irrational" (*Summa*, at "De debito conjugali"). A number of lesser authors developed the attack, condemning *amplexus reservatus* on the basis that a venereal act not directed to generation was always immoral. For this reason the practice was found to be mortal sin by Bartholomew Fundo, a Dominican inquisitor (d. 1545); by the Italian Dominican, Ignatius Conradi (d. 1606); by the Spanish Jesuit John Azor (d. 1608) and the Portuguese Jesuit Henry Henriquez (d. 1608).[47] A more significant author, Lessius, was ambiguous in condemning "withdrawal before semination": it is not clear whether he meant coitus interruptus or *amplexus reservatus,* or both (*Justice and Law and the Other Cardinal Virtues* 4.3.13).

Some important authors compromised and treated the act as venial sin: in the seventeenth century, Paul Laymann (3.4.19); in the eighteenth

[47] These authorities are collected and quotations from them set out in Hyacinth M. Hering, "De 'amplexu reservato,' " *Angelicum* 28 (1951), 326–327.

century, both Billuart (*Summa* 5, "Temperance," 6.17) and St. Alphonsus (*Moral Theology* 6.918). Underlying this position seems to be not an objection to the contraceptive effect — for then the act would be condemned as mortal — but to the seeking of pleasure by this sexual means.

There was general agreement that the act was seriously unlawful if the woman was provoked "to seminate" (Cajetan, *On the Summa theologica* 2–2.154.11.10, reply 6; Sanchez, *The Holy Sacrament of Matrimony* 9.19; Liguori, *Moral Theology* 6.918). This qualification had originally been made by Palude; no more than he had done did these authors explain what they meant. The expression "female seed" is a medical, not a theological, creation. The work of the first-century Roman physician Galen entitled *Seed* was still an accepted authority in the sixteenth century.[48] Book 2, chapter 1, is devoted to "the female seed." Galen describes the female *testes* (apparently the ovaries) and says "they emit seed into the vulva." According to chapter 4, coitus would not be possible without "female seed"; moreover, female seed, which is colder and wetter than male seed, helps the latter to pass to the uterus.

Exactly what physiological process the theologians have in mind when they use the phrase "female seed" is hard to determine. They may have Galen's description in mind, or something vaguer.[49] But they are convinced that there is a female seed and that its release coincides with orgasm. They believe that there is a parallel between male ejaculation and pleasure and female ejaculation and pleasure. Cajetan, for example, speaks of the pleasure for a woman in emitting seed as an indication that nature put the pleasure there to stimulate the reproduction of the species. By the theologians "female semination" is used to designate both what they believe is the discharge and what they believe is the pleasure accompanying the discharge. As late as 1750, for instance, Liguori says of "female seed" that "according to all, it contributes greatly to the perfection of offspring . . . it is necessary, or at least very helpful, to genera-

[48] Galen, *De semine*, in *Opera*, trans. Johannes Bernardo Feliciano (Venice, 1560). Some twenty-two Latin translations of Galen were published during the sixteenth century.

[49] Some theological writers in the twentieth century have assumed that what the older writers had in mind was the discharge from the glands of Bartholin (see, e.g. Benedict Merkelbach, *Quaestiones de castitate et luxuria* 1.2.2, 5th ed., Bruges, 1944). Whether anything so specific was had in mind, or whether the theologians were merely relying on Galen, is hard to tell.

Modern writers differ as to whether orgasm should be described primarily in terms of physical movements or in terms of psychic satisfactions. Compare John W. Huffman, *Gynecology and Obstetrics* (Philadelphia, 1962), p. 230, giving a strictly medical definition, with the definition of social anthropologists such as Alfred C. Kinsey, *Sexual Behavior in the Human Female* (Philadelphia, 1953), p. 627; Clellan S. Ford and Frank A. Beach, *Patterns of Sexual Behavior* (New York, 1951), p. 282. The medieval and Renaissance writers were even less precise, and their failure to be precise contributed to their stumbling treatment of the subject.

tion." Here he is apparently talking about the discharge. He goes on to say that "nature does nothing in vain," and he seems to have in mind the stimulus to intercourse provided by orgasm (*Moral Theology* 6.918–919). The theologians thus have a double confusion. They speak of an "emission of female seed," which does not correspond to any identifiable process, and they make this emission the equivalent of orgasm.

The relevance of this double confusion is that it is for several authors the chief objection to acceptance of *amplexus reservatus*. Cajetan assumes, without argument, that the act will be lawful, unless the woman "seminates." Sanchez defends the act unless there is danger of female semination. Liguori says he believes the act is, in practice, mortal sin because of the danger of "effusion of seed," and a cross-reference to Sanchez indicates that he means female seed. Approval of the act is thus withheld on the basis of a false biology, not because of the interruption of the process of generation which the act involves.

With the reservation noted, Sanchez still must be counted a supporter of the practice. Like Palude, he adds one other qualification: that there must be "a just cause." An example of such a cause is that "the couple are poor and abound in offspring which they are not feeding," and *amplexus reservatus* will "quiet their concupiscence." It is not clear why a "just cause" is particularly required, but the qualification may not be very restrictive.

At the end of this period of development, *amplexus reservatus* has been rejected by some authors as contrary to the assumption that every genital act must have a generative end. But the main authorities — Cajetan, Sanchez, Liguori — have not accepted this point of view. Their reservations are based on a misunderstanding of feminine biology. As far as the action of the man is concerned, there is no claim by these authorities that there is something unnatural in beginning coitus and then restraining the act. Consequently, in theory, *amplexus reservatus* remained a challenge to the logic which insisted that every male genital act must be generative. In practice, there was probably enough authority, old and new — Palude, Nider, Angelus, St. Antoninus, Sanchez, Diana — so that a confessor would have hesitated to condemn its use, and the practice may have seemed to some couples an acceptable alternative to continence or to procreative intercourse. Diana said that it was "frequently" employed (*Moral Resolutions* 3.4.227). The general discussion, and partial approval, of such an alternative, involving the controlled use of sexual faculties, was part of the shift from pure Augustinianism, part of the shift toward values favoring more direct control of conception.

In some Catholic areas the practice existed of inducing boys to submit to castration in order to preserve their voices for singing in the church choir. Such custom was contrary to the teaching of most moralists on what was permissible mutilation. Of the writers who specifically discussed the practice, those of any stature, such as Paul Laymann, Herman Busenbaum, Antonio Diana, John Lugo, and the Salamancans, condemned it unequivocally. However, a few theologians, of whom the best known is the Sicilian Jesuit Thomas Tamburini (1591–1675), defended the practice on the ground that it was for the common good "to hear the divine praises more sweetly sung in churches," and that the boys willingly changed their condition "for the better and through their whole life obtained noble and fat support." The theologians further argued that the Church tolerated the practice (Liguori, *Moral Theology* 3.4.1).

Writing in the mid-eighteenth century, Liguori gave the balance of authorities in the way just summarized and concluded that "the more probable" opinion was that the practice was mortal sin. The decisive argument was that if "it is not lawful for the good of the soul, how much less is it for temporal profit"? But his use of the phrase "more probable" implied that in his judgment the other opinion could be held as "probable." Moreover, he did not challenge the claim that the Church tolerated the practice. In short, however doubtful the prestige of the moral theologians supporting the practice, however contrary their opinion was to the more fundamental statements on man's right over his body, there was a tolerated belief that, for purely economic advantage, a man might permanently incapacitate himself from procreating. The reasoning employed in this very special case was never brought into relation with the problems presented by the married poor. But a minor challenge to the analysis of contraception existed in the tolerance extended to the treatment of the choirboys.

Between 1450 and 1750 there was a substantial rejection of the Augustinian view that intercourse may be initiated only for procreation. A broad range of values in intercourse, from health to pleasure, had been defended by some authorities. More significantly, Sanchez had taken an approach eliminating the different categories of purpose. Love had been introduced as a value increased through some sexual acts, although love had not been related to coitus. At the same time that procreative theory had been impaired, the economic or educational welfare of existing offspring had been found reason for not only practicing continence, but actually suspending the old theology's most basic duty of marriage. In *amplexus reservatus*, a technique of sexual pleasure without generation had been criticized by the major writers not for its interruption of coitus, but for its stimulation of a process wrongly believed to be the emission of female seed. The assumption that every sexual act must be oriented toward generation had been further weakened. Voluntary permanent incapacitation for procreation in order to achieve an economic benefit had not been treated as undeniably sinful by the leading moralist of the eighteenth century. In these ways the sexual acts and organs of man were not treated as sacred, as immune from alteration, as absolute values.

Despite these innovations and developments, the prohibition against contraception was maintained. In the next chapter I propose to examine why.

CHAPTER XII

THE RULE PRESERVED

I
F, IN THE PERIOD between 1450 and 1750, the leading theologians ceased to insist on procreation as the exclusive lawful purpose for initiating intercourse; if the need to educate existing children was recognized by some theologians as a good reason for not wanting more; if some value was assigned to pleasure in intercourse; if the interruption of intercourse short of insemination received some support; was not the condemnation of contraception affected? The new values and analyses bore on the assumptions underlying the condemnation. A rethinking of these assumptions would seem to have been in order.

In some ways the conditions were particularly favorable to reconsideration. Since the demise of Catharism there had been no substantial, organized movement attacking all procreation on religious grounds. The need to react strongly to a fundamental challenge to the perpetuation of life no longer existed. Until the nineteenth century there was no important group, alien to the Catholic Church, urging the control of births.

Not only was there absence of alien pressure; within the Church the intellectual corps available to conduct a reconsideration was of a particularly high quality. Catholic moral doctrine was a subject of concern for a large part of western Europe. The serious attention given to its study reflected its importance not only to the Church but to society. Beginning with moralists like Le Maistre and Major in the fifteenth century and ending with Liguori in the eighteenth century, there were a significant number of men devoted to the study of moral theology whose knowledge, thoroughness, and acumen were evident.

This body of moralists did effect a substantial revision of another patristic and medieval prohibition — the prohibition of seeking profit on a loan, an act labeled usury by medieval theology and canon law. From improvisation of daring alternatives in the late fifteenth and early sixteenth century, the innovating moralists advanced by 1600 to positions that undermined the old rule altogether. Between 1600 and 1700 there was great debate on the theories involved in the new position, and as late as the early eighteenth century there were attempts to revive strict medieval restrictions. By the time of Liguori the battle was over, and the sixteenth-century innovations appeared as commonplaces.[1] Why did the same process of evolutionary adaptation not occur with the prohibition of contraception?

The answer lies both in the different structures of the doctrines and in the different degrees of pressure for revision. I shall consider, first, the pressures to modify the doctrine on contraception, then the factors confining them. Then I shall set out by what arguments and sanctions the old rule was continued.

PRESSURES FOR CHANGE

The standard reason approved by the moralists for refusing marital intercourse or practicing *amplexus reservatus* was oppressive poverty. The references to this reason are evidence of an appreciation that the doctrine on contraception did impose a serious burden on the very poor. The willingness of the theologians to consider alternatives to the forbidden ways of contraception is evidence of pressure on the doctrine. The devising of alternatives to achieve a result, the obvious means of reaching which are proscribed by existing rule, is almost infallibly a sign of discontent with the bite of the law.

The theologians may also have had in mind the problems of the middle class. They may have chosen the case of the very poor as the best case for establishing in principle that economic reasons could justify avoidance of procreation. In Ledesma, this recognition of bourgeois interests is evident. When he refuses to admit that potential fragmentation of an inheritance is a good reason for refusing intercourse, he is admitting the existence of this bourgeois motive for birth control. When he declares that income in relation to education is properly considered in determining the duty of intercourse, he is speaking of values of the greatest interest to the bourgeoisie. Sanchez goes from the case of the poor to the case of the bourgeoisie and even the case of the nobility when he approves avoiding intercourse "to avoid great detriment or to obtain great advantage in property or fame." Dilution of inheritance and decline of family status would seem to have been recognized by these writers as dangers properly leading to the control of offspring (see above, pp. 332–333).

There is, then, some perception by the theologians that socioeconomic reasons exist to limit children. There is also some recognition that parenthood may be a burden which may be rejected simply because burdensome. Le Maistre, writing about 1480, sees only a hedonistic motive for

[1] See my *Scholastic Analysis of Usury* (Cambridge, Mass., 1957), pp. 359–362.

contraception: it is practiced in marriage by "those of looser life" "in order to experience greater delight in coitus" (*Moral Questions* II [Paris, 1490], fol. 56r). A more practical but still selfish reason for contraception is touched on in the earliest book I have encountered which is addressed by a theologian to married laymen in order to instruct them in moral aspects of their state of life. This book, the *Rule of Married Life*, written in the late fifteenth century, is in the vernacular and is apparently designed for a bourgeoisie educated enough to read.[2] Its author is Cherubino of Siena, a Franciscan and an admirer of his fellow townsman, St. Bernardine, "that new star, our father, who of these matters amply preached." Like Bernardine, Cherubino sometimes conceives of his readers as wicked sinners in need of strong rebuke, sometimes as pious Christians requiring only information.

Cherubino deals with contraception under the heading of "Outside Semination" (*De seminatione extrinseca*). He declares that God instituted marriage principally "to make children" (*fare figlioli*). "Many women" try to avoid pregnancy; they should, rather, "have patience" in the cares and tasks of bearing and nurturing. Similarly, some men don't want "to make children" because they are "so fainthearted that they do not have the spirit to nurture them." They commit the act condemned by Genesis (*The Rule of Married Life*, "The Fourth Rule"). Cherubino was not disposed to encourage contraception by listing good reasons for avoiding children. But it seems significant that the motive he does assign to women is the desire to avoid the burdens of motherhood. That this motive strikes him as a probable one suggests that already in the late fifteenth century the women of the Italian bourgeoisie were restive in being given only a maternal role.

Over a century later, Francis de Sales's work in the vernacular reflects more vaguely a recognition of the desire of some laymen to avoid procreation. The *Introduction to the Devout Life* is more clearly aimed at a spiritual elite than *The Rule of Married Life*, and it is not devoted solely to marriage. Yet even a laity seeking perfection must be warned of sins in marriage. In what doubtless seemed a spirit of delicacy at the time, De Sales develops his analysis of marital sins by a comparison with sins of overeating; he abandons the simile to speak directly of "Onan's action," which was "detestable before God" (*Introduction* 3.39).[3] In another chapter, De Sales warns the married that they need the virtue of chastity not only when they are away from each other, but "for moderation when they are together in their ordinary life" (*ibid.* 3.12). The point is made

---

[2] Cherubino, *Vitae matrimonialis regula* (n.p., n.d.). Hugo Hurter, *Nomenclator litterarius recentioris theologiae catholicae* (Innsbruck, 1903–1913), II, 1091, says that the work was published in Florence in 1487.

[3] François de Sales, *Introduction à la vie dévote*, in *Oeuvres* (Annecy, 1843–1925), vol. III.

emphatic by recalling St. Catherine's vision of the married as the only special class in hell (above, p. 227). The call to "moderation" may mean that De Sales has in mind only the "too ardent lover" condemned by the Stoics and St. Jerome. But his insistence in chapter 39 that procreation is the "primary and principal end of marriage," coupled there with the reference to Onan's sin, suggests that he believes the sins of the married, which St. Catherine found so common, include contraceptive acts. Recognizing a desire to practice contraception, De Sales does not analyze the basis of the desire, or, rather, leaves the implication that the basis is a selfish hedonism.

Later in the seventeenth century, another writer in the vernacular for the laity, John Cordier, reports complaints made by "the best families" about bearing many children (*The Holy Family*).[4] The motivation of this attitude appears partly socioeconomic, partly psychological. Cordier's contemporary, James Marchant, a Belgian pastor writing for the clergy, says that the sin of "Onan and Er" is "sometimes" practiced by married couples "lest they be bound to feed more children" (*The Mystic Candelabrum* 8.9.1).[5]

The use of potions is more often connected with contraception outside of marriage. Marchant says that "frequently" girls who fornicate use "herbs or other poisons" "lest they conceive" (*Garden of Pastors* 3.4.6). The bull *Effraenatam* of Sixtus V in 1588 is directed against both abortion and contraception by poison.[6] Among the penalties laid down is the penalty of irregularity, a punishment which only a cleric could incur, so that the Pope must have clerical sinners particularly, though not exclusively, in mind. This kind of indication of motives for practicing contraception outside of marriage affords, of course, no evidence on how much contraception might have been practiced in marriage.

That, in fact, some decline in childbearing occurred is indicated by the limited studies of population trends which have been made. The higher the social status, the fewer the children, is found in one impressionistic account of Renaissance women.[7] A review of birth records of certain French noble families between 1650 and 1700 finds the fecundity of this aristocratic group to be comparable with that of a modern population voluntarily limiting reproduction.[8] Most striking of all, perhaps, is a study of

[4] Jean Cordier, *La Famille sainte* (1643), quoted in Helen Bergues, *La Prévention des naissances dans la famille* (Paris, 1960), p. 217.

[5] Jacques Marchant, *Candelabrum mysticum*, in *Opera* (Paris, 1868), vol. IV.

[6] Sixtus V, *Effraenatam*, in *Codicis iuris canonici fontes*, ed. Peter Gasparri (Rome, 1923), I, 308.

[7] René de Maulde La Clavière, *Les Femmes de la Renaissance* (Paris, 1898), p. 98.

[8] Jean Sutter, "Propos d'un démographe," in Michel Chartier et al., *La Régulation des naissances* (Paris, 1961), p. 41. A study of certain bourgeois families in Calvinist Geneva about 1600 shows a similar declining birth rate (Alfred Sauvy, "Essai d'une vue d'ensemble," in Bergues, *La Prévention des naissances*, p. 380).

Venice from 1563 to 1790. Within that span, the birth rate of Venetian nobles dropped from 34.8 to 20.0 per thousand.[9]

Why the upper classes in these instances had few children has not been demonstrated. In 1509 John Major asked, "What is the cause that kings and princes rarely have children, while farmers and poor men generate multitudes?" His answer was moralistic, but did not refer to contraception. Too much drink, too much delicate food, and too much intercourse unfitted the royalty for breeding. Their lack of progeny was, moreover, punishment for their sins (*On the Sentences* 4.34.1). In any event, the royalty and nobility were special cases. Lowered fertility due to inbreeding could have seriously affected the fertility of these closely interrelated groups.

On a wider scale, the recent study by Mols of urban populations in western Europe between 1400 and 1800 suggests that postponement of marriage was common and was consciously chosen as the chief means of avoiding large families.[10] Good statistics on marriages, however, are lacking before 1700. By this date Mols detects in the principal cities what he calls a "crisis of nuptiality." At the end of the eighteenth century, he finds the average age for marriage in the cities to be "close to thirty." [11]

These pieces of demographic evidence, fragmentary though they are, confirm the impression derived from the theologians. There was among the poor, the bourgeoisie, and the nobility some desire to avoid large families. This desire was reflected in adoption of one of the possible alternatives to contraception — continence in marriage, *amplexus reservatus*, postponement of marriage. To the extent that the desire could not be satisfied by one of the alternatives, there was present a pressure which worked toward a modification of doctrine.[12]

[9] Roger Mols, *Introduction à la démographie historique des villes d'Europe du 14ᵉ au 18ᵉ siècle* (Louvain, 1954–1956), II, 328.

[10] *Ibid.*, II, 542.

[11] *Ibid.*, II, 269.

[12] As in each era we have considered, the most important evidence on practice is the comments of the theologians themselves, for we can be sure that such evidence has played some part in their reactions. Apart from the observations of the theologians that have been reviewed, the evidence on contraceptive practice is not extensive.

Two sixteenth-century writers mention the use of contraceptives in illicit love affairs: Henri Estienne, *Apologie pour Hérodote* (La Haye, 1735), II, 310, 449; Pierre de Bourdeille, Seigneur de Brantôme, *Vies des dames galantes* (Paris, 1841), p. 195.

As for contraception in marriage, it has been argued that a passage in one of Marie de Rabutin-Chantal de Sévigné's letters to her daughter, Madame de Grignan, December 18, 1671, is of significance, because in this letter by a respectable mother (herself the granddaughter of St. Jane de Chantal) to her daughter — a letter designed to be read by an audience wider than her daughter — use of a contraceptive is perhaps recommended. Philippe Ariès, "Deux contributions à l'histoire des pratiques contraceptives," *Population* 4 (1954), 697; Bergues, *La Prévention des naissances*, p. 157, citing Sévigné, *Lettres*, I (Paris, 1953), 433. The word employed

LIMITING FACTORS

Pressure for modification was never translated into doctrinal argument. There are several converging reasons which explain this negative result and its contrast with the development of the doctrine on usury.

Lack of institutional involvement. In the matter of usury, the ecclesiastical organizations were themselves very much involved in the use of credit. They bumped into the problems of lending, both as borrowers and as creditors. Centralized financial structures requiring credit were important to a centralized church. The papacy, the bishops, the orders, used bankers in the daily conduct of their ordinary business. The theologians who dealt with the moral issues involved in profit on a loan were usually not the members of the ecclesiastical organizations who borrowed or lent. There was, however, free access to the theologians by the clerics involved in credit transactions. There was some disposition to believe that methods of finance which the Roman church found indispensable could not be wrong.[13]

Where the problems of marriage were concerned, the theologians dealt with an area in which no ecclesiastical organization acted. Celibates themselves, they had no identity of practical interests with the married laity. Unlike usury, questions involving marriage were not the personal concern of a theologian's colleague, or superior, or bishop.

Lack of public representation. The married laity were a silent group. They did not write on birth control. Women, who might have had the most to say, were not heard from. If Madame de Sévigné wrote to her daughter on contraception, she did not write to Bishop Bossuet. This silence is striking in an age when literacy was no longer confined to clerics. It seems accounted for by the strong inhibitions against speaking candidly on sexual behavior stamped as unnatural.

There was no organization to represent the laity, no group to spearhead a movement for change. With usury, in contrast, there were identifiable bankers who were willing to argue for revision of the law. The largest banking firm in sixteenth-century Europe, the house of Fugger, labored hard for changes in the usury rule with which it could live. There was nothing like this banking lobby acting for the married.[14]

by Madame de Sévigné is *restringents*. It is admitted by Ariès that the meaning of the word is not at all clear.

Norman E. Himes, *Medical History of Contraception* (Baltimore, 1936), p. 190, notes another ambiguous reference, to what may be a condom, in the 1671 De Sévigné correspondence with De Grignan.

From the small and debatable evidence of the December 1671 letter, both Ariès and Sauvy (in Bergues, *La Prévention des naissances*, pp. 315–316, 381) infer a change in attitude among the upper French bourgeoisie.

[13] See my *Scholastic Analysis of Usury*, p. 183.

[14] *Ibid.*, pp. 208–217. One of the rare writings on marriage by a Catholic layman in

When revision of the usury rule was being debated in the sixteenth century, a substantial contribution to the debate was a long critique by one who was professionally interested in the area affected by the rule, the lawyer Charles du Moulin. The one group which might have had a professional interest in contraception was the doctors. They showed no concern. Indeed, in contrast to the medieval books such as Avicenna's or Gaddesden's, a number of works now published on gynecology contained no information on contraception. Some examples are the first full treatment of obstetrics in the Renaissance period, *Der schwangern Frauen und Hebammen Rosegarten* of Eucharius Roesslin in 1513; the writing of Ambroise Paré (1517–1590), a leading authority of his day on obstetrics; the *Observations diverses sur la stérilité* by Louise Bourgeois, midwife of Marie de Médicis; the *Traité des fausses couches* of Charles de Saint-Germain in 1655.[15]

The complaint of the laity was heard occasionally. Cherubino and Cordier are witnesses. But at least as it reached the theologians, it did not have a strong social grounding. The educational reasons for limiting offspring were not seriously and dispassionately argued by lay representatives. There was a general intellectual acquiescence in the rule. Even in the eighteenth century, the rationalists who were openly critical of many of the teachings of the Church did not attack the prohibition of contraception.[16]

Absence of technological improvements. No contraceptives were developed which were substantially different from those already considered and condemned. As late as 1709, *The Diseases of Women* by Carlo Musitano prescribed to prevent conception only a willow drink and the use of saffron or mint in the vagina.[17] These were types of contraceptives as ancient as Avicenna.

One new contraceptive did appear about the middle of the seventeenth century: the condom. But this device, aimed at preventing emission of male semen into the vagina, did not present a different question in principle from coitus interruptus. It was, moreover, not cheaply and efficiently

---

the sixteenth century, and by one powerful enough to be heard, is Henry VIII's refutation of Luther. Although polemical purpose largely determines the content, Henry does treat of the love of a husband for his wife as a sign of the love of Christ for his Church, but he makes no connection between love and intercourse (*Assertio septem sacramentorum adversum Martinum Lutherum*, London, 1521, at "De sacramento matrimonii").

[15] These works are analyzed in Bergues, *La Prévention des naissances*, pp. 84–93.

[16] There was no public advocacy of contraception in France before the nineteenth century (*ibid.*, p. 388). In significant contrast to this acceptance of the rule on contraception by persons openly antagonistic to the Church, the Church's position on the indissolubility of marriage was under constant attack, first by sixteenth- and seventeenth-century Protestants, then by eighteenth-century rationalists. For a summary of these criticisms, see Gabriel Le Bras, *Mariage, DTC* 9²:2224.

[17] *Ibid.*, p. 96.

produced; and it won no medical support. References to it occur chiefly in nonmedical books, and according to these accounts the use of the condom appears to have been usually in illicit, extramarital affairs.[18]

The technical knowledge of the contraceptive means of the past was more widely diffused simply by the discovery of printing. Avicenna's *Canon of Medicine* was, for example, frequently reprinted. But this dissemination of knowledge, with no discrimination as to which means were effective, represented no advance in medicine and presented no new question to theology. The contraceptive methods in use, as dealt with by the theologians, were principally, although not exclusively, coitus interruptus and potions. The usual description of one type of contraceptive behavior is "emission," or "semination," "outside of" or "omitting" "the due vessel." This medieval terminology is employed in the sixteenth century by Sylvester, Cajetan, Soto, Navarrus, Ledesma, Lessius, and Sanchez.[19] The terms used are broad enough to cover both coitus interruptus and anal or oral intercourse. Occasionally, as in Cherubino, "outside semination" is directly linked to the act described in Genesis (*The Rule of Married Life*, "The Fourth Rule"). Cajetan, in his commentary on the *Summa* of St. Thomas, uses the cumbersome description "semination within the natural vessel where steps are taken that conception will not follow" (2–2.154.1.12). A pessary or more probably a douche is meant. Lessius also speaks of "intentionally preventing the emission of what will be born" (*Law and Justice* 4.3.13). This language would seem to describe the effect of a condom. If so, it is the earliest reference to this device in any work, and the first theological condemnation of it in express terms. Possibly only a potion is meant.

Postcoital expulsion of the seed by urination or movement is referred to by Angelus (*Summa*, at "Debt"), Sylvester (*Summa*, at "Debt"), and Sanchez (9.20) — all discussing the case attributed to Palude (above, p. 298). Sanchez also refers "to doing something else by which the received seed is expelled." Alphonsus speaks of postcoital expulsion by urination or immediate movement (*Moral Theology* 6.954).

On artificial contraceptives, the conventions established in medieval theology generally prevail. They are not referred to in works intended for the laity, such as the books of Cherubino and Francis de Sales. In writing

---

[18] James Boswell in his *London Journal, 1762–1763*, ed. Frederick A. Pottle (New York, 1950), p. 49, refers to "armor." Casanova (1725–1798) refers to it several times as "la redingote anglaise" (Himes, *Medical History of Contraception*, pp. 190–191).

[19] Sylvester, *Summa*, at "Luxuria"; Cajetan, *On the Summa theologica* 2–2.154.11.9, *ad* 5, and *Little Summa of Sins*, "The Sin of Matrimony as to the Vessel"; Soto, *On the Sentences* 4.31.1.4, appendix; Navarrus, *Manual for Confessors* 16.33; Ledesma, *Great Sacrament of Matrimony* 49.6; Sanchez, *Holy Sacrament* 9.17.

for clerics, the canonical phrase "poisons of sterility" is preferred. The term is used by Angelus, Sylvester, Cajetan.[20]

In the sixteenth century the Roman Catechism revives the classical Latin term "medicines" or "drugs" (*medicamenta*) to describe pharmaceutical means of preventing conception (2.8.13). The chairman of the catechetical commission, Borromeo, in legislation for his own diocese, uses a variant of *Si aliquis* which speaks of "doing something or giving something to drink" to prevent conception (*Milan Penitential*, "The Fifth Commandment").[21] Similarly, Navarrus in his *Manual for Confessors* speaks of "potions" or "something else" (16.33). Sixtus V, acting against contraception in the bull *Effraenatam*, speaks of both "potions" and "poisons." Ledesma, apparently referring to potions and not a douche, speaks of a woman "after coitus taking a drink of water, which, as it is said, impedes generation, or something similar" (*The Great Sacrament of Matrimony* 49.6).

In the seventeenth century Sanchez speaks of women "using a potion by which conception of offspring is obstructed" (*The Holy Sacrament of Matrimony* 9.20). Laymann revives an ancient term, "drug" (*pharmacum*), to describe a means for preventing conception (*Moral Theology* 5.10.3.1). But the change is purely verbal.

In the eighteenth century there is, if anything, less concern with concrete description of contraceptives. Vitus Pichler (1670–1736), an Austrian Jesuit, speaks of impeding conception "by poison" (*Canon Law* 5.12). Alphonsus speaks of "poisons" in commenting on *Effraenatam* (*Moral Theology* 3.395), but otherwise does not refer to artificial contraceptives at all. General descriptions are now also used which seem calculated to catch all possible forms of contraceptive behavior. Alphonsus speaks of acts "impeding generation of offspring" (*Moral Theology* 6.954). Pichler refers to impeding conception "by design" (*Canon Law* 5.12).

In the entire period from 1480 to 1750, only a single prominent theologian breaks from convention to mention the contraceptive for men which, since Aristotle describes it, would seem to have been at least generally known by name and function. Le Maistre speaks of "oiling" of the genitals with "a certain unguent which would induce sterility" (*Moral Questions* II, fol. 48v). But even he does not specify the unguent or make clear whether the sterility caused is permanent or temporary.[22]

---

[20] Angelus, *Summa*, at "Debt"; Sylvester, *Summa*, at "Debt"; Cajetan, *Little Summa of Sins*, "The Interrogation of Penitents by Confessors," at "The Fifth Commandment."

[21] *Milan Penitential*, in *Die Bussordnungen der abendländischen Kirche*, ed. F. W. H. Wasserschleben (Halle, 1851).

[22] Presumably Le Maistre is referring to unguents like the cedar gum of antiquity, and the effect would be temporary.

A belief in magical methods of contraception also continues. In his usually well-informed work, Le Maistre speaks of copulation at the time of a constellation which will induce perpetual sterility in a wife (*ibid.*). In the notorious *Hammer of the Magicians*, written in 1486 by two Dominican inquisitors, Henrich Krämer and Jacob Sprenger, who were as credulous of marvels as they were obsessed by sex, the devil's power to prevent semination is affirmed (2.2.2), and witches' ways of impeding procreation are said to include "the eating of herbs" and the use of "images" or "cocks' testicles" (2.1.6).[23] A century later, Sixtus V, after legislating against astrologers and magicians in the bull *Coeli et terrae*, referred in the bull *Effraenatam* to contraception "by means of magical evil deeds" (*maleficiis*) and "by cursed medicines" (*maleficiis medicamentis*).[24] The magical practitioners of contraception may be friendly to the person affected, as in Le Maistre's example, or hostile, as Krämer and Sprenger suppose. Interest in witchcraft is reflected as late as 1760 in a work by the Franciscan Lucius Ferraris, where, among the powers attributed to *malefici*, are those of making "women sterile and spouses impotent." [25]

The vague and stereotyped references to contraception often raise the same questions of interpretation already raised in relation to the terminology of the medieval theologians. For the reasons stated above, p. 223, I believe that the vagueness is due to convention rather than to ignorance, and that use of the convention is understandable only if the means are not generally well known. The continuation of the conventional terms is further proof of the absence of challenge to the doctrine by technological improvement. The persistence of the belief that magic may accomplish sterilization not only reflects a failure to develop certain, rational techniques of achieving contraception, but also continues to be a barrier prejudicing the consideration of artificial control of conception.

Absence of significant environmental change. The failure of the laity to speak, of the doctors to assert an interest, of scientists to develop new contraceptives, has some relation to the fact that in this period there were no significant population pressures on western Europe. There was a slow

---

[23] Heinrich Krämer and Jacob Sprenger, *Malleus maleficarum* (Lyons, 1604).

[24] Sixtus V, *Coeli et terrae*, in *Codicis iuris canonici fontes*, I, 281–285. The bull is chiefly against telling of fortunes, but refers also to the use of *veneficia* "to perpetrate other crimes" in league with the devil.

[25] Lucius Ferraris, *Prompta bibliotheca*, ed. J. P. Migne (Paris, 1865). Ferraris has this discussion under the heading "Superstitio," but it is not evident that he views belief in the power of magicians as superstitious; rather it is recourse to magicians which he finds superstitious. As late as the middle of the eighteenth century in Liège, it was a sin reserved to the bishop to use *maleficium*, that is, "poisoning, by which men are made infirm, women sterile, offspring sickly, beasts diseased, trees dry" (Billuart, *The Summa of St. Thomas Accommodated to Today's Academic Customs* VII, diss. 6.6, "Reserved Cases").

expansion of the cities. The largest city of medieval Europe, Paris, roughly doubled its population in three hundred years from 1300 to 1600. It more than doubled it in the next two centuries, from 200,000 in 1600 to 550,000 in 1800. Milan doubled in size from 100,000 in 1500 to close to 200,000 in 1600, but, largely as a result of the great plague of 1630, declined to 100,000 by 1700. Venice numbered 100,000 in 1500, increased to 168,000 in 1600, but, as a result of plague, declined to 130,000 by 1700. Florence was at 50,000 in 1500, increased slowly to 70,000 by 1600, and declined slightly to 65,000 by 1700. Rome went from 50,000 in 1500 to 100,000 in 1600 and increased slowly to 135,000 by 1700. Naples was at 100,000 in 1500, 200,000 in 1600, and then, owing to plague, fell to 185,000 by 1700.[26]

These figures on the larger cities in the Catholic world do not reflect the kind of population growth that could generate serious pressures. What is striking and relevant is how often population growth was not only checked but seriously reversed by disease. A quarter, even a third, of city populations was swept away by seventeenth-century plagues. Milan is estimated to have lost 40 percent in 1630.[27] Sanitary control, maintenance of a completely pure water supply, infant hygiene, vaccination — all these measures which were to reduce mortality at a later date were unpracticed.[28] Consequently, the ordinary mortality rate, especially for infants, was high, and the vulnerability to disease great. In this environment, where life was challenged by forces not yet subjected to control, there was little basis for regarding overpopulation as a danger to society. These considerations are not urged by the theologians, but they partly account for the absence of any lay concern with population growth.

One layman to discuss questions of population was St. Thomas More. In his *Utopia*, written in 1516, it is suggested that the ideal city should have no more than six thousand inhabitants — a number much smaller than the London More knew and very much smaller than Paris.[29] But the Utopians' solution for overpopulation is not any form of birth control, but simple territorial expansion. If their neighbors are unwilling to let them occupy empty land, the Utopians go to war. The Utopian formula for the ideal size of a city is coupled with regulation of the size of individual families. Each family is to have at least ten and no more than sixteen children; those who have more assign their surplus to those whose numbers are under the minimum. This prescription is designed for a society whose primary occupation is agriculture; More remarks earlier of the England of his time that "country business requires many hands" and so the country poor are numerous (1.2). It is difficult to be

[26] Mols, *Introduction à la démographie historique,* II, 504–513.
[27] *Ibid.,* II. 507.
[28] *Ibid.,* II, 541.
[29] Thomas More, *Utopia* 2.5, ed. J. H. Lupton (Oxford, 1895).

sure how seriously More intended to recommend any particular scheme he ascribed to Utopia. At the time a busy lawyer himself, he delightedly reported that Utopia had no lawyers (2.7). Yet it may be argued that he was willing to advance in this description of an imaginary land any social reform he considered to be of great importance. Divorce by mutual consent, for example, is a practice of the Utopians (2.7). There is also an indirect rein on population by a drastic raising of the legal age for marriage established by Roman law (fourteen for boys, twelve for girls) to twenty-two for men, eighteen for women (2.7). The measure is suggested as a way of reducing difficulties in marriage; More could not but have been aware that it would have some effect on births. There is, in sum, a curious, gingerly turning over of the problems of optimal population, the regulation of family size, and the relation of family size to economic occupation. There is already, at this comparatively early date, hostility to urbanization. But there are no strongly pressed proposals for population control. More's basic solution, colonize empty land, was exactly the course taken by the leading European powers for the next three hundred years.

Half a century later an Italian observer, John Botero, found no reason to be concerned about overpopulation. Botero, a Piedmontese priest who was secretary in 1582 to St. Charles Borromeo and then in 1586 consultant to his nephew Cardinal Frederic Borromeo, wrote a treatise entitled *The Greatness of Cities*, which in the scientific spirit of a Machiavelli attempted to evaluate what made cities powerful. He speculated as to why Milan and Venice were failing to increase in numbers. Some attributed the phenomenon to plagues, wars, famines. But these were equally bad in days of old. Men were just as fit to generate today as in former times. Why was there, then, not an indefinite increase? Botero concluded that it was owing to "the defect of nutriment and sustenance sufficient for it." In the same way the ancient Romans, "finding much want and less means to supply their lack of victual, either forbare to marry or, if they did marry, their children oppressed with penury . . . fled their own country." In the New World the Aymores of Brazil are so poverty-stricken that they devour fetuses (3.2). Here is a skirting of the connection between a stationary population, poverty, and some means of birth control. Writing in the same year in which Sixtus V issued *Effraenatam*, Botero refers to ancient or exotic lands to illustrate how poverty may result in voluntary limitation of offspring. Yet this candid and dispassionate observer did not believe that limitation of population was desirable. Against "Aristotle and the ancients" he held that the strength of a city was in its numbers, "for force prevails above reason" (3.1).[30]

This substantial absence of environmental change relevant to doctrine

---

[30] John Botero, *Greatness of Cities*, trans. Robert Peterson, ed. P. J. and D. P. Waley (New Haven, 1956).

on contraception is in marked contrast to the economic changes affecting the usury rule. There, the commercial revolution of sixteenth-century Europe multiplied the opportunities for the investment of money. The old assumption that money not lent was idle money stored unproductively "in a chest" was no longer maintainable. The changed economic facts provided objective reason and support for a new appraisal of the usury doctrine. New theological analyses were necessary, but they did not take place without objective alteration in the conditions affected by the rule. No similar palpable change occurred with regard to population.

Absence of change among the Protestants. On usury, Calvin urged an entirely new approach. On contraception Calvin stayed explicitly with the old Catholic doctrine, and Luther held an Augustinian view of sexuality that did not encourage change.[31] Paradoxical as it may be, Protestant rigidity helped to keep the Catholic position stiff. The Catholic moralists were not eager to appear to abandon a moral doctrine of the Fathers if the Protestants still held it. With particular force this feeling held as to sexual sins. The Lutheran exposition of Augustine did produce a Catholic reaction. The moralists were, however, not prepared to face a Protestant charge of countenancing the sin of Onan. This factor was an intangible one, and by no means controlling. Yet I do not think the indirect influence of the Protestant position was so negligible that it can be ignored, even though it was not referred to by the Catholic writers.

Another possible factor was the competition between Catholics and Protestants in areas such as Germany, the Low Countries, and France. In these areas serious shifts in population growth could have affected religious and political control. This consideration was not mentioned by the theologians. Yet if Botero's theory of what made a city strong was typical of the thinking of politically inclined leaders in the Church, the importance of maintaining numerical strength would not have been overlooked. It is plausible that some perception of the political consequences made Catholics hesitate to consider modification of their rule, and operated as a reinforcement to the doctrinal stand.

Interconnection of sexual sins. There was one additional, internal factor present in the case of contraception which was not present in the case of usury. The usury doctrine affected only one small sphere of human con-

---

[31] Calvin said that purposely to practice coitus interruptus was "doubly monstrous": "It is to extinguish the hope of the race and to kill before he is born the son who was hoped for." Onan both defrauded his brother of his right and "no less cruelly than foully" committed this monstrous crime. *Commentarius in Genesim* 38.8–10, *Opera*, ed. J. W. Baum et al., vol. XXIII (Brunswick, 1882).

Luther was less specific, but in his German Catechism, under the sixth commandment, he said that the purposes of marriage were for a husband and wife "to live together, to be fruitful, to beget children, to nourish them, and to bring them up to the glory of God." *Werke*, ed. J. K. E. Knaacke et al., vol. XXX (Weimar, 1910).

duct. The prohibition of contraception was locked into a series of other doctrines affecting the vast range of human conduct which could be considered sexual.

The central difficulty may be seen by an examination of the most severe internal critique the scholastic sexual ethic has ever received, the controversy of Le Maistre and Cajetan over the reason for condemning fornication. Le Maistre attacked the main Thomistic argument that fornication always involved injury to "the child about to be born," in that this child was deprived of definite parents and particularly of paternal education.[32] Admitting that the argument proved that fornication with a fertile prostitute was evil, Le Maistre put four cases where there would be no injury to "the child about to be born": (1) the woman was the king's concubine, and hence would be amply provided for; (2) the woman was known to be sterile; (3) the couple swore to be faithful to each other and to bring up any children born of their intercourse; (4) the state provided for the nurture and education of the children (*Moral Questions* II, fol. 56v).

Focusing on the weakest point of the Thomistic argument, Le Maistre pressed: Where was the sin if the intercourse were sterile? At most the Thomistic reasoning proved the possibility of injustice to a potential child. But many fornicators did not intend to generate a child. If no injustice is intended, and no injustice occurs, there is no sin. If the intercourse is intended to be sterile, and is sterile, who is harmed? (*ibid.*, fol. 57v). St. Thomas had said that the case of sterility is *per accidens* and proves nothing against the general rule. But, Le Maistre argued, this answer assumes the existence of the rule to be proved. If there were a rationally grounded rule against all fornication, St. Thomas could dismiss these particular cases as "accidental," as not affecting the soundness of the rule. But it first must be shown rationally that there is a universal rule (*ibid.*, fol. 61v).

In the Thomistic framework, where love was not a value related to intercourse, Le Maistre's questions posed a challenge. After Le Maistre's death, Cajetan, both as a devoted Thomist and as an old opponent of the latter-day Paris theologians, undertook to answer them.[33] It is evident that he considered Le Maistre's critique of the sexual ethic of St. Thomas to be the one most worthy of his attention and refutation.

[32] Le Maistre also questioned the interpretation of the biblical texts against fornication, but held that by virtue of the constant teaching of the Church it was clear that by divine law there was a flat and absolute prohibition of fornication (*Moral Questions* II, foll. 58v–59r).

[33] Cajetan had already crossed swords with the Paris school over the authority of the Pope. Major's pupil, Almain, had in 1511 written an attack on Cajetan's placing of the Pope above a General Council (*Liber de auctoritate ecclesiae et conciliorum adversum Thomam Caietanum*).

Why would God have forbidden fornication if it were not evil? Cajetan asks. "God does not envy man. And other lawful pleasures He has granted man." There is no precept of the divine law which is not "in this one word fulfilled: Love your neighbor as yourself." "If fornication is against the divine law, it is against a human good." "And we give thanks to divine Thomas, who has taught us these things" (*On the Summa theologica* 2–2.154.2.13).

Le Maistre's fundamental error is a

confusion of that which is *per se* with that which is *per accidens* . . . Moral precepts depend on what is according to nature, and not on what is *per accidens* found in this temperament or that age.   (153.3.2)

This error of Martin is intolerable, destructive of all moral philosophy by mixing the *per se* and the *per accidens,* and from what is *per accidens* falsifying the universal which arises from the *per se* . . . All doctrine perishes, unless one stands on what is *per se.*   (154.2.14)

Human semination is in itself naturally ordained to the generation, upbringing, and education of offspring. This is easily evident from the nature of the seed, and from the offspring's needs of body and soul.   (154.2.4)

Any departure from this order is intrinsically deformed. The subsequent possible injustice is not in dispute; what is intrinsically wrong is the act of semination outside of marriage. Provision for the child by the mother is accidental, as would be provision for the child by the state. The intention of the parties not to generate offspring is equally irrelevant. "Looking at the intention of the act in itself, nature intends semination for generation" (154.2.10, reply 1).

It would be facile, and incorrect, to analyze this debate as controlled by the alleged nominalism of Le Maistre and the epistemological realism of Cajetan. It is not that Le Maistre is insisting on the particularity of every moral act, as Cajetan implies. Le Maistre, as much as Cajetan, accepts moral universals; his argument against certain species of fornication assumes their existence. At stake between Le Maistre and Cajetan are three issues of the utmost relevance to the doctrine on contraception. Abstracting from the language of the controversy, I formulate them in these terms:

1. How is the norm established for sexual acts?

2. In the sexual, generative, and educative process, what part of the process is taken as a unit for moral judgment?

3. Is the teleology of seminal ejaculation such that it cannot be affected by human intention?

Cajetan appears to answer the first question by looking at the sexual process, finding that it sometimes produces offspring, and concluding that this generation is the most important accomplishment of the sexual act. This is the method of the Stoics and most of the Fathers. He does not attempt to answer how, if several purposes are found accomplished in intercourse, one is more normative than others. Intercourse by sterile married persons, intercourse in pregnancy, intercourse to avoid incontinence, intercourse to pay the marital debt, must be assumed by him to be abnormal. It is obviously important to the position against contraception that Cajetan's approach should prevail.

The second question is implicitly answered by the statement quoted above, where Cajetan takes as the unit for moral judgment the entire process of intercourse, insemination, conception, birth, and education: "Human insemination is in itself naturally ordained to the generation, upbringing, and education of offspring." The contention is that every act of intercourse is naturally ordered to the education of the child-to-be. Not only are ejaculation, insemination, and procreation asserted to be naturally inseparable, but education is made part of this process. The notion of "ordination" or "order" in a single act is thereby expanded to include not only the immediate end of the act itself, its purpose of insemination, but also a goal of generation and education. The natural end of the act is not reached when unwilled biological processes take over, but in a rational process requiring a whole series of discrete human acts. The unit considered for moral judgment is not a single physical movement, but a process. To follow this approach to its logical conclusion is to recognize values not recognized in the argument that contraception is against the natural purpose of coitus; for in this approach the natural purpose of coitus includes education of offspring. The same tension which we have explored in Chapter X, "Counter Approaches," is met: if the moral perfection of the child is stressed, the argument against contraception is undercut.

The third question is resolved for Cajetan by his assumption that whatever the intention of a particular person, the act of ejaculation is ordered by nature, that is, by God, to the generation and education of a child. Le Maistre believes that human intention could change the orientation, and so the moral quality, of the act. If a person does not intend to generate a child, and no child is in fact generated, no injury to any being has been done, and so God has not been offended. If Le Maistre's reasoning is followed, the Thomistic ground for prohibiting fornication disappears when contraceptives are used. On his reasoning, the prohibition against fornication is maintained only by maintaining that contraception is never permissible.

There was no spelling out of a position which asserted, "Not to undermine the doctrine on fornication, we must not change the doctrine on contraception." But the interconnection of the two doctrines is evident enough so that the influence of such thinking may be supposed. As long as there was no argument against fornication based on the demands of love, as long as the main rational case against fornication rested on the treatment of the fornicating act as normally generative, to allow the lawfulness of contraception would have been to favor fornication. Similarly, the argument establishing all the sins against nature — masturbation, bestiality, sodomy — rested on the assumption that any prevention of insemination was unnatural. The argument was seriously disturbed if coitus interruptus was in any case admitted. Again, as long as there was no ethic based on the requirements of love between persons, it seemed dangerous to disturb the rational foundation of a whole range of sexual morality.

The reluctance to draw in question the whole "natural" basis of the sexual ethic affects Le Maistre himself. He does go as far as to question the traditional classification of coitus interruptus with the other sins against nature. The sin of a man with his wife, he maintains, can properly be classified as a separate form of lechery. He would call it "conjugal lechery" (*Moral Questions* II, foll. 54v–55v). In this seemingly slight change in classification there might have been the beginning of a shift in doctrine — an examination of contraceptive behavior as a sin only against marriage, not against nature. But Le Maistre immediately retreats from his advanced position. He finds conjugal lechery, despite its new name, to be a sin against nature. He does raise the question why coitus interruptus is unnatural, when "the matter is not unnatural, the organ is not unnatural, the way of copulating is not unnatural." But he at once answers that the seed is not emitted "into the organ which nature has deputed for its reception, and it is a most grave sin against nature" (*ibid.*, fol. 56r).[34]

In short, Le Maistre, critical and skeptical of much of the scholastic sexual ethic, will not surrender the basic notion which had guided the approach to the sins considered unnatural. This approach rested on the appropriateness of the female vessel to receive the masculine seed. To modify the stand against coitus interruptus and anal intercourse would have been to abandon the basis upon which not only these marital acts but bestiality, sodomy, and masturbation were condemned. If Le Maistre was not bold enough to try to rework the scholastic ethic, no one else was likely to make the attempt.

Le Maistre's age was an age in which speculation in these matters at a Catholic university was easier than in the more austere and rigid times after Trent. Sexuality was the most sensitive area for a moralist to ex-

---

[34] Le Maistre is very strong in condemning sodomy in the strict sense. What the Creator and nature have provided as the proper matter for the sexual act — the body of the opposite sex — is lacking. However, he is much in advance of his time in his suggestion that sodomitic inclinations may be due to sickness or to defective physical qualities (*Moral Questions*, fol. 79r).

plore in the post-Tridentine Church. One symptom of its peculiar status is an order issued April 24, 1612, by Claudius Aquaviva, general of the Jesuits, to all Jesuits. Under the precept of obedience, and under penalty of excommunication and removal from any teaching office, Aquaviva enjoins the Jesuits not to teach or counsel that there is generically any "smallness of matter," *parvitas materiae*, in sexual sins.[35] In other words, unlike, say, the sin of theft, where the theft of a penny would ordinarily be a light matter, a sexual sin must be presented as always generically involving matter of mortal sin. Aquaviva's action did not affect directly the teaching of Jesuit moralists on the purposes of marital intercourse. But the intervention of high authority, terminating speculation, overriding theologians like Thomas Sanchez, and threatening severe penalties for disobedience, suggests the particular stress which analysis of sexual sins created and the limitations which authority was likely to place on their analysis.

The lack of institutional involvement, the lack of interest by professional groups, the absence of invention, little change in population pressures, Protestant rigidity, the close connection of the arguments against contraception and against other sexual sins — all were reasons why the doctrine on contraception resisted the impact of the new valuations of procreative purpose, pleasure, and education, and the feeble pressure of the laity for revision. All these factors distinguish the treatment of contraception from that of the usury rule. One reflection of the difference is the volume of theological references to usury in the sixteenth and seventeenth centuries in comparison with the theological references to contraception. The disparity is roughly that of elephant to mouse. The difference is not, I think, evidence that a sin which could be committed only by persons with money to lend was more widely perpetrated than a sin which any married person could commit. It reflects rather the difference in the pressure to revise the usury doctrine. With the help of new analyses and a new attitude toward the financiers, that revision was accomplished. The rules against contraception, meanwhile, stood without modification. The doctrine had been largely shaped in reaction to Gnostic, Manichean, and Cathar repudiations of the perpetuation of life. The dialectical opposite had disappeared. The old doctrine was in peaceful possession of the field.

THE ARGUMENTS AGAINST CONTRACEPTION

The prohibition against contraception resisted modification. It was, indeed, not merely passively retained and transmitted, but actively main-

---

[35] Claudius Aquaviva, letter of April 24, 1612, Archivum romanum Societatis Iesu, Epp. NN 115, fol. 498.

tained and defended by arguments. The repetition, variations, and patterns of argumentation are the best internal index to the doctrine's strength.

THE SCRIPTURAL ARGUMENT

On the level of biblical authority, apart from rational demonstration, the story of Onan was cited with some frequency to show that contraceptive behavior had been condemned by God.

The critical Le Maistre appealed to the story to show the sinfulness of using "mode or time or place to prevent the generation of offspring" (*Moral Questions* II, fol. 48v). In his commentary on Genesis, Denis the Carthusian explained that Er was slain by God because of "abusing the vessel of his wife and pouring out seed outside of it," an "enormous crime" that, he said, Augustine had taught was worse than sleeping with one's mother. On Onan, he merely noted, with some indication of surprise, that the levirate law apparently antedated Moses, and that Onan "knew his wife uselessly and unnaturally" (*On Genesis* 38). But when writing explicitly for the laity he did not mention the story, although alluding vaguely in his treatment of the Decalogue to its condemnation of "every libidinous contact, even in the married, where the natural order instilled by nature is not kept" (*The Praiseworthy Life of the Married* 26). A different estimate of his lay audience was made by Cherubino. Onan was referred to specifically by him in order to instruct the married lay people on the sin of coitus interruptus (*The Rule of Married Life,* "The Fourth Rule").

In the sixteenth century Cajetan used the story specifically as an objection to ejaculation outside the vagina. This act, performed by the husband of Thamar, was "manifestly a great crime" (*Little Summa of Sins,* "The Sin of Matrimony in Regard to the Vessel"). Peter Canisius was far less emphatic and specific. In a citation of twenty passages from Scripture on the purity required by the Sixth Commandment, the Catechism of Canisius gave Genesis 38:8–10 without comment (Canisius, *Summa of Christian Doctrine,* "The Ten Commandments," 6).

On the other hand, some significant authorities omitted any reference to Onan at points in their discussion where reference would have been relevant and even mandatory if the scriptural argument were dominant. The story was not cited by Angelus, Sylvester, Soto, Navarrus. Most significant of all, the Roman Catechism did not appeal to it in condemning contraception. The Catechism used both Tobias and the example of Jacob's choice of Rachel, in stating the purposes of marriage (2.8.13, 14), so that the omission of such a famous Old Testament text as Genesis 38 seems deliberate de-emphasis, due, perhaps, to a desire not to specify this method of contraception.

Later in the sixteenth century, an exegesis was made which focused on Onan's state of mind, rather than his act. This is the work of the Capuchin preacher, St. Laurence of Brindisi (1559–1619). Intercourse, he said, "to satisfy lust alone so that generation is not desired" is a mortal sin. For this reason, Er and Onan, sons of Juda, were struck by God (*Explication on Genesis*, c. 4).[36] Not the contraceptive act as such, but the desire to avoid children and satiate lust is seen as the grounds for Onan's punishment. Intercourse as a "remedy for concupiscence," accompanied by a contraceptive act, would not fall literally within St. Laurence's definition of the sin. But the tone of his remarks leaves little doubt, I think, that he would have swept such child-avoiding action within the condemnation exemplified in Onan.

At the beginning of the seventeenth century, there were the first stirrings of biblical criticism, but the old story was still relied on. The influential Louvain exegete, Cornelius a Lapide, S.J. (1567–1637), stated that both Er and Onan "sinned by the sin of autoerotic softness [*mollities*] and withdrawal, which is against the nature of generation and of marriage" (*Commentary on the Pentateuch of Moses*, at Genesis 38.7). Lapide added, "Let confessors take note." [37] Francis de Sales criticized "some heretics of our age who said Onan had been blamed for his perverse intention and not his act" (*Introduction to the Devout Life* 3.39). The acute Lessius took the story as an objection to withdrawal in intercourse (*Justice and Law* 4.3.13). On the other hand, Peter de Ledesma, Paul Laymann, and, above all, Thomas Sanchez did not include the story in their discussions of contraception. In the eighteenth century, the most important of moral treatises, the *Moral Theology* of St. Alphonsus, did not cite the story.

The biblical anecdote influenced, but did not dominate, the view of contraception; it was usually interpreted as a condemnation of coitus interruptus, sometimes as a condemnation of all contraception. It was never used alone without reference to the "unnaturalness" of the behavior which God punished in Onan.

CONTRACEPTION AS HOMICIDE

Le Maistre retained the substance of the treatment of contraception as homicide when he estimated the gravity of sexual sins. Coitus interruptus and the use of contraceptive poisons were worse than fornication, for such acts were "against the life of a man to be born" (*Moral Questions* II, foll. 62v–63r). Angelus paraphrased *Si aliquis* in his discussion of

---

[36] Laurence of Brindisi, *Opera omnia*, ed. Capuchin fathers of the Venetian Province (Padua, 1940), vol. III.

[37] Cornelius a Lapide, *Commentarius in Pentateuchum Moysis* (Venice, 1717).

homicide (*Summa*, at "Homicide," 2.10). Although Cajetan did not mention the decretal in his commentary on St. Thomas, in his less refined work for confessors he accepted the analysis of *Si aliquis*. Under the Fifth Commandment, the confessor was told to ask about murder, abortion, and infanticide, and finally to inquire, Did the penitent "take or give poisons of sterility?" (*Little Summa of Sins*, "Interrogations"). As St. Antoninus had broken from the canon law in not putting such a question under the Fifth Commandment in his *Summa for Confessors*, so Cajetan's restoration of the question may be interpreted as endorsement of the canonical theory.

On the other hand, Denis the Carthusian, Major, Sylvester, Soto, and Navarrus did not invoke the decretal. Especially striking was the omission of contraception by Peter Canisius when he spoke of the Fifth Commandment in his great catechism and in his two shorter catechisms. The ancient rhetoric, deserted by so many influential authors, seemed to have lost its appeal.

The Roman Catechism, however, emphatically restated the teaching. Treating of "Holy Matrimony," the Catechism quoted the verses, today recognized as spurious, from Tobias 6:16 and 22 on marrying not to satisfy lust, but to have children. It continued, "And this is one reason why God had constituted it [marriage] from the beginning. Therefore it is a most grave crime for those joined in matrimony to use medicines to impede the conceptus or to abort birth: this impious conspiracy in murders must be extirpated" (2.7.13).[38] The classification made by *Si aliquis* was thus reasserted, not in canon law, but in a work designed to convey the essentials of Catholic doctrine to the faithful. Contraception was declared to be a form of homicide. The force of the old decretal had been qualified by the neighboring presence of the canon *Sicut ex*, refusing to treat the abortion of a young fetus as homicide. No such softening qualification existed in the Catechism. The description was singularly blunt, brought into a statement of the purposes of marriage, and directed specifically at married couples. It was, however, restricted to the use of medicines. Unlike St. Bernardine, the Catechism did not categorize coitus interruptus as homicide.

That the Catechism's classification coincided with *Si aliquis* was scarcely accidental. In the penitential composed for his own diocese by the Catechism's chief editor, Borromeo, a form of *Si aliquis* was used. Sins of contraception by potion or by "doing something" to prevent generation

---

[38] The phrase here translated "impede the conceptus" is *conceptum impediunt*. The phrase might be understood as meaning, prevent the birth of a fetus already conceived. But this interpretation makes the phrase surplusage, as abortion is separately condemned. It seems better, therefore, to understand the phrase as applying to impeding the existence of a conceptus. It is in this sense that Cornelius a Lapide speaks of Onan. He destroyed "the conceptus in his seed" (below, p. 364).

were sins against the commandment, Thou shalt not kill (*Milan Penitential*, "The Fifth Commandment").

A second Roman act, even more stringent than the Catechism but of less permanent significance, was the bull *Effraenatam* of Sixtus V, issued on October 29, 1588. This decree began with a paraphrase of Augustine in *Aliquando:*

Who does not abhor the lustful cruelty or cruel lust of impious men, a lust which goes so far that they procure poisons to extinguish and destroy the conceived fetus within the womb, even attempting by a wicked crime to destroy their own offspring before it lives, or if it lives to kill it before it is born? Who, then, would not condemn with the most severe punishments the crimes of those who by poisons, potions, and *maleficia* induce sterility in women, or impede by cursed medicines their conceiving or bearing?

All the penalties against homicide of both canon and secular law were invoked against those producing an abortion. Ecclesiastics so doing were declared irregular, were to be treated as laymen, and were to be handed over to the secular power. The decree then continued: "Moreover, we decree that they should by the same penalties be wholly bound who proffer potions and poisons of sterility to women and offer an impediment to the conception of a fetus, and who take pains to perform and execute such acts or in any way counsel them, and the women themselves who knowingly and voluntarily take the same potions." Here were the strongest sanctions ever prescribed against contraception, by any ruler, ecclesiastical or lay. The giving or taking of contraceptives was to be treated literally as murder for all purposes of the canon law and the law of the states of the Church. The limitation on *Si aliquis* introduced by the canonists was ended. All abortion and all contraception by potion or poison were to be treated as murder. The ultimate ecclesiastical penalty of excommunication was invoked, and, to make the penalty even more stringent, only the Holy See could release the excommunication unless the sinner were *in articulo mortis.*

What accounts for this sudden shift to a literal application of the treatment of contraception as homicide? The answer would seem to lie almost wholly in the personality of Sixtus V. This Franciscan pope set about to reform Rome and the Church in a draconian way. Men who had committed crimes twenty years before his accession were now brought to trial. An extremist in the pursuit of virtue, he displayed toward sins connected with sexual intercourse a severity which would have done credit to a New England Puritan. In Renaissance Rome he made adultery a hanging matter, and he actually had carried out the execution of a woman who had been a procurer for her daughter.[39] There seems no doubt that

---

[39] On the violent enforcement of law by Sixtus V, see Ludwig Pastor, *History of the Popes* (St Louis, 1899–1953), XXI, 90. Pastor remarks, on these law-en-

he meant the penalties of *Effraenatam* to be literally applied. If they had been, the equation of contraception with homicide would have passed from moral rhetoric to criminal law.

Like most of the efforts at righteous reform of Sixtus V, however, *Effraenatam* overshot the mark. Within a year of Sixtus V's death in 1590, his successor, Gregory XIV, noted with suave understatement that "the hoped-for fruit" had not resulted from the bull, but that instead its rigor had led to sacrilege: those affected by it ignored their excommunicated status. Accordingly, the new Pope repealed all its penalties except those applying to abortion of an ensouled, forty-day-old fetus. The other penalties were retroactively annulled, and the decree of Sixtus V was "to be in this part as if it had never been issued" (*Sedes Apostolica*, May 31, 1591).[40]

Effraenatam was thus the rule of the Church for no more than two and one half years. Because of the unusual personality of Sixtus V, it is hard to say that his literal treatment of contraception as homicide embodied a new theological insight. Yet if there had not been a current of theology supporting his approach, if the Roman Catechism of Borromeo had not spoken of contraception as homicide only two decades before, it is unlikely that Sixtus V would have sought to impose such a law on the universal Church.

Effraenatam was in fact, however, not liked by the theologians and canonists. The leading canonist of Sixtus V's day, Navarrus, did not adopt it. Neither did Ledesma, who took care to point out Gregory XIV's recent action annulling this *motu proprio* of Sixtus V (*The Great Sacrament of*

---

forcing activities, "It cannot be denied that Sixtus V went too far." A recent historian of sixteenth-century Rome treats of *Effraenatam*, "a terrifying constitution against abortion," as part of the effort begun by Pius V, and continued by Sixtus V, to lessen adultery and prostitution in Rome. Jean Delumeau, *Vie économique et sociale de Rome dans la seconde moitié du XVI⁵ siècle*, I (Paris, 1957), 430. Prostitution was, in fact, a phenomenon of Roman life that drew the remarks of both diplomats and saints who visited Rome. In 1527 a conservative estimate of the number of professional prostitutes in Rome, then a city of 55,000, was 1,500. In 1600, after two major campaigns against the prostitutes by Pius V and Sixtus V, a governmental census put professional prostitutes, in a city now grown to over 100,000, at 800. As Delumeau remarks, these numbers are only of persons making an occupation of prostitution (*ibid.*, I, 421–424).

Other socioeconomic facts are of some relevance to Sixtus V's bull. Rome was struck by plague in 1581. It suffered badly from wheat shortages in the last quarter of the century. Conditions described as famine prevailed in 1578, 1583, and 1590–1593 (Giampiero Carocci, *Lo Stato della Chiesa nella seconda metà del sec. XVI*, Milan, 1961, pp. 153–156). Although the population of Rome increased substantially in the sixteenth century, the famines made the poor feel the burden of offspring, while the plague and famines made human life all the more evidently precarious and in need of protection. Botero in 1595 discussed the depopulation of the States of the Church in *Relazioni universali*, Part 6, *Discorso intorno allo Stato della Chiesa* (Rome, 1595), cited in Delumeau, II, 540.

[40] *Codicis iuris canonici fontes*, I, 330–331.

Matrimony 49.6). The bull was not cited in argument after its repeal, even to show what one pope had held. *Effraenatam* may indeed have led to a reaction. In the seventeenth century, St. Francis de Sales and Leonard Lessius ignored the homicide argument altogether. Even more strikingly, the foremost Catholic authority of the age on marriage, Sanchez, cited *Si aliquis* not on contraception but only in regard to a case of abortion (*The Holy Sacrament of Matrimony* 9.20.12).

On the other hand, the ancient approach of St. Raymond, treating contraception and abortion of a young fetus as quasi homicide, was taken by Paul Laymann. Speaking of the sin of voluntary homicide, he wrote, "Whoever maliciously prevents conception of a human fetus, or ensoulment of an embryo, commits not a true but a quasi homicide, and sins mortally" (*Moral Theology* 3.3.3.2). He cited both *Aliquando* and *Si aliquis*. Treatment of contraception as homicide was not confined to moral theologians. It was adopted by a leading exegete, Cornelius a Lapide. In commenting on Genesis 38, he had nothing in the text before him to suggest that the sin of Onan was murder. But he noted that Onan's act "destroyed the fetus and the conceptus in his seed." "Hence," he continued, "this sin is compared by the Hebrews to homicide" (*Commentary*, at Gn 38:7). Talmudic tradition was thus invoked to support the canon law (cf. above, p. 50). More practical manuals also embodied the doctrine. In his book for parish priests, James Marchant treated the taking of "herbs or poisons of sterility." Such an act he labeled a sin against the commandment, "Thou shalt not kill" (*Garden for Pastors* 3, "Charity," 4). In the eighteenth century, the canon law kept the interpretation alive. Vitus Pichler, commenting on *Si aliquis*, made the conventional remark of the canonists that anyone practicing contraception or causing an abortion of a fetus before ensoulment was not a "true homicide." He added that in the external forum the penalty for murder would not apply (*Canon Law* 5.12).

Liguori dropped this line of analysis totally. Nowhere in his *Moral Theology*, that comprehensive treatise of sins, is contraception linked to homicide or related to the provisions of *Si aliquis*. Nor did Liguori, like Cajetan, abandon the approach in theory, only to keep it in his works for confessors. In his two Italian handbooks, he had nothing on the subject under the Fifth Commandment, where so many of his predecessors had treated of contraception by the "poisons of sterility." The first of these vernacular manuals, *Practical Instructions for Confessors*, discussed only abortion (c. 8), sodomitic marital intercourse (c. 9), and coitus interruptus (18.50). The second, *Practice of the Confessor That He May Well Exercise His Office*, had nothing on contraception.[41] A tradition as

---

[41] Alphonsus Liguori, *Istruzione pratica per i confessori* (Turin, 1895). *Pratica del confessore, per ben esercitare il suo ministero* (Venice, 1771); in Latin: *Praxis con-*

old as Regino of Prüm and Burchard, indeed as ancient as St. Jerome, had fallen into disuse. With St. Alphonsus the homicide approach ended its theological life.

Liguori was, of course, familiar with *Si aliquis* in the canon law. Moreover, he does give the form of it in the *Milan Penitential* of Charles Borromeo, which he introduces into a history of moral theology at the beginning of his own work (*Moral Theology,* "Prologemena," 1.5). If homicide no longer seemed an appropriate analysis, what accounted for the change? I suggest that it was linked both to the discovery of spermatozoa in 1677 and to a shifting position on the ensoulment of the fetus. In 1620, Thomas Fienus, a Louvain physician, in his *De formatione et animatione foetus,* had maintained the revolutionary thesis that a human soul was infused not on the fortieth day, but on the third day following conception. In 1658, the Franciscan Jerome Florentinius argued that a fetus in danger of death should be baptized, however little time had elapsed since conception, thereby postulating a human soul in young embryos. In 1661 Paul Zacchias, physician of Innocent X, taught that the human soul was infused at the first moment of conception. By the eighteenth century this was a common belief among medical men on the Continent. The first theologian to defend it was Thomas Roncaglia in 1736.[42] Liguori did not himself accept it, preferring the traditional forty-day, eighty-day rule and citing St. Thomas thereon (*Moral Theology* 3.4.394). Nonetheless, with the medical profession distinguishing between the fetus, human at conception, and the nonhuman spermatozoa, the ancient rhetoric of homicide must have been more strained than when it was generally believed that the fetus after conception was, for a period of time, no more human than the seed.

In the period 1450 to 1750, the analysis of contraception as homicide was far from universal. It was ignored by Denis, Major, Cherubino, Sylvester, Soto, Navarrus, Lessius, De Sales, Ledesma, Diana, Liguori. It was invoked by Le Maistre, Angelus, Cajetan, the Roman Catechism, Sixtus V, Laymann, Lapide, Marchant, Pichler. It was rarely applied to coitus interruptus. Its survival in any form was owed principally to the canon law and the Roman Catechism. To the extent that the canonical and catechistical classification was followed, the designation as "homicide" remained an objection to contraception by potion and poison.

VIOLATION OF THE ORDER OF NATURE

The simplest form of argument against contraception consisted of pointing to the appropriateness of the vagina to receive male semen. It

---

fessarii ad bene excipiendas confessiones, in *Theologia moralis,* ed. Leonard Gaudé (Rome, 1905–1912), vol. IV.

[42] In this summary of development I follow an anonymous article, "De animatione

was the classic argument contained in the description of coitus interruptus, anal intercourse, and oral intercourse as sins against nature.

Le Maistre put this analysis forward formally as an objection to contraception. The argument was merely implicit in Denis the Carthusian's description of Onan as acting "uselessly and unnaturally"; in Cajetan's definition of "the sin of matrimony in respect to the vessel" as "semination outside the natural vessel"; in Angelus' treatment of the sin against nature as not keeping the "natural way of copulation"; and in Sylvester's statement that sin in marriage consisted of "not keeping the vessel." The most emphatic form of this argument, treating "semination not in the due vessel or organ" as sodomy, was used as late as 1600 by Lessius.[43]

The argument did not have much force unless it were assumed that the inseminating act was normally generative. With the interesting exception of Le Maistre, wherever there was not mere definition but formal discussion, the argument was expanded to an objection to "preventing generation." Such expansion was, of course, necessary if the argument was to apply to contraception by douche or potion where insemination was not prevented.

The expanded version was classically put by Cajetan: "Suppose there is semination within the natural vessel and either the man or the woman takes steps, by art or activity, that conception may not follow, then semination is intentionally impeded from attaining its normal end, and . . . there is generic mortal sin, for by intention intercourse is contradicted in its natural end" (*On the Summa theologica* 2–2.154.1.12). This argument rested on the same assumption made by Cajetan in his case against fornication. The normal act was generative. It was "ordained by nature to the conservation of the human species." It might not be disturbed. The same approach was adopted by Ledesma (*The Great Sacrament of Matrimony* 49.6) and by Lessius (*Law and Justice* 4.3.13). Both had in mind the need to show the evil in contraceptive acts which did not interfere with insemination.

A variant version emphasized the ordination of the seed to generation. The difference was, I believe, only rhetorical. The assertion of the ordination of the seed echoed the old tradition of the "sanctity of the seed," but did not postulate an identity of seed and human being. In Cajetan, the rhetorical intent in insisting on the ordination of the seed was clear (*On the Summa theologica* 2–2.154.2.4). In the next century even greater stress was placed on the seed by John of St. Thomas, a leading

foetus," *Nouvelle revue théologique* 11 (1879), 163–186, and A. Chollet, "Animation," *DTC* 1²:1310–1312.

[43] Le Maistre, *Moral Questions*; Denis, *On Genesis* 38; Cajetan, *Little Summa of sins*, at "The Sin of Matrimony in Regard to the Vessel"; Angelus, *Summa*, at "Lechery"; Sylvester, *Summa*, at "The Conjugal Debt"; Lessius, *Justice and Law and the Other Cardinal Virtues* 4.3.13.

Spanish Thomist (1589–1644).[44] The use against nature, he said, was so called because of "the abuse of the seed; it is thus opposed to the sensitive nature itself." The argument was spelled out only in relation to autoerotic ejaculation: such action violated the ordering of "the seminal humor" to "generation alone" (*On the Summa theologica* 2.2.154).[45]

Emphasis on emission of semen was associated with a view that found no difference between coitus interruptus and masturbation. Characteristic of this way of thinking was the collective moral theology of the Salamancans. Under "The Vice Against Nature" they treated of autoerotic action (*mollities*) and cited the story of Onan to condemn it, without noting any distinction between acts performed in a marital context and acts performed alone. The example of Onan served equally against both. The Salamancans were aware that the objection based on Onan was an awkward way of condemning postcoital expulsion of semen by a woman. To the question whether such expulsion was "a sin against nature," they answered only, "It is a sin." The reason was not given.[46]

ENCOURAGEMENT OF EXCESS IN SEXUAL PLEASURE

In Le Maistre's opening discussion of the sin of lechery, he undertook the conventional task of showing that lechery was a capital vice. It was, he said, capital, because the inordinate use of one's body did injury to God, and the sensual delight sought in lechery blinded man to the love of God, "and after we cease to love God, it is necessary that we turn all our love to ourselves" (*Moral Questions* II, fol. 53r). Against this proposition, the old objection was noted that seminal emission was no more a sin than the emission of other superfluous fluids, and Le Maistre answered with St. Thomas that the emission must be ordered to the end for which nature ordained it. He could not stop at this answer, for, unlike St. Thomas, he did not accept the case of the sterile couple as accidental.

[44] The importance of the seed had been emphasized by the bull *Cum frequenter* of Sixtus V, issued June 22, 1587. The bull held "incapable of marriage" eunuchs who have sound and whole genitals but "lack both testicles." In the introductory portion of the bull, restating the question which gave rise to it, reference was made to "the power of emitting true seed" within the feminine vessel. Influenced by the bull, Sanchez held that a person lacking "true seed" could not marry (*The Holy Sacrament of Matrimony* 7.92.17). He then had to deal with the marriage of the aged, and fell back on the assertion that the aged had "true seed," although "per accidens" they were incapable of generation. Sanchez also taught that the meaning of "become one flesh" was "semination in the due vessel" (*ibid.* 2.21.5). On the whole subject, see Felix Trösch, "Das *Bonum prolis* als Eheziel bei Thomas Sanchez S.J. und Basilius Ponce de Leon O.E.S.A.," *Zeitschrift für katholische Theologie* 77 (1955), 9–13.

[45] John of St. Thomas, *Isagoge ad divi Thomae theologiam*, in *Cursus theologici*, ed. the Monks of Solesmes (Paris, 1931).

[46] College of Salamanca, Discalced Brothers of the Primitive Observance of Blessed Mary of the Mountain, *Cursus theologiae moralis* 26, "The Sixth and Ninth Commandments," 7 (Venice. 1728).

Hence he developed the objection, Suppose the seed were "not fit for generation," and answered as follows: "In the emission of other superfluities there do not happen such delights as happen in the emission of seed; in fact men would not think of their emission unless nature of its own accord or considerations of health induced them. And therefore no law was set as to the emission of other superfluities. In the emission of seed because of the vehement pleasure almost everyone is inclined to use it excessively" (fol. 54r).

This argument was not directed at contraception, which Le Maistre criticized directly as unnatural. But the argument was relevant to contraception in terms of his treatment of sexuality as a matter for temperance, in which excess was to be avoided. In this framework, the danger of "vehement pleasure," leading to excess, could have been invoked against intercourse where sterility had been intentionally obtained. He did not, however, make the application, and it was not made until the great specialist in matrimonial ethics, Thomas Sanchez, considered the possible cases involving semination.

On contraception itself, Sanchez adhered to the analysis insisting on natural ordination: "Is it lawful to impede conception after lawful coitus? . . . As long as copulation is contravened in its natural mode so that from the nature of the deed generation cannot follow, there is a lethal sin against nature; for the seed is frustrated of the end for which nature destined it" (*The Holy Sacrament of Matrimony* 9.20.1).

This conventional approach did not exhaust Sanchez' examination. Indirectly, dealing with two other cases, he raised a question relevant to this argument. It is universally held, he said, that a man may not voluntarily ejaculate healthy seed, outside of proper marital intercourse, even to save his life. Why is this proposition sound? "To assign a reason is most difficult." One may amputate diseased sexual organs to save one's life; one may expel seed causing disease.[47] These acts are justified on the principle that the members of the body may be sacrificed for one's good.

---

[47] Lessius provides a discussion of the general principles on mutilation as accepted by the seventeenth-century moralists: (1) A man may mutilate himself when it is necessary for the welfare of his body, for "members are for the good of the whole" (*bonum totius*). (2) Mutilation is permitted, although no evil comes from the affected member; for example, one may cut off one's own hand, if a tyrant orders one to do so on pain of death. "Such a mutilation is not disposing of one's body by one's naked will," but is necessary for the welfare of the whole. Soto is to the contrary. (3) It is "strongly probable" that one may mutilate oneself for the welfare of the state. Again, the action is not "at will," but for a cause of "great moment." (4) One may not mutilate oneself for the welfare of one's soul, for it is "never a necessary means." If a member of one's body endangers one's soul, the malice comes not from the body, but from the will. To cut off a member for this reason is a "tacit injury and blasphemy against God" (Lessius, *Justice and Law*, 2.9.14). Soto's contrary opinion on the second principle appears in Soto, *De justitia et jure decem libri* 5.2.1 (Venice, 1573).

Why does not the same principle sometimes justify voluntary ejaculation? The answer is this: the pleasure of semination is so vehement that man, if permitted to seek ejaculation in any case outside of marriage, would seek the pleasure as "his sovereign good." Hence, "administration of the seed" is in all cases denied to man. The risk of abuse, not the intrinsic unlawfulness of the act, is made the reason for the universal prohibition (*ibid.* 9.17.15).

Sanchez' conclusion was reached in a rare, untypical hypothetical, where contraception was not directly at issue. Academic as his speculation was, its importance may not be ignored. The absolute, intrinsic, always necessary orientation of ejaculation to generation was not affirmed. The absolute prohibition of nongenerative uses was maintained only by invocation of a reason of an extrinsic and prudential character. The very phrase chosen by Sanchez, "administration of the seed," suggested a breaking of the essential tie between the act of semination and generation. Seed, the rhetoric implied, could be administered for other purposes if man could be trusted.

The second case posed by Sanchez tested the necessity of linking insemination and generation. May a woman who is raped expel the seed? The factual assumption of the question is that expulsion can be effected before fertilization occurs; the act will be contraceptive, not abortive. In an answer distinguished by its legal terminology, Sanchez held contraceptive expulsion to be permissible. The act, he said, is "defensive," just as stopping a thief running with stolen goods is "defensive" although he is already possessed of the goods. If a woman may resist insemination by rape — as all agree — so she may expel the seed (*ibid.* 2.22.17).

The relation of this case to contraception in marriage is not developed. But Sanchez here ignored the old argument that "seed" is always ordered to generation. Here the belief appeared that ejaculation and generation were not naturally inseparable. In this unusual case human intelligence might separate them. How account for this divergence from the approach to contraception in marriage? Patently, Sanchez might have answered, here there is no risk of abuse in the concession of power over the seed. Here the person permitted to make the separation between insemination and generation, the victim of the rape, achieves her moral power involuntarily. The vehemence of pleasure, leading to excess, cannot under these circumstances be an objection to the contraceptive act. Here, Sanchez seems to assume, the seed may be administered.

Sanchez never brought these two unusual cases into his general discussion of contraception. It would be rash to insist that in talking about ejaculation of the seed or about a rape he had the intention of putting the argument against contraception on a new ground, the intention of working toward a less absolute rule than that required by "the ordination of the seed to generation." Yet did not Sanchez show an interest, not necessarily limited to rare cases, in the question: When is "administration of the seed" possible? Was he not a master at the use of the hypothetical to test doctrine?

In the next generation, indeed, Sanchez' approach was adopted by one of the most influential of Jesuit moralists, Paul Laymann, and applied in an argument against contraception in a case where the moralists had not produced a good reason for the prohibition. The case was that of therapeutic contraception, brusquely dismissed by Peter Cantor (above, p. 177), and not discussed after that early dismissal. "Can a woman," Laymann asked, "take a drug to prevent conception, if a doctor says or her own previous experience indicates that birth of a child may cause her death?" No, he replied, contraception is contrary to the principal end of marriage. But, sensible that this reason was not very persuasive in a case where conception would end the marriage by death, he added: "If in some cases such permission to prevent conception were given to women, it would be wonderfully abused with great loss to human generation . . . For a similar reason, the doctors of divinity commonly say that in no case is it lawful to procure emission of seed or pollution" (*Moral Theology* 5.10.3.1). Here, in substance, is adoption of the principle of "administration of the seed." Man cannot be trusted to discriminate between cases if sexual pleasure is at stake. Contraception must always be forbidden if it is not to be practiced frequently.

In form this argument may seem harsh and reactionary: it proclaims so directly a distrust of human self-control. But in making an argument against contraception which does not rest on the ordering of the act to generation, Laymann was taking a position more open than the classical one. If the real objection to contraception was extrinsic, prudential, based not on rational ordination but on the probabilities of human abuse, the prohibition of contraception might be reconsidered in the light of new probabilities, new prudential judgments. A casuist as experienced as Laymann could not have been unaware of the perspective he opened up when he chose to discuss contraception in these terms. His position, ignored by major writers later, is evidence that one of the best of seventeenth-century moralists did not find an inescapable ordination of semination to generation, even when contraception within marriage was at issue.

Sanchez' case of contraception after rape was not discussed by Laymann, but it was debated by some of the lesser seventeenth-century moralists. As reported by St. Alphonsus, the lawfulness of the contraceptive act was defended by Diana, Bossius, Marchant, and Raynaud; it was denied by Ponce, Tamburini, Escobar, and Leander. Liguori himself discussed the case under the pointed title, "Is it sometimes lawful to prevent generation of offspring?" He ranged himself with the negative opinion. Using the same legal jargon as Sanchez, he found the seed, once insemination had occurred, to be "in peaceful possession." It could not be expelled without "bespeaking injury to nature or to the human race whose propagation would be impeded" (*Moral Theology* 6.954). The deliberate personification of the seed which this terminology suggests is not as interesting as the refusal of Liguori to separate insemination and generation. The ordination of the sexual process is treated as absolute, even in rape. Generation is here insisted on, although education, in the sense required by the usual argument against fornication, will be lacking. In his anxiety not to admit a case where moral, rational, human intervention interrupts the generative process, Liguori necessarily separates generation and education.

The rejection of Sanchez implied a continuing commitment to the argument that contraception violated the "natural order." The suggestion of Laymann that contraception could not be permitted without abuse of sexuality was not further explored. The standard proposed by Le Maistre that only excess was sinful in sexual acts was not adopted. The notion of Sanchez that "administration of the seed" might be entrusted to man, were it not for the "too vehement pleasure" attached thereto, was not developed. The case against contraception continued to be made on more traditional grounds.

DESTRUCTION OF THE PURPOSES OF MARRIAGE

There was a final basis for the opposition to contraception, a basis as old as Augustine, and originally tied to Augustinian doctrine on the purposes of marital intercourse. As Augustinian doctrine on intercourse declined, one would expect this argument to decline. But it was discovered that the argument could be anchored, if not so firmly, in Augustinian doctrine on the purposes of marriage.

The argument in these terms is phrased by Le Maistre as follows: "Every conjugal copulation in which, by mode, or time, or place, one intends to impede the generation of offspring is an act opposed to conjugal chastity. Proof: the principal end of marriage is offspring" (*Moral Questions* II, fol. 48v). Like so much of Le Maistre, this text was anticipation, not precedent. No one cited it. The approach, at a much later date, became common.

In the Roman Catechism there was some suggestion of this line of attack; its vigorous denunciation of contraception followed a statement that God's intention was for men to marry "led more by the love of children than by lust." "Therefore," the Catechism continued, contraception is "a most grave crime." But the emphasis shifts as the Catechism described the contraceptive act as conspiracy in homicide (2.8.13).

In a clearer way the argument was used by Francis de Sales. The "primary and principal" end of marriage, he declared, was "the procreation of children." "Never may one laudably depart from the order it requires." He went on to denounce the act of Onan (*Introduction to the Devout Life* 3.39). The purpose of marriage was invoked later in the century by Henry Busenbaum, and his text was adopted verbatim by St. Alphonsus: any prevention of offspring by the married was "against the principal end of marriage" (*Moral Theology* 6.954).[48]

Related to this analysis was the contention that contraception was against that fidelity which was another of the three goods of marriage. A wife was not a wife where conception was avoided; therefore by contraception fidelity to one's wife was breached. The argument was rooted in *Aliquando*. It was adopted by three important authorities: Cajetan (cited by Ledesma); Ledesma (*The Great Sacrament of Matrimony* 49.6); and St. Alphonsus, quoting Busenbaum (*Moral Theology* 6.954).

The argument based on the purposes of marriage was far less absolute than that based on the nature of intercourse or on the nature of semen. If the purposes of marriage were not violated by coitus which was naturally sterile, as the non-Augustinian theologians admitted, it was not apparent why the purposes of marriage were violated by intentionally making particular acts of intercourse infertile. To frustrate all procreation was to frustrate the purposes of marriage; to frustrate particular acts of intercourse seemed to have no necessary effect upon the purposes of marriage. This kind of criticism or observation, however, was not made by the authors using the argument. Nor did any of these authors contrast their thesis with the claim that contraception violated the order of nature. In Le Maistre and Liguori both theses were asserted. The prohibition of contraception had not been subjected to such severe criticism that rigorous clarity was believed necessary. In 1750 as in 1480, the two arguments stood intertwined, natural supports of the absolute prohibition of contraception.

THE SANCTIONS AGAINST CONTRACEPTION

On the assumption, which I have advanced before, that the most potent sanction against contraception was the designation of it as a sin, a prime question is the extent of dissemination of this teaching. Printing

---

[48] Jacques Joseph Duguet, a far less famous French spiritual adviser of the eighteenth century, also gives counsel on marriage in much the same way as De Sales. To a female correspondent he cites the words of St. Paul and stresses the primary motive of marriage in the language of the Roman Catechism. He adds, "All that is contrary to the institution of the Creator, all that departs from the natural law, is shameful and abominable." J. J. Duguet, *Lettres sur divers sujets de morale et de piété* (Paris, 1733), IV, 122–123.

made possible the diffusion of canon law, books of theology, instructions for the laity, and catechisms, in a way unknown to the age of manuscripts. The educated classes now had available on a much larger scale the books containing the doctrine. Not only did books multiply, but, although literacy was far from general, the number of those capable of reading them and interested in doing so increased. As the Tridentine decrees on the seminary education of priests were slowly carried out in the middle of the seventeenth century, the written teaching of the theologians and canonists was communicated to a great number of secondary dispensers of doctrine, and a more literate local clergy made the transmission of basic information more secure.[49] Moreover, the educated seventeenth-century layman had a great interest in theology; Montaigne and Pascal were not atypical in their taste for theological works. If a layman was intellectual, he could read the master moralists themselves; if he was merely pious, he could get the doctrine digested in authors like Cherubino or De Sales.

Yet, to reach the mass of people, oral communication was still necessary. Preaching on contraception, I would guess, was even less customary than in the time when St. Bernardine could say a sermon on marriage was "a rare bird in the land." In St. Laurence of Brindisi, for example, I have found nothing comparable to the rough, frank language of Bernardine on marriage. In this famous preacher of the Counter Reformation, a sermon on marriage is a mild exhortation to love of one's spouse, in which the duties of having intercourse and procreating children are not mentioned (*Sermon on St. Joseph's Day*).[50] Sermons on the subject, albeit more restrained than St. Bernardine's, may be found. At Saint-Nicholas du Chardonnet, Paris, in the early eighteenth century, a priest with Jansenist leanings, Philip Boucher, preached against "the execrable crime of Onan," not further described; sodomy, that is, anal intercourse; and the use of potions to prevent the conception of children. Poverty, he said, was not a ground for a woman overburdened with children to refuse the marital debt.[51] Despite occasional examples of this kind, it seems probable that preaching against contraception was infrequent.

[49] A seminary system was established with the greatest difficulty. In France, forty years after Trent, particularly zealous bishops began to take steps to form seminaries. But it was only in the second half of the seventeenth century that any measureable accomplishments were made. Then John James Olier founded Saint-Sulpice, and the societies started by St. Vincent de Paul and St. John Eudes began to establish a number of diocesan seminaries. (Paul Broutin, *La Réforme pastorale en France au 17ᵉ siècle*, Paris, 1955, II, 189, 296.) Without this seminary education the average diocesan priest must have been very badly educated. In a number of areas, gross immorality on the part of the clergy was added to great ignorance (*ibid.*, I, 31).

[50] St. Laurence, *Alia homilia*, in *Opera omnia*, vol. IV.

[51] Philip Boucher, *Conférences ecclésiastiques de Paris sur le mariage*, ed. Jean Laurent Le Semelier (Paris, 1741), I, 372–373, 397. Quoted in Bergues, *La Prévention des naissances*, pp. 222–223.

The Roman Catechism contained directions to pastors as to how the faithful were to be instructed on marriage. No word should fall which would "be unworthy of pious ears or injure pious minds." Two things were especially to be inculcated: that marital acts were not to be undertaken for pleasure or lust, and that sometimes abstinence from intercourse for prayer was good (2.8.33–34). The subject of contraception, if these instructions were followed strictly by a pastor, would have been skirted, although implicitly condemned in the rejection of intercourse for pleasure. Similarly, in directing priests how to treat of sins against the Sixth Commandment, the Catechism said that the prohibition of adultery and the Lord's words against lusting after a woman were to be proclaimed publicly, but there were "to be omitted the many and various other forms of immodesty and lust, of which each one should be admonished by his pastor, as time and person require" (3.7.5). Under these instructions, contraception would have been a matter for individual warning.

A reader of the Catechism would, of course, learn that contraception by drug was a form of homicide. Not all catechisms gave even this much information to their readers. The large catechism of Canisius, as we have seen, buried the story of Onan in a mass of texts under the Sixth Commandment, and his two smaller catechisms had nothing on contraception. The catechism of Bartholomew dos Martyres (1514–1590), archbishop of Braga, had nothing either. This catechism, drawn up for the use of the diocese of Braga, was afterward much used in Portuguese-speaking lands. Homicide, fornication, and sins in marriage were all dealt with, but the usual subsumption of contraception under one of these heads was not made.[52]

If neither public preaching nor catechistical works said much of contraception, what of practice in the confessional? If the authors who were still taken as authorities were obeyed, inquiry on contraception must have occurred. Denis the Carthusian, writing for a pious laity in an age of transition, recommended frequent confession — in Advent, on or about the four principal feasts, at the beginning of Lent, Holy Week, and on special feasts of the Virgin; he added that the married should "particularly confess" whether they went beyond measure in the marital act "knowing each other out of predominating concupiscence" (*The Praiseworthy Life of the Married* 35). In a formula for confession which he provided, he included under the deadly sin of lechery these phrases to be spoken by a penitent if they fitted his case: "[I have sinned] by mixing, as it is said, with my own spouse in a forbidden way or by a sin against nature" (*ibid.* 36). At the close of the fifteenth century, the *Confessional* of St. Antoninus was the most popular guide for confessors. This work, along

[52] Bartholomeu dos Martyres, *Cathechismo ou Doutrina christiãa e praticas spirituaes* 1.8 and 9; 1, "The Sacraments," 7 (Lisbon, 1656).

with the summas of Trovamala and Angelus, was recommended to the clergy by episcopal synods of the Empire down to the middle of the sixteenth century.[53] More ancient works were also in use: St. Raymond's *Summa for Confessors* was printed in the sixteenth, seventeenth, and eighteenth centuries, not for reasons of historical scholarship but as a guide to usage. Works like those of Trovamala and Angelus assumed that the confessor would have to deal with contraception. Works like St. Raymond's and St. Antoninus' directed him to inquire about the sin. Confessionals of somewhat later date continued this tradition. I have already remarked on questions about intercourse in Savonarola's *Confessional* under the heading "Things Which Occur in Matrimony" and in Cajetan's *Little Summa of Sins* under the headings "Interrogations of the Penitents by Confessors" and "The Sin of Matrimony in Regard to the Vessel."

Beginning about the time of the Council of Trent, however, greater caution was apparent in the new books for confessors. The *Roman Ritual*, the authoritative book for administration of the sacraments, directed the confessor to inform himself on moral doctrine from the Roman Catechism.[54] To the extent that this direction was observed, the confessor might have been led to ask about a sin described as a form of homicide. The *Roman Ritual* itself, however, did not say that confessors should inquire on the subject. Rather, its sole passage on inquiry as to sexual sins admonished the priest to avoid "imprudently questioning the young of either sex, or others, about matters of which they were ignorant, lest they be scandalized and learn thereby to sin (*The Roman Ritual*, "The Sacrament of Penance"). In the same cautious vein, St. Charles Borromeo advised confessors that they should interrogate a penitent, after he had completed his self-accusation, lest he had forgotten any sin, but on sins of lechery they were to use "the maximum circumspection" (*Instructions on the Right Administration of the Sacrament of Penance*, c. 12).[55]

This cautious reticence about sins in marriage gradually became common, although probably confessors of Jansenist or merely hard-line inclinations were more inquisitive.[56] St. Alphonsus, hostile to Jansenist practices, gave this advice in the eighteenth century: "Ordinarily speaking, the confessor is not bound nor is it fitting for him to inquire about sins of the married in respect to the marital debt, except that, as modestly as he can, he may ask wives if they have rendered it, for example by asking if they have obeyed their husbands in everything. About other

---

[53] Pierre Michaud-Quantin, *Sommes de casuistique et manuels de confession au moyen âge, XII–XVI siècles* (Louvain, 1962), pp. 74–75, 105.

[54] *Rituale romanum* (Rome, 1757).

[55] Charles Borromeo, *Instructiones de recta administratione sacramenti poenitentiae* (Malines, 1850).

[56] See Broutin, *La Réforme pastorale*, II, 397–401, 538.

things, let him be silent unless asked" (*The Practice of the Confessor* 41).[57] Only wives were to be interrogated. They were to be questioned only in terms of obedience to their husbands. About other things, the priest was to be mute. Evidently there was to be no inquiry about contraception. The anticlerical reaction remarked by St. Bernardine where interrogation about marital matters was employed has apparently had its effect. The priests were now to be, in Bernardine's words from Isaias, "dumb dogs."

The main reason for the stand recommended by Alphonsus, however, was not the danger of husbandly irritation, but his entire theory of the duties of a confessor to a penitent in good faith. This theory, developed in seventeenth-century writers, was most authoritatively enunciated by Liguori, and through him had a strong influence on nineteenth-century theology. The key concepts were set out in the tract on "Conscience" which opened his *Moral Theology*. They were the correlative terms "invincible error or ignorance" and "good faith." Liguori wrote, "That [error] is vincible which can and ought to be overcome by a [moral] agent because he now either adverts to the error, or at any rate doubts about the error and at the same time adverts to the obligation of overcoming it, yet neglects to overcome it . . . Invincible is that which morally cannot be overcome, since no thought or doubt of error enters the mind of the [moral] agent, not even confusedly, when he acts or sets the action in motion" (*Moral Theology* 1.1.4). This analysis was applied to the mind of the penitent at the moment of confession. At this moment, did he have any doubt that an act he had committed was right? If he had none at this moment, his error or ignorance was "invincible." It did not matter that doubt could be created by the confessor warning him. Ignorance was vincible only if the penitent felt an obligation of dispelling it. But he would feel no obligation of informing himself further or correcting his error if he did not doubt that he was right. A man who believed that he had been doing the right thing and did not suspect that he might be wrong was "in good faith" or "invincibly ignorant," even if the confessor could give him information which would destroy his good faith or ignorance. The critical thing was the man's state of mind as he confessed (*ibid.* 6, "Penance," 610, reply to obj. 3; *ibid.* 2.36).

A penitent in the state of good faith or invincible ignorance was not to be told by his confessor of the sinfulness of a past act, if the confessor "foresaw" that his admonition would not be profitable. The reason was that such admonition would put the penitent in a state of bad faith; his ignorance would no longer be invincible. If he continued to perform the act in this state of mind, he would commit formal sin. In his earlier

[57] Alphonsus Liguori, *Pratica del confessore, per ben esercitare il suo ministero;* in Latin, *Praxis confessarii ad bene excipiendas confessiones.*

state of mind he was committing acts which, materially, were sins, but which his good faith prevented from being formal offenses to God. Informed of his sin and unlikely to mend his ways, he would become an intentional enemy of God. The confessor was not only a teacher, but a doctor. He should not impose a teaching on a penitent which would only hurt him by putting him in this position (*ibid*. 6, "Penance," 610).

Obviously a great deal depended on the confessor's judgment as to how his advice would be received. If he thought that the penitent would respond to it by abandoning his old practice, he had a duty of instruction. Admonition, Liguori noted, should not be regarded as hopeless if the penitent would briefly object and would then attempt amendment. This view anticipated the normal psychological unwillingness of anyone to admit that he has been ignorant of the evil of his ways. It seemed to favor instruction of the penitent who was in good faith but teachable. But on this difficult question of when instruction should be given, Liguori struck a balance reflecting a fairly low opinion of the likelihood of a man's accepting instruction and reforming. If there was doubt whether he would amend, the ordinary rule was "to avoid formal sins rather than material ones"; correction was to be omitted (*ibid*. 6.616).

There were two exceptions to the rule. Correction was necessary if the error was about "the means necessary to salvation." A penitent, for example, who did not believe it necessary to be sorry for his sins could not be left in his ignorance. Nor might the confessor keep silence if silence would harm the public good: "Although the confessor is bound by his office principally to occupy himself with the good of the penitent, nonetheless, since he is part of the state and constituted a minister for the good of the Christian state, he is bound to prefer the public good to the private good of the penitent" (*ibid*. 6.615). At the point where harm was done to the public, the social aspect of sin became more important than the welfare of the individual penitent. This limitation on the rule tolerating good-faith sins was later to be of great importance. All depended on what sins were considered to affect the public good. To judge from the one example given by Liguori, he himself interpreted such a sin to be one committed by a man with official responsibilities: for the public good, he said, bishops and governors and others in authority were not to be left in invincible ignorance of their duties; their ignorance was rarely inculpable, and their failings were dangerous to others. In Liguori's understanding, the sins of private persons, although they affected the life of others in the society, were not sins affecting the public good.

Contraception, then, did not fall within either of the two exceptions. Ignorance of the sinfulness of contraception was not ignorance about a means necessary for salvation. The sin did not appear to be a sin harming the public good. Consequently the confessor had no duty to inquire about the sin if a penitent were practicing contraception innocent of its sinfulness. Did Liguori believe that such good faith was possible where the sin against nature in marriage was concerned? He did not deal explicitly with this vital question, but from his treatment of the knowledge of moral rules in general the conclusion may be drawn that he believed such innocent ignorance entirely possible. He taught that without sin a man might be ignorant of the more remote conclusions of natural law — not the first principle, such as "What you do not want done to you, do not unto others" — but the propositions of natural law reached by reasoning. After all, he observed, many of the great theologians of the past had been invincibly ignorant of particular propositions of natural law. An anonymous critic assailed his teaching, contending that ignorance of the natural law must be due to some fault such as lack of diligence or lack of prayer. Liguori replied, "When we see that so many learned and pious men, even those numbered among the saints, were opposed to each other in so many matters relating to natural law, ought we perhaps to say that some of them sinned and suffered damnation?" (*Moral Theology* 1.2.174).

In the theory expounded in the *Moral Theology*, he limited his position by saying that one could not without "a fault of positive negligence" be ignorant of the Ten Commandments or even of the duties of one's state in life. However, in practice he seemed inclined to believe that simple and uninstructed persons might without mortal sin be ignorant of such obligations. In the *Practice of the Confessor*, written for Italian confessors, he warned them that the peasants "did not know the malice of adultery." Further, "it is foreseen that admonition will profit little." Hence it was not expedient to admonish those who customarily committed the sin (no. 39).[58] With this attitude toward admonition about a sin expressly condemned by the Decalogue, it seems probable that St. Alphonsus did not believe in active inquiry into practices which might have been more readily believed to be innocent than adultery by those engaging in them.

---

[58] Edition cited in note 41. Alphonsus has been speaking of mental sins, but the thrust of his statement seems to include acts of adultery as well as the desire for it. Speaking not of confession, but more generally of the Christian's duty to correct his brother, he says that where one is sinning against the natural law, he should be advised of his sin, unless "fruit is despaired of or it is feared that evil acts will become formal instead of material" (*Moral Theology* 2.36).

Two earlier instances of invincible ignorance in sexual matters are given by Jacques Marchant. A "common and uneducated man" could be invincibly ignorant of the sin of fornication, seeing that prostitutes were publicly tolerated, and being unable to distinguish between the lawful and the tolerated. "Frequently" the uneducated are invincibly ignorant of the evil of voluntary pollution. *Summarium resolutionum et responsionum ad quaestiones pastorales frequentius recurrentes circa praecepta decalogi et capitalia vitia* (Cologne, 1694), "On the Sixth Commandment," 7. It is not clear whether Marchant includes coitus interruptus under "voluntary pollution."

According to Liguori's standard, if contraception was practiced in ignorance of the teaching of the theologians, in the belief, say, that coitus interruptus was no more a sin than *amplexus reservatus*, a confessor should not disturb the contraceptor's innocence by rebuke if he foresaw that the rebuke would be little heeded.

The impression left by the *Roman Ritual*, Borromeo, and Liguori is that there was no strong effort to communicate the doctrine on contraception to the faithful. This impression — it is no more than that — would have to be varied with the religious state of particular classes and countries. Doubtless persons educated by Christian schools and the small class of the devout who enjoyed spiritual directors would have been given some indication of the basic sins against nature and marriage among which contraception was numbered. The laymen instructed in this way, by the Roman Catechism, or by special tracts like *The Rule of Married Life*, were probably more numerous than in the Middle Ages, for now schools, spiritual directors, and books for the laity were more common.

Where instruction was given, not only was the spiritual sanction of sin evoked, but the familiar technique of sanction by classification was employed. Contraception was repeatedly designated as not only a sin, but a crime, a vice against nature, a form of homicide, a kind of infidelity, a violation of marriage. The arguments by which contraception was shown to be a sin also stamped upon it the brand of infamy.

THE CONTROL OF CONTRACEPTIVE INFORMATION

In the age of printing, efforts to prevent the dissemination of information about contraception might be expected. But the effort was weak. The Council of Trent authorized the Index of Prohibited Books. In the bull of Pius IV, *Dominici gregis*, setting up the general classes of books whose reading incurred automatic excommunication, Rule 7 condemned all books "of necromancy or containing sorceries or poisons" (*veneficia*). The wording was broad enough to catch the standard medical works such as the *Canon of Medicine*. But the Rule made an immediate exception for books "of assistance to the medical arts." [59] The many medieval medical textbooks, containing contraceptive and abortifacient recipes, were thereby exempted. Nor were works like the *Canon of Medicine* placed by individual name on the list of condemned books.

In 1588, *Effraenatam* excommunicated all those aiding contraception "by writing private letters or prescriptions, or otherwise by words or signs." Taken literally, this prohibition caught not only doctors but authors of medical textbooks. But the context limited the decree to those writing something equivalent to a prescription for a particular individual.

[59] *Index librorum prohibitorum* (Rome, 1596).

The law was not long enough in force to be tested, for it was included in the general repeal of *Effraenatam* two years later by Gregory XIV.

ANNULMENT

Si conditiones was still on the books. A marriage could be annulled for a prenuptial condition against the goods of marriage, including the good of offspring. The decretal was faithfully noted by a sixteenth-century summist like Sylvester (*Summa*, at "Marriage," 3). It was discussed by a seventeenth-century casuist like Sanchez, who concluded that "the more probable opinion" was that the condition put by one spouse, the other not consenting, was sufficient ground for annulment (*The Holy Sacrament of Matrimony* 5.13.5). It was commented on by an eighteenth-century canonist like Pichler, who added to the list of typical conditions an agreement to avoid children by "imperfect coitus or exclusion of ejaculation of the seed" (the medieval writers had mentioned explicitly only the use of artificial contraceptives). Pichler also treated as nullifying a condition against the "upbringing [*educatio*] of the offspring," namely, "if you will kill a child that is born" (*Canon Law* 4.5.12). This addition, of some theoretical significance because it looked to acts affecting not only conception but the growth of the child, was not developed.

The decretal was applied, in what became the classic case, in the treatment of a marriage between a Catholic and a Protestant where the Calvinist ritual followed had contained a condition against the indissolubility of the marriage.[60] The marriage was annulled for this condition against the good of *sacramentum*. Instances of annulment for a condition against the good of offspring may have occurred, but I have not met them. Again the teaching of the decretal was of more importance than its enforcement.

REFUSAL OF INTERCOURSE

According to some medieval authors, a wife had the duty to refuse intercourse if her husband sought intercourse outside the vagina. This sanction for contraception was not much discussed in the later period. Such writers as Angelus, Cajetan, Savonarola, and Soto made no explicit analysis of the questions involved. Denis and Cherubino, writing so frankly for married folk, did not mention the matter. At the middle of the sixteenth century, the Roman Catechism, the catechisms of Canisius, and the catechism of Dos Martyres had no instruction on the point. At the turn of the century Francis de Sales, again writing for the laity, failed to mention what a wife should do if confronted by a husband accustomed

---

[60] Decree of the Holy Office, December 2, 1680, directed to Bosnia, *Codicis juris canonici fontes*, IV, no. 755.

to practice contraception. The important authorities, Ledesma and Lessius, also passed over the point.

The only position with support in the old authorities was, however, re-asserted by Sylvester. If the husband did not "keep the vessel," the wife was excused from mortal sin in cooperating with him only by absolute violence, that is, only by force overcoming her free will (*Summa*, at "The Conjugal Debt").

An entirely different position was taken by Le Maistre in the fifteenth century, by Sanchez in the seventeenth century, and by St. Alphonsus in the eighteenth century. Le Maistre treated two situations. If a husband intended "to induce perpetual sterility" or to cause an abortion, then his wife, by the virtue of conjugal chastity, was bound not to have inter-course. But if a husband sought simply to prevent conception in the instant act of intercourse, there was a different case. Here "the husband seeks only what is his own, and the wife by rendering it does not suffer substantial harm." If his contraceptive intent would probably change, the wife might put her husband off "by feigning sickness or by the pretext of some respectable business." If these subterfuges failed, the marital debt took precedence. "She ought, therefore, to render it, and rendering it so lead him to love of her that she can persuade him to desire children" (*Moral Questions* II, fol. 48v). Without benefit of analysis of the kind of cooperation involved, Le Maistre struck bluntly for a result giving pre-eminence to the personal relationship between the spouses.

Sanchez dealt explicitly with cooperation by a wife in coitus interruptus. He held her act to be lawful, if she did not assent to her husband's with-drawal. "The malice of the man is entirely extrinsic and alien to her act." He even implied that a wife had the duty of engaging in intercourse even if her husband was accustomed to engage in withdrawal and ejacu-lation: she "returns the debt lawfully exacted" (*The Sacrament of Holy Matrimony* 9.17.3).

Liguori, writing a century and a half later, approached the case with the terminology he used to analyze all problems of cooperation in sin. His central distinction was between formal cooperation and material co-operation: "An act is *formal* which concurs in the evil will of the other and cannot be done without sin. That is *material* which concurs only in the evil act of another, beyond the intention of the cooperator" (*Moral Theology* 4.59). Formal cooperation was always sinful. Material coopera-tion was sinful if the act the cooperator performed was itself a sin. But material cooperation might be without sin if the act he did was good or indifferent. To be without sin, material cooperation required justification. Justification was relative; in any particular situation, justification had to be determined by a prudential weighing of such elements as the serious-ness of the sin cooperated in, the degree of cooperation given, the harm done to an innocent third person, and the cause or reason for cooperating. In his analysis of such prudential estimates, Liguori customarily distinguished between "grave" and "very grave" reasons for cooperating. A "very grave" reason was "fear of such evil that according to the laws of charity no one is required to undergo it to avoid evil to another" (Laymann, quoted by Liguori, 4.59). A man, for example, might lawfully open the strongbox of someone else for a robber when his life was threatened: his material cooperation in the sin of robbery was justified by the very grave reason of danger to his life. A "grave," as opposed to a "very grave," reason could be economic. A man in the business of selling swords might lawfully sell swords to all customers, although he knew some would misuse them; he would suffer grave economic loss by refusing this remote cooperation in their sin. These categories, developed in the seventeenth century, run through later analyses of cooperation.

With these distinctions in mind, Liguori's treatment of the role of the wife in coitus interruptus may be considered. Four alternatives were possible. The wife's part in this kind of intercourse might have been viewed as a sin in its own right, or formal cooperation in the sin of another, or material cooperation, or no cooperation at all. The first two alternatives were not stated. A "probable" opinion was that her act was not cooperation of any kind, "for she does not cooperate in the semination outside the vessel, but only in the beginning of the copulation, and that is entirely lawful for both." If the wife, however, sought coitus, knowing from experience what her husband would do, then she was giving material cooperation to an act which she knew would lead to sin by her husband. From a charitable concern for his salvation, she should not seek; this charitable duty, however, could give way to a "just and grave reason" on her part. She might seek coitus if in danger of incontinence. Suppose she were unsure if she was in such danger of incontinence that she should occasion her husband's sin? If she suffered "perpetual scruples" on this point, Liguori said, that in itself was a sufficiently grave reason to justify her seeking intercourse. The "more probable" opinion was also that the wife was bound to cooperate if her husband sought intercourse, although she knew that he intended to practice coitus interruptus (*Moral Theology* 6.947).

The benign toleration of Liguori was remarkable. It led him to say that there was not even material cooperation in having intercourse when the husband "wants to seminate outside the vessel after the beginning of copulation." To most persons the wife's act would seem to have been a sine qua non of the husband's objective and therefore some form of cooperation. Left unexplored and unmentioned was whether the rules on material cooperation justified intercourse where the husband used a condom or the wife used a douche or potion.

The difference between the old opinion so strenuously maintained by authors such as Gerson, St. Bernardine, and Sylvester and the position taken broadly by Le Maistre and Sanchez, and more narrowly by Liguori, was measurable. Can the difference be accounted for by supposing that the older authorities meant only cooperation in anal or oral intercourse? The language they used — "omission of the due vessel" — was broad enough to cover coitus interruptus. There was a perceptible difference in evaluation when Liguori expressly approved cooperation in the beginning of an act of intercourse in which ejaculation would occur outside the vagina. Le Maistre's view, which led logically to permitting approval of a wife's cooperation with a husband using a condom, was even more radically a departure from the old approach. Change, then, had occurred. If Le Maistre was not generally accepted, Liguori's opinion represented a new latitude allowed a woman whose husband was bent on contraception.

The sanctions against sin were better organized in the seventeenth century than in the thirteenth. Probably more persons were informed of their marital duties as a result of spiritual books and schooling than in a less educated age. At the same time the sanctions were softened by the development of two doctrines: the teaching that good faith should be respected in the confessional, so that inquiry should not disturb the penitent ignorantly violating natural law and unlikely to amend; and the teaching that a wife might cooperate in coitus interruptus. In these two doctrines, the bite of the law on contraception was considerably weakened.

By the mid-eighteenth century the shift in analysis whereby contraception was viewed not as homicide but as a violation of the purposes of marriage had diluted the stringent teaching of the canon law and the Roman Catechism. Despite the continuance of a strong pro-Augustinian current among the French and Belgian "hards," the trend was away from the rigors of the medieval position on sexual intercourse. Contraception was still unmistakably condemned. But at the end of the period 1450–1750 the reasons for opposing the contraceptive act, and the application of sanctions against it, seemed to lack the vitality and urgency which the denunciations of contraception by St. Augustine or St. Bernardine had once communicated.

PART FOUR

DEVELOPMENT AND CONTROVERSY

1750–1965

CHAPTER XIII

THE SPREAD OF BIRTH CONTROL:
THE RESPONSES OF THE BISHOPS
AND THE POPE

A NEW PERIOD in the history of the doctrine on contraception began near the end of the eighteenth century. It was marked by two phenomena: the decline in the birth rate of France, the most populous country in Europe, and the open advocacy, especially in England and the United States, of birth control as a socially desirable practice. Of these two phenomena, the first had the greater immediate impact on Catholic teaching. France was the largest of Catholic countries; what happened in it was bound to be of intense concern to the Church.

THE PRACTICE OF BIRTH CONTROL

According to estimates accepted by demographers as reliable, the French birth rate per thousand persons was 38.6 in 1771 and had been falling slightly since 1750. By 1800 it had dropped to 32. The significance of the fall for France at the very height of her expansion geographically is described provocatively by Alfred Sauvy, the present director of the Institut National des Etudes Démographiques, as "the most important fact of all her history." [1] The precipitous 17 percent drop was only the beginning of a phenomenon that appeared in France almost a century before it occurred in other European countries. For the rest of the century, the French decline continued to be marked. By 1829, the birth rate had fallen below 30 per thousand. It was never to be as high again. By 1851–1860, the rate was 26.3. [2]

[1] Alfred Sauvy, *La Prévention des naissances* (Paris, 1962), p. 13.
[2] Charles H. Pouthas, *La Population française pendant la première moitié du 19ᵉ siècle*, Institut National des Etudes Démographiques (Paris, 1956), p. 21. After 1800, reasonably reliable statistics are used instead of estimates.

Proof of a declining birth rate is not necessarily proof of the spread of contraception. In this case, however, there is reason to believe that contraception was the decisive factor. The hypothesis that postponement of marriage with growing industrial urbanization occasioned the decline seems to be disproved by the case of England, where industrialization tended to encourage earlier marriages and a higher birth rate.[3] The hypothesis that the French became less fertile for genetic reasons seems disproved by the history of French stock in nineteenth-century Canada, where no diminution of fertility is observable.[4] Emigration of couples of a child-bearing age does not seem to be the key, for such emigration was less common from France than from England or Germany. Sweeping generalizations are necessarily tentative — other factors cannot be excluded — but the spread of contraception seems to have been principally responsible for the fall.[5] The evidence is especially impressive where particular French towns have been studied, as Henry has studied Crulai.[6]

The decline thus brought about in natality had a serious effect on the population of France in an age when infectious fatal diseases were still uncontrolled. Vaccination had been introduced as a preventive in the mid-eighteenth century; it became widespread, however, only in the latter part of the nineteenth century, and smallpox and typhus did not begin to disappear as substantial threats to life until after 1870. Tuberculosis and cholera continued to cause the death of thousands throughout the century.[7] Mortality was lower in 1850 than 1800, but there was no steady improvement. The worst years were 1832–1834 — dramatic testimony to the impact of cholera. Major diseases threatened adults. Major diseases and unsanitary methods of treatment menaced babies and young children. Infant mortality remained very high in the first half of the century, with even less improvement than the adult rate.[8] As late as 1840, more than half the children born in Paris and Manchester died under the age of five.[9]

With a sharply declining birth rate and a slightly declining mortality rate, the point was reached at which the net rate of reproduction fell below 1. By 1850 the French nation was failing to reproduce itself.[10] A

[3] On the effect of industrialization on marriage in England, see J. T. Krause, "Changes in English Fertility and Mortality, 1781–1850," *Economic History Review* 11 (1958), 52, 67.

[4] Alfred Sauvy, "Essai d'une vue d'ensemble," in Helen Bergues, *La Prévention des naissances dans la famille* (Paris, 1960), p. 382.

[5] Sauvy, in Bergues, *La Prévention*, p. 382.

[6] Louis Henry, "L'Apport des témoignages et de la statistique," in Bergues, *La Prévention*, p. 375.

[7] William L. Langer, "Europe's Initial Population Explosion," *American Historical Review* 69 (1963), 5, 6.

[8] Pouthas, *La Population française*, p. 26.

[9] Langer, "Europe's Initial Population Explosion," p. 6.

[10] Pouthas, *La Population française*, p. 28.

more drastic reduction in mortality in the later nineteenth century again produced a surplus of births over deaths. The birth rate continued to decline.

The statistics on births and deaths may serve not only to demonstrate the seriousness of the new problem, but to challenge one hypothesis about the connection between contraception and religion. The improvement of medicine and the spread of contraception, it has been asserted, accompanied each other. With the control of death by medicine, there arose the belief that life could be controlled as well. A rationalistic faith underlies both the perfecting of medical technique and the practice of contraception. Irrational folklore had associated sexual pleasure and the life force. Theology had confounded the ends of nature with the purposes of God. Both folk belief and theology had treated sexuality as sacrosanct. But the new rationalism began to treat nature, including man, as a machine. Improvement and control were possible.[11]

It is difficult to deny that this hypothesis offers valuable suggestions. The age of birth control begins in the age of *l'homme machine*, of the perfectibility of man, of a clear-eyed rationalism that is impatient with the mysterious, the sacred, the numinous. Rationalism existed in England, Germany, and America too, but nowhere as in France was it the philosophy of the day, destroying the institutions which elsewhere tempered its impact. Yet the hypothesis must be qualified. Control of nature, of diseases, of death, had not been achieved in the late eighteenth century. Such control was at most a program. Birth control was more readily achievable. The deists, the encyclopedists, the revolutionaries, were not themselves open advocates of birth control. If their philosophy led themselves and others to practice it, practice responded to a silent logic and an unachieved hope.

The hypothesis must also be supplemented. France was still predominantly rural. As late as 1850, 70 percent of the population was nonurban.[12] These people were largely dependent on uncontrolled forces like the weather. They lacked the rationalistic sophistication of the cities. Yet they, too, must have practiced contraception extensively, if the birth rate was so seriously affected. What accounted for their behavior?

Its roots may be found in the spiritual malaise that affected France as profoundly as the rationalistic spirit. The Church in mid-eighteenth century France was officially supported, but rejected in many hearts. There resulted, at first, not open defiance, but acts of disobedience to the laws of the Church in an area of conduct which the Church could control

---

[11] This hypothesis is proposed by Philippe Ariès, "Interprétation pour une histoire des mentalités," in Bergues, *La Prévention*, pp. 325–327.

[12] Pouthas, *La Population française*, p. 196.

only if it retained spiritual allegiance.[13] When the Revolution occurred and the Church was rejected openly, there was not merely a repudiation of an official ecclesiastical establishment. There spread at the same time a pervasive and destructive cynicism toward all efforts to regulate conduct by intangible ideals. If the Church was a lie, then it was each man for himself — this is the kind of radical individualism much more characteristic of bourgeois Latin anticlericals than of less disillusioned Anglo-American agnostics. It was not part of the program of revolutionary rationalism, but it was often the result. It is this difference in spiritual reaction, I suggest, which is paramount in the puzzling fact that France experienced the spread of contraception before England or the United States.[14]

Why France more than Italy? I would suspect from the Italian moralists and from the demographic data already cited in Chapter XI that contraception had spread in Italy before it took hold in France, so that in nineteenth-century Italy the changes were not so dramatic. Moreover, in Italy, despite a spiritual malaise comparable to that of France, the Church never ceased functioning. In contrast, in much of France the ecclesiastical organization was annihilated. As late as 1815, thirteen thousand French parishes were without priests.[15] For forty years — two generations — large numbers of Frenchmen were without any priestly instruction whatever. In France lack of religious education of the believers added to the consequences of disaffection and open rejection in half the nation.

The predominant factors in the spread of birth control in France were, then, of an intellectual, ideological, religious character. There were other less intangible forces. France experienced the effects of the Industrial Revolution. A rising standard of living, a greater number of chances at middle-class prosperity, marked the nineteenth century. As can be observed in such societies as Japan today, it is often a prospect of economic betterment, rather than a reality of utter destitution, which is the most powerful incentive to family limitation.[16] The French bourgeois and the French peasant responded to emancipation from the restraints of the

[13] Sauvy, in Bergues, *La Prévention*, p. 389.

[14] Sauvy points to the eighteenth-century rationalists' insistence on moral law, and suggests that as the traditional props of morality in religion were abandoned there was all the greater fear of a moral decline. "La pruderie du XIXᵉ siècle trouve peut-être une explication analogue" (Sauvy, in Bergues, *La Prévention*, p. 387). It seems to me that these observations make sense in accounting for official statements, rules, attitudes; often enough, disillusioned individuals must have adopted different rules of conduct for themselves.

[15] Edgar Hocedez, *Histoire de la théologie au XIXᵉ siècle* (Brussels, 1947–1952), I, 69.

[16] Kingsley Davis, *The Theory of Change and Response in Modern Demographic History* (Berkeley, 1963), p. 350.

ancien régime with a keen awareness that their success depended on themselves and that a multitude of mouths to feed was generally a drain. In the special spiritual and ideological conditions of France the economic motivation, surely no more powerful than in the England of the early Industrial Revolution, operated without restraint from ancestral pieties. It was easy and economical to improve one's lot by curtailing one's obligations.

I stress the motivations which seem to have led to the diffusion of contraception in France, because I think it clear that the circumstances under which the diffusion took place in France were of critical importance in determining the reaction of the Church in the nineteenth century. The weight of tradition, to be sure, played a large part in this reaction. But the tradition met no counterweight. The theologians were asked to judge a practice supported by neither scientific opinion nor governmental approval, justified by no pressing social exigencies, and not related by theological analysis to Christian love. Birth control in France first appeared as irreligious, calculating, egotistic.

To say this is not to say that contraception was not practiced by believers. A study correlating birth rates and areas where a majority of the population remained practicing Catholics shows that, in the course of the century, the birth rate of the faithful also declined. Religious conviction acted as a brake, but not as an absolute barrier, to population decline: the average birth rate in the believing areas was as high as the maximum birth rate elsewhere in France.[17] Such a result, of course, does not by itself demonstrate that the faithful were using contraceptive methods rather than practicing continence. But the comments, complaints, and questions we shall shortly examine suggest that contraception was the common form of control.

The French experience was the critical one for the nineteenth-century Church. At the same time a movement was starting in England which was at length to be of even greater significance for doctrinal development. In the early nineteenth century, the "movement" was scarcely more than a few voices. They were only a portent; they had no substantial impact upon either marital conduct or upon the teaching of the Church. But for the first time since the Cathars there were persons in Europe teaching that the prevention of birth was good. In sharp contrast to the Cathars, these persons were not opposed to all procreation, but only to uncontrolled procreation. They acted without any metaphysical or religious hostility to creation. Their motives, as proclaimed by themselves, were economic, political, social, and moral.

---

[17] Philippe Ariès, *Histoire des populations françaises et de leurs attitudes devant la vie depuis le XVIII° siècle* (Paris, 1948), p. 470.

Overpopulation itself had become the subject of intellectual concern with the publication in 1798 of *An Essay on the Principle of Population*, by Thomas Malthus. According to Malthus, "population when unchecked goes on doubling itself every twenty-five years, or increases in a geometrical ratio." Malthus did not believe that the food supply could be increased faster than arithmetically. Accordingly, he supposed that the unregulated population of England would be 176,000,000 by 1900, while the food supply would be sufficient to feed 55,000,000.[18] Similar results were predicted for the world as a whole. Clearly the situation would become intolerable, and a solution was mandatory. The solution of Malthus was to check population by "moral restraint," that is, by the postponement of marriage. Contraception he did not recommend or even consider, merely alluding to "violations of the marriage bed and improper arts to conceal the consequences of irregular connections [which] clearly come under the head of vice." [19] The work of this young Anglican clergyman was, nonetheless, to be the foundation of respectable advocacy of birth control in the nineteenth century.

Contraception as a social remedy was publicly, though cautiously, proposed by certain Englishmen interested in social reform, utilitarian in ethics, and consciously free of any allegiance to traditional Christian beliefs. Among the first, if not the first, was Jeremy Bentham. In 1797 he hinted, in awkward circumlocutions, at the use of "sponges" to limit the poor, with the ultimate objective of reducing the poor rates.[20] Twenty years later, in an article on colonies for the *Encyclopaedia Britannica*, James Mill declared that, instead of the inefficacious expedient of colonization as an outlet for excess population, a way "neither doubtful nor difficult" could be found, if "the superstitions of the nursery were discarded and the principle of utility held steadily in view." [21]

Direct and explicit advocacy was undertaken by Francis Place (1771–1854). A remarkable self-educated workingman, Place was at the center

[18] Thomas Malthus, *An Essay on the Principle of Population*, 2nd ed. (London, 1803), pp. 5, 8.

[19] *Ibid.*, p. 11. A utopian proposal for birth control by abstinence was made by Jonathan Swift in *Gulliver's Travels* 4.8, published in 1726, after Swift had spent years in Ireland. The perfectly rational Houyhnhnms act "to prevent the country from being overburdened by numbers." The superior class of Houyhnhnms cease from intercourse after they have had a child of each sex; the inferior Houyhnhnms are permitted to produce three to provide a supply of domestic servants.

On the steady growth of discussion about the relation between population and food in the eighteenth century, see Charles Emil Strangeland, *Pre-Malthusian Doctrines of Population* (New York, 1904), pp. 224–351.

[20] Jeremy Bentham, "Situation and Relief of the Poor," in Arthur Young, ed., *Annals of Agriculture and Other Useful Acts* 29 (1797), 423.

[21] "Colony," *Supplement to the Fourth, Fifth and Sixth Editions of the Encyclopaedia Britannica* (Edinburgh, 1824), p. 261. The author is identified in the article "Birth Control," by Frank H. Hankins, in the *Encyclopedia of the Social Sciences*, II, 560–561.

of English liberalism in the first part of the century; he was described by Robert Owen as "the real leader of the Whig Party." He met James Mill in 1808 and through him Bentham; he became a friend of Owen in 1813. He himself at nineteen had married a seventeen-year-old girl and, in a life marked in its early years by desperate poverty, had fathered fifteen children. The emphasis put on education of children by Mill and Bentham impressed him. In 1820 he began openly advocating birth control, which his friends believed in but hesitated to support openly, and which the other leaders of the working classes turned from supporting. In 1822, he took the opportunity of commenting on an earlier controversy between Malthus and William Godwin by writing a book of his own, *Illustrations and Proofs of the Principle of Population,* in which his views were discreetly stated: "If means were adopted to prevent the breeding of a larger number of children than a married couple might desire to have, and if the laboring part of the population could thus be kept below the demand for labor, wages would rise so as to afford the means of comfortable subsistence for all, and all might marry." [22] It was essential to understand "that it was not disreputable for married persons to avail themselves of such precautionary means as could, without being injurious to health or destructive of female delicacy, prevent conception." [23] Place's book did not describe these means. But in anonymous handbills, distributed to workingmen, he recommended the use of coitus interruptus and occlusive sponges.[24] The social and moral restraints on discussion of the subject were still such that neither Bentham, Mill, nor Place in his own name actually recommended particular contraceptive devices: Bentham spoke ambiguously, Mill in generalities, and Place anonymously.[25]

In the United States open advocacy of birth control was undertaken in 1830 by Robert Owen's eldest son, Robert Dale Owen, in *Moral Physiology: or A Brief and Plain Treatise on the Population Question.* Owen recommended the use of coitus interruptus, a method he had

[22] Francis Place, *Illustrations and Proofs of the Principle of Population* (London, 1822), p. 176. On the incidents in Place's life just referred to, see Graham Wallas, *The Life of Francis Place* (New York, 1898), pp. 1–5, 63–72, 169–170.

[23] Place, *Illustrations and Proofs,* p. 165.

[24] Norman E. Himes, *Medical History of Contraception* (Baltimore, 1936), pp. 212–218.

[25] The state of English sentiment on the subject may be gauged from a letter of April 24, 1831, from Bentham to Place. Addressing Place as "Dear Good Boy," he tells of a conversation with Archibald Prentice: "I asked him why he called you a bad man; his answer was because of the pains you had taken to disseminate your anti-over-population (I should have said your over-population-stopping) expedient . . . As to the point in question, I took care not to let him know how my opinion stood; the fat would have been all in the fire, unless I succeeded in converting him, for which there was no time." (Bentham to Place, in Wallas, *The Life of Francis Place,* p. 81.)

heard from French physicians to be widely and successfully used in France. In its first year his book went through several editions, and in fifty years it had sold over 75,000 copies. Another American book of the same era, *The Fruits of Philosophy: or The Private Companion of Young Married People,* by Charles Knowlton, both advocated contraception and taught how to practice it. Knowlton, a doctor, placed emphasis on post-coital douching, stating that he was "quite confident that a liberal use of pretty cold water would be a never-failing preventative." [26]

The advocacy of birth control preceded technical developments facilitating its practice. The methods of Place, Owen, and Knowlton were as old as the Greeks. In 1843, however, the vulcanization of rubber led to the possibility of manufacturing inexpensive rubber condoms, and this form of contraceptive became increasingly distributed.[27] Coitus interruptus remained the most common way of practicing contraception in continental Europe. Referring to this usage, the French Jesuit, John Gury, wrote in 1850: "In our days, the horrid plague of onanism has flourished everywhere" (*Compendium of Moral Theology* 2.705).[28] It continued to be the most usual way. Even a century later Jean Sutter found it the most widely diffused and most widely used of contraceptive practices.[29]

What Rome reacted against, then, was neither a new technique of control nor a new teaching on the purposes of control. The English and American works were not before the ecclesiastical authorities. The new arguments on the benefits to society obtainable through contraception were not presented to the theologians. In 1806 the first French writer to defend contraception in a published work, Jean-Baptiste Etienne de Senancour, had recommended "precautions" to women for purely personal reasons, such as avoiding unpleasant consequences in fornication.[30] Contraception was not set out as a solution for overpopulation in any French literature before the middle of the nineteenth century. Even in England and America the few voices raised in favor of birth control on economic grounds were not a chorus. Medical, scientific, and sociological backing had not yet been given to the birth control movement. What the Church encountered and judged in the first half of the nineteenth century was the widespread individual decision to limit births, chiefly by coitus interruptus, and chiefly in France.

[26] Himes, *Medical History of Contraception,* pp. 224–227.
[27] *Ibid.,* p. 227.
[28] John Gury, *Compendium theologiae moralis* (Tournai, 1852).
[29] J. Sutter, "Sur la diffusion des méthodes contraceptives," in Bergues, *La Prévention,* pp. 345–346.
[30] Senancour, *De l'amour,* quoted in Bergues, *La Prévention,* p. 305. Sauvy states that this reference seems to be the first recommendation of contraceptives by a French author writing for the public at large (*ibid.,* p. 388).

RESPONSES OF ROME, 1816–1876

The new pressure on the old rule occurred in a period when moral theology was at its nadir. The reasons for this state were both institutional and intellectual. The institutional decline began before the Revolution, with the fall of the Jesuits. Some six thousand of them, responsible for over two hundred *collèges,* had been expelled from France by Louis XV in 1762; the order was suppressed altogether by Pope Clement XIV in 1778. In these moves the institution was eliminated which for two centuries had played the principal part in Catholic education, and which had nurtured the greater number of Catholic moralists. The Revolution completed the havoc. Not only in France itself, which since 1100 had been the center of Catholic intellectual life, but in Germany, Spain, the Low Countries, the Church lost its centers of higher learning.[31] Institutional deprivation was paralleled by the degradation of theology. Looking back, twentieth-century historians can describe theology in 1800 as "almost dead" or as reduced to "profound decadence." [32] The rationalism dominant in intellectual life outside the Church was not acceptable within it, and the intellectual resources of the Christian past were neglected. The Bible was little known. The Fathers were forgotten. Scholasticism was discredited.[33] If theology as a subject was at a mean and apathetic level, the misery of moral theology was acute. Of all subjects this was studied scientifically the least. As the most practical of topics, it was dominated by timidity, conventional prudence, and a bourgeois prudery. Theology as a whole began to revive in post-Napoleonic Europe. Moral theology was the last branch of the subject to be affected. In the entire nineteenth century it is difficult to name a single person who displayed genius in its study and exposition.

While Catholic universities and university theology were lacking, some seminaries existed, and more were added. The typical intellectual formation of a nineteenth-century theologian was that of the seminary, and the typical book on moral theology was the manual for instruction of students. A seminary system, standardized and controlled from Rome, was fed on a diet of manuals. This fare did not consist of original intellectual works. The manuals were statements of conclusions with citation of authority and a minimum of reasoning. They were composed on the theory that moral principles could be learned like a code, and the detailed argumentation that gave depth to a work like Aquinas' *Summa theologica* or Liguori's *Moral Theology* was lost in them.

[31] Hocedez, *Histoire de la théologie au XIX⁰ siècle,* I, 67–69, 132.
[32] The first description is that of Henry Pesch, S.J., quoted *ibid.,* I, 21; the second is that of Hocedez himself, I, 13.
[33] *Ibid.,* I, 20.

Of these works the most successful, as it was the most typical, was the *Compendium of Moral Theology* by John Gury (1801–1866), a French Jesuit. This work, based on Liguori, was developed by Gury in teaching at the Jesuits' Roman College. It appeared in 1850 and quickly swept the seminary world. Editions appeared in Germany, England, Belgium, and Spain, as well as Italy. By 1865 it had gone through sixteen editions.[34] Revisions and up-datings of it have continued to the present; a revised Gury has been brought out as recently as 1950 in Naples.

In addition to Gury, two French bishops presented adaptations of Liguori and enjoyed a reputation as moral theologians: Thomas Gousset (1792–1866) wrote, in 1832, *Justification de la théologie morale de St. Alphonse de Liguori*; John Baptist Bouvier (1783–1854), bishop of Le Mans, wrote, in Latin, *Dissertation on the Sixth Commandment of the Decalogue and Supplement to the Treatise on Marriage*, a practical work for confessors.[35] In the United States, the first American to write as a Catholic moralist, Francis P. Kenrick, bishop of Philadelphia, wrote in 1839 a *Theologia moralis* largely based on Liguori.

Liguori, indeed, was the cry of most writers who undertook to expound Catholic moral doctrine in the nineteenth century. Bitterly criticized by conservatives in his lifetime, St. Alphonsus became unassailable after his death. In the process of beatification in 1800, his works were examined, and the examining commission of Roman ecclesiastics pronounced them "free from error." He was beatified in 1816. In 1831, at the instigation of Gousset, then vicar-general of Cardinal Rohan, the Penitentiary was asked, Might confessors be "undisturbed" who, when in doubt, followed Liguori's opinions, "not weighing the elements and reasons on which his various opinions depend?" The Penitentiary answered affirmatively.[36] This extraordinary statement did not entirely substitute Liguori for reason or the Gospels: the confessor had to be "in doubt" before Liguori could be invoked as an absolute guide. The answer, moreover, dealt only with practice. But for practice here was a decisive official commitment to the use of his teaching. He was canonized by Gregory XVI in 1839 and declared a doctor of the Church by Pius IX in 1871.

Each step in the elevation of Liguori might be read as a mark of the decline of French Jansenism and the "hard" attitudes loosely described

---

[34] P. Bernard, "Gury, Jean-Pierre," *DTC* 6²:1994.

[35] J. B. Bouvier, *Dissertatio in sextum decalogi praeceptum et supplementum ad tractatum de matrimonio*, 18th ed. (Paris, n.d.) (hereafter cited as *Supplement to the Treatise on Marriage*), p. 127. There are at least eighteen editions in the nineteenth century of this work. According to a "Notice" at the front of the book, it would be sold to a person presenting authorization from the superior of a major seminary or the vicar-general of the diocese. Its circulation was thus presumably restricted for the most part to priests.

[36] Text of decree in *Vindiciae alphonsianae* (Rome, 1873), p. xvii.

as Jansenistic. The loss of institutions in the Revolution was a disaster. But it had permitted a fresh start. The new French church was neither so Gallican nor so Jansenist as that of the *ancien régime;* the Roman authorities who, for a century, had tended to associate the two attitudes, were determined that neither Gallican independence of the pope nor Jansenistic rigor should revive. The exaltation of Liguori assured the ultimate extinction of Jansenist morality. In the course of this process, Augustinianism suffered a partial decline in official moral theology on marriage, while surviving in many regions such as French Canada as a tradition and an outlook. In the manuals St. Augustine was replaced without much struggle by St. Alphonsus.

Intellectual torpor ameliorated by a Liguorian tolerance: it is against this background that the first Roman responses to birth control must be seen. The congregations who were asked to pass on the new questions were staffed by men who had learned the inadequate theology of the day in seminaries of a quality no better than the theology. Their knowledge of history was small. Sociology and psychology were unknown disciplines. The men in the congregations looked at the textbooks for their answers and transplanted to the nineteenth century rules worked out for other ages.

The Roman congregations responded to inquiries from the clergy, chiefly the French clergy. The restored Church in France had some awareness of confronting a new situation. The French clergy realized that the widespread practice of birth control was a new problem. Rome slowly, even sluggishly, replied to their request for guidance.

The inquiries and the replies centered about "onanism" and "onanists." What was meant by these terms? "Onanism" was used to designate contraceptive behavior as early as the middle of the eighteenth century.[37] The first use of either term I have encountered in an ecclesiastical document is in a question addressed by Thomas Gousset to the Penitentiary in 1822. Gousset spoke of a husband known to be an "onanist." He did not explain the term. The Roman tribunal answering him took the word to refer to one who, "instead of consummating, withdraws and ejaculates outside the vessel."[38] Ecclesiastical usage in the middle of the nineteenth century continued to equate onanism with coitus interruptus. It was so defined in terms of withdrawal and extravaginal ejaculation in 1850 in Gury's *Compendium of Moral Theology* (2.702). In this sense, onanism was contrasted with artificial means in a decree of the Inquisition in 1853,

---

[37] Philippe Dutoit-Mambrini, *De l'onanisme ou Discours philosophique et moral sur la luxure artificielle et sur tous les crimes relatifs* (Lausanne, 1760), cited in Bergues, *La Prévention,* p. 266.

[38] *Decisiones Sanctae Sedis de usu et abusu matrimonii,* ed. Hartmann Batzill, 2nd ed. (Rome, 1944), p. 15.

which spoke of a man acting "onanistically or by condom" (*onanistice sive condomistice*).[39] The thirteenth edition of Gury, edited by A. Ballerini and B. Palmieri in 1898, still preserved the 1850 definition. At least until 1900, Roman documents using "onanist" or "onanism" without further qualification may be presumed to refer only to coitus interruptus.

The inquiries of the clergy dealt with two practical problems: the responsibility of a spouse cooperating in contraception, and the responsibility of a confessor to inquire about the sin. Let us examine first the decisions on cooperation.

COOPERATION

The cooperation asked about was always the cooperation of a wife in the contraceptive act of her husband. This approach not only reflected the belief that the male took the initiative in marital matters, but it focused on a key aspect of the ecclesiastical control of morals. In France, and in many of the Latin countries, the Church had lost its hold on the allegiance of the majority of the men while it retained the allegiance of the majority of the women. The answers on cooperation were concerned with the moral status of the sex likely to respond to directions from the confessional.

Between 1816 and 1823 there were three responses from the Penitentiary, the Roman tribunal for questions arising in the administration of the sacrament of penance. The first decision, dated November 15, 1816, responded to the inquiry of one Blain, vicar of Chambéry. Some theologians were maintaining that it was mortal sin for a wife to engage in intercourse where she knew her husband would practice coitus interruptus.[40] Blain, apparently troubled by this rigorist doctrine, asked what the obligations of the wife were. The Penitentiary replied that a woman might have intercourse although she knew by experience that her husband would withdraw and ejaculate outside the vagina, if by refusing intercourse she would be badly regarded [*habenda*] by her husband and therefore fears serious detriment to herself." The decree added that the woman "should not cease prudently to warn her husband to desist from this baseness." In the light of existing authorities, the tribunal did not feel able to decide whether a woman could seek intercourse with a husband likely to practice coitus interruptus. The head of the tribunal, Cardinal Michael De Petro, added as his personal opinion that she might, if she were in danger of committing a sin of incontinence.[41]

A second interrogator, this time anonymous, asked the Penitentiary if a wife might have intercourse with a husband known to conduct himself

[39] *Ibid.*, p. 21
[40] Bouvier says that "a number" of authors held this view, but he cites only a few authors of little weight; *Supplement to the Treatise on Marriage* 2.1.3.4, pp. 172–173.
[41] *Decisiones Sanctae Sedis*, pp. 11–12.

"in the wicked manner of Onan," when by denial she risked "cruelties" or her husband's deserting her for prostitutes. On April 23, 1822, the Penitentiary said that the wife could "offer herself passively" if she feared "beating, death, or other serious cruelties." "Serious reason" of this kind excused her, for charity bound her to prevent the sin but "not with such great detriment." No specific answer was given for the situation in which the wife feared her husband would be driven to adultery.[42]

In a third inquiry, Thomas Gousset, then a professor at the seminary in Besançon, posed a similar case, of a wife with a husband she knew to be an "onanist." She feared "very serious evils" to herself from denying him intercourse. Could she "at any rate sometimes permit the abuse of marriage"? On February 1, 1823, the Penitentiary said that if "the husband presses threatening blows, death, or other very serious evils," the wife might "hold herself permissively."[43]

These answers were distinguished more by circumspection than by clarity. The Penitentiary appeared to assume that the woman's part was not intrinsically evil. To this extent it followed Liguori and rejected the extreme rigorists. But it did not accept the indulgent Liguorian view that the wife's acts did not amount to cooperating in any act that was itself sinful. Her participation, the Penitentiary seemed to believe, was a form of material cooperation in sin. It could be justified only as a way of avoiding detriment to herself. Whether this detriment must be "very serious" or merely "serious," actual physical violence or moral injury, was not made precise. Nor did the Penitentiary explain what it meant for a wife to behave "passively" or "permissively."

The three interrogations between 1816 and 1823 are the only ones to have been given publicity; there may have been others. The Penitentiary did not seek to publicize its answers. Gousset published the 1816 and 1823 answers in his 1832 work on moral theology. The 1822 reply seems to have been first printed for the public by Bishop Bouvier.[44] The answers functioned more as guides to Roman thinking and as precedents than as a program for action by the clergy.

Bishop Bouvier himself sought clarification of the decrees, only to meet with a repetition on June 8, 1842, of the rules of April 23, 1822.[45] The uncertainty of these generalities left much to individual judgment, as Bouvier made clear. "Serious detriment," he wrote, varied with the woman involved. "Even some blows do not weigh much with peasants," while "passing quarrels would be unbearable to a timid woman, in-

---

[42] Ibid., p. 13.

[43] Ibid., p. 15.

[44] I am not certain of the date of the edition of Bouvier which first carried this decree. By 1864 it is included.

[45] Ibid., p. 18.

structed in refined conduct and accustomed to civility." [46] Sufficient cause for cooperation would, therefore, according to this analysis of the Penitentiary's decrees, vary from person to person.

On May 27, 1847, the Penitentiary answered an anonymous bishop inquiring about the responsibilities of a wife. Suppose a husband seeks normal intercourse, but the wife "vehemently desires that [he] withdraw because she fears to have offspring." Could she be absolved? Suppose a wife could, "by her blandishments," persuade her husband not to withdraw, but fails to do so. Could she be absolved? [47] The Penitentiary answered both questions negatively, without elaboration. The second negative implied a definite duty for a wife to prevent her husband's sin.[48]

On April 19, 1853, a different congregation, the Holy Office of the Inquisition, charged with the supervision of Catholic doctrine, spoke on a form of contraception never before treated by an official Roman document: contraception by condom. It answered the question "May a wife passively offer herself in intercourse where a condom is used?" The Congregation answered, "No. For it would be participation in what is intrinsically unlawful." [49] The Congregation discerned a difference between coitus interruptus, where wifely cooperation preceded the sinful ejaculation, and the case presented, where cooperation coincided with the sinful act.

INQUIRY

Cooperation in coitus interruptus had received limited toleration. An even greater toleration was accorded those who in good faith practiced contraception. The first Roman instruction on inquiry about the sin occurred as late as 1842 and was occasioned by the inquiry of Bishop Bouvier. As he later described the situation which prompted his question, some of the faithful could "scarcely be persuaded" that there was an obligation under penalty of mortal sin either to be chaste in marriage or "run the risk of generating countless offspring." In good faith these Christians, particularly the wives, believed their acts to be innocent. They acted because they could not otherwise "provide decent and respectable education" for their existing children, or because of the health of the wife, or simply not to have "too many children." They did not see why intercourse with withdrawal was worse than intercourse at times when procreation was impossible, as in pregnancy. The sexual act between spouses still extinguished concupiscence "and favored mutual love." They appealed to the "more common feeling" of Christian fathers, otherwise

[46] Bouvier, *Supplement to the Treatise on Marriage* 2.1.3.4.
[47] *Decisiones Sanctae Sedis*, p. 19.
[48] *Ibid.*, p. 19.
[49] *Ibid.*, p. 21.

men of probity, in support of their action (Bouvier, *Supplement to the Treatise on Marriage* 2.1.3.4).

The attitude of French Catholics so sympathetically perceived by Bouvier convinced him that in many cases contraception was indeed practiced by those who were in good faith. What should he do about it? He addressed a memorial to Rome, weighted with his sympathy. "Almost all the younger couples" of his diocese, he reported, did not want "an overgenerous progeny" and yet "were morally not able to abstain from the conjugal act." If confessors inquired about their marital habits, they were seriously offended, and they were not likely to follow the instructions given. "In many places the number of those who approach the sacred tribunal declines from year to year, especially for this reason." What their ancestors did was as much a mystery to them as it appears to be to modern American Catholics: "'How did confessors use to act?' many ask. For in earlier times no more children than today were born in any given marriage; nor were the married more chaste. Yet still they did not default on the precepts of annual confession and Easter communion."

After this prelude setting out the moral crisis in France, Bouvier asked the Penitentiary three questions:

1. Do spouses who use marriage in such a way as to avoid conception commit an intrinsically evil act?
2. If the act is held intrinsically evil, can spouses not accusing themselves of it be considered as being in good faith, which excuses them from serious fault?
3. Should approval be given the way of acting of confessors who, lest they offend spouses, do not interrogate them about the way in which they exercise their marital rights? [50]

The Penitentiary replied to the first question with the answer tolerating cooperation by the wife in the circumstances already noted. This reply does not seem responsive to the question, unless one supposes that Bouvier had given up on the men and that his real concern was about women ceasing to confess. The answer does imply that the husband is committing sin.

The Penitentiary answered the second and third questions with remarkable leniency. It said merely that confessors should keep in mind what St. Alphonsus Liguori, "a learned man, most skilled in these matters," had taught in section 4 of *The Practice of the Confessor*: as to sins in marriage, ask the wife only whether she paid the marital debt; "about other things be silent, unless asked" (above, p. 375). Other authors should also be consulted. But only Liguori was named, and the Penitentiary strongly committed itself to Liguori's tolerant position. It seems probable that Bouvier, himself a follower of Liguori, put the questions to the

[50] *Ibid.*, pp. 17–18. The answer of the Penitentiary follows on p. 18.

Penitentiary with some assurance that its answers would adopt Liguorian principles. The Penitentiary thereby gave tacit approval to the confessors who did not lose penitents by questioning about contraception. It accepted the position that contraception could be practiced in innocence of its malice. In the face of the description of a diocese where the practice was widespread, the Penitentiary did not consider the social evil to be such that education should be attempted in the confessional.

The tolerant approach of the Penitentiary was disseminated by authors like Bouvier and Gousset. In his book designed only for priests, Bouvier stated that "the majority" of married persons practicing coitus interruptus were in good faith, at least as to the gravity of their sin. Good faith excused "if not from all, at least from such great" sin (*si non a toto, saltem a tanto*). The counsels of Liguori on preserving good faith were set out now with particular reference to contraception. Confessors, especially young confessors, were told to be careful that "they do not destroy good faith without any fruit for souls." Even if asked, the confessor "ought to reply with the same discretion; sometimes he can be silent about the degree of malice, that is, when the hope does not shine forth of obtaining a better way of acting." If asked directly, however, he cannot be silent, but must speak out. Outside of this situation, prudence is the rule (*Supplement to the Treatise on Marriage* 2.1.3.4).

The same stand was taken by Thomas Gousset, now cardinal-archbishop of Rheims. Quoting the passage from Liguori's *Practice of the Confessor* referred to by the Penitentiary, Gousset continued, "It is certainly better that the married sin materially than be exposed to the danger of sinning formally. Further, should not confessors fear lest they offend penitents by interrogating them importunely and either imprudently or maliciously complaining about these deeds as if they were done impudently and without shame, whereby sacramental confession is made odious?" (*Moral Theology for the Use of Curés and Confessors*). This rather severe rebuke to confessors disturbing those who practiced contraception in good faith was joined with a statement looking to the behavior of future married couples. Confessors should instruct fiancés or newly married couples on their duties. This teaching, Gousset suggested, should emphasize mutual love. There was to be a single specific instruction on contraception: "That they use matrimony moderately, so that together they may grow old healthily and as Christians, as in the sight of God and his angels, doing nothing which prevents conception or harms the conceived offspring." [51] Gousset, in short, would tolerate existing practice, but try to teach the coming generation. Presumably, if the newlyweds were deaf to the advice

[51] Gousset, *Théologie morale à l'usage des curés et des confesseurs* 2.846, 896 (Paris, 1874).

given them, they too could be found to be in invincible ignorance of the law.

The leading contemporary moralist, Gury, interpreted the Penitentiary in the same spirit, if slightly more severely than the words the Penitentiary had quoted from Liguori would indicate. Admitting that "onanism" flourished everywhere, Gury noted that confessors differed in their approaches. But to follow St. Alphonsus there should be "some kind of questioning," by general questions of this order, "Does your conscience give you remorse on anything concerning the sanctity of marriage?" If the penitent answered negatively, no further questions were to be asked (*Compendium of Moral Theology* 2.705). The suggested questioning was not to proceed to a challenge to good faith.

The mild reply to Bouvier by the Penitentiary under Gregory XVI may have encouraged a belief that the Church was about to modify its position on contraception. On usury, between 1822 and 1836 a series of responses of the Penitentiary had tacitly abandoned the formal scholastic positions by instructing confessors that persons charging interest on the strength of the civil law permitting interest "were not to be disturbed." These responses had not touched on the theoretical questions, but admitted only that Christians might, in good faith, believe that they had a basis for taking the legal rate of interest. Refusing to disturb their good faith, the practical decisions of the Penitentiary facilitated a new approach to the theory of what constituted usury.[52] Was the same kind of shift about to occur in respect to birth control, through the medium of practical toleration in confession?

The Inquisition on May 21, 1851, under Pius IX, acted to dissipate any such speculation or doubt. It dealt with two propositions which were apparently gaining currency and which the Congregation said were argued "keenly" before it. (1) For decent reasons it is lawful for spouses to use marriage in the way which Onan used it. (2) It is probable that this use of marriage is not prohibited by natural law. The first proposition was characterized as "scandalous, erroneous, and contrary to the natural law of marriage." The second was said to be "scandalous, erroneous, and elsewhere implicitly condemned by Innocent XI, Proposition forty-nine."[53]

This act of the Inquisition was firm, but comparatively restrained. The strongest note of censure applied was "erroneous," rather than "heretical." The propositions were thereby characterized as untrue in terms of Christian theology, but not formally contrary to the faith. "Scandalous" was

---

[52] Noonan, *The Scholastic Analysis of Usury* (Cambridge, Mass., 1957), pp. 378–382.

[53] *Decisiones Sanctae Sedis*, pp. 19–20.

a note bearing not on the truth or falsity of the proposition, but on its likely effect on other persons. The reference to Innocent XI did not intensify the condemnation, for the minimal note of censure applied by him to the "laxist" propositions, of which Proposition 49 had been one, was "offensive to pious ears" (above, p. 327). Proposition 49 itself had read, "An autoerotic act [*mollities*] is not prohibited by natural law. Whence, if God had not forbidden it, it would often be good, sometimes obligatory under mortal penalty." [54] The invocation of this old condemnation to condemn contraception reflected the persistence of the view that contraception was a form of masturbation. The argument of Bouvier's "younger couples" that coitus interruptus could express love was implicitly rejected.

Having struck at any modification of theory, the Inquisition then turned to the pressing practical question of inquiry in the confessional. It acted upon this extreme expression of a laissez-faire approach: "It is never expedient to interrogate spouses of either sex about this matter, even if it is prudently feared that the husband, or the wife, or both, abuse marriage." This proposition "as it stands" was branded as "false, too lax, and perilous in practice."

This response substantially undercut the 1842 decision of the Penitentiary. The very situation which Bishop Bouvier had described was one in which it could be "prudently feared" that "almost all the younger couples" were engaged in contraception, and yet interrogation was not to be made. Formal distinctions between the Inquisition's reply and the Penitentiary's could be drawn. It might be said that the Inquisition did not deny that good faith could exist. It might be said that "prudent fear" was to be determined on an individual, not statistical, basis, so that even in a diocese like Le Mans prudent fear would have to exist in an individual case before interrogation was proper. Formal consistency between the two decrees can be found. Two different attitudes, however, are reflected, and the predictable result was confusion in practice.

This confusion was to be revealed in documents of the next pontificate. To summarize what has already been noted, the official directives from Rome in the period from the restoration of the Church in France to the end of the reign of Pius IX showed no special concern to combat birth control. There was a marked tolerance of good faith, a tolerance cut short at the point where doctrinal modification appeared to suggest itself. By 1851 a slight stiffening of attitude was perceptible. Cooperation with the condom was strictly forbidden. Some interrogation was urged. Yet as birth control swept France, the Church was not yet its active and tireless adversary.

[54] H. Denzinger, *Enchiridion symbolorum*, 21st ed., no. 1199 (Freiburg, 1937).

Pius IX, absorbed by other battles, did not concern himself with the forces operating in favor of birth control. When in 1869 he reviewed and revised the reserved excommunications, he continued in effect the excommunication provided by *Effraenatam* for those procuring an abortion (*Apostolicae Sedis moderationi*). [55] He made no attempt to reinstate the short-lived treatment of contraception as a reserved sin. Pius IX was not distinguished in his later years by the mildness of his response to "modern civilization." But apparently contraception was a modern problem which he preferred to leave to the local episcopates.[56]

ARGUMENTS AGAINST CONTRACEPTION

The arguments against contraception at this period were focused upon coitus interruptus. They were traditionalist rather than closely reasoned. Like the earlier condemnations of contraceptive acts as "homicide" or "sodomy," the peculiarly nineteenth-century designation of the act as "onanism" served a double function: to denounce the act as odious and ugly, and to be a capsule form of argument. There was a corresponding tendency to dwell on the sin of Onan. In authors normally dependent on Liguori, this emphasis is a striking reaction to contemporary problems, for Liguori had ignored Onan utterly. In Gousset's *Théologie morale à l'usage des curés et des confesseurs*, no other argument against coitus interruptus was given than that it was the act of Onan (*Théologie* 2.892). The same was true in the American Kenrick's *Moral Theology* (21.3.2.84).[57] Bouvier relied partly on the argument that contraception is "opposed" to the primary end of marriage, that is, procreation of offspring, and partly on Genesis. He admitted that doubts could arise on the interpretation of the reason for Onan's punishment, but the "authority of a great multitude of doctors" constrained him to hold that the punishment was for the act of withdrawal (*Supplement to the Treatise on Marriage* 2.1.3.4).

Like Bouvier and Gousset, Gury dealt only with coitus interruptus. One major argument against the act was "that it was strictly prohibited by the supreme Legislator and Author of nature, as is clear from the text of Genesis [38:8–10] just cited" (*Compendium of Moral Theology* 2.703).

[55] *Codicis iuris canonici fontes*, ed. Peter Gasparri (Rome, 1923), III, 28.

[56] According to Michael Rosset, bishop of St. Jean-de-Maurienne, one French bishop circulated, anonymously, a pamphlet to the Fathers of Vatican I, urging that the Church permit contraception. Rosset, *De sacramento matrimonii* (St. Jean-de-Maurienne, 1895), V, 375.

[57] Francis P. Kenrick, *Theologia moralis* (Philadelphia, 1841). Kenrick's work was much used in American seminaries in the second part of the nineteenth century, although the Sabetti revision of Gury became the most popular American textbook near the end of the century. Paul E. McKeever, "Seventy-Five Years of Moral Theology in America," *American Ecclesiastical Review* 152 (1965), 17–19.

Gury also condemned contraception because it "plainly wars with the primary end of marriage and tends per se to the extinction of society." This sentence implied that the act was unnatural, and it suggested that the act of coitus must be viewed per se as directed to the conservation of society.

These arguments were perfunctory and undeveloped. A vigorous attack on birth control began only in the last quarter of the nineteenth century. This development was the fruit of the Franco-Prussian war, the pontificate of Leo XIII, the revival of Thomism, and the increased momentum of the promotion of birth control. The development reached its climax in the encyclical *Casti connubii* in 1930. Outside of the Church, birth control became a cause, a movement enlisting first social reformers, then medical, scientific, and religious authorities. I shall sketch the course of this movement, and then describe the ecclesiastical reaction to these events.

THE BIRTH CONTROL MOVEMENT

In the 1860's a Malthusian League had been founded in England by George Drysdale, the author of *The Elements of Social Science: or Physical, Sexual, and Natural Religion*. This league, designed to foster contraceptive practice, did not flourish.[58] In 1877 the first change in public opinion occurred. The English government prosecuted Annie Besant and Charles Bradlaugh for distributing Charles Knowlton's American text on contraception, *The Fruits of Philosophy*. The prosecution was unsuccessful, and the publicity was immense.[59] In the four years following the trial the book, which had been selling 1000 copies a year, sold over 200,000 copies.[60] The mass spread of contraceptive information had begun. A new Malthusian League was formed in 1878, and this organization proved viable. It at once began the work of winning a hearing with the English public for contraception as a remedy for miseries attributed to over-population and "over-childbearing." The leaders of the League were also instrumental in spreading abroad the ideal of birth control. English example and influence led to the forming of "Malthusian Leagues" with the purpose of promoting birth control as socially desirable in countries such as these: Germany (1889); Bohemia (1901); Spain (1904); Brazil

---

[58] Himes, *Medical History of Contraception*, p. 238.

[59] Bradlaugh and Besant v. The Queen, 3 Queen's Bench Division 607, reversing 2 Q.B.D. 569 (1877). The defendants were charged with distributing an "indecent, lewd, filthy, bawdy and obscene book, called 'Fruits of Philosophy.'" The Court of Appeals held the indictment defective in failing to charge what particular words were obscene.

[60] Himes, *Medical History*, pp. 243–244.

(1905); Belgium (1906); Cuba (1907); Switzerland (1908); Sweden (1911); Italy (1913).[61]

Next to England, the Netherlands was of particular importance in the birth control movement. In 1875 and 1876 birth control was proposed as a solution for population problems by Greven and Van Houten. George Drysdale's *The Elements of Social Science* was translated into Dutch in 1876. In 1882, with Drysdale's help, a Malthusian League was formed. Aletta Jacobs, the first woman doctor in Holland, was a supporter of the cause. In 1881 she pioneered in a method which was a forerunner of modern birth control clinics: the instruction of midwives so that they could teach contraceptive methods in the home.[62] In France, a Malthusian League started in 1865, but vigorous leadership of the movement did not occur until 1898, when Paul Robin founded "La Ligue de la Régénération Humaine," a French-Belgian association with both eugenic and contraceptive objectives. Periodicals favoring contraception began to appear in the 1880's.[63]

In the twentieth century the birth control movement became consciously international. International congresses were held in Paris in 1900; in Liège in 1905; in the Hague in 1910; in Dresden in 1911; after the war, in London in 1922; in New York in 1925.[64] In 1927 the proponents of birth control organized a World Conference on Population at Geneva, which gave substantial impetus to the organization of population studies. In 1930 the first international clinic on contraceptive methods was held at Zurich.[65] These international gatherings were milestones in the diffusion of publicity in favor of birth control, in the mobilizing of public opinion for birth control, and in the establishing of birth control as a social objective in the Western world.

Organized promotion of contraception also spread in more countries. In the United States Margaret Sanger in 1913 began the movement which was to lead to the National Birth Control League and then to the American Birth Control League. Sanger brought the message of birth control to Japan in 1921 and to India in 1936.[66] In 1931, birth control societies were formed in Czechoslovakia and Poland. During the 1920's, birth control clinics, dispensing instructions on ways of controlling conception, were established in Great Britain, Germany, Holland, and some American states.[67]

[61] Maurice Chachuat, *Le Mouvement du "Birth Control" dans les pays Anglo-Saxons* (Lyons, 1934), p. 453.
[62] *Ibid.*, p. 454; Himes, *Medical History*, p. 309.
[63] Chachuat, *Le Mouvement du "Birth Control,"* p. 195.
[64] *Ibid.*, pp. 196–213.
[65] Himes, *Medical History*, pp. 315–316.
[66] Margaret Sanger, *An Autobiography* (New York, 1938), p. 318.
[67] Chachuat, *Le Mouvement du "Birth Control,"* p. 475; Himes, *Medical History*, pp. 357–358.

New forms of old contraceptive methods were developed in this period of expansion. In 1880 Wilhelm Mensinga developed a diaphragm for use as a pessary in the vagina, a method which came to be preferred by the birth control clinics of the later period.[68] By 1935 some two hundred types of mechanical devices, either condoms or pessaries, were being used in Western societies. In addition there was a wide range of chemical solutions employed as spermicides or occlusive agents. The business of manufacturing contraceptive devices became a substantial trade.[69]

Slowly the birth control movement won the approval of a substantial number of doctors. In the United States the first discussion of contraception in medical journals began in the 1880's, and there was considerable debate as to its desirability. By 1933, a majority of the better medical schools not under Catholic auspices regularly gave instructions in indications and techniques of contraception, or both.[70] In France, contraception became a subject for respectable medical discussion with a symposium in 1905 in *La Chronique médicale,* but did not yet win overwhelming medical support. In England in 1922 a survey of gynecologists indicated that a substantial majority approved the use of contraceptives. A sizable body of medical opinion had thus swung to their acceptance.[71] This was a clear shift of articulate opinion since the nineteenth century, when contraception was viewed by leading doctors as medically and morally suspect if not obviously dangerous.[72]

The change in medical opinion paralleled changes of opinion in the learned worlds of science, sociology, and economics. Here the humanistic arguments of the advocates of birth control received attention and won much support. These arguments were directed partly to the social good, partly to personal happiness. Margaret Sanger had been particularly moved by the misery and ill health caused by undesired pregnancies among the very poor.[73] A theme as old as Place was that contraception would make early marriage possible and thereby reduce prostitution. It was restated in a resolution of the Fourth International Congress at Dresden. The relation between overpopulation and war was often emphasized. The Fourth International Congress in 1911 said that the "rational regulation" of population would produce peace. The Sixth International Congress in 1925 said, "Overpopulation produces war." In England Marie Stopes "stressed birth control as a health and eugenic measure." [74]

[68] Himes, *Medical History,* p. 321.
[69] *Ibid.,* p. 210.
[70] *Ibid.,* pp. 265–360.
[71] *Ibid.,* pp. 305–306.
[72] *Ibid.,* pp. 281–283.
[73] Sanger, *An Autobiography,* pp. 88–90.
[74] Chachuat, *Le Mouvement du "Birth Control,"* pp. 205, 213; Himes, *Medical History,* pp. 258–259.

The basic proposition of Malthus that population tends to increase faster than food resources was frequently repeated. In a representative statement of this proposition, *Mankind at the Crossroads,* Edward M. East, a professor at Harvard University, wrote in 1923, "The world confronts the fulfillment of the Malthusian prediction here and now." East predicted that, unless checked, world population would reach an insupportable three billion by the year 2000, and that the United States population by 1964 would be 214,000,000, a population "beyond the maximum agricultural possibilities set by the calculations made a few pages before." [75]

Not only medical and academic opinion shifted. There was a notable change in position by the Anglican Church. Both in 1908 and in 1920 the Lambeth Conference of bishops of the church had condemned contraception. [76] In America, in 1925, the House of Bishops of the Protestant Episcopal Church had also condemned it. At the Lambeth Conference of 1930, despite the determined opposition of a minority led by Bishop Gore, the following resolution was adopted on August 14, by a vote of 193 to 67 (46 not voting).

Where there is a clearly felt moral obligation to limit or avoid parenthood, the method must be decided on Christian principles. The primary and obvious method is complete abstinence from intercourse (as far as may be necessary) in a life of discipline and self-control lived in the power of the Holy Spirit. Nevertheless in those cases where there is such a clearly-felt moral obligation to limit or avoid parenthood, and where there is a morally sound reason for avoiding complete abstinence, the conference agrees that other methods may be used, provided that this is done in the light of the same Christian principles. The Conference records its strong condemnation of the use of any methods of conception control from motives of selfishness, luxury, or mere convenience.

(*The Lambeth Conference*, 1930, Resolution 15)

The bishops of the church whose theology was closest to that of the Roman Catholic Church no longer adhered to an absolute prohibition of contraception.

These shifts in learned opinion were after the fact. The people of western Europe had already acted. As far as statistics of a falling birth rate can suggest, birth control was widely practiced by the end of the nineteenth century. The statistics alone do not exclude other factors, and they say nothing as to the means used. They do show falling European and North American birth rates tending to become uniform, and this uniformity implies control of procreation.

Consider, first, the population of a country with a large number of believing Catholics, Belgium. Its total population increased from 3.7

[75] East, *Mankind at the Crossroads* (New York, 1923), pp. viii, 340, 167.
[76] The Lambeth Conference, 1908 (Resolutions 41, 43); The Lambeth Conference, 1920 (Resolution 68). *The Lambeth Conferences* (*1867–1948*) (London, 1948), edition of the Society for Promoting Christian Knowledge.

million in 1830 to 8.1 million in 1930. About 1880, however, its birth rate began to fall, and it fell, with small spurts upward in particular years, from 31 per thousand in 1880 to 18.1 in 1929. This result is not due to a decline in marriages, but to a decline in births per marriage. Whereas in 1880 the births per marriage were 4.49, they were 2.29 by 1930.[77] In Europe as a whole, the French birth rate continued to fall, the English began to fall about 1880, the Dutch about 1885, the Austrian, German, and Italian about 1890. The low point was reached in the 1930's. By 1936 Belgian, French, German, Austrian, Dutch, Swedish, British, Danish, Canadian, and American birth rates were all less than 20 per 1000.[78] Germany in 1931–1934, England, Switzerland, and Sweden in 1935–1937, all had net rates of reproduction below 1. Belgium and France in 1939 had rates slightly over 1. Western society seemed to be seeking stability of population and achieving it. In most countries, this achievement appears to have been through contraception.[79]

There were secular pressures counter to this sweepingly successful movement. In France, warning voices had been raised before 1870. Proudhon had predicted in 1858 that Malthusianism would depopulate France as it had done the Roman Empire.[80] The legislature under Napoleon III discussed proposals for stimulating births. But only the debacle of 1870–1871 caused substantial public concern with the birth rate. In the wake of the shattering defeat by Prussia, analysts of French society and journalists gloomily predicted the eclipse of France as a great power as her population growth continued to sag below that of the rest of Europe.[81] Little, however, was done about it. New obscenity laws in 1882 were invoked against certain journals promoting birth control, but the check administered was slight.[82]

It was only after the next war with Germany that France took more rigorous steps to check the promotion of contraception. In 1920 a combination of nationalist and Catholic deputies enacted a law forbidding the dissemination of "contraceptive propaganda" under penalty of six months' imprisonment. The law did not attempt the impracticable end of discouraging the usual French methods of contraception, coitus interruptus and the douche. The law, moreover, was interpreted not to apply to the giving of medical advice nor to prevent the state from paying for

[77] Valère Fallon, S.J., "La Population Belge," *Population* 1 (1933), 65–69.

[78] Michel Cépède, François Houtart, and Linus Grond, *Population and Food* (New York, 1964), p. 146.

[79] Himes, *Medical History*, p. 392.

[80] P. J. Proudhon, *De la justice dans la révolution et dans l'église* (Paris, 1858), I, 348–349.

[81] Joseph J. Spengler, *France Faces Depopulation* (Durham, N.C., 1938), pp. 118–122.

[82] Chachuat, *Le Mouvement du "Birth Control,"* p. 462.

advice on contraception tendered to a person receiving state aid. The law did, however, inhibit the spread of birth control by an organized movement and prevent the opening of birth control clinics. In the thirties France adopted on a large scale the idea, discussed since 1860, of promoting natality by a system of allotments from the state based on family size.[83]

In Germany and Italy state action to discourage contraception occurred only when they had become controlled by nationalistic dictators. In Nazi Germany birth control clinics were closed, and bonuses were given by the state for children.[84] At the same time a stringent law decreeing sterilization for certain classes of the population was adopted. In Italy the Fascist ideology and program favored population growth. In 1926 a law forbidding written advocacy of contraception was enacted. In 1927 Mussolini told parliament that "the demographic rejuvenation" of Italy was an imperative. The new Penal Code, drafted over a period of several years, went into effect July 1931. Title Ten, "Crimes Against the Integrity and the Health of the Race," had two relevant provisions. Article 552, designed according to the report of the draftsmen to meet the needs of "the political demography of the new Italian state," prohibited sterilization ("procuring impotence to procreate"). Article 553, explained as necessary "to defend the continuation and the integrity of the race," provided a fine and imprisonment of a year for "whoever publicly incites to practices against procreation or propagandizes in favor of them." [85]

Some Catholic influence may be discerned in the basically nationalistic legislation of France and Italy. Only in Belgium, Ireland, and Spain, however, was there legislation of Catholic inspiration. In Belgium a law of June 20, 1923, made it a crime to distribute "objects specifically designed to prevent conception" or to distribute commercial writings describing means of preventing conception. In Ireland, section 16 of the Censorship of Publications Act of 1929 made it a crime to print, publish, sell or distribute "any book or periodical publication which advocates or might reasonably be supposed to advocate the unnatural prevention of conception." In Spain the Penal Code of 1928 made it a crime to propagate contraceptive theory or practice.[86]

---

[83] The basic law on contraception is the Law of July 31, 1920, *Recueil général des lois, décrets et arrêtés*, 12th series, Vol. 502 (Paris, 1920), pp. 549–550. On its interpretation, see Sauvy, *La Prévention des naissances*, p. 102. On its effect on clinics, see the arguments presented against the law by Catherine Valabrègue, *Contrôle des naissances et planning familial* (Paris, 1960), pp. 142–144. On the allotment system, see Sauvy, *La Prévention des naissances*, p. 96.

[84] Himes, *Medical History*, p. 390.

[85] *Codice penale* 10.552–553. For the history of the law, with the quotations from Mussolini and the drafting commission, see Eugenio Jannitti Pirimallo, *Il Codice penale* (Milan, 1936), III, 160–162.

[86] Belgium: *Code pénal*, 383, *Les Codes et lois spéciales les plus usuels en rigueur*

In the United States the efforts of a young Protestant moral reformer, Anthony Comstock (1844–1915), the secretary of the New York Society for the Suppression of Vice, led to a comprehensive federal statute entitled "An Act for the Suppression of Trade in and Circulation of Obscene Literature and Articles of Immoral Use." The purposes of the bill were not debated in Congress, but a qualification in the draft of the act permitting the possession, sale, or mailing of contraceptives on a prescription of a physician in good standing in good faith was struck from the bill on motion of Senator Buckingham of Connecticut. As enacted, March 3, 1873, the so-called Comstock law forbade the sending through the mails of "any drug or medicine or any article whatever for the prevention of conception"; the advertisement of such articles through the mails; their importation into the United States; or their manufacture, sale, or possession in the District of Columbia and federal territories. Up to ten years' imprisonment was provided for violation of the section on mailing, with lesser penalties for the other acts.[87] In penalizing the possession of contraceptives Congress went further than any Pope or canonist. Following the federal example, and responding to the efforts of Comstock and his followers, many individual states adopted laws controlling in some measure the sale, promotion, or prescription of contraceptives. The New York state law was enforced against Margaret Sanger in 1918.[88]

The opponents of birth control were strong enough in 1930 to secure

à Belgique, ed. J. Servais and E. Meckelynck, 23rd ed. (Brussels, 1937). Ireland: Censorship of Publications Act, sec. 16, The Public Acts Passed by the Oireachtas of Saorstát Éireann (Dublin, 1930). Spain: for the history of the Spanish law, see Federico Piug Peña, Derecho penal (Madrid, 1955), III¹, 431. The present law, enacted under Franco, forbids the sale or "public divulging in any way of means or procedures to avoid procreation, as well as any kind of contraceptive propaganda" (Codigo penal, 416).

Catholics cooperated with Protestants in three other countries to pass legislation on birth control. In Switzerland an ambiguous law was adopted. To advertise or put on sale "objects intended to prevent pregnancy or to prevent venereal infection" became a crime if done "so as to offend good morals," Code pénal, 211 (Lausanne, 1942). In 1909 Canada enacted a law punishing with imprisonment of two years anyone advertising or selling "any means or instructions or any medicine, drug, or article intended or represented as a means of preventing conception." The crime was committed only by one acting "without lawful justification or excuse." In 1937 it was held that an employee of the Parent's Information Bureau visiting women to give them instructions on birth control was acting for the public good, and a criminal complaint against him was dismissed (Rex v. Palmer, 3 Dominion Law Reports 493, affirming 2 D.L.R. 609 [1937]). In the Netherlands legislation on contraception was also enacted.

[87] 17 Stat. 598–600 (Forty-Second Congress). The present form of the law appears in 18 United States Code, secs. 1471–1462, and 19 United States Code, sec. 1305 (1958). For legislative history, see Peter Smith, "The History and Future of the Legal Battle Over Birth Control," Cornell Law Quarterly 49 (1963), 275–277.

[88] People v. Sanger, 222 New York Reports 192 (1918). On the development of state legislation, see Robert William Haney, Comstockery in America (Boston, 1960).

the re-enactment of the provision against importation of contraceptives in the Tariff Act of that year,[89] but already judicial opinion was shifting. In the same year the most professionally respected of American courts, the Court of Appeals for the Second Circuit, held that a manufacturer of condoms was not engaged in an illegal activity precluding recovery of damages in a civil case. In 1936 the same court permitted the importation of contraceptives by a doctor, holding that Congress had meant only to prohibit the "immoral use" of contraceptives and that use by a physician was not immoral. In 1939 the federal district court in Puerto Rico followed this precedent in permitting a doctor to possess contraceptives in the federal territories.[90] The final step in abandonment of attempt to enforce the federal law was taken by the Post Office Department in 1958 when it announced that it would not ban the mailing of contraceptives if they were not destined for "unlawful purposes."[91] In each situation the impracticability of distinguishing between medical uses and "immoral" or "illegal uses" made enforcement of the law impossible once the distinction was accepted between medical uses and unlawful ones. Just as in Roman law there were good *medicamenta* and bad *medicamenta*, so now there were good and bad contraceptives in the United States.

State laws and city ordinances, rarely enforced, still existed against the distribution of contraceptives. As of 1964, seventeen states regulated or prohibited the advertising of contraceptives or their sale by vending machines; eight states prohibited the sale of contraceptives except by licensed physicians or pharmacists; two states (New York and Minnesota) prohibited their sale, but permitted doctors to prescribe them; two states prohibited their sale, but permitted the sale of medical works describing contraceptive methods. Massachusetts prohibited the sale absolutely. Connecticut went further than any government since Sixtus V by making it a criminal misdemeanor to "use any drug, medicinal article or instrument for the purpose of preventing conception."[92]

The federal and state income tax laws with provision for deductions for dependents and lower rates for married persons filing joint returns

[89] 46 Stat. 688 (1930).

[90] The cases were, respectively, Youngs Rubber Corp. v. C. L. Lee and Co., 45 *Federal Reporter* 2d, 103; United States v. One Package, 86 *Federal Reporter* 2d, 737; United States v. Belaval, unreported decision, see Smith, "History and Future," p. 285.

[91] Smith, "History and Future," p. 284.

[92] *Ibid.*, pp. 277–278. The most stringent laws, then, enacted by Protestant legislatures and now retained by Catholic support were 272 *Massachusetts General Laws Annotated* 20–21 (1956), and *Connecticut General Statutes, Revised* 53–32 (1958). The Supreme Court twice avoided pressing on the constitutionality of the law: Tileston v. Ullman, 318 *United States Reports* 44 (1943); Poe v. Ullman, 367 *United States Reports* (1961). Pending before the court in 1965 was Griswold v. Connecticut, probable jurisdiction noted, 33 *United States Law Week* 3208 (1964).

in effect penalized celibacy and childlessness, and were probably no more effective deterrents than the more celebrated laws of Augustus; at least they lessened the effect that a high tax rate might have of discouraging large families. Even in England, where no law restrained the promotion of contraception, a similar tenderness for the family appeared in the deductions and rates of the tax law.

The legal measures taken to check contraception were neither vigorous nor many. The most successful were the positive efforts to reward procreation or to keep it from being too burdensome; and these efforts, of course, did nothing to prevent the use of contraceptives for such purposes as the spacing of offspring. Since Western society accepted contraception as a usual practice, its law could scarcely be more stringent. By 1930 the birth control movement had in most countries overcome most restraints upon its freedom.

RESPONSE OF THE POPE AND THE BISHOPS, 1876–1930

Faced with an international movement promoting contraception to control the size of individual families and of national populations, and faced by falling birth rates in countries with substantial numbers of Catholic believers, the hierarchy of the Church reacted.

PUBLIC TEACHING

In the aftermath of the Franco-Prussian war, there was outspoken ecclesiastical comment on what birth control was doing to France. Were these remarks inspired by nationalism or by a desire to use the opportunity afforded by the disaster to drive home a lesson? Probably both motives were influential. In oratory on ceremonial occasions, and in theological tracts, contraception was decried. In a Bastille Day speech in 1872 at Beauvais, Gaspar Mermillod, a Swiss cardinal, declared to the French people: "You have rejected God, and God has struck you. You have, by hideous calculation, made tombs instead of filling cradles with children; therefore you have wanted for soldiers." [93] In a multivolume treatise on marriage, Bishop Rosset of St. Jean-de-Maurienne pointed to the falling French birth rate and argued that France would sink to seventh place among European nations if the comparative trends continued.[94] In Ballerini's 1874 edition of Gury, Gury's arguments were retained, and the danger of injury to society was expanded upon. Prevention of generation in the conjugal act or voluntary ejaculation outside the vagina was gravely

[93] Quoted in B. Deppe, "Théologie pastorale," *Nouvelle revue théologique* 31 (1899), 455–456.
[94] Rosset, *De sacramento matrimonii*, V, 389.

sinful, because "if men could enjoy that pleasure without the consequent burden of feeding and educating children, the generating of offspring would be easily postponed, indeed purposely avoided, and so society it-self would decline to ruin" (Gury-Ballerini, *Compendium* 2.730). This argument combined the thesis of Sanchez that man cannot be trusted with "the administration of the seed" with the related contention that the social consequences of contraception would be disastrous.

There was, still, in France much restraint in the episcopal reaction. The bishops might speak individually, but they took no collective action. In 1876 an anguished curé from Anjou set out the different styles of con-fessional practice which prevailed and asked the Penitentiary for advice as to what practice was correct. He elicited an answer which reflected hesitation, but seemed stronger than the 1842 response to Bishop Bouvier. Confessors acted unlawfully who "favored" the belief of their penitents in good faith that contraception was not a mortal sin. Confessors who generally doubted that contraception was practiced in good faith might lawfully follow the practice of "sometimes" making interrogations if within the limits set by approved authors and the *Roman Ritual*.[95] This qualifying cross-reference created ambiguity in the answer. The *Roman Ritual* warned against questioning which would scandalize and lead the ignorant to sins they did not know (above, p. 375). Was someone commit-ting contraception in good faith in the class of those "ignorant" within the meaning of this admonition? The Penitentiary did not say.

In 1876 there appeared the first theological work solely devoted to a study of contraception, *Dissertation on Conjugal Onanism*, by Maurus Nardi. Nardi took the position that coitus interruptus was so clearly un-natural that good faith could never be found in a man practicing with-drawal. He urged that the confessor inquire as a matter of course into the contraceptive practice of a married penitent. An anonymous reviewer of the book in the Belgian *Nouvelle revue théologique* observed that Nardi's rule was directed to France, where "everyone admits onanism is very common."[96]

It is against this background of uncertainty as to practice in the con-fessional and of knowledge of widespread contraception in France that the action of Leo XIII should be judged. On February 10, 1880, scarcely a year after his election, this Pope, so sensitive to the moral needs of contemporary society, issued a major encyclical on marriage, *Arcanum Divinae Sapientiae*. In view particularly of the situation in France, civil divorce was the preoccupation of the encyclical. The Pope had not a single express word to say on contraception. Not a sentence indicated

---

[95] *Decisiones Sanctae Sedis*, pp. 22–24.
[96] Maurus Nardi, *Dissertatio de onanismo conjugali* (Toulouse, 1876), p. 84, quoted in *Nouvelle revue théologique* 8 (1876), 650.

directly that it was a major problem. Under "duties" of spouses it was not mentioned. Even when the Pope turned to the bishops to urge them to instruct the faithful on the nature of marriage, nothing specific was said against it.[97]

Yet this document, whose Victorian reticence or Liguorian tolerance on what seemed to be a major problem is so puzzling, was a reassertion of the basis for the Church's right to speak about contraception and anything else affecting marriage. Marriage, the encyclical insists, may not be "naturalistically" conceived as a merely human arrangement. It was founded by God. Even among the pagans it is religious; even among pagans it is a sacrament. For the Christian, marriage is "wonderfully conformed" to the pattern of the mystical union of Christ with his Church; for the Christian, it is "an image of the Incarnation." There is in it, for Christian and non-Christian, something sacred, something innately holy. It is because of this that the Church has in the past "wanted to assure and to maintain intact the holy modesty of the marital bed." It is for this reason that the Church has "surrounded this divine institution with so many strong and farsighted laws." [98] In short, never speaking explicitly against contraception as an evil of the day, Leo XIII set out the foundation of the Church's competence and, proclaiming the holiness of marriage, indirectly invited the faithful to observe the laws necessary to keep it holy.

A new attempt to achieve a more rigorous and uniform approach to contraception in the confessional was made in 1886. An anonymous French bishop wrote to the Penitentiary that "the wicked crime of Onan" was widespread in France, that almost no province was immune, that, whereas in earlier times couples tried to prevent too many children, now their practice might exclude "almost any acceptance of children." The matter was made worse by the divergent practice of confessors. "The nub of the difficulty," the bishop said bluntly, "is the necessity of interrogating and warning penitents." Some confessors believed that among "such a number of the faithful" who practice onanism there must be good faith. Their belief has been ironically confirmed, for a number of married persons, on being openly told of the sinfulness of the act, promptly stopped frequenting the sacraments; the inference drawn is that these persons formerly thought that they were acting innocently, and now will not sacrilegiously participate in the sacraments if unable to refrain from what they have been informed is a vice. Other confessors think the right rule is that, "if a penitent is ignorant of crimes which he ought to know," he should be told. Moreover, if not told, he may frequent the sacraments to

[97] Leo XIII, *Arcanum Divinae Sapientiae*, ASS 12:385–402.
[98] ASS 12:386–391.

the scandal of those who know of his sin. As often as founded suspicion is present they interrogate. If a sinner is found to be only in probable good faith, the common good requires that he be told that he is sinning. But even these more severe confessors will leave undisturbed the penitent who, it is morally certain, is in good faith. From the responses of the Roman Congregations to date, the bishop observed wryly, various rules had been derived. He therefore framed two questions:

1. When there is a founded suspicion that the penitent is addicted to the crime of onanism, about which he is silent, is it lawful for the confessor to abstain from prudent and discreet interrogation, in that he foresees that some in good faith will be disturbed and many will desert the sacraments? Or, rather, is not the confessor bound to interrogate prudently and discreetly?

2. If, from spontaneous confession or prudent interrogation, the confessor knows the penitent to be an onanist, is he bound to warn him of the gravity of this sin just as of other mortal sins; to rebuke him, as the *Roman Ritual* says, with paternal charity; and to confer absolution on him only when it is clear from adequate signs that he is sorry about the past and proposes not to act onanistically again? [99]

The Penitentiary, agreeing that the sin in question was widely prevalent, said that "regularly" confessors should not abstain from interrogation in the first case and that there was a duty to inquire prudently and discreetly. It said that the answer to the second question was Yes. According to this answer, good faith of the penitents would not "regularly" be a defense; for the question noted that "some in good faith will be disturbed," yet the Penitentiary replied that inquiries were to be "regularly made." There is measurable stiffening of attitude from the responses of 1842.

A key ambiguity in the question lay in the phrase "founded suspicion." The Penitentiary did nothing to make the phrase precise. The leading contemporary Jesuit moralist, Augustine Lehmkuhl, said in his *Moral Theology* that the "general rule" was that a confessor should be modest and sparing in his inquiry about marital sins.[100] Lehmkuhl may have had in mind chiefly his own country, Germany, where contraception was not yet as widespread as France. Did, then, "founded suspicion" turn on statistical probability in a given area, or on the circumstances of the particular penitent? No authoritative answer existed.

In a thorough, practical discussion of the question in 1898 in *L'Ami du clergé*, a paper published in Langres, Haut-Marne, and widely read by French priests, the anonymous author gave as his "nub of the problem" the practice of contraception in good faith. Such good faith was common. The notion that "all is permitted in marriage" was widespread.

---

[99] *Decisiones Sanctae Sedis*, pp. 27–29. The Penitentiary's answer follows, p. 30.
[100] Augustine Lehmkuhl, *Theologia moralis*, 5th ed. (Freiburg im Breisgau, 1888), II, no. 859.

Instruction to the contrary was rare. Public opinion and articles in the press encouraged the belief that contraception was desirable. The example of others confirmed this opinion. There were often good personal reasons for wanting to limit one's family. All of these factors concurred to establish good faith in the husband, wife, or couple practicing contraception. But this good faith must be destroyed. It must be destroyed for the common good, the one consideration which overrides the welfare of the individual penitent. Depopulation and the bad example furnished others were injuries which must be prevented. Consequently, the author recommended that the confessor inquire and instruct. He cannot act at once with everyone, if most of the married men in the parish are practicing contraception. But let him interrogate one or two penitents, then several. The word will spread. True, there will be some angry reactions. But gradually the belief that contraception is not sinful or at least not gravely sinful will disappear. Even when he has no suspicion about a particular penitent the confessor may ask, "Have you anything to reproach yourself for in your intimate relations with your wife?" If there is founded suspicion — and a family no bigger than one or two children does not by itself create suspicion — then the confessor should ask, "Have you abused marriage in any way, in order not to have children?" Admittedly the practice of confessors now varies widely. Pastor and curate may disagree in the same parish. The 1886 answer of the Penitentiary is only gradually being known or followed. But it at last has established a norm which should, prudently and slowly, be put into practice.[101]

The kind of reaction L'Ami du clergé so clearly anticipates is described in the letter of an anonymous parish priest to the Penitentiary in 1901. The priest has interrogated "Titius," whom the priest finds it relevant to describe as "rich, honorable, educated," and "a good Christian." On being interrogated in the confessional, Titius said that he practiced coitus interruptus lest he lower the status of his family (he had a boy and a girl) and lest he exhaust his wife by repeated pregnancies. The priest reproved him. Titius replied that another confessor, a professor of moral theology in a seminary, had approved his conduct. Titius left the confessional and spread the report that the parish priest was proud and ignorant. To the curé's request for counsel, the Penitentiary replied on November 13, 1901, that he "had acted rightly": he could not have absolved an impenitent onanist.[102] The response is particularly striking because there was nothing in the exposition of the case which suggested that there was "founded suspicion" or that Titius was not acting in good faith. Interrogation without suspicion of the individual penitent and

---

[101] "Une grosse question de morale contemporaine," L'Ami du clergé, December 1, 1898, p. 1075; December 8, 1898, pp. 1108, 1111.

[102] Decisiones Sanctae Sedis, pp. 32–33.

destruction of his good faith were approved, presumably on the theory that the common good demanded this rigorous action.

France had been the chief area provoking questions over contraception. But by 1880, when Leo XIII wrote on marriage, birth control was already a European phenomenon. There was some time lag between the event and the clerical reaction. In Austria, for example, by 1902, the Jesuit moralist Jerome Noldin taught that in a region where contraception was widespread a confessor "can almost always reasonably suppose that the penitent has been silent about this sin." A duty of inquiry arose.[103] The real battleground was Belgium, where a particularly vigorous Catholic faith flourished in part of the nation while the rest of the population was influenced by anticlerical and socialist ideologies. Between 1889 and 1909 the pages of the *Nouvelle revue théologique* testify to an increasing awareness of the spread of contraception. Belgian priests, especially in the country, tried to resist the new practices by strenuous means.[104] Unlike the French clergy, observed L. Roelandts with satisfaction, "We do not practice the system of tolerant *mutisme*": that is, we don't shut up when we should be interrogating penitents.[105] One writer in 1899, B. Deppe, recommended inquiry into contraceptive practice if the penitent complained about the number of children he had, saying, for example, "We have five, six, seven, or eight children, and we are not yet forty." Deppe admitted that good faith, which should not be disturbed, could be found among younger and simpler women, who had been initiated into contraceptive intercourse by their husbands.[106] Roelandts, in 1906, thought that good faith was rare. He also recommended interrogation of the mothers of recently married girls. Have they told their daughters "to be prudent"? If so, they have sinned.[107]

In France the bishops had never sought to instruct the faithful or even to achieve unity of confessional practice by a joint letter. Some contributors to the 1898 symposium in *L'Ami du clergé* had proposed such a course, but nothing had happened. It became evident that public episcopal action would be necessary if Belgium was not to go the way of France. For thirty years the Belgian birth rate had fallen; the international birth control conference had been held in 1905 in Liège. The leading Belgian moral theologian, Arthur Vermeersch, sounded the tocsin in an article

---

[103] Jerome Noldin, *De sexto praecepto et de usu matrimonii* (Innsbruck, 1911), p.86.

[104] See, e.g., Deppe, "Théologie pastorale," p. 465. Deppe, deprecating the crude way of country clergy of requiring the penitent to have marital intercourse without contraception before absolution would be given, says himself that absolution, or at least communion, is to be deferred until the penitent has destroyed the instruments by which contraception is practiced (*ibid.*, p. 460).

[105] L. Roelandts, "Théologie pastorale," *Nouvelle revue théologique* 38 (1906), 309.

[106] Deppe, "Théologie pastorale," pp. 459, 462.

[107] Roelandts, "Théologie pastorale," pp. 312, 320.

grimly entitled "A Grave Moral Peril." In 1909, prodded by Vermeersch, Cardinal Mercier, primate of Belgium, issued a pastoral letter, "The Duties of Married Life," and on June 2, 1909, the bishops of Belgium issued to curés and confessors their "Instructions Against Onanism." [108]

The bishops began forthrightly by saying that according to the testimony of economists, doctors, and confessors it was incontestable that "the very evil sin of Onan" was being practiced in Belgium, by rich and poor, in cities and in the country. "In this common danger" they would be remiss in their duty if they did not speak out and denounce onanism, as a violation of the primary purpose of marital intercourse, as a vice against nature, as a sin crying out to heaven. The sin now flourished in Belgium because of the acceptance of a materialistic conception of life; to this false philosophy priests should oppose the Christian view of life as a way to the heavenly fatherland and a time of probation; they should recall the teaching of St. Paul in 1 Corinthians 7:29–39 that "the time is short." If a person practiced contraception from fear of having more children than he could feed, he should be encouraged to have a greater faith that Providence would provide, that no one would starve. If a person practiced contraception because of fear of danger to his wife from pregnancy or delivery, the fear should be calmed. If there was real danger, heroic continence should be recommended. Outside of confession, the priest should work against contraception by blessing large families. There was to be no direct preaching on the sin, with two important exceptions: such preaching was desirable in giving special missions to segregated audiences of men or women, and in giving instructions on marriage to groups of engaged persons.

Within the confessional, particularly vigorous battle was to be waged. In his article Vermeersch had analyzed the duty of the confessor in terms of "the common good." The confessor was bound to consider the effect which his silence might have on others than the penitent. The penitent might often report the silence of a confessor as approbation, and spread the word. Thus, respect for the good faith of one person would lead everybody into error. Even where contraception was widespread, not every person was suspect; some persons were of a piety which put them beyond suspicion. But in areas where contraception flourished, the general rule should be discreet inquiry about fulfillment of the obligations of marriage. Suspicion, properly speaking, however, would arise "only from the indications given by the penitent himself." [109]

The instructions of the Belgian hierarchy bore the marks of Ver-

[108] "Instruction des Evêques de Belgique sur l'onanisme," Nouvelle revue théologique 41 (1909), 616–622.

[109] Arthur Vermeersch, "Un grave péril moral," Nouvelle revue théologique 41 (1909), 65–72.

meersch's teaching. "Founded suspicion" could arise "from the manner of confessing of the penitent" and also from what he disclosed of his life to the confessor. The kinds of questions which could be asked were, "Do you live in marriage in a truly Christian way?" "Does nothing about the duties of marriage trouble your conscience?" "Do you conform yourself to the divine will as to the number of children?" "Do you commit yourself totally to divine Providence in the generation of children?" The "Instructions" of the Belgian bishops was both a manifesto and a program. It called for strenuous action, of a kind from which the French hierarchy had shrunk, against the danger.[110]

Four years later their example caught fire in Germany. On August 20, 1913, from Fulda, the German bishops issued a pastoral letter which, deploring the sexual immorality threatening the sanctity of the home, specifically decried the spread of contraception. The economic reasons advanced for contraceptive practice were not, they said, the real reasons; contraception was the "consequence of luxury." An industry was now devoted to making artificial contraceptives available. The bishops felt compelled to speak: "It is serious sin to will to prevent the increase of the number of children, so that marriage is abused for pleasure alone and its principal purpose knowingly and willingly frustrated. It is serious sin, very serious sin, with whatever means and in whatever way it occurs." Catholics practicing contraception should know that they could not receive the sacraments. The bishops closed with a slight amendment of the purpose of marriage as proclaimed by the Roman Catechism. The chief end of marriage, they said, was procreation "in order to secure the continuation of the Church and the state." [111]

In France an account of the situation twenty years after the articles in *L'Ami du clergé* does not reflect any change in the practice of French

---

[110] Alois de Smet, a theologian at Bruges, writing in Belgium after the hierarchy's instructions, admitted that the belief, in good faith, could still be found that contraception was not a sin, but he believed such good faith was "rather rare." If a confessor believed questioning would not lead the penitent to amend his life, he could omit it. *Les Fiançailles et le mariage* 2.1.3.1, annex 2 (Bruges, 1912). In 1919, Arthur Vermeersch cited with approval Noldin's teaching that where contraception was widespread, there was "almost always" a rational supposition that the penitent had committed this sin; *De castitate et de vitiis contrariis* (Rome, 1919), no. 270. An anonymous commentator in the diocese of Tournai commented earlier that "founded suspicion" arose "more easily" if the penitent lived a worldly life, if he declared other serious sins against chastity, if he were uneducated and ignorant, if he very rarely approached the sacraments. On the contrary, there was less reason for suspicion if the penitent had numerous children, if his life was otherwise Christian, if he declared all his sins with great care, if he frequented the sacraments, if he went to confession at some time other than Easter or on the occasion of a mission (*Collationes dioecesis tornacensis* 15 [1910], 411).

[111] Citations here are from quotations in the analysis of the letter by Joseph Laurentius, S. J., "Das Bischofswort zum Schutze der Familie," *Theologisch-praktische Quartalschrift* 67 (1914), 517–528.

confessors. Writing in 1918 in the *Revue du clergé français*, E. Jordan stated that there had been little instruction in the confessional. He quoted a priest from southwestern France who said that "complete silence" on "any sexual question" was maintained by both confessors and penitents. He quoted a Breton priest who said that for a century "duty in marriage" had been passed over in the confessional.[112] Such comments are impressionistic, and possibly exaggerated. They are not, however, countered by any testimony that instruction in the confessional was common.

On May 7, 1919, as World War I drew to a close, the French bishops finally acted. Like the Germans, they mixed the appeals of religion and patriotism:

> The principal end of marriage is the procreation of children; for this God honors the spouses by associating them in his creative power and paternity. It is to sin seriously against nature and against the will of God to frustrate marriage of its end by an egotistic or sensual calculation. The theories and practices which teach or encourage the restriction of birth are as disastrous as they are criminal. The war has forcefully impressed upon us the danger to which they expose our country. Let the lesson not be lost. It is necessary to fill the spaces made by death, if we want France to belong to Frenchmen and to be strong enough to defend herself and prosper.[113]

At the war's end the Austrian hierarchy issued a pastoral, chiefly on the indissolubility of marriage, but noting that the "profanation of marriage" was "the greatest moral scourge of our day." [114]

In the United States concern by the hierarchy with contraception was also voiced after the war. Before 1915 textbooks like Kenrick's had touched on the question, but indicated no awareness of a pressing issue. The 1884 pastoral letter of the hierarchy, written by Archbishop Gibbons of Baltimore, spoke of the sacredness of marriage but dwelt only on religiously mixed marriages and divorce as current problems.[115] The first full discussion of the matter as an issue of the day by an American moral theologian occurred in 1916 in the *Ecclesiastical Review*, a journal published at The Catholic University of America and directed to the American clergy. This analysis by John A. Ryan (1869–1945), a priest who was a professor at the university, may be taken as a good example of the kind of thinking which, in the first half of the twentieth century, the American church was to contribute to the development of moral doctrine. Ryan had a strong regard for the authority of Roman decisions and the teaching of Thomas Aquinas. At the same time he was not bereft of common sense or

---

[112] E. Jordan, "Religion et natalité," *Revue du clergé français* 97 (1919), 48, 40.
[113] *Documentation catholique* 1 (1919), 578–579.
[114] *Ibid.*, p. 519.
[115] Pastoral Letter of the Archbishops and Bishops of the United States, dated December 7, 1884, in *The National Pastorals of the American Hierarchy, 1729–1919*, ed. Peter Guilday (Washington, 1923), pp. 247–248.

blind to the needs of modern society. He was at his best on social and economic questions, where the broad lines of papal teaching left much room for interpretation and where American experience could be most forcefully invoked. In general, he was not inclined to speculation, and he used his homely observations to shore up his authorities in preference to developing new hypotheses. On marital matters, he avoided innovation, yet he did not like to be more rigorous than he felt constrained to be by authority.

In his article, "Family Limitation," Ryan noted that "birth control" and "contraception" had become topics of the press in America in the past two years (a reference to the early work of Margaret Sanger). This introductory remark brought into use in moral theology the American expressions "birth control" and "contraception," and so increased the technical vocabulary. It also marked an American preference for these words to the European term "onanism," which probably seemed less apt for a description of contraceptive practice in the United States. Ryan went on to say that, despite some complacent official assumptions that the sin was not a problem for the American church, contraception was practiced by a substantial number of American Catholics. From his own knowledge of families doing this, however, he doubted that the practice was engaged in with a knowledge that it was mortal sin. His conclusion was not that of Bishop Bouvier in 1842: tolerate what is done in good faith. He had confidence that, if properly instructed, American Catholics would desist. He said, therefore, Tell them that it is wrong.[116]

Ryan's reasoning probably led to the statement on contraception made by the American bishops in their first joint pastoral since 1884. This letter, in the name of Gibbons, now a cardinal, individually and in the name of all the bishops, was a review of the prosperous state of the Church in America as America assumed world political leadership. In the course of seventy pages, two paragraphs were devoted to birth control. Having spoken of idealistic illusions about joy in marriage, the bishops said,

On the other hand, it is idealism of the truest and most practical sort that sees in marriage the divinely appointed plan for cooperating with the Creator in perpetuating the race, and that accepts the responsibility of bringing children into the world, who may prove either a blessing or a curse to society at large.

Where such ideals prevail, the fulfillment of marital duties occasions no hardship. Neither is there any consideration for the fraudulent prudence that would improve upon nature by defeating its obvious purpose, and would purify life by defiling its source. The selfishness which leads to race suicide with or without the pretext of bettering the species, is, in God's sight, "a detestable thing." It is the crime of individuals for which, eventually, the nation must suffer. The harm which it does cannot be repaired by social

[116] John A. Ryan, "Family Limitation," *Ecclesiastical Review* 54 (1916), 684–696.

service, nor offset by pretending economic or domestic advantage. On the contrary, there is joy in the hope of offspring, for "the inheritance of the Lord are children; and His reward, the fruit of the womb." The bond of love is strengthened, fresh stimulus is given to thrift and industrious effort, and the very sacrifices which are called for become sources of blessing.[117]

The hierarchy in America was henceforth to be known for its vigilant opposition to the birth control movement.[118]

The series of actions by national hierarchies which began in 1909 reached their climax in 1930. At last the Pope spoke specifically on contraception. On December 31, 1930, Pius XI issued *Casti connubii*. The immediate causes for the Pope's action were three: reaction to the Lambeth Conference vote of August 15, 1930; a call for revision of the teaching in the German Catholic periodical *Hochland* of June 1930; and a growing uneasiness among Roman theologians that in practice priests were not enforcing the teaching. The actual timing of the encyclical seems to have been affected by the Pope's desire to speak on the mixed marriage of King Boris III of Bulgaria to Princess Giovanna of Italy.[119]

The action of the Anglican bishops at Lambeth had been met by strong denunciation from the Catholic archbishop of Westminster. On October 4, 1930, Cardinal Francis Bourne declared that these bishops, by their vote, had forfeited any claim to be "authorized organs of Christian morality." [120] The cardinal, no doubt, was anxious that Rome support his vigorous stand.

In Rome, at the height of his prestige, was Arthur Vermeersch, the most influential moral theologian of the first part of the twentieth century. Vermeersch, who had played such a large role in the statement of the Belgian bishops in 1909, now helped to initiate a definitive Roman state-

[117] Pastoral Letter of the Archbishops and Bishops of the United States, dated September 26, 1919, in Guilday, ed., *The National Pastorals*, pp. 312–313. The letter, or part of it, was to be read at all masses on Washington's Birthday, Sunday, February 22, 1920 (*America* 22 [1920], 407).

[118] See Margaret Sanger's account of the closing of the meeting of the first National Birth Control Conference, in New York in 1921, at the instigation of Patrick Hayes, the Catholic archbishop of New York (*An Autobiography*, p. 304).

[119] Pius XI, Sermon to the Cardinals and Prelates of the Roman Curia, December 24, 1930, AAS 22:537–538.
The connection (for the third time) of Bulgaria and the development of doctrine on marriage came about in this way. The marriage of Boris and Giovanna on October 30, 1930, had been a major problem of Vatican diplomacy. Mussolini wanted the marriage, to further Italian aspirations in the Balkans; the couple were also in love; but the heir to the Bulgarian throne had to be reared in the Orthodox faith. Pius XI stood firm, and Boris finally agreed that all children of the marriage would be Catholics. The wedding at Assisi took place two weeks after his agreement. For the popular stir occasioned by the royal romance, see *Time*, October 13, October 27, and November 3, 1930.

[120] Quoted in Arthur Vermeersch, "La Conférence de Lambeth et la morale du mariage," *Nouvelle revue théologique* 57 (1930), 850.

ment and to draft the text. His strategic place in doctrinal development makes it appropriate to add some comment on his character.[121] Vermeersch (1858–1936) came from a small Flemish town. At twenty-one he entered the Jesuit order, and went on to both theological and legal studies. At thirty-five he became a professor of theology at the Jesuit scholasticate of theology in Louvain. For twenty-five years he exercised a strong influence on the Belgian hierarchy. He then moved to a wider field, becoming professor of moral theology at the Jesuits' Gregorian University in Rome. From 1918 to 1934 he dominated Roman moral theology. No narrowly academic man, but a moralist used to solving hard problems of conscience and telling bishops what to think, endowed with an excellent legal mind and a strong sense of what was morally right, Vermeersch was a force to be reckoned with. His exposition of principle is characteristically clear, terse, strong, and uncompromising. Now, twenty-one years after the campaign in Belgium, at the age of seventy-two, he saw birth control as a worldwide menace. Enthusiastically, he backed Cardinal Bourne: Could the Church of England be believed any longer by anyone to be the Church of Jesus Christ? [122]

Apart from the Anglicans, there were the German Catholics. The *Hochland* article, "Revolutionizing of Marriage," was not a major cause of the encyclical but, appearing in an influential and old Catholic periodical, it had caused a stir.[123] It was an index of a growing German discontent with the old doctrine on marriage. Moreover, the worldwide situation was such that Vermeersch and other theologians of his mind believed that strong papal action alone could dispel the uncertainty and doubt. In

[121] Vermeersch's role in stimulating the encyclical is evident from what follows. His part in the drafting of the encyclical is not only known from its close conformity to his work, but may be inferred from the annotations he was able to publish on it within a month of its issuance: "Annotationes," *Periodica de re morali, canonica, liturgica* 20 (1931), 44. On his life see J. de Ghellinck, S.J., and G. Gilleman, S.J., "Arthur Vermeersch," *DTC* 15²:2687; Joseph Creusen, S.J., "In Memoriam," *Nouvelle revue théologique* 63 (1936), 817–838.

[122] Vermeersch, "La Conférence de Lambeth et la morale du mariage," p. 859.

[123] In this article Matthias Laros stated that, in Germany, "we are already in the midst of a revolutionizing of marriage." He asked for a firm foundation for the Catholic position. He noted that Lindner's book, *Der Usus matrimonii*, had demonstrated a complete change of position by the moral theologians on intercourse in pregnancy. He asked if the natural law on contraception knew no exceptions or modifications. He noted that peace in the family and education of the offspring, also objectives of marriage, might conflict with the rule on procreation, and asked how natural law bound one in this conflict. He noted the teaching of the nineteenth-century German theologian Linsenmann, *Lehrbuch der Moraltheologie* (1878), that the first purpose of marriage is the common life of the spouses, and contended that this was also the teaching of the Roman Catechism. He suggested that "the personal end" in marriage might, under some circumstances, take precedence over the biological end. He asked how theologians could speak of an act of contraception as "intrinsically evil and unlawful," adding that this was the question "of thousands today." ("Revolutionierung der Ehe," *Hochland* 27² [1930], 193–207.)

Belgium, where such strenuous efforts had been made by the hierarchy to instruct the faithful, one "could meet educated laymen and even priests, who would deny or put in doubt the opposition of these [contraceptive] practices to natural law." [124] Vermeersch had been stung by Lambeth's reference to Liguorian doctrine on good faith, in the Conference Report's declaration that Rome "recognized that there are some occasions where the rigid maintenance of principle is impossible." Yet while he denied that principle could ever be sacrificed, he admitted that confessors could be observed who, as to sins of contraception, did not conduct even prudent interrogation of their penitents, skillfully avoided questions on its sinfulness, and "by ambiguous words rendered more or less secure" those penitents who actually accused themselves of the sin.[125] *Casti connubii*, then, was not only intended to answer the Anglicans; it was to answer the questions from Germany, to encourage confessors, to dissipate all doubts. It became the strongest papal statement on contraception since the bull *Effraenatam* of Sixtus V.

The encyclical was a small summa on Christian marriage. The holiness of marriage, the Pope declared, was endangered by ignorance and by the false principles of a new and absolutely perverse morality. Pernicious errors and depraved morals had even begun to spread among the faithful. As vicar of Christ, as supreme pastor, as teacher, the Pope spoke "to turn sheep from poisoned pastures." The grand lines of *Arcanum Divinae Sapientiae* were insisted on. Marriage was of divine institution; all errors flowed from treating its laws as adjustable by human will. Marriage was a great sacrament, whose care had been committed by Christ to the Church. Divorce and such innovations as "trial marriage" and "companionate marriage" were denounced. The goods of marriage were summarized in the ancient Augustinian formula: offspring, fidelity, sacrament. Offspring was the primary good. God had spoken to all spouses when He said, "Increase and multiply and fill the earth." Christian parents should understand that not only were they to propagate the human race, but "to bear offspring for the Church of Christ, to procreate saints and servants of God, that the people adhering to the worship of God and our Saviour should daily increase." The use of the phrase from the Roman Catechism and *Arcanum* on the purpose of using marriage to multiply Christians did not amount to saying "the more children the better." Still,

---

[124] Joseph Creusen, S.J., "L'Onanisme conjugal," *Nouvelle revue théologique* 59 (1932), 132. In the United States, in a book which appeared in 1930, two rather strict Dominican moralists taught that invincible ignorance about the sin of onanism could be present "when married persons are poor or the woman sickly." John A. McHugh and Charles J. Callen, *Moral Theology* (New York, 1930), II, 510, sec. 2496.

[125] Arthur Vermeersch, "Annotationes" [on the encyclical *Casti connubii*], p. 51.

the additional phrase "daily increase" provided an emphasis that seemed to favor large families if the children could be educated as Christians.

Those who erred in their view of marriage claimed that "the act of nature might be vitiated." They acted either because they wanted pleasure without burden or because owing to their own situation or that of their wives or families they could not accept children. "But," the Pope said,

Assuredly no reason, even the most serious, can make congruent with nature and decent what is intrinsically against nature. Since the act of the spouses is by its own nature ordered to the generation of offspring, those who, exercising it, deliberately deprive it of its natural force and power, act against nature and effect what is base and intrinsically indecent.   (AAS 22:559)

As St. Augustine recalled, Scripture attested that God had punished this wicked crime with death.

"Certain persons," the Pope said, referring to the Anglican bishops, "have openly withdrawn from the Christian doctrine as it has been transmitted from the beginning and always faithfully kept." Consequently,

The Catholic Church, to whom God himself has committed the integrity and decency of morals, now standing in this ruin of morals, raises her voice aloud through our mouth, in sign of her divine mission, in order to keep the chastity of the nuptial bond free from this foul slip, and again promulgates:
Any use whatever of marriage, in the exercise of which the act by human effort is deprived of its natural power of procreating life, violates the law of God and nature, and those who do such a thing are stained by a grave and mortal flaw.   (AAS 22:560)

This condemnation was reinforced by a statement that every sin "against offspring" was "in a way" a sin against fidelity. The famous passage of Augustine on the cruel lust of couples avoiding procreation, who consequently could no longer be considered man and wife — the passage preserved in *Aliquando* and paraphrased by *Effraenatam* — was also invoked, although in a paragraph where it was made to tell against abortion.

Here, in the small compass of a single document, was a synthesis of themes which this book has explored at length: the Hebrew emphasis on procreation, the anti-Gnostic teaching of Timothy, the Augustinian doctrine of the marital goods, the Thomistic view of the nature of the coital act, nineteenth-century theology on the sin of Onan. The encyclical reverberated with classic citations. As a distillation of past doctrinal statements, the encyclical was a masterpiece. At the same time, its composers were indifferent to the historical contexts from which their citations came, and uninterested in the environmental changes which differentiated the present context. The encyclical was a synthesis, it was not history. Yet if not history, it had immense doctrinal authority as a solemn declaration by the Pope.

How great was that authority? By the ordinary tests used by the theologians to determine whether a doctrine is infallibly proclaimed, it may be argued that the specific condemnation of contraceptive interruption of the procreative act is infallibly set out. The encyclical is addressed to the universal Church. The Pope speaks in fulfillment of his apostolic office. He speaks for the Church. He speaks on moral doctrine that he says "has been transmitted from the beginning." He "promulgates" the teaching. If the Pope did mean to use the full authority to speak *ex cathedra* on morals, which Vatican I recognized as his, what further language could he have used?

Some theologians (Cappello, Ter Haar, Piscetta, Gennaro, and Vermeersch himself) held the condemnation to be infallible by virtue of the *ex cathedra* exercise of papal authority.[126] Other theologians, with whom Vermeersch's disciple Joseph Creusen seemed to associate himself, noted that the Pope says he "again promulgates" the doctrine.[127] On this interpretation, the Pope purports to be only repeating the teaching of the Church, not defining doctrine. This reading leads to two slightly varied positions. The first is that, while repeating the teaching of the Church, the Pope puts it as infallibly true; so held in 1951 the Jesuits Zalba and Cartechini, and in 1963 Ford and Kelly.[128] The other position was taken by Joseph Fuchs, who wrote: "It is regarded as such a solemn, authentic declaration, renewing previous decisions and itself afterwards often confirmed, that anyone who did not want to accept it would sin against the virtue of faith, although he would not lose the faith." [129] It must be added that, according to the constitution on the Church enacted by Vatican II in 1964, infallibility extends "only as far as the deposit of divine revelation extends" (3.25, *AAS* 57:30). The formulas used for defining a dogma usually either have included anathematization of those denying the truth proclaimed or, as in the definition of the Assumption, have been explicit: "We pronounce, declare, and define to be divinely revealed dogma" (*Munificentissimus Deus, AAS* 42:770).

What did the condemnation of *Casti connubii* embrace? In the period between 1880 and 1930 the term usually used by theologians to describe contraception was "onanism." But the meaning of this term had been expanded from its earlier meaning of coitus interruptus. This expansion is not explicit in the documents, but it is clear in the definitions given by the moral theologians. Thus in 1880 Augustine Lehmkuhl defined "onanism" as withdrawal followed by ejaculation, or "prevention of the

---

[126] Authorities are collected in John C. Ford, S.J., and Gerald Kelly, S.J., *Contemporary Moral Theology* (Westminster, Maryland, 1963), II, 263–264.

[127] J. Creusen, "L'Onanisme conjugal," p. 132.

[128] Ford and Kelly, *Contemporary Moral Theology*, II, 277. See p. 264 for a résumé of Zalba and Cartechini's position.

[129] Joseph Fuchs, *De castitate et ordine sexuali: Conspectus praelectionum theologiae moralis ad usum auditorum* 2.6.2.3, 2nd ed. (Rome, 1960), p. 66.

seed from reaching the vessel by other wicked means" (*Moral Theology*, "Marriage," 2.1.8.4.1.1.1, *ad* 5). In their instructions to confessors in 1909, the Belgian bishops said that "the sin of onanism is committed in every conjugal act so exercised that by some positive method generation is impeded." In this context "some positive means" was used to designate mechanical means or chemical means. In a response from a Roman congregation in 1916, the broad use was adopted without comment: the Penitentiary spoke of "onanism by instrument." [130]

It is evident that the condemnation of *Casti connubii* cannot be restricted to coitus interruptus. The encyclical does, however, focus on contraception performed "in the exercise" of the marital act. A strict reading would confine the condemnation to coitus interruptus and the use of a condom: by these methods coitus, in its exercise, is deprived of its procreative force. Other methods do not affect coitus in its exercise. As will be seen, however, a broader reading of the condemnation was favored by Pope Pius XII. In this interpretation, at least the use of diaphragms or postcoital douches would also fall within the express condemnation.

It seems probable, however, that the condemnation of *Casti connubii* did not, in its terms, reach contraception achieved by sterilizing surgery or drug. To understand this silence a review of the authorities who preceded the encyclical is in order. General principles governing castration had been set out by the classical moralists. But sterilization that would achieve a contraceptive effect without preventing coitus had not been analyzed. Nor was the operation discussed by such nineteenth-century writers as Gury, Ballerini, Lehmkuhl, or Capellmann. The method was not unknown. In 1894, Peter Gasparri could speak of "excision of the Fallopian tubes or extraction of both ovaries or the uterus" as means which might be specified in a condition antecedent to marriage, and which would invalidate the marriage.[131] But I find no discussion of the moral position of married persons who have sterilized themselves.

In the twentieth century, De Smet noted that a vasectomy or ovariotomy might be sought to achieve the end of "onanism." He did not say whether the operation itself was a sin of contraception, or whether intercourse after the operation was sinful (*Les Fiançailles et le mariage* 2.1.3.1.1, annex 2). Ampler and more exact analysis was undertaken by

---

[130] For usage by the bishops, see "Instruction des Evêques de Belgique sur l'onanisme," p. 617; cf. Alois de Smet, *Les Fiançailles et le mariage* 2.1.3.1.1, annex 2. For the usage of the Penitentiary see *Decisiones Sanctae Sedis*, p. 35.

After *Casti connubii*, the broad use of "onanism" continued. Thomas Iorio, an Italian Jesuit, noted in 1939 that coitus interruptus was an old-fashioned form of contraception, and that the common forms today were by "instruments": the condom, pessary, pseudo-vagina, and vaginal lotion (John Gury, *Theologia moralis*, ed. Thomas Iorio, Naples, 1946, p. 1202). Like most theologians, however, he kept the old term. In 1952, Francis Hürth used a hybrid term "onanismo condomistico," contraception by condom (*Periodica de re morali, canonica, liturgica* 41 [1952], 267).

[131] Peter Gasparri, *Tractactus canonicus de matrimonio* (Rome, 1894), II, no. 856.

Vermeersch. If a spouse sought and achieved permanent sterility by surgery, he could repent the act and then lawfully have intercourse. If the sterilization were reparable, lawful intercourse must await restoration of the affected organ. Otherwise the couple were guilty of onanism. If there was necessarily a short delay in repairing the effect, an innocent spouse might lawfully seek intercourse, which the sterilized spouse should grant (*Chastity and the Contrary Vices,* no. 23). The approach of Vermeersch emphasized, broadly rather than technically, the effect achieved. Coitus in a sterilized state was clearly not regarded as intrinsically sinful — otherwise intercourse by a repentant or innocent spouse would not have been permitted. But Vermeersch viewed intercourse in a sterilized state as sinful if the sterility could be removed. The precise basis for this opinion was not developed.

If Vermeersch's work was the sole guide to the interpretation of the encyclical, or if the document itself had used the broad term "onanism," sterilization would have fallen within the encyclical's condemnation. But in the late 1920's the main issue involving sterilization was the lawfulness of compulsory sterilization. Beginning with Indiana in 1903, twenty-three of the American states had adopted laws permitting the sterilization for eugenic reasons of persons classified as feeble-minded or insane, and in 1927 the Supreme Court had upheld the constitutionality of this kind of legislation. American Catholics had deplored this trend, and the National Catholic Welfare Conference issued a pamphlet by John A. Ryan, *Human Sterilization,* decrying compulsory sterilization, although not absolutely denying the hypothetical right of the state to sterilize if confronted with the danger of multitudes of defective offspring. In 1928 eugenic sterilization spread to Europe with the adoption on September 3, 1928, of legislation authorizing sterilization of the feeble-minded by the Swiss canton of Vaud. On June 1, 1929, Denmark adopted a similar law.[132]

Against the background of this recent question *Casti connubii* spoke specifically and separately on sterilization. The section was principally drafted by Francis Hürth, a German Jesuit. It took an even stronger stand than Ryan. The right of the person over his sexual faculties was asserted to be superior to the welfare of the community, as long as he had committed no crime. The state was denied to have the right to sterilize an innocent person (*Casti connubii,* AAS 22:564–565). The encyclical went on to deal with private, voluntary sterilization. An individual, it said, had

---

[132] For the American laws on sterilization see J. N. Landman, "The History of Human Sterilization in the United States — Theory, Statutes and Adjudication," *Illinois Law Review* 23 (1929), 463. The decisive case was *Buck v. Bell,* 274 *United States Reports* 200 (1927). For American Catholic reaction see John A. Ryan, *Human Sterilization* (Washington, 1929). For European laws see Walter Kopp, *Gesetzliche Unfruchtbarmachung* (Kiel, 1934), p. 28.

no dominion over his members, except what "belonged to their natural ends." Self-mutilation was unlawful, and bodily organs should not be "rendered unfit for natural functions except when the good of the whole body cannot otherwise be provided for." This succinct statement was notable in four respects. It spoke very broadly of making an organ unfit (*ineptus*) to function. It made no special reference to sterilization as an operation governed by any principle distinct from those relating to mutilation in general; onanism was not mentioned. It made the standard for permissible mutilation the good of the "body" (not the person). It did not make as solemn a claim to be the teaching of the Church as the encyclical's express condemnation of an act in the course of coitus preventing procreation.

The authority of the encyclical, then, on contraception was great. Its scope was not unlimited, and has been debated. At all events, its issuance was of immense relevance to the question whether a Catholic could practice contraception in the innocent conviction that it was not a sin. The publicity of the encyclical itself in an age of rapid diffusion of the news made such innocence less likely. Moreover, the encyclical itself had a program. Vermeersch's view was that the common good demanded that good faith be destroyed in the confessional. "Let not confessors," the encyclical declared, "permit the faithful to err about this most serious law." The Pope severely admonished confessors "conniving in the false opinion of the faithful" or by silence "fraudulently" confirming them in their errors (*AAS* 22:560).

This language seemed to point to a positive duty of education in the confessional even where "founded suspicion" of the individual penitent's practice of contraception did not exist. Read in this way, *Casti connubii* overruled or reinterpreted the 1886 response of the Penitentiary. Writing in 1936, the Belgian Dominican Benedict Merkelbach (1871–1942) said that the Penitentiary had meant that a confessor could leave no one, whatever his good faith, in the belief that contraception was not a serious sin. The injury to the common good outweighed the consideration due to the individual (*Questions on Chastity and Lechery* 8.4.5).

Casti connubii had not completely resolved the question of the duty to inquire. After it, however, there was general agreement that practice of the sin in good faith might not be permitted. The tolerant days of the 1842 answer to Bishop Bouvier were past. The Pope had made clear that, for the common good, the sinfulness of contraception must be made known to all.

The instructions from Rome from 1816 to 1930 had interacted with the acts of the national hierarchies. It would be a mistake, I believe, to see the national statements against contraception as dictated from Rome, or the Roman interventions as brought about by national demands. A common tradition and theological training, supervised from Rome, suffices to explain the harmony of action. *Casti connubii* was the high-water mark. It guided action for the next thirty-four years. It has remained the most solemn, complete, and authoritative presentation of Catholic doctrine on contraceptive practice.

OTHER SANCTIONS: COOPERATION; ANNULMENT OF MARRIAGE

As the tempo of the campaign against birth control increased, other sanctions besides public denunciation and inquiry in the confessional were invoked. Substantial reliance was placed on the principles governing cooperation in sin; greater attention was given the teaching that the intention not to procreate invalidated the marriage.

In his call to action in 1909 Arthur Vermeersch dwelt on the duty not to cooperate in sin. He did not challenge the standards set by the nineteenth-century responses of the Penitentiary; rather, he urged that these standards be enforced. Passive cooperation with coitus in which withdrawal with ejaculation was foreseen was permissible. But an obligation should be "imposed" by confessors on women with husbands practicing such contraception: an obligation to dissuade them. Moreover, Vermeersch added, a wife did not have a duty of intercourse with a husband practicing coitus interruptus. As for cooperation with contraception by "instrument," since the act was intrinsically evil, passive cooperation was not permissible. Resistance must be to the point of being physically overpowered or to sacrificing some good "equivalent to life." The threat of divorce or the knowledge that the husband would seek sexual intercourse elsewhere was not sufficient grounds. The resistance must be the resistance offered to rape. Vermeersch was prepared to contemplate the consequences which enforcement of this rule might entail for marriages: "domestic unhappinesses, disorders, abandonments, divorces, alienation from the sacraments." If the act was intrinsically sinful, no other position was open: "Why should it be astonishing that conjugal chastity, like all the Christian virtues, claims its martyrs?" [133]

Vermeersch was also prepared to have the confessor take the steps necessary to discover whether a husband was committing contraception by coitus interruptus or condom. He noted that artificial means of contraception had become widespread, but that in some areas only coitus interruptus was practiced. Except in these areas, if a woman confessed that she had cooperated in contracepted intercourse, the confessor had an obligation to inquire as to the means of contraception.[134]

[133] Vermeersch, "Un grave péril moral," pp. 75–78.
[134] *Ibid.*, p. 76.

The Belgian bishops in their instruction to confessors later in the year repeated the basic standards. The confessor should impose on women cooperating in coitus interruptus "an obligation" to use "prayers and blandishments" to dissuade their husbands. Severity, rather than leniency, on cooperation was to be adopted, "Lest it come to this, that, husbands being excluded from the sacraments, by a subtle distinction there be admitted to them women who are passively indulging in onanism." As to cooperation with a husband using an instrument: "For the gravest reason, that is, fear of death or an equivalent evil, it is lawful not to resist the attacker."[135]

The views of Vermeersch and the Belgian bishops were incorporated in a response by the Penitentiary, dated June 3, 1916, to this question: "That this whole matter be set out and taught and in a safer way, is a husband using such instruments to be equated with a rapist, to whom a woman must then oppose the resistance which a virgin must offer to an attacker?" The Penitentiary answered, Yes.[136]

It is against this background of theological severity that Casti connubii made allusion to cooperation. Pius XI said "the Church well knows" that often a spouse "suffered rather than perpetrated a sin when, for a truly grave reason, she permitted a perversion of right order which she did not will." There was no sin in submitting, provided that the duty imposed by charity was observed of attempting to persuade the other not to use the sinful contraceptive method (AAS 22:350). No reference was made to the distinction between different kinds of contraceptive acts. A controversy developed over this ambiguity. John A. Ryan at the Catholic University of America contended that the Pope had obliterated the distinction: wifely cooperation was permissible both where coitus interruptus was practiced and where a condom was used. Monsignor Ryan added that he saw no real difference between the wife's state of mind cooperating with an act that from experience she knew would not terminate in intravaginal semination and cooperating with the use of a condom.[137]

Ryan's interpretation was attacked by several Jesuit theologians: in

[135] "Instruction des Evêques de Belgique sur l'onanisme," p. 623.
[136] The Penitentiary, two months earlier, had somewhat obscurely indicated that any involvement in anal intercourse involved greater culpability than unwilling involvement in intercourse with a condom. On April 3, 1916, it declared that when a husband desired to commit "a sodomitic crime," he must be resisted by his wife and she could not cooperate "even to avoid death," as the act would be "against nature" on the part of both. The Penitentiary expressed "great astonishment" that "some priests" had taken a milder view. At the same time the Penitentiary repeated that a wife could cooperate in coitus interruptus for a grave reason such as "death or serious vexations" (Decisiones Sanctae Sedis, p. 35).
[137] John A. Ryan, "The Moral Teaching of the Encyclical Letter on Christian Marriage," American Ecclesiastical Review 84 (1931), 266; "Reply," ibid. 85 (1931), 72–73.

the United States by James H. Kearney; in Europe by Arthur Vermeersch and Joseph Creusen.[138] These writers contended it would be surprising if the Pope had departed from both the 1916 rulings of the Penitentiary and the general teachings of the theologians without being more explicit; they intimated, indeed, that since what the theologians had taught was obviously true, the Pope could not have meant anything else.

The views of Vermeersch on cooperation by a wife seemed, then, to have general acceptance by the theologians. A similar approach prevailed at this time as to cooperation by a husband in his wife's contraceptive act. This question did not begin to concern the theologians until the 1920's. Then use of a contraceptive such as a pseudo-vagina, preventing completion of insemination, was treated as intrinsically evil, like the use of a condom. Use of a contraceptive such as a postcoital lotion, operating after ejaculation, was analogized to coitus interruptus as a sinful act not involving participation by the other spouse. There was doubt as to how a diaphragm should be categorized. The German bishops issued an *Instruction for Confessors* which said a husband should try to remove any "instruments or means inserted in the vessel" and used by his wife to prevent conception. If he could not succeed in doing this, he was permitted to have intercourse for "a serious reason." The bishops added that a serious reason was present "as often as it is serious for him to lack the conjugal act." [139] In 1926 Vermeersch asserted that a woman whose vagina was occluded was impotent by the canonical tests of impotence for marriage.[140] Intercourse with her was "intrinsically illicit." Vermeersch questioned whether the German bishops would want to stick to their permission of cooperation. Shortly after his article, the bishops rescinded their limited acceptance. Writing in 1932 on cooperation with a wife using a diaphragm, Creusen could say, "not one author defends its lawfulness." [141]

Where a condition of a marriage had been the avoidance of children, the old decretal, *Si conditiones,* said that the marriage was null. In the twentieth century, this sanction against premarital agreement to practice contraception received its most substantial application. In the new *Code of Canon Law,* which in 1917 replaced the *Decretum* and the *Decretals,*

---

[138] James H. Kearney, "Sinned Against Rather Than Sinning," *ibid.* 84 (1931), 502–508; Arthur Vermeersch, "Annotationes" [on *Casti connubii*], *Periodica* 26 (1936) 56; Joseph Creusen, "L'Onanisme conjugal," pp. 406–408.

[139] The quoted part of the German instruction and its Latin translation are both given in "Occlusio vaginae estne casus impotentiae an sterilitatis?" *Periodica de re morali, canonica, liturgica* 14 (1926), 65.

[140] *Ibid.,* pp. 65–66. The article is anonymous. Its author is identified by Creusen, "L'Onanisme conjugal," p. 409. A controversy on this point in reference to the grounds for annulment of a marriage occurred between Vermeersch and Agostino Gemelli at the Catholic University of the Sacred Heart (Milan).

[141] Creusen, "L'Onanisme conjugal," p. 409.

canon 1092 stated that a condition "concerning the future and contrary to the substance of marriage" and not revoked at the time of marriage invalidated the marriage.

The old commentators on *Si conditiones* had disputed whether an intention not to have offspring invalidated a marriage.[142] In a decision dated February 7, 1914, annulling a marriage where only one party had not intended to have children, the Rota said, "Whatever distinguished authors once wrote, today it is certain among all that to contract validly there is required at least implicit consent to the substance of the marriage, that is, to the three goods of marriage." [143] This position was enacted into the new *Code of Canon Law.* Canon 1086 read:

Sec. 1 Internal consent is presumed to be in agreement with the words or signs used in the marriage ceremony.
Sec. 2 But if either party or both parties by a positive act of the will exclude marriage itself, or all right to the conjugal act, or any essential property of marriage, the marriage contract is null.[144]

Between 1909 and 1940 the Sacred Roman Rota, the marriage appeals court of the Church, handled 148 cases where nullity of marriage was sought on the grounds of exclusion of the good of offspring. These cases were about 10 percent of the Rota's caseload. Nullity was found to exist in 47 cases. Proof of the actual use of contraceptives was not demanded, but often was made in the course of showing that the premarital condition or intention actually existed. Proof of the motive for excluding offspring was required as a check on credibility.[145]

[142] Orville N. Griese, *The Marriage Contract and the Procreation of Offspring* (Washington, 1946), p. 14. Before the Rota had had exclusive jurisdiction, marriage cases were heard by the Congregation of the Council. An example of their practice is the annulment of the marriage of Anne de Crosmières and Edward de Maricourt because Anne, a widow with two children, had agreed to marry Edward only if they had no children. "Parisiensis Matrimonii," July 16, 1904, *Thesaurus resolutionum Sacrae Congregationis Concilii*, vol. 163, ed. Caietano De Lai (Rome, 1904), p. 801.

[143] *Sacrae Romanae Rotae decisiones seu sententiae* (Rome, 1916–), 6.5. This decision was contrary to a decision rendered in 1909 holding that there must be "a condition in the true and proper sense, to which each party offers his consent" (*ibid.* 1.18, before G. Persiani). This statement was made in the case of one "Patroclus" and "Felicitas," a kind of curial Jarndyce v. Jarndyce. Annulment was finally granted, under the new canon law, on July 30, 1924, eighteen years after the suit for nullity had been brought (*ibid.* 15.32, before Raphael Chimenti).

[144] *Codex juris canonici* (Rome, 1918). The leading decision applying the rule that intention by one party not to have offspring is grounds for nullity is *Decisions of the Sacred Rota* 19.35 (1927, before Massimo Massimi), affirmed 20.5 (1928, before Francis Guglielmi).

[145] Griese, *The Marriage Contract*, pp. 111–112. Among the motives which, according to the testimony in cases before the Rota, have led to the avoidance of children are the following: avoidance of injury to the offspring through infection, 20.53 (1928); antipathy to husband, 14.14 (1922); danger to career of husband, 21.50 (1929); belief that life is unhappiness, 21.50 (1929); fear for health and beauty,

The phenomenon encountered before in canon law recurred here. The canon law was rather a statement and teaching than a system of sanctions comparable to secular law. Concretely, two factors checked strong enforcement of the canon: the Rota's desire not to have its process abused by persons who had acted in bad faith; and the desire not to annul marriages easily. It was expressly provided by canon 1094 that a marriage was presumed to be valid; the contrary had to be proved. The official attitude in practice was embodied by a letter of the Apostolic Delegate, Amleto Cicognani, to the bishops of the United States on September 23, 1938: leniency was not to be encouraged.[146]

A more practical attempt to give meaning to the old rule was by a more thorough examination of the state of mind of the parties at the crucial point before marriage. In the course of a general directive, issued June 29, 1941, on steps to be observed by a priest before marrying a couple, the Congregation on the Administration of the Sacraments recommended to the discretion of bishops a form question and instruction. Their use, the Congregation said, was desirable since, "especially in large cities," there were those who entered marriage "with an added condition or intention

---

19.35 (1927); economic condition, 15.32 (1923), 17.34 (1925).

Among the means used to carry out the condition or intention have been the following: coitus interruptus, 21.45 (1929), 15.16 (1923); use of acids by husband, 20.58 (1928); pessary, 23.30 (1931).

[146] Amleto G. Cicognani, Letter to the Bishops of the United States, September 23, 1938, in T. Lincoln Bouscaren, S. J., *Canon Law Digest. Officially Published Documents Affecting the Code of Canon Law, 1933–1942* (Milwaukee, 1943), II, 531-533.

The first factor found embodiment in canon 1971, section 1, providing that the person who was the "culpable cause" of an impediment of marriage could not initiate a proceeding of nullity. The Commission for the Authentic Interpretation of the Code of Canon Law held on March 12, 1929, that "impediments of marriage" in this canon included the impediments of condition or intention contrary to the substance of marriage (*AAS* 21:171). The Congregation for the Sacraments affirmed this rule (*Instructio* 3.38.2, *AAS* 28:313 [1936]). This disqualification applied, however, only if a person was the "direct" and "malicious" (*dolosa*) cause of the impediment, that is, if the person married knowing that his intention would invalidate (*AAS* 34:241 [1942]). Another procedure also existed. The parties could and should bring the alleged nullity to the attention of the promoter of justice, an official of the diocesan tribunal. His duty was to urge the spouses to remove the impediment "by a new consent rightly tendered." If, however, the nullity of the marriage would become "public and scandal in truth is present" (e.g., if civil divorce has been sought), and the spouse denouncing the marriage gives signs of repentance, and the arguments for nullity are "so clear and valid that the nullity of the marriage is entirely probable," then the promoter of justice has "the right and duty" of beginning proceedings to have the marriage declared null (*AAS* 28:313). This decree leaves considerable discretion in the hands of diocesan officials, and the key terms — "public" nullity, present "scandal," "clear and valid arguments" — are taken with varying degrees of seriousness. The Letter of the Apostolic Delegate in 1936 says that the case where the promoter of justice can act is "very rare indeed." The net effect of the rule is to check the number of cases where canons 1089 and 1092 are applied.

nullifying the marriage," to be invoked if escape was sought from the purported marriage to contract a new one. As a routine matter, the couple should be asked if they wished to contract marriage according to Catholic doctrine, "that is, as it is universally in use among the faithful — single, indissoluble, and ordained to the procreation of offspring, without any contrary intention or condition." If the engaged persons responded to this question affirmatively, nothing more was to be asked. If their replies or other information aroused doubt or suspicion of a nullifying condition or intention, the priest was to recall to them the teaching of the Church that their marriage would be null and that they would be putting themselves in a status where a multitude of sins would occur. If a nullifying condition or intention indeed existed, the priest could not witness the wedding unless the condition were revoked and repented (*AAS* 33:297–304). This procedure, where followed, has been probably the most effective and practical embodiment of the theological teaching that a condition or intention to avoid offspring is a bar to marriage.

When the clergy had first encountered the practice of birth control by Christians on a wide scale, in the form of coitus interruptus engaged in for bourgeois, individualistic motives, the response had been not to change the judgment on the act, but to refrain from disseminating the judgment. Contraception spread in France and was tolerated as a lesser evil by Rome. In the pontificate of Leo XIII a stronger stand began to be taken. Inquiry in confession was urged. Cooperation was denounced. Led by Belgium, five national hierarchies spoke vigorously. The climax was *Casti connubii.* As the birth control movement emerged from infancy to adolescence, it stood confronted by the international organization of the Church. Mutual hostility, open war, prevailed. To the idealistic advocates of birth control as an urgently necessary solution of social problems, the Church appeared to reiterate, in obscurantist fashion, an incomprehensible and irrelevant doctrine on nature. To the Pope, the bishops, and the theologians, the birth control movement appeared to rationalize and foster hedonistic irresponsibility and to challenge the wisdom handed down from Christian antiquity. The positions seemed irreconcilable. Yet there were other factors at work in the consciousness of the Church and in the social environment which might have made an impartial observer suspect that the enmity was not, in all respects, eternal.

CHAPTER XIV

PERMITTED AND DISPUTED MEANS OF CONTROLLING CONCEPTION

W HEN MEANS ARE DEVELOPED to reach a result whose achievement by other means is prohibited, several questions arise. Does the logic of the prohibition require condemnation of the new alternatives, or does the existence of the alternatives require rethinking of the prohibition, or can prohibition and permitted alternatives coexist? Is it the means and not the end which is objectionable? What is the purpose of the prohibition? All of these questions, so characteristic of the development of rules, appeared in the course of controversy over the means by which conception might be regulated.

Prior to the mid-nineteenth century, it was admitted that conception might be avoided by abstinence; no obligation to procreate was ever imposed. It was debated whether *amplexus reservatus* was permissible, and this debate continued. But never had it been admitted by a Catholic theologian that complete sexual intercourse might be had in which, by deliberation, procreation was excluded. It was, then, a capital event when use of a sterile period, even one wrongly calculated in fact, was permitted in theory. In the twentieth century the significance of this permission was to become apparent.

USE OF THE STERILE PERIOD

In 1845, Felix Archimedes Pouchet had won the prize for experimental physiology of the French Royal Academy of Sciences for his report, on the basis of observations of animals, that conception in all mammals occurred only during menstruation and one to twelve days after menstruation.[1] In 1853, Antoine de Salinis, the bishop of Amiens, reported that

[1] F. A. Pouchet, *Théorie positive de l'ovulation spontanée et de la fécondation des*

some married persons, "relying on the opinion of skilled doctors," were persuaded that there were "several days each month in which conception by a woman could not take place." The bishop asked the Penitentiary if those who had intercourse on such days were to be disturbed, "if at any rate they had legitimate reasons for abstaining from the conjugal act." The Penitentiary replied that "those about whom you ask are not to be disturbed provided they do nothing by which conception is prevented." [2] Evidently there was no one who recalled St. Augustine's opinion that intercourse only on sterile days was a prime way of doing something to prevent conception. The Penitentiary did not restrict its answer to those who in good faith believed they were acting lawfully, so that its decision seemed to indicate more than mere tolerance. The practice was accepted although its apparent purpose was to make conception impossible.

The reply of 1853 was not given publicity, and in 1867 a Dr. Avard of La Rochelle asked Cardinal Gousset whether it was lawful for couples to use the period they believed to be absolutely sterile according to the Pouchet theory. Noting that the question needed further study, Gousset replied that such couples should not be disturbed; he seemed himself to favor permitting such usage, but did not commit himself. [3]

There was no theoretical development of support for deliberate use of the sterile period before 1873. Then a theologian at Louvain with a knowledge of biology, Auguste Joseph Lecomte (1824–1881), published *L'Ovulation spontanée de l'espèce humaine dans ses rapports avec la théologie morale*. [4] This was the first attempt to take theological account of the nineteenth-century discoveries about ovulation. In 1827 Karl Ernst von Baer had published his discovery of the human ovum, which revolutionized the understanding of human reproduction. [5] But the moral theologians were still speaking about female "seed" and female "semination." Part of Lecomte's work was directed to showing the consequences of the new account of reproduction for the traditional theological views

---

mammifères et de l'espèce humaine, basée sur l'observation de toute la série animale (Paris, 1847). Pouchet was an admirer of St. Albert the Great and later wrote a book on his contributions to experimental science.

[2] *Decisiones Sanctae Sedis de usu et abusu matrimonii*, ed. Hartmann Batzill, 2nd ed. (Rome, 1944), p. 130.

[3] Answers of Gousset summarized in *Revue de thérapeutique médico-chirurgicale*, February 15, 1867, and July 15, 1867.

[4] Paris and Louvain, 1873. My citations are from the excerpts therefrom in *Analecta juris pontificii*, Recueil de dissertations sur différents sujets de droit canonique, de liturgie, de théologie, et d'histoire, 12th series (Paris, Brussels, Rome, 1873). Lecomte published his book anonymously as by "Abbé A. L., docteur en sciences naturelles." He is identified as the author in the Index to the *Nouvelle revue théologique* for the years 1869–1880. Lecomte also had written a work on human evolution.

[5] Charles Singer and E. Ashworth Underwood, *A Short History of Medicine*, 2nd ed. (Oxford, 1928), p. 204.

on feminine "pollution," part to showing that menstrual blood had no effect on offspring and that intercourse in menstruation was not certain to be sterile, and part to relating the Pouchet theory to moral theology.[6]

Citing Pouchet and other medical authors, Lecomte concluded that in the period which was sterile by Pouchet's calculations fecundation was improbable, although exceptions had been noted and their cause debated. He then argued that married couples having "reasonable and proportionate causes" for avoiding children might morally choose to have intercourse only in this period.[7] Lecomte emphasized the dilemma presented by the large number of ovulations which might occur if, "as often happens," a girl married under the age of twenty. Either she would be burdened "by a most numerous abundance of offspring" or the couple would practice "onanism." Lecomte believed that use of the sterile period was the way out of the dilemma. Confessors should insinuate the method in discreet language, not appearing "over-learned" in these matters.[8]

Lecomte's book was published with the permission of the archbishops of Malines and Bourges.[9] Large extracts from it were reprinted in the Analecta juris pontificii, a clerical journal addressed to a clerical audience. That a book presenting such a breakthrough in theory then received comparatively little attention must be attributed to the prevailing torpor in moral theology. Its thesis on the intentional use of the sterile period was well received by an anonymous reviewer for the Nouvelle revue théologique.[10] It was, however, violently attacked in 1874 by an anonymous priest in a Madrid weekly, Consultor de los parrocos. This critique is an index to the continued existence of one current of thought in the Church. The anonymous author accused Lecomte of defending intercourse in marriage "not to generate children, but only to have pleasure. This pernicious sensualism is entirely contrary to the laws of God and the good of society. It constitutes the horrible crime against nature." The vital point was made: "Coitus indeed takes place, but at a time at which conception is known to be almost impossible. And is this not to prevent generation? Without doubt." The author admitted that intercourse might lawfully be had by the pregnant or the aged for the lawful purpose of quieting concupiscence. What was the difference between such intercourse and the use of the sterile period? He answered that the obstacle to procrea-

---

[6] Lecomte noted that the ancient theory by which intercourse in menstruation had been treated as a mortal sin had been refuted in 1774 by De Lignoir, De l'homme et de la femme consideré physiquement dans l'état du mariage (Lille, 1774).

[7] Lecomte, in Analecta juris pontificii (1873), col. 721.

[8] Ibid., cols. 722–723.

[9] Ibid., col. 706, n. 1.

[10] "Bulletin bibliographique," Nouvelle revue théologique 5 (1873), 527. The reviewer notes that he himself defended the same theory in 1857, but that there were and are substantial doubts about its scientific foundation.

tion in the former cases was not put by human design, whereas "in this will of avoiding generation is found the great difference between the two cases." The author's parting shot was to invite Lecomte to submit his theses to the Roman congregations.[11]

Another review of the book in 1874 in the *Revue des sciences ecclésiastiques* (27:594ff), published in Amiens, was more restrained. The reviewer, one Craisson, former vicar-general of the diocese, said that the deliberate choice of the sterile days in order to avoid children "was contrary to the principal end which the Creator had in view in authorizing the conjugal act." However, as a lesser evil, the method might be suggested by a confessor to lead habitual onanists from their mortal sin.

Lecomte was apparently under more serious pressure than from these two unfavorable reviewers. "By order of his superiors," he withdrew his book from circulation.[12] He also submitted his thesis on the sterile period to the Penitentiary. He asked a series of questions:

I. 1. Is it permitted to act in this way without sinning mortally?
    2. Is there any venial sin because of the intention of not conceiving?
II. May a confessor counsel use of this means:
    1. To a wife who detests and reproves the onanistic action of her husband without being able to correct it?
    2. To two spouses who are willful onanists in order not to have the care of a numerous family?
III. 1. Is there any danger which decency [*l'honnêteté*] reproves in counseling this means which would procure the diminution of the family more surely than onanism?
    2. Would not the resulting danger be compensated for by the advantage of avoiding mortal sin and of giving tranquillity to numerous Christian women who are alienated from the sacraments by the fault of their husbands or their own fear?

The Penitentiary replied on June 16, 1880. Without characterizing them, it referred to the positions of Gousset, the *Analecta juris pontificii*, and the two reviews. It then said: "Spouses using the aforesaid way of marriage are not to be disturbed, and a confessor may, though cautiously, insinuate the opinion in question to those spouses whom he has vainly tried with other reasons to lead from the detestable crime of onanism."[13]

[11] Anonymous review of *L'Ovulation spontanée de l'espèce humaine dans ses rapports avec la théologie morale*, reprinted from *Consultor de los parrocos* in *Analecta juris pontificii*, 13th series (1874), cols. 995–997. This anonymous critic was even more shocked at Lecomte's view that a woman could commit a mortal sin of autoerotic excitement, but that this sin could not be described as a "sin against nature" because no emission of seed for generation was involved (col. 997).

[12] *Ibid.*, col. 993. It is not clear whether the withdrawal was ordered because of the thesis on the sterile period or the thesis on "the sin against nature" in the case of women.

[13] The French text of the questions is given in *Decisiones Sanctae Sedis*, p. 26, and *Nouvelle revue théologique* 13 (1881), 459–460. In its answer, the Penitentiary puts the questions in Latin (*Decisiones*, pp. 24–26).

This answer was indirect and ambiguous. In saying that confessors could recommend use of the sterile period, the Penitentiary could have meant to indicate that the practice was not sinful. On the other hand, some authority supported the position that a confessor might tolerate a sinful act to lead a penitent from a greater sin. This was the position of Craisson, which the Penitentiary refers to in the preliminary discussion. Consequently, it may also have meant to adopt his view. Grudging as the answer seemed, this official Roman act gave the theologians enough ecclesiastical backing to enable them to maintain the new position.

No advance beyond the cautious position of the Penitentiary appeared in such typical works as Lehmkuhl's *Moral Theology* (2–1.8.4.1.1.1, *ad* 5) or De Smet's *Les Fiançailles et le mariage* 2.1.3.1.1, annex 2). Both authors observed that the method was not certain, and followed the Penitentiary in saying that its use was not to be recommended indiscriminately to everyone. Somewhat greater enthusiasm appeared in the work of C. Capellmann, an Aachen doctor, who wrote one of the first treatises explicitly devoted to the moral theology of medicine. He said that "he and others" had observed that impregnation was improbable, although not impossible, in the third week after the beginning of menstruation. No moral law prevented coitus at that time.[14] On the other hand, by 1900 it could be noted in the *Nouvelle revue théologique* that "the improbability of fecundation at the so-called sterile times had been exaggerated by the doctors." "Who has not heard penitents who adhered to the observance of these times and yet did not avoid fecundation?"[15] As the formula for sterility involved having intercourse at the time subsequent research indicated that fertility would be apt to be greatest, it was perhaps fortunate that no greater attention was paid this method.

By the time of *Casti connubii* the lack of success with the Pouchet period made it far from a burning question. New discoveries had been made, but they had not made their way into practice. Accordingly, Pius XI made only a passing reference to couples who have intercourse "even though, through natural causes either of time or of certain defects, new life cannot thence result" (*AAS* 22:561). Such intercourse, the Pope held, was lawful, "provided always the intrinsic nature of that act is preserved, and accordingly its proper relation to the primary end." There was nothing in the Pope's address dealing with the deliberate avoidance of births through such use in a systematic way.

Meanwhile, research had been going on which made the use of a truly

---

[14] C. Capellmann, *Medicina pastoralis* (Aachen, 1890) D.4.1.

[15] E. de Gryse, "Théologie pastorale," *Nouvelle revue théologique* 32 (1900), 581.
In the United States the method was apparently recommended by some priests to parishioners even in the 1920's, for Monsignor John A. Ryan comments wryly on the complaints and jokes about the method's failure to work; "The Moral Aspects of Periodical Continence," *Ecclesiastical Review* 89 (1933), 29.

sterile period a possibility. In 1924 Kyusaku Ogino published in Japan a work presenting new data on the time of the sterile period. His work was not at once known in Europe, and in 1929, independently of Ogino's research, Hermann Knaus, an Austrian doctor, published the results of research reaching the same conclusion.[16] According to these studies, ovulation occurred sixteen to twelve days before the anticipated first day of the next menstrual period. For a woman with a regular menstrual cycle it was possible to avoid intercourse at the time when fecundation of the ovum might occur.

These results were widely circulated in Europe and the United States in the early 1930's. In Europe, J. N. J. Smulders was the chief popularizer. His *Periodische Enthaltung in der Ehe: Methode Ogino-Knaus* was published in Regensburg in 1931. In the United States there appeared Leo Latz's *The Rhythm of Sterility and Fertility in Women* (Chicago, 1932) and Valère Coucke and James J. Walsh's *The Sterile Period in Family Life* (New York, 1933). The first two works were by doctors; the last was written in collaboration by Canon Coucke and Dr. Walsh. All carried imprimaturs from the dioceses in which they were published.

The principal Roman authority was still the 1880 response of the Penitentiary. Writing for American priests, John A. Ryan recognized that this response dealt with a different question: Could intercourse be sought on days when fertility was improbable? What was proposed now was a method whereby sterility was certain. If successfully employed, the method might substantially decrease the population. But, pending that time, and stressing the ideal of fecundity, Ryan thought that deliberate use of the method was acceptable. Further, Ryan believed that the 1880 answer of the Penitentiary could be liberally construed to permit confessors to suggest the sterile period not only to those already practicing contraception, but to any married person with a serious reason for avoiding offspring.[17] Asked directly about the new method, the Penitentiary on July 20, 1932, replied by simply citing the response of 1880. This answer was not, however, immediately published.[18]

From the cautions that soon followed, it is apparent that many priests found in the Ogino-Knaus method an answer to pressing pastoral problems. In reaction, Ignatius Salsmans, a Belgian Jesuit, protested against the "rash promotion" of "Oginoism," a system which Salsmans seemed to

[16] Ogino's work appeared in an English translation by Yonez Miyagawa ten years later: *Conception Period of Women* (Harrisburg, Penn., 1934). Hermann Knaus, *Die periodische Fruchtbarkeit und Unfruchtbarkeit des Weibes: Der Weg zur natürlichen Geburtenregelung* (Vienna, 1934), translated into English by D. H. and Kathleen Kitchin as *Periodic Fertility and Sterility in Woman* (Vienna, 1934).

[17] Ryan, "The Moral Aspects of Periodical Continence," p. 28.

[18] Text of the reply of the Penitentiary in Francis X. Hürth, *De re matrimoniali*, Pontificiae universitatis Gregorianae series theologica, 30 (Rome, 1955), p. 111.

feel was but one remove from onanism. Pius XI in *Casti connubii*, he contended, had not thought of rhythm when he approved the use of a sterile "time"; he had had in mind only intercourse after the menopause.[19] A still more influential warning voice was raised by Arthur Vermeersch. He quoted the outraged cry of an American priest that the "heresy of the empty cradle" was now being promoted by the Church as priests recommended use of the sterile period to space births. He noted as an evil the dissemination of the view that the Church had its own method of achieving sterility contrary to the primary end of marriage. He further observed that widespread use of the method would diminish the population, contrary to "the common good of men and the particular good of states." In the light of these risks, Vermeersch taught that the subject should not be treated in special books devoted to the Ogino-Knaus method, but only in the context of a treatise on marriage where the Church's ideal of fecundity was set out. He did not move an inch beyond the 1880 answer of the Penitentiary. Confessors should, cautiously and prudently, suggest the method to obstinate onanists, not commending the method to them but permitting it as a lesser evil.[20]

Several bishops followed Vermeersch's lead and counseled restraint in the diffusion of the rhythm method. As enlightened a body as the provincial council of Malines under Cardinal Van Roey said in 1937 that (1) the use of the sterile period presents dangers, such as the encouragement of egotism, the unilateral denial of marriage rights in the fertile period, the lessening of conjugal love, the willingness even to abort a child conceived by mistake; (2) the method is consequently not to be proposed except to onanists, to wean them from their sin, and to others who have adequate reasons for avoiding conception; (3) adequate reasons for avoiding conception are danger to the wife from childbirth, or "truly serious economic difficulty in feeding numerous offspring." [21]

A doctoral dissertation in 1942 at The Catholic University of America by a diocesan priest, Orville N. Griese, reviewed the authorities and concluded that the Church neither approved nor disapproved the use of rhythm. Griese himself contended that the use of rhythm was per se illicit,

[19] Ignatius Salsmans, "Sterilitas facultativa licita?" *Ephemerides theologicae lovanienses* 11 (1934), 563–564.

[20] Arthur Vermeersch, "De prudenti ratione indicandi sterilitatem physiologicam," *Periodica de re morali, canonica, liturgica* 22 (1934), 246–247.

[21] Fifth Provincial Council of Malines, Resolution 47, set out in J. Goeyvaerts, "De moralitate usus matrimonii ad tempus ageneseos restricti," *Collectanea mechliniensia* 33 (1948), 704. Somewhat similarly, Patrick Cardinal Hayes in September 1936 sent to every priest of his diocese a letter entitled "Official Monitum on the Rhythm Theory," in which he said that in teaching and preaching priests "must insist on the Church's ideals of the purpose of marriage, rather than what is allowed in particular cases for upright and holy motives." Quoted in Orville N. Griese, *The Morality of Periodic Continence* (Washington, 1942), p. 41.

but under some circumstances might be justified.[22] In the face of criticism, he later explained that he was speaking of rhythm chosen as "a way of life." [23] His position was generally rejected. However, in rejecting it, one of the leading American Jesuit moralists, Gerald Kelly, professor of moral theology at St. Mary's Seminary, Kansas, wrote: "Only exceptional couples can take up the practice of the 'rhythm-theory' without exposing their married lives to grave dangers; and even these couples usually need the special grace of God. If this is true, and I believe it is, then the *per se illicitum, per accidens licitum* is also true — though not, it seems, in the sense in which he [Griese] explains it." [24]

There was recognition among the theological writers that the method would not work in all cases to prevent procreation. Confessors were counseled not to try to tell the penitent when the sterile period occurred.[25] An instruction from the Holy Office, dated May 16, 1943, reminded confessors that they were not to give medical advice.[26]

Medical doubts, pastoral caution, general suspicion, still surrounded the practice of rhythm two decades after it had been popularized. In 1950, however, the fourth national convention of the Association of Italian Catholic Physicians, recognizing that the method was not secure, approved the method in particular cases where it was desirable to avoid childbirth.[27] A year later, on October 29, 1951, Pius XII spoke to the Italian Catholic Society of Midwives, a group of nurses specializing in maternity cases. The Pope chose the occasion to make the fullest statement on marriage since *Casti connubii*. In this address a new spirit was visible.

[22] Griese, p. 18. Griese said that if a newly married couple asked a priest, they should be told that the practice can be justified, but only in cases where married persons are in such unfavorable circumstances as poor health or genuine poverty (*ibid.*, p. 110). The actual use of the method should be adopted only with the approval of a confessor (*ibid.*, p. 95).

[23] Orville N. Griese, "Objective Morality of the Rhythm Practice," *Ecclesiastical Review* 120 (1949), 475.

[24] Gerald Kelly, "Notes on Moral Theology, 1946," *Theological Studies* 7 (1946), 105–106. See also John C. Ford, S.J., "Notes on Moral Theology, 1944," *Theological Studies* 5 (1944), 509. Hugh J. O'Connell, C.SS.R., "Is Rhythm *Per Se* Illicit?" *Ecclesiastical Review* 119 (1948), 336; Gerald Kelly, S.J., "Notes on Moral Theology," *Theological Studies* 11 (1950), 71–77; J. McCarthy, "The use of the 'Safe Period,'" *Irish Ecclesiastical Record* 67 (1946), 259–263.

[25] John C. Ford, S.J., "Current Moral Theology and Canon Law," *Theological Studies* 2 (1941), 537; P. Ahearne, "The Confessor and the Ogino-Knaus Theory," *Irish Ecclesiastical Record* 61 (1943), 1–14.

[26] "Normae quaedam de agendi ratione confessariorum circa VI decalogi praeceptum," *Periodica de re morali, canonica, liturgica* 33 (1944), 130. John Ford interpreted this instruction as not preventing the confessor from answering to a direct question by indicating "when the sterile period generally takes place, making it quite clear that only professional advice can give any real assurance in the matter." "Notes on Moral Theology, 1943," *Theological Studies* 4 (1943), 584.

[27] "L'Opinione dell'Associazione de' Medici Cattolici Italiani sulla continenza periodica," *Perfice munus* 26 (1951), 8–14.

For the first time rhythm was referred to by Roman authority not as an alternative to be cautiously proffered to onanists, but as a method open to all Christian couples. The group Pius XII addressed were specialists, but the public character of the address and its publication in the *Acta Apostolicae Sedis* proclaimed that Pius XII had moved far from the 1934 counsels of Vermeersch. The Pope taught that rhythm, for a reason, could be used. To have intercourse and avoid the duty of procreation without serious reason would, he said, be a sin. But there might be serious motives (*seri motivi*) for avoiding procreation. These motives might be "not rarely present in the so-called 'indications' — medical, eugenic, economic, and social." Given these serious motives, "it follows that observance of the sterile period can be licit" (*AAS* 43:845–846).

The papal statement was not only public approval of rhythm. It recognized "economic" motives without restricting them to serious poverty. It recognized "social" motives, and such motives would seem to have embraced consideration of the world population or at least consideration of the population of a given society. The Pope's speech was far from being as serious or solemn an act as, say, the adoption of the decretal *Si aliquis* or the approval of the Roman Catechism. But as the sign of a new attitude it was a major step.

One month later Pius XII underlined the authoritativeness of the October statement and at the same time left no doubt of his intention by using the word *regolazione*, regulation, to describe what might be accomplished by use of the sterile period. This was the first time that a Pope had spoken with approval of the regulation of birth. Referring to the October address, Pius XII declared, "We have affirmed the lawfulness and at the same time the limits — in truth quite broad — of a regulation of offspring . . . Science, it may be hoped, will develop for this method a sufficiently secure base" (*AAS* 43:859). This second address, of November 26, 1951, was given to an even more significant audience than the midwives: to two Italian societies, the Association of Large Families and the Family Front. Not only was regulation of births publicly expounded to these lay groups; the Pope hoped that the method for securing sterility would be made certain.

A dozen years after the Pope had asserted leadership in approval of regulation of births, the American Jesuit John Lynch in an address to the Catholic Theological Society reviewed the evolution from 1930. Up until the allocution of Pius XII the "standard authors [were] still treating quite gingerly the pastoral aspects of periodic continence." Even after the allocution, theologians "lagged." It was still, "often carelessly," stated that a large family is the Christian ideal. "However, this maxim is not universally applicable to each individual marriage; it obtains, in truth, only in circumstances wherein the decent raising of a large family is reasonably possible." It was time to recognize that the education of children might require spacing of births, time to recognize that "the average couple of normal fertility over the average span of married life can virtually always adduce more than sufficient reason for at least periodic recourse to periodic continence." Lynch called attention to the operation, beginning in 1961, of a Family Life Clinic by the Catholic diocese of Buffalo. He plainly implied that instruction in the use of rhythm should be undertaken with the support of ecclesiastical organizations.[28]

Use of the sterile period, once attacked by Augustine when used to avoid all procreation, approved in 1880 for cautious suggestion to onanists, guardedly popularized between 1930 and 1951, was now fully sanctioned. The substantial split between sexual intercourse and procreation, already achieved by the rejection of Augustinian theory, was confirmed in practice.

AMPLEXUS RESERVATUS

Amplexus reservatus as a form of birth control would seem in the United States to be of greater theoretical than practical interest. The testimony of Europeans, however, indicates that it is of practical significance in some groups. The theoretical justification of it, moreover, casts light on the reasons for condemning contraception.

Throughout the nineteenth and into the twentieth century, theological opinion continued to be divided on the morality of the practice. Gury did not mention it, but his revisers, Ballerini and Palmieri, did, quoting Diana's remark that the "case can happen frequently" (*Compendium of Moral Theology*, 1898 ed., no. 730, note 11). Lehmkuhl, accepting the theoretical lawfulness of the case, pronounced it "rarely useful" in practice; rather than satisfying the sexual appetite, he said, it usually aroused it (*Moral Theology* 2-1.1.8.4.1.1.1, *ad* 4). Capellmann, in his book on medico-theological questions, strongly attacked the whole theory: "What, I ask, can be intended by an uncompleted copulation?" he asked rhetorically. "The direct and proper end of the act is excluded." He suggested that, in fact, most couples using this method practiced coitus interruptus (*Pastoral Medicine* D4.2).

[28] John J. Lynch, S.J., "Changing Pastoral Emphases on the Practice of Periodic Continence," in *The Catholic Theological Society of America, Proceedings of the Eighteenth Annual Convention* (St. Louis, 1963), pp. 110, 112, 114–115.
  It was widely felt by doctors experienced with rhythm that many people who were instructed in its use were badly instructed, and that much greater accuracy in its use could be obtained by combining the simple method of keeping track of the dates of menstruation with the taking of temperature in order to note the slight temperature rise indicative of ovulation. The first international symposium on the use of rhythm was held October 20–22, 1964, in Washington, D.C.; see Martin Boler, O.S.B., "Symposium on Rhythm," *American Ecclesiastical Review* 152 (1965), 13.

In the twentieth century, De Smet accepted the practice as a last resort; "as a lesser evil," confessors might recommend the practice to spouses practicing contraception, if the spouses know from experience that ejaculation will not occur (*Les Fiançailles et le mariage* 2.1.3.1.1, annex 2). The weightiest modern authority in its favor was Arthur Vermeersch, who said that some persons "know from experience that pollution is not risked if they withdraw from copulation which has begun." For them such an act was lawful; they might even treat occasional ejaculation as accidental and not willed. Generally, however, freedom from such risk was not experienced, and so for most persons the practice was sinful (*Chastity and the Contrary Vices,* no. 277).

Casti connubii said nothing on the matter, nor was there official Roman action until a controversy broke out in the 1950's over *L'Art d'aimer* and *Art d'aimer et continence conjugale* by Paul Chanson, a Catholic layman. In these books, printed in Paris in 1948 with the imprimatur of the archdiocese, *amplexus reservatus* was set out not only as a lawful means of avoiding children, but as a desirable "humanization of the flesh" and "mastery of love." The practice, lasting from ten to thirty minutes, was said to foster mutual love. The Holy Office by letter of August 12, 1950, ordered the books removed from commerce and prohibited new editions "on account of the general orientation and practical counsels given." Nothing was said on the truth or falsity of the doctrine taught. Chanson wrote two more books defending the practice: *L'Accord charnel* (Paris, 1950) and *L'Etreinte réservée: Témoignage des époux* (Paris, 1951).[29]

In 1951 Hyacinth M. Hering, the leading Dominican authority on moral theology at the Angelicum, made a full-dress attack, the most thorough critique the practice had ever received. Hering refused to assimilate the act to kisses and embraces which could lawfully be used to favor marital love. Any act involving the genital organs, he said, must be classified as "shameful" (*turpis*). Shameful acts were not "of their nature" ordained "to manifest or to foster love." Some such acts might be justified for a good end — for example, the examination of the organs for a medical purpose was justified. But if the genital act in question was actual copulation, it could only be justified by being an exercise of the marital right; and the marital right, as the Code of Canon Law, c. 1081, sec. 2, proclaimed, and as St. Thomas taught, was only the right to an act "per se apt to generate offspring." *Amplexus reservatus* was not such an act, and was therefore "a grave sin, reductively pertaining to the vice against nature."

Besides violating strict Thomistic doctrine, the theory and practice of *amplexus reservatus* had several other defects. The theory exalted carnal

[29] John C. Ford and Gerald Kelly, *Contemporary Moral Theology,* vol. II: *Marriage Questions* (Westminster, Md., 1963), pp. 216–217.

pleasure to the level of a "sacred rite, as an effort at spiritual ascension." Chanson's books "practically forgot the primary end of marriage." In practice, many couples, unable to achieve control, engaged instead in coitus interruptus. In teaching the method, a number of truths of the faith were neglected, such as "the doctrine of original sin and its consequences, especially concupiscence." [30]

On June 30, 1952, the Holy Office issued a *monitum* warning authors not to "describe, praise, and urge" *amplexus reservatus*. Priests were instructed that they should never speak "as though there was nothing to be objected to against *amplexus reservatus* on the part of Christian law" (*AAS* 44:546). The decree may have reflected a compromise in a quarrel between Hering at the Angelicum and Francis Hürth, the leading Jesuit moralist at the Gregorianum. Apparently unconscious of its early sponsorship by Dominicans like Palude and St. Antoninus, Hering had made out that most defenders of the practice, from Sanchez to Vermeersch, had been Jesuits. Not long after the decree came a magisterial article from Hürth showing that in theory the practice of *amplexus reservatus* was still licit. Some incomplete genital acts were defensible. Not all were lawful, he said, for some, such as anal intercourse, were contrary to "human dignity." But some by their "natural structure" — that is, "by the natural union of bodies" — were "evidently in the natural line of sexual activity." They were appropriate means to serve "dispositively" to the end of human generation, for their result was "the conservation and vigorous animation of sexual affection between the spouses." [31]

This controversy may illustrate the relevance of the doctrine on *amplexus reservatus* for the history of contraception. If *amplexus reservatus* is not condemned,[32] it can only be because some genital acts need not result in insemination. Why, then, is coitus interruptus sinful? The distinction suggested by Hürth's response is that an incomplete act like

[30] Hyacinth M. Hering, "De 'amplexu reservato,'" *Angelicum* 28 (1951), 333, 338–340.

[31] Francis Hürth, "Inquisitio critica in moralitatem 'amplexus reservati,'" *Periodica de re morali, canonica, liturgica* 41 (1952), 265.

[32] Among recent moralists there are degrees of acceptance. The German theologian Bernard Häring does not recommend *amplexus reservatus*, but does not absolutely forbid it if the couple observe respect for each other and love for God. Häring, *Das Gesetz Christi* 2.2.4.3.2.6.d.4, 4th ed. (Freiburg im Breisgau, 1957), p. 1107. It is hard to see how Häring, who condemns coitus interruptus as an offense against love, distinguishes *amplexus reservatus*, and it may be that his own theory would condemn it utterly. Joseph Fuchs essentially follows Hürth's defense of the act in some circumstances for some persons. Fuchs, *De castitate et ordine sexuali* 11.2, 2nd ed. (Rome, 1960). Cardinal Suenens is a strong defender. He declares that "ordinarily conjugal continence means that the husband and wife may use every legitimate means of expressing their love physically, without going as far as the act's ordinary conclusion." He even appears to recommend it as a good solution where, for good reason, impregnation must be avoided. Leo Joseph Suenens, *A Crucial Problem*, trans. George Robinson (Westminster, Md., 1960), pp. 81–82.

amplexus reservatus is not frustrated by remaining incomplete. A limited human freedom to use the genital organs in marriage short of ejaculation is defended, if a rational purpose is served. Suppose it were argued that coitus interruptus also serves "dispositively" to aid some later act of generation by increasing "conjugal sexual affection." The answer assumed is that, at the point where disposition of the semen occurs, a special divine mandate prevents the use of this act as an aid to some later act of generation. The line drawn between coitus interruptus and *amplexus reservatus* shows more importance attached to the use of the semen than might be suspected from the argument that "the act of coitus is ordered by God to generation." It is only where ejaculation occurs that the process is regarded as so ordered.

OTHER PERMITTED MEANS

By *copula dimidiata* is meant partial penetration of the vagina with insemination. In 1921, the bishop of Haarlem, acting for the Dutch hierarchy, informed the Holy Office that some confessors were recommending use of this form of coitus as a lawful substitute for contraception and a way which would substantially diminish the probability of conception. Some of the clergy and laity, including doctors, had been scandalized by this advice. The bishop asked if the method could be taught "promiscuously" to all penitents, and if a confessor should be rebuked for recommending the method to one he had vainly tried to turn from contraception. On November 23, 1922, the Holy Office answered the first question negatively and the second affirmatively. These questions and answers centered on the danger of scandal, rather than on the truth or falsity of any moral proposition.[33]

Subsequent theologians divided on the lawfulness of *copula dimidiata*. The question is of some theoretical interest: was it considered lawful to reduce the chance of conception? In 1934 Merkelbach held the practice to be at least venial sin if used without a sufficient reason; he would accept physical infirmity, but not the desire to avoid children, as such a reason (*Questions on Chastity and Lechery* 8.1).[34] The Italian Jesuit Thomas Iorio said in 1946 that it was mortal sin if there was an intention "to impede" conception (*Moral Theology*, no. 1201). In 1963, the American Jesuits John Ford and Gerald Kelly, doubting that the method worked, held that there would be no sin if the couple had reason to avoid having children.[35]

A practice raising a similar question of the lawfulness of reducing the

[33] *Decisiones Sanctae Sedis*, pp. 40–41.
[34] Benedict Merkelbach, *Quaestiones de castitate et luxuria*, 4th ed. (Bruges, 1934).
[35] Ford and Kelly, *Contemporary Moral Theology*, II, 222–223.

probability of conception is a diet which would reduce fertility. On the supposition that it would not make procreation "impossible," Lawrence L. McReavy, an English theologian teaching at St. Edmund's College, the diocesan seminary for Westminster, held that such a diet would be lawful for persons with good reason to avoid having children. Its use would be like "going to live in a climate which had been observed to be less favorable to fertility."[36]

A similar response was given by Francis Connell, an American Redemptorist teaching at the Catholic University of America, on the use of anaphrodisiacs. To use them to produce sterility or impotence would be sinful. But, assuming that there was no unjust denial of marital rights, their use "merely to lessen sexual inclinations" would be lawful. Ford and Kelly in 1963 spoke of sexual depressants which "may cause temporary impotence." Without citing authorities, they said, "we think that many moralists would not consider the use of such drugs as intrinsically immoral." Their own position was not clear. They only observed, "Nevertheless, the use of such drugs seems to involve some kind of control of or interference with the reproductive function."[37]

STERILIZING OPERATIONS

Casti connubii had condemned self-mutilation in general and compulsory sterilization in particular. A year later, in response to the question, "Is direct sterilization lawful?" the Holy Office answered, No.[38] In the thirties Nazi Germany embarked on the largest sterilization campaign in human history.[39] Against the background of this campaign, the Holy Office under Pius XII, on February 21, 1940, again answered the question, "Is the direct sterilization of man or woman, perpetual or temporary, lawful?" The Holy Office replied, "No; it is forbidden by the law of nature" (*AAS* 32:73). The condemnation was twice repeated by Pius XII in contexts which clearly did not restrict the condemnation to involuntary operations. "Direct sterilization, that is, that which seeks as means or end to render procreation impossible, is a serious violation of the moral law" (Address to the Italian Catholic Society of Midwives, October 29, 1951, *AAS* 43:843). "We have stated in substance that direct sterilization is

[36] Lawrence L. McReavy, "Protein Diet and Fertility," *The Clergy Review* 45 (1960), 482–484. A diet affecting fertility by its effect either on seminal plasma or on the estrogens had been noted in 1953 by Henshaw. Such a diet, he said, might be deficient in vitamin A or E or in arginine. Paul S. Henshaw, "Physiologic Control of Fertility," *Science* 117 (1953), 572.

[37] Francis Connell, "The Use of Anaphrodisiacs," *American Ecclesiastical Review* 136 (1957), 55. Ford and Kelly, *Contemporary Moral Theology*, II, 365.

[38] Hürth, *De re matrimoniali*, p. 105.

[39] For theological reaction, see the anonymous article "Sterilization Law in Germany," *Ecclesiastical Review* 95 (1936), 50.

not authorized by man's right to dispose of his own body . . . by direct sterilization we mean an act whose aim . . . is to make procreation impossible" (Address to the Seventh International Congress of Hematology, September 12, 1958, *AAS* 50:734). None of these condemnations was of the solemn authority of *Casti connubii* on interference with the procreative function in the exercise of coitus. They were, however, taken by the theologians to control discussion.

The full meaning of these papal pronouncements can be understood only when one considers the development which was simultaneously occurring in the teaching on self-mutilation in general. Some forms of self-mutilation for one's own good had always been held to be lawful (above, p. 368n). During the regime of Pius XII three questions on this topic were explored. Was the good for which mutilation might be inflicted physical good, or might it be the good of the person as a whole? Must the good be simply average well-being, or could it be the attainment of bodily perfection? Did the mutilation have to be necessary, or merely useful?

Casti connubii had spoken of permissible mutilation for "the good of the whole body." In 1952 Pius XII used somewhat different language. In a talk on the morality of surgery to a medical congress, he declared, "by virtue of the principle of totality, by virtue of his right to use the services of his organism as a whole, the patient can allow individual parts to be destroyed or mutilated when and to the extent necessary for the good of his being as a whole" (Allocution to the First International Congress on the Histopathology of the Nervous System, *AAS* 44:782). It is not clear how deliberately the expressions "organism" and "being as a whole" were meant to contrast with "good of the body." In a later address he used "good of the whole body" as the test (*AAS* 45:674 [1953]). His remarks, however, provided an opportunity for the theologians to get away from the Cartesian language of *Casti connubii* which seemed to separate body from soul. Gerald Kelly, the leading American theologian on matters of medical morality, argued that the "good of the whole" was "the good of the person." This was what the Pope had meant. This was the only proper test in a philosophy which did not divide man into soul and body, but regarded him as an integrated being.[40]

The second question was closely related to the first. If the good of the person was what might be sought, average physical health was not the only good for which mutilation might be inflicted. Speaking to an Italian congress on plastic surgery on October 4, 1958, Pius XII discussed the moral questions which plastic surgeons might encounter. The principles ruling self-mutilation, the Pope declared, did not forbid surgery to maintain physical beauty. But suppose one sought by surgery to accom-

[40] Gerald Kelly, "Pius XII and the Principle of Totality," *Theological Studies* 16 (1955), 373.

plish "the perfection of attributes which already conformed to the canons of normal aesthetics." Such an act would not be intrinsically evil. It could be done for a good motive. For example, a person "dedicated to public life or to art" might need to correct some imperfection which handicapped his activity. Mutilation to achieve this correction would be lawful (Address to the Tenth National Congress of the Italian Society of Plastic Surgery, *AAS* 50:958–959).

The Pope's words to this limited audience scarcely constituted irreversible teaching. His approach did favor the notion that not the body one received from nature, nor even the "nature" which was established by averages, was the standard by which the lawfulness of bodily mutilation might be measured. The standard was nature as it might be perfected by reason for the good of a particular person. In the Pope's statement, mutilation for this purpose was still restricted to removal of "imperfections." But the theologians were left free to ask what was an "imperfection."

How necessary to the achievement of the desired good did the mutilation have to be? *Casti connubii* said that mutilation was lawful only "when no other provision can be made." Pius XII himself used the unqualified term "necessary" ("Address to the First International Congress on the Histopathology of the Nervous System," *AAS* 44:782 [1952]). But Gerald Kelly queried whether the popes meant their language literally. To preserve life itself, according to the common teaching, extraordinary measures did not have to be taken. It was unlikely that the popes meant to say that extraordinary measures had to be undertaken to preserve part of the body. Moreover, the line between the strictly necessary and the merely useful was blurred. It would be better to understand "necessary" in the papal documents as meaning "useful" with the qualification that the "useful" here required a weighing of the loss of a part of the body against the evil of choosing other ways of achieving the same end.[41]

Discussion on a fourth question further enlarged the criterion for mutilation. Suppose the act were useful not for the good of one's own person, but for the good of one's neighbor. The transplantation of organs such as kidneys from one human being to another was first considered by the moralists in the later thirties. Early opinion was condemnatory.[42] An American Vincentian, Bert J. Cunningham, took a different view of the matter in a doctoral dissertation in theology at the Catholic University of America in 1944. Mutilation, he argued, must be regarded as an act which was good or evil depending on its purpose. If one cut off one's hand in order to escape imprisonment, one properly sacrificed the part for the

---

[41] *Ibid.*, p. 380.
[42] J. Noldin and J. Schmitt, *Summa theologiae moralis* 2.328.4, 12th ed. (Innsbruck, 1935); Thomas Iorio, ed., John Gury, *Theologia moralis* 2.200 (Naples, 1946).

good of the whole, even though the hand itself was not diseased. Similarly one could morally sacrifice part of one's own healthy body for the good of another. The justifying principle here was not the subordination of part to whole, as in the case of the hand, but the charity which bound all men together. Men were related to each other in the mystical body of Christ as members of the human body were related to each other. One might rightly sacrifice part of oneself to aid another human being.[43]

Cunningham's basic position on transplantation was accepted by Gerald Kelly. Was the language of Pius XI in *Casti connubii* an objection? Kelly said that the words restricting mutilation to the good of one's own body should not be extended beyond their context: Pius XI was talking the theology of self-mutilation current in his time; he had not envisaged the case of organic transplantation and did not consider the role mutilation could play in such a case.[44]

In 1948 Pius XII, in a speech to a group of blood donors, used language of some pertinence to the problem. Saying that blood donors in a special way followed Christ, "the divine donor of His blood," he continued, "and this admirable transfusion transfers with your blood, with your vigor, something of your own life, which gives you, so to speak, a kind of paternity in relation to them." [45] This teaching appeared to accept the principle that one might voluntarily sacrifice part of one's body for one's neighbor, and to approve the intentional disruption of an organic natural process in one's own body on behalf of another.

In his talk to the congress on histopathology in 1952, however, the Pope said that a bodily organ had "no finality" outside the body in which nature had placed it (*AAS* 44:786). Organic transplantation was now a well-known operation. Was this statement a condemnation of the operation? Kelly again urged that the talk be restricted by a context, in this case the context provided by modern history. Speaking in the light of knowledge of the medical practices of the fallen Nazi regime, Pius XII, he argued, was condemning a totalitarian principle that would support the involuntary mutilation of one man's body for the benefit of another's. The Pope, he contended, did not purport to deal with transplantations voluntarily undertaken from fraternal charity.[46]

On each of these four questions final answers had not been given. Yet for each the way of probable development seemed marked. If this development were accepted, mutilation might be done for the good not merely of the body, but of the person as a whole. It might be done for his

[43] Bert J. Cunningham, *The Morality of Organic Transplantation* (Washington, 1944), pp. 100–104.

[44] Gerald Kelly, "Notes on Moral Theology, 1946," p. 101.

[45] Pius XII, Allocution, in *Les Enseignements pontificaux: Le Corps humain*, ed. the Monks of Solesmes (Le Mans, 1953).

[46] Kelly, "Pius XII and the Principle of Totality," p. 373.

personal perfection. It might be done for the good of his neighbor. It might be done if relatively less harmful than some other alternative. These principles seemed to suggest the permissibility of sterilization to prevent conception endangering one's or one's spouse's health or personal development. If sterilization were merely a form of mutilation, then direct sterilization seemed in some cases to be lawful.[47]

Why was this conclusion not reached? One line of thought took the position that all mutilation was justified only by the principle of double effect, and that in the case of sterilization appeal could not be made to double effect. This classic tool of scholastic moral analysis rested on the fact that most acts have more than one consequence.[48] In an imperfect world, action would be paralyzed if every effect had to be good. It was therefore permissible, all scholastic moralists agreed, to act, although one effect of the action would be evil, provided that the evil was not disproportionate to the good. To be lawful, the subjective intention of the person must be directed to the good end; if he posits an external act which also has a bad effect, the bad effect must be "beyond his intention." An evil means might never be justified by a good end. But if the evil were not a means but the inevitable consequence of a good act, the act might be performed and the evil tolerated. This was the principle of double effect. Some authors seemed to understand mutilation as justified only by this principle. One cut off a gangrenous leg with the good effect of removing the limb and the bad effect of losing the leg. The good consequence outweighed the simultaneous bad effect. But in the case of sterilization the evil means preceded rather than followed the good result. On this basis in 1937 Merkelbach condemned sterilization to cure satyriasis: the bad means of mutilation preceded the effecting of the cure; hence double effect did not justify.[49] On this basis the European opponents of organic transplantation in the thirties, the Jesuits Jerome Schmitt and Thomas Iorio, analyzed or-

[47] Cunningham was aware that his analysis, if extended to the sexual organs, raised the question of the morality of sterilizing oneself for the good of one's neighbor. That such an act was moral "might seem to follow." However, as the Holy Office had condemned direct sterilization without exception, Cunningham was unwilling to state the affirmative opinion here as "an absolute conclusion." In sexual matters, moreover, there was always present a danger of abuse which called for a prudential limiting of principle (*The Morality of Organic Transplantation*, p. 103).

[48] For two different accounts of the history of this principle, see Joseph T. Mangan, "An Historical Analysis of the Principle of Double Effect," *Theological Studies* 10 (1949), 41, and J. Ghoos, "L'Acte à double effet: Etude de théologie positive," *Ephemerides theologicae lovanienses* 27 (1951), 30. Mangan rightly insists that the germ of the idea can be found in Aquinas, where he says that a man killing another in self-defense acts lawfully, intending only the preservation of his own life (*Summa theologica* 2-2.64.7). Ghoos points out that the technical development of the principle as a tool in moral theology begins with Navarrus and is established by 1630 with the Portuguese Thomist, John of St. Thomas.

[49] Benedict Merkelbach, *Quaestiones de embryologia* 1.2 (Bruges, 1937).

ganic transplantation as the use of a bad means (mutilation) to serve a good end (a neighbor's life). They saw no difference between killing oneself, which all would agree was unlawful to save one's neighbor, and mutilating oneself. In both cases, they argued, double effect failed to apply; in both cases a good end would be unlawfully sought by a bad means. In the same way in 1953 Louis Bender, a Dominican teaching at the Angelicum, condemned a hysterectomy which would remove a uterus unable to stand further pregnancies: the removal of any organ not itself diseased was an intrinsically evil act. In other words, where the good effect was not simultaneous with the mutilation, the principle of double effect failed to apply, and the act become unlawful.[50]

This approach to mutilation in general was criticized by Cunningham in his defense of organic transplantation and by Ford and Kelly in their analysis of sterilization. Mutilation, they contended, was good or bad depending on the subordination of the mutilating act to the good of the whole. To excise part of the body to save the rest was good if the sacrifice was relatively necessary for the good of the whole. Double effect did not have to be invoked.

If this approach were followed, it became even more difficult to see why sterilization was not, in some cases, lawful. If sterilization was only one type of removal of an organ, and if such removal might be lawful for the welfare of the organism, there seemed to be situations where direct sterilization was justified. Faced with this conclusion, running squarely against the teaching of Pius XII, Gerald Kelly proposed this solution. The principle of totality permits one to subordinate a part to the whole good of the person. But the reproductive organs exist not only for the good of the person, but for the good of the human race. They are, therefore, subject to more rules than other parts of the body. Their removal or impairment for the good of the person is not an unqualified good; it is always accompanied by an evil, namely, their loss to the human race. Sterilization is, of all forms of mutilation, the one form which can be justified only by the principle of double effect. The bad effect (elimination of the capability of reproduction) must not be a means, but can only be justified if it is accompanied by a good effect, such as the removal of a diseased organ.[51] Kelly's analysis was concurred in by John Lynch, who put the matter succinctly: "Of no less practical importance is the seemingly inescapable conclusion that what the principle of totality allows under these conditions [of danger to the person] is *direct* mutilation, and that it does not of itself require recourse to double effect. There

[50] For Schmitt and Iorio, see note 42 above. Louis Bender, "Extirpatio uteri morbosi ut actus coniugalis tuto fieri possit," *Angelicum* 30 (1953), 274.
[51] Kelly, "Pius XII and the Principle of Totality," p. 383.

are admittedly cases where the further effects of mutilation (e.g. sterility) can be justified only by applying both principles in combination."[52]

Within the framework provided by Kelly, it is possible to arrange four types of cases in which sterilization was considered by the theologians: (1) an organ involved in reproduction is presently diseased and will endanger the health of the person if not excised; (2) a reproductive organ is healthy, but disease related to it will endanger health unless it is removed; (3) a reproductive organ will result in danger to health only if pregnancy occurs; (4) all reproductive organs are healthy, but pregnancy will endanger health by affecting other parts of the body.

In Kelly's framework, the first case is easy. The good effect of sterilization occurs at the same time that the evil is done by removing the diseased organ. This is the way Vermeersch in 1928 analyzed removal of sexual organs causing "morbid concupiscence," and hence reached a different conclusion from Merkelbach on sterilization as a cure for satyriasis.[53] In the second case sterilization is also lawful. The first instance I have encountered of its discussion is a note in 1942 by Thomas V. Moore, then a Benedictine priest teaching at the Catholic University of America. He put the case of a sterilizing irradiation of the testicles when a cancerous prostate is removed, the healthy testicles being treated in order to lessen the danger of the spread of the cancer. Moore defended the lawfulness of the sterilization. The same conclusion was reached by John J. Clifford, an American Jesuit, as to the lawfulnss of castration in the form of orchidotomy in the case of cancer of the prostate.[54] This opinion on orchidotomy was adopted by Pius XII in 1953, who restated the general principle that a healthy organism may be sacrificed for the good of the whole "if the maintenance or function of an organ provokes serious damage in the whole organism or constitutes a threat to it" (Address to the Twenty-Sixth Congress of the Italian Society of Urologists, AAS 45:674–675).

The third case was confined to the case of a uterus believed unlikely to stand further pregnancies. Was a hysterectomy lawful? John Ford, a Jesuit professor of moral theology at the Catholic University of America,

---

[52] John Lynch, "Notes on Moral Theology," *Theological Studies* 17 (1956), 180.

[53] Arthur Vermeersch, *Theologiae moralis principia, responsa, consilia* (Bruges, 1922–1923), vol. II, no. 323. The same position was taken by the Carmelite Peter Kremer in a short note, "Some Ethical Considerations in X-Ray Treatment of Irradiation of Ovaries in Cancer of the Breast," *Ecclesiastical Review* 108 (1943), 271–273. A second note by a Franciscan, Honoratus Bonzelet, did not challenge the principle, though it raised doubt as to medical opinion on the use of radiation of the ovaries to treat breast cancer: "The Morality of Indirect Sterilization," *Ecclesiastical Review* 109 (1943), 125–127.

[54] T. V. Moore, "The Morality of a Sterilizing Operation," *Ecclesiastical Review* 106 (1942), 444–446; J. J. Clifford, "The Morality of Castration in Carcinoma of the Prostate," *Theological Studies* 5 (1944), 452.

suggested that the operation might be an illicit means to a good end, and concluded that it was unlawful. Three years later Gerald Kelly argued to the contrary. The uterus was already damaged. It might be regarded as pathological in its prime function of gestation, and lawfully removed. In effect, it was a situation of the first type. In 1954, in a joint article, Kelly and Ford rejected Bender's aberrant framing of the issue and agreed that if the medical judgment was that the uterus was pathological it might be removed, although the opposing opinion was also probable.[55]

In the fourth case a sterilizing operation was firmly rejected. As early as 1919, Vermeersch condemned a hysterectomy performed because pregnancy would endanger the general health of the woman (*Moral Theology* 2.323). In 1924 an anonymous commentator in the *Ecclesiastical Review* repeated this opinion.[56] The same view was advanced by Pius XII in his address to the urologists: excision of the oviducts to prevent a pregnancy likely to be dangerous to other organs such as the heart was not lawful (*AAS* 45:675 [1953]). Here sterilization was considered to be the evil direct means to a good end. The differentiation between this case and the third case seemed to represent a highly arbitrary form of line-drawing. In each case the organism as a whole could no longer support a pregnancy; a difference was found only by isolating the reproductive system from the whole.

The casuistry developed in this drawing of lines raised the question whether Kelly was right in his reason for distinguishing impairment of the sexual organs from other forms of mutilation. His reason rested on the orientation of these organs toward the social good. Yet the state was denied any right to sterilize for the common good, just as the individual was denied the right to sterilize for his individual good. Moreover, the reason did not explain the fourth case, where the common theological position was that only abstinence from intercourse was permissible: here the sexual organs were not allowed to function for the social good, yet their excision was prohibited. It would seem that the real grounds for treating sterilization differently from other forms of mutilation of the body lay in the general arguments against contraception. If the sexual functions were sacral, in a special way God's, they were immune from human attack on their procreative function as such. If any intentional interference with the sexual functions would lead to abuses dangerous both to the sanctity of human life and to chastity, then no interference could be tolerated. It was general arguments of this kind that seemed to be implicit in the theologians' prohibition of direct sterilization. It was

[55] John Ford, "Notes on Moral Theology, 1944," p. 516; Gerald Kelly, "Notes on Moral Theology, 1946," *Theological Studies* 8 (1947), 103; Gerald Kelly and John Ford, "Notes on Moral Theology, 1953," *Theological Studies* 15 (1954), 68–70.
[56] "Studies and Conferences: Moralitas Sectionis Chirurgicae Tubae Fallopianae," *Ecclesiastical Review* 71 (1924), 95.

this kind of thinking that made them treat the third case leniently and the fourth case severely. The drawing of lines, of course, is the moralists' business; it is no refutation of a moral judgment to say that it is but one step removed from an opposite result. Line-drawing for no reason at all is insupportable. But if there is a reason for drawing a line at some point, the precise point chosen may seem arbitrary and yet be reasonable. In their judgments on sterilization, the moralists had to draw the line somewhere if they were to preserve their general case against contraception.

The casuistry on sterilization opened up another area of problems for the general prohibition. Contraception was forbidden because the act of intercourse in which conception was prevented was viewed as intrinsically evil. It was apparent, however, in the analysis of sterilization that the captions "direct" or "indirect" depended solely on the intention with which an act was performed; the physical operation and result were the same whatever the intention. Consequently, in recognizing a number of cases in which indirect sterilization was permissible, it was tacitly admitted that what made direct sterilization sinful was the intention and not the physical operation or result.

It had been accepted, ever since the general rejection of Augustinian doctrine on procreative purpose, that intercourse with a sterile person was not itself a sin. The same position held true of intercourse with a sterilized person. Vermeersch had argued that if a person sterilized himself and then had intercourse, the acts formed a moral unit and the act of intercourse was affected with the malice of a sin of contraception (above, p. 430). But here the sin in intercourse seemed to arise from the earlier intention to prevent procreativity, not from anything in the act itself. Vermeersch had agreed the sinful intent might be repented, and intercourse resumed without sin. But he had insisted on the duty of restoring the sterilized organ to its function if possible. A new position was reached when a study in 1944 indicated division of theological opinion on the obligation of untying a simple ligation of the Fallopian tubes. A respectable number of theologians believed that the obligation constituted an extraordinary burden which should not be placed on a penitent. Given this division of opinion, a confessor could not in practice impose the obligation under pain of sin or refusal of absolution. As to reparation of a vasectomy, it was argued that here the medical evidence did not warrant any expectation of success; a fortiori, there could be no obligation imposed to attempt the operation.[57]

Sterilization, it was apparent, presented problems of moral analysis distinct from those presented by coitus interruptus or the condom. It was against the background of casuistry developed to treat sterilizing opera-

[57] John L. Clifford, S.J., "Marital Rights of the Sinfully Sterilized," *Theological Studies* 5 (1944), 141, 158.

tions that the controversies of the 1950's and 1960's over "the pill" occurred.

PILLS

In the early 1950's the first contraceptive pill appeared in commercial usage. This was hesperidin, an anti-enzyme which affected the hyaluronidase present in the semen; taken orally by both husband and wife for a prescribed period, it was supposed to prevent infecundation of the ovum.[58] Thus what was affected was not an organ of the body, as in conventional sterilization, but constituents of the generative process. Moral distinctions between this pill and surgical sterilization might have been suggested. The theological reaction, however, was unanimously condemnatory. In 1953, André Snoeck, a professor at the Jesuit scholasticate of theology in Louvain, pronounced the use of hespiridin to be "direct sterilization" of the conjugal act and as such condemned by *Casti connubii*; to use it and have intercourse was also "onanism," the use of marital intercourse while interfering with the process. Similar judgments on hesperidin were proffered by the American Jesuit John Lynch and the French Jesuit Stanislas de Lestapis.[59]

By 1953 a progesterone pill had been developed which, taken orally by a woman over a period of days, would make conception impossible. The effectiveness of the pill for human beings was first tested on a large scale in Puerto Rico in 1956. In 1960 it was approved in commercial form by the Food and Drug Administration for marketing in the United States.

The means by which the progesterone pill was virtually 100 percent effective in preventing pregnancy were not entirely established. As described by John Rock, one of the first physicians to test the pill and the first defender of its use as consistent with Catholic theology, the pill acted upon the thalamopituitary complex in such a way as to prevent the secretion of hormones which would cause the ovary to release an ovum. Its effect was analogized to the suspension of ovulation brought about in pregnancy by progesterone naturally secreted.[60] Further tests of the pill in the dosages usually taken by women indicated that the pill also had two other effects. The pill seemed to change the physical consistency of the cervical mucus, which normally speeded the spermatozoa to the ovum, and to render the mucus hostile to sperms. Further, the endometrium, or inner lining of the uterus, in which was implanted the fertilized

---

[58] Henshaw, "Physiologic Control of Fertility," p. 576.

[59] André Snoeck, "Fécondation inhibée et morale catholique," *Nouvelle Revue théologique* 75 (1953), 702; John J. Lynch, "Fertility Control and the Moral Law," *Linacre Quarterly* 20 (1953), 83–89; Stanislas de Lestapis, *La Limitation des naissances* (Paris, 1960), p. 182.

[60] John Rock, *The Time Has Come* (New York, 1963), pp. 167–168.

egg, or conceptus, was affected. The progesterone taken by pill seemed to make the endometrium unfavorable to implantation of the egg.[61] Hence, if the pill failed to prevent ovulation, it might still prevent pregnancy either by preventing fecundation or by preventing nidation. Prevention of nidation would be described by most modern Catholic theologians as abortion. That, in fact, an abortive effect occurred was not proved. If the pill failed to affect a particular woman's ovulatory responses, it might be equally ineffective in affecting her endometrium. At this stage of research one could only label as unknown the consequences of the pill where ovulation was not suspended. Prevention of fertilization would present the same question as hesperidin. However, in the discussion of the pill which took place among theologians from 1957 to 1964, it was regarded solely as an anovulant, that is, as an agent preventing conception by preventing ovulation.[62]

The cases of sterilizing surgery already allowed by the theologians suggested at once that there could be lawful uses of an anovulant for medical purposes. Although sterility was produced, if the direct intention was to cure a disease, both means and intention were lawful. Permissible medical uses included interruption of the ovulatory process in the treatment of endometriosis, excessive menstrual bleeding, and painful menstruation. These uses were accepted by the moralists without dispute and recognized in principle by Pius XII in 1958: "If a woman takes this medicine, not to prevent conception, but only on the advice of a doctor as a necessary remedy because of a disease of the uterus or the organism, she provokes an indirect sterilization, which is permitted according to the general principle of actions with a double effect" (Address to the Seventh International Congress of Hematology, September 12, 1958, AAS 50:735).[63]

[61] Edward T. Tyler and Henry J. Olson, "Fertility Promoting and Inhibiting Effects of New Steroid Hormonal Substances," *Journal of the American Medical Association* 169 (1959), 1843–1854; P. M. F. Bishop, "Oral Contraceptives," *Practitioner* 185 (1960), 158–162; Joseph W. Goldzieher et al., "Study of Norethindrone in Contraception," *Journal of the American Medical Association* 180 (1962), 359–361; Alan F. Guttmacher, "Oral Contraception," *Postgraduate Medicine* 32 (1962), 552–558; anon., "Today's Drugs," *British Medical Journal* 2 (1963), 489–491; Council on Drugs of the American Medical Association, "An Oral Contraceptive: Norethindrone with Mestranol (Ortho-Novum)," *Journal of the American Medical Association* 187 (1964), 664.

[62] A report prepared for the Family Life Bureau of the National Catholic Welfare Conference, July 1964, by Frank J. Ayd, Jr., "The Oral Contraceptives: Their Mode of Action," was the first work to gather statements of medical opinion on the effects of the progesterone pills and to argue that the "extreme effectiveness" of the drugs in preventing pregnancy was due not simply to their causing anovulation, but to their effect on the sperm as contraceptives and their effect on the endometrium as abortifacients.

[63] The position was supported by: Francis J. Connell, "The Contraceptive Pill," *American Ecclesiastical Review* 137 (1957), 50 (recognizing the use of the anovulant to relieve painful menstruation); William J. Gibbons and Thomas K. Burch, "Phys-

More difficult cases of indirect effect on ovulation were posed. The pill might be used to remove a fear of pregnancy which was causing heart disease or sexual impotence. Joseph Fuchs, followed by Joseph Farraher, an American Jesuit, analyzed this case as one involving direct suppression of fertility (a bad means) to achieve the good end of eliminating the physical dangers.[64] But suppose the fear of pregnancy was itself treated as a pathological condition. Then the removal of the fear and the suppression of ovulation were simultaneous, and the use of the pill could be justified by the principle of the double effect. That the fear was a psychic rather than a bodily evil made no difference, according to the theory that the criterion was the good of the person as a whole. This position was adopted by Louis Janssens, professor of theology at the University of Louvain, and by canon Paul Anciaux, professor of moral theology at the seminary of Malines.[65]

A much more difficult case was the use of the pill to regulate the menstrual cycle. The usual purpose of such regulation would be to make possible the practice of rhythm. In a very brief note in July 1957, Francis Connell at the Catholic University of America took the position that the pill could be used "to give a woman a normal cycle of twenty-eight days for ovulation and menstruation." In an article addressed to a popular audience in 1957, William Gibbons, S.J., noted that such use needed "further consideration both medically and morally." In April 1958 Louis Janssens at Louvain interpreted Gibbons as favoring the use, and seemed to approve it himself. In the same month, Gibbons joined with Thomas Burch, a layman and American sociologist, in an article which reviewed current opinion on the pill. Without giving their own opinion, they noted that "some" thought irregularity of cycle, with accompanying nervous strain, could be regarded as pathological. Others, they said, "argue that

iologic Control of Fertility: Process and Morality," *American Ecclesiastical Review* 138 (1958), 265–266 (recognizing the general principle of indirect use of the anovulants); Ford and Kelly, *Contemporary Moral Theology*, II, 346 (recognizing the use of the anovulants for endometriosis and painful or excessive menstruation); John J. Lynch, "Moral Aspects of Pharmaceutical Fertility Control," *The Catholic Theological Society of America, Proceedings of the Thirteenth Annual Convention* (St. Louis, 1958), p. 134 (premenstrual tension recognized). Joseph J. Farraher noted that there was ambiguity in the application to premenstrual tension. If the progesterone has "as an immediate effect a feeling of relief," then it operates like a tranquilizer on the tension and is lawful. But if "the medication will remove the fear of pregnancy from acts of intercourse," then a bad means is being used ("Notes on Moral Theology," *Theological Studies* 21 [1960], 602).

[64] Joseph Fuchs, "Nota de aliquo casu recentiore sterilizationis therapeuticae," *Periodica de re morali, canonica, liturgica*, 50 (1960), 35; Joseph Farraher, "Notes on Moral Theology," p. 601.

[65] Paul Anciaux, "Regulation des naissances et thérapies hormonales: Aspects normaux des traitements à base de substances progestatives," *Saint-Luc médical* 32 (1960), 67; Louis Janssens, "Morale conjugale et progestogènes," *Ephemerides theologicae lovaniensis* 39 (1963), 790.

one cannot define a 'normal' cycle for a given individual in terms of a statistical average." [66]

At the June 1958 meeting of the Catholic Theological Society of America, the question of what constituted a "normal" cycle was debated. John J. Lynch proposed as a test "that degree of irregularity which would preclude a reasonably effective use of rhythm — in other words, an irregularity which would prompt a competent gynecologist in a particular instance to advise against rhythm as an effective means of avoiding pregnancy." [67] Commenting on Gibbons and Burch's article later in the year, John Connery, another American Jesuit, interpreted Gibbons and Burch as permitting the use of drugs "to correct a pathological condition." He went on: "Would it be licit (if it were medically feasible) so to regularize the period that it would always be twenty-eight days and ovulation would always take place on the fourteenth day? I really do not see why it would not. I see no moral reason why one must be limited to what is normal. It seems to me that perfect regularity is as legitimate a goal as perfect health or perfect vision." [68]

In 1960, in a thorough discussion of the question, Denis O'Callaghan, an Irish theologian, defended the use of the drug "to correct a pathologically irregular cycle," "pathological" being liberally defined as the description of a condition which would prompt one to consult a doctor. The defense was in terms of double effect. But O'Callaghan went further. Might "hormonal therapy" be used to achieve complete regularity of ovulation? O'Callaghan abandoned the appeal to double effect and approved the use on a different principle: "When one considers how the delicate endocrine mechanism is geared to effect a uniform pattern, it seems ridiculous to regard the more precise adjustment of this pattern as suppression of function." [69] In other words, O'Callaghan joined Connery in finding perfection of function a lawful direct end.

In 1961, Lawrence L. McReavy, in England, stated that gynecologists were reluctant to admit that "irregularity, however pronounced, is a malady at all." "Logically," he concluded, the pills could not be used to regulate the cycle. This opinion he found to be "the common conclusion of moralists" and "the safer doctrine." Yet McReavy seemed unwilling to close discussion with this conclusion. "In favor of freedom," he suggested

[66] Connell, "The Contraceptive Pill," p. 50; William Gibbons, S.J., "Antifertility Drugs and Morality," *America* 98 (1957), 346, 347; Louis Janssens, "L'Inhibition de l'ovulation est-elle moralement licite?" *Ephemerides theologicae lovanienses* 34 (1958), 360; Gibbons and Burch, "Physiologic Control of Fertility," p. 268.

[67] John J. Lynch, "Digest of the Discussion," following "Moral Aspects of Pharmaceutical Fertility Control," *Proceedings of the Thirteenth Annual Convention*, p. 137.

[68] John Connery, "Notes on Moral Theology," *Theological Studies* 19 (1958), 550.

[69] Denis O'Callaghan, "Fertility Control by Hormonal Medication," *Irish Theological Quarterly* 27 (1960), 13.

that irregularity could be regarded as "a notable physical handicap to women who have a just cause for exclusive use of the infertile period." He concluded, "and to judge from Pius XII's ruling on the morality of plastic surgery for beauty's sake, it can be lawful to remove a physical handicap at the expense of a minor mutilation which, as in the present instance, involves no lasting impairment of functional integrity." [70] With McReavy, as with Lynch, the cycle appropriate for the effective use of rhythm became a way of defining the menstrual irregularity which it was lawful to correct.

In the same year, M. Thiéffry, a Belgian Jesuit, challenged this kind of approach. He appeared unwilling to accept the implicit postulate of Lynch and O'Callaghan that impossibility of using rhythm was itself a "medical anomaly or pathological case." [71] His challenge raised the question of what was meant by "pathological" in this context. "Pathological" did not seem to mean a disease threatening life; it seemed here to mean a condition which prevented a woman from functioning at her best, and, of course, "best" or "perfection" introduced the question of the standard for such evaluation. This question was intertwined with the determination of what was normal. Menstrual cycles varied by the age of the woman and from woman to woman; even in a given year one woman might have considerable variation in her cycle. Cycles as short as 17 days had been found, and as long as 40 days. If statistics were to establish the norm, the average cycle would be 30.1 days for women aged 19 to 23, and 27.4 days for women aged 34 to 38. But did statistics establish the norm or the natural? Without exploring these questions, however, in June 1962 Lynch reviewed the state of opinion and found "the majority" of moralists in favor of use to regulate the cycle.[72] Writing in 1963, Louis Janssens said the moralists were "practically unanimous" in admitting this use.[73]

As Thiéffry brought out, and as Lynch and Connery admitted, what was at issue here was not "normalcy" of menstruation, but a predictability that would permit rhythm. It seemed to be assumed by the proponents of the argument that some kind of predictability could be called "normal"

[70] Lawrence L. McReavy, "Use of Steroid Drugs to Regulate Menstrual Cycles," *The Clergy Review* 46 (1961), 750.

[71] M. Thiéffry. "Stérilisation hormonale et morale chrétienne," *Nouvelle revue théologique* 83 (1961), 149.

[72] John J. Lynch, "Notes on Moral Theology," *Theological Studies* 23 (1962), 244. Data on short and long menstrual cycles, on variations by age and person, and statistics on the norm are set out in Paul Vincent, "Données biométriques sur la conception et la grossesse," *Population* 11 (1956), 71–77. At the symposium of Catholic theologians and doctors on rhythm, the doctors present denied that, by taking the progesterone pill, women with irregular menstrual cycles achieved regularity (Boler, "Symposium on Rhythm," p. 15).

[73] Janssens, "Morale conjugale et progestogènes," p. 787.

or natural. To the objection, If you permit use of the pills to make rhythm easier, why do you not allow their use to put rhythm on a yearly, rather than monthly, basis? they would probably have answered, We permit predictability only within the 25–35 day range which observation shows to be natural for most women; we do not defend changing the natural limits of the cycle. But there was a more difficult question for them to answer. If it was lawful to suppress ovulation to achieve a regularity necessary for successfully sterile intercourse, why was it not lawful to suppress ovulation without appeal to rhythm? If pregnancy could be prevented by pill plus rhythm, why not by pill alone? In each case suppression of ovulation was used as a means. How was a moral difference made by the addition of rhythm? The moralists favorable to the use did not ask these questions; they were implicit in Thiéffry's negative judgment. The favorable position was close to acceptance of direct, intentional suppression of fertility by pill. A serious crisis in the prohibition of contraception was at hand.

When the anovulants first became the object of theological analysis in 1957, the early reaction, in the very articles which accepted their therapeutic use, had been to class their direct use to suppress ovulation as "contraceptive" and "sterilizing." Thus Francis Connell said that to use the pill "directly as a contraceptive" was "a grave sin"; "for it is a serious transgression of God's law to interfere directly and positively with the process of human generation." William Gibbons analyzed such use as an "attack" on "the role of nature in reproduction." "Hence the new methods are morally wrong and their use must be judged seriously sinful." In the more scientific article of Gibbons and Burch in 1958, the effect of the pills affecting ovulation was classified as "sterilization" and as therefore morally unacceptable.[74]

Louis Janssens, however, commented on the use of the anovulants only in a favorable way. In his June 1958 article entitled "Is the Inhibition of Ovulation Morally Lawful?" he found lawful not only the indirect use of anovulants, but their direct use to produce sterility in the period of lactation. He built on a theory that had first been expounded by Dr. Raoul de Guchteneere in connection with rhythm. De Guchteneere in 1950 had maintained that the normal period of lactation was nine months and that during this period ovulation was inhibited by nature; nature thereby spaced births at least at eighteen-month intervals; "if the natural mechanism was in default," rhythm could be used to space the births. Now Janssens argued that the same theory could be invoked to justify the use of anovulants. Here, too, was a case of "sustaining

---

[74] Connell, "The Contraceptive Pill," p. 50; Gibbons, "Antifertility Drugs and Morality"; Gibbons and Burch, "Physiologic Control of Fertility," p. 269.

natural mechanisms which are in default." [75] Carefully building a case for particular uses of the anovulants, Janssens at no point condemned their general use. His note, making suggestions rather than developing an elaborate case, had the marks of a trial balloon.

Three months later, on September 12, 1958, Pius XII took the occasion of his address to the hematologists to speak on Janssens' suggestions. The Pope compared himself to Innocent XI (whom he had recently beatified), forced to reprove the laxist theologians of the seventeenth century. As Innocent XI had acted at the instigation of the theologians of Louvain, there was a nice historical irony in the allusion. Some Catholic moralists, the Pope declared, proceeded with a praiseworthy intention not "to exclude too quickly new possibilities for solutions." But "this effort at adaptation" was undertaken unhappily when "certain principles are poorly understood or given a significance they cannot have." The Pope proceeded to "the case often discussed today among moralists and doctors": "Is it licit to prevent ovulation by means of pills used as remedies for exaggerated reactions of the uterus and of the organism, although this medication, by preventing ovulation, also makes fecundation impossible?" The form of the question, modeled on Janssens' title, served to recall it. The Pope went on to admit the indirect use to prevent disease of the organism. He continued:

> But one provokes a direct sterilization and therefore an illicit one, whenever one stops ovulation [*arrête l'ovulation*] in order to preserve the uterus and the organism from the consequences of a pregnancy which they are not capable of supporting. Certain moralists assert that it is permitted to take drugs to this end, but this is a mistake. It is equally necessary to reject the opinion of several doctors and moralists who permit their use whenever a medical indication renders an early conception undesirable or in other similar cases which it would not be possible to mention here; in these cases the employment of drugs has as its end the preventing of conception in preventing ovulation; it is therefore a matter of direct sterilization.
>
> To justify it they quote at times the moral principle, correct in itself, but wrongly interpreted: "It is lawful to correct the defects of nature." Since, in practice, it suffices, in order to use this principle, to have reasonable probability, they assert that it is a matter here of correcting a natural defect. If this principle had unqualified validity, eugenics could without hesitation utilize the drug method to stop the transmission of a defective heredity. But it is still necessary to consider by what means the natural defect is corrected and to take care not to violate in any respect other principles of morality.
>
> (Address to the Seventh International Congress of Hematology, *AAS* 50:735-736)

The Pope's address responded to more than Janssens' article. Janssens had not spoken of the use of an anovulant when the uterus could not

[75] Janssens, "L'Inhibition de l'ovulation est-elle moralement licite?" p. 359. Janssens referred to R. de Guchteneere, "Raisons de santé," in *Limitation des naissances et conscience chrétienne* (Paris, 1950), p. 117.

support a pregnancy; nor had Janssens spoken of "medical indications" rendering conception undesirable. Nonetheless, by alluding to Janssens' title and by speaking of the correction of natural defects, Pius XII seemed to have his article in view. Whether he also had in mind the oral opinions of other moralists is conjectural.[76]

One earlier pronouncement of Pius XII must be noted in order to understand his full position on the anovulants. In 1951, well before the anovulants were an issue, in his address to the Italian Catholic Society of Midwives, he had substantially expanded the teaching of *Casti connubii*. In that encyclical his predecessor, he said, had

solemnly proclaimed again the fundamental law of the marital act and relations: any attempt by the spouses in the completion of the conjugal act or in the development of its natural consequences, having the aim of depriving the act of the force inherent in it and of impeding the procreation of a new life, is immoral; and no alleged indication or need can convert an intrinsically immoral act into a moral and lawful one.

This precept is as valid today as it was yesterday; and it will be the same tomorrow and always, because it does not imply a precept of the human law, but is the expression of a law which is natural and divine.   (*AAS* 43:843)

The important clause here is *nello sviluppo delle sue conseguenze naturali*, "in the development of its natural consequences." By these words, Pius XII asserted that not only did Pius XI condemn the impeding of coitus — a prohibition of coitus interruptus, the condom, and the pseudo-vagina — but he condemned such means as the douche and other postcoital efforts to destroy or expel the spermatozoa. Pius XII's interpretation was not put forward as infallible, but it was later asserted by him to be an example of the Pope "intervening authoritatively in moral questions" (Radio broadcast, March 23, 1952, *AAS* 44:275). In the light of his own view of the teaching of Pius XI, Pius XII apparently believed that the anovulants were a condemned interference "in the development of the natural consequences" of coitus.

The authority of the explicit papal statement on anovulants, delivered in the course of an informal address, and before either the bishops or the theologians had the opportunity to reach a mature judgment, was far from that of an *ex cathedra* pronouncement. The analysis of the use of the anovulants by Pius XII was not an infallible declaration of moral truth. It was, however, the only papal statement on the subject. As such, it commanded respect.

For four years the words of Pius XII were taken by the moral theologians as controlling. Throughout the world the proposition was re-

---

[76] Eugene Tesson knew of no French theologians who had written anything on the pills; "Derniers enseignements de Pie XII aux médecins," *Etudes* 299 (1958), 246. John Lynch reported that he knew of no theologian who had defended them; "Notes on Moral Theology," *Theological Studies* 20 (1959), 240.

peated that the direct use of the anovulants to prevent procreation was an immoral interference with the generative process. A survey of countries showed condemnations by the following theologians: Australia, Nicholas Crotty, C.P.; Belgium, M. Thiéffry, S.J.; England, L. L. McReavy; France, Stanislas de Lestapis, S.J.; Germany, Bernard Häring, C.SS.R., Joseph Fuchs, S.J.; Ireland, Denis O'Callaghan; United States, John J. Lynch, S.J., Joseph J. Farraher, S.J.[77]

There was apparent unanimity. There were also signs of strain. Despite the criticism of Pius XII directed at the principle "it is lawful to correct the defects of nature," this very principle seemed to be invoked by the several writers we have noted who, after September 12, 1958, argued that anovulants might be used to perfect the menstrual cycle. The papal condemnation was in fact restricted, and, to this extent, disregarded, by the theologians. Even more significantly, the direct use of anovulants to produce sterility during lactation was considered an open question despite the apparent papal repudiation of any direct sterilization. Thiéffry vigorously attacked the practice, doubting that there was proof of any natural mechanism preventing ovulation in lactation which the anovulants could be said to supplement. But Crotty believed the issue arguable. Denis O'Callaghan defended the practice, provided the mother was breast-feeding. In that case the mother using anovulants "is aiding nature rather than frustrating it." Reviewing the controversy, Joseph Farraher, who condemned the usage, pointed to the implications of permitting it. Who is to say, he asked, "when nature intends sterility"? "Is it natural for a woman to be sterile for twenty-five days out of every twenty-eight? So may she use anovulants to be sure that she cannot be fertile except on a given three days each month?" [78] As Farraher saw, if the direct use of anovulants were licit to produce a sterility equivalent to nature's, the field of their application would be wide.

In the seven years from the beginning of debate on the anovulants, no theologians had defended their lawfulness to regulate fertility except in the special cases of correction of the cycle and in lactation. In 1963 this situation was drastically altered. The change began with a book entitled

[77] Nicholas Crotty, C.P., "The Moral Issues in Hormonal Control of Fertility," *Australasian Catholic Record* 35 (1958), 102; M. Thiéffry, S.J., "Stérilisation hormonale et morale chrétienne," pp. 143–144; L. L. McReavy, "Why Direct Temporary Sterilization Is Wrong," *Clergy Review* 45 (1960), 743; Stanislas de Lestapis, S.J., *La Limitation des naissances*, p. 182; Bernard Häring, C.SS.R., "Verantwortete Elternschaft — aber wie?" *Theologisches Digest* (1959), 56; Joseph Fuchs, S.J., *De castitate*, sec. 6; Denis O'Callaghan, "Fertility Control by Hormonal Medication," p. 14; John J. Lynch, S.J., "Notes on Moral Theology," *Theological Studies* 20 (1959), 240; Joseph J. Farraher, S.J., "Notes on Moral Theology," *Theological Studies* 21 (1960), 599.

[78] Thiéffry, "Stérilisation hormonale et morale chrétienne," p. 156; Crotty, "The Moral Issues in Hormonal Control of Fertility," p. 108; O'Callaghan, "Fertility Control by Hormonal Medication," p. 14; Joseph J. Farraher, "Notes on Moral Theology," *Theological Studies* 22 (1961), 630.

The Time Has Come by John Rock, a Boston doctor who had played a major role in the development of the progesterone pill. Rock, describing himself as a Catholic doctor, argued that use of the anovulants was equivalent to a " 'pill-established safe period' and would seem to carry the same moral implications." No organ was mutilated. No natural process was damaged. An analogy was advanced: ovulation was naturally inhibited by secretions of progesterone during pregnancy; nature thereby prevented a new pregnancy endangering the existing fetus. Why could not man similarly inhibit ovulation when a new pregnancy might endanger the education of existing offspring? To admit this position would only be to substitute rational control for the automatic functioning of hormones. A mother's intellect should be able to achieve a proper end by means analogous to nature's, "so that as responsible parents, she and her husband will be able to nourish, physically and mentally, the children they already have." [79]

Rock's thesis was immediately rejected by several American theologians — Connell, Lynch, Ford, and Kelly — who commented on it. None of his arguments changed their opinion that here was a direct interference with the generative process, naturally wrong and specifically condemned by Pius XII. Richard Cushing, cardinal archbishop of Boston, issued a statement on April 30, 1963, also rejecting Rock's contention. [80]

In the Netherlands, individuals had, since 1960, doubted the teaching on the pill. [81] The first sign of reconsideration by the hierarchy of any country appeared in a television speech by William Bekkers, bishop of 's-Hertogenbosch, on March 21, 1963. Describing "birth regulation" as part of the normal responsibility of married couples, Bishop Bekkers emphasized personal responsibility in deciding the means of regulation; the Church, he said, "knows that what one man can achieve is not necessarily within the reach of another." In a statement issued to meet the criticism, especially the charge of "too great vagueness," that this address evoked in the Netherlands, Bishop Bekkers noted that there was necessarily vagueness when it was unclear whether the traditional statements applied to the progesterone pill. These pills were not contraceptives in the usual sense. Greater study was necessary before a judgment could be made on them. [82]

More uncertainty and controversy followed in the Netherlands. On

---

[79] Rock, *The Time Has Come*, pp. 168–175.

[80] *The Pilot*, May 9, 1963.

[81] Statements are cited by Willem van der Marck, "Vruchtbaarheidsregeling: Poging tot Antwoord op een nog open Vraag," *Tijdschrift voor Theologie* 3 (1963), 378.

[82] William Bekkers, television speech given on the program "Brandpunt" (text furnished me by Bishop Bekkers). Bishop Bekkers in an article in his diocesan paper, *Analecta*, asked if the pill was in the same category as the older contraceptives ("Herder Correspondence," October 1963, p. 30).

August 10, 1963, the seven bishops of the Netherlands, acting as a national hierarchy, issued this statement:

New views of man and his existence, of sexuality and conjugal love, as well as the continuous evolution of the biological and biochemical sciences, procuring new means for regulation and control of human fertility, confront the Church with questions on which, in view of the new and varied problems, it cannot immediately have the answer in all situations.

Even if the oral, chemical means which are now being disseminated to prevent conception cannot be a generally used solution of need in marriage any more than the long-known mechanical means, Catholic ethics discusses the question whether, in special situations, the use of these means might be accepted.[83]

The bishops concluded with the hope that the question might be discussed in a wider context at the Vatican Council.

The Dutch hierarchy left open all the major questions, with their statement that use "in special situations" was being discussed. In this atmosphere of free discussion, the direct use of anovulants to regulate birth was now defended in three different theological periodicals by three European theologians. Louis Janssens wrote "Conjugal Morality and Progesterones," which appeared in the December 1963 issue of the magazine of theological studies published by the University of Louvain. William van der Marck, a Dutch Dominican at the Dominican house of studies at Nymegen, wrote "Fertility Control: An Attempt to Answer a Still Open Question," which appeared in the leading Dutch theological journal, whose editor was the Dominican Edward Schillebeeckx. Joseph Mary Reuss, auxiliary bishop of Mainz, wrote "Marital Sacrifice and Procreation," which appeared in the organ of the Catholic faculty of theology at the University of Tübingen and in a French translation in the supplement to *La Vie spirituelle*.[84]

In reaching their common conclusion, that it was lawful to use anovulants to regulate births when the regulation of births in a family was rationally desirable, the three authors took different routes. Van der Marck redefined the act being judged. When one took an anovulant, one might, he insisted, be performing one of three possible acts: (1) using hormonal compounds to deprive the act of intercourse of its generative power; (2) using hormonal compounds for a therapeutic purpose such as correction of an irregular menstrual cycle; (3) using hormonal compounds to regulate fertility. The Pope and the theologians had condemned

---

[83] "Publikatie van de Bisschoppen aan de Priesters van Nederland over de Momentele Huwelijks-Problematiek," *Katholiek Archief* 18 (1963), 937.

[84] Janssens, "Morale conjugale et progestogènes," p. 787; Van der Marck, "Vruchtbaarheidsregeling"; Josef Maria Reuss, "Eheliche Hingabe und Zeugung," *Tübinger theologische Quartalschrift* 143 (1963), 454; French translation "Don mutuel des époux," Supplement to *La Vie spirituelle* 17 (1964).

the first use and permitted the second. The morality of the third was an open question. He undertook to defend this act. The structure of coitus was not attacked by the pills. The subjective intention of the user could be good. The act itself, intrinsically, was good: to regulate fertility was objectively lawful. Earlier writers, Van der Marck argued, had not seen that the use of anovulants could be defined in this third way as an act of regulating fertility. He drew a parallel with the analysis first made of organic transplantation. As long as the act of excision was analyzed as an act of mutilation committed to help a neighbor, it appeared to be a bad means to a good end. But when it was seen that the act of excision could be defined as part of the act of "transplantation," it was possible to accept the act as moral. "The typical quality of the human act is precisely that the physically separated elements can, by human giving-of-meaning, become one by reason of the intended end." [85]

Bishop Reuss did not redefine the act. He merely took the position, implicit in Van der Marck, that biological and physiological acts were not immune from interference. Everyone agreed that this was true of non-sexual processes. Reuss refused to treat the sexual process, aside from the coital act itself, differently. For a proportionate good, the factors making the act fertile could be altered. Reuss went further to argue that such prevention of fertility could be a duty. Suppose that a couple with children should not have more children, suppose that for them the denial of all intercourse produced a tension. This tension was harmful to the welfare of the existing children. The solution of this "situation of conflict" might be found in the use of the drugs producing sterility. Here Reuss, too, invoked the principles involved in organic transplantation. The use of sterilizing means was "commanded not only by the fact that a part can and even ought to be sacrificed to the whole, but also by the fact that such interventions can be permitted and commanded in order to come to the aid of one's neighbor." [86]

Reuss spoke of use of the already accepted sterile period as a way of excluding fecundity by human calculation. Janssens pressed this point. If "every human interference limiting the generative power" was to be called "directly sterilizing," then use of the sterile period was "directly sterilizing." Time, he pointed out, was a major element in human acts. Ask a hunter if time was not important in his shot. When one changed the time that one performed an act, one thereby introduced human calculation into what one did. If one had intercourse only at sterile times, one placed a temporal obstacle to procreation, as much as one placed a spatial obstacle by coitus interruptus. But Pius XII had approved family planning by the use of the sterile period. The placing of a temporal ob-

<hr/>

[85] Van der Marck, "Vruchtbaarheidsregeling," pp. 403–413.
[86] Reuss, "Don mutuel des époux," p. 122.

stacle, as long as the structure of the act was respected, was not illicit. Neither, then, was the placing of an obstacle by the progesterone pills.[87]

A special emphasis was given by Janssens to the fact that the pills destroyed nothing. In this respect they were implicitly distinguished from postcoital douches. Even use of the sterile period, Janssens noted, resulted in letting an ovum come to maturity and go to waste unfertilized. Use of the progesterone pill postponed ovulation and not only did not destroy the ova but kept them from a wasteful process of destruction.[88]

All three writers rejected contraception committed for hedonistic purposes. Such an intervention in the biological process was "arbitrary." Nor did any of them defend interference with the act of intercourse itself. Janssens contended that the "nature and structure of the conjugal act" must be respected. Van der Marck wondered whether the earlier judgments of the popes, congregations, and theologians "really touched any more than the intention and mentality which were felt to be realized and concretely manifested in these methods at a given time." It was "possible" that the same methods "with a different intention and mentality might be entirely unobjectionable." [89] But he did not develop this point. Reuss merely said that he was putting aside the question of methods interfering with the integrity of the act. However, he did go further than the others by speaking of medicines or of an "operation" which would produce temporary sterility.[90] Apparently his defense of anovulants had led him to believe that a sterilizing operation such as ligation of the Fallopian tubes was lawful. But he did not specify what he had in mind. The general thrust of Van der Marck's argument would also have supported the lawfulness of temporary sterilization by surgery; but he did not mention this point. In each of the three authors the main objection to contraception seemed to be to means which would destroy the "integrity" of the conjugal act and interfere with the expression of love in coitus.

The pill became the center and symbol of effort to modify the Catholic position on birth control. In April 1964 an article by Thomas D. Roberts, former archbishop of Bombay, questioning the rationality of the entire Catholic position on contraception, set off an immediate reaction in England.[91] On May 7, 1964, John Heenan, archbishop of Westminster, issued a statement in the name of the bishops of England and Wales. He said, "It has even been suggested that the Church could approve the practice of contraception. But the Church, while free to revise her own positive laws, has no power of any kind to alter the laws of God . . . Contracep-

---

[87] Janssens, "Morale conjugale et progestogènes," pp. 817–821.

[88] *Ibid.*, p. 822.

[89] Van der Marck, "Vruchtbaarheidsregeling," p. 408.

[90] Reuss, "Don mutuel des époux," p. 122.

[91] Thomas D. Roberts' article which first appeared in *Search* (April 1964) is reprinted in *The Pill and Birth Regulation*, ed. Leo Pyle (Baltimore, 1964), p. 85.

tion . . . is not an open question, for it is against the law of God." [92] The English bishops quoted a single sentence from the statement of the Dutch hierarchy: "The new contraceptive pill now being advertised can be no more acceptable as the answer to the problem of married people than the contraceptive instruments hitherto in use." This sentence was not only an inaccurate translation of the original statement;[93] it was removed from its context and quoted without the important qualification that study was being made of the pill's use in "special circumstances." The seven bishops of the Netherlands and the twenty-three bishops of England and Wales were, in fact, at odds.

At this critical juncture, with theologians and bishops divided, Pope Paul VI, on June 23, 1964, announced that "the Church" was studying the subject. The Pope asked for preservation of the status quo, pending the outcome of this study: "In the meantime we must say openly that up to now we have not sufficient reason to consider the rules laid down by Pius XII in this matter to be out of date and therefore not binding" (*AAS* 56:588). Discussion had advanced to the point where the Pope could think that "the rules" laid down by his predecessor on sterilizing agents might be only of a contingent and therefore mutable character.

The campaign of the Church to outlaw some forms of contraception must be read in conjunction with this doctrinal development, in a little over a century, on the means of controlling conception. At the very time the campaign began to increase in tempo, in the regime of Leo XIII, greater official approval was given to the use of the sterile period to avoid procreation. At the climax of the campaign, sterility became relatively ascertainable, thanks to new scientific discoveries, and the theologians, albeit with misgivings, accepted rhythm. In the last twenty years, as sterilization was condemned for some purposes, so it was accepted for others. In short, only by considering the full range of means condemned, approved, and tolerated by the Church could one accurately determine what the Catholic position on controlling conception had become, and what constituted its core.

If the progesterone pill was accepted to the extent advocated by Janssens, Van der Marck, Reuss, and others, rethinking of the entire prohibition of contraception was required.[94] Even if only the uses of the pill ad-

[92] John Heenan, Statement of the hierarchy of England and Wales in *The Universe*, May 7, 1964, reprinted in *The Pill and Birth Regulation*, ed. Pyle, p. 95–99.

[93] The quotation was made from a translation furnished Archbishop Heenan by Cardinal Alfrink and published in *The Clergy Review* 114, February 1964.

[94] One American priest, Michael O'Leary, chairman of the philosophy department of Sacred Heart Seminary, Detroit, also expressed himself in sympathy with a position permitting use of the pill by married couples who had a right to use rhythm but found it a practical impossibility (O'Leary, "Some Thoughts About the Oral-Steroid Pill," *Jubilee*, March 1964, pp. 44–45). A Belgian professor of moral theology stated that although one could not yet be certain of the hormonal effects, one might reach

mitted by the more conservative authors were considered, along with the current doctrine on surgical sterilization, a problem was raised. Prevention of fertility by certain kinds of acts antecedent to coitus was now admitted by everyone to be lawful under some circumstances. In the case of surgery, however, most authors held that the intent to prevent fertility was a sinful intent; some other intent had to exist for the operation to be justified. Why was the intention to prevent fertility sinful when one employed surgery, but not when one employed a choice of time? As to the anovulant pill, a majority seemed to support its use to regulate the menstrual cycle, and a minority accepted its use to produce sterility in lactation. Why was it lawful to intend to suppress the capability of procreating in order to make rhythm work or in order to be "normal" in lactation, but not lawful to suppress ovulation in order to avoid a pregnancy fatal to health? Finally, if the full use of the pills was accepted, the questions arose, How was the pill different from hespiridin? Was it really different from postcoital douching? Could the line be effectively drawn between acts interfering with the exercise of coitus and acts antecedent to it? [95] All

the conclusion that "techniques of this kind, 'sterilizing pills,' require permanent spiritual dispositions and qualities [in their users] in order to be *secundum naturam,* that is, at the service of persons." Michel Dagez, "Le Recours aux pilules stérilisantes est-il légitime?" *Revue diocesaine de Tournai,* December 1963, p. 594.

Bernard Häring had condemned "infertility drugs" in the 3rd edition of *Das Gesetz Christi* (Freiburg im Breisgau, 1961), III, 355. However, after the declaration of the English hierarchy, he gave an interview to the Manchester *Guardian,* printed in the *Guardian* May 9, 1964, in which he indicated that the question of the pill was distinguishable from the use of contraceptives. He followed this with an article in the *Catholic Herald* (London) of May 29, 1964, in which he said that theologians should not condemn an act as mortal sin unless they were sure of their ground. He said that at the moment it was uncertain whether the pill was a positively acceptable method of birth regulation.

In 1964 Alphonse Auer joined Bishop Reuss in support of the pill because it did not destroy the natural structure of the coital act. "Eheliche Hingabe und Zeugung: Zu einem Diskussionsbeitrag des Mainzer Weihbischofs Dr. J. M. Reuss," *Theologisch-praktische Quartalschrift* 112 (1964), 121–132. Commenting on the discussion, Felix Cardegna concluded with the hope that the Church would reject all forms of contraception which destroyed "the natural structure" of the marital act between husband and wife, "but that it will refrain from pronouncing on the question of intervention in the generative system, i.e., that it will allow theologians to reflect further on the meaning of human sexuality and the concept of sterilization." Cardegna, "Contraception, The Pill, and Responsible Parenthood." *Theological Studies* 25 (1964), 636. Cardegna, a Jesuit at Woodstock College, Maryland, was the first American Jesuit to write so sympathetically on the Janssens-Reuss theory.

[95] An even more difficult question as to means was presented by one analysis of the mode of operation of the intra-uterine ring. This ring composed of silk threads bound by silver wire had been invented by Ernst Gräfenberg, a Berlin doctor, in 1928. Medical opinion was hostile to it as relatively ineffective and as sometimes causing injury to the wearer. However, Japanese doctors continued to prescribe it, and in 1959 American doctors took a second look. The new medical evaluation discounted the health dangers and found it had a very high efficiency as a contraceptive. (Christopher Tietze, "Intra-Uterine Contraceptive Rings: History and Statistical Appraisal," in *Intra-Uterine Contraceptive Devices,* ed. Christopher Tietze and Sarah Lewit, Amster-

of these questions faced resolution in the light of the development of Catholic theory and the change of the intellectual and social environment.

---

dam, 1962, pp. 9–12.) What was not clear was how the ring worked. One analysis was that it prevented implantation of the fertilized ovum. Treating it as operating in this way, De Lestapis denounced it as an abortifacient (Stanislas de Lestapis, "De 'pillula contraceptiva': An eius usus florere iam desierit?" *Periodica de re canonica, morali, liturgica* 53 [1964], 447–449). However, Tietze noted in the article cited that "ectopic pregnancies occur far less frequently than would be expected if the contraceptive action consisted in preventing implantation, but not fertilization of the ovum" (p. 14). It was possible that the ring merely accelerated the passage of the ovum, so that fertilization was prevented. If this was the mode of action, a new case was presented, that of a contraceptive which did not attack the spermatozoa, did not stop the functioning of part of the body, did not interfere with the coital act; it could be argued that it made very probable what was already statistically probable, viz. that spermatozoa and ovum would not meet.

CHAPTER XV

THE DOCTRINE AND THE CONTEXT

THE PERIOD from 1880 to the present — in which contraception spread throughout the world, the planning of births became a generally accepted ideal in Western and Western-influenced cultures, and the Catholic Church waged war on contraception — was also marked by changes whose impact on the Catholic position was inescapable. The changes created a new context for the teaching on contraception. At the same time developments within the Church and an internal evolution of doctrine on marriage affected the inner constituents of the teaching. The question of permissible means of regulating birth could not be decided by the simple inspection of alternatives. It was set within the context of a changed environment and an evolved theology of marriage.

THE CHANGED ENVIRONMENT

Population. Until about 1650, the population of the world had increased at an annual rate of no more than .1 percent. At this date the world population was about 500 million. The annual rate of growth then began to increase and rose to about .5 percent. By 1850 the world population had doubled to one billion. The rate of growth now began to accelerate. By 1900 it was nearly 1 percent per year. By 1930 the world population had, in eighty years, doubled to two billion. In 1964 the rate of growth was nearly 1.75 percent, or double the rate in 1880. It was predicted that, unless there were major checks, the world population would reach four billion by 1980, and that the rate of growth would probably continue as high as 2 percent.[1]

The principal factor bringing about these increases in the total world population and in its rate of increase was the control of disease. The creation of healthful environments, the development of public health

[1] M. Cépède, F. Houtart, and L. Grond, *Population and Food*, (New York, 1964), pp. 10–12; Julian Huxley, *The Human Crisis* (Seattle, 1963), p. 50.

measures, a vast improvement in the care of infants and young children, and the discovery and use of means to cure infectious diseases first increased life expectancy in western Europe and North America, and then, in the twentieth century, had the same beneficent effect in eastern Europe and much of Asia, Latin America, and Africa. The preservation of millions of human beings through childhood into child-producing ages meant that the population grew not only because people were living longer, but because there were more child-producing people. In areas where modern health measures were suddenly introduced, such as Ceylon and Brazil, there were dramatically sharp climbs in life expectancy and in population. The changes in western Europe occurred more gradually; but a comparison of nineteenth- and twentieth-century mortality and life expectancy rates is equally dramatic. From a crude death rate of 30 per year per thousand in western Europe in 1800, the death rate fell to 11 by 1960. Even between 1913 and 1955 there was an impressive gain in life expectancy for Western countries. In 1913 life expectancy at birth in the Netherlands was 52; in 1956 it was 75; in the same period in Italy it rose from 45 to 70, and in Canada from 45 to 70. By 1964 life expectancy in northwestern Europe, North America, Oceania, and the U.S.S.R. was nearing 75.[2]

The rate of growth, projected, created a hypothetical situation in which avoidance of procreation could seem mandatory: "a two percent growth rate will result in one square yard of land area per person 600 years hence, an obvious absurdity."[3] But most moralists probably did not feel bound to deal with this hypothetical, believing that against it could be played off other hypothetical possibilities, such as the colonization of outer space. In short, immediate moral judgments were difficult to obtain on a situation in a remote and contingent future.[4]

[2] Cépède, Houtart, and Grond, *Population and Food*, pp. 152–156.
[3] Hudson Hoagland, "Mechanisms of Population Control," *Daedalus* 93 (1964), 814.
[4] The point was also made that "overpopulation" in the sense of too many persons per unit surface was not, in the present context, "very useful, except in situations where the primary resources are extractive, such as mining, the most primitive types of agriculture (independent of industry for fertilizers, machines, etc., and hence essentially dependent on area), and forestry" (Jean Mayer, "Food and Population: The Wrong Problem?" *Daedalus*, Summer 1964, pp. 835–836). Mayer also points out that as to food shortage, the problem now is not lack of production, but lack of rational distribution and even destruction of food "surpluses." There seems to be little correlation between population density and present shortages. The 14,000-square-mile area from Boston to Washington has more than 2000 persons per square mile, more often suffering from overweight than starvation. A small population is not necessarily a better fed one. In the foreseeable future, moreover, no absolute shortage of food appears probable. Only 3.4 billion acres, or less than 11 percent of the total land area, is now cultivated; 13 to 17 billion acres could be made arable. Increase in the use of fertilizers could easily double the low yield now realized in underdeveloped countries. The possibilities of making synthetic food from oil have been recently enhanced. Food through the photosynthesis of algae appears to be a

The real bite of the population increase was in its effect on the countries characterized as underdeveloped because of their low per capita incomes, low rate of saving and investment, and low industrial output. In these African, Latin American, and Asian countries the drastic reduction of mortality by modern health measures resulted in expansions of population which consumed their resources and made economic accumulation and improvement difficult or impossible. In some of these countries, dependent on forestry, mining, or primitive agriculture, the diminution of space per person had an immediate impact which it would not have in a modern industrial society. In countries with millions of very poor workers, such as India, the increase of people was accompanied by a danger of malnutrition which would not have threatened a population whose density was greater but whose wealth was more equitably divided.[5] In the underdeveloped countries, the increase of population also sometimes overloaded inefficient educational systems to the point of endangering them. In none of these countries could the influx of numbers alone be said to be causing the disappointment of educational and economic aspirations. Existing systems of economic allocation, political patterns, social organizations, cultural ideals, were also responsible. But given the existence of these factors, the influx had serious consequences. In specific underdeveloped countries, "overpopulation" acquired a meaning and became a menacing reality.[6]

The status of women. The same period, from the last part of the nineteenth century to the present, in which population so enormously expanded, was independently characterized by the emancipation of women. This emancipation was embodied in four remarkable changes. Economically, women in the West became income-earning members of society on a large scale. Husbands lost most of their earlier legal controls over their wives' property. In capitalistic countries like the United States women came to own a major share of the national wealth. Equality with men in the economic world, if not totally attained, was in the way of being realized. Politically, in most of the democracies by the mid-twentiees, women had acquired the right to vote. Intellectually, women gained access to higher education, and by the 1960's countries like the United States and the U.S.S.R. were educating many girls at a college level and beyond. Women began to write on a variety of subjects, including contraception, hitherto man's exclusive domain. Finally, with a substantial effect on a wife's

likely possibility. "A breakthrough in this field [of photosynthesis] could for centuries altogether remove food as a limiting factor to population growth" (*ibid.*, pp. 836–842).

[5] See Ansley J. Coale and Edgar M. Hoover, *Population Growth and Economic Development in Low-Income Countries* (Princeton, 1958).

[6] A vigorous presentation of the dangers of overpopulation was given by Huxley in *The Human Crisis*, pp. 50–80.

position in marriage, divorce became easier for women to obtain and less socially disastrous if obtained.[7]

These familiar phenonema of freedom, characteristic in varying degrees of Western or Westernized cultures, gave women a status of near or complete equality with men, and necessarily affected the relationship possible in marriage. No longer was the average wife bound by economic chains and condemned to educational inferiority. More often than was objectively possible before, marriages could be the meeting of equal persons. What was true of marriage itself was also true of courtship. The meeting of relatively free and relatively equal persons became possible on a large scale. Modern Western society became the first society in history where individual decision consciously played a major role in the choice of a spouse. In the great slave systems of Greece and Rome, a large segment of the population could not marry; in feudalism, much of the population had little choice as to marriage; in aristocratic and bourgeois Europe, and even in the class- and property-conscious Victorian era, personal choice was largely fettered; only in the twentieth century did personal decision become predominant. The confining influences of religion, race, wealth, social status, family, were not eliminated, but while they frequently guided decision they were infrequently strong enough to override personal choice, and were seldom set forth as ideals more important than personal response. Marriage by personal choice was the system. The "great mystery" of St. John Chrysostom's day and La Tour Landry's day and St. Alphonsus Liguori's day — how two persons who had never met before could love each other for life — was replaced by more complex mysteries of personal interaction.[8]

With women relatively free and equal, rules for marriage developed in an age of slave concubinage and continued in a feudal era when women generally lacked education, were put in a new setting. Much of the traditional teaching had tried to prevent exploitation of the wife as an object. Much of the teaching had tried to safeguard personal values in unions formed with a minimum of personal consent. The assumptions, the social framework, of the rules had altered.

Methods of education. Partially as a corollary of feminine independence, partially as the result of urban industrial life, Western families became "single-cell" units, rather than including ancestors and collaterals. The

[7] See *The Potential of Women*, a symposium held at the University of California San Francisco Medical Center January 25, 26, and 27, 1963, ed. Seymour M. Farber and Roger H. L. Wilson (New York, 1963); Eric J. Dingwall, *The American Woman: An Historical Study* (New York, 1956).

[8] For sociological study of this change, see Alain Girard, *Le Choix du conjoint: Une enquête psycho-sociologique en France* (Paris, 1964); for an interpretive study, see Denis de Rougemont, *Love in the Western World*, rev. ed., trans. Montgomery Belgion (New York, 1956), pp. 291–302.

early care and raising of children became the task for man and wife alone with little help from other kin. Western man was usually the sole material and moral support of his children.

The raising and education of children not only became a more personal responsibility, it became a more expensive one. A technical society required more education, and a democratic society made it possible, at some cost to the family, for every child to attend grammar school and for many children to attend high school and college. The stage reached by the United States, where in 1964 over 4,500,000 students were engaged in higher education after twelve years of school, could be seen as the one likely to become common. Formal education could be expected to last sixteen or more years.[9]

The medieval theologians had seen education as an essential constituent of parental duty to offspring, and they had meant by education a spiritual training. They had not envisaged a formal process of sixteen years as the norm. Yet nothing in the old teaching had limited the parental obligation to a stationary minimum; on the contrary, implicit in the notion of education was that it be such as would meet the spiritual and intellectual needs of a man of the age. As the age set higher standards of education, so a new content was given the requirement of education. In the medieval and Counter-Reformation theologians, the tension between the demands of procreation and the demands of education had already been evident. Yet the formula had been unchanged: the primary purpose of marriage was the procreation and education of offspring. The new substance to "education" in the old formula gave a different weighting to the issues where the two duties clashed.

Scientific knowledge and philosophy. The sheer physical number of people increased, one of the two sexes emerged from inequality to equality as persons, the education of millions became better — not only did these well-known changes in the social environment occur, but the most relevant physical data changed. The ovum had been discovered in 1827, but an understanding of the joint role of spermatozoa and ovum in generation was obtained only in 1875. The existence of several hundred thousand potential ova in the ovaries of every woman was established only in the twentieth century. That fecundation was possible in only a fraction of the menstrual cycle was known only in 1923. Only very recently have studies been made of the number of children women were likely to have who made no effort to restrain their fecundity.[10]

---

[9] For a development of the points in the two paragraphs above, see Cépède, Houtart, and Grond, *Population and Food*, pp. 216–227.

[10] See Paul Vincent, "Etude d'un groupe de familles nombreuses," *Population* 16 (1961), 105–112 (report of a study of 14,000 families who had been candidates for the Prix Cognacq-Jay, a French prize for fertility).

These facts, discovered since 1875, were relevant to what the purposes of sexual intercourse could be said to be. The theologians had shaped their arguments and conclusions in the light of the biology of their day. Relying on erroneous biological data, they had made intercourse in menstruation or in pregnancy mortal sin. Their arguments against contraception had also been constructed in the light of the biology they knew. Until well into the twentieth century, some theologians continued to believe that their predecessors, who had known nothing of the basic constituents of generation, spermatozoa and ova, had been enlightened as to the only way in which the natural law of reproduction could be observed. There were signs, however, as will be observed, that this confidence in ancient misconceptions was becoming obsolete.

Psychology also presented relevant fresh data — less unassailable than the biological information, but better verified than the casual observations of human behavior made before empirical psychology existed. The penetration of personality by sexuality was suggested. The focus of the old theological approach on distinct genital acts as the chief criterion of marital virtue was implicitly challenged. A greater understanding of the interaction of persons in marriage and the place of sexual intercourse in their relationship was obtained.[11]

Sociology, another science to develop only at the end of the nineteenth century, brought information on the growth and decline of populations where rough guessing had formerly sufficed. Anthropology provided new information on human sexual behavior. The kinds of data these new sciences offered were not to be mistaken for moral judgments. In trying to prescind from their own prejudices, the sociologists and anthropologists often claimed to offer only statistics or observations. Moral theologians could not determine the good way of behavior merely from the average way that was described. But neither could they make judgments about the ideal requirements of man without attention to these data. "Before the age of sociology," wrote Canon Jacques Leclerq, professor of moral and social philosophy at Louvain, "these questions have never been studied"; and by "these questions" he said he meant "the natural conditions of the family order."[12]

It is platitudinous to remark that the modern consciousness is historical. But it may not be superfluous to observe that the development of this consciousness was of immense importance for a subject so immersed in history as moral theology. Sensitive as a writer like Liguori had been to differences of opinion among his predecessors, he treated the dif-

---

[11] E.g., Ignace Lepp, *The Psychology of Loving*, trans. Bernard B. Gilligan (Baltimore, 1963), pp. 21–24, 133–166.

[12] Jacques Leclerq, "Natural Law the Unknown," *Natural Law Forum* 7 (1962), 10–13.

ferences as though they were talking of the same case. In his introduction to his *Moral Theology* he reviewed earlier works of moral theology from patristic times to his own day. He noted that the scholastic treatment of moral topics was "by far better and fuller" than that of the penitentials; he rebuked the rigorists of his age who "boast much of the Fathers, value the Popes little, and esteem more recent theologians not at all" (*Moral Theology*, Prolegomena, 1.66). But although he was aware that methods had changed, and although he defended the right of modern theologians to contribute modern solutions, Liguori ignored the environmental context. For him all writers of the past stood on the same flat line; all were supposed to have sought the same abstractly rational result. In the nineteenth century, moral theology had immunized itself from excesses of German historicism by conceding nothing to history, first copying eighteenth-century casuistry, then attempting a literal restatement of St. Thomas. Occasional apologetical necessities led to historical discriminations, as in the case of Francis X. Funk's *Zins und Wucher*, which tried to explain the evolution of the doctrine on usury. But moral theology in general, and the sexual ethic in particular, were proof against the historical spirit. Only when Western society was saturated by it, only when no respectable intellectual process could be undertaken without it, did the moral theologians succumb. The consequence began to be clear in the books which, beginning with *Der Usus matrimonii* of Lindner in 1929, sought to explore historically the development of doctrine on sexual ethics.[13]

Developments in philosophy also had a substantial effect on the framework of the old prohibition. About 1850 Thomism began to be thought of by some Italian ecclesiastics as a solution to the evils of the day. After the encyclical *Aeterni Patris* of Leo XIII, issued August 4, 1879, Thomism was the cry in Catholic circles. At Louvain in 1882 Désiré Mercier instituted a course in Thomistic philosophy, capping it with the establishment in 1895 of the Higher Institute of Philosophy.[14] The 1917 Code of Canon Law represented the apogee of the movement Leo XIII had launched. Canon 1366, sec. 2, prescribed that the teaching of philosophy and theology must be "according to the arguments, doctrine, and principles of St. Thomas, which they [the professors] are to hold inviolately." The Catholic University of America was committed to a literal Thomism and remained so, as did the Angelicum and the Lateran University in Rome. In other parts of Europe, however, in the 1920's the phenom-

---

[13] The pioneer work was Dominikus Lindner's *Der Usus matrimonii: Eine Untersuchung über seine sittliche Bewertung in der katholischen Moraltheologie alter und neuer Zeit* (Munich, 1929).

[14] On the slow rebirth of Thomism and the work of Mercier at Louvain, see Louis de Raeymaeker, *Le Cardinal Mercier et l'Institut Supérieur de Philosophie de Louvain* (Louvain, 1952), pp. 40, 47–62.

enology of Edmund Husserl and Max Scheler and the existentialist personalism of Gabriel Marcel became fecund influences on Catholic thought. A personalist conception of natural law came to compete with a literally Thomistic view. Thus, by 1962, a contemporary Dutch Dominican, M. Plattel, could note that natural law at one time was conceived of by analogy with a static world order in terms which emphasized the givenness of biological imperatives. Today, in a personalist perspective, natural law "appeals to the authentic choice of man, who, from his very being as a person, must fashion a concrete universal image of man, more in the manner of a creator than of a conformist . . . [It possesses] a dynamic, functional character because of its active orientation toward the ideal personal community." As biological regularity became less emphasized than the freedom of the spiritual person, so, Plattel said, it became more difficult to insist that biological norms should completely govern human acts.[15] As this concept of natural law was advanced, so the most basic concepts in the analysis of the law prohibiting contraception were affected.

All of this intellectual development — biological, medical, psychological, sociological, historical, and philosophical — created a world of data and of mental attitudes very different from the world in which contraception had been analyzed since the second century after Christ. Both the facts and the methods of analyzing them were fresh.

The internal structures of the Church. The teaching on contraception might have remained static, immunized against the social and intellectual changes, if the institutional life of the Church had not also been modified. This modification, itself partially the product of the new environmental forces, made it more probable that the Church would consciously respond to the environmental developments.

Catholic higher education began to recover from the nadir of 1800. In the 1820's Catholic faculties of theology were established at Tübingen and Munich. In the 1830's Louvain was refounded with some claim to moral continuity with the medieval university. It was only in 1876, however, that Catholic universities became legal in France and only in 1876 that the Institut Catholique was founded. In the United States a beginning was made in 1889 with the founding of the Catholic University of America as a center for graduate study. In the nineteenth century, Louvain and the theological faculties at the German universities proved the most fruitful institutions. The French centers were first buffeted by the fierce anticlerical battles of the 1880's and 1890's, then shaken by the crisis of the Modernist errors from 1900 to 1908. The Catholic University of America became, for the most part, an enlarged seminary. None of these institutions had much immediate impact on the work of moral

[15] M. G. Plattel, "Personal Response and the Natural Law," *Natural Law Forum* 7 (1962), 36–37.

theology; its status in 1900 was almost as low as in 1800.[16] The problems engaging attention seemed more fundamental: the existence of God, the truth of the Catholic claim, the relation of the Church to society. Lecomte's work on ovulation stands out as an exception. It was not until the 1920's that much influence of the German and French faculties, Louvain, and the Catholic University of America on moral theology could be discerned. The consequences were more indirect than direct. The universities did provide bases where the advances in knowledge could be related to Catholicism. The universities did form a community of men interested in developing the self-consciousness of the Church in its incarnation in the world. Only in the 1960's, however, did the existing Catholic universities, joined now by Nymegen in the Netherlands, St. Michael's College at Toronto, and Notre Dame, St. Louis, and Georgetown in the United States, contribute substantially to what had been the province of the seminaries. The importance for the development of moral doctrine of Catholic institutions not encumbered by the job of providing practical training for priests became evident. The universities showed promise of bringing an academic detachment, a speculative boldness, and an historical perspective to matters where pastoral and apologetical needs had played a dominant role.

The slow and uncompleted growth of the Catholic universities was intimately connected with another growth within the Church, the expression of loyal, critical, and free opinion. The counter forces within the Church were strong. Even before the Reformation, ecclesiastical authority had been suspicious of a free press. Since the Fifth Lateran Council in 1515, a form of prior restraint on books had existed in the requirement that any book bearing on Catholic doctrine carry the imprimatur of the bishop of the diocese of the publisher; the old rule was continued in substance, but without the earlier severe penalties, in canon 1385 of the 1917 Code of Canon Law.[17] In addition to this theoretical commitment

---

[16] By the end of the nineteenth century the state of Catholic moral theology was not perceptibly improved in comparison with its state in 1800. Cardinal d'Annibale could observe, "What the old theologians considered broadly and at length we scarcely touch with our fingertips" (Summula theologiae moralis, 3rd ed., Rome, 1892, I, 12). An anonymous reviewer in the Jesuits' Civiltà Cattolica could agree, adding that "with few exceptions, we have a mass of compendiums made and fashioned with a somnolency almost senile" (Civiltà Cattolica, series 14, 6 [1890], 443). Thomas Bouquillon (1840–1902), a professor at the Catholic University of America, found that moral theology had "failed to put itself in touch with new currents of thought, failed to anticipate problems of life." "Moral Theology," he concluded, "is all but an outcast." Bouquillon, "Moral Theology at the End of the Nineteenth Century," Bulletin of The Catholic University of America, April 1899, pp. 246–248.

[17] The bull of Leo X, Inter sollicitudines, May 4, 1515, after rejoicing in the benefits of printing, observed that a number of books were being printed which led people into errors of faith or morals. The Pope, with the approval of the ecumenical council, decreed, under penalty of the burning of the book and the fining and excommunica-

to the right of authority to restrain free expression by any Catholic, there were special restrictions on members of religious orders. Members of a religious order were subject not only to the bishop's imprimatur but, according to the law established by Trent and reaffirmed by canon 1385, to censorship from their own order. Not only were they bound to respect Catholic dogma; often they were prevented from writing anything which would disturb the posture or image which their superiors believed appropriate to their order. Beyond the canonical requirements of censorship, administrative sanctions existed. Removal from a teaching position could be used by a bishop or a religious superior against any priest teaching in a seminary if he expressed unsound or unwelcome opinion. The mere existence of this power of removal, subject to little practical restraint, was generally sufficient to impose silence on priests with dangerously new ideas. The effect of this censorship was especially severe on moral theology because so much of it was written by members of the orders. With a few exceptions at Paris and Louvain — Le Maistre, Major, Sinnich — almost all the moral theology on sexual matters from the second quarter of the thirteenth century to the first quarter of the twentieth was written by priests under the special discipline of a religious order.

Administrative control of theological speculation produced a situation in which no one could pretend that what was written represented what

---

tion of the author, that no book should be published without the approval of the bishop of the diocese and the approval of the inquisitor of the diocese (*Inter sollicitudines,* in *Codicis iuris canonici fontes,* ed. Peter Gasparri, Rome, 1923, I, 115–116). This legislation was renewed as to the requirement of approval of the bishop by the Council of Trent, April 8, 1546, Session IV, *De editione et usu sacrorum librorum,* as to books "on sacred matters," in a context which arguably restricted the law to books on sacred scripture, but was more broadly interpreted by the canonists. This legislation also made it mandatory for members of religious orders to have the approval of their superiors (Mansi 33:22–23). The penalty of excommunication was renewed in the same terms, as to "books treating of sacred matters," by Pius IX in the constitution *Apostolicae Sedis moderationi, Fontes* III, 28. The Constitution of Leo XIII, *Officiorum ac munerum (Fontes* III, 502–512), of January 25, 1897, expanded the term to include explicitly "books regarding the sacred Scriptures, sacred theology, ecclesiastical history, canon law, natural theology, ethics, and other religious and moral disciplines of this kind, and generally all writing of special interest to religion and decent morals." The penalty of excommunication was dropped. The 1917 Code followed this approach, eliminating the phrase "all writing of special interest to religion and decent morals." The license could be given by the bishop of the diocese of the author or of the printer or of the place of publication. Laymen were explicitly included by the canon. The additional obligation of permission from their major superior was imposed on members of religious orders (canon 1385). As recently as 1941, the Holy Office exhorted bishops to be more careful in granting permission for publication (*AAS* 33:121), and in 1943 the Holy Office called attention to the obligation imposed by canon 1397 on all the faithful, but especially clerics, to report pernicious books to the local bishops or the Apostolic See (*AAS* 35:144). There is no express penalty now provided for disobedience to canon 1385, and in practice in the last twenty years it has often been ignored by Catholic laymen.

was thought by all theologians. The result was not insincerity on the part of those who wrote openly with a strong conviction of the rightness of their views, but silence, involuntary or voluntary, from those who disagreed. An unhealthy climate for discussion was created when it was not certain that all the thinking of theologians was being communicated. This climate, characteristic of many seminaries in which university influences were absent, prevailed particularly from 1800 to the very recent past. It was notable that in the controversy over the progesterone pill Van der Marck could remark that "many opinions" on the issue did not appear in print, and that Bishop Reuss found it necessary to begin his article with a strong plea for candor: "Despite all the fidelity which is due the common doctrine, the theologian should teach nothing as absolutely valid when he is not himself convinced that it is legitimate." [18] It was common knowledge that in private some theologians were freer and bolder in their expressions on the subject of contraception than they dared to be in any publication.[19]

Despite the continuation of restraints on discussion, a new trend in the theological defense of freedom was apparent. A pioneer essay was "On Consulting the Faithful in Matters of Doctrine," by John Henry Newman. Writing in 1859, Newman drew on the process by which Pius IX had reached the decision to promulgate the dogma of the Immaculate Conception: "Pope Pius has given us a pattern, in his manner of defining, of the duty of considering the sentiments of the laity upon a point of tradition, in spite of whatever fullness of evidence the bishops had already thrown upon it." [20] Newman added that in the fourth century it was the faithful who had preserved the true doctrine on the Trinity when the majority of the bishops had gone over to the Arian heresy. This occasional piece, designed to vindicate an expression of Newman's, necessarily vindicated the freedom of all members of the Church. In the pontificate of Pius IX it was received with cold hostility in Rome.[21]

Newman was the outstanding Catholic theologian of the nineteenth century. His thesis was neglected in his time. But, as often in the history

[18] Willem van der Marck, "Vruchtbaarheidsregeling," *Tijdschrift voor Theologie* 3 (1963), 378; Josef Maria Reuss, "Don mutuel des époux," *La Vie spirituelle* 17, Supplement (1964), 104.

[19] Cf. Louis Dupré, *Contraception and Catholics: A New Appraisal* (Baltimore, 1964), p. 86: "In their personal convictions, many moralists are far more advanced than in their publications. It is regrettable that at least the technical publications do not reflect more of the doubts concerning the traditional position which are so widespread in theological circles."

[20] John Henry Newman, "On Consulting the Faithful in Matters of Doctrine," *Rambler,* July 1859; reprinted and amended in Newman, *The Arians of the Fourth Century* (London, 1879); separately published, ed. John Coulson (London, 1961). The quoted passage is on p. 104 of the Coulson edition.

[21] John Coulson, Introduction to *On Consulting the Faithful in Matters of Doctrine,* pp. 36–42.

of theology, a principle was reasserted by the Church when the world had most absolutely denied it. In reaction to the totalitarian Nazi and Communist regimes, the idea of freedom was vindicated. Speaking on February 17, 1950, to an International Congress of Writers of Catholic Newspapers, Pius XII brought out the evil of a totalitarian society in which only the opinion of the leaders is heard. To reduce citizens to silence is, he said, "an attack on the natural right of man, a violation of the order of the world as God has established it." He concluded with a word on "public opinion in the very breast of the Church (naturally, in matters left to free discussion)." The Church, he said, "is a living body, and something would be lacking in its life if public opinion defaulted in it, a default for which the pastors and the faithful would be responsible" (*AAS* 42:251, 256). Pius XII's reservation, "naturally, in matters left to free discussion," was an exception that could have swallowed the rule. But a new note had been sounded by a Pope: a free public opinion was a natural part of every society. The Pope also recognized that "the Church" could not be identified with the authorities — Pope, bishops, theologians. The laity, he told the college of cardinals on February 20, 1946, "are the Church" (*AAS* 38:141).

Using the remarks of Pius XII to the press as a springboard, a leading Catholic theologian of the twentieth century, the Austrian Jesuit Karl Rahner, in 1953 wrote *Free Speech in the Church*. Fifty years before, he noted, one would hardly have expected the words of Pius XII on the lips of a Pope. Rahner went on to distinguish two kinds of opinion within the Church. First, he noted that the Holy Spirit "can breathe upon whomsoever he will in the Church — even the poor, the children, those who are 'least in the kingdom of God.' " The Church which teaches and the Church which is taught are the same Church. "The 'Church taught' has its own understanding of the Faith, its own kind of 'infallibility' — in the sense that not only the teaching Church but the 'Church taught,' as a whole, will always remain within the orbit of divine truth, safe under the power of the Holy Spirit." [22] This kind of supernaturally protected opinion, of which Newman wrote, was to be distinguished from another kind of public opinion to which Rahner addressed himself, which was not necessarily the effect of the guidance of the Holy Spirit: "Its justification is simply that this is the sole means of discovering what is really going on. If there is any real desire to know the current situation — spiritual, psychological, social, etc. — then Catholics must be allowed (within the limits already laid down) to talk their heads off." [23] The limits of discussion were what "comes into conflict with the Church's dogma and her

[22] Karl Rahner, *Das freie Wort in der Kirche* (Einsiedeln, 1953); English translation, *Free Speech in the Church* (New York, 1959). The quotation is on pp. 18–19 of the English translation.

[23] *Ibid.*, p. 25.

divinely willed constitution." But, Rahner added, "there is always a strong tendency to narrow down far too closely the range of what parts of the Faith can be legitimately discussed." He observed, "If there is, as there should be, a real public opinion within the Church, not merely an unthinking reflection of the Church's official views, a certain tension is likely to exist around all those matters that are subject to change and hence to free discussion." [24]

With some theological and ecclesiastical encouragement, then, free speech became more prized in the Church. The universities embodied the principle and at the same time provided persons capable of exercising the right. Finally, "the spirit of Pope John," and the climate of freedom from bureaucratic surveillance created by the open discussion at the Second Vatican Council, produced an atmosphere in which frank discussion of the basic prohibition of contraception could occur. Whether the speakers were only Catholics talking their heads off, or whether their witness constituted the *consensus fidelium*, the divinely protected expression of Christian faith, was not immediately determinable.

The emergence of the universities and the later development of articulate discussion were closely associated with an increasing role for the laity in the Church. Before the founding of magazines edited by Catholic laymen but not under ecclesiastical control, there was no institutional form designed to express the opinion of the laity on matters in the Church. In the United States, the way was led by *Commonweal*, founded in 1924, followed by *Cross Currents, Jubilee, The Critic,* and *Ramparts*. These magazines were both symbols of and outlets for an educated Catholic laity which was seriously concerned with the teaching of the Church. The articulation of lay sentiment had special significance for the analysis of contraception. [25]

In declaring evil an act of contraception performed by lawfully wedded persons, the theologians had condemned an act which was literally beyond their experience. The number of married men who had written as Catholic theologians on contraception could be numbered on a hand — Joannes Andreae is the only prominent name. Obviously, experience is not a precondition for judging the morality of an act intelligently. All condemn murder, though few are murderers. Observation, empathy with the experience of others, reasoning, can be the process of moral judg-

---

[24] *Ibid.*, pp. 27, 42.

[25] On the new phenomenon of an educated, articulate, and concerned laity in the United States, see Daniel Callahan, *The Mind of the Catholic Layman* (New York, 1963); Donald Thorman, *The Emerging Catholic Layman* (New York, 1963); Michael Novak, *A New Generation: American and Catholic* (New York, 1964). The Christian Family Movement, an essentially lay organization designed to study Christian principles and apply them to family life, numbered 11,000 couples in 1956 (John L. Thomas, S.J., *The American Catholic Family*, Englewood Cliffs, N.J., 1956, pp. 428–430). By 1965 it numbered over 40,000.

ment. At the same time the characteristic problems and joys of one occupation or state of life are usually more acutely perceived and feelingly expressed by those who experience them. To judge rightly of the morality of particular acts may require close listening to those who have had experience of the way of living in which the questions arise.

The theologians of the past had heard the sins of many married folk recounted in confession, but the context in which communication occurred did not invite impartial evaluation of the experience. The theologians may also have had limited and probably inhibited conversations on the subject with spiritual advisers, friends, and kin. But there is a uniqueness to random individual testimony that could easily cause it to be discounted in the face of any strong official position. The lay voice on marriage was never entirely lost after the late fifteenth century, when it played a part in framing the new doctrine on the purposes of marital intercourse. It was not much listened to. When Bishop Bouvier cited the belief of the younger couples of Le Mans that contraception was not a sin, the testimony of the laity never rose to the dignity of an argument that contraception was lawful, but was used to support the plea that their good faith not be unsettled. The laity spoke, but their testimony was individual, oral, unsystematic, and not expressed in theological categories. To most theologians it failed to be persuasive or even relevant.

It was, then, a capital event in the development of testimony when in the fall of 1964 there appeared *The Experience of Marriage*, edited by Michael Novak, in which thirteen Catholic couples stated their own experiences in attempting to observe the theological doctrines on contraception and on rhythm. There had been harbingers within the preceding twelve months in the form of magazine articles by laymen. The book, open to criticism from all sides, was a limited pledge that the experiences reported were not idiosyncratic. It preserved in a form available to all future theologians the voices of educated married American Catholics in 1964.

Not only did the direct written testimony of laymen add new data. The testimony of women was added. In twenty centuries no Catholic woman had written on contraception. The emancipation of women in the late nineteenth century was particularly resisted by some Catholic churchmen who identified a given social structure with the Gospel; as late as 1930 a portion of *Casti connubii* gave a caricature of feminine emancipation and deplored the consequences. But by the 1960's there were many Catholic women who had been sufficiently emancipated by education to be able to articulate their views on marriage and contraception. There was testimony now not only of the experience of the married, but of those who bore the children.

Finally, a factor, partly external, partly internal, began to be of importance in the light of ecumenical developments. This was the testimony of the other Christian churches. As long as hostility to "the heretics" marked Catholic relations with these bodies, there was a negative reaction to doctrinal development by Protestants. But with the inauguration of a new approach by John XXIII and the institution in 1961 of the Secretariat for Christian Unity as a Roman office, a new appreciation became apparent of the many Christian beliefs, signs, and values shared by Catholic and non-Catholic Christians. In this era of dialogue, the testimony of the other churches became important.

Beginning with the Anglican decision in 1929, a large number of churches publicly abandoned the absolute prohibition of contraception by married couples. What was especially striking was the change in position of the bodies whose general theology was closest to Catholic thought: the Anglican, Lutheran, and Calvinist communions. The bodies changing their stand were as follows: the Congregational Christian General Council (1931); the General Council of the United Church of Canada (1936); the Methodist Conference of Great Britain (1939); the British Council of Churches (1943); a special commission of the Church of Scotland (1944); the bishops of the (Lutheran) Church of Sweden (1951); the General Synod of the Netherlands Reformed Church (1952); the Augustana Evangelical Lutheran Church (1954); the General Conference of the Methodist Church in the United States (1956); the United Lutheran Church in the United States (1956); the National Council of the Reformed Church of France (1956); the (Lutheran) Church of Finland (1956); the International Convention of the Disciples of Christ (1958); the World Council of Churches (1959). A similar position against any absolute prohibition of contraception was taken by such leading theologians as Derrick Sherwin Bailey, Karl Barth, Emil Brunner, Jacques Ellul and Reinhold Niebuhr.[26] A substantial consensus of Christian

---

[26] The positions of the churches and the theologians is set out in Richard M. Fagley, *The Population Explosion and Christian Responsibility* (New York, 1960), pp. 195–208. An international study group, convened at the instance of officers of the World Council of Churches and the International Missionary Council, met at Mansfield College, Oxford, April 12–15, 1959, and adopted a statement on "Responsible Parenthood and the Population Problem," otherwise known as the Mansfield Report. The Report said that married persons in deciding how many children to have should act after deliberation together in love, valuing children as persons in their own right, recognizing the witness a Christian family offered of the fruit of the Spirit even in the most adverse physical conditions, and taking into account the social needs, including the population pressures, of the region in which they lived. If the decision was reached not to have a child, there was no moral difference between use of the infertile period, artificial barriers to the meeting of the sperm and ovum, and drugs regulating ovulation ("Responsible Parenthood and the Population Problem," paragraphs 19 and 22, printed in Fagley, pp. 231–233).

The Lambeth Conference in 1958 also emphasized the duty of responsible parenthood in the light of "a thoughtful consideration of the varying population needs and problems of society and the claims of future generations" (The Lambeth Conference,

thought in the West outside the Catholic Church now approved of some form of contraception.[27]

The consciousness of the Church itself could not but be affected by the new institutional forms, the new voices, the new freedom within it, and the Christian testimony outside it. These developments produced new data on the question of contraception; they brought into being new attitudes; they created a demand for greater clarity and rationality in the rules against contraception.

THE DEVELOPMENT OF DOCTRINE

Between 1850 and 1964 the teaching of the Church on the purposes of marital intercourse experienced substantial evolution. The process partly reflected the environmental changes, partly reflected the new voices speaking in the Church, partly represented a work of self-criticism by the theologians. This evolution reached the point where the question was asked: Is contraception sometimes permissible? And the broad question met the technical question raised by surgery and the pill: When is sterilization permissible?

PLEASURE AND LOVE AS VALUES IN COITUS

In the age of St. Alphonsus Liguori, pure Augustinianism, represented by writers like Billuart, still held a strong position. By 1850 the triumph of St. Alphonsus had banished Augustinian doctrine on the sole lawful intent with which intercourse might be initiated. But the Augustinian distrust of pleasure and indifference to love as purposes of intercourse remained. A new step was taken by the humble compendium of Gury.

Gury declared that marital intercourse was lawful for any one of four purposes: "the generation of offspring"; "the satisfaction of the obligation"; "the avoidance of incontinence in oneself or one's partner"; "the desire of fostering or bringing about decent friendship, of manifesting or promoting conjugal affection, and so forth." No reasons were given for this conclusion, but authority was cited as follows: "So commonly with Liguori, n. 881, Sanchez, and others, against others who eliminate the

---

1958, resolution 115). Nothing was said as to means of contraception. The Committee which had prepared the report which led to the resolution had said, "The *means* of family planning are in large measure matters of clinical and aesthetic choice, subject to the requirement that they be admissible to the Christian conscience." The Anglican bishops did not go so far as the Committee.

[27] On the other hand, the Greek Orthodox Church, as far as can be judged, still opposes all contraception. A letter of the hierarchy of the Church of Greece in October 1937 condemned the "unnatural evil" of "escape from begetting children and nurturing them." In 1956 Archbishop Michael of the American archdiocese also condemned contraception (Fagley, *The Population Explosion*, pp. 164–166).

last two ends." [28] The names cited suggest how Gury had proceeded. He had taken the approach hesitantly adopted by Liguori himself of looking to the purposes of marriage to determine the purposes of intercourse. In his *Moral Theology* 6.881, Liguori had listed among the lawful extrinsic reasons for marrying the purpose "to effect peace among kingdoms and illustrious families." This social motive for marriage was the slender basis for Gury's "fostering or bringing about decent friendship." The awkwardness of the phrase came from its transfer from being the description of a motive for marriage to being the description of a purpose of intercourse. By the 1874 edition the inappropriate term "friendship" had been replaced by "love." Gury's other inspiration had been the proposition set out by Sanchez, and accepted by Liguori, that some acts short of coitus were lawful among spouses "to foster or show mutual love" (above, pp. 325, 329). This thesis was boldly, but logically, applied to coitus itself.

If the fostering of love or the manifesting of conjugal affection could be a lawful purpose of coitus, the old dispute over pleasure as a purpose lost some of its significance. As long as only procreation and avoidance of concupiscence were recognized as lawful purposes, the spontaneous desire for intercourse was suspect. The new theory meant that there were no longer only three possible categories, of which two were dutiful and virtuous and one was pleasure-seeking and mortally or venially sinful. Gury himself said of the pleasure purpose merely that the condemnation of Innocent XI applied to intercourse sought for pleasure alone. His reviser, Anthony Ballerini, developed this point by saying that to act for pleasure meant "positively excluding" the other ends of action so that one placed one's "last end" in the pleasure. Without such positive exclusion of other ends, it was lawful to seek pleasure in marital intercourse (Gury-Ballerini, *Compendium of Moral Theology* 1.28; 2.908). This almost complete acceptance of pleasure was attacked by the anonymous Redemptorist authors of the *Vindiciae Alphonsianae;* they urged that the old authorities stood to the contrary.[29] Ballerini answered them with a thorough defense of pleasure, joy, and enjoyment as proper human ends (Gury-Ballerini, *Compendium,* 1887 ed., 2.908). Ballerini was then followed in substance by the leading moralist of the day, Augustine Lehmkuhl (*Moral Theology* 2.850).

At the turn of the century a long review of the controversy by John Becker concluded with a vigorous defense of pleasure as a proper purpose in sexual intercourse — as proper a purpose as seeking pleasure in intellectual activity. But there was one caveat: to seek pleasure, excluding

---

[28] Gury, *Compendium of Moral Theology* (Turin, 1852), "Marriage," no. 688.

When Bouvier is reciting the arguments of the married laity in favor of coitus interruptus, he notes that it is said to "favor mutual love" (*Supplement to the Treatise on Marriage* 2.1.3.4).

[29] "Certain Redemptorist Theologians," *Vindiciae alphonsianae* (Rome, 1873), 7.8.

other objectives, was mortally sinful, because this rare state of mind excluded any relation of the act to God.[30] That pleasure was a proper end in marital intercourse, if other ends were not willfully excluded, was then supported by Jesuits such as Jerome Noldin and Arthur Vermeersch, Dominicans such as Dominic Prümmer and Benedict Merkelbach, and secular priests such as Alois de Smet. It would be fair to describe the position as common after 1900.[31]

The position was still subject to qualification. In his address to the Italian Catholic Society of Midwives on October 29, 1951, Pius XII said, "The Creator who in His goodness and wisdom has willed to conserve and propagate the human race through the instrumentality of man and woman by uniting them in marriage has ordained also that, in performing this function, husband and wife should experience pleasure and happiness in body and spirit. In seeking and enjoying this pleasure, therefore, couples do nothing wrong. They accept that which the Creator has given them" (*AAS* 43:851). This passage was followed by a strong warning against attributing a value to sexuality as such independently of the end of the procreation of a new life. The Pope's words taken alone could be read as saying that pleasure might be sought only when man and wife were performing "this function" of propagating the species. However, this reading would not be justified by the larger context of the allocution; the Pope had already admitted the lawfulness of intercourse on the basis of rhythm. His words were simply a rebuke to "anti-Christian hedonism" which would "obey blindly and without check the caprices and impulses of nature."

In the *Law of Christ*, the German Redemptorist Bernard Häring drew a different distinction. If one generally sought only pleasure in marital intercourse, one would be behaving with sinful hedonism; such was the teaching of Innocent XI's condemnation of the proposition on intercourse for pleasure alone. But the "sudden need" of pleasure might be the "occasion" for intercourse, and intercourse to meet this need was lawful.[32]

In 1963, the American Jesuit theologians John C. Ford and Gerald Kelly made this wry comment:

> If sexual pleasure is to serve as an inducement to propagate, then God must want men to choose the act because of the pleasure, not the other way round.

[30] Becker, "Die moralische Beurteilung des Handelns aus Lust," *Zeitschrift für katholische Theologie* 26 (1902), 679, 689.

[31] De Smet, *Les Fiançailles et le mariage* 2.1.1.3.1.1.; Noldin, *De sexto praecepto et de usu matrimonii*, 19th ed. (Innsbruck, 1923), no. 78.2; Vermeersch, *Theologiae moralis principia, responsa, consilia* (Bruges, 1922–1923), vol. IV, no. 53; Merkelbach, *Questions on Chastity and Lechery* 8.1.2.; Dominic Prümmer, *Manuale theologiae moralis* 3.701.5 (Freiburg im Breisgau, 1923).

[32] Bernard Häring, *Das Gesetz Christi*, 5th ed. (Freiburg im Breisgau, 1961).

If they were to choose the pleasure because of the act (a process psychologically difficult to envision), the pleasure would not be an inducement at all. The older authors seemed oblivious of this psychological aspect of the matter.

Ford and Kelly concluded that

those who consciously act for the pleasure of sexual intercourse, apprehended as something permissible, need no further explicit legitimating motive to escape the imputation of acting *ob solam voluptatem*. In other words, if their conduct in marital intimacies is such that it preserves the inherent purposes or values which belong to conjugal intimacy, the pleasure they seek is well-ordered.[33]

Pleasure was not unqualifiedly recognized as an independent value. But the opinion dominant from 1880 to the present was closer to Le Maistre and Major than to Augustine.

Pleasure as a purpose, then, received guarded acceptance. Love was to be given complete recognition. Gury's adaptation of Sanchez had been made without theoretical underpinning. In the later nineteenth century a more reasoned development was attempted. In Germany in 1850 Ferdinand Probst, in his vernacular *Moral Theology*, spoke of the sharing of life by husband and wife and said, "In the conjugal act alone this sharing finds its highest expression. By it the principal end of marriage becomes other [than procreation], to wit, precisely the sharing of undivided life of the spouses." [34] In 1878, also writing in the vernacular, Francis X. Linsenmann, professor of theology at Tübingen, distinguished between the subjective and objective purposes of coitus. Objectively, the primary purpose was procreation. Subjectively, the primary purpose was that "through the ordered appeasement of the natural drives the spiritual union of the spouses be consolidated." Making these distinctions, Linsenmann sought to integrate the end usually expressed as "satisfaction of concupiscence" into an account which found a positive spiritual value in intercourse.[35] At the turn of the century De Smet spoke as Trent had spoken of love in marriage, but added the un-Tridentine thought, "The marriage act itself, by which the partners are made one flesh, cultivates and nourishes this love" (*Les Fiançailles et le mariage* 2.1.3.1.4).

It was only after World War I, however, that there was a substantial development of the relation of intercourse to love. This advance in speculation occurred principally in Germany, and principally under the influence of the phenomenology of Edmund Husserl and Max Scheler. The most prominent of the early writers on the relationship was Dietrich von Hildebrand, professor of philosophy at the University of Munich, the

[33] Ford and Kelly, *Contemporary Moral Theology*, vol. II: *Marriage Questions* (Westminster, Md., 1963), pp. 192–193.
[34] Ferdinand Probst, *Katholische Moraltheologie* (Tübingen, 1848–1850), II, 180.
[35] Francis X. Linsenmann, *Lehrbuch der Moraltheologie* (Freiburg im Breisgau, 1878), p. 630.

first married layman to make a substantial contribution to Catholic doctrine on marriage. In lectures delivered to the Federation of Catholic Students at Innsbruck in 1925, Von Hildebrand spoke in lyrical terms of coitus. He rejected "the purely biological approach." The intention to propagate would not, by itself, "organically unite physical sex with the heart and spirit." The marital act, he declared, "has not only a function, the generation of children; it also possesses a significance for man as a human being (*in quantum homo*) — namely to be the expression and fulfillment of wedded love and community of life — and, moreover, it participates after a certain fashion in the sacramental meaning of matrimony." For the first time, a Catholic writer taught that love was a requirement of lawful, marital coition. He tied this novel demand to an ancient term — *fides*, fidelity. Fidelity required that person meet person in a giving of self. The old and long-used Augustinian comparison of intercourse to eating was rejected. The significance of eating was exhausted by its objective end. In eating it made no difference if one paid attention to the process of eating. But, in the marital act, "a fully deliberate, conscious attention is demanded." "The act of wedded communion has indeed the end [*Zweck*] of propagation, but in addition, the significance of a unique union of love." [36]

This evaluation of marital intercourse, where ideal aspirations were set out as guides, made an extreme contrast with Augustine and the whole patristic and medieval tradition. Yet Von Hildebrand was not an advocate of sexual activity deprived of religious criteria. His position was linked to the Catholic tradition by the special, sacral value assigned to the act of coition. The tradition had made coitus a sacral act free from human interference; Von Hildebrand first fully emphasized its content of love. With St. Albert, he saw a sacramental value in it; but, unlike St. Albert, he cut away completely from the Augustinian and scholastic approach that made procreation and a remedy for concupiscence the only values present. Not confusedly like Albert, not grudgingly like Gury, but enthusiastically, with conviction coming from the heart, Von Hildebrand made love central to the moral meaning of conjugal coitus.

The new approach, if not warmly accepted, was not attacked by *Casti connubii.* The encyclical quoted the Roman Catechism that "matrimonial fidelity" demanded a union in love. Love held in Christian marriage "a kind of primacy of excellence." The encyclical added that the "especial task" of this union was that "the spouses aid each other in more fully perfecting and conforming the interior man" (*AAS* 22:548). The emphasis on interior spiritual perfection scarcely responded to Von

[36] Dietrich von Hildebrand, *Reinheit und Jungfräulichkeit* (Munich, 1928); English translation, *In Defense of Purity* (New York, 1931), pp. 20, 22. Quotations are from the English translation.

Hildebrand's emphasis on coitus as expressive of love. But love, even if not considered in its physical expression, was given a place in marriage which the sixteenth-century teaching had ignored. Where the Roman Catechism had said that the primary reason for marriage was mutual aid in bearing the burdens of life, the encyclical made a reinterpretation and enlarged the teaching: "This mutual interior formation of the partners, this earnest desire of perfecting one another, can be said in a very true sense, as the Roman Catechism teaches, to be the primary reason and cause for marriage, if marriage is not considered strictly as instituted for the proper procreation and education of children, but is more broadly taken as a sharing, way, and partnership of all of life."

To this point, the encyclical had exalted the importance of love, but only in relation to spiritual development. It went on: "This same charity ought to harmonize with all the rest of the rights and duties of the spouses; and so it is not only the law of justice, it is the rule of charity that must be recognized in the word of the Apostle, 'Let the husband render to his wife the debt, and equally the wife to her husband'" (*AAS* 22:548–549). In this restrained reference to charity and "the debt," the thesis of Von Hildebrand, that love must animate intercourse, was faintly reflected. No attempt was made to develop the relation between coitus and the perfection of the other spouse and the communion of lives. But, for the first time in a papal document, coitus and love were linked. The proposition owed to Gury and ultimately to Sanchez was restated, if not emphasized: among the "secondary ends" of marital intercourse was "the fostering of mutual love." Provided "the intrinsic nature" of coitus was safeguarded, spouses were "not forbidden" to have this secondary end in view (*AAS* 22:561). This lukewarm teaching marked a stage in the absorption of the new approach. The encyclical was not a vigorous affirmation of the personal values attainable in intercourse, and in stressing that procreation was the primary end of intercourse it ran counter to some personalist thought. But it was only the beginning of discussion.

Five years later Von Hildebrand's ideas were restated and enlarged by Herbert Doms in *The Meaning and End of Marriage*.[37] Doms was to have, in a different way, as great an influence on the next quarter century of Catholic thought on marriage as Vermeersch had had on the first quarter. Doms, born in 1890 in Regensburg, had been a student of zoology before becoming a priest; he earned doctorates in both philosophy and theology; and in 1935 he was a *Privatdozent* teaching Catholic

---

[37] Herbert Doms, *Vom Sinn und Zweck der Ehe* (Breslau, 1935); French translation by Paul and Marie Thisse, *Du sens et de la fin du mariage*, revised and augmented by the author (Paris, 1937); English translation, *The Meaning of Marriage* (New York, 1941). Citations are to the French edition. A brief biography of Doms is given at the end of a second book by him, *Dieses Geheimnis ist gross* (Cologne, 1960).

theology at the University of Breslau. In his book he said eloquently what serious Catholic laymen were waiting to hear: not only marriage, but marital intercourse, was a means of achieving holiness. The theory sketched by Von Hildebrand was given solidity and buttressed by scholarship. Doms provided biological data; a critique of St. Thomas' analysis of marriage; an explicit evocation of the passages from St. Albert on the sacramental significance of intercourse; and a discussion of the related ideas of Max Scheler. *The Meaning and End of Marriage* was the most comprehensive attempt yet made to develop a theory of Catholic marriage different from that of Augustine. It did not succeed in wholly winning the professional moral theologians, but its influence on later Catholic writing on marriage was inescapable.

The biological end, Doms argued, could not be the primary end. The sperm might or might not meet the egg, whose production did not depend on the sexual act. The Thomistic theory rested on the belief that the active form, the male seed, immediately acted on the female matter; of course, this was a biological misconception (*The Meaning and End of Marriage* [French edition, 1937], pp. 73–74). Doms's own thesis was as follows: "In the perfect act, worthy of human beings, the two partners grasp each other reciprocally in intimate love; that is, spiritually they reciprocally give themselves in an act which contains the abandonment and enjoyment of the whole person and is not simply an isolated activity of organs" (*ibid.*, p. 27). The act of marital coitus was an ontological act, that is, an act affecting the being of the persons who interacted; a true, not symbolic, abandonment of oneself; a completion of oneself in the other. The elementary human desire to have relationship with a person was realized in the actuation and completion of the two partners (*ibid.*, pp. 48, 54–55).

Doms's theory was comprehensive enough to account for at least seven practices in the life of the Church which the Augustinian-Thomistic theory made incomprehensible. Four of these practices related to sterile intercourse. If ontological completion of the person, not procreation, was the end of marriage, the marriage and the intercourse of the sterile could be understood. Similarly coitus in pregnancy had an understandable end. Sterile marriages were indissoluble, because the ontological union held although procreation was impossible. The fornication of the sterile was illicit, for ontological union could be realized only in the way ordained by God, although no offspring would result (*ibid.*, pp. 104, 97, 101, 191). The rule on sterility was explicably different from that on impotency; for the impotent, union was impossible (*ibid.*, p. 172). The Pope's long-recognized power to dissolve sacramental unconsummated marriages when one spouse wanted to enter religious life was also given a rationale: the absence of completed ontological union made dissolution possible (*ibid.*, p. 107). Finally, the ancient and still existing disfavor for remarriage on the death of a spouse was also accounted for: the second ontological completion was unnecessary and in a sense diminished the first (*ibid.*, p. 172). All of these common practices in the Church were anomalies in a theory which said that procreation was the primary purpose of marriage. All were at least harmoniously explained by Doms. Again and again Doms offered a better explanation of the treatment of sterility; again and again he hit the weakness of the Augustinian position. To touch the keys of an organ when the pipes are not working, he observed, is not to play the organ; nor can one pressing the soundless keys be said to have the primary purpose of playing. To say coital acts were directed to offspring by persons who because of their physical condition could not have offspring was, Doms declared, nonsense (*ibid.*, p. 180).

The theory of Doms had four additional merits. The old approach treated pleasure like bait, and the spouse seeking intercourse like an animal lured by the bait to procreate. Doms said that the pleasure and sentiment experienced were great, not as bait to action, but as reflections of the profound ontological change involved. The old theory took little account of the ordinary absence of a conscious desire to procreate in any given act of intercourse. Doms's position reflected the primacy of the consciousness of personal fulfillment. Even when spouses consciously desired children, he observed, the emphasis on personal accomplishment was often reflected by the statement "I am becoming a parent." The old theory treated the generative organs as though they had a finality of their own apart from the human person. Doms's theory rested on the fact that sexuality marked the whole human person. What was involved in the sexual exchange was not the finality of the genital organs alone, but the finality of the person. Finally, the old theory had nothing to say on the sacramental structure of marital intercourse. Doms boldly developed the parallel with the Eucharist. The physical union in marriage completed the moral participation in the life of the other just as physical union with Christ in the Eucharist completed the believer's moral union with Christ (*ibid.*, pp. 23–27, 127).

Doms proposed an integrated new approach to Catholic marriage. No one would have supposed that anything so new and so complete would win instantaneous acceptance. In fact, Doms was met by one of those official reactions which so often have checked enthusiasm without fundamentally stopping progress. Doms had discarded the classic terminology of "primary" and "secondary" ends in marriage. Marital intercourse had an "immanent" end or meaning, the realization of interpersonal union. It had a procreative end, which Doms called the *finis operis* and treated as the end for which coitus might be accomplished. In the work of another personalist writer, Bernhardin Krempel, a Swiss Passionist, marriage was said to have only one essential end, the perpetual union of the lives of two persons of opposite sex. On April 1, 1944, the Holy Office noted that in some recent writings "a meaning is attached to words which occur in the teaching of the Church (for example, *end, primary, secondary*) which is not appropriate to these words according to their common use among theologians." With this word of explanation, the Holy Office answered the question: "Can the opinion of certain modern writers be admitted, who either deny that the primary end of marriage is the generation and education of children or teach that the secondary ends are not essentially subordinate to the primary end, but are equally principal and independent?" (*AAS* 36:103). The answer was, No. There was no note of doctrinal censure attached. Doms was not mentioned by name, and, arguably, Krempel's book rather than his contained the propositions criticized. Nonetheless, Doms was asserted to be the object of the decree by the *Nouvelle revue théologique* (67:839), which seemed to have access to unidentified but highly placed sources. The official rebuke addressed to a particular aspect of his book weakened its prestige as a whole. In the long run, however, the moral theology of the Church is determined not by decrees but by a more complicated process of reasoning by the theologians and response by the faithful. In the evaluation of marriage and marital intercourse after 1944, the book of Doms continued to play a preeminent part.

Reinforcement of the personalist position came in an unexpected way and from an unexpected quarter only seven years after the action of the Holy Office. To understand the development, it is necessary to return to 1897. In this year the Inquisition had acted on a very simple question, "May artificial insemination be applied to a woman?" The answer of the Congregation, approved by Leo XIII on March 26, 1897, had been negative (*ASS* 29:704). The question put was extraordinarily abstract; it did not introduce the supposition that the semen came from the woman's husband. At this time theologians such as Lehmkuhl (*Moral Theology* 2.835) and Ballerini and Palmieri in their revision of Gury (*Compendium* 6.1304) were teaching that semen resulting from marital coitus might lawfully be placed by instrument in the vagina, while it was unlawful to obtain semen by the ejaculation of the husband apart from intercourse. An anonymous commentator in the *Nouvelle revue théologique* (29:324) observed that the decision did not change this teaching.

In his book Doms argued that the 1897 decrees supported his position. The sexual act was there regarded not merely as a means to a biological end. It was regarded as an act meaningful in itself; and this meaning imposed restraints even upon an action which achieved the biological end of generation (*The Meaning and End of Marriage*, p. 187). Doms had an argument. But could the decree be accounted for only by a personalist theory of intercourse? Francis Hürth, who had succeeded Vermeersch as the leading Jesuit authority on sexual matters, thought not. Artificial insemination was immoral because nature had determined the manner of reproduction "in the smallest details," and "it would be absurd to abandon to the good pleasure of man the right of choosing this manner or of replacing it by another he has invented." His line of reasoning barred even the insertion by instrument of semen emitted in lawful coitus.[38] The insistence on the rigidity of the natural order paralleled the Thomistic argument against contraception based on the natural structure of the act, and avoided any concession to the personalist perspective.

In the light of this rejection of Doms by an influential Roman theologian, the evolution of teaching by Pius XII was instructive. In 1949 Pius XII condemned artificial insemination, not mentioning insemination by semen obtained in normal coitus (Address to the Fourth International Congress of Catholic Doctors, September 29, 1949, AAS 41:559). Two years later, in his comprehensive Address to the Midwives, he explained that his objection had been based on personalist considerations. Referring to the 1949 statement, he said that in it he had "formally excluded" artificial insemination, because the family is not "a biological laboratory." He continued, "The conjugal act, in its natural structure, is a personal action, a simultaneous and immediate cooperation of the two spouses, which, by the nature of the participants and the quality of the act, is the expression of the reciprocal gift, which, according to the word of the Scriptures, effects the union 'in one flesh alone'" (AAS 43:850). This language sounded more like Doms than Hürth. Five years later, on May 19, 1956, Pius XII repeated his personalist objections to artificial insemination. The biological result cannot be lawfully separated, he declared, from "the personal relation of the married couple," who "surrender themselves to each other and whose voluntary self-donation blossoms forth and finds its true fulfillment in the being which they bring into the world" (Address to the Second World Congress on Fertility and Sterility, AAS 48:470). In both talks the Pope insisted that the personal purposes of the spouses were subordinate to "what surpasses them, paternity and maternity." But the papal statements aimed at the manipulation of nature by insemination had the effect of emphasizing the personal values of intercourse and giving official approval at least to the personalist rejection of a narrow interpretation of procreative purpose. The significance of intercourse for the person had been expounded by the Pope. The self-donation of the spouses had been championed by him as a value of coitus.

The leading theologians on marriage in the 1950's also embraced a qualified personalist understanding of intercourse. Bernard Häring said in 1954 that he did not agree with Doms that "conjugal love was the first

[38] Francis Hürth, "La Fécondation artificielle: Sa value morale et juridique," *Nouvelle revue théologique* 68 (1946), 415, 406.

end of marriage." But he formally abandoned Doms only to combine a modified version of Doms's theory with the old teaching on procreation. Love was seen as the fundamental, although not the final value, in every act of the spouses (Häring, *The Law of Christ* 2–2.4.3.2.3.a). It was a love sacramentally established and vivified: conjugal love he described as "the accomplishment of a sacramental mission in virtue of a sacramental grace" (*ibid.* 2–2.4.3.2.6.c). In this perspective marital intercourse itself became "a fundamental mediation of charity." Apart from procreation, one of its permissible purposes was "the augmentation of love" (2–2.4.3.2.6). The loving union of spouses was not directed, however, to their own completion but to the child, whose "virtual presence" was somewhat vaguely said to be "inscribed in the ontological act of total union." But while this orientation to the child was acknowledged, Häring spoke in Doms's terms of a "completion of persons" in coitus. Only, he added, the completion was not ultimate; it "surpasses the dyad and in the image of the Trinity produces a third" (2–2.3.2.1.1.a). The old insistence on "the debt" was transcended in a statement which carried the seeds of development: as a sacramental community of persons, marriage was "infinitely richer than all categories of personal justice" (2–2.3.2.1.3.a).[39]

A new stage was reached when the new doctrine was expounded in 1960 by Joseph Fuchs, who had succeeded to the mantle of Vermeersch and Hürth as the leading Jesuit authority in Rome on marital morality. Fuchs found the expression of love to be an objective purpose of intercourse as much as procreation was an objective purpose: "Sexual actuation is in itself ordered to the generation of offspring"; it is also "in itself ordered to the intimate expression of love between joined persons of different sexes." At last the neglected thought of St. Thomas that fidelity (*fides*) was an objective end of intercourse was revived, with "love" substituted for fidelity. To have intercourse without love was declared to violate the objective order or purpose of the marital act. Like Häring, Fuchs did not formally abandon the teaching that the good of the offspring was primary. But he added a considerable gloss to the statement of this purpose in documents such as *Casti connubii*: "This love, together with all the consequences of common life, entirely (although not solely or as a mere means) serves and is subordinated to the education of off-

---

[39] The first three citations are to the fifth edition of *Das Gesetz Christi*; the last two are to the French translation of the fourth edition. The translators, Francis Bourdeau, Armand Danet, and Louis Vereecke, have, with Häring's approval, made additions to the original text (*La Loi du Christ*, Paris, 1959).

Doms himself in his new work in 1960 synthesized the doctrine on love and procreation: "Conjugal coitus intends not simply offspring, but a new human person as the direct, substantial reproduction of the permanent community of life of the spouses, who have become a bodily unity — a new human person who is by this engendering through unity a faint image of the Incarnation, that is, of the relation of Christ to Church" (*Dieses Geheimnis ist gross*, p. 112).

spring, to whose generation such an act expressive of love is evidently ordered" (*Chastity and the Sexual Order* 2.4.1). The good of the offspring was maintained as primary by pointing to the relation of conjugal love to the education of the children. This love itself was no longer seen "solely or as a mere means" at the service of the child.

The doctrine now seemed solidly established. It was vigorously affirmed in 1963 by Ford and Kelly in their book in the vernacular: "Marital intercourse is immoral when love has ceased," because conjugal acts are properly "expressions of love." They added, "It is hardly stressing sex too much to say that in the ordinary providence of God, the marriage act is one of the chief means by which Christian spouses are to attain God together, just as it is the central act of that state of life to which God has called them." [40]

At Vatican II in 1964 four major addresses by fathers of the Council related the new theory of love to the question of contraception. They spoke on Schema 13, "The Church and the Modern World," drafted by a commission of which Bernard Häring had been the secretary. Cardinal Leger, archbishop of Montreal, said that the schema was too hesitant in affirming the place of conjugal love: "It should clearly present human conjugal love — I stress human love which involves both the soul and the body — as a true end of marriage, as something good in itself, with its own characteristics and laws." The schema should "proclaim the two ends of marriage as equally good and holy. Once that is done, the moral theologians, doctors, psychologists, and other experts can much more easily determine for particular cases the duties both of procreation and of love." Cardinal Alfrink, archbishop of Utrecht, stated that conjugal love was essential both to the motive for procreation and to the education of one's children. This love was "sustained and increased by sexual intercourse." It was endangered if abstinence was the only way of regulating offspring. The Church must examine if "the only efficacious, moral and Christian solution to such conflicts" is continence. Maximos IV, patriarch of Antioch, declared, "The development of personality and its integration into the creative plan of God are all one. Thus, the end of marriage should not be divided into 'primary' and 'secondary.' This consideration opens new perspectives concerning the morality of conjugal behavior considered as a whole." The patriarch added that there was now a "break between the official doctrine of the Church and the contrary practice of the immense majority of Christian couples." [41]

[40] Ford and Kelly, *Contemporary Moral Theology*, II, 117–119, 157. For an analysis of marriage in philosophical terms, finding in it a "vertical" finality of love, see Bernard Lonergan, S.J., "Finality, Love, Marriage," *Theological Studies* 4 (1943), 477–510.

[41] English translations of the speeches of Leger, Alfrink, Maximos IV, and Suenens appeared in *The National Catholic Reporter*, November 11, 1964, p. 6.

Cardinal Suenens, archbishop of Malines-Brussels, spoke with particular authority. As an auxiliary bishop in 1956 he had already suggested a new approach to the old doctrine on the primary end. The end of generation, he had written, was "objective and inherent in all genital activity." This end could be characterized as "primary" in the sense of "the most specific" but not in the sense of "the most important." "On the psychological plane, the immediate end, experienced as first, will be the mutual perfection and complementation of the couple." In this view of intercourse, he had stated, "God's first demand of the act of love is that it be based on love." [42] Now, in the Council, Suenens asked if the Church had maintained "a perfect balance" between "Increase and multiply" and "they will be two in one flesh." These scriptural doctrines must illuminate each other. "This 'two in one' is a mystery of interpersonal communion given grace and sanctified by the sacrament of marriage." Suenens urged that the commission set up by the Pope "tell us whether we have excessively stressed the first end, procreation, at the expense of another equally important end, that is, growth in conjugal unity."

Schema 13 itself, as circulated to the Council Fathers in April 1964, adopted Häring's position that love was linked to procreation. "Such is the nature of conjugal love that matrimony is essentially ordered to the procreation and education of offspring." At the same time it was recognized that "the good of the offspring requires that the spouses truly love each other." In procreation the spouses were not to be "bound by blind instinct" but to act "with full and conscious responsibility." It was further recognized that there might be a serious conflict between responsible procreation and the demands of love. "In particular," the schema recognized "the frequent difficulty of harmonizing the responsibility of not being able, at least for a time, to increase one's offspring, and of the tender cultivation of love; and if love ceases, the spouses often become as strangers to each other, and the good of fidelity is called into question and the good itself of offspring is subverted, either in relation to the education of the existing offspring or in relation to the live and open spirit to be kept toward offspring to be later procreated in less adverse circumstances." The treatment of the schema concluded with a plea to anthropologists, psychologists, sociologists, and experienced and virtuous couples to collaborate with the theologians in seeking "practical solutions for many conflicts" by exploring more profoundly "the complex order given to nature by Providence." In its frank admission of conflicts, in its insistence on inquiry, in its deliberate avoidance of any specific

[42] Leo Joseph Suenens, *Un problème crucial: Amour et maîtresse de soi* (Bruges, 1956), trans. George J. Robinson, *Love and Control* (Westminster, Md., 1961). Quotations are from the English translation, pp. 68, 94–95.

statement on contraception, Schema 13 marked a new era in the history of the Church's thought on the subject.[43]

CHANGES IN DISCIPLINE

Three modifications or mitigations of the law enforcing the teaching on contraception reflected resistance by some of the faithful. Each change was a reason for re-examination of the theory being enforced. They occurred as to the duty of inquiry, the treatment of cooperation, and the annulment of marriages.

Pius XI had inculcated a duty of inquiry about contraception in the confessional so that confessors would not leave the faithful in good faith practicing contraception. The instruction of the Holy Office in 1943 entitled "Certain Rules for Action by Confessors About the Sixth Commandment" did not withdraw from this position; neither did it reaffirm it. Its studied avoidance of a stand, however, might be read as a retreat. It told confessors not to interrogate about "material sins" (that is, acts committed in good faith) "unless the good of the penitent himself or the averting of the danger of a common evil requires or prompts admonition." [44] Confessors were not told that contraception was such a "common evil."

In 1960 the German Jesuit Joseph Fuchs, teaching at the Gregorian University in Rome, observed that "conjugal onanism" was found almost everywhere, even in "truly Christian homes" (*Chastity* 5.16.1).[45] Yet he suspected that the practice of contraception in good faith was rare. True, "not a few faithful" took the position that "onanism, exercised because of difficulties which are, in some fashion, real," cannot be a serious sin. It was hard to say whether these Catholics were in good faith. However, for the common good, "lest this opinion be spread," their good faith, if it exists, must be destroyed by telling them the true Catholic doctrine (*ibid.* 5.16.3). Fuchs added that many theologians held that in some regions contraceptive practices might be so prevalent that "all married persons" were to be treated as suspect of committing contraception, unless the confessor had reason to believe to the contrary. In these areas, there was

---

[43] Documents of the Second Vatican Council, Schema 13, "The Church and the Modern World," chapter 4 (draft, April 1964). The idea that the number of children in a family should depend on the family's circumstances, and that the decision should be made by the family, had been strongly urged by Bernard Häring in his book *Ehe in dieser Zeit* (Salzburg, 1960), p. 365.

[44] *Periodica de re morali, canonica, liturgica* 33 (1944), 131.

[45] Two Italian priests observed that "conjugal onanism" was almost universal in Italy; *Perfice munus* 36 (1961), 555. In Spain, too, it was believed that a majority of couples practiced contraception (Bernard Häring, *Ehe in dieser Zeit*, p. 374). A study of a southern Dutch group of Catholic churchgoers found that a majority practiced contraception, almost always by coitus interruptus (L. A. G. J. Timmermans, *Huwelijksbeleving van Katholieke Jonggehuwden*, Utrecht, 1964).

an obligation on the confessor to interrogate those who were silent about the sin (*ibid.* 5.16.3).

On the other hand, there was still dissent on the meaning of "founded suspicion." John J. Lynch, an American Jesuit teaching at the Jesuit college in Weston, Massachusetts, held that "founded suspicion" did not rest on statistics. Rather, he wrote, "It seems to me that the references of the Sacred Penitentiary to a founded suspicion or prudent doubt in this matter of birth control are not only legitimately, but far more prudently, understood as applying to the individual penitent and not to married people in general." [46] If Lynch's theory was followed, as it probably was by many priests, there was little inquiry about contraceptive practice in the confessional. There was created a situation where contraception might be practiced without challenge to the good faith of the penitent. This possibility was particularly likely to be realized in countries when there had been public debate about the progesterone pill, and many persons might in good faith take the pill to prevent pregnancy.

A second disciplinary change had been realized earlier. The canon law had committed itself to the proposition that any intention to exclude "any essential property of marriage" was a ground of nullity of marriage (canon 1086, above, p. 435). Theoretically, an antecedent intention to avoid procreation even for a period of time was an exclusion of an essential property of marriage. The Rota in 1931 said, "What is said as to the invalidity on account of the exclusion of the right to procreation and education of offspring or to conjugal acts applies equally whether the exclusion happens perpetually or for a time." [47] If this logic were followed, many marriages where the couples intended to avoid offspring for a year or two might be considered void. The Rota was unwilling to come to this conclusion, and, in the same case in which the dictum quoted occurs, it went on, "In practice, however, exclusion of offspring or of the conjugal act for a limited time is regarded as a proposal [*propositum*] of abstaining from the use of the conjugal right or of abusing or violating conjugal obligations, and so is no obstacle to the validity of marriage." [48] In fact, not only has the intention to avoid procreation for a period usually been labeled a mere proposal to violate the conjugal right, but the in-

[46] Lynch, "Notes on Moral Theology," *Theological Studies* 17 (1956), 192.

[47] *Sacrae Romanae Rotae decisiones seu sententiae* (Rome, 1912—), 23.30, before Francis Morano, June 23, 1931.

[48] The theory was applied in a case begun in 1903 where the Rota first held the marriage valid (14.14, before Parrillo, April 29, 1922); and then determined that nullity existed on the grounds of a premarital intention of the wife not to have intercourse with her future husband, for whom she felt antipathy, until she came to love him (16.14, before Chimenti, March 14, 1924). However, this was a short-lived victory for the principle that intention to exclude offspring temporarily nullifies a marriage. On March 23, 1925, the Rota held finally for the validity of the marriage (17.18, before André Julien).

tention to avoid offspring permanently has also been customarily analyzed as something less than an intention to exclude an "essential property of marriage." [49] One may conclude that, in order to prevent fraud on the court and to favor the stability of marriages, the Rota has refused to annul some marriages which are theologically invalid.[50] Alternatively, one might draw a theological conclusion from the living law of the Rota: the intention to exclude offspring is not necessarily destructive of the essence of marriage.

A third development occurred as to cooperation. The early thirties had been the high point not only of active teaching against contraception, but of an absolute stand against cooperation with instruments. The next thirty years saw questioning and modification of the position. Vermeersch's teaching on the diaphragm was the first to be challenged. In 1936 the Dominican moralist Merkelbach argued that intercourse by the husband when his wife used a diaphragm could not be intrinsically evil: coitus took place, and in pregnancy coitus was lawful although the pas-

[49] The policy has been given practical effect by the application of a distinction as old as Sanchez. Sanchez had taught that there was a distinction between an intention contrary to the obligation of having children and an intention contrary to the execution of this obligation. According to this distinction one can intend to assume the obligation and at the same time intend to violate it. Comparison is made with someone taking an oath intending to violate it. He sins in his intention, but he is bound by the oath. Similarly, he who intends to assume the obligations of marriage, but to violate them, sins; yet he is held to the obligations assumed, and his marriage is valid (Sanchez, The Holy Sacrament of Matrimony 2.29.11).

This distinction has been criticized as unintelligible when the question is one of internal assent. Gerard Oesterle, O.S.B., "Animadversiones in sententiam S.R.R. diei 23 Februarii 1951 coram Staffa," Il Diritto ecclessiastico 62 (1951), 730, defending the judgment of nullity given by him as a member of the tribunal for the vicariate of Rome and published in Il Diritto ecclessiastico 60 (1949), 159–169. This decision had been overruled by the Rota. For a response by the Rota auditor responsible, see Dino Staffa, "De iure et eius exercitio relate ad bonum prolis," Il Diritto ecclesiastico 62 (1951), 1059. Staffa cited as decisive the words of Pius XII quoted below. Oesterle reasoned that marriage demands internal consent, and one cannot at the same time intend to assume an obligation and intend to violate it. The intention not to have offspring contradicts the intention to assume the obligation of having offspring. The comparison with oath-taking does not hold, because there a man is held by what he externally manifests: if he swears, then his subsequent falsehood will be punished as perjury, whatever his state of mind in taking the oath. On the other hand, Pius XII adopted the distinction in his celebrated talk to the midwives. He said that a premarital agreement to practice periodic continence did not vitiate matrimonial consent, for it did not exclude the perpetual marriage right, but only "the use of the marriage right" during certain periods (Address to the Italian Catholic Society of Midwives, AAS 43:845 [1951]).

[50] This is the conclusion of Raoul Naz, "Les Empêchements de mariage improprements dits (can. 1081–1103 d'après l'opinion populaire et d'après la jurisprudence de la Rote)," L'Année canonique 1 (1952), 126. According to the statistics published annually in L'Année canonique since 1952 there has been a small rise since the 1920's in the number of annulments for a condition against offspring, but the increase does not seem large enough to establish a trend.

sage to the uterus was closed. Hence, cooperation by the husband in his wife's sin was lawful for him on the usual grounds permitting material cooperation (*Questions of Chastity and Lechery* 8.2.2). Merkelbach's views received limited Roman support twenty years later in a letter dated April 21, 1955, from the Holy Office to certain unnamed bishops. The letter dealt with the case of a husband "cooperating materially" with a wife using a diaphragm. Material cooperation, the Holy Office warned, could not itself be regarded as lawful as a matter of course. "Ordinaries shall not permit the faithful to be told or taught that no serious objection may be made [to it] according to the principles of Christian law." [51] Yet the very description of the act as "material cooperation" accepted Merkelbach's contention that formal participation in an evil act was not at issue.

The shift from Vermeersch on cooperation with a diaphragm can be explained in terms of lines drawn centuries ago between inability to ejaculate semen and inability to impregnate. The doubts and difficulties experienced over implementing the rules on cooperation by a wife with a husband using a condom pointed to more fundamental weaknesses of theory. Almost all moral theologians who wrote on the subject felt bound to maintain the analogy with rape. Resistance by the wife was required unless it was impossible "without very grave physical consequences to her here and now." [52] Yet the communication of this apparently logical but strangely harsh rule was difficult. It was noted by an English priest that the analogy with rape "was not intended to be used as a direct pastoral admonition to the wife." [53] In this view the analogy was merely a technical device for bringing out the principles involved. But if theologians needed a dramatic illustration to understand that something terribly serious was involved in cooperation, how could housewives get the principle without the illustration? It seems entirely probable that in practice most confessors felt that it went beyond the bounds of prudential decency even to inquire about the resistance to cooperation offered.

The emotional difficulty in enforcing the principle caused doubt about the principle itself among those who were not professional moral theologians. A London priest, Wilfred Stibbs, probably spoke for many when he wrote, in the course of a running discussion in *The Clergy Review*, "One cannot but feel that anyone, even when dealing formally with

[51] See Ford and Kelly, *Contemporary Moral Theology*, II, 214.
[52] See the survey of authorities by Lawrence L. McReavy, "Cooperatio in Copula Condomistica," *The Clergy Review* 48 (1963), 119.
[53] Maurice O'Leary, Letter to the Editor, *The Clergy Review* 48 (1963), 651. Father O'Leary is a leading member of the Catholic Marriage Advisory Council of London.

the *finis operis* of the act of intercourse, who seriously equates a loving wife with a virgin in danger of rape, is out of touch with real people and real human problems." [54]

In 1956 a questioning of the casuistic on cooperation was suggested by Suenens. He noted that a survey of a "large number" of wives who were practicing Catholics had found that they considered "repugnant" the "moral distinction" permitting their cooperation in coitus interruptus. He added, "They are the more offended by this moral 'dualism' because the passivity in question implies a minimum of active cooperation. They know they are not sinning mortally, but they are unanimous in saying that the solution seems to be spiritual mediocrity." Suenens suggested that the theologians reexamine the whole question of cooperation. As a guide to such reconsideration, he quoted with approval the statement of one spouse: "I accuse us of my partner's sin, and we must do all we can together to leave it behind us." [55]

At first glance, the thrust of Suenens' remarks would seem to favor a more stringent rule on cooperation. But was he not, in effect, pointing to the lack of realism in the existing rule? The distinctions drawn to permit cooperation by one spouse in the contraceptive act of the other were of an abstract kind which seemed to ignore the psychological realities of the situation, and to define as "passivity" what most people would call "activity." The teaching, moreover, was of a character so repugnant to the emotions of ordinary married couples that it was evident that many priests felt unable to communicate it. The practical difficulty of making reasonable distinctions, the practical difficulty of communicating the doctrine, raised the possibility that there was some defect in the analysis which made everything turn on whether or not in a given sexual act ejaculation was completed within the vagina. The narrow focus on this aspect of conjugal relations seemed to distort the more fundamental question of love between the spouses.

CONTROVERSY

The April 1964 draft of Schema 13 of Vatican II not only avoided any direct condemnation of contraception; it also said that the number of children to have was the decision of each couple, to be made not by blind instinct, but "with full and conscious responsibility." In an Appendix, circulated with the draft of the schema, some issues were amplified or explained without seeking to put conciliar authority behind the proposals. Under the heading "Fecundity of Matrimony" it was observed, "And if according to the ordination of nature not each and every conjugal

[54] Letter, *The Clergy Review* 48 (1963), 322.
[55] Suenens, *Love and Control*, p. 72, p. 67.

act is directly destined to lead to procreation, yet the character and expression of this act and the mind of the spouses ought to be such that the generous disposition to procreate and educate children is favored." This language was only another way of saying that love between the spouses had a link to procreation. The Appendix went on to say that the Council warned all men of good will: "Every deliberate intervention of men which vitiates the work proper to the conjugal act of the person is contrary to divine law and the order of matrimony; nor can such a way of acting be consonant with the integrity of conjugal love." Here was an explicit but very carefully qualified condemnation of some forms of contraception. What were condemned were means affecting "the act of the person," that is, coitus interruptus and the condom. It was not clear whether pessaries, douches, diaphragms, or pills were included in these words. A proposed footnote referred to methods "falsifying the conjugal act itself, which *Casti connubii* had in contemplation, to wit, deliberate interruption of copulation, the condom, and so forth"; the footnote added that no judgment was given as to the use of progesterones. The entire footnote was struck from later versions of the text.[56]

The draft of Schema 13, with its emphasis on love in marriage, and its clear but qualified condemnation of contraceptives put in a subordinate document, suggested that development of doctrine was about to receive conciliar approval. The suggestion created tension. New stages have rarely been reached in the life of a doctrine without partisans of the old position insisting that the ancient letter be preserved, while partisans of the new point to a spirit whose law is organic growth. The commitment of the papacy, hierarchy, and theologians to a condemnation of contraception made the crisis particularly acute. The momentum of the great campaign which had been climaxed with *Casti connubii* had carried over into the allocutions of Pius XII. John XXIII, in *Mater et magistra*, issued May 15, 1961, had included a rejection of the solution of the population problems of underdeveloped countries by measures "by which, in addition to violation of the discipline of morals determined by God, there is violation of the procreation of human life itself." He described these measures as "means and plans [*rationes*] which are alien to the dignity of man; which those are not ashamed to advocate who think man himself and his life can entirely be reduced to matter" (*AAS* 53:446–447). The Pope's words, to be sure, did not have the same juridical cast as *Casti connubii*, and the methods he condemned were unspecified; but, taking account of the pastoral, paternal style in which John XXIII couched his strongest rebukes and bearing in mind the background of the theological description of contraceptive methods, it would be a feat

[56] Schema 13, "The Church and the Modern World," appendix 2 (draft, April 1964).

of reinterpretation to say that at least some forms of contraception were not in his mind. The present Pope, Paul VI, when Prosecretary for Ordinary Affairs in the Secretariat of State under Pius XII, had also written strongly against "the diffusion of neo-Malthusian practices which violate the divine laws presiding at the transmission of life."[57]

Not only the papacy but several national hierarchies had also taken strong stands in the late 1950's and early 1960's when the population problem was already altering the context of the question. In November 1957, the bishops of India, gathered at Bangalore, solemnly warned the faithful of India against Communism, immoral movies, and contraception: "Family limitation by unnatural means is an offense against natural and divine law. It is against the primary ends of the holy state of matrimony. The deliberate destruction of life in potency is a crime close to murder, as St. Thomas stated in the thirteenth century." After disuse for over a century, a reminiscence of the homicide analysis appeared again. The Indian bishops added to St. Thomas a statement of Mahatma Gandhi in *Harijan*, March 28, 1936, where Gandhi spoke of procreation as the sole end of intercourse. The bishops closed with an evocation of "the traditions of our country and the sacred character of family life." [58]

On March 3, 1961, the Assembly of Cardinals and Archbishops of France issued a statement on contraception. The Church was not "nataliste à tout prix." The primary end of marriage, it reminded the faithful, is "not only the procreation but the education of children." Responsible regulation of birth was lawful and desirable. But man is forbidden "to violate the natural order established by God, who is the sole Master of human lives." "That is why it is necessary to reject every manipulation which, by contraceptive procedures or sterilizing products, has the purpose of artificially preventing the coming of children into the world." [59]

In the United States, the hierarchy acted after the President's Committee to Study the U.S. Military Assistance Program (the Draper Committee) had issued a report on July 13, 1959, recommending cooperation with underdeveloped countries in "plans designed to deal with the problem of rapid population growth." This vague statement caused much speculation that the United States government would aid birth control

---

[57] Letter of G. B. Montini to Cardinal Siri, September 19, 1954, trans. in *Les Enseignements pontificaux: Le mariage*, ed. the Monks of Solesmes (Le Mans, 1956). In 1939, in one of the first acts of his reign, in congratulations addressed to the American hierarchy on its sesquicentennial, Pius XII noted that among the evils flowing from neglect of the law of God was "avoidance of the procreation of offspring" (*Sertum laetitiae*, AAS 31:639).

[58] "Birth Control," Declaration of the Bishops of India, *Documentation catholique* 55 (1958), 210.

[59] "La Limitation des naissances: Déclaration de l'Assemblée des cardinaux et archévêques de France," *Documentation catholique* 58 (1961), 371.

programs abroad.[60] At the annual meeting of the bishops of the United States, November 26, 1959, a strong statement was issued in the name of all the bishops by the five cardinals and cardinals-designate and ten bishops constituting the Administrative Board of the National Catholic Welfare Conference. The bishops stated that the population increase in the underdeveloped countries should be met by international economic measures, not programs of artificial birth control, abortion, or sterilization. They deplored the propagandist use of the term "population explosion." They rebuked persons who had stated that "artificial birth prevention within the married state is gradually becoming acceptable even in the Catholic Church." "This," they said, "is not true." "The Catholic Church has always distinguished artificial birth control, which is a frustration of the conjugal act, from other forms of birth regulation which are morally lawful." The only true solutions were "those which are morally acceptable under the natural law of God."[61]

The statement of the hierarchy of England and Wales on May 7, 1964, quoted the condemnations of contraception of St. Augustine in *Adulterous Marriages*, of Pius XI in *Casti connubii*, of Pius XII in the Address to the Midwives. Contraception, they concluded, "is not an open question, for it is against the law of God."[62]

In the debate in the Council, the statements of Leger, Alfrink, Suenens, and Maximos IV in favor of re-examination of the doctrine drew a strong reaction. Three cardinals, identified with the conservative wing of the curia, and opposed to the liberal majority on issues ranging from methods of biblical exegesis to the collegial constitution of the Church to freedom of conscience from coercion by the state, challenged these speakers who, on the other issues too, had been their opponents. Cardinal Browne, an Irishman who had been general of the Dominicans, appealed to classic scholastic theology, to *Arcanum Divinae Sapientiae*, to *Casti connubii*, and to the Address to the Midwives. He brought into play an old Thomistic distinction between two kinds of love, the love of friendship (*amor amicitiae*) and the love of concupiscence (*amor concupiscentiae*), "concupiscence" being used here in a morally neutral sense. By the love of concupiscence one used another person for one's own good; by the love of friendship one sought the good of another. In the analysis of St. Thomas both forms of love are good, although the love of friendship is higher (*Summa theologica* 1–2.26.41). In Cardinal Browne's application, he

[60] See, e.g., *America* 101 (1959), 583.

[61] Statement of the administrative board of the National Catholic Welfare Conference, in *The New York Times*, November 26, 1959, p. 43.

[62] Statement of the hierarchy of England and Wales in *The Universe*, May 7, 1964, reprinted in *The Pill and Birth Regulation*, ed. Leo Pyle (Baltimore 1964), pp. 95–98.

suggested that intercourse involved the love of concupiscence, and that this use of one's spouse was destructive of the love of friendship that should develop between man and wife. Cardinal Browne's exercise in the application of a Thomistic text was supported by Cardinal Alfred Ottaviani, the head (under the Pope) of the Holy Office. Speaking now, as he said, as the eleventh of twelve children, he declared, forthrightly, "The freedom granted by the schema to married couples to determine for themselves the number of their children cannot possibly be approved." He expressed his amazement at hearing doubt expressed about whether until now a correct stand had been taken on the principles governing marriage. He asked if the inerrancy of the Church was being called into question. Cardinal Ottaviani was followed by Cardinal Ernest Ruffini, archbishop of Palermo. He noted critically the passages in the schema leaving the number of offspring to the judgment of the parents. He then quoted, not by name, *Aliquando*, the famous text on contraception in St. Augustine's *Marriage and Concupiscence*, which had been the canon of Gratian, the locus classicus of Peter Lombard, the law of the Church from 1150 to 1917, the inspiration of *Effraenatam*. Once more the words "Sometimes lustful cruelty or cruel lust" were employed to describe the motives for contraception, and the ancient formula rang in the basilica of St. Peter and in the councils of the Church.[63]

Battle had been joined. Popes, cardinals, and bishops had, from 1951 to 1964, reaffirmed that contraception was against God's law; they had pointed to no exceptions. Some of the leading fathers of the Council had asked for re-examination. No Catholic writer before 1963 had asserted that the general prohibition of contraception was wrong. In late 1963 and in 1964, however, in addition to the writers favoring the direct use of the progesterone pills, in addition to Bishop Reuss's defense of sterilization, there appeared Catholic writers challenging the doctrine itself. Of these the most prominent was Thomas D. Roberts, a leading English Jesuit, who, as former archbishop of Bombay, was free of the censorship of his order and now acted as a gadfly in the Church. In his article in *Search*, which alarmed the English hierarchy, Roberts said that he was constrained by the authority of the Church, but that he could not see any rational argument against contraception. In the fall of 1964, Archbishop Roberts introduced a collection of essays, *Contraception and Holiness*, and declared, "on the grounds of reason alone, one can conceive of many cases in which a husband and wife might, after having examined their consciences, decide that contraception was the only means for preserving the health of one or the other spouse, or for preserving the marriage itself. If that is so, then, with the most spiritual of motives such

[63] English translations of the speeches in the *National Catholic Reporter*, December 16, 1964.

a husband and wife might be convinced that contraception was necessary for the growth in holiness which is the aim of the sacrament of matrimony." [64] Finding no reason for the Church's absolute prohibition, Roberts asked the Church to clarify and reconsider its position.

The possibility and rationality of a less than absolute prohibition were urged by the other contributors to *Contraception and Holiness*: E. R. Baltazar, assistant professor of philosophy at the University of Dayton; Gregory Baum, an Augustinian of St. Michael's College at the University of Toronto; Kieran Conley, a Benedictine professor of dogmatic theology at St. Meinrad's Seminary, Indiana; William V. D'Antonio, associate professor of sociology at the University of Notre Dame; Elizabeth A. Daugherty, a zoologist; Leslie Dewart, associate professor of philosophy at St. Michael's College at the University of Toronto; Justus George Lawler, professor of humanities, St. Xavier College, Chicago; Julian Pleasants, research associate in the Lobund Laboratory, University of Notre Dame; Rosemary Reuther, a teacher of classics at Scripps College, California. In another book appearing in the fall of 1964, *Contraception and Catholics*, Louis Dupré, a layman who was associate professor of theology at Georgetown University, also criticized the existing arguments for an absolute prohibition.[65] In a third work of the same date, *What Modern Catholics Think About Birth Control*, entirely written by married laymen, the existing rule was upheld by Vernon Bourke, professor of philosophy at St. Louis University, but criticized by William Birmingham, an editor of *Cross Currents*, Mary Louise Birmingham, an editor of a publishing house, Sydney Cornelia Callahan, a writer, Eugene Fontinell, an editor of *Cross Currents* and teacher at Queens College, New York, James Finn, editor of *Worldview*, Michael Novak, author of *The Open Church*, and Sally Sullivan, a writer. Daniel Sullivan, a student at the Institut Catholique, outlined the development of Catholic thinking on the subject; Frederick E. Flynn, professor of philosophy at the College of St. Thomas, Minnesota, showed how the natural law was capable of development.[66] A fourth book, *The Experience of Marriage*, edited by Michael Novak, was composed of statements by thirteen anonymous Catholic couples, American and mostly engaged in intellectual work; the book was a compelling presentation of injury and strain in the marital relation by the attempt to regulate birth by the use of rhythm.[67] The devotion of these writers to the Church was evident. They wrote not as enemies or as rebels, but as witnesses. Only one couple in *The Experience of Marriage*,

[64] *Contraception and Holiness*, by Archbishop Thomas D. Roberts et al. (New York, 1964), p. 10.
[65] Louis Dupré, *Contraception and Catholics: A New Appraisal* (Baltimore, 1964).
[66] *What Modern Catholics Think About Birth Control*, ed. William Birmingham (New York, 1964).
[67] *The Experience of Marriage*, ed. Michael Novak (New York, 1964).

only two contributors to *What Modern Catholics Think About Birth Control*, used contraceptive methods which had been condemned; these asserted respectfully their free right to obey their consciences when it seemed wrong to have more children, wrong to abstain from intercourse altogether, and impracticable to use rhythm. While some attention was given to population pressures, the main thrust of the critics of the absolute rule was to justify in theory what these two couples had done in practice. As the good of parents and of existing children demanded both family planning and sexual intercourse, and as rhythm was unreliable and destructive of the free expression of love, the critics urged the Church not to condemn all forms of contraception.

The success of the critics' plea for revision depended, at least in part, on the strength of the rational arguments supporting an absolute prohibition. Rational arguments in moral matters are, perhaps, never absolutely decisive. Too many intuitions, too many sentiments, escape articulation. It is possible to be wise without arguments to justify one's wisdom. Yet arguments are the usual means for examining doctrinal position, and, if only as indices, they point to the health of a teaching. Of the arguments against all contraception, Dupré quoted La Fontaine's words on the animals in the plague, "They did not all die, but they were all struck." The arguments had been affected by the changes in environment. They had undergone some criticism by the theologians. They were now subjected to direct attack by the advocates of modification. The arguments purported to show that contraception was injurious to society, family, and self, and against the will of God. Did they still hold?

INJURY TO PARTICULAR POPULATIONS AND TO THE HUMAN RACE

The argument that contraception injured society had a double aspect. Sometimes it was viewed as endangering particular groups, sometimes the race as a whole. In the declarations of the German hierarchy in 1913 and the French hierarchy in 1914 the notion appeared that it was good to procreate citizens for the state; the standard was a nationalistic one. Similarly, depopulation of a particular nation appeared to be the evil evoked by Belgian theologians like De Smet and Merkelbach, and by an American like Ryan, who pointed to the French example.[68] What weakens the national state was, in these presentations, assumed to be evil. This assumption was least likely to be challenged between 1870 and 1940. Thereafter, in a world increasingly conscious of its unity, a yardstick based on the nation, although not wholly abandoned, did not have much status as a moral guide.

[68] De Smet, *Les Fiançailles et le mariage* 2.1.3.1.1, annex 2; Merkelbach, *Questions on Chastity and Lechery* 8.4; John A. Ryan, "Family Limitation," *Ecclesiastical Review* 54 (1915), 693.

An interesting variant of this argument, substituting the Church for the state, was doubtless often enough in the back of some ultraclerical minds. The position was that contraception would deprive society of a fair share of Catholics, or, put more imperially, that the Church might grow if Catholics controlled their procreative activities less than other people. The traditional doctrine that the purpose of marital intercourse is the generation and *religious* education of offspring could be given this emphasis; and such emphasis does occur in *Casti connubii*, with its language on procreation as a way of making "the people of God increase day by day." Similarly, the argument seemed to Ryan a reason to restrict the use of rhythm: "A large proportion of Catholic couples would be under specific and particular obligation to discard the practice of periodical abstinence so far as would be necessary to maintain at least the previously existing proportion between Catholics and non-Catholics."[69]

As nationalism declined, so also did competition of this kind among the churches; and within religiously divided areas like Canada and the Netherlands, ecumenicism softened competitive anxieties. It was doubtful if a respectable moral theologian could have been found in 1964 to maintain that contraception was forbidden to Catholics because they had a duty to increase their numbers by births in order to best other religions or irreligious groups.

A mutation of these arguments was based on the observation that in a typical underdeveloped country contraception was more often practiced by the urban elite than by the least educated. The practice thereby effected a disproportionate reduction in offspring of the leading elements in a society.[70] This argument, however, might be read as merely suggesting the need to intensify propaganda for contraception among the uneducated. At most, it showed that contraception practiced without a sense of social responsibility might harm a particular nation.

The argument directed to the social evil of depopulation was given a more metaphysical attire by some writers. Arthur Vermeersch argued in 1919 that the person practicing contraception violated the subordination of his act to the species: "The human race, as it is a moral person, provides for its perpetuity by conjugal copulation. The onanists positively exclude this perpetuity by the manner in which they couple" (*Chastity and the Contrary Vices*, no. 258). Here each act of contraception was treated as an act against the species. In 1946 the same argument appeared in Iorio's revision of Gury: the contraceptive act "tends *per se*

[69] John A. Ryan, "The Moral Aspects of Periodical Continence," *Ecclesiastical Review* 89 (1933), 34.

[70] Stanislas de Lestapis, *La Limitation des naissances*, 2nd ed. (Paris, 1960), p. 69. De Lestapis urged this phenomenon not as a general argument against birth control, but as an objection to the claim that birth control could help the population of underdeveloped countries.

to the extinction of society" (*Moral Theology*, no. 1206). A Kantian variant of the argument was chosen by Creusen: if contraception became "a general principle" of action — that is, if everyone practiced it — the human race would be destroyed.[71]

This metaphysical form of the argument was criticized by Herbert McCabe, an English Dominican, in 1964. What the race required was "a whole complex of acts which go to make possible the birth and survival of a child." Not every sexual act in this complex had to be generative. Using an analogy which only an English writer would invoke, he compared the complex of required acts to the complex of acts necessary to score in a game. Not every single act had to tend toward the goal: the player may be "occasionally making a move which is the opposite of the crucial one — making a move which if invariably employed would make success impossible."[72] *On recule pour mieux sauter*, both in games and in the preservation of the race, was McCabe's suggestion.

A difficulty in the older theology which had indirectly lent plausibility to the "race suicide" argument was removed by a theological development. The old theory, in its anxiety to preserve the lawfulness of virginal marriages, had recognized no obligation in marriage to procreate. A marriage was lawful and valid in which intercourse, and consequently procreation, were abstained from. "The Anglicans assuredly err," taught Vermeersch in 1934, when they say there is a duty for married persons to have children: "The multiplication of the human race is sufficiently provided for so that no precept is given that it be undertaken."[73] In this traditional analysis, the obligation to procreate attached to the exercise of the marital act, not to the entrance into matrimony. It might have seemed, if this analysis were pursued, that to eliminate the absolute obligation not to render particular acts of intercourse infertile would mean that married couples would be morally free to have intercourse without ever having children, and in the long run the preservation of the race would be threatened.

The same child-avoiding result was also possible, in the old analysis, merely by the use of rhythm. To reach a more acceptable conclusion, some theologians in the 1940's, led by Gerald Kelly, found an affirmative obligation for married persons engaging in intercourse to have some children.[74] This tentative theory was accepted by Pius XII in his discussion of the sterile period in the Address to Midwives:

[71] Joseph Creusen, "L'Onanisme conjugal," *Nouvelle revue théologique* 59 (1932), 308–309.

[72] Herbert McCabe, "Contraceptives and Natural Law," *The New Blackfriars* 46 (1964), 89, 93.

[73] Arthur Vermeersch, "De prudenti ratione indicandi sterilitatem physiologicam," *Periodica de re morali, canonica, liturgica* 23 (1934), 242.

[74] Gerald Kelly, "Notes on Moral Theology, 1949," *Theological Studies* 11 (1949), 74.

On partners who make use of matrimony by the specific act of their state, nature and the Creator impose the function of providing for the continuance of the human race. This is the characteristic debt [*prestazione*] from which their state of life derives its peculiar value, the *bonum prolis*. The individual and society, the people and the state, the Church itself, depend for their existence, in the order established by God, on fertile marriage. Consequently, to embrace the state of matrimony, to use continually the faculty proper to it, and allowed in it alone, and on the other hand to withdraw always and deliberately, without a grave motive, from its primary duty, would be to sin against the very meaning of conjugal life. (*AAS* 43:845–846)

Some questions concerning the extent of the duty to procreate were left open; Kelly and Ford, for example, found a limit to the duty in the population needs of a time and country: "a family of three children would sufficiently provide for the needs of the United States." But while analysis remained to be done, the theologians followed the papal lead, and the new position seemed accepted.[75] It provided a moral basis for opposing contraceptive practice which made a couple completely childless. The indirect result was to put less weight on the argument that every act of intercourse must be immune from human interference if the race was to survive.

Arguably, society still might be endangered by the attitudes bred of contraception. The old fear that if there were approval of contraception there would be approval of other forms of nonprocreative sexual activity

[75] See the discussion by Ford and Kelly, *Contemporary Moral Theology*, II, 400–430. Ford and Kelly pointed out that Pius XII left open four questions: Is the obligation to procreate derived from the state of marriage or from habitual intercourse? Is the obligation traceable to the virtue of legal justice or to some other virtue? Is there a limit to the duty? Is violation of the duty a mortal sin? Francis Hürth, clearly desirous of preserving a place for virginal marriage, taught that the duty to procreate arose only from exercise of the marital act (Hürth, *De re matrimoniali* [Rome, 1955], pp. 112–115). Ford and Kelly rejected this analysis, believing it to be a reminiscence of the Augustinian view that intercourse needed an excuse. They held that the obligation arose from the state of marriage, and that the higher good of a virginal marriage could excuse from this kind of affirmative precept (pp. 404–409). On the second question Ford and Kelly found it unlikely that society had, in legal justice, a right to require procreation, and suggested that the governing virtues were piety toward family and fatherland, and chastity (pp. 411–417). On the fourth question, the gravity of the obligation, Fuchs held that "the more probable opinion" was that the practice of rhythm without justification, for the duration of the marriage constituted mortal sin (*Chastity and the Sexual Order* 10.4.2). Hürth held that use of the sterile period "sometimes" became serious sin. Ford and Kelly, however, argued that omission of the duty "in any individual instance would rarely have any damaging effect." They continued, "It may be objected that if everyone refused to have children the common good would suffer grave damage. Therefore it is necessary to impose a grave obligation on individuals even if individual omissions would not of themselves be seriously damaging. This line of reasoning is not conclusive. If everyone lied habitually, the common good would suffer grave damage; if everyone refused to go to the polls, the common good would suffer grave damage. Yet individuals do not ordinarily sin gravely by lying (even habitually) or by failing to vote" (*Contemporary Moral Theology*, II, 427–428).

was voiced in 1960 by Stanislas de Lestapis. He asked, as a rhetorical question, "If in fact erotic activity between two persons has a complete meaning in itself, if its purpose is purely psychological in the service of the couple, if the reference to the work of the flesh is only incidental, why should we wish at all costs to limit mutual erotic activity to heterosexuality?"[76] This question had already been answered by theologians like Fuchs and Häring who had refused to treat "erotic activity" and "conjugal love" as identical. It was also answered by the new critics like Michael Novak, who defined lawful intercourse as "that act of two persons which physically symbolizes the permanent union of their mutual good will, and which, when the biological imperative so commands, is apt for the generation of children."[77] The new answers were, in fact, more satisfactory than the old position, which could never explain why the fornication of the sterile was wrong or why the intercourse of the pregnant was right.

The heart of the "race suicide" argument was removed by the demographic changes since 1850. Vermeersch and Creusen had come from Belgium; the popes had come from Italy. Yet none of these inhabitants of densely populated areas had remarked that a high density of population in relation to economic resources might threaten society or race as much as avoidance of procreation. Indeed, the Belgian bishops in their 1909 Instructions told priests to combat contraception by blessing large families.[78] Pius XII, on January 20, 1958, told the Association of Large Families, an Italian society, that large families were "those most blessed by God and specially loved and prized by the Church as its most precious treasures" (AAS 50:90). In the 1960's, however, the impact of population growth was evident in the theological discussion. Joseph Fuchs rejected Creusen's contention that "if everyone practiced it, the human race would be destroyed." The argument failed to show why, under particular circumstances, particular acts of contraception were not permissible. Moreover, he said drily, that the existence of the race would be threatened if every sexual act was not per se generative "could be doubted" (Fuchs, *Chastity and the Sexual Order* 5.2). In the United States, at the annual meeting of the Catholic Theological Society in 1963, Gerald Kelly dismissed the race suicide argument as obsolete.[79]

A different kind of argument from social consequences was provided by the statistics on abortion. It was alleged that dissemination of contraceptive methods with official sanction brought about a "contraceptive

---

[76] De Lestapis, *La Limitation des naissances*, p. 97.

[77] Novak, "Toward a Positive Sexual Morality," in *What Modern Catholics Think About Birth Control*, p. 113.

[78] "Instructions," *Nouvelle revue théologique* 41 (1909), 623.

[79] Gerald Kelly, "Contraception and Natural Law," *Catholic Theological Society of America, Proceedings of the Eighteenth Annual Convention* (St. Louis, 1963), p. 38.

state of mind": parents who did not want a child, who therefore practiced contraception, and who failed in their effort at avoidance, were often led to resort to abortion. In England, for example, the Royal Commission on Population noted that in 1949 the proportion of procured abortions was 8.7 times as high among couples who habitually practiced contraception as among the others. In Sweden, after contraception had been fully sanctioned by law, legal abortions increased from 703 in 1943 to 6,328 in 1951.[80] In Switzerland, where contraception was almost unrestricted, abortions by 1955 were alleged to equal or outnumber live births.[81] In Hungary, a Communist country with a Catholic tradition of eight hundred years, legal abortions rose from 1,600 in 1949 to 163,700 in 1962; in 1962 legal abortions, at the rate of 16.3 per thousand, exceeded the birth rate of 12.9 per thousand. In Poland, a country with a large Catholic population, legal abortions rose from 1,400 in 1955 to 140,400 in 1962. Japan was the chief example. Under the Influence of the United States army of occupation, the Japanese Diet passed the Eugenic Protection Law in 1948. Overtly eugenic in purpose, its actual intent was to control the population. It permitted legal abortions for reasons of health, and it set up Eugenic Protection Consultation Offices, to be run in conjunction with governmental health centers or private associations, to furnish contraceptive advice and train midwives and nurses in the methods of contraception. From 1948 to 1955, contraception, already known and practiced to some extent by the more educated Japanese, spread rapidly through urban Japan and with some difficulty in rural Japan. But much more dramatic was the rise in abortions. The law was amended in 1949 to permit legal abortion if the mother's health was endangered "for economic reasons," and by a 1952 amendment a requirement that the operating physician first consult an official medical committee was eliminated. Legal abortions rose as follows: 1949 — 246,104; 1950 — 489,119; 1951 — 638,350; 1952 — 798,193; 1953 — 1,068,066; 1954 — 1,143,059; 1955 — 1,170,143. The numbers were a minimum, because legal abortion required the disclosure of income, which could be used for tax purposes; it was consequently estimated that the actual number of abortions might be twice that reported. The number of abortions was higher in the higher income groups, and the total number increased as Japan experienced economic prosperity.[82]

It was, of course, impossible to conclude from the case of Japan that "a

[80] De Lestapis, *La Limitation des naissances*, pp. 63–65.
[81] "Le Droit à la vie," Pastoral Letter of the Bishops of Switzerland, *Documentation catholique* 55 (1958), 205.
[82] The figures and description of the developments in Japan are taken from Irene B. Taeuber, *The Population of Japan* (Princeton, 1958), pp. 269–276. The figures on Hungary and Poland are taken from Christopher Tietze, "The Demographic Significance of Legal Abortion in Eastern Europe," *Demography* 1 (1964).

contraceptive mentality" led to abortion on a mass scale. What would have happened if abortion had received no official encouragement could not be determined. The figures did show that availability of contraceptive means was not necessarily a substitute for abortion.[83] Beyond that, they suggested on a grand scale what the Hungarian, Swiss, and Polish statistics suggested on a smaller scale: it was dangerous to create the idea that offspring were to be avoided. Japan could be written off as a "pagan civilization"; Switzerland was more difficult to explain. The statistics suggested that the evil dreaded in the Roman Empire had still to be feared in the modern world: the greatest threat to the life of a human being was his own parents. In the presence of this evil, any revision of the universal and absolute prohibition of contraception had to take into account the degree to which it might be a necessary outer protection to fetal human life.

INJURY TO THE FAMILY

Children in a small family grow up spoiled, selfish, effete. This result is true especially of the child who is an only child, but to a lesser degree of children in families with two or three children. Considerations of this kind were advanced in the nineteenth century by Michael Rosset. They were given a homely American presentation in the twentieth century by John A. Ryan. Their authors did not attempt to establish their observations by any statistical survey of small families. Ryan anticipated the obvious rejoinder, What of families who were small because the couple practiced sexual continence? His answer was that in these families the discipline and self-control of the parents was exemplary and counterbalanced the lack of many children.[84]

This kind of guessing, unsupported by systematic empirical inquiry, was never indulged in by the major theologians. The flimsiness of a case for an absolute prohibition of contraception built on this ground was evident. By 1964 the argument was no longer used.

Some writers urged that contraception was a factor leading to divorce. They cited statistics showing dissolution of a higher number of marriages with one child or none than with two or more children.[85] This argu-

---

[83] This was the main purpose for which such statistics were cited by De Lestapis, *La Limitation des naissances*, pp. 63–66. A sharp conflict had been going on since 1955 in France to revise the French laws against the promotion of birth control. The claim had been advanced that more contraception would reduce the number of abortions. This claim, in particular, many Catholic spokesmen doubted. For an account of the French controversy in 1955 and 1956 see *Documentation catholique* 53 (1956), 873–887.

[84] Michael Rosset, *De sacramento matrimonii* (Saint-Jean-de-Maurienne, 1895), V, no. 3336; Ryan, "Family Limitation," pp. 691–692.

[85] Suenens, *Love and Control*, pp. 16–17; De Lestapis, *La Limitation des naissances*,

ment suffered from several defects. It was not established how often the sterility of the divorced was due to natural causes and the divorce sought because of the sterility. It was not clear whether, in a country like France where the women were more often practicing Catholics than the men, the refusal of the women to practice contraception did not result in contention, making divorce more probable. It was not shown to be more likely that the absence of children was the reason for the divorce than that other causes producing tension in the family had led to the avoidance of children. Moreover, divorce allowed less time for a family to have children.

A third argument, advanced by Anthony Zimmerman, an American priest of the Society of the Divine Word, asserted that contraception injured the family by increasing the number of sins of extramarital intercourse.[86] Like the other two arguments, this one suffered from a lack of supporting evidence. It was also unconvincing unless comparative statistics were obtainable on the extramarital sins committed in a society where contraception was not practiced but the birth rate was kept low by late marriages. Such statistics — short of an Irish Kinsey report — were not likely to be obtained.

More specific injury to the family was claimed by many writers who found contraception to inflict an injury on a spouse. One argument invoked medical testimony to show that contraception inflicted injuries on the health of the wife. Coitus interruptus was said to cause nervous difficulties and pelvic disorders; other contraceptives were vaguely connected with uterine cancer. This kind of argument was never used by the leading theologians, but it does appear in writers such as Rosset and Roelandts.[87] As late as 1930, Richard de Guchteneere, a Belgian doctor, devoted an entire chapter of his *Judgment on Birth Control* to reports of medical injury.[88] In the light of the acceptance of contraception by the medical profession in most countries, the theological concern on grounds of health seemed misplaced, and this line of attack was largely abandoned.

More subtle psychological damage to a spouse was argued by many

---

pp. 98–99. De Lestapis argued that the Netherlands, France, and Belgium, whose laws did not permit the promotion of contraception, had lower divorce rates than the United States, Sweden, Switzerland, and Denmark. But his argument did not hold, as he failed to show that contraception was practiced less in fact in one set of countries than in the other.

[86] Anthony Zimmerman, *Catholic Viewpoint on Population* (Garden City, N. Y., 1961), p. 148.

[87] Rosset, *De sacramento matrimonii*, V, no. 3336; L. Roelandts, "Théologie pastorale," *Nouvelle revue théologique* 38 (1906), 316.

[88] Raoul de Guchteneere, *Judgment on Birth Control* (New York, 1931), pp. 152–165. There is still some medical opinion supporting the contention that the practice of coitus interruptus can result in serious emotional disturbances; William S. Kroger and S. Charles Freed, *Psychosomatic Gynecology* (Glencoe, Ill., 1956), p. 276.

theologians. Characteristically they assumed that the injured spouse was the wife, and that the contraceptive act was performed against her will. Thus John A. Ryan restated the ancient Augustinian contention in mild American terms: contraception involved a "loss of reverence" for one's spouse.[89] In 1954 Bernard Häring quoted Augustine himself: in the contraceptive act a wife was treated as a harlot. In such an act, Häring added, a wife "was not loved as a companion for salvation, but rather sought as an instrument for the release of passion" (*Das Gesetz Christi* 2–2.4.3.6.7. [5th ed., p. 1093]).

The old Augustinian approach, as indeed was evinced by Häring's acceptance of it, was strikingly close to the position taken by the Catholic personalists. Von Hildebrand had indirectly touched on this point when he declared that the act of married intercourse was "perfect self-surrender and self-revelation"; any other use was a "desecration of the other person."[90]

The most influential of all the writers of the new school, Herbert Doms, wrote in 1935:

> Every artificial alteration of the normal biological act, which ends in making impossible the biological end of generation inscribed in the form of the sexual organs and processes, constitutes a falsification of an act which is profoundly mysterious and extremely complex, an act which carries with it the mutual abandonment of the persons and the consequences of this abandonment . . . If a person mutilates the biological process anatomically or physiologically, before, during, or after the act, he gives himself only with an arbitrary reservation, which is contrary to the immutable meaning of the sexual act and the most profound intention of conjugal love.[91]

In this exposition by Doms, the focus was not on "the desecration of the other person," but on the destruction of love. A closely related contention was made by Suenens: "Contraception is an essential denial of conjugal communion, which it secretly disintegrates and turns into self-seeking."[92]

Another variant of this approach was developed in an essay written in 1961 by an American Jesuit, Paul Quay. Coitus, he argued, is a natural, not conventional, symbol of love. As a "natural symbol," the structure of the coital act cannot be altered without violence to the truth. When contraception is practiced, the communication which coitus should be is distorted; coitus becomes "lying," in the sense of telling an untruth. The partners "take that which says perfect union and corrupt it till it can express only mutual pleasure."[93]

[89] Ryan, "Family Limitation," p. 690.
[90] Von Hildebrand, *In Defence of Purity*, p. 36.
[91] Doms, *Du sens et de la fin du mariage*, pp. 177–178.
[92] Suenens, *Love and Control*, p. 103.
[93] Paul Quay, "Contraception and Conjugal Love," *Theological Studies* 22 (1961), 35.

Contraception was thus variously characterized as selfish, as an exploitation of the spouse, as a denial of love, as a destruction of the natural meaning of coitus. The characterizations may be distinguished in the consequences they focused on and the perspectives from which they were made. They shared a common ground: from Augustine to Suenens the essential contention was that contraceptive intercourse violated love. To reject this line of argument as did André Snoeck, with the statement that "the moralists have considered this value as important only in the last twenty-five years," [94] was to fail to perceive the identity of principle in the development of doctrine.

The various forms of the contention that contraception violated love did, however, share one weakness. It was not evident who was injured. In an approach like Häring's, a psychological aspect seemed to predominate: the wife, it was implied, was humiliated. In Suenens the emphasis was an injury to the husband himself: he became "self-seeking." Yet no demonstration was attempted of why the wife was injured if she consented, or why the husband was self-seeking if he had good reason to avoid more offspring. Neither writer showed why intercourse which was intentionally rendered sterile was more degrading or selfish than intercourse which was naturally sterile. In an approach like Doms's or Quay's an ontological injury was alleged; the entitative completion of the act, or its structure, was said to be denied. This contention was puzzling. In terms of the usual Christian approach, an act was a sin only if it hurt oneself, one's neighbor, or God. If the arguments centered on love were to hold, either injury to onself or one's neighbor, or violation of some order directly identified with the will of God, had to be shown. The alleged ontological injury seemed to be no injury to self or neighbor. If injury there was, it was offense to the will of God, and the argument resolved itself into the contention, soon to be examined, that coitus was sacral.

The experimental basis of the arguments appealing to love was also open to question. They appeared to assume that the only lawful intercourse was that in which the person gave himself totally. Michael Novak commented on this assumption: terms such as "'total surrender' or 'total self-donation' are not the language of ordinary human life. We learn to love only gradually. Perfect love is not attained so easily as the invocation of the simple criterion of the nonuse of contraceptives seems to imply. The language of 'total surrender' concludes to a sense of moral superiority that perhaps has not been earned. Some who use contraceptives may love one another more than some who do not." [95] Somewhat

[94] André Snoeck, "Morale catholique et devoir de fécondité," *Nouvelle revue théologique* 75 (1953), 898.
[95] Novak, "Toward a Positive Sexual Morality," in *What Modern Catholics Think About Birth Control*, p. 117.

similarly, Louis Dupré observed that no single act could express the gift of self in marriage; the gift was necessarily made in a repetition of acts over a period; there could be no "total" expression in a single act of intercourse, and hence there was no contradiction of a total expression of love if contraception were occasionally practiced.[96]

Another argument analyzable in terms of injury to the family was the Augustinian statement that contraception violated the purposes of marriage. The statement was retained in the later editions of Gury, and was invoked by such a writer as Rosset (*Marriage*, V, no. 3333). It was used in the 1909 Instructions of the Belgian bishops. *Casti connubii* affirmed, "First place among the goods of marriage is held by offspring"; and the Pope quoted from St. Augustine on Genesis (*AAS* 22:543).

Again, the question was presented, Who was injured by violation of the primary purpose: self, neighbor, or God? If neither injury to self nor to neighbor appeared, the argument, to be successful, had to assert that in the institution of marriage God had set up an order inviolable even when violation would injure no man. Moreover, it was not evident how the primary purpose of marriage became the necessary purpose of every marital act. Once it was admitted that no procreative purpose was required for lawful coitus, it became extremely difficult to find in the primary purpose doctrine any absolute barrier to contraception. At most the doctrine created a state of mind in which contraception was regarded as undesirable; no complete prohibition was established, and, as an argument against contraception, the primary purpose rule was invoked with increasing rarity.

INJURY TO SELF

The Christian tradition of asceticism is strong: "If anyone wishes to come after me, let him deny himself and take up his cross, and follow me" (Mark 8:34; cf. Matthew 10:38, 16:24; Luke 14:27). In describing the contribution of different factors in shaping the doctrine on contraception, I have alluded to this tradition only as it was embodied in the exaltation of virginity. Now Christian asceticism was brought into more direct relationship with the prohibition of contraception. Contraception was opposed because of the materialistic, unascetic reasons often adduced for practicing it. Remind the faithful, said the Belgian bishops in 1909, that Christian life is "a way to the fatherland," that is, to the Christian fatherland which is heaven. Contraception, said the German bishops in 1913, is "the consequence of luxury."[97] The run-of-the-mill theologians sounded

---

[96] Dupré, *Contraception and Catholics*, pp. 77–78.

[97] "Instruction des Evêques de Belgique sur l'onanisme," *Nouvelle revue théologique* 41 (1909), 618. Letter of the bishops of Germany, quoted in Joseph Laurentius, "Das Bischofswort zum Schutze der Familie," *Theologisch-praktische Quartalschrift* 67 (1914), 519.

the same note. Materialism was at the root of the desire to practice contraception, wrote Bishop Rosset in 1898. "The impelling principle" of contraception is "dislike of sacrifice," said John A. Ryan in 1915.[98]

To the person not holding Christian convictions this appeal to sacrifice, asceticism, and the cross was foolishness. Even for the Christian it was difficult to see that failure to practice self-sacrifice, either through continence or through raising a large family, necessarily constituted a mortal sin. If the Christian was *homo viator*, a wayfarer in "a vale of tears," carrying his cross, it was not established that refraining from contraception was the particular cross inflicted on every married Christian under pain of serious sin. The refusal to sacrifice might be injurious to one's spiritual welfare; but specific sacrifices were not shown to be mandatory. The argument based on Christian asceticism was a counterargument to bourgeois reasons for practicing contraception. It did not attempt, by itself, to show that every act of contraception was a mortal sin.

INJURY TO NATURE

A new and substantial form of the Stoic and Thomistic contentions that contraception was contrary to nature was made in 1964 by Germain G. Grisez, a married layman and associate professor of philosophy at Georgetown University. Grisez postulated in man's rational constitution the prescription, "Procreation is a good which should be pursued." This principle, like the principle, "Life is a good which is to be sought," or "Truth is a good which is to be sought," was a first principle of human action and therefore indemonstrable; it was postulated because demanded by the fact that rational beings did, in fact, procreate. Basic principles of this kind were not rules externally imposed by a superior, nor were they always being implemented. Man was not always engaged in truth-seeking activity; man was not always procreating. But because these principles were part of the radical, rational constitution of man, the goods they set for human action could not be directly attacked by man without his doing violation to his rational nature. To act against truth, to act against life, to act against procreation, was to deny part of man's rational nature.[99]

In distinguishing from the lawful use of rhythm a contraceptive act which attacked the procreative first principle, Grisez was compelled to distinguish between "individual acts" and "policy acts." Individual acts of contraception were always evil; acts setting a policy to practice rhythm might be good.[100] It was not clear, however, why a decision to avoid con-

---

[98] Rosset, *De sacramento matrimonii*, V, no. 3336; Ryan, "Family Limitation," p. 691.

[99] Germain G. Grisez, *Contraception and the Natural Law* (Milwaukee, 1964), pp. 78–86.

[100] *Ibid.*, pp. 162–163.

ception, executed by a series of acts, was less directly opposed to the procreative principle than a decision to perform a discrete contraceptive act. Moreover, in concentrating purely on a philosophical presentation of what his system postulated in the human constitution, Grisez did not focus on the requirement of Christian morality that for an act to be sinful it must be shown to be contrary to charity. In criticizing "situationist" ethics for selecting a "controlling value," which was treated as "an absolute end in itself," Grisez seemed to ignore the implication his criticism had for Christian ethics based on love as the absolute value.[101] At one point, however, he seemed to posit an unconceived entity as the neighbor to whom love was not shown: "The objection that the unconceived child has no actual rights is narrow-minded legalism." [102] But generations of Catholic theologians had taken that position: there are no souls waiting to be born; if a being has not been conceived there is no "unconceived child" to talk about. The current of thought which held contraception to be homicide had been itself a legal, rhetorical way of speaking. To emphasize the protection of life, the prevention of conception had been "interpretively" homicide. But when the canon law was codified in 1917 most rules of substantive morality had been dropped from the code; *Si aliquis* was among the provisions eliminated. Nothing now in the canon law supported, even rhetorically, the notion that the child-to-be-conceived had rights that justice or charity should lead a potential parent to take into account.

It appeared, in fact, in Grisez's analysis, that the person injured by the contraceptive act was the person performing it. But to maintain this analysis Grisez was required to suppose that a conflict could not exist for a parent between procreation and education. His statement of principle, "Procreation is a good which should be pursued," omitted one element which Christian moralists had traditionally insisted on: procreation and education had always been linked as the good of Christian intercourse. By omitting the educational element Grisez's analysis suppressed the tension built into the traditional statement. If man were not free to ignore the basic postulate which Grisez's analysis attributed to him, it had to be because God himself would be offended by the departure from His order. Offense against nature, then, became analyzable as offense to God.

OFFENSE TO GOD

Some theologians, assuming that contraception was evil, argued against its practice because of the punishments that would overtake its perpetrators. They seem to have believed that they had found a punishment peculiarly suited to the crime and that God would back them up: the

[101] *Ibid.*, p. 56.
[102] *Ibid.*, p. 95.

perpetrators would be punished by the premature death of their children. The contention was made by Bishop Rosset and by Adam Tanquerey, the Sulpician author of a manual for seminaries. It was recommended by the Belgian Roelandts as a threat to be used by confessors, and Tanquerey was cited with approval by Merkelbach as late as 1944.[103] Most strikingly of all, the threat was endorsed by the Belgian bishops in their 1909 instructions to confessors. The somewhat similar approach of Ferreres, predicting other evils for the children of those who practice contraception, was cited with approval by Thomas Iorio as recently as 1946 (*Moral Theology*, no. 1221).

Most reputable theologians have never engaged in these efforts to anticipate divine justice. I should suppose that almost everyone today who read them would feel keenly the cruelty of these arguments *ad terrorem* and be struck by the absurdity of men assuming that they were privy to the judgments of God. But I can imagine one pressing further: Is it essentially different for the theologians to proclaim that they know God's will as to the purpose of coitus? Is not there here an equally farfetched claim to be the spokesman for God, and is not the result as arbitrary and cruel as the more primitive case of the preaching *ad terrorem?* For one who did not share the convictions of Catholics as to the authority of the Church, there would be no answer to the claim that here man presumed to know what God wanted. A Catholic, however, might discriminate between the first case of men playing God, and the second case, where he believed the Church indeed spoke with divine authority. Nor would the assertion of such authority be either arbitrary or cruel if it was necessary in a given environment to safeguard human life and protect the holiness of marriage. The question would remain, How does the Church know it is God's will? It makes no claim to a "pipeline to God," no claim to a crude infusion of knowledge. What it has, it has from a revelation which closed with the Apostles.

That contraception was a direct offense to God might, theoretically, be proved by a text of Scripture saying so. This was the way, in fact, that many Catholic exegetes in all ages had read Genesis 38:8–10. It continued to be the reading of late-nineteenth-century writers such as Rosset and the revisers of Gury. Two of the leading theologians of the mid-twentieth century followed this ancient path. Häring, in 1954, cited Genesis 38 to condemn contraception and described Onan's act as constituting sacrilege, a sin against the Creator, and a display of lack of love for his wife. Hürth, in 1955, asserted that Onan was punished for his contraceptive act.[104] The most authoritative interpretation of Genesis 38

[103] Roelandts, "Théologie pastorale," p. 315; Benedict Merkelbach, *De castitate et luxuria* 8.4.3 (Bruges, 1944).

[104] Häring, *Das Gesetz Christi* 2.2.4.3.6.6 (5th ed., p. 1093); Hürth, *De re matrimoniali*, pp. 101–103.

was given by Pius XI in *Casti connubii*: "It is, therefore, not remarkable that Holy Writ itself testifies that the Divine Majesty pursued this wicked crime with detestation and punished it with death, as St. Augustine recalls" (*AAS* 22:559).

The argument from Genesis was not used by a good many theologians, including St. Jerome, St. Thomas, St. Albert, St. Alphonsus. It was not used by all twentieth-century theologians. The term "onanism" was itself not an exegesis; it was merely the conventional term for the sin of contraception. The difference of exegetical opinion was clear in the early twentieth century. De Smet wrote, "From the text and context it seems that the criticism of the sacred author is less directly and formally attached to the spilling of the seed than to the frustration of the levirate law which Onan intended to achieve" (*Les Fiançailles et le mariage* 2.1.3.1.1, annex 2, n. 5). It seems unlikely that *Casti connubii* intended to resolve definitively a point of exegesis where there was respectable exegetical authority on both sides. The interpretation given by Pius XI was by quotation of Augustine, not by independent papal determination.

In 1953 André Snoeck, professor of theology at the Jesuit scholasticate at Louvain, rejected the controlling force of Genesis. The sin of Onan "obviously consisted in the fact that he did not observe the levirate law." [105] The argument was dismissed with similar brusqueness on the same grounds by Louis Janssens in 1963.[106]. More cautiously, Joseph Fuchs said in 1960 that many modern exegetes "understand Onan to have been condemned only for his failure to observe the Mosaic law" (*Chastity and the Sexual Order* 2.6.2.2). Fuchs did not endorse these opinions; neither did he reject them. In the present state of exegetical opinion, it would not seem that the argument based on Genesis is heavily relied on to sustain the condemnation of all contraception.

That an act offends God, though not man, might be proved by reason alone. An unspoken blasphemous thought is at least one case of an act offensive to God, although arguably doing harm to no man. Analogously, desecration of the Eucharist would be principally an offense against God and demonstrably so by reason, once the premise of Catholic faith was accepted that the Eucharist contained the Body and Blood of Christ. Was contraception an act which reason alone or reason in conjunction with the premises of faith showed to be offensive to God?

A medieval line of thought had stressed the value of procreation as a way of replenishing heaven, which had lost the fallen angels. A more modern form of this thought contended that God was given glory by the multiplication of men. Thus in 1933 John A. Ryan commented on the command of Genesis to increase and multiply: "And the purpose of this

---

[105] Snoeck, "Morale catholique et devoir de fécondité," p. 909.
[106] Louis Janssens, "Morale conjugale et progestogènes," *Ephemerides theologicae lovanienses*, 39 (1963), 816.

injunction was not merely that the earth should be populated but that God should be increasingly glorified both on earth and in heaven." [107] If this view were taken literally, it would be an offense to God to limit the number of beings glorifying Him. The trouble with this contention was that it proved too much: if glory was given by the multiplication of men, then the value of virginity and the condemnation of extramarital procreation were both drawn in question. Granted that God was glorified by man, it was evident that the main line of Catholic thought held that mere multiplication of men was no absolute value, that other values were higher, and that among the higher values was the perfection of existing men.

There was, however, one argument which offered an absolute bar to contraception because of its departure from the order established by God. As has already been shown, the Thomistic argument that intentional prevention of generation is unnatural essentially embodied this contention: to interfere with the procreative act is to offend God, although no injury is done to man. The essence of this argument was frequently obscured by its rhetoric, which focused on the injury to "nature." But, as was observed by thousands of skeptical critics, "nature" as such possessed no special immunity from interference; dams and irrigation projects were never considered immoral. Nor was human nature itself ordinarily regarded as immune from improvement or from mutilation for the good of the person; the principles permitting surgery were deeply embedded in Catholic moral thought. If, in the one case of the sexual act, nature could not be interfered with, it was because in this one case the natural order was treated as special, as sacral, as in some extraordinary way God's.

The new critics subjected this argument to three basic attacks. Julian Pleasants took it at face value as a defense of what was natural in man. The argument, he said, "implies that inhibiting one purpose of an act while achieving another is unnatural." But biology shows that "a biological action is ordinarily multifunctional, and that inhibition of a function which is not needed is the typical means of achieving the integrated control required by living things." He gave as examples the action of the kidneys and the action of the nervous system: in their functioning action was initiated and then frustrated in some of its effects. "Life would be impossible if the body were at the mercy of any action which, once started, had to be allowed to achieve all its possible effects. On the contrary, the body commonly overdoes things, and then inhibits or frustrates any excessive results. If this seems untidy, it certainly cannot be called unnatural." [108] If such frustration of some effects was the ordinary biology of man, what was unnatural in frustrating the procreative function of

[107] Ryan, "The Moral Aspects of Periodical Continence," pp. 33–34.
[108] Julian Pleasants, "The Lessons of Biology," in Roberts et al., *Contraception and Holiness*, pp. 97–98.

intercourse while permitting the achievement of its purpose of expressing love?

Secondly, the critics observed that no showing had been made that procreation was the natural purpose of each act of intercourse. The evidence was just the other way. "Nature" sought to achieve its end by a plurality of acts, of which only a few could be meant to be procreative. Once more in the history of this doctrine animal behavior was invoked to explain a point, but this time the invocation was made after close observation. "Conception as a result of mating," Elizabeth Daugherty noted, "holds primacy of purpose only among the subprimate forms." The freedom of human beings from physiologically dominated sexual desires related to procreation was a human characteristic.[109]

A third line of criticism was tellingly developed by Louis Dupré and Michael Novak. To treat the act of intercourse as absolute, Dupré argued, was to isolate it from its normal context in a marriage. There was no reason to value the attainment of the biological end of the act as absolute, and to sacrifice to it the welfare of spouse or existing children. "To absolutize one particular value, even the most basic, at the expense of all the others is precisely what we call moral evil."[110] Similarly, Michael Novak objected to the narrow focus of the moralists on the integrity of the biological act: "The act of intercourse is not only defined by its biological externals; it reaches out into the total texture of our lives. This total texture is a 'good of the whole' more important than the good of any part — i.e. the biological placement of the act. The part must sometime yield to the good of the whole."[111]

These criticisms left the defenders of the Thomistic argument in this position: they could accept the characterization of their position made by Dupré: "To build an argument against contraception on the sacredness of nature (understood in such a way that the 'natural' course of the marriage act excludes any deliberate interference) is to withdraw the act from the sphere of the properly human, even for the attainment of its natural, biological end."[112] They could say, that is exactly what we mean. The act of coitus is sacred, is invested with a nonhuman immunity. It is sacramental for Christians and non-Christians alike. Why is it thus? Because by means of it God permits two human beings to join in the creative task of producing human life. The unique power of this act is such that every instance of its exercise must be treated reverently, as one would treat a sacrament. The criticisms based on the function of the

[109] Elizabeth A. Daugherty, "The Lessons of Zoology," in Roberts et al., *Contraception and Holiness*, pp. 112–126.

[110] Dupré, *Contraception and Catholics*, p. 44.

[111] Novak, "Toward a Positive Sexual Morality," in *What Modern Catholics Think About Birth Control*, p. 114.

[112] Dupré, *Contraception and Catholics*, p. 87.

biological system, the analogies drawn from animal behavior, even the arguments showing that to absolutize this value destroys other marital values — all these miss the point. This act is absolute, interference with its natural function is immoral, because it is the act from which life begins.

It would be possible to read the teaching of the theologians and canonists, popes and bishops, for over seventeen hundred years, as embodying this position. To do so would require isolating a single strand of the teaching from other reasons and treating it, abstracted from all contexts, as dispositive of the morality of any act which, in the exercise of coitus, "intentionally deprives it of its natural power and strength." This interpretation of the requirements of the tradition would reaffirm the teaching of *Casti connubii*. It would, however, be consistent with a position which permitted the use of anovulants as agents not affecting the sacral act of coitus itself. To predict that this position would not be the option adopted by the Church would be to presume beyond the purview of history.

A sense of option was at least present. Paul VI had summed up the state of thought in the Church when on June 23, 1964, he addressed the cardinals on "the problem which everyone is talking about, that is, birth control." "The problem," he said,

is extremely complex and delicate. The Church recognizes in it multiple aspects, multiple competencies, among which certainly the first is that of the spouses, their liberty, their conscience, their duty. But the Church has also to affirm her own competency, which is that of the laws of God. The Church has to proclaim such laws of God in the light of scientific, social, and psychological truths which, in recent times, have received new and most ample studies and documentation. It will be necessary to pay attention to this development of the question both in its theoretical and practical aspects. And this is precisely what the Church is doing. (*AAS* 56:588)[113]

[113] The Pope was referring to the commission on problems of population, the family, and natality set up to advise the Holy See. Established under John XXIII with a membership of six, it had been expanded to fifteen by May 1964, and to fifty-two by March 1965. The commission was international. There were nine members from the United States, seven from France, six from Germany, five from Belgium, five from Italy, two apiece from Canada, England, India, Japan, the Netherlands, and Spain, one apiece from Brazil, Chile, Jamaica, Madagascar, the Philippines, Senegal, Switzerland, and Tunis. Theologians — nineteen in all — were a plurality, but not a majority; there were fifteen demographers or economists, a dozen doctors, six representatives of the married laity, including the leaders of the Christian Family Movement. There were five women. The first plenary session of the commission was held March 25–28, 1965, in Rome. Addressing this group, Pope Paul VI pointed to the Church's guardianship of life and of love, and said, "In the present case, the problem posed may be summarized as follows: in what form and according to what norms ought spouses to accomplish in the exercise of their mutual love that service of life to which their vocation calls them?" (*L'Osservatore romano*, March 29, 1965, p. 2).

The recorded statements of Christian doctrine on contraception did not have to be read in a way requiring an absolute prohibition. The doctrine had been molded by the teaching of the Gospels on the sanctity of marriage; the Pauline condemnation of unnatural sexual behavior; the Old Testament emphasis on fertility; the desire to justify marriage while extolling virginity; the need to assign rational purpose and limit to sexual behavior. The doctrine was formed in a society where slavery, slave concubinage, and the inferiority of women were important elements of the environment affecting sexual relations. The education of children was neither universal nor expensive. Underpopulation was a main governmental concern. The doctrine condemning contraception was formulated against the Gnostics, reasserted against the Manichees, and established in canon law at the climax of the campaign against the Cathars. Reaction to these movements hostile to all procreation was not the sole reason for the doctrine, but the emphases, sweep, and place of the doctrine issued from these mortal combats.

The environmental changes requiring a reconsideration of the rule accumulated only after 1850. These changes brought about a profound development of doctrine on marriage and marital intercourse: love became established as a meaning and end of the coital act. Before women were emancipated and marriages in the West came to be based on personal decision, writing like that of Von Hildebrand, Doms, Häring, Suenens, Fuchs, Ford, and Kelly would have seemed chimerical. Their work responded to the change in conditions. Their teaching on marriage was in many ways different from that of older theologians. Huguccio would have marveled at the teaching of Ford and Kelly, Jerome would have been astounded at Häring. Suppose the test of orthodoxy were, Would Augustine or Thomas be surprised if he were to return and see what Catholic theologians are teaching today? By this criterion, the entire development on the purposes of marital intercourse would have been unorthodox. But it is a perennial mistake to confuse repetition of old formulas with the living law of the Church. The Church, on its pilgrim's path, has grown in grace and wisdom.

That intercourse must be only for a procreative purpose, that intercourse in menstruation is mortal sin, that intercourse in pregnancy is forbidden, that intercourse has a natural position — all these were once common opinions of the theologians and are so no more. Was the commitment to an absolute prohibition of contraception more conscious, more universal, more complete, than to these now obsolete rules? These opinions, now superseded, could be regarded as attempts to preserve basic values in the light of the biological data then available and in the context of the challenges then made to the Christian view of man.

At the core of the existing commitment might be found values other than the absolute, sacral value of coitus. Through a variety of formulas, five propositions had been asserted by the Church. Procreation is good. Procreation of offspring reaches its completion only in their education. Innocent life is sacred. The personal dignity of a spouse is to be respected. Marital love is holy. In these propositions the values of procreation, education, life, personality, and love were set forth. About these values a wall had been built; the wall could be removed when it became a prison rather than a bulwark.

INDEX

Abaye, Rabbi, 10

Abelard, Peter, 174, 193–194, 252n

Abellán, Pedro, 177n, 223n

Abigail, wife of David, 33

Abortion: and age of fetus, 86–88, 90; condemned by Ambrose, 99, Ancyra, 88, *Apocalypse of Paul*, 87, *Apocalypse of Peter*, 87, Athenagoras, 87, Augustine, 136, *Barnabas*, 87, Basil, 88, Caesarius, 146, *Casti connubii*, 427, Chaucer, 215, Clement of Alexandria, 87, council at Elvira, 88, Cyprian, 87, Decretals, 232, *Didache*, 87, Gerbald, 158n, Jerome, 88, Lactantius, 87, Liguori, 365, Minucius, 93, penitentials, 157–158, 164, Philo, 87, Pius IX, 405, Septuagint, 86, Sixtus V, 362, Tertullian, 87; confusion with contraception, 14; and "contraceptive mentality," 519; penalties for, 88, 164, 217, 232–233, 362–363, 405; and pill, 460–461; practice of, by clerics, 221, in England, 519, Hungary, 519, Japan, 519, Poland, 519, Roman Empire, 27–28, 86, Sweden, 519, Switzerland, 519; relation to contraception, 520n; and Roman law, 27; taught by Albert, 211, Avicenna, 203, Rhazes, 204, Soranos, 18

Abraham, 31, 121

Accursius, 217

Act, moral, determination of, 355–356

Adam, 41, 67, 68n, 109, 133, 134, 185, 189, 195, 316

Adeodatus, son of Augustine, 125

Adrian VI, Pope, 312n

Adulterii malum, 174, 260, 304

Adultery, 53; and contraception, 521; and invincible ignorance, 378; objection to, 244

Aeterni Patris, 482

Aetios, 13–19

Africa: Manichees in, 107, 117; population of, 24, 478

Agape, abuse of, 64

Aged, marriage of, 129, 289–291, 310, 497

Alan of Lille, 188, 258, 271

Albanians, 186

Albania, 168n

Albert the Great, St.: on abortifacients, 211; on absence of sin in marital intercourse, 287–288; on anaphrodisiacs, 205; argument against contraception, 247; and Avicenna, 222; on coital positions, 238n, 241; on confession, 272; on contraceptive means, 205–206, 211; on cooperation, 263; criticism of homicide theory, 233–234; on immoderate love, 251; influence of, 288, 303, 439n, 495; 497–498; on intercourse in pregnancy, 284n; on love and marriage, 256n; on the marital debt, 284, 285; on sacramental intercourse, 286–288; on virginity, 277

Albi, 183, 192, 193

Albigensians: see Cathars

Alexander Lombard, O.F.M., on cooperation, 262

Alexander of Hales, O.F.M., 235, 247; on cooperation, 261; on immoderate love, 251; on intercourse for pleasure, 250; on intercourse in pregnancy, 284n; on marriage of aged, 290; on procreative purpose, 248; on unnatural intercourse, 224–225

Alexander, Natale, 318, 326

Alexander III, Pope, 192, 232, 262

Alexandria, 60, 64, 117

Alexandrian rule, 105

Alfaric, Prosper, 124n

Alfrink, Bernard, Cardinal, 473n, 502

Algasia, letter from Jerome to, 90

Note:

For various religious orders, the following abbreviations are used:

C.S.B. — Basilians
C.S.C. — Holy Cross Fathers
C.P. — Passionists
C.SS.R. — Redemptorists
F.S.C. — Christian School Brothers
O.E.S.A., O.S.A. — Augustinians

O.F.M. — Franciscans
O.P. — Dominicans
O.S.B. — Benedictines
S.D.B. — Salesians
S.J. — Jesuits
S.S. — Sulpicians